THE OFFICIAL® PRICE GUIDE TO

# AMERICAN ARTS AND CRAFTS

David Rago and Bruce Johnson

**HOUSE OF COLLECTIBLES**

Random House Reference, New York

© 2003 David Rago and Bruce Johnson

Published by House of Collectibles, 1745 Broadway, New York, New York 10019. Distributed by the Random House Information Group, a division of Random House Inc., New York, and simultaneously in Canada by Random House of Canada Limited, Toronto.

(HOC logo) House of Collectibles is a registered trademark and the colophon is a trademark of Random House, Inc.

www.houseofcollectibles.com

Printed in the United States of America

Design and composition by North Market Street Graphics

ISBN 0–609–80989-X

10 9 8 7 6 5 4 3 2 1

First Edition

# ACKNOWLEDGMENTS

We collaborated on this third edition in an effort to give the work a single voice. Nevertheless, we chose to pull on our respective strengths when we felt it would be to the benefit of the final product. Bruce Johnson wrote the furniture, metalware, textile, and woodblock chapters. David Rago wrote the market survey, updated the pottery and lighting chapters from Bruce Johnson's second edition, and provided the photographs for the third edition.

Most of the prices were gleaned from David Rago/Craftsman Auction results.

## DAVID RAGO:

I would like to thank my wife, Suzanne Perrault, for too many things to mention here. The efforts of my staff members were instrumental in getting all this together, including Anthony Barnes, Denise Rago, Meaghan Roddy, Regina Pelligrini, and Miriam Tucker. I would like to thank my parents for getting me into this in the first place. While I simply cannot include all the collector friends who've supported me over the years, I would like to express my gratitude to Jordan Lubitz, Bob Ellison, Bob and Betty Hut, Rosalie Berberian, Dr. Martin and Esther Myers, and Bob and Mim Klein. And a special thanks to Robin Crawford, may he rest in peace.

## BRUCE JOHNSON:

The completion of this, the third edition of *The Official Price Guide to the Arts and Crafts Movement*, marks my 26th year as an Arts and Crafts collector and writer. In looking back over the past 26 years, I am pleased to see that not only has interest in the Arts and Crafts movement continued to grow, but the wealth of knowledge and research now available to new collectors is nothing short of astonishing. In addition to the journals and periodicals that now recognize and promote the Arts and Crafts philosophy and style, we have web sites, regional and national conferences, non profit organizations, tours, restored historic structures, newsletters, catalogs, and a steady stream of new books at our disposal. Authors Michael Clark, Jill Thomas-Clark, Marilyn Fish, David Cathers, Scott Braznel, Robert Winter, Beth Cathers, Stephen Gray, Thomas Maher, Bruce Smith, Yoshiko Yamamoto, David Surgan, Patricia Bartinique, Paul Duchscherer, Su Bacon, Kitty Turgeon, and Don Marek, plus scores of others who have written for *Style: 1900* and *American Bungalow* magazines have taken the time to research their field of interest and have unselfishly shared that information with all of us.

To all of them and to others too numerous to mention a special thanks goes out from the authors of this book.

# CONTENTS

## PART 1    Art Pottery

## PART 2   Arts and Crafts Furniture

# AN INTRODUCTION TO THE ARTS AND CRAFTS MOVEMENT IN AMERICA

*by Bruce Johnson*

Born in England and raised to maturity in the United States, the Arts and Crafts movement inspired a style of decorative arts that included furniture, pottery, metalware, art, linens, and lighting fixtures, which, while distinctively American in style, combined crucial elements from several countries. From England came the philosophy in the books of John Ruskin and William Morris, who established the principles upon which the movement was built. From America came the entrepreneurs and industrialists, such as Gustav Stickley, Charles Limbert, and Elbert Hubbard, who embodied those principles in a new style of furnishings made affordable to the middle class through carefully controlled mass production. And from Europe came the designers, Josef Hoffmann, Charles Mackintosh, and C F A. Voysey, whose influence brought grace and sophistication to the furniture, metalware, and decorative arts that have emerged as the best of the Arts and Crafts movement. Each individual had many goals, but all shared one desire: to raise the level of the craftsman to that of the artist, hence the name Arts and Crafts.

Like the roots of a towering oak tree, the origins of the Arts and Crafts movement in America can be traced to several sources, none more important than the classroom of the Oxford scholar and author John Ruskin in the year 1853. Although first and foremost an academic, Ruskin decried the evils of the Industrial Revolution, which, he believed, threatened to transform England's pastures into factories and craftsmen into laborers. In his 1849 book, *Seven Lamps of Architecture*, Ruskin called for a return to quality craftsmanship, the implementation of honest materials, simple forms based on purpose rather than popularity, and the involvement of the craftsman in every aspect from design through completion.

Ruskin and other social reformers of his era sought "to improve the quality of life for everyone by restoring integrity to the objects common to daily living."[1]

Among their concerns were: (1) the restoration of the dignity of the worker, including a sensitivity to working conditions and the artistic involvement of the workers in the entire project; (2) the integrity of the product, taking into consideration how well it was made, its usefulness, and its artistic merit; and (3) the impact of the product on the home and the family, insuring that it both be affordable and a contribution to the artistic harmony of the home.

Among his many students was William Morris, who in 1853, inspired by the writings and lectures of John Ruskin, dedicated his entire life to the implementation of the ideals of what was to be known as the Arts and Crafts movement. Trained initially as an architect, Morris turned to art and eventually to the means by which art could be merged with craft to create beautiful objects for the home. While social reformers fought to improve both the working conditions and housing for the lower class, Morris and his followers attacked the factory system from another direction. Dismayed by the crumbling quality of goods being mass produced in England's factories, Morris and other reformers, such as A. H. Mackmurdo and Charles Robert Ashebee, established guilds and cooperatives in which craftsmen and women could work under ideal conditions, selling their crafts to the English public. They believed that by raising the status of the craftsman, they would also increase the quality of the objects being produced. And by approaching each object, regardless of how utilitarian it might be, as a work of art, they hoped to also bring beauty, serenity, and happiness to the homes in which the objects would be used. "We should at all events take as our maxim 'the less, the better,' " Morris declared. "Have nothing in your houses that you do not know to be useful, or believe to be beautiful."[2]

By 1875 Morris & Co. was firmly established in the production of hand crafted furniture, wallpaper, rugs, draperies, fabrics, pottery, and books. What soon became evident, however, was that the time and materials required by quality craftsmanship inflated the price of each article. Rather than placing their products in the homes of the lower and middle classes, Morris & Co. discovered that the only people who could afford their handcrafted wares were wealthy members of the upper class. While the quality of their materials remained high, their impact was lessened by the limited availability and restrictive prices of their products.

William Morris discovered that he had run into a problem that he was never able to resolve: How is it possible to produce hand crafted, artistic, high-quality furnishings—whether they be furniture, wallpaper, textiles, metalwork, or pottery—and simultaneously increase the wages of the worker and make the products affordable for the lower and middle classes?

So while the English provided the philosophical foundation on which the ideals of the Arts and Crafts movement were built, they never succeeded on a national scale in resolving this conflict. And it was almost as if, for that reason, the Arts and Crafts movement nearly stalled in England. It began to flounder and instead of a national reform, took the form of scattered guilds, which succeeded in only isolated instances in solving the problem that neither Ruskin nor Morris could solve: how to make handcrafted items affordable for the working class without decreasing the wages or diminishing the working conditions of the craftsman.

Shortly before the turn of the century, the message broadcast by Ruskin and Morris had crossed the Atlantic, where Americans were wallowing, in the words of Gustav Stickley, in "badly-constructed, over-ornate, meaningless furniture that was turned out in such quantities by the factories. . . that its presence in the homes of the people was an influence that led directly away from the sound qualities which make an honest man and a good citizen."[3] The seeds of the movement first took root and flourished in areas such as Boston, New York, Chicago, and California and eventually anywhere people had grown weary of the excesses of the Victorian era, including shoddy workmanship, unnecessary forms, and elaborate ornamentation.

Proponents of the Arts and Crafts movement in America faced the same challenges William Morris did in their attempt to make artistic furniture, pottery, and metalware affordable for the middle class and yet profitable for the craftsmen and craftswomen. But whereas the English remained steadfast in their attempt to form craft guilds based on medieval models, American entrepreneurs, most notably the five Stickley brothers, adapted the existing factory system to produce quality Arts and Crafts furniture in a pleasant workshop setting.

While there is no doubt that the majority of Arts and Crafts furniture collected today was produced in what, by definition, would be called a factory, the more conscientious furniture manufacturers utilized woodworking machinery, such as joiners and planers, to reduce time spent on non creative stages in the process, thus freeing their craftsmen to apply their skills to the selection of boards, the assembly of the machined pieces, and the coloring and finishing of the completed piece. And while a certain amount of propaganda regarding the degree of handcraftsmanship that went into each piece was evident in their advertisements and catalog introductions, the fact remains that Arts and Crafts furniture represented better-quality materials, a higher degree of craftsmanship, and more pleasing designs than the American public had been offered previously.

Gustav Stickley himself had been on both sides of the issue. During the 1880s, he and his brothers produced and marketed several lines of inexpensive period reproductions imitating the styles of Chippendale, Sheraton,

Hitchcock, and whoever else was popular at the time. Discontented with his role as a furniture salesman, Stickley left the family business and, for more than a decade, experimented with various styles of furniture in search of one that would embody the ideals of William Morris in a form that was honest, simple, and attractive. His debt to Morris was later reflected in the first issue of his monthly magazine, the *Craftsman* (1901–16), which was dedicated to the English philosopher.

It is difficult to fully appreciate the radical departure of the new furniture style that characterized the Arts and Crafts movement in America without first visualizing that which had previously been popular. While the industrial factory system did not demoralize a class of people in America to the extent that it did in England, the mass production of inexpensive goods did manifest itself in a number of garish, often bizarre furniture aberrations. Manufacturers invented elaborate machines to carve ornate scrollwork, turn bulbous table legs, slice paper-thin veneers, mold ornaments from plaster and pulpwood, cut recessed and raised panels, stamp out thin hardware, press designs into chair backs, and turn dozens of identical spindles simultaneously. Mass-produced, machine-spawned, inexpensive furniture reached its ignominious glory in the 1890s and early 1900s with what is now referred to as the Era of Golden Oak. Unfortunately, not all that glittered was golden oak, as manufacturers freely substituted ash, hickory, and even pine and poplar under the disguise of an oak stain and an amber shellac finish.

Gustav Stickley was not alone in the search for an honest furniture style that would appeal to a large part of the population. While Stickley was still making period reproductions, a young Chicago architect named Frank Lloyd Wright had already designed an oak dining room set in the style that would later be called Arts and Crafts. Wright, however, was first and foremost an architect who insisted on designing the interior furnishings for each of his clients' homes; he appeared uninterested in manufacturing a line of Arts and Crafts furniture. Nevertheless, several other individuals were, and by 1900 the McHugh Company, the Michigan Chair Company, and the Roycrofters were each producing and selling a line of sturdy, simple, plain oak furniture.

It remained for Gustav Stickley, though, to improve their early, almost crude forms, to promote the ideals of the Arts and Crafts movement through his magazine, and to develop an efficient, yet worker-conscious factory system that would produce moderately priced "simple, strong comfortable furniture."[4] Stickley was the first American industrialist to manufacture Arts and Crafts furniture that appeared to have been entirely built by hand, yet that depended on electric- or steam-powered woodworking machines to saw, plane, and sand the lumber. Workers then assembled, pegged, stained, and finished each piece by hand, thereby promulgating the principles of the

Arts and Crafts movement while using modern technology to reduce production costs.

Stickley and the dozens of other furniture manufacturing firms that soon introduced their own lines of Arts and Crafts furniture or, as it was often called, "Mission oak" (tracing its heritage back to the California missions and their simple, sparse furniture), most often used white oak in their shops. Whereas early 19th-century furniture designers had often worked in mahogany, and the Victorian manufacturers who followed selected walnut for some of their best work, oak was the first choice of the Arts and Crafts designers. In addition to being both plentiful and less expensive than either Honduras mahogany or American black walnut, the dynamic flaking in quartersawn oak provided the furniture with the only decoration designers such as Stickley and Wright felt the furniture required. Quartersawn oak, however, was more expensive than plain sawn oak and has emerged as one of the distinguishing features between mediocre Mission oak and quality Arts and Crafts furniture.

Designers of the Arts and Crafts style were not limited to furniture. Just as quartersawn oak and pegged joints were associated with Arts and Crafts furniture, hand-beaten copper and brass, with a dark, chemically induced patina, became characteristic of the metalware of the era. Once again, manufacturers attempted to achieve the look of medieval hand craftsmanship while utilizing, as much as possible, the technology available to reduce production costs. Lighting fixtures, whether of oak or copper, incorporated mica shades or amber slag glass for a mellow glow similar to that of the satin furniture finishes. Art pottery firms gradually saw the demand for their high glaze vases dwindle as the public turned to matte glazes to complement the low-gloss finishes on their furniture. While firms such as Rookwood, Weller, and Roseville remained popular with their hand-painted vellum glazes, other firms such as Teco, Grueby, Marblehead, and Hampshire produced simple, vertical forms featuring subtle, naturalistic decorations under matte glazes that became—and have remained—associated with the movement.

While the English provided the basis for the philosophy of the Arts and Crafts movement and the Americans popularized it, designers such as Arthur Mackmurdo, Baillie Scott, and C. F. A. Voysey in England, Charles Mackintosh in Scotland, and Josef Hoffmann in Austria provided models that led American designers such as Gustav Stickley, LaMont Warner, Harvey Ellis, and Dard Hunter beyond the early massive forms and into a realm of design that brought lightness, grace, and sophistication to what otherwise might still be known as the "chunky charm" of Mission oak furniture.[5] Subtle touches, such as arched toeboards and stretchers, thin overhanging tops, cutout designs, tall chair backs, and long, delicate corbels, have proved that they can turn a formidable piece of furniture into a graceful, moden design.

The Arts and Crafts star burned brightly for the first quarter of the 20th century, although it never pretended to be a mainstream movement. It always was and remains today an alternative philosophy, style, and lifestyle for those who appreciate elegant simplicity, quality materials, and handcraftsmanship. And while many historians previously declared that the Arts and Crafts movement had burnt out either with the bankruptcy of Gustav Stickley in 1915, with America's involvement in World War I in 1917, with the introduction of the Art Deco craze in 1924, or even with the paralysis of the Great Depression in 1929, the fact remains that in 1938 people could still buy books and metalware from the Roycrofters; lamps from the Dirk Van Erp Studio; furniture from J. M. Young, Stickley Brothers, and Charles Limbert; art pottery from Dedham, Fulper, Newcomb, Saturday Evening Girls, Rookwood and Van Briggle; and metalware from Kalo, Shreve, Samuel Yellin, and Arthur Stone.

The Arts and Crafts movement did not end as meekly nor as quickly as many have assumed. In fact, throughout the 20th century, people retained a respect for simple elegance, honest construction, native materials, artistic design, and practical function. The principles and the philosophy of the Arts and Crafts movement were never rejected, even during the Great Depression and the second World War. They were simply put on hold until the American public could appreciate them again.

# ARTS AND CRAFTS MARKET REVIEW

*by David Rago*

The revival of interest in the American Arts and Crafts period is now into its fourth decade, and the market for this material has finally entered its mature phase. Because of this, Bruce Johnson and I believe that a book that prices these objects is most timely. What we feel is even more important is assisting you in learning how to price such pieces on your own.

The reasons for this are many. First, while you will find over 1,000 prices accompanied by hundreds of photos, these pages cover but a small fraction of the material available today. Second, many of these objects, especially the decorative ceramics, are one-of-a-kind pieces that clearly show the hand of the artist. Even the best of these artists had good days and bad days, and the most reliable of kilns offered varied results.

In addition, issues of condition, availability, and regional interest often have a profound influence on current pricing. We might say, for example, that an Arequipa Pottery vase is worth $25,000, but a buyer in California might pay more, and another in New York might pay only a fraction of that price. Similarly, most collectors of high-end/academic Mission furniture are insistent upon original finishes on wood and patinas on hardware in nearly all cases; such pieces with new finishes might be worth only 20 percent of a mint one. However, middle-range examples, such as a standard Gustav Stickley 60 inch sideboard with a good, new finish, might bring 75 percent of what a perfect original one would fetch.

When the first edition of this book came out in 1988, the market was then in its middle phase and, even though I was selling hundreds of pieces of Mission furniture a year, my own place in the field was primarily centered on ceramics and decorative objects.

With this new edition, Bruce and I have worked together to provide you with the fullest possible picture of the market. Between us, we have over 50 years of experience with Arts and Crafts furniture and objects, and we would like to share some of that information with you. Toward that end, we would like to begin by giving a brief history of the revival market for Arts and

Crafts, from the earliest days to its mature phase, detailing both the growth in pricing, and the objects and events that served as landmarks along the way.

## The History of the Market for Arts and Crafts

The earliest days of collecting Mission furniture, art pottery, and wrought copper began around 1970. While we often hear collectors and dealers today sighing in hindsight about "the good old days," those first years were not necessarily the best time to form an Arts and Crafts collection. Each phase, as in life, had its plusses and minuses.

It is certainly true that there was much to buy prior to 1975, and most of it was priced at what seems like ridiculously low numbers when compared with today's market. But who knew what to buy? Who could determine whether one piece of Gustav Stickley was better than another? How would damage from use and abuse affect value and collectibility in 30 or even 50 years down the road?

The early collectors of Arts and Crafts were truly pioneers. There was precious little knowledge to be had back then, and those first buyers were as inclined to purchase a bad piece as a good one.

Consider that there were virtually no revivalist books on the Arts and Crafts movement prior to Princeton University's *The Arts and Crafts Move-*

Fine and early Gustav Stickley writing desk #518 with gallery top, through-tenon construction to paneled case, drop-front door with riveted hammered copper strap hinges and escutcheon enclosing full gallery interior, over two lower shelves. Refinished. Unmarked, 52" × 26" × 11", $5,750

*ment in America,* published in 1974, based on its exhibition of arts and crafts material. There were several art pottery books published before 1975, but excepting the Herbert Peck *Rookwood Pottery,* and the more general Kovels' *Collector's Guide to Art Pottery,* most available information existed in the form of archival work from the turn of the century.

The Princeton exhibition was the first major showing of this material within a scholarly framework, and had an impact similar to a large stone being dropped into a placid pond. At the time most buyers/collectors were schoolteachers and academics who had far more knowledge than money, but from this point on, buyers with money started to enter the market.

In those early years, most furniture collectors bought only Gustav Stickley pieces, turning away from those by L. and J. G. Stickley and Limbert Furniture. Even great Gustav pieces with minor imperfections were shunned. Similarly, pottery buyers mostly prized Victorian-influenced ceramics such as Japanese-styled Rookwood or Zanesville pottery with photo-like portraits. Even slightly damaged pieces were nearly worthless.

The belief at this time was that these academic relics, those which best displayed the influences of European and Oriental precedents, were the most interesting of the Period. With little revisionist scholarly work, and relatively few comparative objects providing contrast, there was little else to believe.

Things changed briskly after 1975. Museum shows opened, one on top of another, and new books on the field were published in quantity. Many of these shows and tomes were general studies of the Arts and Crafts move-

Large blue "Pine Cone" urn (12"–15"). Restoration to rim chip. Impressed mark, $2,185

ment, but a good number of them were monographs, exploring in depth the oeuvre of a single artist or company. These had the dual effect of educating buyers and bringing greater awareness and credibility to the field.

Also at this time the earliest galleries and important private dealers began to work the market. The Jordan-Volpe Gallery, for example, opened its doors in 1975. For the first time, in their ads, pieces of art pottery and Mission oak were advertised in prestigious magazines. Imagine, if you can, how startling it was to pick up an old school publication like *Antiques Magazine* and see a piece of square brown Stickley alongside Chippendale and Meeker masterpieces.

Private dealers too began flexing their muscles. I recall in 1978 one such dealer, Rosalie Berberian, telling me about how uninteresting the portraits and derivative Japanese work would surely become. She advised, instead, to look for pieces where the decoration blended with the vase, and where glazes were harmoniously organic and vegetal. The ceramic base was from, and of, the ground, after all.

This confluence of information and interest created secondary markets for things not Rookwood or Gustav Stickley. Collectors, albeit cautious and outside the mainstream, emerged with a taste for Limbert and L. and J. G. Stickley furniture and Fulper and Newcomb College pottery. Although their time was not to come fully for another decade, their existence marked the first blush of credibility for a broader collecting base.

The decade of the 1980s was a curious time for collecting Arts and Crafts, earmarked by the highs and lows, the agony and the ecstasy, resulting in a jumble of serious knowledge and opportunistic acquisition. The decade began with the uncertainty of the Carter recession, with money and interest both frighteningly short. As the economic turndown eased, the Arts and Crafts market experienced unprecedented growth in interest, information, and pricing.

It was during this time that the specialty auction house first established itself as a market standard. Prior to the 1980s there were mostly auctions of general "stuff" that happened to contain some art pottery and/or Arts and Crafts material. While there were some exceptions to this, perhaps 99 percent of all Arts and Crafts at auction were represented in general sales. This changed dramatically between 1980 and 1985, with no fewer than eight firms holding at least one all-Arts and Crafts session a year. While some of these were established major houses who adopted specialty sales as part of their program, such as Christies' or Sotheby's, most were new specialty firms such as ARK Antiques and Biff Taylor Art Pottery Auctions. It was in 1984 that I began my own specialty Arts and Crafts auction.

Specialty auctions brought several novel ideas to the table, putting them in direct opposition to the established houses. For one, these firms were

Rare and exceptional Grueby two-color cylindrical vase decorated with tooled and applied stylized flowers in chartreuse alternating with broad leaves, covered in an excellent leathery dark green matte glaze. (Perfectly fired.) Circular pottery mark ER/12/3/4, 10" × 4¼", $9,775

headed by people who had a great deal of knowledge in the Arts and Crafts area. Secondly, most of them offered unprecedented guarantees to the buyer, ones that promised authenticity and accurate descriptions of condition.

Nearly all auctions prior to this time were headed by well-schooled experts whose range of knowledge spanned many fields, and their clearly stated business practices were of the "buyer beware" kind. While this was a perfectly acceptable way to auction material, it did little to assuage Arts and Crafts buyers who had relatively little expertise or who were unable to attend

Large and fine Fulper hammered urn covered in a frothy indigo and light blue glaze. Stilt-pull bruise. Incised racetrack mark, 11¾" × 11¾", $1,495

a sale in person. How much would they risk on an object sold without guarantee?

Almost overnight specialty auctions, which had commanded a minor share of the overall market for Arts and Crafts, grew to virtual parity with the nationwide surfeit of dealers, who had long dominated the field. Coinciding with this was the closing of the field's most preeminent dealership, Manhattan's Jordan-Volpe Gallery, in 1986. While dealers might not have welcomed the emergence of auctions, for it threatened their dominance of the market, the overall impact expanded and developed the field as never before.

The auctions, by their nature, were far more public a marketplace for Arts and Crafts material. Even if you weren't interested in buying at auction you could, for $10 or $15, purchase a catalog showing several hundred pieces of pottery, furniture, and metal, with presale estimates and post-sale results. If you bought catalogs from all the major auctions you could, over the course of a single year, for the cost of only about $150, have pricing information for thousands of pieces.

This affected not only how collectors bought objects, but also how they chose to sell them. Collectors often bought and sold to the private gallery dealers with whom they had the closest relationship. It was convenient and relationship-based, after all. But once the auctions took hold, those same collectors (and the dealers they worked with) had far more marketing information with which to work. Perhaps both the collector and dealer had always

The second Rago Auction catalog

thought a Limbert cut out table worth $2,500. But, if one sold in New York or California for $4500, the price of tables just went up.

Dealers have always been the cornerstone of any good market. Just as with auctions, there are good and bad ones, honest and dishonest ones. But in a relatively small field, such as the Arts and Crafts market in the mid–1980s, word traveled sufficiently to offer its own sort of checks and balances. Dealers usually maintained a regional base from a gallery, shop, or show circuit, cultivating interest at a grass-roots level. While most individual dealers may have influenced only a large handful of collectors, there were several hundred dealers nationwide developing bedrock interest in the period.

A few dealers, such as the Jordan-Volpe Gallery and Michael Carey Gallery, both of New York City, or the Arts and Crafts Shop in Sausilito, California, had taken things to the next level. Their activities included holding gallery exhibitions, publishing books, or helping to organize museum shows. They established a nationally based interest, creating a larger market while at the same time infusing it with their taste and influence.

Major museums, high-end trade publications, and publishing houses increased the interest in the Arts and Crafts. While prior to 1975 there were precious few books found on the subject, it now seemed that there was something else to read every month. Where there had once been a single book on Rookwood Pottery, there were now four or five. When collectors had been able to only guess at the production of Gustav Stickley furniture, Big G Press, for example, offered inexpensive, handsomely printed period catalogs as required reading.

As understanding of the period grew, so did a desire for a variety of objects associated with it. Hand- stitched textiles, for example, were pursued with astonishing vigor. I recall New York dealer Beth Cathers paying $5,500 for a Gustav Stickley linen table runner at a Phillips Auction in Manhattan in 1987. Few events over the years were so shocking to me. And few seem, in retrospect, so appropriate and prescient.

Even established markets were refined and redeveloped. While interest in the Arts and Crafts influence in ceramics had blossomed since Ms. Berberian's decade-old observation, never before had prices for the work of Grueby, George Ohr, and Newcomb College reached their late 1980s levels. At the same time, hand-painted Victorian pottery, including portraitures and quaint Japanese vignettes, stagnated at best and reversed themselves in many cases.

The furniture market was in even more a state of flux. From about 1985—90, buyers emerged who had less interest in developing an academic collection of early Gustav Stickley, for example, than they did in building a reasonable period interior. If their pocket and schedule wouldn't allow for a curator's dream, they were more than happy to make do with an appropriate selection of furniture by Limbert, Quaint, Lifetime, and L. and J. G. Stickley.

Fine and rare Limbert plant stand with quarter-round corbels under the square top, flaring sides with ovoid cutouts, lower shelf, and plank base. Fine original finish, factory edge repair to top and seam separation to side. No visible mark, 29½" × 20" sq., $6,900

Buyers were still rather condition-conscious, and any piece with less than its original surface was severely discounted. But clearly the boundaries of what constituted a "good" collection were being stretched like never before.

It was only a matter of time before the market was inundated with avid new collectors, and only a matter of economics for a percentage of them to have equal amounts of money and interest. Hollywood was suddenly at-

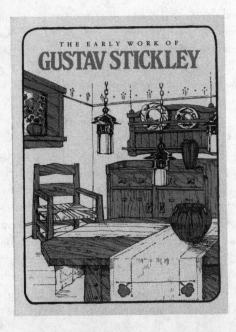

*The Early Work of Gustav Stickley* by Stephen Gray (Turn of the Century Editions)

tracted by both the beauty and relative obscurity of the material. Arts and Crafts might have been more popular than any time in its past, but it was still seen as an "undiscovered" field when compared with the likes of Tiffany and Chippendale. The movie industry entered the fray and bought with expendable income previously only the narcotic dreams of dealer and auction alike. Barbra Streisand was the most visible buyer, though she was one of a legion in the entertainment field attracted to the clean lines of the period.

The high-water event of the market in the 1980s was the sale at Christie's in Manhattan of Gustav Stickley's own furniture (well, nearly all of it was, anyway…). The star of the day was an important sideboard from the master's home, selling to Ms. Streisand for a staggering one-third of a million dollars. Whether or not you liked auctions, and whether or not you liked Christie's, there was no denying the enduring impact this event would have on buying Arts and Crafts material for years to come.

Also in 1987 co-author Bruce Johnson created an event, catering to Arts and Crafts enthusiasts of all kinds, called the Conference at Grove Park Inn. I do not include this here as either a sop to an author or an easy plug for the event. Neither would be sufficient to advance the credibility of this book. Instead, the conference proved to be the cornerstone of a burgeoning market.

Prior to that first Grove Park Inn Conference, there were a number of general and specialty dealer shows held across the country. For several years Roycroft enthusiast Boice Lydell, for example, held a small and elegant show

Exceptional and large Newcomb College scenic ovoid vase by A. F. Simpson, 1930, crisply carved with a full moon shining through oak trees and Spanish moss in blue and green matte glazes. (First rate.) Three small flat manufacturing chips to base. NC/SN43/131/JH/AFS, 11¼" × 5", $16,100

Unusual Stickley Brothers drink stand with square inset top and three round-bottom slats to each side. Good original finish and condition. Paper label and stenciled number, 24¼" × 15" sq., $1,380

at the Roycroft Inn in East Aurora, New York, attracting high-end, nationally based dealers, and presenting a show in a period environment.

But none of these efforts featured the facility or space on a grand scale, which could be the most critical component of the event. Bruce's idea was so radical that, when asked to exhibit at Grove Park Inn as a dealer, I told him I would be glad to do it, but I doubted it would be successful. I contended that the show was too far off the beaten path and that February was the wrong time of year to host such an event. I was soon introduced to how wrong I could be.

What happened that first year is history, and that history is rewritten in larger letters, and larger numbers, with each new offering. While the quality of the material offered for sale and the scope of lectures, workshops, and exhibitions held during the event are all part of its success, there is really only one reason for Grove Park Inn's staying power, and that is the spirit of the Grove Park Inn itself.

Year after year I've endured the emotional ravings of first-year attendees about the natural stone this and the period furniture that. But what I'm hearing between the lines is their inner reactions to the faint echo of lingering spirit manifest on the grounds. Those sensitive to the Arts and Crafts can understand the emotional content of a great piece of Stickley furniture or a handcrafted George Ohr pot.

But seldom have any of us had the opportunity to actually walk through and experience firsthand the feeling that was intended by period masters. It is an indefinable quality, a combination of a bold surroundings made by hand with the simplest ingredients, with the best of intentions. Grove Park Inn offered, and still offers, this, and it is bringing the community of collectors and dealers together, under one roof, for one weekend each year, that establishes it as the quintessential event.

I am allowing myself this digression because it is exactly this kind of understanding that attracts, and keeps people connected to, the Arts and Crafts. I know collectors and dealers in many fields, having been introduced to dozens more through my tenure as an appraiser appearing on *Antiques Roadshow*. Certainly, there is love and passion in every field, from Pez collectors to advanced Tiffany glass and lamp buyers. But the passion that is borne through the connection to the timeless, hopeful spirit of a different era is the thing that sets Arts and Crafts people apart.

It is also worth noting that several of the largest dealers in the field, the Jordan-Volpe Gallery and Michael Carey Antiques, both of New York City, were both out of business by the end of the decade. Other private dealers commanded the top of the market in their absence, and the latent strength of California collectors began to show.

The decade ended with the dull thud of the Bush recession, and it is worth noting that the impact was most immediately felt at the Grove Park Inn convention of 1991. It was there, during the assemblage of dealers and collectors, that the ground war in Iraq kicked in. That was the one conference where people were far more interested in watching CNN than in seeing what high-end dealers such as Geoffrey Diner or David Rudd had for sale in their booths. It was a painfully memorable week, the low-water mark for a market that had advanced perhaps fourfold over the previous 10 years.

The irony was that, in spite of all signs to the contrary, there may never have been a better time to buy Arts and Crafts. The 1980s, in retrospect, had all the traits of a developing market. There was more knowledge and information than ever before, but perhaps only enough to get into a great deal of trouble. There were more buyers than any time in the past, but relatively few of them understood the period enough to remain in it for the long haul. People were beginning to understand that there was more to collecting Arts and Crafts than Gustav and Dirk Van Erp and Grueby, but not enough to delve, with confidence, into Rhead Pottery and Charles Rohlfs furniture and Jarvie metalware.

The 1980s, in short, provided the road signs but not the road. It would probably have been too much to expect that then. Fifteen to 20 years is just not enough time to fully develop a market. Whatever the case, all was put to rest in 1990 when the recession hit. Amid signs that Arts and Crafts furniture and accessories were dead, the slate of expectations was wiped clean for the next decade of collecting.

The 1990s began inauspiciously with prices at their lowest levels since the beginning of the 1980s. Auctions were reeling from the blow; Skinner Gallery, one of the major players the last decade, lost its department head and

The Grove Park Inn, Asheville,
North Carolina

refocused on the more traditional antiques on which it originally built its reputation. Even Christie's, which at one point had built a high level interest, scaled down its Arts and Crafts sales, pushing much of the material to its second-tier block, Christie's East.

Dealer sales were abysmal. This was a time of consolidation in the private sale sector. Shows, even the illustrious Grove Park Inn, saw total sales of perhaps half their collective gross only a few years earlier. As a whole, however, the market and the players in it struggled forward, changing strategies to remain in business.

The market languished for about three years. Though there were few high points at that time, pieces sold with some consistency and prices for most things remained stable. Ironically, the years from about 1993 to 1995 were to prove the best time ever for collectors at all levels.

It would be true to say that prices for the best pieces in good condition seldom tapered off and, in most cases, even increased somewhat. But during this time there were few great leaps in value of high-end goods.

What remained the strongest were solid, mid range objects and furniture in excellent condition. This was largely due to the infusion of interest from West Coast collectors and the dealers who serviced them. Specialty stores like Lifetime Gallery and Circa 1910 flourished in Los Angeles like California poppies, providing this new crop of collectors with a broad and varied selection of furniture and objects in professional settings. It would have been impossible to understand then how critical this was in breathing life into the field. In hindsight, it seems the market across the nation turned on this new interest.

The decade was also a time for a correction of a more difficult sort, with two major players disappearing from the scene entirely. Todd Volpe, former co-owner of Jordan-Volpe Gallery in New York City, was indicted for fraud surrounding a number of spurious deals with California gentry. According to a *New York Times* article, Volpe created a sort of "Ponzi scheme" which, by the paper's calculations, siphoned over $6 million from the likes of Jack Nicholson.

Fine large and early Dirk Van Erp hammered copper table lamp with four sockets, four riveted armatures on a bulbous base, and four-panel mica shade with riveted strapwork. Enhanced original patina on base, original patina and mica on shade. Closed box mark, 22½" × 21¼", $25,875

Fine and rare Jarvie brass Omicron three-branch candelabra with curled riveted brackets inset with torch-shaped inserts. Original untouched naturally occurring patina, a few scratches. (Found in a basement in Orange County, California.) Incised Jarvie, 10½" × 7", $24,150

Fine and massive Charles Rohlfs mahogany sideboard with five drawers flanked on either side by a small drawer over cabinet, with faceted front legs and pulls. Refinished top, some replaced hardware, screw holes inside both doors. Branded mark, 41¼" × 68¾" × 22¼", $5,175

Another of the nation's leading dealers, D. J. Puffert of the Arts and Crafts Shop of Sausilito, California, filed for bankruptcy, taking with him over $2 million in funds from collectors and fellow dealers alike. Only a few years prior, Puffert managed one of the most creative and interesting Arts and Crafts auctions in the country. The catalogs to these sales, in spite of his business practices, remain icons of the market's past.

But many determined collectors and institutions entered the market at this time, and their impact sustained the field during this difficult period. Their emergence was a clear sign of the maturity and longevity of the Arts and Crafts. One was Gustav Stickley's rustic home in Parsippany, New Jersey, Craftsman Farms, and the other was the formation of the Sarah Lee Corporate collection, Crabtree Farms, outside of Chicago.

Craftsman Farms was not a major buyer of Arts and Crafts material, depending mostly on donations to either buy back pieces that had left the building or replace lost objects with similar acquisitions. But the field now had a spiritual base, in an honest period setting, to bring new people into the fold. Gustav's country home was a living, ongoing testament to his eye and his heart. Unlike the Greene and Greene masterpiece, Pasadena, California's Gamble house, which was as elitist as it was Arts and Crafts, Craftsman Farms was an explanation of the simple rusticity of Gustav's vision.

While it may not have been intended this way, the rebuilding of the exterior of the Farms, and the replenishing of its interior, became a rallying point for serious enthusiasts. Some people, upon their initial visit to the Farms, express disappointment at how "simple" the place appears at first blush. The more seasoned traveler, especially those who had a hand in the project, leaves with each visit somehow fuller.

Crabtree Farms created Arts and Crafts authenticity in a whole different way. While the complex augmented period standing buildings with the construction of new ones, the emphasis was on the complete and accurate re-creation of period life. A walk though the private compound is like stepping

The Craftsman Farms Foundation, Parsippany, New Jersey. Courtesy of Ray Stubblebine

through a time warp, thanks to a combination of corporate funding, flawless direction, and unbridled passion.

The easiest part of Crabtree Farms was the matching of wall textures and colors, detailing with stencils, and proper lighting. The attention to detail brought the idea to an even greater level, however. Period sinks and stoves were built into the homes. Dinnerware and stemware are all antique in the Arts and Crafts style. Linen clothes hanging in bedroom closets are of the time, design, and construction one might expect to see in 1910. Even the sundries in the kitchen, down to the box of drinking straws in the cupboard, are appropriate.

The corporation's openness to specialized tour groups allows growing numbers of individuals to experience that which before had been available only in words. This is one of the landmarks of this new, mature market.

Concurrent with these icons were a spate of new museum and gallery shows, the publication of many new books, and the development of more specialty dealer shows across the country. No single event can claim responsibility for the steady resurgence of interest, and pricing, for the Arts and Crafts. But, by 1996, the sum of these disparate strands began to show clearly in prices that increased steadily and didn't look back for years.

In 1993 Grueby Pottery, for example, sold for about the same prices as it sold for in 1986. Then, a piece of Grueby, which was sold in 1996 at a Cali-

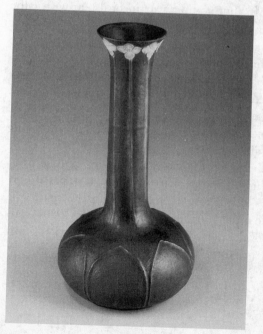

Exceptional and large Grueby vase by Wilhelmina Post with squat base and tall neck, decorated with tooled and applied leaves around the base alternating with long stems and yellow trefoils around the neck, and covered in a superior leathery matte green glaze. Perfectly fired and very sharply modeled, even the stamens of the flowers are detailed. Mint condition. Pottery stamp/WP/188A, 17¾" × 8½", $92,000

fornia pottery show for $21,000, sold again at one of my auctions in 1991 for a record $92,000. By 2001, prices for average pieces tripled and, for the best work, increased five fold. Newcomb College Pottery prices trebled. High-end Gustav Stickley pieces doubled, doubled again, and then nearly doubled again within a seven-year span.

Much of the increase in values was directly tied to the robust economy of the Clinton era. The stock market nudged to unprecedented highs, and the high-tech sector and *NASDAQ*, made paper millionaires of thousands of new potential buyers. A feeling of invincibility could be felt on the floors of auctions and dealer shows alike, and record prices at both were broken, and broken again with regularity.

This new market took its first hit in the spring after the dot-com crash. Some of the biggest collectors simply disappeared, while others chased fewer pieces at auction and privately. Prices for all the most advanced Gustav Stickley pieces mostly reflected the downturn. Art pottery remained strong for two reasons. First, there was a broader collector base dictated by individual markets for nearly 200 makers. Second, as co-author Bruce Johnson once said to me, "You can buy a Gustav Stickley bookcase, or thirty pots to fill it with."

Whatever the case, 2001 marked the first time in nearly a decade that more prices steadied than rose. Things trundled along until the terrorist attacks on New York and Washington in September, 2001. Buyer confidence was bent, but it didn't break. The first months after the attacks saw a drop in sales and prices for Arts and Crafts, but not in a way inconsistent with sales of just about everything else across the country.

The year 2002 began with frenzied buying which, at the time, was inexplicable. In hindsight, it seems that a dearth of material on the market (people were loath to part with objects in what appeared to be a stalled atmosphere), coupled with a pent up demand to buy durable goods, contributed to this rush.

This brings us to the present, a time in which the market for Arts and Crafts appears solid in nearly all categories. While furniture prices have dipped, they are still substantially higher than they were a decade ago. I believe that things are "soft" only if you had the expectation that prices would never back up. Based on 30 years of working in, and studying, this market, I think these watershed periods do much more good than bad. The 1990s were a breathless time. The sobriety of the dot-com crash, the stock market's fall, and 9/11 may ultimately prove to be the healthiest turn the field has ever taken.

PART 1

# ART POTTERY

# EVALUATING ART POTTERY

*By David Rago*

Accurately evaluating art pottery today is both easier and more difficult than ever before. Since I first wrote the art pottery chapter to this book back in 1988, there is more information available to even the casual enthusiast. Thousands of pieces are pictured and priced on the Internet, selling publicly on ebay and other sites with or without a fixed price.

In addition, there have been hundreds of specialty auctions focusing on art pottery at all levels. Nearly all these pieces are pictured in catalogs, accurately described, and accompanied by presale estimates and post-sale results. Many of these catalogs are still available today in print form, and a good portion are available online for free.

Moreover, there have been nearly 100 new books written about the Arts and Crafts movement and the decorative ceramics used to outfit period, and now contemporary, interiors. Many of these tomes have accompanied museum and private gallery exhibitions, which provide greater context for the material.

Finally, there are a number of specialty shows and conferences across the country, such as the Grove Park Inn, in Asheville, North Carolina, and the California Art Pottery Show in Glendale, California, where dealers periodically exhibit their inventories, providing realistic pricing and hands-on experience to anyone paying the price of admission. So much for the good news.

The downside of this older and wiser market for art pottery is that this font of information is often as confusing as it is clarifying. At best, it can be ephemeral and incomplete. For example, niche markets often rise or sink to new levels based on the participation of a single new buyer. While collectors of pottery by George Ohr, for example, are plentiful, the same cannot be said for those who are looking for pieces by Chicago Crucible or W. J. Walley. If, tomorrow, three more people decided to collect pieces by Walley, prices would increase by perhaps 50 percent within six months. Yet, if one of the current collectors of Walley's work dropped out, prices might fall by 25 percent almost immediately for all but his best work.

W. J. Walley vase covered in a
brown and green semimatte glaze,
with speckled blue interior.
Stamped W.J.W., 5¾" × 6",
$500–$750

A case in point is the current pricing for matte green pottery by Thomas Wheatley, one of the potters featured later in this chapter. Wheatley's matte work had been a favorite of Arts and Crafts collectors for most of the last decade. Well made, distinctively designed, covered with rich (usually green) glazes, and available at only a fraction of what similar pieces of Grueby Pottery would cost, this ware filled a growing need for more moderately priced decorative art compatible with Arts and Crafts interiors.

Prices for Wheatley's work increased steadily through the 1990's until 1999, when two major collections reached the auction market at nearly the same time. The first of these, the smaller of the two, performed fairly well, selling mostly within auction estimate ranges. The second collection, which was considerably larger and fell on the heels of the first grouping, did not do nearly as well. Many pieces sold for about one-third less than normal, and a lofty percentage failed to meet their auction minimums.

Another problem with the current market is that, because of the nation-wide interest in decorative ceramics, regional markets have developed unique, and sometimes counterintuitive pricing structures and evaluation standards. For example, within the last five years, prices for high-end California art pottery have risen by as much as 400 percent because a handful of savvy, West Coast buyers have entered the fray. Yet, if you're a New York buyer or seller of Arequipa pottery, which is originally from Fairfax, California, you're less likely to be attuned to the current market structure. (It is important to note that this is more relevant to private sales than the auction market because of the national reach of most specialty auctions. Their catalogs, both print and online, tend to reach buyers at most locations.)

We will address some of these nuances within the individual chapters that follow. The purpose of this brief study is simply to apprise you of the complexity of the market for pottery and to assure you that this is as positive a situation as it is a negative one. The access to information has never been

Fine Wheatley vase with four
flaring buttresses, covered in a rich,
curdled matte green glaze. Minor
glaze nick to one foot. Incised
WP/640, 8¼" × 9", $1,840

more important, and if you become a student of the market, you will find
your research and the application of it well rewarded.

Before we examine each of the Arts and Crafts companies, I would like
to outline the essential factors that ultimately determine the value of a pot.
The guidelines that follow are intended to instruct without being too specific. It is more important at this point to understand the concepts stated
below than to immediately understand how they relate to specific pricing.

Exceptional, rare and large
Arequipa vase, 1912, decorated in
squeezebag with stylized yellow-
orange irises and green leaves on a
deep purple ground. (The best
example of Arequipa we've seen.)
One small bruise to base. In cobalt
on white, 670 Arequipa/California,
10" × 5", $74,750

## MAKER OR PRODUCER

Some potteries/potters developed a style of ware and others copied it. Some of the originators of those styles did it better and charged more for it when it was made. Some of the imitators made similar looking but less qualitative work and charged less. Current pricing almost always reflects these disparities. Rookwood Pottery, for example, was the premier factory for the Ohio Valley school of decorative ceramics. It was so successful in hand painting designs on art pottery that many other Ohio companies, such as the Roseville and Weller Potteries, made a name for themselves producing similar, but less expensive, work. As such, a vase by the Rookwood pottery will always be worth considerably more money than a similar piece by any of its imitators.

This is not to say that simply because a company or an artist invented a style that their work will automatically be worth more. Some would argue that pottery by Susan Frackelton is rarer, earlier, and more germinal than similar early work by the Newcomb Pottery. However, Frackelton's work seldom brings as much as good pieces by the latter, if only because it is so rare that building a consistent market for her work is difficult.

However, Rookwood and most of the originators of specific, regional styles such as Grueby or Teco Potteries have much more to offer than just being first. Rookwood, for instance, owned a corner of most of the best ceramic decorators, chemists, designers, and technical capabilities. It had a

Fine and large Rookwood Vellum vase, 1906, painted by Carl Schmidt with lavender and purple irises on a pink to celadon ground. Fine glaze bubbles around rim, pitting inside rim. Flame mark/VI/artist cipher/950C/V, 10¼" × 4½", $1,725

two-decade head start over its competitors and in every possible way manufactured a consistently superior ware.

## ARTIST/ARTISTRY

This is a tricky area of evaluation because the artist of an Owens vase or an Arequipa bowl is critically important. A. F. Best was one of the best slip decorators in Zanesville, Ohio for example, and his work at the Owens Pottery is consistently better than that of his peers.

Yet the designer of a Grueby or a Newcomb piece is far less essential than the eye appeal of the piece itself. You would be correct in thinking that the two notions should be linked, and they may well be, but this often has more to do with which pottery we're evaluating.

For example, Kataro Shirayamadani was arguably Rookwood's best artist, someone who designed a pot in the round instead of visualizing the surface as a flat canvas. Few of Rookwood's artists painted with such vision and few of them were comparable to Shirayamadani on even his worst day. You can be reasonably sure that if you have a vase decorated by this master, you are likely to have at least a very good pot. Yet, if you have a handsome piece of Rookwood with no artist signature, even if it appears to be by Shirayamadani, the value of the vase drops significantly.

On the other hand, if you compare 50 pieces of Grueby sitting juxtaposed on a shelf there is virtually no visual clue as to which artist's initials, if any, appear incised into the bottom. In fact, the total lack of an artist's signature will have no impact on the value of any of the pieces. While the artists who

Fine and unusual Rookwood Vellum bulbous vase by Kataro Shirayamadani, 1907, decorated with dragonflies on tall grasses in gray and white on a shaded yellow and blue-green ground. Seconded mark for glaze scaling around rim and glaze misses around base. Flame mark/VII/1097C/V/artist's cipher/X, 9¼" × 5½", $2,415

worked at Newcomb College have a slightly larger following, there are no collectors who are more concerned with what's under a Newcomb pot than what's happening on its surface.

## STYLE

The market for art pottery matured along with the taste of its collectors. While the Oriental and Classical precedents of the early, Victorian years were once in favor, the flowing lines of Art Nouveau and the bold simplicity of the Arts and Crafts have ultimately won out. Perhaps the easiest way to say this is that, once America's designers developed their own style and relied less on outside influences, they began to establish their own mastery of the medium. Today's best buyers are more than capable of distinguishing between the two.

If, for example, you compare a single blossom, a poppy, painted at the Rookwood Pottery in different styles over a 40 year period, you'll see in that image alone the maturation of the pottery's style and its development from imitator to innovator. A Victorian painter, circa 1890, will render a photorealistic flower, crisply detailed, in slip relief, under a brown overglaze. A decade later, reacting to the influence of Art Nouveau, the same flower would be painted, or perhaps lightly carved, into and above the surface of the pot, with the curving lines more exaggerated and the color bright under a clear, glossy finish.

A few years later, in about 1905, that poppy would be carved back in high relief, less florid in style, and finished unusually with only one or two matte colors. And, by 1925, you would see a starkly rendered, flat painted, simplified blossom in a way more consistent with contemporary graphic design. In short, Rookwood grew in its craft from copying to innovating ceramic design, and it is exactly this quality that kept it at the top of the field.

With this in mind, it is essential to remain abreast of what is currently revered by contemporary collectors, looking for decorative motifs and styles that are commanding the highest prices.

Rare Rookwood Limoges-style humidor with double-lid by Maria Longworth Nichols, 1882, painted with spiders and bats on a mottled ground. Base has 2" tight hairline from rim, outer lid has glaze bubble. Stamped Rookwood/1882/MLN, 6" × 6", $2,185

Fine Rookwood iris glaze bulbous vase by Lenore Asbury, 1905, painted with delicate pink dogwood blossoms and green leaves on a shaded gray-to-white ground. Seconded mark for 1" overglaze scratch. Flame mark/V/909BB/L.A./X, 10½" × 5½", $1,265

## FORM AND SIZE

This is one of the easiest areas to understand when determining the value of a pot. Open bowls, for example, show only a limited amount of artwork from a single vantage point, take up a good deal of space on a collector's shelf, and have to be placed at eye level to be appreciated. These are usually the least valuable form.

Fine and unusual Rookwood matte painted corseted vase by C. S. Todd, 1911, painted with three panels of flying birds in a blue sky on a brown ground. (Very nice). Flame mark/XI/1358E/C.S.T., 7" × 3¾", $1,495

Floor vases, those tall pots over 18" or 20", are usually the showiest and most attractive. The artists who labored over them, many years ago, knew they were designing a "statement" piece and seldom missed the opportunity to show off. And these same pots, often pulled "off the line" for exhibitions, usually sold for a great deal more than the average piece. For these reasons and more, they had to be better than average.

The average pot, however, is usually between 8" and 9" tall, and most of what we'll be working with in this book will use that as a standard. It is worth mentioning here that you can have an 8" pot that is 3" at its widest and one that is 6" or more across. Obviously, the more surface you have to look at, the more valuable it is likely to be.

Finally, it is worth noting that some forms are just prettier, and more desirable, than others. While the cylinder was used by all potteries, and often with satisfying results, it's seldom as valuable as the same painted idea on an undulating pot of the same dimensions.

## CONDITION

It's obvious that a perfect pot will always be worth at least something more than the same piece with even a minor defect, but not all damage is created equally. There are many kinds of damage, some occurring while the pot was being made and some imparted once it left the kiln. And there are all kinds of collectors, some who insist upon perfection and others who have learned to accept damage. Understanding various condition issues, and the expectations of collectors of such work, is a critical part of your learning curve.

Fine and large Rookwood scenic vellum bulbous vase by Ed Diers, 1922, depicting an autumn landscape with red-roofed buildings in the background. Three small chips to base. Flame mark/XXII/2523/V/ED, 17¾" × 8", $5,175

Rookwood iris glaze ovoid vase by
Caroline Steinle, 1906, painted
with an indigo iris and green leaves
against a shaded blue-green, ivory,
and yellow ground. Overall crazing.
Flame mark/VI/904E/artist's
cipher, 6¾" × 3", $1,610

Rookwood buyers, for example, are traditionally the pickiest collectors
in the market. In fact, the nature of the Rookwood Pottery and the work it
usually produced contribute to this mindset. A typical Rookwood vase, as described above, depicts a design hand painted onto the side of the ceramic vessel. While there were diversions into abstraction and impressionism, their
pottery's central thrust was focused on photo-realistic depictions of flowers,
landscapes, or whatever.

A Rookwood "Iris" glazed vase, for example, is crisply painted in relief
and coated with a clear, glossy finish. These were intended as lovely, show-
case pieces. If you pick one up and handle it you'll mar it with fingerprints.
Collectors who are attracted to this aesthetic have always been intolerant of
anything that interferes with their notion of visual perfection. The company
itself was one of the few that "seconded" pieces that had manufacturing
flaws, the sort of maladies that occasionally happened in the heat of the kiln.
A relatively minor surface flaw might reduce the value of a Rookwood vase
by 50 percent.

Grueby collectors, however, are an entirely different breed. Their understanding of, and attraction to, the organic naturalism of Arts and Crafts
pottery is more forgiving of minor imperfections, whether imparted before
or after manufacture. In the case of the Arts and Crafts potter George Ohr,
for example, whose goal was to make "no two pots alike," collectors have the
option of accepting a piece as it is or not having the "idea" at all. A small im-
perfection on an Ohr or Grueby vase might not even cause a reduction in
value by 10 percent.

Fine and large Grueby vase with five tooled and applied curled handles alternating with full-height leaves, under an excellent frothy matte green glaze. Small nick to one handle, 1" grinding chip. Circular pottery mark, 11¼" × 6½", $12,000–$16,000

There were over 200 art potteries working during the period, producing innumerable types and sizes of work, each capable of bearing countless flaws and imperfections. To provide some general pricing information to get you started, we'll end this section by focusing on seven of the major companies. In order to be practical, we are going to work with the following fixed variables:

*Form and size.* The average pot, as stated earlier, is about 8" tall and has some undulation of form (we're not talking about cylinders here…). You can assume, if you are trying to evaluate a larger or smaller piece, you should raise or lower the price accordingly.

George Ohr pinched and folded bisque pitcher of scroddled terra cotta and buff clays. Two large sanded chips to rim. Script signature, 4¼" × 5¼", $3,737

*Condition.* The following "examples" we'll be studying should be considered free of all post-manufacturing flaws and have only minor manufacturing defects, if any, as described below.

*Style.* The Grueby Pottery worked almost entirely in a single style. Rookwood, however, kept changing with the times. When the style of the pot we're examining is an issue it will be described as such.

*Quality of decoration/production.* All artists and potteries had good and bad days, and uneven kiln production. If we try to describe them all this book, it would be insufferably boring and of little value to you. For the sake of this exercise, let's assume the examples to follow are above average in quality. In the parlance of the trade, they rate a 7 on a 10 scale.

*Subject matter.* The design of a pot can vary greatly, especially with Ohio School companies which might choose anything from a fuzzy rabbit to an old master portrait to a bunch of roses. We'll stick with what you're most likely to find: in the case of Rookwood, a cluster of flowers; in Grueby, applied leaves and buds.

*Marks.* The purpose of this book is not to make experts of beginners but rather to assist beginners in their quest to establish some expertise. We can deal with unmarked pieces in another book. For now, assume the following examples are all clearly marked or possess enough distinguishing characteristics to make a formal mark unnecessary.

## Rookwood Pottery

Rookwood is the most difficult American pottery to evaluate for many reasons, but mostly because it worked for so many years in a variety of styles, each attracting different buyers and selling at different price levels. We'll

Rare Rookwood Limoges-style humidor with double-lid by Maria Longworth Nichols, 1882, painted with spiders and bats on a mottled ground. Base has 2" tight hairline from rim, outer lid has glaze bubble. Stamped Rookwood/1882/MLN, 6" × 6", $2,185

break this subchapter into several sections, giving pricing criteria and current market information for each.

## EARLY, VICTORIAN STYLED WORK

How the mighty have fallen. Thirty years ago, these early and historically important pieces were the darlings of collectors across the nation. Now, with rare exception, they have been relegated to a position just above production (nonartist decorated) work, with no change in sight.

I have covered in the Arts and Crafts Market Review section the reasons for this, so there is no need to repeat it here. Suffice it to say that these naive interpretations of French copies of Japanese and Chinese ceramics say much more about where Rookwood came from than where it was ultimately headed.

Nevertheless, Rookwood produced masterpieces from every period, and even average work from this time remained superior to that of it's American contemporaries. It is because of this that no Rookwood collection would be complete without at least an example or two of their Victorian creations.

For this brief study, let's work with a few assumptions. Once again, all pieces are 8" tall vase forms with no handles. Second, they are decorated by Rookwood factory employees, and not by local club members who purchased Rookwood blanks for out-of-factory production. Next, they should be totally free from defects, since Rookwood buyers are usually unreasonably implacable concerning damage.

Vase 1 is of average quality, with a smeared background in browns and smudges of black and white. The decoration is of birds and/or bats flying over black, painted bulrushes against an open sky. It is a typical piece, like the majority you'll see from this period: $450–$650.

Vase 2 is similar to vase 1 but the definition of the painted decoration is much crisper and a bit more imaginative. Rabbits, or perhaps a school of fish, are set against a background that works with, rather than against, the decoration. The overglaze is bright and crisp, setting a professional, polished look. The design encompasses the entire surface of the pot: $650–$950

Vase 3 has some of the attributes of the first two examples, but it employs another early technique, slip painting on a bisque ground. Instead of the smeary darker colors of most early work, the decoration here is set against a white, buff, or sometimes salmon pink field that is matte and coarse to the touch. The clarity is striking and the crispness of the painting is unhampered by overglaze. Values here rise and fall on background color (pinks and blues are best, creams and browns least valuable), decoration (puffy Japanese fish and Asians playing paddleball are better than a flock of bats swirling into the horizon), and quality of artistry. This piece is soft blue, and painted nicely with a small school of fish: $1000–$1500.

## LATER VICTORIAN ROOKWOOD

Much of the Rookwood available on the market is from this period. We call it standard glaze, or brown glaze ware, because it is typified by slip painted decoration under a clear, orange-brown overglaze. This technique was developed around 1885, and Rookwood continued its production until about 1910, though the use of it was on the decline after about 1903.

Brown glaze work bridges the naiveté of Rockwood's first period and the brilliance of its Art Nouveau work. The overall quality of the work is exceptional, the painting is the best in the country, if not the world, and the imagination of the artists shows some much-needed restraint. You will not see during this time, for example, pieces with crabs dancing with fishermen painted onto the side of a vase.

Prices for brown glaze Rookwood had languished for over a decade. It is just recently that they have shown signs of life, and even damaged pieces are regularly traded (though at no more than 50 percent of what perfect examples would bring). Assume that our three pieces have nicely shaded backgrounds of brown, green, and orange, bear normal crazing, and are otherwise typical of this ware.

Vase 1 is painted by Lenore Asbury, who was one of their reliable, if only average, artists. A spray of roses crosses the front and the painting is reasonably good, if not sharp and crisp: $300–$400.

Vase 2 is by Ed Diers, one of Rockwood's better artists, and he has chosen the same subject matter. His rendition of roses, however, is far more realistic, with detailing on leaves and a raised quality to the stems and thorns: $500–$600.

Vase 3 is by Kataro Shirayamadani and is the best example not only because his artistry is so good. In addition to the photo-realistic quality of the blossoms, the spray of roses is wrapped around the pot in a 360-degree dis-

Early Rookwood standard glaze light two-handled spherical vessel by Albert Valentien, 1888, decorated with floral swags. A couple of tight lines to rim, shallow spider lines to body (do not go through), overall crazing and some glaze bubbling to decoration. Flame mark/411/W/ A.R.V./L., 9" × 10¼", $1,000–$1,500

play of beauty and craft. This may be an 8" piece of brown glaze Rookwood, but you may not see another of this quality: $1000–$1500.

## ART NOUVEAU

Rookwood really hit its stride approaching 1900, at least partially because of a desire to compete at the Paris Exposition, introducing the new century. It was during this time, from about 1895 until about 1910, that Rookwood introduced, developed, and perfected a series of new lines and glazes, firmly establishing it as the premier hand-painted pottery in America, on par with the best Europe had to offer.

The lightly colored glazes Rockwood began using were a significant part of this change. Iris, which was its name for a clear high glaze finish, and Sea Green, a clear gloss with a light green tint, were two such innovations. Both of these allowed for more colors than the brown overglaze because the darkness of the latter masked the decoration.

The stylistic qualities of the artwork were an even greater factor. Instead of a straightforward painting onto the side of a pot, Art Nouveau work was more whiplash and curvilinear in nature. Also, it was during this time that the modeling, or carving, of the decoration became widely used. It is not hard to imagine the relative clarity of a flower that is painted in reds and yellows, under clear high glazes, and raised with gentle modeling. And it is also no surprise that such pieces have always brought so much money.

Assume here that our three examples are flawless, excepting minor crazing. We'll stick with clear high glazes, though the same idea might be found with a sea green or an aerial blue finish. Those would be worth from about three to five times more.

Exceptional Rookwood iris glaze bulbous vase painted by O.G. Reed, 1900, with fleshy mauve poppies with yellow centers on a shaded mauve-to-amber ground. (Pan American Exposition paper label.) Flame mark/900B/O.G.R./W. 9½" × 6" $9,775

Vase 1 is a handsome Iris glazed vase with tulip blossoms on a ground shading from black to gray to white. It was decorated by Sallie Coyne and dates to about 1900. $850–$1250.

Vase 2 is considerably better, with wisteria blossoms painted by Sara Sax, one of Rockwood's best decorators. The background is also more interesting and shades from green to yellow. This is a handsome pot: $2250–$2750.

Vase 3 is exceptional, even for an 8" vase. Painted by Carl Schmidt, a premier artist, the pot is covered with poppy blossoms and pods on a pink to cream to pastel green ground: $4000–$5000.

## ARTS AND CRAFTS

Rookwood was not an Arts and Crafts company, though it worked in this popular style for about a decade. It understood the look, even if it was unwilling to undertake the expense of a totally handmade production. Pots, for example, were molded rather than hand thrown. And even though individual decorators designed pieces, they were still products of a production line where different people cast, decorated, finished, and fired pieces. A true Arts and Crafts studio attempted to minimize the number of hands involved in the making of a piece.

Not all of Rookwood's artists worked in the Arts and Crafts style, and there were several types of this ware, including painted mattes, modeled mattes, and incised mattes. We'll use modeled mattes for pricing examples, since these are readily available and most consistent with Arts and Crafts design.

Fine Rookwood Carved Matte vase by Rose Fecheimer, 1905, deeply modeled with oak branches in green, brown and burgundy on a brown butterfat ground. Flame mark/V/951C/R.F., 10½" × 4¼", $3,220

Vase 1 is a relatively sedate piece, decorated by Albert Pons in tones of green with a single large blossom deeply carved on one side. There is very little color variation: $650–$950.

Vase 2 is also by Pons, though there are deeply modeled fish and the use of secondary coloring to highlight details: $850–$1,250.

Vase 3 is by Rose Fecheimer, one of Rookwood's best modelers, and the pot is covered with hollyhock in reds and yellows on green stalks on a brown matte ground. The definition and modeling are excellent: $1,750–$2,250.

## Grueby

Grueby is one of the premier potteries of the Arts and Crafts movement, and its work is almost completely different from that produced by Rookwood. Where Rookwood was attempting a photo-realistic approach, hand painting decoration onto a pot's surface, Grueby was exploring the organic naturalism of the ceramic arts, employing vegetal forms and finishes.

We'll describe Grueby's work a bit more in the corresponding chapter later in this book. For now, it is important to know that its ware is always hand thrown, and almost always covered with matte glazes, which are green 90 percent of the time. Further, when these pieces are decorated, the designs are always imparted entirely by hand.

Minor damage has little impact on the value of a Grueby pot. The modeling on leaf edges is often so sharp, and the relatively low fire employed by the company left pots so "soft," that at least minor edge damage is inevitable. We'll do two studies of the most common decorated ware, those with two or more colors and those of a single color. Single-color Grueby pieces outnumber multiple-color pots by about eight to one.

### SINGLE COLOR

Vase 1 is a simple, cylinder form with tall, spade-shaped leaves tooled and applied to the surface. They cover about 80 percent of the pot: $2,000–$3,000.

Vase 2 is similar to Vase 1, though the vase has a bulbous middle and there are now small, tooled flower buds alternating with the rows of leaves: $2,500–$3,500.

Vase 3 is a more interesting shape, flaring gently to a flat shoulder, which closes quickly to a small, rolled lip. The leaves overlap, and the glaze is rich and even: $4,000–$5,000.

### MORE THAN ONE COLOR

Vase 1 is exactly like Vase 2 in the single-color category above, except the yel-

Unusual Grueby spherical vessel, crisply decorated with tooled and applied pointed leaves under a curdled dark green matte glaze. Remnant of paper label, 4¼" × 4½", $4,600

low bud between each leaf is a crisp, soft yellow. This vase is now worth $4,500–$6,500.

Vase 2 is more of the same, though the form is more bulbous at the bottom and it has a flared rim. What makes this better is the iris blossom at the top, which is far more complicated, and rarer, than a simple bud. It too is crisply fired in light yellow: $8,000–$12,000.

Vase 3 is a special piece of Grueby, with three panels of narcissus, one in yellow, the second in blue, and the third in red. The color is fairly even, with only a trace of color run from the heat of the kiln: $12,500–$17,500.

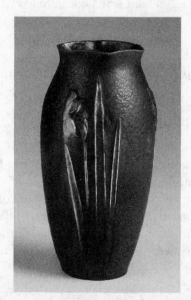

Exceptional and rare Grueby four-color ovoid vase with floriform rim, decorated with tooled and applied daffodils in yellow, blue and burgundy, with narrow leaves, covered in a frothy matte green glaze. Paper label and LFH, 11" × 5", $12,650

## Newcomb College

An adjunct of Tulane University, Newcomb produced art pottery for nearly 50 years. This has been a collector favorite since 1970, and prices have risen steadily since that time. Work by no other makers have so consistently increased in value, and it is considered one of the Blue Chip American potteries.

Newcomb College produced primarily two types of work, early high gloss (prior to about 1910) and the later matte (until closing). There are exceptions to this but, for now, this is sufficient to get some handle on pricing.

Newcomb's work did not employ a large range of colors. Most pieces from all periods favor tones of blue, with white and/or green often added for contrast. The addition of yellow, pink, or violet is unusual and always adds some value.

One of the more interesting trends in pottery collecting over the last decade is increased collector tolerance toward damage. Newcomb was a true Arts and Crafts ware; each piece was hand thrown and handcrafted. While the pottery certainly repeated designs, especially during its later years, each piece is one of a kind. Because of this, small chips, drill holes, interior lines that barely migrate to the rim or foot, and bruises to edges might decrease the value of a piece by only 25 percent. If you really like the way a piece looks, you have to either buy it or learn to do without it. If the pot is a masterpiece, it may lose only 10 percent of its value.

Damaged Newcomb is very collectible, and it's nice to know that a damaged pot is worth 75 percent of what it would bring in perfect condition. But that does you little good if no one wants to buy it at the price. During the 1990's , flawed Newcomb became easy to sell and prices for damaged work increased by 300 percent.

We'll examine pricing for the two main types of Newcomb ware available on the market. The early high-glazed work is relatively rare and nearly always expensive. Matte Newcomb was made for decades and outnumbers the early work by about 10 to 1.

### MATTE NEWCOMB POTTERY (FROM ABOUT 1912–35)

Vase 1 is a typical floral pot, the shape of an elongated corset. It is fairly narrow, and the work is gently carved around the top. The background is light blue and the blossom, a jonquil, is in soft white: $1,500–$2,000.

Vase 2 is a more bulbous form but the decoration is better, depicting a stylized bayou scene carved with some strength, giving the illusion of depth. The colors are bolder, with medium to dark blues and hints of feathered green for the moss in the trees. This is better than most of these plentiful "moon and moss" scenes: $5,000–$7,500.

Vase 3 is a most lovely piece of Newcomb, another bayou scene, with top-

Newcomb College transitional corseted vase by A. F. Simpson, 1917, carved with jonquils under a lavender glaze; 2½" × 2" glaze inconsistency, NC/AFS/272/JM/IN91, 5¾" × 5", $2,070

to-bottom, 360-degree decoration of live oaks and dripping moss. There is great depth to the carving, and the detailing in the bark of the tree and the modeling in the leaves is exceptional. The colors in the trees, dark blues and contrasting greens, are nicely offset by the limited use of soft pink in the horizon: $7,500–$10,000.

## HIGH GLAZED NEWCOMB POTTERY (FROM ABOUT 1896–1908)

Vase 1 is a relatively simple piece, another corset form with decoration surface painted around the upper third. The decoration, of medium blue freesia outlined in cobalt, is rendered flat against a white ground: $4000–$5000.

Fine and early Newcomb College high-glaze tapering bud vase by Leona Nicholson, 1906, decorated with a band of cicada in ochre and green against a blue ground. In ink, NC/AZ84/LN, 6¼" × 2½", $13,800

Vase 2 is better than our first example in several ways. First, the pot is more bulbous in form, allowing for more surface to decorate. Next, the iris blossoms on the pot are fleshier and provide a romantic remembrance of the fleur-de-lis of which New Orleans remains proud. The decoration is not restricted to just the top, as the stems and leaves reach the bottom rim. More important, there is gentle modeling to the design, giving it dimension and clarity. The colors remain blue on a white ground: $10,000–$15,000.

Vase 3 is short of a masterpiece, but not by a lot. Large lily blossoms, in soft yellow, are carved deeply into the top of this pot. Their stems, in medium green and outlined in dark green, reach the bottom. The background color is soft blue: $20,000–$30,000.

## George Ohr Pottery

Pricing Ohr's work is mostly an exercise in futility. Each piece was intentionally different; this was a point of pride for George. This becomes more complicated when throwing into the mix the individual tastes of the people collecting his work. People who buy Ohr are not your average pottery collectors.

These are collectors who have an eye for the abstract, and who are more interested in being challenged by this master's strange and beguiling style. Ohr played with glazes and forms, with an inquisitive and sometimes bawdy mind. These quirks resulted in a body of work that was as likely to include teapots as it was puzzle mugs or brothel tokens.

Minor damage has relatively little impact on the value of an Ohr pot. There are several reasons for this. Ohr's work was disregarded for six decades, where for much of that time it sat unprotected in the attic above his sons' auto repair shop. More was damaged while shipping it north when it was bought en masse by a New Jersey barber/antiques dealer. Further, Ohr is the thinnest of the American potteries and was fired at low temperatures. It is easily chipped or cracked.

But these are reasons why you're likely to find some damage on an Ohr pot. These flaws have little impact on value because of the uniqueness of each vessel. Ohr was mostly a one-on-one kind of guy, involved with the process of each piece from digging the clay to stacking the kiln. If you like the way a piece looks, buy it at some price because you'll not likely see another.

We'll explore three types of Ohr pottery here, to give you some idea of pricing structure and the difficulty establishing that. Though he created many masterpieces, about 60 percent of his work was just good. Our first grouping will focus on these. We'll contrast these simple pots with a selection of teapots and finally a trio of interesting, hand-sized vase forms.

One more note: Ohr's pots average about 4–5" in height. For this category only, I'll provide dimensions.

## OHR'S MORE COMMON WARE

Vase one is a 5" tall straight-sided vase with a gently flaring rim, covered in a matte, pebbly black finish. It is well thrown and the condition is excellent, but it is simple and unchallenging: $800–$1,200.

Vase 2 is slightly better, with a mottled brown and green high-gloss finish over a more tapered body. It too is 5" tall and there is a gentle waviness to the top rim: $1,500–$2,000.

Vase 3 is the best of the lot, with a bulbous top that has been dimpled by Ohr's fingertips. The glaze is black but it has a glittery gunmetal quality. It is bigger than most at 6" tall: $2,500–$3,000.

## OHR'S MORE INTERESTING POTS

Vase 1 is only 4" tall, but there is a deep twist in its body, and the flared rim is crimped. The basic glazing is yellow but there are large brown polka dots over the surface: $3,000–$4,000.

Vase 2 is slightly larger at 5", and the body also has a twisted center. The glaze is light blue, however, and there are some red and green spots drizzled down its side. This pot has a lot of eye appeal: $4,500–$6,500.

Vase 3 is an excellent, if small, piece of Ohr. Bulbous in form, there is a twist in its center and the top is folded and pleated in a complicated but pleasing manner. It is encased in a rich red finish with some black and dark green drippings. It is only 4 1/2" tall, but it feels like a much larger piece: $7,500–$10,000.

## BISQUE WORK

About a quarter of Ohr pottery was never glazed, mostly because he seemed to think it was fine as it was.

Exceptional George Ohr pinched and folded pitcher covered in a rare amber and green-speckled purple leathery matte glaze. A couple of minor nicks and two small chips (restored) on rim. Script signature, 4½" × 5½", $17,250

Fine and large George Ohr bulbous vase with crimped rim, of buff bisque clay. A couple of small nicks to rim and restoration to two chips at base. Script signature, 5½" × 5¾", $3,220

Vase 1 is a simple globular form of buff clay with no damage and a clear mark. It measures about 5" tall: $650–$950.

Vase 2 is not much larger at 6", but there is a deep in-body twist and there is some black and brown toning from the heat of the kiln, giving more life to the simple buff finish: $2,000–$3,000.

Vase 3 is scroddled, or of mixed clays of brown, red, and cream. You might want to consider the piece a vase, but it's hard to tell what the shape was meant to be or how you would even use it. It is about 4" tall by 5" across: $4,000–$6,000.

## TEAPOTS

Ohr explored the teapot form, playing with the idea in novel ways.

Teapot 1 is a simple piece with a body the size of a large navel orange. Attached to one side is a simple "pulled" handle and, to the other, a molded serpentine spout. It is covered in a deep, mirrored brown: $3,000–$4,000.

Teapot 2 is a "cadogan," or a bottom-loading pot that was never really intended for use. Ohr made a selection of perhaps 20 of these and this one falls in the middle in quality. There is some decorative tooling to the surface and the piece is covered in a rich royal blue glossy finish. The top is fused to the body of the pot to render it unusable. It is about 7" tall: $7,500–$10,000.

Teapot 3 is a larger form with an elongated serpentine spout and a double-kink handle. The glaze is pink with an orange peel texture, with feathered orange running through it. It is short of a great teapot, but better than 90 percent of these studies. It measures about 5" high by about 9" to the tips: $30,000–$40,000.

# Fulper Pottery

Ceramics by Fulper are one of the most collectible of the American art potteries for several reasons. Fulper made mostly handsome and creative ware, produced in quantity for over 20 years. It produced pottery in several styles during that time, ranging from austere Arts and Crafts pots to Oriental and then finally Art Deco works.

Prices vary considerably based on style, size, and glazing but, even at their most expensive, holloware pieces have remained available on the market and reasonable in price. There are exceptions here, such as their early ceramic and leaded glass lamps. But 95 percent of what Fulper made sells for under $1,000.

We'll chronologically examine the three major types of Fulper pottery. It is worth noting that most of the best work was made prior to World War I, and that most of the least interesting ware was produced during, and after, the Great Depression.

## EARLY FULPER VASEKRAFT WARE

Vase 1 is a faceted, cylindrical vase with a gunmetal to beige flambé glaze. Like nearly all early Fulper, the piece is molded and fairly heavy: $200–$300.

Vase 2 is broader than our first example, with two handles at the top. The finish is more interesting, employing one of Fulper's best combinations. A white semigloss glaze drips unevenly over a mustard matte ground: $400–$600.

Fulper "Mushroom" vase covered in an ivory-to-elephant's breath flambé glaze. Restoration to two hairlines at rim to top of windows. Rectangular ink mark, 9¾" × 4¼", $575

Vase 3 is only about 8" tall but nearly 10" around. There is a mirrored black finish dripping in sheets over a deep Chinese blue flambé. It has the appearance and feel of a "serious" piece of their work: $1,000–$1,500.

## MIDDLE-PERIOD FULPER WARE

Vase 1 is bulbous with faceted sides and a short, faceted neck. It shows a thin, light green cucumber crystalline finish ending in flambé with a light brown high glaze. This is a good, but not a great, rendition of this combination: $300–$400.

Vase 2 is a bulbous three-handled piece with a footed base and a collar rim. It shows a brilliant copper dust crystalline finish, one of the pottery's premier glazes. Again, about 8" high, it is about 8" across: $650–$950.

Vase 3 is the pick of the litter, nearly 14" tall with gently flaring sides and a rolled rim. It also has one of their best glaze combinations, a deep rich cat's eye flambé of browns and creams: $1,000–$1,500.

## LATER FULPER WARE

All these pieces, in addition to bearing the later, horizontal mark, weigh about 25 percent less than the earlier examples. This is typical of its late pottery.

Vase 1 is an adaptation of an earlier form, with flaring sides and two small handles at the top. It has a later, thinner, blue flambé with some crystals. It's pretty dull: $150–$250.

Vase 2 is a flaring vase with a reticulated collar and a flaring foot. There is vertical fluting to the body and the glaze is a pale green flambé: $200–$300.

Fine and large Fulper tapering vase covered in a mirror black-to-copper dust crystalline flambé glaze. (Perfectly fired.) Incised racetrack mark, 12½" × 7", $2,990

Two Fulper pieces: a two-handled bowl and a spherical vessel, both covered in Chinese blue crystalline flambé glaze. Restoration to hairline on bowl. Ink racetrack and horizontal marks, 3½" and 4½", $258

Vase 3 is one of Fulper's best later works, with embossed decoration of women and fruit covering its body. It is about 11" tall. The glaze is also a later version of the moss to rose flambé: $500–$750.

The above examples are intended to augment the specialized sections, and the prices, that follow. I again encourage you to buy books and auction catalogs and go online, to see as many examples and prices as you have the appetite for. And remember that all of these markets are moving targets, with prices changing from year to year.

# THE POTTERIES

## Arequipa Pottery

SHOPMARKS: Early: Painted, in blue, on white, with a pot under a tree. Early: Incised into bottom, with a pot under a tree. Later: Impressed, with a pot under a tree.

PRINCIPAL CONTRIBUTION: Decorated and undecorated pottery and tiles

FOUNDERS: Dr. Philip King Brown and Henry E. Bothin, benefactors of the Arequipa Sanitorium. Frederick H. Rhead, first director. Albert L. Solon, second director.

STUDIOS AND SALESROOMS: Arequipa Pottery, Arequipa Sanitorium, Fairfax, California 1911—18.

> "All the work is done by hand; everything, throwing the vase, drying, baking, decorating being done slowly, with individual interest. The larger pieces are thrown by a man, but the rest of the work is done by the girls, who when they first come are not able to work more than an hour a day."
>
> —the Craftsman, 1913.[1]

There are many similarities between the Arequipa Pottery of Fairfax, California, and the Marblehead Pottery of Marblehead, Massachusetts. The Marblehead experiment, which began in 1904, introduced potting, woodworking, weaving, and other crafts, as therapies for patients recovering from nervous breakdowns. Dr. Philip Brown and Henry E. Bothin were initially inspired by that experiment's success. Further, and the remaining materials from both these ventures bears this out, the pottery each produced was easily the most artistically successful aspect of their output.

Unfortunately, Arequipa was dissimilar in two important ways which ultimately led to its demise. For one, the Marblehead Pottery, under the supervision of Arthur E. Baggs, was separated from the medical institution. This allowed Baggs to both become an owner of the venture and ensure consistent leadership throughout his tenure there. When Arequipa tried this in 1913, things did not go as smoothly.

Frederick Rhead, one of the stalwarts of the American art pottery movement, came to Arequipa with an impressive background. He worked first in the Ohio valley as a designer and decorator at famous companies such as Roseville, Weller, and Avon. He then cut a swath through the decorative arts community, partnering a pottery with William P. Jervis in New York and sharing a wheel with the likes of Adelaide Robineau and Taxile Doat at the University City Pottery in St. Louis, Mo. By the time he arrived in Fairfax, Rhead was a formidable presence in American decorative ceramics.

In spite of his pedigree, however, Rhead experienced problems with the transition from workshop within the sanitarium to a work force of young female patients recovering from tuberculosis. He left a few months later, and the corporation was dissolved in 1915. The sanitarium's directors again assumed responsibility for the venture, which continued in their hope that the "sale of the pottery would help finance (the patients') hospitalization at the Arequipa Sanitorium."[2]

The pottery's second director, Albert L. Solon, improved the glazes it employed. Pieces from the end of Rhead's stay at Arequipa bore dull matte, and often listless, finishes. While using the same local clays that Rhead employed, Solon introduced an array of coatings, including a fairly modern high gloss crackled flambé. Also, Rhead specialized in squeezebag decoration, a technique he brought to America from England and continued to perfect at his stops between Ohio and California.

Solon, however, was equally challenged by the turnover of patient-workers at the pottery. The time required for the young women to become competent at making pottery was usually equal to that required to recover from the ailments that brought them to Arequipa in the first place. Since the

Early Arequipa mark

Late Arequipa mark

Exceptional, rare and large Arequipa vase, 1912, decorated in squeezebag with stylized yellow-orange irises and green leaves on a deep purple ground. (The best example of Arequipa we've seen.) One small bruise to base. In cobalt on white, 670 Arequipa/California, 10" × 5", $74,750

facility tended to treat only mild cases of tuberculosis, a majority of its patients remained there for less than half a year.[3]

    The quality of Arequipa work varied greatly for several reasons. First, Rhead was a world-class decorator and innovator, and by the time he got to California he was doing the best work of his career. Pieces bearing his hand are of superior quality and bring often startling prices. The bulk of work at Arequipa, however, was done by the facilities newly trained patients. As one might expect, these are uneven at best, and seldom remarkable. Finally,

Tall and unusual Arequipa baluster vase, ca. 1916, from the Salon period carved with arabesques and curlicues under a sheer green and turquoise glossy glaze. Hand-incised GC/Arequipa/illegible markings, 13½" × 6", $3,500–$4,500

Solon's creations were second only to Rhead's, though of a style that spoke more of what Arts and Crafts had become, rather than what it had been. Contemporary collectors of Arequipa's work have yet to warm to Solon's pieces, and prices reflect this limited interest.

Solon left in 1916 to accept a teaching position at what is now known as California State University at San Jose. Fred H. Wilde, his successor, brought considerable experience in the development of new glazes and established Arequipa as a resource for fine decorative tile. The outbreak of World War I soon brought the venture, like many American producers, to a close.

### SELECTED PRICES

Vase, 1912, decorated in squeezebag w/yellow-orange irises on purple ground; bruise to base, 10" × 5"; This piece brought a record price of $74,750.

Vase, baluster ca. 1916, Solon period, carved w/arabesques and curlicues under sheer green and turquoise glossy glaze, 13½" × 6", $4,000.

Vase, gourd-shaped covered in matte olive green glaze, 6" × 5", $750.

Four-tile section designed by Frank Ingerson, in Cuenca w/bird of paradise in blue, green, orange w/flowers and vinery on ochre matte ground each 6" × 6½", $12,500.

Bowl w/tin-glazed border and central medallion of fruit/leaf motif on white semi-matte ground; couple short lines to rim 2½" × 6½.", $2,150.

Arequipa bulbous vase carved with eucalyptus leaves and covered in a seafoam green matte glaze, the brown clay showing through. Stamped AREQUIPA/ 10?/136, incised B.L., 5¼" × 3¾", $4,312

Large vase designed and executed by Frederick Rhead, 1912, carved w/full length lotus leaves under matte blue-grey glaze; minute nick to edge of one leaf $12\frac{1}{2} \times 7\frac{1}{4}$", $15,500.

Bulbous vase carved w/eucalyptus leaves and in seafoam green matte glaze, brown clay showing through, $5\frac{1}{4}$" $\times 3\frac{3}{4}$", $1,250.

Bulbous vase possibly by Frederick Wilde, carved w/blossoms and leaves under speckled light blue matte glaze, $6\frac{1}{4}$" $\times 5\frac{1}{2}$", $1,250.

Cabinet vase by Frederick Rhead, decorated in squeezebag w/holly leaves and berries against matte, mottled blue ground, $3\frac{1}{2}$" $\times 2\frac{1}{2}$", $2,500.

## Brouwer Pottery

SHOPMARKS: Incised or impressed arch formed by two whale jawbones, over the letter M and/or FLAME incised in script and/or incised "flames" and/or the incised name Brouwer (which appears after 1903)

PRINCIPAL CONTRIBUTIONS: Ceramic vases, bowls, and teapots, mostly covered with Brouwer's brilliant orange and gold lustered, usually glossy, finishes

FOUNDER: Theophilus A. Brouwer, 1864–1932. Pottery from 1894 to 1946.

STUDIOS AND SALESROOMS: Middle Lane Pottery, East Hampton, New York, 1894–1902. Brouwer Pottery, West Hampton, New York, 1903–1946.

"With regard to the manner of my discovering this 'Fire Painting', I am frequently asked if it was by accident. It certainly was not, unless one considers seeing a bit of iridescent color on the bottom of a little sand crucible an accident. I saw this bit of color and determined to find out how it got there. It took me months of hard work, literally day and night before my muffle furnace door."
—T. A. Brouwer, 1917[1]

One would learn much by comparing the work of Theophilus to that of Hugh C. Robertson, of the Chelsea and Dedham potteries. Both seemed more interested in their craft than in the marketing of it. Moreover, they were primarily concerned with glazing rather than potting, and the quality of the vessels they used were clearly the least of their contributions. Both men oversaw small operations, though Robertson did have some assistance at Dedham and was in business with his brothers at Chelsea Keramic.

Brouwer was also similar to other major figures on the horizon: Henry Mercer, of the Moravian Tile Works in Doylestown, Pennsylvania, and Charles Rohlfs, the furniture maker from Rochester, New York, because his interest extended beyond the kind of art for which he became most famous. Mercer, like

Brouwer, was also an architect and a potter, and they both constructed at least part of their homes using the same reinforced concrete technique.

His vibrant, revolutionary glazing is where Brouwer was in a class of his own. His fire-painting technique, as described years ago in a conversation with a descendant, was to grasp a vessel with a pair of tongs, dip it into a glaze solution, and then expose the piece directly to the fire of the kiln. It was said that Brouwer could put a white clay pot into the kiln and, by reintroducing the piece again and again to the fire, could change the colors from gold, to orange, to green, and back to the white clay of the body. Contrary to what we had believed for years, it was a very controlled process.

Brouwer separated his work into five categories:

*Fire Painting:* The most available of his work, though still quite rare. Would produce a variety of mottled colors under a high glaze.

*Iridescent Fire Painting:* A similar technique resulting in one primary color with a rougher texture, with more iridescence.

*Kid Surface:* A matte finish of solid colors such as brown, white, blue, and gray.

*Sea-Grass Fire Painting:* With lines that look like sea grass in tones of green, brown, and gray on a plain ground.

*Gold Leaf Underglaze:* The rarest, and most attractive, of Brouwer's work, where real gold leaf was applied between two layers of colored glaze before the final firing.

Brouwer moved his pottery in 1903 into a structure he designed and partially built. He soon developed his flame painting technique, which is his most consistently fine and available creation. Brouwer was said to have destroyed the molds of pieces he felt were successful, though the large number of shapes that remain in modern day collections, and their repetition, suggests otherwise.

Large and exceptional Brouwer baluster-shaped vase flame-painted in orange, yellow and brown lustered glaze, with a thick bronze glaze dripping on the neck and shoulder. Firing line and flat chip under base, minor scratches to body, glaze flakes to rim. Incised wishbone mark and Flame, remnant of paper label, 12" × 7¼", $8,625

It should also be noted that, on rare occasion, Brouwer attached modeled flower or vegetal forms to his pots. These are usually larger pieces and often bear his very best glazes. They continue to command great interest from collectors.

After 1911 Brouwer's interests focused elsewhere. While a corporation was formed in 1925 to promote his fire painted pottery, it does not seem to have been successful in increasing production of Brouwer's ware. The corporation folded in 1946, 14 years after Brouwer's death.

## SELECTED PRICES

Vase, baluster-shaped, flame painted in orange, yellow, brown lustered glaze, w/thick bronze dripping to neck; firing line and chip under base, minor scratches to body, glaze flecks to rim, 12" × 7¼", $8,500.

Vase, classically shaped with flat shoulder, in flame painted vermillion glaze; several small flecks to rim and base, 6¼" × 5¾", $1,250.

Spherical cabinet vase in flame painted chartreuse and brown glaze, 3¾" × 3", $850.

Bulbous vase with closed-in rim, flame painted in amber, orange, yellow, and brown; minor flecks to rim and base 5¼" × 5½", $600.

Tapering vessel, flame painted in yellow, amber and bright brown glaze. Restoration to drill hole in base and side, shallow flakes and touch-up to rim, 5½" × 5½", $400.

Elongated vase w/flat shoulder, flame painted in purple, amber and yellow. Small nicks around rim, 6" × 4", $650.

Vase w/flat shoulder, flame painted in amber, green and yellow, 3½" × 4", $500.

Squat vase, flame-painted in yellow, orange and purple; chip to rim, glaze flakes to shoulder, 4" × 5", $350.

## Byrdcliffe Pottery

PRINCIPAL CONTRIBUTIONS: Handmade pottery bowls, vases, and tiles.

The Byrdcliffe Colony was one of a number of artists' havens that sprung up in different parts of America during the 20th century. Started by Ralph Radcliffe-Whitehead in about 1903, it was similar to other communities such as Rose Valley, in Delaware County, Pennsylvania, that produced ceramics, paintings, furniture, and other handmade goods.

The furniture shop eventually failed, but the pottery operation, headed by Edith Penman and Elizabeth R. Hardenbergh, operated until 1928. They fired some of the pottery in the nearby kilns of fellow artist Charles Volkmar.[1]

Studio ventures are small by nature and ceramic output is relatively small. Byrdcliffe was no exception to this, and its work remains relatively rare. Sometimes, however, rarity helps to keep prices down, particularly if the work is less than extraordinary. It's difficult to generate collector interest

Fine and rare Byrdcliffe faience tile, hand painted with a cottage and its lush garden in polychrome glaze. Signed Byrdcliffe, 5½" sq., $1,092

if there is little to buy, and less to get excited about when the opportunities arise. This is the best way to describe the market for Byrdcliffe ware.

About half of the pottery made by the firm was undecorated, and most of its decorated ware is surface painted with flowers or fruit, to blurry effect. The best pieces have stylized landscapes.

Damage significantly affects pricing, with a single chip reducing value by about 50 percent

### SELECTED PRICES

Faience tile, hand-painted w/a cottage and its lush garden in polychrome glaze, 5½" sq, $1,150.

## Clewell

SHOPMARKS: Etched "Clewell" into the metal jacket under the pot. Impressed Clewell Metal Art/Canton, O.

PRINCIPAL CONTRIBUTION: Line of bronze- or copper-coated pottery, often on blanks from other companies such as the Weller and Owens potteries.

FOUNDER: Charles Walter Clewell. Born: ca. 1876, died: 1965, founded: ca. 1906, closed: 1965.

STUDIOS AND SALESROOMS: Clewell Ware, Canton, Ohio, 1906-55.

> "A number of years ago, while visiting the Wadsworth Atheneum in Hartford, I saw a small bronze wine jug in the J. Pierpont Morgan Memorial Collection. The bronze had been found at Boscoreale during the excavations, which led to the finding of the famous silver treasure of the Louvre, was accredited to the Romans and dated 200 B.C. It was blue; a wonderful blue varying from the very light tones through turquoise to almost black with flecks of green and rustlike brown and spots of bare darkened metal."
> —Charles W. Clewel[1]

Unlike nearly all of the most respected craftsmen, artists, and designers associated with the art pottery movement in America, Charles Walter Clewell was not a potter. In truth, he was a metalsmith who developed a secret formula and technique for adhering thin layers of copper, silver, or bronze on the outside of fired earthenware vases, bowls, mugs, bookends, and similar wares.

The idea was not novel. Metalsmiths had for centuries applied copper, silver, and other metal overlays to pottery and ceramics, but according to Paul Evans, "Clewell's work appears to have been the first of the period to to-

tally mask the ceramic body with a metal coating (a technique later employed in the production of Tiffany's Bronze Pottery)."[2]

Judging from the forms and marks, it appears that Clewell purchased biscuit wares (earthenware that has been fired once in the kiln) from a number Ohio potteries, including Cambridge, Weller, and Owens. Using a process that has never been revealed, Clewell would then deposit a thin coating of metal, either copper, bronze, or silver, over the entire exterior of the piece. As he perfected his technique, Clewell was able to duplicate both the hand-hammered effect that was popular during the Arts and Crafts movement and the appearance of metal rivets.

Not content with simply achieving a durable bond between the metal and the pottery, Clewell initiated experiments that he continued throughout his career in an attempt to achieve a variety of natural-looking patinas on the metal. In referring to the bronze wine jug in the L. Pierpont Morgan Collection, Clewell said, "Seeing this little jug cost me more than two years of experimenting and a number of trips to Hartford to compare results, but finally the perfect blue appeared. It was a long hunt and particularly difficult; textbooks gave me no help."[3] The particular blue patina he had been seeking began appearing on his bronze coatings after 1923, but he continued to work at perfecting his techniques for both the bluish green patina on bronze and a matte green oxidation on copper.

Since he preferred to work alone and at his own pace, Clewell's production was quite limited. His technique and his patination formulas were, according to his wishes, destroyed upon his death in 1965.

Clewell values are most often judged by the condition of the colored patinas applied to the metal. The most valuable of these are orange or blue, or particularly a combination of the two. Wear, scratches, or peeling will re-

Fine and rare Clewell tall copper-clad vase with reticulated collar embossed with three poppy pods in high relief and blooming poppy (on Weller blank). Medium dark patina. Clewell stamp mark and remnant of paper label, 13¼" × 5½", $4,887

duce value by nearly 50% unless it's minor. Cleaning of the patina, to the point of revealing the brown of the copper, will reduce value by 60% and render a piece virtually unsaleable.

It is important to note that some Clewell pieces, particularly those on exceptional Art Nouveau blanks, didn't come with brightly colored patinas. Such vases,with heavily embossed decoration of poppies, Egyptian women, or stark, futuristic stylization, were patinated simply in dark brown.

## SELECTED PRICES

Copper-clad ovoid vessel w/verdigris patina, 11" × 7½" $1,250

Copper-clad tall baluster vase w/verdigris patina, 11" × 5". $1,000

Copper-clad classically shaped vase w/verdigris patina, 12" × 5" dia. $1,400

Copper-clad classically shaped vase w/bronze and verdrigris patina; scarring to surface, 8½" × 3½" $550

Copper-clad tapering vessel w/verdigris patina, 4½" × 4½", $600

Copper-clad punchbowl w/10 cups, w/faux-riveted exterior and porcelain interior, 9½" × 13", $1,000

Copper-clad mug w/riveted texture; minor dent to rim, 4½" × 5" $40

Tall copper-clad faceted vase in excellent verdigris and bronze patina, 10" × 3½", $1,400

Classically shaped copper-clad vase w/fine brown to verdigris patina, 8½" × 7". $1,250

Large copper-clad vase w/flat shoulder in fine verdigris patina, 10" × 5", $1,150

Copper-clad classically shaped vase in fine verdigris patina, 8¾" × 7", $1,250

Copper clad vase w/squat base in verdigris patina. 10¼"x4½", $1,000

Copper-clad ovoid vase in verdigris patina, 6" × 3", $500

Copper-clad spherical vase in verdigris and bronze patina, 5" × 4¼", $875

Copper clad small jardiniere in good verdigris and bronze patina, 5¼" × 6½", $1,000

Copper-clad vase w/reticulated collar embossed w/three poppy pods in high relief and blooming poppy. Medium dark patina, 13¼" × 5½", $3,000

Copper-clad classically shaped vase, good bronze and verdigris patina; some scarring to surface, 8½" × 3½", $550

Copper-clad vessel w/bronze and verdigris patina; pea-sized colored spot near base, 8½" × 5", $800

Copper-clad ovoid vase in verdigris patina; couple of small patina flakes near base, 7½" × 3¾", $750

Copper-clad ovoid vase w/fine bronze and verdigris patina, 7½" × 3½", $875

Copper-clad bulbous vase w/flaring rim, in bronze to verdigris patina, 7½" × 3½", $625

Copper-clad classically shaped vase w/bronze to verdigris patina; few small flakes to verdigris and some splits to copper on neck, 14½" × 6¼", $2,650

Copper-clad vase w/flat shoulder, in striated gold, green, and copper patina; minor ceramic loss inside rim 11" × 7¾", $750

## Clifton Art Pottery

SHOPMARKS: Incised or impressed CLIFTON or CLIFTON POTTERY/ NEWARK.

Indian ware may have reference to the location of the tribe from which the form originated.

Cipher marks "1906/First Fire."

PRINCIPAL CONTRIBUTION: Standard art pottery forms featuring clear glazes, underglaze decorations, or Indian motifs.

FOUNDERS: William A. Long. Born: 1844, died: 1918.

Fred Tschirner (dates unknown), founded: 1905, closed: 1914.

STUDIOS AND SALESROOMS: Clifton Art Pottery, Newark, New Jersey, 1905-14.

After having organized, operated, and sold Lonhuda Pottery,[1] William A. Long first went to work for J. B. Owens from 1896 until 1900 and then moved to Colorado where he formed the Denver China and Pottery Company.[2] In 1905 he returned east, where the 60-year-old Long and Fred Tschirner, a college graduate chemist, opened the Clifton Art Pottery.

From the very beginning of their partnership Long and Tschirner produced a line called Crystal Patina, which featured "a dense white body, subdued-crystalline glaze; its likeness to the green oxidation of bronze suggested the line name."[3] In 1906 Long also created a number of Native American-influenced vases and pottery forms. Although both Weller and Owens soon began creating similar lines, Long's Clifton Indian Ware marked the first significant production of this style. Using local New Jersey red clay for the body, Long incised Native American Indian designs, which were then generally treated with a glossy black glaze to make them waterproof.

Although their Indian Ware line and their other forms proved to be popular, Long and Tschirner chose not to expand their work force beyond the dozen assistants they had working in their small pottery.[4] In 1909 Long left their New Jersey pottery and moved back to Ohio, where he worked for Samuel Weller again, the Roseville Pottery Company, and the American Encaustic Tiling Company before his death in 1918 at the age of 74. The Clifton Art Pottery company produced decorated wares for only two additional years after Long's departure, gradually switching its emphasis to floor and wall tiles, which in 1914 led to a name change to the Clifton Porcelain Tile Company.

The most valuable of Clifton ware is the Crystal Patina line, particularly when vibrantly colored in gold, brown, and green. These are occasionally found with a thin silver overlay, and this adds more value to the ware. Damage severely reduces value, with a single chip costing as much as 50 percent or retail.

Exceptional Clifton crystal patina spherical vase, covered in an unsual green and mirrored caramel glaze. Signed and dated 1906, 5½" × 6½", $575

## SELECTED PRICES

Tirrube vase w/stovepipe neck and squat base, decorated with yellow and orange nasturtium on terra cotta ground, 12" × 8¼", $650

Tirrube bottle-shaped vase decorated with white nasturtium, 8½" × 5¼", $500

Two Crystal Patina vases, 1905 and 1906; restoration to rim of one, 8½" × 9½", $350

Tirrube flaring vessel decorated w/white wild rose, 6" × 3¼", $250

Two Crystal Patina pieces: one bulbous vase and one squat chamberstick; bruise to rim, line to base of vase, 5½" and 4", $250

Crystal Patina spherical vase covered in unusual green and mirrored caramel glaze, 5½" × 6½", $800

Indian jardinière "Four Mile Ruin, Arizona," incised and painted w/motif I buff and black on brown ground; hairline to rim, 8½" × 11", $500

Indian bulbous vessel w/collared rim and geometric chain pattern, "Homolobi, no. 233"; a few shallow scratches, 7½"x10", $1,250

Indian bulbous vessel w/stovepipe neck and swirls on base, "Mississippi, no. 227," 12" × 9¼", $1,250

Indian bulbous vessel, "Homolobi, no. 235," w/dark birds in flight, 8" × 9", $1,2050

Indian squat vessel w/diamonds on crosses, "Little Colorado, Ariz.", 5", $350

Two Indian squat vessels, "Shumodow, Arizona no. 218", the other unmarked (no. 29); fleck to rim of smallest, 3¼" and 2¾", $350

Indian tall gourd-shaped vessel w/contrasting ovals at base, "Middle Mississippi Valley, no. 231," 11½", $875

Clifton Indian bulbous vessel with stovepipe neck and swirls on base, "Mississippi" (#227). Marked, 12" × 9¼", $1,092

Indian squat vessel w/flaring rim, "Arkansas, no. 206," 4¾", $350

Indian gourd-shaped vase w/wave pattern, "Arkansas, no. 238," 6", $350

Indian squat vessel w/stylized feathers, "Four Mile Ruins, Ariz, no. 160," 5½", $350

Indian cooking ware bowl w/black-glazed interior; minor flake to rim, 9" dia, $150.

Double gourd-shaped vase in pale green glaze, 4", $100

Pair of Crystal Patina two-handled squat vessels, 1907; grinding chips 4" × 6½", $350

Crystal Patina vase, 1906, w/stovepipe neck and bulbous base, 8¼" × 5¼", $350

## Dedham Pottery and Chelsea Keramic Art Works

SHOPMARKS: (1875-89) Impressed CHELSEA KERAMIC ART WORKS/ ROBERTSON AND SONS or stacked letters *CKAW*, often with incised initials of decorators.

(1891-96) Paper label CHELSEA POTTERY/US/TRADEMARK or impressed letters C.P.U.S. in cloverleaf.

(1896-1928) Stamped mark of a resting rabbit beneath the words DEDHAM POTTERY; Volcanic Ware will have DEDHAM POTTERY incised along with initials H.C.R.

(1929-43) Addition of the work REGISTERED beneath the stamped outline of the rabbit.

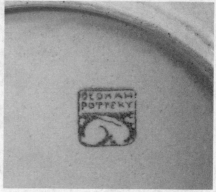

**PRINCIPAL CONTRIBUTIONS:** Early art pottery, crackle glaze tablewares, and Volcanic Ware.

**FOUNDER:** Hugh Robertson. Born: 1844, died: 1908, founded: 1867, closed: 1943.

**STUDIOS AND SALESROOMS:** A. W. and C. H. Robertson, Chelsea, Massachusetts, 1867-72.

Chelsea Keramic Art Works, Chelsea, Massachusetts, 1872-89.

Chelsea Pottery U.S., Chelsea, Massachusetts, 1891-96.

Dedham Pottery, Dedham, Massachusetts, 1896-43.

"Owing to the hand-made feature, there is usually a slight variance from the sizes of the pieces listed herein. Our firing is done in the old

Large and exceptional Dedham experimental bulbous vase by Hugh Robertson, covered in a fine frothy oxblood glaze. (A particularly strong example.) Two small nicks to rim. Incised Dedham Pottery in script and HR., 10" × 7", $5,750

Large Dedham crackleware plate in the "Elephant" pattern. (Very dark.) Firing glaze bubbles around rim. Ink and impressed marks, 12½" dia., $300–$500

style kilns and there again is a slight variance in color, which adds rather than detracts from the appeal of the ware."
—*Catalog introduction, 1938*[1]

## THE CHELSEA KERAMIC ART WORKS

The Robertson family was a family of proficient potters. James Robertson (1810-80), was the father of three potters (Alexander, Hugh, and George), and worked alongside his father in a small pottery in Scotland. He rose to become the manager of a northern England firm before bringing his new family to America in 1853 and settling near Boston, where he once again served as a pottery superintendent.

All three of his sons followed him into the pottery profession, Alexander (1840–1925) forming his own pottery in Chelsea in 1865, where he was joined by Hugh (1844–1908) by 1867 and in 1872 by his father and brother George (1835–1914). The newly named Chelsea Keramic Art Works began offering a line of artware for sale in 1875, but it was discontinued shortly thereafter when the public failed to respond to their fine red earthenware designs, many of which were polished with boiled linseed oil in a unique process. In 1877, however, the Robertson family responded with a hand-thrown faience line "which brought Chelsea to the attention of connoisseurs of the day. Shapes were classically simple; glazes for the most part were soft in color and have proven remarkably free from crazing."[2] The elder Robertson died in 1880, but not before the Chelsea Keramic Art Works had begun to receive recognition for the many glazes that he and his sons had developed over his last 15 years.

In 1878 John G. Low, a local artist who had joined the firm to learn ceramic techniques, left to form his own tile business, the Low Art Tile Works,

also in Chelsea. George Robertson accepted Low's invitation to work for him in the building Low's father had financed. In 1884, four years after the death of James Robertson, Alexander decided to move to California, leaving management of the family firm to Hugh.

Robertson dedicated his efforts to the discovery of various glazes; one in particular was inspired by a red Chinese glaze he had seen at the Philadelphia Centennial Exhibition. As his grandson later described it:

> At the Centennial Exhibition in Philadelphia in 1876, Hugh saw the Korean Exhibit, including the Chinese Crackle and "Dragon's Blood" vases, which so intrigued him that on his return to Chelsea, he set out

Fine Chelsea Keramic experimental bottle by Hugh Robertson, covered in a rich, deep oxblood glaze. Stamped CKAW/in glaze, E/A29, 7½" × 3½", $2,300

to produce this red. The final result was the production of Chinese Dragon's Blood, which was the same as those from the Ming Dynasty. The cost of these experiments left Hugh penniless, but during the stages of experimentation for the red color, he discovered the process of making crackle ware.[3]

Robertson preferred to work with undecorated forms, which would permit his "superb glazes and simple shapes to be appreciated unmarred. Glazes developed included sea-green, apple-green, mustard-yellow, and turquoise, in addition to the rich and very successful oxblood, which was first obtained in 1885 and finally perfected in 1888."[4] It has been estimated that only 300 examples of what Robertson considered authentic oxblood glazes were produced, although many of his near-successes have been touted as being equal to his greatest work.

While Robertson was diligently working with his award-winning glazes, the family pottery business was crumbling around him. In 1889, one year after he had perfected the "Robertson's Blood" glaze, the kilns sat cold. Without money for the fuel to fire them, Robertson was forced to end his experiments and close the pottery.

## CHELSEA POTTERY U.S.

The closing of the Robertson pottery did not go unnoticed in Boston circles. Within a matter of months a group of local supporters had formed a board of directors to fund and oversee a new pottery by the name of Chelsea Pottery U.S. In 1891 Hugh Robertson was named manager, but "learning from the financial failure of his earlier pottery, Robertson and his directors decided that the firm should try making salable tablewares and avoid the expensive time-consuming art wares. Robertson remembered the crackleware glaze that he had achieved earlier on a few large vases. He worked on the process and within a few months after the formation of the new firm, he developed what is now the famous crackleware."[5]

The site of their pottery proved unsuitable; however, as smoke from nearby factories ruined several batches of tableware, and the moisture from the Chelsea marshes affected the performance of the kilns. In 1895 one of the directors purchased a tract of land along a canal near Dedham, Massachusetts, and a new four-story pottery was constructed. With the move in 1896, the name of the firm was changed to the Dedham Pottery Company.

## DEDHAM POTTERY

The crackleware technique that Robertson had discovered years earlier and developed at the Chelsea Pottery provided the technical basis for an extensive line of dinnerware that served as the trademark of Dedham Pottery for nearly 50 years. Ironically, it was the popular success of his crackleware glaze that enabled Hugh Robertson to resume his work with various other glazes. While one of the plant's two new kilns was kept busy firing plates, cups, saucers, platters, bowls, and related tableware the other was reserved for Robertson's experiments with his line of Volcanic Ware (1896–99).[6] His new glaze technique involved a process in which a vase could conceivably be fired as many as 12 times, causing a thick glaze that had been applied around the top to run down the sides in unpredictable patterns. The failure rate was high and his experiments costly: Robertson died in 1908 from lead poisoning contracted from his lifelong work with pigments and glazes. William Robertson (1864–1929), his son, who had worked with him for years, took over the duties of plant superintendent, though he too had paid dearly for his profession. A kiln explosion in 1905 had permanently damaged both of his hands, leaving William incapable of designing pottery. As a result, the firm continued to use the dinnerware patterns designed by Hugh Robertson between 1891 and 1908. Despite the lack of new designs, the crackleware continued to grow in popularity through the 1920s and 1930s, but in 1943 J. Milton Robertson, the grandson of Hugh Robertson, was forced to close down the famous kilns, citing a drop in sales and extensive repairs as the reasons for the firm's failure.

The line of Dedham crackleware designed by Hugh Robertson proved to be charming, artistic, and practical. The combination of the classic blue and white colors beneath a finely crackled glaze gave the dinnerware the appearance of being much older and much more fragile than it actually was. In fact, the "ware was fired at a high temperature so that a true porcelain was made."[7] Part of the closely guarded secret of the fine crazing in the final glaze was explained years later. The dinnerware was quickly removed from the hot kiln and rushed to the elevator that led to the top of the four-story building. As the cool air in the shaft enveloped the warm tableware, "a very audible crackling could be heard."[8] What captured the hearts of thousands, however, were the hand-painted Dedham borders: plump rabbits, parading elephants, outstretched butterflies, and graceful swans were among the two dozen patterns listed in the only catalog the firm released.[9] The drawing of the now-famous Dedham rabbit was submitted by a Boston art teacher in response to a contest Hugh Robertson sponsored in 1892 for a trademark for the newly-formed firm. The Dedham rabbit pattern remained in production every year from 1892 until the plant closed in 1943.

As Marilee Meyer observed in her preface to the 1987 reprint of the original 1938 Dedham catalog, "purchases may be directed by motif, searching for various sizes and forms of one particular pattern, such as the Azalea or Butterfly, Others choose one specific form, perhaps the six inch plate, and collect several different patterns. Whatever the approach, the present collector has sparked an interest in Dedham pottery that is rapidly kindling in antiques shops, shows, and auctions thoughout this country."[10]

While the crackled pattern ware can be very expensive, especially for center design pieces and such oddities as baby chicks and clover, the most expensive pieces will always be Robertson's extraordinarily glazed art ware.

Much of this is fairly uninteresting, with thin flambés of brown and apple green. Look for rich blues, bright greens, and the addition of red. Even a single splash of this bright red will double the value of a pot and make it that much easier to sell.

Further, since this is a very desirable studio ware, damage does not seriously reduce value. Robertson spent more time on glazing than potting, and the vessels are often clunky and thick. Because of their bulk, they often "cracked" in the heat of the kiln. You will find more examples with these firing lines than without, and some piece will have multiple firing lines.

A short post production crack will knock about 35 percent off the price of a piece. A chip to the base will reduce value by about 25 percent. Even more important, if the piece is a strong example, it will still find a ready market.

## SELECTED PRICES

### CHELSEA

Experimental porcelain crackleware vase, white flowers on indigo ground; restoration to several cracks, $5^{1}/_{2}$" × $4^{1}/_{4}$", $1,250

Experimental bottle by Hugh Robertson, oxblood glaze, $7^{1}/_{2}$" × $3^{1}/_{2}$", $2,500

Bottle-shaped vase embossed in honeycomb pattern under teal glaze; restoration to rim, $8^{1}/_{2}$" × 4" $650

Bottle-shaped vase embossed in honeycomb pattern, carved w/three daisy medallions under teal glaze, $8^{1}/_{2}$" × 4" $650

Charger by Hugh Robertson, w/modeled butterflies in relief and draped classical nude on high waves, in glossy green glaze, $10^{3}/_{4}$" dia. $2,500

Covered pilgrim flask by Hugh Robertson after popular printed image by L. Knauss of a little girl feeding geese, under glossy blue-green glaze, set in a green vase; stilt-pulls to back from manufacture $9^{1}/_{4}$" × $10^{1}/_{2}$" $1,500

Pilgrim flask by George Ferrety, incised w/pine bows and flowers under a speckled amber glaze $7^{1}/_{2}$" × $6^{1}/_{4}$" $750

Bottle in unusual oxblood and slate gray glaze $6^{1}/_{2}$" × 4" $1,650

## DEDHAM

Experimental bulbous vase by Hugh Robertson, covered w/oxblood glaze; two small nicks to rim, 10" × 7", $5,000

Experimental bulbous vase by Hugh Robertson, covered in dripping white and brown glaze over green ground, 6" × 3¾", $1,500

Experimental vase by Hugh Robertson, w/thick crackled green glaze over pearl gray ground, 8¾"x 5", $2,000

Crackleware bottle decorated in Chinese style w/apple blossoms in cobalt; firing inconsistency to shoulder, pitting around rim, $6^{13/4}$" × 3¼", $1,650

Experimental bulbous vase by Hugh Robertson, covered in feathered crackled green, brown and red glaze 6½" × 7", $2,000

Experimental bulbous vase by Hugh Robertson covered in dripping beige, ivory and blue lustered glaze, 8" × 4½", $1,750

Crackleware plate in "Elephant" pattern; firing glaze bubbles around rim, 12½" dia., $400

Experimental crackleware plate w/green sponged decoration to rim. 8¾" dia., $550

Experimental vase by Hugh Robertson, covered in brown and green flambé glaze, 8" × 4", $1,250

Two crackleware pieces: a small plate in grape pattern and small bowl in azalea pattern; restoration/flake, 6" and 4" dia., $250

Crackleware plate commemorating Dedham Tercentenary, decorated w/band of ducks, 8¼" dia., $200,

Experimental vase by Hugh Robertson of bulbous form in rich lustered oxblood glaze; 2½" hairline from rim, 7" × 5¾". $1,250

Crackleware bulbous pitcher decorated w/band of rabbits and one of apples, 8½" × 7", $1,050

Crackleware bread plate w/rabbit pattern, 6" dia., $150

Crackleware large bowl in rabbit motif, 3" × 8" dia., $550

Cabinet vase by Hugh Robertson in thick, dripping oxblood, green, and blue mottled glaze; short opposing firing lines to rim, 2¾" × 2", $750

Volcanic vase by Hugh Robertson w/straight neck and slightly protruding shoulder, uniquely thick and organic glaze, bubbly, cratered, and dripped in lustered red, green and cobalt blue, 11¾" × 7", This piece brought $47,150

# Denver China and Pottery Company

SHOPMARKS: Impressed DENVER over initials *L.F.* (Lonhuda Faience) in shield.

Impressed DENVER over initials *C. & P. Co.*

Impressed DENAURA over arrow and DENVER.

PRINCIPAL CONTRIBUTION: Wide range of forms featuring underglaze decorations.

FOUNDER William A. Long. Born: 1844, died: 1918, founded: 1901, closed: 1905.

STUDIOS AND SALESROOMS: *The Denver China and Pottery Company, Denver, Colorado, 1901–05.*

By the year 1900 William Long had started and sold one pottery company, had formed an ill-advised and short-lived partnership with Samuel Weller, and had revealed his technique of underglaze slip painting to both Weller and J. B. Owens.[1] It would not seem unusual for any man to then want to find a new home.

Long moved to Denver, where he started the Denver China and Pottery the same year that Artus Van Briggle opened his new pottery. Long continued to produce his Lonhuda line of underglaze decorated pottery as well as an inexpensive line of household pottery. In addition, he introduced a line called Denaura, revealing an attraction for Art Nouveau designs "similar in concept to some of the early Van Briggle work"[2] and also for native Colorado flora. Many of his art ware pieces were molded by his staff of approximately 20 workers. In 1905 the Denver China and Pottery Company merged with the Western Pottery Manufacturing Company, and Long moved to New Jersey, where he formed the Clifton Art Pottery.

Rare Denver Denaura column-shaped vase with flaring rim and base, covered in shaded semi-matte green glaze. Stamped Denaura, and numbered, 9¼" × 4¼", $1,840

The value of Long's work varies with the company. While he developed and help produce interesting ware from each venture, his Denaura line is the rarest and most valuable. It's an odd interpretation of the Arts and Crafts, with a semi gloss green finish covering mostly static floral designs. Curiously, the best example of Denaura work seen to date is a large, flat, closed pot with two handles, decorated with embossed mermaids and fish.

Minor damage, such as a small chip at the rim or base, will cause a reduction in price of about 20 percent.

## SELECTED PRICES

Column-shaped vase w/flaring rim and base, in shaded semi matte green glaze, 9¼" × 4¼". $875

Denver Pottery squat vase with small opening, decorated with embossed florals under a waxy deep green finish, 3" × 6", $2,000

# Frackelton Pottery

SHOPMARKS: Incised initials *S.F.,* occasionally with year
PRINCIPAL CONTRIBUTION: Salt-glazed stoneware, occasionally with under-
glaze decoration.
FOUNDER: Susan Stuart Frackelton. Born: 1848,
died: 1932, founded: ca. 1882, closed ca. 1903.
STUDIOS AND SALESROOMS: *Frackelton Pottery,*
*Milwaukee, Wisconsin, ca. 1881–ca. 1903.*

Susan Frackelton was a pioneer in the development of china painting, establishing the Frackelton
China Decorating Works in 1893. She also experimented in salt-glaze stoneware, creating award-
winning examples at numerous exhibitions. Unfortunately, she never
possessed the necessary equipment or kilns to develop a line of art pottery;
thus, examples of her work are considered quite rare. As a review in the
*Craftsman* mentioned, "The product is small and no duplicates are made."
The same author gave Mrs. Frackelton "the distinction of being the first
American who has raised stoneware from the most common utilitarian uses
to the rank of an artistic product."[1]

"At the same time," a modern observer recently noted, "Susan Frackelton was the first in a succession of pottery and china decorators to give up
decorating for the lure of carving and modeling in wet clay. Her large, richly

Fine and rare Frackelton salt-glazed
stoneware bottle-shaped vase,
modeled and incised with poppies
in cobalt on a gray ground. (Inch
for inch, as good a piece of
Frackelton as we've seen.) Some
scaling to body in the firing.
Incised SF, 6" × 4", $8,625

carved, and modeled 'Olive Jar' in saltglaze stoneware was exhibited in Chicago at the 1893 World's Columbian Exhibition to great acclaim."[2]

Frackelton's work remains as one of the rarest of the American art potteries. Nevertheless, about a new piece is found once a year and enough have been marketed to give some consistent idea of value. Minor damage has only limited impact on pricing. A small chip will reduce pricing by only about 10%. Frackelton is marketable in nearly any condition.

## SELECTED PRICES

Salt-glazed stoneware bottle-shaped vase, modeled and incised w/poppies in cobalt on grey ground. Some scaling to body in the firing, 6" × 4", $10,000

Gourd-shaped salt-glaze stoneware vase, ca. 1905, decorated w/abutilon blossoms alternating w/stylized leaves and vines in indigo on ivory ground; chip and nick to rim 6¾"x 3¾", $6,250

Bulbous stoneware vase, 1900, painted in Delft style w/indigo poppies against gray ground, on an overall stippled surface; short tight line and minor flecks to rim 5¼" × 5", $5,000

# Fulper Pottery

SHOPMARKS: (1909–14) Ink-stamped circle VASEKRAFT/FULPER around potter at his wheel.

(1909–ca. 1915) Ink-stamped vertical rectangle around vertical *FULPER*.

(Ca. 1915–20) Smaller ink-stamped box around vertical *FULPER*.

(Ca. 1922–55) Impressed horizontal *FULPER* (no rectangle), generally with three- or four-digit number.[1]

PRINCIPAL CONTRIBUTIONS: Vases, bowls, and lamps utilizing a variety of quality glazes.

Early Fulper mark

Middle period Fulper mark

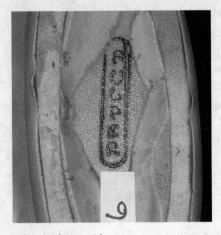

1920s Fulper mark                    Late FULPER mark

FOUNDER: Samuel Hill. Born: 1793, died: 1858, founded: 1814, sold: 1930.
STUDIOS AND SALESROOMS: Samuel Hill Pottery, Flemington, New Jersey,
   1814–60.
Fulper Pottery, Flemington, New Jersey, 1860–81.
Fulper Brothers, Flemington, New Jersey 1881–89.
Fulper Pottery, Inc., Flemington, New Jersey, 1889–55.

> "The use of natural clays, not over-refined, gives an element of the un-
> expected, for the glaze 'steals' from the body in firing, particles of min-
> eral in the body, producing variations in color or crystalline effects in
> the glaze."
> —*Evelyn Marie Stuart, 1914*[2]

In 1860 the Fulper family assumed possession of the pottery that was to bear
their name for nearly 100 years. At the outset they maintained the manufacture of a line of utility household pottery and continued in this fashion under
the management of three brothers: George W. Fulper, Edward B. Fulper,
and William H. Fulper (1872–1928), who was largely responsible for the introduction and development of Fulper's art pottery production.

The Fulper entry into an already crowded art pottery market came in
the middle of the Arts and Crafts era. In 1909, utilizing the same heavy New
Jersey clay they had used for decades in their commercial production, the
Fulper brothers introduced a line of art pottery by the name of Vasekraft. Recent research, however, has revealed that experiments with various glazes for
the new line may have started as early as 1900, with experimental pieces
being produced by 1906.[3] The new line was manufactured, according to a

Large Fulper table lamp, believable marriage of a mushroom-shaped shade covered in a brown, celadon, and blue glaze inset with green and amber slag glass, on a cucumber green matte base. (Originally came from a private New Jersey estate. While the shade and base would appear to have been married, it would have been done decades ago. In any case, it seems a happy union.) Both have rectangular ink mark, 21½" × 17", $17,250

1912 article, "from the same clay, in the same factory, and in some cases by the same workmen that are working on the more common articles."[4] The wares developed at the Fulper Pottery for the Vasekraft line ranged widely, from vases, jardinieres, and lamps to bookends, pitchers, clock cases, and tiles. Although some required hand-throwing, the majority were molded. While the heavy Fulper forms were open to criticism from early reviewers accustomed to Rookwood-inspired vases and ewers, the hundreds of quality glazes developed by William Fulper and his chemists have been credited with the popular and artistic success of the firm's art pottery.

Among the more successful and most popular of the Fulper glazes were the following:

*Mirror*—a high-gloss glaze in either black, green, blue, ivory, or yellow

*Wistaria*—a flowing matte glaze in pastel colors, individually or combined

Fulper effigy bowl covered in a frothy ivory over matte mustard glaze. Ink racetrack mark, 6½" × 10½", $977

*Flambé*—unusual combinations of colors in a flame effect
*Lustre*—an iridescent glaze
*Crystal*—a crystalline glaze
*Matte*—textured dull glazes in a variety of colors, including shades of greens, yellows, and whites

Like Teco and Hampshire, the Fulper Pottery utilized a large number of molded forms to prevent production costs from driving the price of the pottery beyond the reach of potential customers. Grueby, the symbol of hand-thrown art pottery, had entered the first stages of bankruptcy the same year Fulper announced the introduction of Vasekraft, and it appears that the Fulper brothers were determined not to follow in Grueby's footsteps. Emphasis was placed on the development of dozens of classical, yet molded forms. The result was efficient production of a quality art pottery. As observed in the beautifully illustrated *From Our Native Clay*, "while Fulper produced its molded, forms in large quantities, it made a point with its glazing techniques to encourage the fire in the kiln to give each piece unique markings."[5] Specific glazes were often assigned to specific forms but were also used in alternative succession and, in many of the most spectacular wares, in combination with each other. One of the most highly valued of the many Fulper glazes is the crystalline, of which it was said that while "Teco has the distinction of producing the first microcrystalline glazes . . . it was Fulper, a late entrant in the field of art pottery, who produced the more successful and more varied crystalline glazes. Because such glazes tend to flow irregularly,

Fine and unusual Fulper corseted vase covered in a dripping, frothy ivory, blue and mahogany flambé glaze. (Spectacular glaze.) Rectangular ink mark, 7½" × 4", $1,035

and the locations of the crystals cannot be predicted, such glazes were normally used on relatively simple, Oriental-inspired vessels."[6]

Among the many varied Fulper forms that are destined to become prized members of fine collections are those with deep, rich glazes. Unlike other potteries, which worked in numerous shapes but utilized only one or two particular types of glazes, the size and form of Fulper pottery is often of less importance than the quality of its glazes. Dull, lifeless glazes can be found and should be recognized as such. Strong, well-distributed crystalline glazes, along with deep Mirror and rich Flambè, are among the most highly sought of the firm's many glazes.

One of the rarest of the Fulper glazes was the famous Famille Rose, which William Fulper may have first developed as an exhibition rather than a production glaze. "Fulper considered this the rediscovery of the ancient Chinese secret, and hence the glaze was applied to classical Chinese shapes."[7] The various red hues were time-consuming to duplicate, as reflected in both their rarity today and their original cost. At a time when an average worker was earning $10 a week, a fine example of Fulper's famille rose could cost as much as $100.

Nevertheless, present-day collectors do not exactly share the Fulper Pottery's love of this glaze. While there were one-of-a-kind pieces covered with Famille Rose variations that can sell for thousands of dollars, this is not the case when this red matte finish is covering a standard, molded, production form.

It would be wrong to suggest that only Fulper's glazes are of interest to modern collectors. While many of their shapes are less interesting than the glazes that coat them, there are some important (mostly early) forms that are eagerly sought by collectors. These include their Germanic, seccessionist vessels and several rarer, larger vaes with embossed decoration. Of particular note is a 12" corseted vase with embossed rings around the opening. That it is nearly always seen with a magnificent copper dust Crystalline finish is not to its disadvantage. Nevertheless, it is the glazing and form in consort that make this such an important piece.

The now-famous Fulper mushroom lamps were first offered in 1910, coinciding perhaps with the arrival of Martin Stangl, who had created several new designs and numerous glazes by 1915. While stoneware lamp bases were not unusual, as Grueby, Tiffany, Teco, Hampshire, and Rookwood had all demonstrated, Fulper created a pottery shade as well, with as many as two dozen hand-incised openings for irregularly shaped pieces of stained glass. The lamps were praised for the "unity of base and shade in the same material, the utility of the lamp for reading, and the harmony of the glazes and forms within 'the general scheme of artistic home furnishing.' "[8] Like much of the Vasekraft line, lamp bases and even the pierced shades were often molded rather than hand-thrown, but the quality of the glazes and the relative rarity of the lamps ensured their popularity, not only between 1910 and 1920 but 70 years later as well.

Stangl's appointment as technical superintendent followed the retirement of George W. Fulper in 1911. Stangl oversaw the infusion of several new glazes into the Vasekraft line, which was awarded a medal at the 1915 San Francisco Exposition; but Stangl's departure that same year, coupled with a declining interest in art pottery, forced the company to accept a contract for the production of bisque doll heads, which were mass produced under the Fulper trademark between 1918 and 1921 at a rate of nearly 1,000 per day.[9] Stangl returned to the pottery in 1920 and purchased the business from the Fulper family in 1930, one year after a fire destroyed the main plant and most of its inventory. Art pottery was produced on a reduced scale for five more years until 1935, when production was completely switched to dinnerware, ceramic gifts, and figurines. Although the name of the corporation was not changed until 1955, the production of important Fulper art pottery had, in effect, ended in the fire of 1929.

Because Fulper is almost always molded, damage will have more than average impact on value. A single chip might reduce the cost of an average piece by 50 percent. However, as with nearly all art pottery, the better the piece, the less damage reduces value. This is particularly true of the ceramic lamps. Rare and expensive when made, susceptible to damage because of the cutouts in the shade and the unwieldy nature of a top-heavy form, minor damage is almost expected on these.

## SELECTED PRICES

Large table lamp, mushroom-shaped shade covered in a brown, celadon and blue glaze inset w/green and amber slag glass, on cucumber green matte base, $21\frac{1}{2}$" × 17", $12,500

Bulbous floriform vase w/embossed panels, covered in mirrored cat's eye Flambé glaze, $11\frac{1}{2}$" × 9", $3,500

Cattail vase covered in Leopard Skin crystalline glaze, $12\frac{3}{4}$" × $4\frac{3}{4}$", $3,500

Bulbous jug w/loop handle, in perfectly fired copper dust crystalline glaze; $\frac{1}{4}$" grinding chip from manufacture, $11\frac{1}{2}$" × $7\frac{3}{4}$", $3,500

Mushroom-shaped lamp, shade inset w/leaded slag glass pieces, covered in strong leopard skin crystalline glaze; hairline to one ceramic bridge between two pieces of slag glass, $18\frac{1}{2}$x$15\frac{1}{4}$", $12,500

Porcelain covered dresser box w/Egyptian figure on orange ground, 8" × 5", $250

Silver-overlaid jug covered in blue crystalline glaze w/stopper; area of overlay missing, 10" × $5\frac{1}{2}$", $150

Urn w/hammered texture, covered in Leopard Skin crystalline glaze; $\frac{1}{2}$" abraded area to one handle, $12\frac{1}{4}$" × $11\frac{1}{2}$", $1,650

Bulbous, tapering urn covered in turquoise and blue Flambé glaze; line to base from firing, 11" × 8", $1,050

Bottle w/salamander covered in green and blue Flambé glaze, 8" × 4", $850

Flag vase covered in fine mahogany, ivory, and turquoise Flambé semi-matte glaze, 8" × $5\frac{1}{2}$", $875

Flower frog of medieval castle; several nicks around base, 5" × $5\frac{1}{2}$", $350

Penguin flower frog covered in blue, gray, and ivory matte glazes; re-glued base, repaired break, 7" × $4\frac{1}{2}$", $300

Flower frog of Pocahontas in canoe, covered in a green matte glaze; minor restoration to edge of canoe, $3\frac{1}{4}$" × 7", $350

Two flower frogs, one w/fish and one w/goose, covered in polychrome matte glazes; grinding chips, $3\frac{1}{2}$" and 2", $350

Effigy bowl covered in frothy ivory over matte mustard glaze, $6\frac{1}{2}$" × $10\frac{1}{2}$", $825

Hexagonal vase in moss-to-rose Flambé glaze; restoration to stilt pull chip inside bottom ring, 11" × $5\frac{3}{4}$", $500

Bulbous vase covered in frothy gunmetal and blue flame over Famille Rose ground, 8" × 8", $875

Corseted vase covered in dripping, frothy ivory blue and mahogany Flambé glaze, $7\frac{1}{2}$" × 4", $500

Bulbous vase in mirrored cat's eye Flambé glaze, $9\frac{1}{2}$" × 6", $500

Corseted vase in lustered green and frothy mahogany Flambé glaze, $7\frac{1}{2}$" × $4\frac{1}{2}$", $350

Bottle-shaped vase in mirror black crystalline Flambé glaze, 8" × 6", $350

Pair of hearth bookends in dark matte green glaze; several chips along top edges only, 8" × 6", $350

For Prang, tall pitcher covered in matte mustard glaze, 10" × $5\frac{1}{2}$", $350

Baluster vase embossed w/dots on shoulder and covered in Mirrored Black glaze, 7", $350

Two chambersticks, one covered in moss-to-rose Flambé glaze, the other in café-au-lait; several chips to base and rim, $4\frac{1}{2}$" and 6", $200

Footed flaring bowl covered in blue-green crystalline glaze, 3" × $7\frac{1}{2}$", $150

Three-sided vase, in Chinese Blue Flambé glaze, 8" × 3", $150

Two urns, one with flaring rim covered in frothy blue and beige Flambé glaze (opposing hairlines), and one colonial covered in a mottled green and yellow glaze (firing crack), 7" and $8\frac{3}{4}$", $150

Bud vase w/squat base covered in mustard cat's eye Flambé glaze, 5¼" × 3½", $200

Two vases, one squat cabinet with scrolled handles covered in caramel crystalline glaze and one teardrop-shaped covered in mustard and turquoise glossy glaze. Latter has cracked handle and small bruise to rim, 3" × 3¾" and 6", $200

Two small vessels, one pillow vase embossed w/wavy lines under Chinese Blue and olive glaze, and one squat vase in glossy green over blue matte glaze, 3½" and 3", $150

Pair of Buddha bookends covered in speckled blue and green matte glaze; restoration to both necks and one base, 5½" × 4", $150

Gourd-shaped factory lamp base w/buttressed handles, covered in leopard skin crystalline glaze, 6¼" × 7½", $250

Tapering vessel w/buttressed handles covered in an ochre-to-Rose Famille matte Flambé, 4¼" × 5¾", $250

Tall milk can shaped vase covered in Leopard Skin glaze; restoration to three stilt-pull chips and to several lines at rim, 12" × 5½", $425

Buttressed vase w/squat base, covered in cat's eye Flambé glaze over a speckled mustard matte ground; hairlines around rim, 8½" × 6", $250

Effigy bowl with cat's eye Flambé glaze interior and mustard matte Flambé exterior; short hairline from rim, touch-ups to base, 7½" × 10½", $550

Buttressed vase w/squat base covered in a turquoise and mustard crystalline Flambé glaze, 8½" × 6", $300

Bulbous vase covered in unusual moss-to-wisteria Flambé glaze; grinding bruise and chips to base, 7" × 5½", $200

Two pieces, a corseted vase and squat vessel, both w/matte blue exterior and Flambé rim, 5" and 3", $250

Two pieces, a small vase w/Chinese Blue Flambé over matte blue, and a chamberstick in wisteria glaze, 5" and 6" dia., $250

Classically shaped vase covered in Leopard Skin crystalline glaze; few tight lines from rim, 7½" × 5¼", $200

Pair of tall candlesticks covered in bright yellow matte glaze, 15½" × 5", $750

Rare and early pair of bookends molded w/lions standing back-to-back and covered in café-au-lait matte glaze; chip to corner of one, 4¾" × 6" × 3¼", $250

Bulbous vessel w/two angular handles, covered in Chinese blue crystalline Flambé glaze; restoration to small rim chip, 6¼" × 7¾", $150

Large tapering vessel w/two ring handles, covered in moss-to-rose Flambé glaze; restoration to one handle, small bruise to base, 12¾" × 7¾", $350

Bulbous vessel w/two angular handles, covered in mirrored mahogany, blue, and olive green Flambé glaze, 6¼" × 7½", $350

Two pieces, squat cabinet vase in turquoise and mustard crystalline glaze and a tapering bud vase in blue matte glaze, 2¾" and 5¼", $200

Bulbous urn covered in famille rose glaze, 7½" × 5½", $250

Squat vessel w/two scroll handles, covered in Leopard Skin crystalline Flambé glaze, 5" × 6", $250

Bulbous vessel w/two angular handles, covered in Chinese blue crystalline Flambé glaze; some scratches near base, 6¼" × 7¾", $250

Barrel-shaped vase in Chinese blue glaze over frothy medium green and matte white ground, 8½" × 5", $500

Urn covered in fine Chinese blue Flambé over mahogany glossy glaze, 8" × 7", $500

For Prang; flaring four-sided vase in gunmetal green and frothy blue glaze; short lines to rim, 8¾" × 3¾", $350

Bulbous vessel w/flat shoulder in mirror black, indigo, and Famille Rose Flambé glaze, 7½" × 8", $800

Pair of faceted vases embossed w/rectangles at rim, covered in frothy mission verde, turquoise, and ivory Flambé glaze, 7½" × 7", $1,025

Bulbous vessel w/three horn-shaped handles, in ivory, blue and Mirror Black Flambé glaze, 6½" × 6", $750

Hammered urn in frothy indigo and light blue glaze; stilt-pull bruise, 11¾" × 11¾", $1,750

Bulbous vessel w/four short handles, in exceptional Leopard Skin crystalline glaze; restoration to drill hole on bottom, 13¼" × 11½", $1,650

Bulbous vase in frothy blue, ivory and Mirror Black Flambé glaze, 12" × 9", $1,750

Tapering vase in mirror black to copper dust crystalline Flambé glaze, 12½" × 7", $2,000

Table lamp w/two-socket baluster base and mushroom-cap shade inset w/organically shaped blue, green, and red leaded slag glass pieces, the entire piece covered in Chinese blue Flambé glaze; shade has a few very minor scratches and four short hairlines between leaded glass pieces, probably from firing, w/original porcelain sockets. Base: 18", shade: 15", $11,000

Buttressed vase, in Flemington green Flambé glaze; restoration to drilled hole on bottom, 13¼" × 10, $1,500

Tapering vessel in fine green crystalline over elephant's breath Flambé glaze; bottom drilled for lamp base, 12¾" × 7", $550

Vase in cat's eye Flambé glaze; invisible restoration to drill hole on bottom, 16" × 5½", $800

Urn in mottled blue, amber, mahogany and caramel glaze, 11½" × 7¼", $1,000

Bulbous and ridged vase of Chinese form w/two small handles in cat's eye w/blue Flambé glaze, 12½" × 8½", $875

Bulbous vase in Chinese blue Flambé glaze, 10¼" × 10", $1,650

Two pieces: two-handled bowl and spherical vessel, both in Chinese blue crystalline Flambé glaze; restoration to hairline on bowl, 3½" × 4½", $250

Bullet-shaped vase in ivory, mahogany and blue crystalline Flambé glaze, 10" × 5½", $550

Low bowl w/collared rim in black and ivory-to-green Flambé glaze; light abrasion around rim, 4½" × 10¼", $500

Buttressed vase w/squat base in famille rose matte glaze, 8½"x6", $325

Bullet-shaped vase in ivory, blue-gray, and rose Flambé glaze, 10", $450

For Prang, ovoid vase w/closed-in rim, in elephant's breath and Leopard Skin crystalline Flambé glaze, 8½", $625

Pair of tall candlesticks in bright yellow matte glaze, 15½", $625

Spherical three-handled vessel in Butterscotch Flambé glaze, 7", $350

Spherical vessel w/butressed rim, in mirror black, blue, and white Flambé glaze, 5", $250

Corseted vase in mirror black, copper dust crystalline and feathered blue and amber Flambé glaze, 7½", $300

Two low bowls, one w/ivory exterior and blue-green crystalline interior (short hairline from rim), the other covered in mirrored Flemington Green glaze, 8¾" dia., $250

Two center bowls, one w/blue exterior and ivory and blue Flambé interior (restoration to 1" bruise) and Lotus bowl in turquoise and clear crystalline glaze, 8" and 9½" dia., $250

Flaring center bowl, interior covered in flame-pattern mahogany, ivory and green Flambé glaze, w/moss-to-rose exterior; ¾" chip below rim, 12" dia., $300

Lamp base in Chinese blue Flambé glaze; replaced fittings, missing sockets, original light switch, hairline from factory hole to base, 18", $850

Tall vase in leopard skin, white frothy semi gloss, and yellow crystalline glazes; manufacturing bruise to bottom, 16" × 5½", $1,750

Mushroom-shaped lamp in cucumber green crystalline and gunmetal glaze, shade inset w/leaded blue-green slag glass; restoration around rim of shade, 18½" × 15" dia., $6,250

Vasekraft architectural table clock w/Waterbury clockworks, in sheer white and amber glossy glaze, 5½" × 4", $1,150

Garden urn in blue and green microcrystalline Flambé glaze; line inside factory hole, restoration to glaze flaking at base, 23¼" × 17½", $1,550

## Grand Feu Art Pottery

GRAND FEU
POTTERY
L. A., CAL.

SHOPMARKS: Impressed GRAND FEU POTTERY/ L.A., CAL.

PRINCIPAL CONTRIBUTIONS: Simple forms of vases and bowls featuring high-quality glazes.

FOUNDER: Cornelius Brauckman. Born: 1864, died: 1952, founded: ca. 1912, closed: ca. 1916.

STUDIOS AND SALESROOMS: Grand Feu Art Pottery, Los Angeles, ca. 1912– ca. 1916.

The relatively few numbers of examples of Grand Feu pottery that were produced and have survived have demonstrated that the firm ranks with the most highly regarded of all of the art pottery manufacturers. Grand Feu pottery exhibits exquisite glazes in a variety of colors; the decorative effect was left to the unique reaction of the glaze on each piece to the heat of the kiln.

Fine and rare Grand Feu corseted vase covered in a superior tiger eye and green mottled glaze; 4" line in body, may go through. Stamped GRAND FEU POTTERY/L.A. CAL./TT/154, 5¼" × 4½", $1,092

Unfortunately, the firm and its production remained small during the few years it produced art pottery.

Nevertheless, pockets of Grand Feu ware continue to surface in yard and estate sales. One such batch, found in central California in 1995, brought eight newly discovered pieces to the market at one time.

It is much easier to find a successful piece of Grand Feu than one that failed in the kiln. The production standards were extremely high, if we're to judge by the remaining work. Because of the high fire body of the ware, pieces are seldom found with post-manufacturing flaws.

Look for pieces larger in size (over 6"), brightly glazed (as opposed to dull brown mattes), and in near-perfect condition.

## SELECTED PRICES

Cylindrical vase, 1917, in superior matte brown microcrystalline Flambé glaze. 7" × 3¼", $5,000

Corseted vase in superior Tiger Eye and green mottled glaze; 4" line in body, 5¼" × 4½", $1,250

Bulbous vase in mission matte brown glaze, 7" × 4¼", $5,000

Bulbous vase in mission matte brown glaze, 3" × 4¼", $3,250

# Grueby Pottery

SHOPMARKS: Impressed GRUEBY/BOSTON. MASS or GRUEBY POT-TERY/BOSTON/U.S.A. or GRUEBY FAIENCE CO./BOSTON/U.S.A., occasionally around outline of lotus plant
Paper label with lotus plant logo
PRINCIPAL CONTRIBUTIONS: Hand-thrown art pottery vases, lamp bases, bowls, and tiles in matte glazes.
FOUNDER: William H. Grueby. Born: 1867, died: 1925, founded: 1894, closed: 1919.
STUDIOS AND SALESROOMS: Grueby Faience Company, Boston, 1894-1909. Grueby Pottery Company, Inc., Boston, 1907-11. Grueby Faience and Tile Company, Boston, 1909-19.

"Although for many years, dull-finished pottery has been produced by sand-blasting ware with a glossy finish, or by taking a piece of glazed pottery and treating it with acid to make it dull, the Grueby potteries were the first in the history of ceramics to make a dull finish pottery in their kilns. The surface thus obtained has a deep velvety look, unlike any other finish made."

—the Craftsman, 1914[1]

For design pioneers such as Laura Fry, Gustav Stickley, and William Grueby, success proved to be a double-edged sword. No sooner had each developed a popular handcrafted design than a horde of competitors flooded the market with thousands of imitations. In each case the less-expensive imitations found a public excited about the new "look" but willing to sacrifice quality for a lower price. As many of their competitors prospered, the pioneers found themselves struggling not only for recognition but, especially in the cases of Stickley and Grueby, for a means of saving the company each had founded.

As a young man William Grueby received his first extensive training with the firm of J. &. J. G. Low Art Tile Works in Chelsea, Massachusetts. Grueby worked for over 10 years with John G. Low (1835–1907) and his master glaze technician, George W. Robertson (1835–1914), both of whom had been trained by James Robertson at the Chelsea Keramic Art Works. In 1890 both Robertson and Grueby left the Low firm to establish individual businesses. While Robertson formed a new tile company with his brother Hugh in Chelsea, William Grueby moved to nearby Revere to begin manufacturing architectural terra cotta, glazed bricks, and decorative tiles. A brief partnership intended to expand the market for his architectural products failed, and in 1894 Grueby reorganized his sole partnership under the name of the Grueby Faience Company.[2]

Grueby continued producing terracotta ornaments, but his interest in glazes (inspired, most likely, by George Robertson) soon led to experimentation with pottery forms, as he utilized the center portion of the kiln that grew too hot for the firing of the terracotta panels. In 1897 Grueby formally incorporated his firm to raise the capital necessary to expand into the lucrative, but risky, art pottery market. Two of his principal stockholders also became working partners: William H. Graves, a young architect from a prominent Massachusetts family, assumed the responsibilities of the corporation's business manager, while George P. Kendrick, a noted silversmith, became the chief designer of the Grueby Faience Company's early line of vases, lamp bases, and bowls. William Grueby remained the firm's general manager, but the addition of these two gifted individuals freed him to experiment with and develop a line of matte glazes.

Grueby's initial pottery experiments had utilized the same clay that had been ferried across from Martha's Vineyard for use in producing his terracotta ornaments. Although additional clay was shipped from New Jersey, the pottery produced by the newly organized firm retained some of the coarseness associated with its terracotta products—a circumstance that did not escape notice by at least one of their early critics.[3] Despite this questionable "flaw," the hand-thrown Grueby pottery garnered numerous awards and medals at major exhibitions in Boston, Paris, Russia, and St. Louis within the first seven years of its formal existence.[4] Their richly textured, flowing, matte green glaze set in motion a trend that influenced the art pottery movement for years to come. "Immediately upon its appearance," the *Boston Globe* reported, "examples of the ware were bought by museums around the globe from Philadelphia to Berlin to Budapest to Tokyo."[5] Their immediate success, according to respected scholar Paul Evans, was due as much to the "shapes (that) distinguished Grueby ware every bit as much as the glaze, as they depended not on intricacy or elaborateness of design and ornamentation, but rather on integrity and contour."[6]

Exceptional and large Grueby vase by Wilhelmina Post with squat base and tall neck, decorated with tooled and applied leaves around the base alternating with long stems and yellow trefoils around the neck, and covered in a superior leathery matte green glaze. Perfectly fired and very sharply modeled; even the stamens of the flowers are detailed. Mint condition. Pottery stamp/WP/188A, 17¾" × 8½", $92,000

In 1899, in an attempt to distinguish between its two principal lines, the firm established two loosely defined divisions. The Grueby Faience Company continued to manufacture terra cotta, while the Grueby Pottery (formally incorporated in 1907) concentrated on art pottery. Despite the departure of chief designer George Kendrick in 1901, the pottery branch continued to excel. Addison B. LeBoutillier assumed design duties in 1901 and was succeeded years later by Julia H. Bradley. Although much of the decorating was assigned to female graduates of Boston-area art schools, the quality and the forms remained consistent, for the decorative design of each vase, bowl, and lamp base was dictated by the chief designer and by William Grueby as operations manager. "One might wonder, though," Robert Ellison has speculated, "whether the lack of novelty and change did not ultimately lead to the pottery's downfall."[7]

In the process the designer would determine both the form of the hand-thrown vessel and the decoration—most often leaves or a simple flower—before turning the barely dry, though not yet fired, piece over to one of the assistants. The decorations would then be pressed into their appointed places, the piece fired, the glaze applied, and the piece returned to the kiln. The glazes included yellow, brown, blue, and white, but the most popular was the famous matte Grueby green—a color that inspired similar glazes at Teco, Van Briggle, Merrimac, and numerous other potteries. In rare instances a second or third color might also be applied to the tips of the leaves or the petals of the flowers; these have risen to become the most highly sought-after of all the Grueby designs.

In 1907, perhaps feeling the first effects of the flood of imitators that threatened to erode its hold on the art pottery market, the Grueby Pottery Company was incorporated and additional stockholders were brought in. The other branch, the Grueby Faience Company, entered into the first stages of bankruptcy two years later. In 1909 William Grueby turned management of the Grueby Pottery Company over to his associates, but within two years the art pottery line was brought to a close. After leaving Grueby Pottery, William Grueby formed a new Grueby Faience and Tile Company in an attempt to reestablish his name in the architectural wares business. As it was beginning to succeed, however, a disastrous fire in 1913 destroyed most of the plant. The factory was rebuilt, sales rebounded, and in 1919 the Grueby Faience and Tile Company was sold to the C. Pardee Works of New Jersey and moved there by 1921. Four years later, in 1925, William H. Grueby died.

Indicative of the respect accorded the Grueby pottery was the early agreement in which the L. C. Tiffany Company (along with several others) purchased Grueby bases for the prestigious line of stained-glass lamp shades at a time when Tiffany had his own art pottery factory. These lamps which

Fine Grueby cuenca tile, "The Pines," with pine trees in brown and green in a landscape of greens and blues. Small glaze bubbles and a couple of nicks to edges. Unmarked, 6" sq., $3,450

have since become the most highly sought-after of all their type produced at the same time as the art pottery, fall into various value categories.

The Grueby Pottery, like its competitors, manufactured vases and bowls that, while always hand-thrown and individually modeled, were less expensive to produce than some of their more expressive and highly organic wares. These less-imaginative examples remain quite moderate in value, especially when compared to some of the more dynamic pieces. Just as not all Gustav Stickley furniture is as highly valued as the inlaid or spindle examples, not all Grueby pottery is as fervently collected as the two- or three-color examples. Grueby collectors continually seek expressive, organic vases demonstrating exquisitely tooled leaves or flowers covered with glazes rich in texture and color. Grueby offered several glaze colors, but its famous matte green remains the most popular today. Although Grueby manufactured only hand-thrown pottery, some of his forms were not as expressive as others. Lifeless or unimaginative vases and bowls, regardless of their size, are less desirable than even small examples with crisp, vibrant decorations.

Although continued success escaped William Grueby and the firm he founded, the pottery he produced has endured as one of the most valued examples of art pottery produced during the Arts and Crafts movement. For, as Robert Ellison has observed, "Grueby's sparse, austere ware were welcomed as a purifying concept in a market burdened with pottery that was either over-ornamented or full of dark, glossy painting."[8]

Remember that Grueby is one of the most important of the Arts and Crafts potteries, and that each piece is one of a kind. Minor damage is almost expected and will have little negative impact on pricing. This is particularly true of the dramatic, organic pieces with wild handles and heavily-embossed decoration.

## SELECTED PRICES

High-fired vessel covered in dripping matte mustard glaze, $3\frac{3}{4}" \times 3\frac{1}{2}"$, $750

Bulbous vessel covered in thick white curdled matte glaze; abrasion around rim, $4\frac{1}{2}" \times 5"$, $500

Vase by Wilhelmina Post w/squat base and tall neck, decorated w/tooled and applied leaves around the base alternating w/long stems and yellow trefoils around the neck, and covered in a leathery matte green glaze; mint condition, finely detailed, $17\frac{3}{4}" \times 8\frac{1}{2}"$. This piece brought a record price of $92,000.

Spherical vase w/tooled and applied squared-off leaves alternating w/buds under leathery matte green glaze; several small nicks to leaf edges, 13" $\times 13\frac{1}{2}"$ dia., $17,500

Squat vessel by Wilhelmina Post, shoulder decorated w/tooled and applied broad leaves alternating w/buds and quatrefoils under blue-gray curdled and oatmealed matte glaze; chip to rim and minor flecks to leaf edges, $4\frac{1}{2}" \times 10\frac{1}{4}"$ dia., $8,000

Vase by Marie Seaman w/tooled and applied full height leaves alternating w/buds and covered in feathered organic matte green glaze; few minor flakes to leaf edges, $11\frac{1}{2}" \times 5\frac{1}{2}"$, $6,250

Vase w/corseted shoulder, incised w/vertical ribs, in matte ochre glaze, $9\frac{1}{2}" \times 5"$, $4,000

Vase w/full-height leaves alternating w/yellow buds on bright green stems, leaves and ground under deep oatmealy matt green glaze; minor flakes to leaf edges, $12" \times 6\frac{1}{2}"$, $7,500

Bulbous vase w/crisply tooled and applied leaves alternating w/full-height buds under a superior leathery matte green glaze; restoration to chip at base, $15\frac{1}{4}" \times 8"$, $10,000

Cylindrical vase w/modeled and applied tulips under leathery matte green glaze, $10"x4\frac{1}{2}"$, $6,250

Gourd-shaped vase w/vertical ribs, in superior feathered matte green glaze, $15\frac{1}{2}" \times 9"$, $6,250

Large vase by Ruth Erickson, 1906, w/rows of tool leaves around its bulbous base, tall stove-pipe neck, under fine feathered matte green glaze, w/original factory bronze lamp mounts and original period leaded glass shade; factory hole near bottom, $20" \times 11"$ dia., $8,750

Bulbous vase by Marie Seaman w/tooled and applied leaves alternating w/buds under leathery matte green glaze; restoration to rim, $9" \times 4\frac{1}{4}"$ dia., $2,500

Three-lobed vase w/full height leaves alternating w/buds under feathered matte green glaze; restoration to chip at rim, 7¼" × 4", $3,000

Cuenca tile, "The Pines," w/pine trees in brown and green in a landscape of greens and blues; glaze bubbles and nicks to edges 6" sq., $3,500

Ovoid floor vase w/tooled and applied broad leaves in leathery matte green glaze; chip to one leaf edge, line from base, 2" string of small glaze bubbles, 23" × 9", $8,000

Small squat vessel w/tooled and applied leaves under curdled matte green glaze; small flecks to leaf edges, 3" × 4½", $3,000

Vase w/tooled and applied full-height leaves under matte green glaze; two small restored chips to rim, kiln kiss to shoulder, 5½" × 4", $2,500

Teardrop-shaped vase by Ruth Erickson, w/tooled and applied pointy leaves under leathery matte green glaze, 6¾" × 4", $5,000

Bulbous vessel w/tooled and applied rounded leaves and in a matte green glaze; chips to high points of three leaf tips, 4½" × 5¼", $2,000

Vase w/floriform top by Ruth Erickson, w/full-height tooled and applied leaves alternating w/narrow buds in green against a superior oatmealed blue glaze, 5½" × 3¾", $16,500

Floor vase decorated w/full-height tooled and applied leaves alternating w/lemon yellow buds under a thick leathery matte green glaze; restoration around rim and touch-ups to nicks on leaf edges, 22"x 8", $16,500

Two-color bulbous vase decorated w/tooled and applied buds alternating w/leaves under leathery matte green glaze; glaze nicks to high points, restoration to several small chips at rim, 4½" × 4", $3,500

Tile decorated in cuenca w/turtle under garland of leaves, in shades of green and brown against a dark brown ground, 6" sq., $4,000

Bulbous vase decorated w/leaves alternating w/yellow buds on an excellent leathery matte green ground, 6¼" × 6¾", $12,500

Bulbous vessel by Annie Lingley, decorated with tooled and applied full-height leaves under a leathery medium matte green glaze, 11" × 8", $8,000

Two-color bulbous vase decorated w/tooled and applied short broad leaves alternating with tall yellow buds under a fine pulled and feathered matte green glaze, 10½" × 3¾", $8,750

Gourd-shaped vase by Wilhelmina Post, w/two rows of tooled and applied rounded leaves under frothy matte green glaze; nicks to edges, 12¾" × 8", $5,000

Pear-shaped vase decorated w/tooled and applied leaves alternating w/buds at rim and covered in dark matte green glaze, 7½" × 4½", $2,500

Grueby small squat vessel with tooled and applied leaves under a fine curdled matte green glaze. A few small flecks to leaf edges. Mark obscured by glaze, remnant of paper label, 3" × 4½", $4,887

Bulbous vase w/tooled panels covered in leathery pale blue glaze, 6¾" × 4¼", $2,500

Barrel-shaped vase by Wilhelmina Post w/tooled and applied alternating short and tall leaves under leathery matte green glaze; restoration to rim and touch-ups to leaf edges, 1" sq. glaze missing, 8½" × 7", $5,000

Bulbous vase w/four-lobed rim, tooled and applied leaves alternating w/buds under pulled leathery matte green glaze; patchiness and nicks to edges, grinding chip, 9" × 5", $3,000

Tile decorated in cuenca w/water lilies in white, yellow, and green, 6", $2,750

Grueby/Pardee tile in cuerda seca w/lion in leathery ivory and blue glaze; minor nick to edge and corner chip on back, 4¼", $750

Ram's head wall hanging covered in matte green glaze, 5½" × 6", $1,500

Ram's head wall hanging in matte ochre glaze; restoration to 1½" chip on ear, 5½"x6", $1,400

Tile modeled w/a bunch of grapes in blue, green and brown on tan ground. 6" sq., $825

Bulbous vessel by Marie Seaman w/tooled and applied leaves to a ridged floriform base and covered in organic matte green glaze; minor nicks to edges, 12½" × 8¼", $10,500

Advertising tile decorated in cuenca w/candle under the words "grueby tile." Minor glaze flake to top, 6" × 4½", $3,500

Tile decorated in cuenca by Marie Seaman w/pink tulip on green matte ground, mounted in bronze Tiffany trivet base. Wear to surface, patina to mount, 6" sq., $5,000

Bulbous vase w/tooled and applied rounded leaves alternating w/irises under curdled medium green matte glaze; restoration to small hole drilled near base; minor glaze slip at top, 13¾ × 9", $11,000

Bulbous vase w/tooled and applied rounded leaves alternating w/buds under medium matte green glaze; small nick to one leaf edge, 7½" × 4½", $2,500

Bulbous vase by Florence S. Liley, decorated w/tooled and applied broad leaves under leathery matte green glaze; small chip to one leaf tip, 8" × 6½", $5,000

Ovoid vase decorated w/crisply tooled broad leaves, covered in leathery dark green glaze; some nicks to high points of leaves, 5½" × 4½", $2,000

Architectural Faience plaque carved and modeled w/family of elephants glazed in black against blue-gray ground, mounted in a box frame; two firing lines to body, restoration to one; small chip to one corner, 14" × 23", $12,500

Two floor tiles w/white backgrounds, one with hart in red clay, the other w/knight on horseback in indigo, 6" sq., $600

Five tiles, including one w/yellow fleur-de-lis on blue ground and brown elephant on ivory ground; chip to corner of elephant tile, 3¾" sq., $350

Gourd-shaped vase by Ruth Erickson w/tooled and applied leaves under green matte ground; glaze misses, bruise to rim, firing chip to base, 8" × 4½", $2,500

Approximately 200 hexagonal floor tiles and 40 half-hex, in matte green glazes, 3" dia., $2,500

Two-color jardiniere w/three rows of curled leaves below nine light blue five-petaled flowers against oatmealed matte green glaze; couple of minor flecks, 7½" × 9", $15,000

Barrel-shaped vase by Wilhelmina Post, 1906, w/tooled and applied daffodils and green leaves in fine pulled leathery matte green glaze; restoration to drilled holes under base is professional and invisible, 1" kiln kiss near base, 12" × 7¾", $20,000

Two-color vase, w/tooled and applied leaves alternating w/yellow buds at the rim and covered in a feathered matte green glaze; touch-up to base fleck and restoration to rim chips, 9" × 4¼", $8,750

Tile decorated in cuenca w/large oak tree against blue sky w/puffy white clouds, pristine condition, 6"sq., $6,000

Tile, "The Pines," in polychrome cuenca; small ½" chip to one corner, 6", $3,500

Tile, "The Pines," in polychrome cuenca, 6", $4,000

Tile decorated in cuenca w/yellow tulip on matte green ground, mounted sterling silver trivet base by Karl Leinonen; very light abrasion to surface, 6¼" sq., $4,500

Two-color cylindrical vase decorated w/tooled and applied stylized flowers in chartreuse alternating w/broad leaves, in leathery dark green matte glaze, 10" × 4¼", $8,750

Three-color squat vessel, 1914, decorated w/tooled and applied waterlilies and lilypads in yellow and green against a leathery dark green ground; very short tight bruise to rim, 4¼" × 9½", $15,000

Two-color ovoid vase w/tooled and applied broad leaves alternating w/yellow trefoils covered in matte green glaze; 1" hairline from rim, 6½" × 3¼", $8,250

Spherical vessel, decorated w/tooled and applied pointed leaves under curdled dark green matte glaze, 4¼" × 4½", $2,000

Vase w/flaring rim, its squat base decorated w/tooled and applied leaves under feathered matte green glaze, 7" × 4½", $2,750

Bulbous vase w/tooled panels in leathery matte brown glaze, 8" × 5", $2,000

Vase w/five tooled and applied curled handles alternating w/full height leaves, under frothy matte green glaze; small nick to one handle, 1" grinding chip, 11¼" × 6½", $14,000

Four-color ovoid vase w/floriform rim, decorated w/tooled and applied daffodils in yellow, blue and burgundy w/narrow leaves in frothy matte green glaze, 11" × 5", $15,000

Squat vessel w/ribbed band in leathery matte green glaze, 3½" × 6", $1,250

Low bowl by Ruth Erickson, 1907, w/tooled and applied square leaves w/curled edge under blue-gray curdled glaze; minor nicks to edges, dark crazing lines to rim, 2" × 6½", $1,250

Low bowl w/closed-in rim, in leathery matte green glaze, 1½" × 4", $500

Small vase covered in feathered matte green glaze; restoration to small chip at base, 4½", $625

Watermelon-shaped vessel, w/tooled and applied leaves under curdled dark green matte glaze, 9½" × 7", $5,500

Bulbous vase in leathery ivory matte glaze; short lines of bubbles and small glaze chips to base from grinding, 15¼" × 10", $3,000

Kendrick reticulated lamp base w/tooled and applied broad leaves under leathery dark green matte glaze, w/original Bigelow & Kennard leaded glass dome shade w/pine cone motif in white, yellow, green, and brown slag glass, 21" × 18" dia., $32,500

Ovoid vase w/tooled and applied full-height leaves under matte green glaze; two small restored chips, ½" kiln kiss to shoulder, 5½" × 4", $2,000

Shouldered vase by Marie Seaman, w/tooled and applied broad leaves alternating w/slender ones under leathery matte green glaze, 8" × 8", $8,500

Gourd-shaped vase by Ruth Erickson, w/tooled and applied leaves under green matte ground; glaze misses to rim, ½" bruise to rim, firing chip to base, 8" × 4½", $3,500

Squat vase w/tooled and applied rows of leaves under fine leathery matte green glaze; minute flecks to leaf edges, 4¾" × 5½", $2,500

Lotus bowl w/tooled and applied leaves, glossy green interior glaze and matte green exterior; glaze flake to rim, couple of glaze misses, 6" × 7" sq., $1,650

Wall pocket w/tooled and applied full height leaves in thick, rich oatmealy matte green glaze, 8½" × 3½", $1,750

Vase w/tooled and applied quatrefoils around rim and broad leaves to squat base in leathery green matte glaze, 17½" × 8½", $10,500

Large scarab paperweight in veined blue-gray matte glaze; small glaze miss to front, 3¾" × 2¾", $650

Lamp base w/original Tiffany acorn pattern leaded glass shade. The bulbous base has tooled and applied leaves alternating w/bright yellow buds and is perfectly fired, oatmealed matte green glaze; minute flecks to leaf edges, 16" × 12", $22,500

Scarab paperweight in matte and sheer caramel glaze, 3" × 2", $500

## Hampshire Pottery

SHOPMARKS: Various combinations of the following: JAMES S. TAFT & CO./J.S.T. & CO./ KEENE, N.H./HAMPSHIRE POTTERY/HAMPSHIRE, printed, impressed, or on a paper label.

PRINCIPAL CONTRIBUTIONS: Matte glaze artware, including vases, bowls, and lamps.

FOUNDER: James S. Taft. Born: 1844, died: 1923, founded: 1871, closed: 1923.

STUDIOS AND SALESROOMS: Hampshire Pottery Company, Keene, New Hampshire, 1871-1923.

J.S.T. &CO.
KEENE. NH.

Hampshire
Pottery

"The 'Witch Jug' made by Hampshire for Daniel Low of Salem, Massachusetts, and which can accurately be dated as produced in 1892, was matt, glazed and established the fact that Hampshire was producing pieces thus glazed at least four years before Grueby began operation."
—*Paul Evans*[1]

In 1871, at the age of 27, James S. Taft purchased an abandoned building in Keene, New Hampshire, long known for its fine clay deposits, and with the help of his uncle transformed it into a budding pottery operation. Unfortunately, it burned down before the first piece of redware was produced. Less than two months later, however, a new building had been constructed, and the partnership had begun selling simple flowerpots produced from local clays. Within the next few years Taft and his uncle increased their line to include stoneware items, buying a neighboring pottery building to aid in their expansion, and by 1876 they were advertising flowerpots, vases, florists, supplies, and related items from one plant and jars, pitchers, jugs, pots, and similar household containers from the other.[2]

The turning point in the development of Keene pottery came in 1879, when Taft hired Thomas Stanley, an Englishman, to oversee the two plants and their continued expansion. Soon after arriving, Stanley initiated a high-glaze majolica tableware that led to improvements in the quality of the firm's clay, decorations, glazes, and equipment. A gifted artist by the name of Wallace L. King was added to the growing staff. King oversaw the production of a Royal Worcester-style line of "plates, dishes, dressing table sets, etc. in a semi-porcelain body with a pink-tinged ivory matt surface"[3] and a popular line of souvenir plates and jugs with transfer-printed scenes including "the famous Longfellow jug and the witch jug made to be sold in Salem, Massachusetts."[4] While the success of their transfer-decorated line paved the way for further expansion in their staff during the last decade of the 19th century, it also overshadowed an achievement in the field of matte glazes that has since been credited to the Grueby Faience Company. As the Kovels observed in their study, confirming Evans's earlier conclusion, the Hampshire pottery's "green matte finish was particularly popular. It is interesting that while Grueby was credited with making the first popular matte finished art pottery in America, the Hampshire Pottery used this glaze in 1883, four years before Grueby."[5]

Cadmon Robertson, Taft's brother-in-law, who joined the firm in 1904, proved to be a crucial addition to the management at a time when Wallace King, their foremost artist, was nearing retirement, "A notable chemist, he introduced no fewer than 900 formulas and was responsible for the great variety of matte glazes from green and peacock (two tone) blue, to old blue, gray bronze, brown and yellow,"[6] The good fortune of "New Hampshire's

Hampshire bulbous vase embossed with stylized flowers under a fine leathery teal blue and green matte glaze. A couple of tight lines to base from firing. Stamped Hampshire Pottery/123, 7¼" × 5¼", $805

most successful commercial pottery"[7] seemed due to three factors: a durable clay body, a variety of affordable molded shapes, and quality matte glazes.

King's retirement in 1908 and Robertson's death in 1914 proved too much for the 70-year-old Taft to overcome. Production continued to decrease until 1916, when the Hampshire Pottery Company was sold to George M. Morton, a former potter at the Grueby Faience Company. Using the molds and glaze formulas included with the plant, Morton immediately fired more than 1,000 of Hampshire Pottery's most popular forms, but his planned infusion into the pottery market was halted by the onset of World War I. Afterward Morton switched Hampshire's focus to restaurant china and mosaic floor tiles, but in 1923 "the saga of the pottery . . . was drawn to a close with the death of the firm's founder, J. S. Taft, the dismantling of equipment and the destruction or scattering of the molds."[8]

The sudden upswing in prices being paid for Grueby pottery has refocused attention on Hampshire pottery—particularly those pieces that have a Grueby-like appearance. Large matte-glazed examples with crisp, detailed features have developed a following of their own. Lamps and large vases in particular have found a new crowd of collectors who, like admirers from their grandparents' era, are less concerned with the fact that Hampshire pottery was formed from molds than they are with its overall appearance—and its reasonable price.

Because Hampshire ware is molded and, for the most part, repeatable, even the slightest damage will decrease value by about a third. Happily, attractive pieces of Hampshire matte are salable with all but serious damage.

## SELECTED PRICES

Ovoid vase embossed w/lotus buds and leaves, covered in mottled green glaze; restoration to hairlines at rim, 7" × 5", $500

Two vases, one bulbous and one cylindrical, both covered in matte blue glaze; spider line to base of latter, 4½" and 5", $250

Two vessels, one covered in fine blue-green leathery glaze (hairlines to rim) and one with Greek key band under leathery brown glaze (minor fleck to rim), 7½" and 5¼", $500

Bulbous vase embossed w/rows of leaves under butter yellow matte glaze; tight line from rim, 8¼" × 6½", $350

Low bowl embossed w/alternating waterlilies and pads, in smooth matte green glaze; restoration to hairline, 3¼" × 10", $250

Ovoid vase covered in matte green glaze, 12½" × 4¾", $625

Bulbous vase embossed w/stylized flowers under leathery teal blue and green matte glaze; tight lines to base from firing, 7¼" × 5¼", $800

Oil lamp complete w/glass chimney and shade painted w/red roses, 19" × 12", $1,250

Ovoid vase in raspberry semi matte curdled glaze, 6" × 3¾", $250

Low bowl embossed w/waterlily pads and buds under fine leathery matte brown-green glaze, 3" × 10", $625

Large bulbous vase impressed w/scroll decoration, in smooth matte green glaze; factory shaved neck to accommodate oil font, 9" × 9½", $875

Bulbous vase in fine mottled blue and rose matte glaze, 7" × 4½", $550

Ovoid vase embossed w/ears of corn under matte green glaze; some burst glaze bubbles to body and around base, 5¾", $875

Ovoid vase embossed w/three panels of stylized leaves under frothy matte green glaze; burst bubbles, 6¾", $350

Two pieces: bulbous vase in matte green glaze and early mug painted w/lady's portrait, 5½" and 6¼", $300

Vase w/tall neck and squat base embossed w/leaves in fine mottled blue and rose matte glaze; spider cracks to base, one branch goes up one side, 10" × 6½", $350

Lamp base embossed w/buds and leaves under matte green glaze, w/original fixture and topped w/wicker shade, 11", $1,150

Tall vase w/frothy blue and green matte glaze; 2½" green spot on side, 12¼" × 5", $1,050

Factory lamp base w/heavily embossed leaves under fine matte green glaze; repainted metal fixture, 12½" × 7½", $1,400

Ovoid vase in good mottled and feathered blue matte glaze, 7½" × 4", $450

Squat vessel w/embossed panels in smooth matte green glaze; 1" line from rim, 2¾" × 4¾", $300

Bulbous vase w/embossed Greek key pattern under fine matte green glaze, 5½" × 5¾", $400

Tapering cabinet vessel embossed w/leaves and covered in matte green glaze; flat grinding chip, 3¾" × 3¼", $350

Tall vase shaped as tired pouch, covered w/ dark green matte glaze, 11" × 5¼", $550

Tall vase w/flaring rim and two handles, in fine dark green matte glaze, 15" × 5½", $625

## Jervis Pottery

SHOPMARKS: Incised vertical JERVIS, occasionally with the letters *O* and *B* (Oyster Bay), or Briarcliff.

PRINCIPAL CONTRIBUTIONS: Incised-decorated vases and bowls.

FOUNDER: James William Percival Jervis (with initial assistance from Frederick H. Rhead). Born: 1849. died: 1925, founded: 1908, closed: ca. 1912.

STUDIOS AND SALESROOMS: Jervis Pottery, Oyster Bay, New York, 1908-ca. 1912.

After having written about and worked for several potteries, William Jervis, assisted by his friend Frederick H. Rhead, whom he had worked with at the Avon Faience Company, opened a small pottery in 1908 in Oyster Bay, New York. Rhead may have designed some of Jervis's molds before leaving around 1910 to join the newly formed University City Pottery. Jervis preferred an incised form of decorative technique for his molded pottery; each piece was coated with a thin white clay slip, which when dry, was carved with incised lines. The unwanted white slip was then peeled away, leaving the design intact on the redware body. The form would then most often be fired with a matte or, on occasion, a metallic glaze. The small pottery, with its limited output, closed around 1912 apparently on the retirement of William Jervis.

It is important to note that Jervis appeared to work out of several locations, including the Rose Valley experiment in Moylan, Pennsylvania. He seems an artist in search of a style, and his work often reflects the talents of his associates and the locale of the kiln.

Fine and rare Jervis (Oyster Bay, New York) vessel with banded closed-in rim, enamel-decorated with daffodils in yellow, green stems, and the inscription "Daffodils That Come Before the Swallows Dare," on a dark blue ground. (A wonderful example of Arts & Crafts pottery.) Incised JERVIS/OB, 6" × 5½", $4,600

His work is very uneven in quality, though the norm is rough and somewhat crude. His best ware is decorated, almost certainly with the assistance of Frederick Rhead, in an excised fashion not dissimilar to the Della Robbia ware Rhead created for the Roseville Pottery in Zanesville, Ohio. The red clay bodies are usually press molded or perhaps even hand built, and the finishing details are short on charm.

Nevertheless, well-decorated pieces are quite rare are highly prized by modern collectors. Minor damage, especially roughness around the low-fired edges, is acceptable.

**SELECTED PRICES**

Jervis/Briarcliff vessel, hand-carved w/stylized trees in dead matte blue and green glazes; a few minute flecks, 3½" × 3¾", $1,400

Tall tapering vase incised w/peacock against railing in shades of blue and green against a deep Persian blue ground; kiln kiss to side, 10¾" × 4¼", $4,000

Squat vessel incised w/stylized leaves in green and white on blue deadmatte ground, 3" × 4¾", $1,400

Jervis/Oyster Bay cylindrical vase w/closed-in rim, w/a squeezebag band of turquoise and white panels on shoulder, in matte green glaze, 5½" × 3", $500

# Losanti

SHOPMARKS: Incised initials *LMcL,* often overlapping *LOSANTI,* occasionally in Oriental lettering. Some marks are painted underglaze in dark blue.

Often the year and the mark of the pottery that produced the blank will appear.

PRINCIPAL CONTRIBUTION: Decorated porcelain vases

FOUNDER: Mary Louise McLaughlin. Born: 1847, died: 1939, founded: 1898, closed 1906.

STUDIOS AND SALESROOMS: Mary Louise McLaughlin, Cincinnati, Ohio, active 1877-1906.

> "Miss McLaughlin, the President of the Club, is the discoverer of the method of decorating under the glaze that is still used as the foundation principle of the work at the Rookwood Pottery. The same method was used at the other Art Potteries of Cincinnati during their existence."
> —*Chicago World's Fair, 1893*[1]

The verbal battle between Mary Louise McLaughlin, Thomas J. Wheatley, and Marie Longworth Storer over recognition as the first American to develop successfully the underglaze technique of decorating pottery with tinted clays (called slips in their creamy consistency) lasted from 1877 until at least 1893, when William Taylor, the president of Rookwood, bristled over the suggestion that his firm was indebted to McLaughlin for the technique that propelled Rookwood toward continued success. By that date Mary Louise McLaughlin had, for the most part, concluded her experiments with underglaze decoration—due in no small part to her eviction from the Rookwood Pottery in 1892 by Taylor.

McLaughlin's talents were eventually turned toward the challenge of creating (for the first time outside a major firm) decorative porcelain. "The obstacles for Miss McLaughlin seemed overwhelming at times: no published technical instruction to follow, the necessity of adapting foreign formulas to American materials, [and] complaints from neighbors about the burning of

Fine and rare Marie-Louise McLaughlin Losanti ware porcelain vase incised with swirling peacock feathers under a superior beige and oxblood crackled glaze. Short, heavy crazing line to rim. Incised artist cipher/Losanti/97, 4¼" × 3¾", $2,645

coal in a backyard kiln,"[2] all of which contributed to an arduous trial-and-error beginning. Although her first public showing was in 1899, little more than a year after her experiments had begun, "it was not until about March 1901 that the best results were secured by a single firing at over 2500° F., wherein the native clay body and glaze matured together."[3]

McLaughlin continued to develop her technique, calling her new line of porcelain Losanti (Cincinnati had once been called Losantiville). Decorations included painting, incising, and/or modeling designs in the clay; the latter occasionally developed into pierced detailing. Her particular style of carving is reflective of Art Nouveau motifs, as she "integrated her designs of gently swirling, conventionalized floral motifs . . . with the forms of the vases. Some leaf designs were carved so as to envelop and become the form of the vase itself, the irregular edges of the leaves jutting out to form the lip."[4] Soft, pastel glazes were used most often, although on rare occasions a bright, colorful glaze, such as red or even purple, will be found.

McLaughlin's experiments with porcelain were drawn to a close in 1906 as she moved on to conquer other challenges.

McLaughlin's porcelain work is extremely rare and remains highly prized among modern day collectors. Each piece is one of a kind and reflects clearly the hand of a master innovator. The best examples are heavily carved, from top to bottom, glazed in brighter colors. Most of her porcelain work is small in size, ranging from about 3" to about 6" tall. While larger pieces surface from time to time, they are clearly the exception.

It is also important to note that, because of the ongoing experimental nature of her work, pieces usually bear some kind of firing flaw or another. These can range from gaping under glaze cracks to "dirty" firing, with ash or kiln dust blemishes in the glaze. Unless they are very obvious, these have little negative impact on value.

## SELECTED PRICES

Marie Louise McLaughlin Losanti ware squat porcelain vessel incised w/scrolled wreath in white against mottled dark blue ground; short hairline from rim, grinding chips, $2\frac{3}{4}$" × $4\frac{1}{4}$", $1,250

Marie Louise McLaughlin Losanti ware circular porcelain trivet embossed w/floral motif under celadon glaze; clay particles stuck to glaze, firing lines and chips to bottom, 6" dia., $625.

## Low Art Tile Works

SHOPMARKS: Name of firm incised or in raised letters on reverse of tile, often with CHELSEA, MASS. USA/ COPYRIGHT and the year.

PRINCIPAL CONTRIBUTIONS: Decorative tiles and art pottery vases.

FOUNDER: John Gardner Low. Born: 1835, died: 1907, founded: ca. 1878, closed: 1902.

STUDIOS AND SALESROOMS: J. & J. G. Low Art Tile Works, Chelsea, Massachusetts, 1878-83, J. G. & J. F. Low Art Tile Works, Chelsea, Massachusetts, 1883-1902.

> "The Lows never imitated other work, either domestic or foreign. They have never made hand-painted, mosaic, printed, encaustic, or floor tiles, and they have never employed men who were trained in other tile works. Consequently, their products are characterized by the marked originality, both in style and design, which has caused them to be extensively imitated, both at home and abroad."
> —*Edwin Barber, ca. 1904*[1]

Educated and trained in Europe as a landscape artist, John G. Low turned his talent to ceramics when it became apparent, at age 35, that he was not going to be able to support himself through the sale of his paintings. Back in his hometown of Chelsea, Massachusetts, Low learned that a local pottery run by the Robertson family was in need of artists to decorate a new line of art pottery. Though inexperienced in this field, Low went to work for the Chelsea Keramic Art Works at the time that James Robertson, the father of the three famous pottery sons, "made what is believed to be the first pressed clay tiles produced in the United States."[2]

Low stayed with the Robertsons for more than a year, learning both the art pottery and the tile trade and experimenting with his own designs before

J. & J. G. Low vertical plastic sketch by Arthur Osborne of a monk holding a rosary, inscribed AVE MARIA, under an olive-green glaze, mint condition, in original frame, velvet worn. Inised AO/remnant of label on back of frame. Tile: 17½" × 7", $1,475

leaving. Like many artists in 1876, Low journeyed to Philadelphia for the Centennial Exposition, returning with plans to form his own tile works. With the help of his father, John Low, the J. & J. G. Low Art Tile works opened in 1878 in a new and fully equipped factory building. One of the first employees was George Robertson, the eldest son of James Robertson and an experienced glazer, whom John had come to know while working at Chelsea Keramic Art Works. They produced tiles in a number of sizes and a variety of colors, but most were either six or four inches square in natural tones of brown or green. Smaller tiles, especially the more common round tiles, were generally designed to decorate cast-iron stoves.

Although decorative tiles had long been produced in England, John G. Low was forced to learn the process through experimentation. The traditional means involved pressing damp clay dust under extreme pressure, using a metal plate decorated with the desired design. Afterward the tile would be glazed and then placed in the kiln to be baked. In another technique, wet clay was pressed into a mold that contained the desired design; it was then allowed to dry slowly, at which time it would shrink enough to permit it to be removed from the mold. After additional air drying, each tile was glazed and sent to the kiln. Low developed a process that he had first observed at the Robertson firm: Actual plant forms, such as grass or leaves, were pressed into tiles, which were then used to form a matching tile with a corresponding raised design.

Another early employee was Arthur Osborne, a sculptor who stayed with the firm for more than 15 years, working as an artist and designer. Osborne developed low-relief "plastic sketches"[3] as Low called them—large square or rectangular tiles with sculpted scenes often depicting people from foreign countries stories from mythology, animals, or plants, though studies of individuals were also popular. Most were signed with the artist's initials, the letter *A* inside the letter *O*.

Recognition came quickly for the young firm, as it received awards both in America and abroad for its fine tile work. A few years later, in 1883, the elder Low retired from the firm, making way for his grandson, John Farnsworth Low, and a new name for the business: the J. G. & J. F. Low Art Tile Works. The firm expanded into pottery, undoubtedly drawing on the experience brought to the firm by both Arthur Osborne and George Robertson. The Low Chelsea Ware had much in common with the Oriental-inspired designs of Hugh Robertson: simple, undecorated forms with glazes that "ranged from dark cream to chocolate; delicate claret to a deep, almost oxblood red."[4] Paul Evans has speculated that "Low's firm was encouraged in the development of this line by Hugh C. Robertson after his Chelsea Keramic Art Works abandoned their similar efforts in favor of the crackle-ware and moved to Dedham."[5]

John Low also marketed a successful line of art tile soda fountains. Low had begun experimenting with tiles for a soda fountain around 1883, but his patent application was not approved until six years later. In 1893 an elaborate 20-foot-long, 16-foot-high model was displayed at the Columbian Exposition in Chicago. It helped spread the fame and the sales of Low art tile soda fountains across the country, but stiffer competition led to the end of both tile and art pottery production around 1902. Low's son, though a trained chemist and capable manager, was unable to save the firm, and in 1907—the year in which John Gardner Low died—the tile and pottery works was dismantled.

Low's tile was the best Victorian ware produced in America. Crisply modeled designs were enveloped in rich, bright, transparent glazes. The pottery's continued production of an "Old World" style of ceramic was the cause of its decline, and certainly not the quality and consistency of its work.

Even the simplest Low tile speaks to the artistic success of it's endeavors. Modern-day collectors, however, are primarily interested in larger (bigger than 6" × 6") tiles with landscapes and town scenes rather than portraiture. Lighter glazes, such as honey or soft blue, are more in demand than darker finishes because they tend to show designs more clearly. Minor damage is acceptable on such pieces.

The laws of supply and demand play an important part in determining value. Even relatively simple tiles, if rare, bring several thousand dollars. And some of their more elaborate designs, if already in the hands of the few major collectors of this work, might sell for as little as $1,000 each.

## SELECTED PRICES

14 tiles w/herringbone pattern under gold glaze, $4\frac{1}{4}$" sq., $200

Tile w/herringbone pattern under teal-blue glaze, $4\frac{1}{4}$" sq., $15

7 tiles w/herringbone pattern in relief, in brown glaze, $4\frac{1}{4}$" sq., $100

Four border tiles w/an Oriental stylized floral pattern under olive green glaze; minor glaze nicks, $2\frac{1}{4}$"x6", $60

Tile w/an Oriental trellis pattern w/branches and fruit under dark amber glaze, chip to one side, in mahogany frame, 6" sq, $65

Japonesque tile w/spider weaving a web off flowering tree, under light caramel glaze, in gilded frame, 6" sq., $185

Large square tile w/stylized plant growing out of a kylex-shaped urn, under a burgundy glaze, 12" sq., $325

Round covered brass box w/circular tile on cover of a classical female profile under blue glaze, tiny glaze fleck at rim, $2\frac{3}{4}$" dia., $345

Brass ring tray w/circular tile in the center, a classical female profile under burgundy glaze, $4\frac{1}{2}$" dia., $245

Large tile w/stylized plant growing out of a kylex-shaped urn, 12" sq., $325

Vertical plastic sketch by Arthur Osborne of a monk holding a rosary, inscribed Ave Maria, under an olive-green glaze, mint condition, in original frame, velvet worn, $17\frac{1}{2}$"x7", $1,475

# Marblehead Pottery

SHOPMARKS: Impressed outline of a ship and the initials *MP*, all enclosed in a circle, occasionally with initials *A.E.B.* (Arthur E. Baggs) and/or *H.T.* (Hanna Tutt).

PRINCIPAL CONTRIBUTIONS: Hand-thrown vases, bowls, and tiles with conventionalized designs under a matte glaze.

FOUNDER: Arthur E. Baggs. Born: 1886, died: 1947, founded: 1904, closed: 1936.

STUDIOS AND SALESROOMS: Marblehead Pottery, Marblehead, Massachusetts, 1904-36.

"The Marblehead Pottery stands for simplicity—all that is bizarre and freakish have been avoided. It stands for quiet, subdued colors, for severe conventionalization in design, and for careful and through workmanship in all details."

—*House Beautiful, 1912*[1]

In 1904 the picturesque fishing village of Marblehead, Massachusetts, provided the overwrought patients of Dr. Herbert J. Hall with a relaxing environment in which they could recuperate. To aid them in their recovery, Dr. Hall established the Handcraft Shops, where each patient could, "under supervision, partake of certain occupational therapy in the form of arts and crafts."[2] As Dr. Hall explained in 1908, his intent was to provide his "nervously worn out patients the blessing and privilege of quiet manual work, where as apprentices they could learn again gradually and without haste to use their hand and brain in a normal, wholesome way,"[3] Among the crafts with which they could experiment in the former clubhouse that served as the Handcraft Shops were metalwork, woodcarving, weaving, tiles, and pottery, the last inspired by the nearby Beverly Pottery (1866–1904).

To help organize and manage the pottery works, Dr. Hall contacted 19-year-old Arthur E. Baggs, who had been recommended by his former ceramics instructor Charles F. Binns (1857–1934). For the first three years Baggs and his patient-potters experimented with various forms and struggled to establish a studio and pottery operation with a consistent style and steady output. By 1908 production of "simple, well-designed shapes and severely conventional decoration,"[4] clearly reflective of both the philosophy of Charles Binns and the current Arts and Crafts movement, had reached nearly 200 pieces per week.[5] Realizing that the pottery's potential could only be hampered by tying it too closely to the sanitarium and its temporary patient help, Baggs began the weaning process by hiring a small staff of full-time designers, artists, and potters. Among them were Hanna Tutt, decorator; Maude Milner and Arthur Hennessey, designers; and Englishman John Swallow, potter; most remained with the pottery for several years. By 1915, it was apparent that Marblehead Pottery had outgrown its original intent, and it was agreed that Arthur Baggs would become its sole owner.

The simple forms and soft, matte-glazed decorations appealed to an Arts and Crafts-conscious public. While popular designs were often repeated, vases and bowls continued to be hand-thrown and individually decorated by the artists, ensuring their clients that no two items (with the exception of tiles and molded bookends) could ever be identical. Early designs occasionally featured incised Indian motifs over a red clay body, and early wares can often be distinguished by their wide foot rims and rough bottoms compared with the narrow, smooth bottoms of the later vases. Early pieces often had designs of nautical influence, such as stylized waves or harpoons.

Other motifs found on Marblehead pottery include insects, flowers, birds, seashells, animals, fish, and sailing ships; but as Martin Eidelberg observed in 1972, "More important than the motif, however, is its treatment: the design is conventionalized into flat, abstract patterns. There is often an insistence on a rigid, vertical stem, and many of the patterns are purely geometrical."[6] Fifteen years later Eidelberg went on to state that "typical of the new, sparse mode, Walrath and Marblehead shrank the design elements into linear, vertical or horizontal patterns and vastly increased the negative spaces of the ground. There was only one step left to take, and Baggs took it. He pushed past conventionalization into non-representational design through the use of geometric motifs."[7]

Essential to the Arts and Crafts style was the matte glaze popularized by Grueby, Hampshire, and Teco potteries prior to Marblehead's entrance. In contrast to Rookwood's version, the popular vellum matte glaze, the matte glaze that Baggs and his associates developed, "is at once the color, the design, and the surface—fused by the kiln into an immutable whole, a three-dimensional object of uniform surface patterned with color and devoid of all depth, gloss, or visual trickery."[8]

While the undecorated Marblehead forms appeal to a wide range of collectors, Arts and Crafts enthusiasts have actively sought the decorated forms

Marblehead bulbous vase covered in matte gray glaze. Illegible mark, 5½", $488

embellished with geometric designs and incorporating several colors. Like Walrath pottery, many times the colors are muted; those that reveal a distinct contrast between the colors have become very popular, as have those vases and bowls in which the form and decoration are in complete harmony. Collectors have also demonstrated a clear preference for those pieces in which the decoration utilized a large portion of the clay body. Finally, the pieces most popular with contemporary collectors are those whose designs are gently tooled into the vase surface, rather than those with only surface-painted decoration.

With the help of a loyal staff, Baggs was able both to continue his own education and to teach at universities in New York and Ohio without jeopardizing the quality of the work at Marblehead. Even the undecorated ware that became more prevalent after 1920 still commands respect for its pure forms and quality glazes. Baggs's experiments with glazes both at Marblehead and with his friend R. Guy Cowan (1884–1957) at Cowan's pottery in Cleveland earned him the respect and admiration of colleagues across the country. Baggs closed the pottery at Marblehead during the Depression and served as professor of ceramic arts at Ohio State University until his death in 1947.

Collectors are fast to distinguish between earlier Marblehead pieces and later examples. Those made before about 1915 tend to have a certain controlled crudeness to them; the glazes are speckled and deep, the designs intense and controlling the surface. Such pieces lose only about 25 percent of their value with minor flaws such as flat base chips and short, tight hairlines.

Undecorated Marblehead, hand-thrown pots with a single glaze color only, are also extremely popular because they are relatively inexpensive and are the perfect accouterment to the Arts and Crafts interior. These, however, will lose half their value with only the slightest flaw.

### SELECTED PRICES

Two low bowls, one w/blue matte exterior, one w/speckled gray; hairlines to rim, 7¼" and 8" dia, $400

Bulbous vase in matte gray glaze, 5½", $350

Small ovoid vase w/matte gray glaze, 4", $350

Large ovoid vase in dark blue matte glaze; drilled hole to base, 8½" × 6, $350

Squat vessel in speckled matte gray glaze; glaze bubbles, 3½" × 4½", $350

Three vases, two in blue matte glaze and one in speckled matte gray w/ blue semi-matte interior; restoration to rim of all three, 4¼", 4¾", 5¼", $350

Low bowl in matte indigo glaze w/blue semi matte interior, 2½" × 6¼", $300

Rare and important Marblehead ovoid vase by Hannah Tutt, carved with tall stylized flowers in umber, black, and cream on a speckled matte green ground. (The only one we've auctioned.) Impressed ship mark/incised HT, 6¾" × 4", $120,750

Ribbed pitcher in dark blue matte glaze; chips to rim, nick to base, 4½" × 5", $250

Pear-shaped vase in gray matte glaze; restoration to small rim chip, 5¼" × 3½", $200

Ovoid vase incised w/stylized green trees and red fruit on speckled dark blue ground, 7¼"x4¼", $5,500

Tile decorated w/potted topiaries in green, brown and blue on speckled gray ground; restoration to corners and to small burst bubbles on pots, 6¼" sq., $2,000

Beaker-shaped vase by Hannah Tutt, carved w/stylized decoration in black on speckled blue-green ground, 6¼" × 5", $5,000

Barrel-shaped vase painted by Hannah Tutt, w/stylized flowers in two tones of indigo on speckled gray ground, 4½" × 4", $2,500

Squat vessel carved w/wreath of flowers in pink and green on dark blue matte ground; restoration to small chip under rim, 3½" × 4¼", $1,650

Ovoid vase decorated w/grapes and leaves in gray and blue on speckled gray ground; small stilt-pull chip, 5¼" × 3¼", $1,550

Tile decorated in wax-resist w/sailboat in blue on speckled gray matte ground. Restoration to corner chip, firing line, 6" sq., $1,500

Ovoid vase covered in speckled blue matte glaze, 8¾" × 5", $350

Cylindrical vase in mauve matte glaze, 9" × 4", $850

Tapering vase in speckled brown matte glaze; minute fleck to rim, 8" × 4½", $1,000

Spherical vase in speckled pink matte glaze, $3\frac{1}{4}$" × 5", $350

Ovoid vase in matte lavendar glaze; minor burst bubbles, $5\frac{1}{4}$" × $3\frac{1}{4}$", $350

Vase in dark blue speckled matte glaze; fleck to inner rim, $3\frac{1}{2}$" × 3", $300

Tapering vase incised w/egrets in flight in dark teal on gray/blue matte ground, 6" × $5\frac{1}{4}$", $1,250

Ovoid vase by Hannah Tutt, incised w/mistletoe in dark grey on speckled light grey ground, 7" × 4", $3,000

Cylindrical vase w/band of stylized flowers in dark brown against speckled matte green glaze, 6" × 3", $2,500

Faceted match holder painted in abstract pattern in dark brown on speckled matte green ground; minute flecks around base, 2" × $2\frac{1}{4}$" dia., $1,050

Tile decorated in cuerda seca w/house and trees in polychrome on matte grey ground; restoration to y-shaped crack, 6"sq., $2,000

Ovoid vase by Hannah Tutt, matte painted w/stylized trees in green, ochre and blue on grey ground, 7" × $3\frac{3}{4}$", $6,250

Cylindrical vase decorated w/incised stylized holly branches w/green leaves and red berries on dark blue matte ground, $4\frac{1}{2}$" × $3\frac{3}{4}$", $5,000

Barrel-shaped vase decorated by Hannah Tutt w/a broad band of incised stylized flowers and leaves in amber, brown and blue on matte mustard ground, 9" × 6", $7,500

Barrel-shaped vase decorated by Hannah Tutt w/full height stylized lilies in amber, brown and blue on matte mustard ground, $4\frac{1}{2}$" × $3\frac{3}{4}$", $2,500

Corseted vase in speckled gray matte glaze; restoration to top, $8\frac{1}{2}$" × $3\frac{1}{2}$", $250

Tapering cabinet vase designed by Arthur Baggs and decorated by Hannah Tutt, w/incised chevron pattern in two-tone mottled matte green glaze, $4\frac{1}{4}$" × $2\frac{3}{4}$", $2,500

Cylindrical vase w/band of stylized palm fronds in gunmetal over speckled matte green ground, $8\frac{3}{4}$" × 4", dia., $6,250

Pair of triangular bookends embossed w/triptych of sailing ship in green, red, and white on indigo ground; minute glaze fleck to corner of one, $5\frac{1}{2}$" × $5\frac{1}{2}$" × $2\frac{1}{2}$", $1,150

Ovoid vase by Hannah Tutt, carved w/tall stylized flowers in umber, black and cream on speckled matte green ground, $6\frac{3}{4}$" × 4". This piece brought a record price of $120,750.

Cylindrical vase w/stylized poppies and leaves in three shades of matte olive green glazes; two hairlines from rim, 9" × $5\frac{1}{2}$", $8,000

Tall ovoid vase by Arthur Baggs, carved w/branches of pine cones in brown on speckled green matte ground; restoration to several cracks, 12" × 4¼", $6,500

Tile in cuerda seca w/bouquet of flowers in purple and teal on white ground; flecks to edges, 6" sq., $1,000

Pair of bookends, each w/different ship embossed in triptych in polychrome matte glazes, on blue ground; two restored chips to one, one additional restored and hairline to other, 5½" × 5½", $1,000

## Merrimac Pottery Company

SHOPMARKS: (1900-1901) Paper label, MERRIMAC CERAMIC COMPANY, with drawing of a sturgeon. (1901-1908) Impressed or incised mark with *MERRI-MAC* over a sturgeon.

PRINCIPAL CONTRIBUTIONS: Decorative garden pottery, plus a line of art pottery featuring quality colored glazes

FOUNDER: Thomas S. Nickerson. Born: unknown, died: unknown, founded: 1897, closed: 1908.

STUDIOS AND SALESROOMS: Merrimac Ceramic Company, Newburyport, Massachusetts, 1897–1902, Merrimac Pottery Company, Newburyport, Massachusetts, 1902–08.

> "These pastes so pleasing to the eye, and withal so varied, since they range from dull to highly vitrified surfaces, are left without painted decoration: beauty, according to the modern principle, being sought in a simplicity which embraces the entire work, extending to the form, as well as controlling the color."
> —*the Craftsman, 1903*[1]

Thomas S. Nickerson spent several years in preparation for the opening of his pottery in Newburyport, Massachusetts, in 1897. After study under Sir William Crookes in England and extensive experimentation at his home in picturesque Newburyport, Nickerson initiated production of florists' wares and glazed tiles under the name of the Merrimac Ceramic Company. Within the next three years Nickerson added a partner, increased the size and production of his plant, and began experimenting with forms of art pottery. His first offerings consisted primarily of flowerpots and vases with, according to Irene Sargent in 1903, "color and glazes obtained by Mr. Nickerson [that] first attracted public attention: both having a wide variety."[2]

As Miss Sargent noted, Nickerson achieved a variety of colors, not

Unusual Merrimac three-handled squat vessel with a dead-matte brown glaze dripping over a mustard ground. Minor flake inside rim. Stamped MERRIMAC with fish, 3¼" × 5", $1,840

through underglaze decoration but through a number of glazes, producing simple forms in greens, dull black, orange, brownish red, blues, and violet, some with an iridescence, others under a crackle surface. As were recently observed, "Merrimac's dense mat glaze and leafy decoration suggest analogies with the work of the nearby Grueby Pottery, but the curling leaves are rhythmic when compared with Grueby's staid rigidity."[3]

In 1902 Nickerson and his partner, W. G. Fisher, changed the name of the company to the Merrimac Pottery Company as an indication to the public of their newly expanded range. His original line of garden pottery was not dropped, but instead the firm increased the quality, the variety of forms, and the total production to meet a growing demand. An additional line of reproduction antique Roman pottery, called Arrhelian, produced from molds of authentic vases, was also added around 1902. In 1904 the firm exhibited at the Louisiana Purchase Exposition in St. Louis, returning home with a silver medal, indicative of the advances Nickerson had made in the development of the glazes that give the work "a cheerful, tender, bright, radiant character."[4]

For reasons yet unclear, Nickerson sold the Merrimac Pottery in 1908, possibly after production had ceased. Before the new owner had an opportunity to resume operations, however, a fire destroyed the plant and most of the inventory. It was never reopened.

Merrimac remains a bit of a cipher through today, in spite of the published information available and the hundreds of pieces that have passed through the marketplace. Its production was inconsistent; the pottery was as capable of producing a great piece as it was a modest one. Glazes similarly run the gamut from extraordinary and intense, to boring and dull.

The best pieces are those with tooled surface designs and rich, flowing matte finishes. The exceptions to these are the metallic finishes, some like the skin of a snake, that surface from time to time. Perhaps it is the abrupt closing of the company that resulted in the scarcity of its most interesting work.

Merrimac spherical bowl decorated with deeply tooled papyrus flowers and alternating leaves, covered in a fine rich leathery matte green glaze. Typical nicks to high points, rim and base. Incised artist's initials (EB), 5" × 9", $1,800–$2,200

We are left to consider that Merrimac was just hitting its stride when it was closed by the fire that destroyed the factory.

Collectors of Merrimac pottery are few and far between, and this paucity of buyers has created a market that does not suffer much damage. While nicks and flakes on the high points of tooled leaves little reduce value, cracks and chips will almost immediately knock 50 percent off the cost of a good piece.

## SELECTED PRICES

Two-handled squat vessel w/matte green glaze over bright matte yellow ground, $4\frac{3}{4}$" × 8", $2,500

Three handled squat vessel w/dead matte brown glaze dripping over mustard ground; minor flake inside rim, $3\frac{1}{4}$" × 5", $1,550

Cylindrical vase w/tooled and applied plants under superior feathered green microcrystalline glaze. Two hairlines, chip to base, several nicks to decoration, $5\frac{1}{4}$" × $3\frac{1}{2}$", $800

Barrel-shaped vase w/dead matte blue glaze over turquoise ground; $\frac{1}{4}$" chip inside rim, 4" × $3\frac{1}{2}$", $825

Squat urn in green and orange mottled matte glaze; small nick to rim, $4\frac{1}{4}$" × $4\frac{1}{4}$", $825

Bottle covered in dead matte yellow glaze over white ground; restoration to shallow chip at rim and base, $6\frac{3}{4}$" × $3\frac{3}{4}$", $875

Baluster vase w/closed-in rim, top covered in waxy forest green glaze dripping over fine green and brown mottled ground; two hairlines and short bruise to rim, glaze flakes to base, 11" × 5", $1,150

Bulbous vase in iridescent copper glaze; restoration around neck and grinding chips, $4\frac{3}{4}$" × $3\frac{1}{2}$", $625

Melon-shaped jardiniere in matte green glaze; restoration around rim and on bottom, $8\frac{1}{4}$" × 12", $1,750

Two-handled squat vessel w/a matte green glaze over bright matte yellow ground; ½" glaze burst to base, 4¾" × 8", $1,500

Baluster vase in feathered matte green glaze; minute flecks around rim, more around base, 4¼" × 3½", $550

Squat cabinet vase in mottled apple green semi-matte glaze, 3" × 3¾", $550

Squat two-handled jug in leathery semi-matte green glaze; several glaze flakes, 4" × 4", $625

Spherical bowl decorated w/deeply tooled papyrus flowers and alternating leaves in rich leathery matte green glaze; typical nicks to high points, rim and base, 5" × 9", $2,000

## Newcomb Pottery

SHOPMARKS: (1894-1899) Paper Words *NEWCOMB COLLEGE*
(1897-1948) Letter *N* within a larger letter *C*, often with date
Code: Letter *M,* mold form; letters *HB,* hand-built.
PRINCIPAL CONTRIBUTIONS: Decorated bowls, vases, candlesticks, mugs, and lamps in both high-gloss and matte glazes.
FOUNDERS: Ellsworth Woodward, William Woodward. Founded: 1895, closed: 1939[1].
STUDIOS AND SALESROOMS: The Newcomb Pottery, the Sophie Newcomb Memorial College (Tulane University), New Orleans, Louisiana, 1895-1939.

> "Our beautiful moss-draped oak trees appealed to the buying public but nothing is less suited to the tall graceful vases—no way to convey the true character of the tree. And oh, how boring it was to use the same motif over and over and over, though each one was a fresh drawing."
>
> —Sadie Irvine, decorator[2]

In New Orleans, as in Cincinnati, Chicago, Boston, and other American cities, the Arts and Crafts movement spawned an interest in improving the lives of young women by giving them training in weaving, leatherwork, metalsmithing, china decorating, and art pottery. As in other cities, clubs and organizations sprang up in New Orleans, but rather than developing into a private commercial enterprise, one such organization, the New Orleans Art Pottery, evolved into a school for pottery decorators at a recognized institution of higher education, the Sophie Newcomb Memorial College.

With the Rookwood Pottery as a model, the president of Newcomb College, acting on a proposal submitted by two members of the art faculty, brothers William and Ellsworth Woodward (both of whom had been involved with the New Orleans Art Pottery), had thrown his whole hearted support behind the project by 1895. Mary Sheerer was persuaded to leave Cincinnati to oversee the pottery decoration department; Joseph Meyer, a friend of the Woodwards and a potter at the new Orleans Art Pottery, assumed responsibility as head potter in 1896, a position he was to retain until he retired in 1927. The early days of "big heartbreaks and bigger dreams"[3] gradually gave way to repeated success. The veteran Meyer was adept at throwing the forms requested by the designers and providing practical experience with glazes, while Miss Sheerer guided the decorators in their quest for both artistic expression and practical skills. Although the pottery may never have been an outstanding commercial success, income from the sale of their work encouraged the young decorators and ensured continued support by the college.

Work from the early period of Newcomb (1895–1901) was marked by a great deal of experimentation with types and colors of decorations, including underglaze slip painting, but in a distinctive style—"favoring bright, clear tones, covered with a clear transparent glaze"[4]—totally unlike that being popularized at Rookwood. Since the goal of the pottery was to train young decorators rather than potters, both the shapes of the pieces and the clear, high-gloss glaze remained relatively consistent, whereas the artwork revealed a good deal of experimentation. Eventually, though, naturalistic Southern motifs in lively blue and green colors emerged as the most popular of the Newcomb Pottery line. It's exhibit at the Pan-American Exposition in Buffalo in 1901 garnered a silver medal and vital national exposure; numerous sources were soon reporting that the student decorators at the pottery could not keep up with the large numbers of orders that were coming in from all parts of the country.

It is interesting to note that, while historically important, pieces made during this first period were quite naive and often clumsy. This was a time when Newcomb College was developing its style, and the work more often displayed a formative, rather than a formidable, hand.

The second period (1902–10) in the development of Newcomb Pottery was ushered in with a series of awards at national exhibitions. The number of student decorators was increased from 10 to 15 for a brief time, perhaps indicative of the pottery's involvement in several expositions, but the temptation to expand into a manufacturing concern never seems to have been a serious topic of discussion at the college. Content to serve as a model for other institutions and encouraged by its artistic recognition and popular success, the pottery entered a period of combined creativity and continued refinements. Clearly defined incised designs under light blue or green glazes emerged, as well as the rare red glazes experimented with between 1903 and 1907. Relief modeling and more subtle incising led a "movement toward a softer, more romantic handling"[5] after 1908.

Clearly, Newcomb's work during this second period was its most creative and succesful. While it would always produce fine art pottery, the designs and decorative techniques from 1901 to 1910 are highly favored among contemporary collectors. Instead of mere surface painting of designs, they were incised and tooled into the surface of the pot. Their color scheme was more dramatic as well, often including bold greens, striking yellow, and occasionally, soft pinks and violet.

The third era (1910–18) was initiated with the arrival of Paul Cox (1897–1970) as perhaps the pottery's single most important decorator. The matte glazes made popular by Grueby, Hampshire, and Teco could not simply be applied to the decorated Newcomb wares; it was left to Cox to adapt and perfect a matte glaze that would please both the public and the pottery's decorators. Sculpted low relief continued to take precedence over the earlier sharply defined incised lines, and the misty, almost mysterious Southern landscapes were complemented by Cox's matte and semimatte glazes. Sadie Irvine had been a student decorator in 1903 and remained with the pottery until she retired in 1952. Credited with the famous bayou scene depicting a moss-draped oak tree illuminated by a full moon, she served as the backbone of the decorating department for more than two decades.

While the year 1919 is used to mark the departure of Paul Cox and the end of the third period of development of the pottery, it coincides with the general decline in interest in the Arts and Crafts movement. The public still responded enthusiastically to Newcomb pottery, but the experimentation and enthusiasm that characterized the earlier periods was largely replaced by the standardized forms and decorations (though still done by hand) that dominated production in the 1920s and 1930s. In 1939 the college changed the emphasis from commercial production to instruction, in effect bringing to a close not only the third period in its development but the Arts and Crafts era of the Newcomb Pottery. The change was marked also by the announcement of the formation in 1940 of the Newcomb Guild, which, while still serving as a pottery outlet for students and staff, was but an echo of its former self.

Although Newcomb collectors dream of someday discovering a rare experimental piece of red Newcomb pottery, most are also quite pleased if they discover a highly valued example of the early high-gloss glaze. Regardless of whether they are early or later, vases and bowls with crisp carving, clear definition, and a rich, warm blend of colors are the most popular among Arts and Crafts collectors. While the Sadie Irvine "Moonlight and Moss" motif is among the most common, it remains representative of the pottery's work and for that reason alone is popular with all art pottery collectors. Advanced Newcomb collectors distinguish between different treatments of this same motif on the basis of how well it fits the particular pottery shape, the depth and dimension of the decoration, and the crispness of the details. While they are almost always colored in hues of blue, soft green, and cream, darker versions are preferred.

Recently, the market for early, high glazed Newcomb pottery has risen so greatly in price that there is a broad acceptance of limited damage. In fact, collectors who bought slightly damaged pieces of early Newcomb a decade ago have seen a 500 percent increase in price. Small chips, discreet holes drilled through the bottom, and interior hairlines have relatively little impact on value. The same cannot be said about the later matte pieces. While still quite valuable, a single chip will reduce value by about 35 percent.

## SELECTED PRICES

Bulbous ribbed vase by Sadie Irvine, 1931, covered in indigo and ivory matte glaze; crack from rim, 4½" × 5", $400

Inkwell by M. T. Ryan, 1903, decorated w/stylized mushrooms under glossy glaze; cracked and missing lid, 2" × 4", $500

High glaze tapered bud vase by Anna Frances Simpson, 1908, carved w/jonquils in yellow and tall green leaves on blue ground, 9" × 3¼", $5,250

Bulbous vase by Anna Frances Simpson, 1929, w/live oaks and Spanish moss, Strong color and carving, 4½" × 4½", $3,000

Transitional ovoid vase by Henrietta Bailey, 1917, carved w/pale blue orchids w/yellow stamens and broad green leaves on denim blue background; 2", firing line inside bottom does not go through, some dark crazing lines to shoulder, and a few exterior firing lines to bottom ring, 13¾" × 7", $8,000

Bulbous vase by Sadie Irvine in the Espanol pattern, 1927, in blue-green, pink and white on a dark denim blue ground, 5½" × 4½", $2,500

Loving cup by Katherine Kopman, 1902, painted w/white clover blossoms and green leaves over pale blue and white ground; 1", chip inside rim, 4" × 5", $2,500

Transitional tapering vase, by Anna F. Simpson, 1912, with stylized pale blue narcissus against a green and blue ground, 8½" × 3½" dia., $2,500

Matte ovoid vase by Corrine Marie Chalaron, 1923, decorated w/broad leaves alternating w/yellow and white stylized blossoms on a denim blue ground, 8" × 4", $2,500

Bulbous matte vase by Anna F. Simpson, 1921, carved w/a wreath of pink trumpet vines and green leaves on a denim blue ground, 9" × 5", $1,500

Transitional squat vessel by Sadie Irvine, 1914, carved w/light bluebell flowers and green leaves on a dark blue ground, 3¼" × 5¼", $1,600

High glaze cabinet vase by Anna F. Simpson, 1926, w/live oak and Spanish moss in blue on gray ground, 4½" × 2", $3,000

High glaze ovoid vase by Roberta Kennon, 1902, deeply carved and incised w/irises in shades of indigo against a pale blue ground; short tight line to rim, 12½" × 7", $20,000

Carved matte bulbous vase by Sadie Irvine, 1919, decorated w/grapes and leaves on a medium blue ground, 8¼" × 6", $2,500

Bulbous vase carved by Sadie Irvine, 1913, w/stylized blossoms under an all-over lavendar glaze; tight line to rim, 7½" × 4¼", $2,250

Carved scenic vase by Sadie Irvine, 1932, w/live oaks, moon and Spanish moss; short, tight line to rim and some glaze running, 3½" × 4½", $2,500

Squat vessel, 1918, carved by Sadie Irvine w/blossoms under an overall lavender matte glaze, 1½" × 3¾", $1,050

Carved bulbous vase by Anna Frances Simpson, 1924, decorated w/pink flowers on a medium blue ground, 4½" × 5", $1,500

Scenic matte covered jar by A. F. Simpson, 1929, carved w/live oaks and Spanish moss on a denim blue ground; ½", firing line to rim of base, 5" × 4½", $3,500

Scenic matte bulbous vase by Sadie Irvine, 1929, carved w/live oaks and Spanish moss on denim blue ground, 5¼" × 4¼", $3,500

Scenic matte ovoid vase, probably by Sadie Irvine, 1928, carved w/willows, Spanish moss, and full moon on denim blue ground, 6" × 3", $3,000

Squat vessel by Mary W. Butler, 1905, carved w/stylized poppy pods in glossy green on cobalt ivory ground, 4½" × 4½", $8,000

Low bowl by Desiree Roman, 1904, carved w/blue water lilies and green leaves on buff ground; restoration to small chip inside rim, 3¼" × 8½", $5,500

Inkwell painted by G. R. Smith, ca, 1902 w/pink thistles and green leaves on an ivory ground, w/original line; glaze misses to pink centers, short and tight line to rim and reglued lid, 2¾" × 4", $3,500

Newcomb College high glaze jardiniere by Harriet Joor, 1902, with yellow daffodils and blue-green leaves on an ivory ground. Four lines to rim, shallow spider lines to base do not go through. NC/JM/R29/HJ. 8" × 10", $12,500

Vase painted by G. R. Smith, ca, 1902, w/pale red thistles and blue-green leaves on glossy ivory ground; glaze misses to pink centers, 1", hairline from rim, 4¼" × 3½" dia., $5,500

Loving cup by Katherine Kopman, 1902, w/white clover blossoms and green leaves over pale blue and white glossy ground; 1", chip inside rim, 4" × 5", $5,500

Scenic vase by Sadie Irvine, 1919, carved w/palm trees and full moon; drilled bottom for lamp, 10¾" × 6½", $8,750

Ovoid vase carved by Henrietta Bailey, 1931, w/tall pine trees in blues and greens and full moon; some glaze dripping, 9¼" × 4", $8,000

Carved bulbous vessel by A. F. Simpson, 1919, w/4 handles depicting mauve crocus blossoms on lavender matte glaze ground, 4½" × 5½" dia., $3,250

Plate, 1906, decorated by Henrietta Bailey, w/a band of carved white and yellow flowers on blue and green ground; restoration to a few small chips around the rim, 8¼" dia., $875

Vessel by A. F. Simpson, carved w/live oak trees and Spanish moss in green and blue on light pink sky, 8½" × 3¾", $4,000

Vase by Sadie Irvine, 1928, carved w/Spanish moss on live oak trees on yellow and red sky, 6½" × 3¼", $3,150

Squat bulbous vessel, 1933, carved by Henrietta Bailey w/Spanish moss, live oaks and full moon on pale blue ground, 4½" × 5½", $2,600

Spherical vessel carved by Sadie Irvine, 1918, w/Spanish moss and live oaks in blue and green against yellow sky, 3" × 3", $2,500

Bulbous vase, 1913, carved by Henrietta Bailey w/tall pine trees in green on blue-green ground, 4½" × 4", $3,000

Transitional vase, 1912, carved by A. F. Simpson w/tall pines under waxy blue-green and light green glaze; 3 cracks to rim and glaze lifting to body, 8¾" × 3¾", $1,500

Fine Newcomb College scenic matte bulbous vase by Sadie Irvine, 1929, crisply carved with live oaks and Spanish moss on a denim blue ground. (Very crisp). NC/RX25/JM/24/artist's cipher, plus original paper label, 5¼" × 4¼", $4,312

Transitional bulbous vase, 1913, carved by Alma Mason w/paper whites and green leaves on blue ground; several hairlines from rim, 9" × 3¾", $875

Squat vessel carved w/live oak trees and Spanish moss in front of a full moon, 3½" × 4½", $2,500

Corseted bud vase by Sadie Irvine, 1927, w/carved band of pink flowers on pale blue ground, 6" × 3", $1,250

Squat cabinet vase decorated by Sadie Irvine, 1933, w/geometric pattern in white on cobalt and green ground, 2¼" × 3", $875

High glaze bulbous vase by Amelie Roman, 1907, decorated w/sailboats reflecting on water in blue and green on an ivory ground; short tight line from rim and two small chips to base, 6½" × 5¼", $13,000

Transitional ovoid vase by Henrietta Bailey, 1915, carved w/Spanish moss on tall trees; a couple of minute flecks to base, 11½" × 5½", $7,500

Vase by Mazie Ryan, 1906, carved w/white chrysanthemums on denim blue ground; hairline and restoration to rim, touch-ups to base, 9" × 6", $19,500

Squat transitional vessel by Cynthia Littlejohn, 1915, carved w/band of white flowers and green leaves on flat shoulder against a denim blue ground; tight hairline from rim, 4" × 6", $1,000

Factory lamp base w/three sockets, in dripping ochre and green crystalline over green matte glaze, 16½" × 8½", $1,250

Transitional corseted vase by A. F. Simpson, 1917, carved w/jonquils under lavender glaze; 2½" × 2", glazy inconsistency, 5¾" × 5", $2,100

Center bowl by Anna Simpson, 1928, decorated w/wreath of white narcissus on medium blue ground; opposing hairlines to rim, $4\frac{1}{2}$", × $10\frac{1}{4}$", $850

Tapering bud vase by Anna Simpson, 1923, carved w/white jonquils and green leaves on denim blue ground, $6\frac{1}{4}$", × $3\frac{1}{4}$", $950

Transitional bulbous vase by Sadie Irvine, 1912, carved w/grape clusters on satin blue green ground, $7\frac{1}{2}$", × $4\frac{1}{2}$", $2,500

Squat cabinet vessel by Sadie Irvine, 1922, decorated w/wreath of pink mespilus and green leaves on medium blue ground; a few glaze bubbles, $1\frac{3}{4}$", × $3\frac{1}{2}$", $1,000

Carved matte cabinet vase by Sadie Irvine, 1920, decorated w/pink orchids on medium blue matte ground, $2\frac{1}{2}$" × 3", $1,150

Transitional vase carved by Sadie Irvine, 1914, w/tall pines covered in Spanish moss; minor chip to edge of foot ring from manufacture, $8\frac{1}{4}$" × $6\frac{1}{2}$", $6,250

Organically shaped vessel by Marie de Hoa LeBlanc, ca. 1905, w/three modeled ginkgo leaf handles and covered in semi-matte olive green and gun-metal glaze, 6" × $7\frac{1}{2}$", $3,000

Matte vase carved by Sadie Irvine, 1924, w/pink and red loquat fruit and leaves around an undulating rim; small chips to foot ring, short tight line to rim, $6\frac{1}{2}$" × $4\frac{1}{2}$", $1,400

Tyge by unknown artist, 1901-02, decorated w/stylized floral band under red lustered glaze; line to base on two handles from firing, $5\frac{1}{2}$" × 7", $11,000,

Tyge by Marie De Hoa LeBlanc, 1905, incised w/band of white flowers at rim, under denim blue glossy glaze; old, tight hairline to one handle, $3\frac{3}{4}$" × 5", $5,500

Squat bowl in dripping green and amber semi matte glaze, 4" × $8\frac{3}{4}$", $1,100

Pitcher attributed to Sadie Irvine, 1909, carved w/paper whites on blue-green ground, $7\frac{1}{2}$" × $5\frac{1}{2}$", $5,500

## Niloak Pottery

SHOPMARKS: (1910–28) Impressed NILOAK.

(After 1928) Impressed NILOAK and patent number.

Paper label, NILOAK POTTERY in a circle.

Paper label, FROM THE NILOAK POTTERIES AT BENTON, ARKANSAS.

PRINCIPAL CONTRIBUTION: Wide range of marbleized art pottery forms.

FOUNDER: Charles Hyten. Born: 1887, died: 1944, founded: 1909, closed: 1946.

STUDIOS AND SALESROOMS: Niloak Pottery Company, Benton, Arkansas, 1909–46

"There have been numerous attempts to imitate the Mission ware . . .
All, however, are inferior copies in comparison to Niloak's Mission
ware, which occupies a distinctive place in the art pottery movement."
—*Paul Evans*[1]

After their father's death, their mother's remarriage, and her subsequent move to Ohio in 1895, Charles Hyten and his two brothers elected to remain in Benton, Arkansas, to continue the operation of their father's Eagle Pottery, which continued to produce commercial stoneware such as crocks, churns, and jugs for more than three decades, in addition the Hyten Brothers Pottery was organized and later renamed the Niloak Pottery.

Around 1909 Charles Hyten began experimenting with several different colors of local clay on the pottery's wheel at the same time. The result was a multicolor, swirling effect that was striking in appearance but that did not come without its own problems. Different types of clay dry and shrink at different rates, and Charles spent several years perfecting a process and a formula that would permit him to utilize several clays in each vessel.

The first pieces were produced in 1910, and their immediate popularity led to the formal organization and naming of the Niloak Pottery Company in 1911. The new name came from the work *kaolin*, a fine white clay that has been used for centuries in the manufacture of quality Chinese porcelain; spelled backward it becomes Niloak. Ironically, kaolin may not have been used in the production of Niloak's most famous line, Mission,[2] but the effect was not lost. "Forms, predominantly classical or Oriental, included small bowls, candlesticks, pitcher and tankard sets, steins, punchbowl and cup sets, fern dishes, clocks, and vases made in a variety of sizes adaptable as lamps."[3]

Some of the early experimental pottery had a glaze applied to both the inside and the outside of the piece, but Charles soon instituted the classic Niloak style, in which the marbleized pieces were glazed only on the inside, making them suitable to hold water but leaving the outside with a natural clay texture. The colors that appeared depended on the types of clays being used at any particular time and the skill of the potter. The later pieces tend to be more colorful than the early examples, perhaps reflective of Charles's experiments with colored pigments and the refinement of his patented mixing and drying process.

The incorporation of the Niloak Pottery enabled the brothers to sell the stock necessary to raise the capital to build a new and larger plant. The unique pottery quickly became popular, first in Benton, then spreading across the country, as the firm employed salesmen as well as additional potters. Production rose to as many as 75,000 pieces per year as seven potters turned out the swirling shapes, no two of which were identical in either color or form, often before a crowd of admiring tourists.[4] By 1918 Charles was able to buy back most of the stock issued in 1911, thus acquiring complete control of the pottery. Soon Niloak pottery was being sold in Europe and the Far East, as well as across the United States and Canada.

The Depression, however, cut into sales of the handmade pottery, leading Charles to introduce a line of molded, less expensive pieces marked Hywood. The new line failed to stave off serious financial problems; Charles soon lost control of the property and the Niloak Pottery and was reduced to being a salesman for the firm he had founded. He died in 1944, two years after the last piece of marbleized Niloak was made and two years before the Niloak Pottery Company finally closed.

Large Niloak Mission ware bulbous vase of brown, tan, terra cotta, and blue marbled clays. Firing lines to base do not go through. Stamped Niloak, 14" × 9½", $1,380

The best pieces of Niloak ware are darker and less colorful. Look for shades of deep brown, deep red, and deep blue. Most pieces are small in size, usually under 6" tall. Large pieces are rare and valuable. Handled pieces, covered jars, and punch bowls are very rare and quite valuable. Minor damage reduces value of most pieces by at least 50 percent.

## SELECTED PRICES

Mission ware bulbous vase of brown, tan, terra cotta, and blue marbled clays; firing lines to base that don't go through, 14" × 9½", $1,150

Two Mission ware vases, one corseted and one cylindrical, in blue, brown, and ivory scroddled clay, 10" and 11", $250

Mission ware cylindrical vase in brown and terra cotta scroddled clay, 10", $200

Two Mission ware classically shaped vases in blue, ivory and brown scroddled clay; chip to each, one also has scratch, 8¼" and 9½", $250

Two pieces, a vase and a low bowl in marbleized blue and gray clay, 4" × 4" dia., $200

Pair of tall candlesticks of blue and grey marbleized clay, 8", $350

Mission ware punch bowl of scroddled brown, tan and blue clays on corseted pedestal base w/glazed interior, 11" × 13½", $1,250

Six Mission ware punch cups, 2" × 3½", $1,750

Two vases of marbled clay, one classically shaped, the other bulbous 8½" and 4", $200

Two vases of marbled clay, one ovoid, the other bulbous, 5" and 8", $200

Two vases of marbled clay, one corseted, the other bulbous, 8½" and 6", $200

Mission ware baluster vase of marbleized blue, brown, ivory, and gray clay, 10" × 4½", $500

Mission ware ovoid vase of marbleized clay, 9¼" × 4¾", $250

## Norse Pottery

SHOPMARKS: Impressed NORSE, with the last four letters within the large letter *N*.

PRINCIPAL CONTRIBUTION: Household pottery finished with a matte metallic glaze to imitate antique bronzes.

FOUNDERS: Thorwald P. A. Samson, Louis Ipson. Born: unknown, died: unknown, founded: 1903, closed: 1913.

STUDIOS AND SALESROOMS: Norse Pottery, Edgerton, Wisconsin, 1903–04, Norse Pottery Company, Inc., Rockford, Illinois, 1904–13.

Inspired by antique bronze bowls excavated in Sweden and Denmark, Thorwald P. A. Samson and Louis Ipson, former potters at Pauline Pottery in Edgerton, Wisconsin, formed a small company to produce and distribute replicas made from local clay in 1903. Hindered by a lack of capital, the pair sold their designs to A. W. Wheelock, who had been their major distributor. Wheelock moved the firm and its two founders to Rockford, Illinois, where he had built a new plant. Between 1904 and 1913 the Norse Pottery Company produced a large number of examples, decorated with incised lines and painted, then "decorated with a dull metallic glaze with highlights in the effect of verdigris in the corners, crevices, and sunken line of the etchings."[1]

Norse ware is difficult to find and, as such, is not easy to collect. This is one of those markets whose prices rise and fall on the interest of a handful of collectors. Larger pieces, and those with molded dragons on their sides are worth the most to modern collectors. Minor damage reduces value by at least 50 percent

## North Dakota School Of Mines

SHOPMARKS: Incised cobalt blue circle UNIVERSITY OF NORTH DAKOTA/GRAND FORKS, N.D./MADE AT SCHOOL OF MINES/N.D. CLAY, also with glaze number.
PRINCIPAL CONTRIBUTION: Art pottery produced from North Dakota clays.
FOUNDER: University of North Dakota. Founded: ca. 1892, closed: current.
STUDIOS AND SALESROOMS: North Dakota School of Mines, University of North Dakota, Grand Forks, North Dakota, ca. 1892-current.

The pottery studio at the North Dakota School of Mines was developed from a study of the suitability of clays found within state boundaries for use

in pottery production. After a successful exhibition at the 1904 Louisiana Purchase Exposition in St. Louis, the university continued to hire experienced potters to instruct and train students in throwing, molding, decorating, and glazing pottery. As a result, the shapes, styles, and quality of the pottery bearing the ink trademark varies considerably, although the tenure of Margaret Kelley Cable, who remained with the pottery from 1910 until 1949, provided the stability and direction required for the production of quality pottery. The university has maintained a detailed record of the glaze numbers often found on the pottery, which can help pinpoint the year of production.

NDSM work ranges from ungainly molded pots with no decoration, to hand-decorated works of art. The most collectible pieces are those signed by teachers, such as Ms. Cable. Look also for pieces with cowboys, indians, haystacks, and other western motifs. Minor damage will have little impact on the value of a unique piece. It will, however, greatly reduce the value of a commercial or student piece.

## SELECTED PRICES

Bulbous vase, 1942, carved by Sorenson w/stylized flowers under matte brown glaze, 7" × 6", $1,250

Vase by Margaret Cable, carved w/jonquils under matte green glaze, 5½" × 5½", $850

Ovoid vase by Julia Mattson, embossed w/cowboys on horseback under matte brown glaze, 7¼" × 5", $750

Prairie Pottery flaring Bentonite clay bowl by Maggie Mud, decorated w/ochre, umber and red bands, 2" × 8¾", $500

Bulbous vase by Flora Huckfield, "Bustin," decorated w/band of prairie roses in beige and black on a brown ground, $4\frac{1}{2}$" × 4", \$750

Classically-shaped vase painted w/trees in silhouette against amber ground, \$2,250

Cabinet vase in Prairie Rose pattern in purple, grey-ish green and rose; small nick to one petal, glaze bubbles around base, $4\frac{1}{4}$" × $3\frac{1}{2}$", \$625

Vase carved w/stylized floral pattern by Flora Huckfield, 1925, covered in brown to blue shaded semi matte glaze, $10\frac{1}{2}$" × $5\frac{1}{2}$", \$1,750

Squat vessel w/closed-in rim by Julia Mattson, incised w/brown acorns and oak leaves against matte green glaze, 4" × $6\frac{3}{4}$", \$875

Squat vessel by Margaret Cable, "Red River Oxcart," covered in matte brown glazes, $3\frac{1}{2}$" × $6\frac{1}{2}$", \$800

Bulbous vase by M.A.S, carved in Prairie Rose motif and covered in brown and green matte glaze, $5\frac{3}{4}$" × $5\frac{1}{2}$", \$875,

Tapered vase by M. Cable, incised w/deer under tall pine trees and covered in smooth matte green glaze, the buff clay showing through, $7\frac{3}{4}$" × 4" dia., \$875

Bulbous vase by Margaret Cable carved w/narcissus under brown and umber matte glaze, $7\frac{1}{2}$" × $5\frac{1}{2}$", \$1,500

Spherical vessel by Margaret Cable, "Covered Wagon," in smooth matte brown glaze, $6\frac{1}{2}$" × $7\frac{1}{4}$", \$1,000

Reticulated flowerpot by I. Kelman, 1952, decorated w/dogwood and covered in lavender and celadon glaze; tight line to rim, $5\frac{1}{2}$" × $6\frac{3}{4}$", \$1,000

Bentonite clay vessel decorated w/Native American motifs in yellow and black on a red ground; small glaze flakes to rim, 4" × 5", \$500

Closed-in bowl by L. Whiting w/birds of paradise and cornflowers in blue, ivory and green; minor fleck to shoulder, $4\frac{1}{4}$" × $7\frac{1}{2}$", \$1,500

Bulbous vase by Flora Huckfield, painted w/band of pioneers and covered wagons in polychrome against glossy brown ground, $4\frac{1}{2}$" × $3\frac{1}{2}$", \$1,250

Squat vessel by Julia Mattson, carved w/band of cowboys under terra cotta and brown matte glaze, $3\frac{1}{2}$" × 5", \$625

Mammy cookie jar by Margaret Cable in dark brown matte glazes; small nick inside lid rim, $10\frac{1}{2}$" × $6\frac{3}{4}$", \$1,500

Spherical vessel w/closed-in rim by R. Skyberg, embossed w/band of stylized geometric forms in charcoal on green matte ground, $6\frac{1}{4}$" × $6\frac{3}{4}$", \$875

Ovoid vase by Steen, in shaded green and brown matte glaze, $9\frac{1}{2}$" × 5", \$400

## George Ohr Pottery

SHOPMARKS: Impressed or incised script signature of G. E. OHR, BILOXI
or GEO. E. OHR/BILOXI, MISS.

PRINCIPAL CONTRIBUTION: Bowls and vases in bizarre forms and twisted
shapes under quality glazes.

FOUNDER: George E. Ohr. Born: 1857, died: 1918, founded: ca. 1883, closed:
ca. 1909.

STUDIOS AND SALESROOMS: Biloxi Art Pottery, Biloxi, Mississippi, ca. 1883–
ca. 1909.

> "I send you four pieces, but it is as easy to pass judgment on my pro-
> ductions from four pieces as it would be to take four lines from Shake-
> speare and guess the rest."
> —*George Ohr, 1905*[1]

While George Ohr certainly had no problem using Shakespeare to illustrate
his work, most of his contemporaries—especially some of his fellow potters—would never have predicted that his bizarre and often grotesque vases
and bowls would someday become prized additions to the collections of
major museums around the world. "He is ever making," a visitor reported in
1900, "and as comparative few are buying, he is accumulating a vast quantity
of pottery, having upwards of 6,000 or 7,000 pieces, no two of which are just
alike in shape and decoration; and every one of these, he is quite satisfied in
his own mind, will some day be worth its weight in gold."[2]

Ounce for ounce, the best work of George Ohr is now worth more than
its weight in gold, but several years before his death in 1918, George Ohr,
frustrated at the public's failure to respond favorably to his life's work,
packed his inventory of pottery in boxes and retired. Most of it remained untouched until 1972, when an astute collector managed to buy nearly the en-

tire inventory from the potter's family. Since that time both the works and the reputation of the infamous "Mad Potter of Biloxi" have spread across the country.

While many of Ohr's contemporaries did not like him or his pottery, none could ignore him. Ohr managed to offend and confuse the austere Arts and Crafts reformers as carelessly as their staunch Victorian predecessors. Early historian E. A. Barber described his work as "twisted, crushed, folded, dented and crinkled into grotesque and occasionally artistic shapes."[3] For many, Ohr's eccentric behavior and his bizarre forms overshadowed the technical aspect of his pottery. Using local clay he dug by hand from a nearby riverbank and hauled to his pottery in a wheelbarrow, Ohr was able to create eggshell-thin vessels of extraordinary quality, but, dissatisfied with their static silhouettes, he proceeded to "dig his fingers into the moist, plastic clay of his perfectly executed, wheel-thrown vessels . . . twisting, crinkling, indenting, folding, ruffling, lobing, off-centering, and conjoining"[4] until he had created forms never before imagined, let alone seen by most people.

Ohr's creations, however, while reflections of a rebellious nature, were the work of a genius rather than a huckster promoting a gimmick. Scholars in search of a source for his inspiration have attributed it to nearly everything from Pennsylvania fold art to Victorian glassware to the pottery of the American Indians[5]; a study in frustration, it is a reflection not so much of their efforts as of Ohr's unbridled creativity. Less concerned than scholars with the inspiration for his work, Ohr was relentless in his task. "No two pieces alike,"[6] he declared at exhibitions where he turned, twisted, and fired vases in a portable kiln before an audience of curious bystanders. Their failure to support his unusual pottery prompted him to declare toward the end of his career, "If it were not for the housewives of Biloxi who have a constant need of flowerpots, water coolers, and flues, the family Ohr would often go hungry."[7]

At least one reviewer found Ohr's pottery to be a sincere and refreshing change from the outpouring of pottery from hundreds of Ohio kilns. " . . . unlovely as they are," the *Clay Worker* reported of Ohr's pottery in 1905, "they appeal more strongly to the person who is genuinely interested in the art of pottery than all the smooth shapes, molded with exasperating mechanical accuracy, which the so-called 'art potteries' turn out by the million to sell to the pseudo-artistic public of our day."[8] Seventy years later, as the Arts and Crafts revival began to sweep the country, the pottery of George Ohr literally came out of the attic to find a receptive and appreciative audience.

The unique nature of Ohr's work has made it difficult for modern collectors to make comparisons between pieces or draw conclusions that will enable them to distinguish between a highly desirable example and one that is less apt to inspire widespread interest. While generalizations are dangerous

Fine George Ohr bisque vessel with deep in-body twist. Script signature, 3" × 3¾", $4,312

when applied to an artist as imaginative as George Ohr, most advanced collectors agree that the twisted, tortured forms are among the most sought-after of his work. Reflective, perhaps, of his personality, the colorful, vibrant glazes are clearly favored over flat blacks or solid browns. Examples with outlandish handles, spikes, spouts, and snakes—especially when combined with multicolored glazes—have collectors scrambling for an opportunity to add one to their collection. The new enthusiast may find the prices paid for premium Ohr as startling as his designs but can be assured that less colorful, less imaginative Ohr pottery can still be found on the market.

The legacy of George Ohr was further enhanced in 1989 with the release of the long-awaited, definitive text entitled *The Mad Potter of Biloxi* (Abbeville Press, New York). Destined to emerge both as a landmark study of George Ohr and his pots, and also as a model for other authors and publishers, *The Mad Potter of Biloxi* proved to be an indispensable guide for anyone interested in the personality and the pottery of George Ohr.

## SELECTED PRICES

Pitcher w/dimpled body, folded side, and single ribbon handle, in striking red, pink, cobalt, green, yellow, and white sponged glaze; one chip and several minor nicks to rim, one small chip to base, 10" × 7". This piece brought a record price of $46,000.

Bulbous vase covered in raspberry and white volcanic glaze (some loss) on glossy blue ground; underglaze firing line inside neck, 6" × 2¾", $8,000

Vase w/straight edges, notched shoulder, folded rim, covered in gunmetal brown glaze, 5½" × 4¼", $4,250

Squat vase w/flaring and folded rim in raspberry and amber glossy glaze; tight line to base, 3¼" × 3", $2,500

Bottle-shaped vase w/in-body twist and ruffled rim, in gunmetal glaze; minute nick to rim, small kiln kiss, 4¾" × 3¾" $3,500

Bulbous vase w/lobed rim and in-body twist, covered in green and amber speckled glaze, 4" × 3¼", $4,000

Small pinched pitcher w/three lobed openings, in speckled gunmetal glaze; repairs to handle and rim edge, 2½" × 4¼", $2,500

Baluster cabinet vase in mottled forest green glossy glaze; touch-up to rim, minor abrasion to base, 4¾" × 2¼", $1,750

Small hourglass shaped pitcher in mirror black and eggplant glaze, 5½" × 3¾", $1,750

Bulbous bisque vase of red clay w/deep in-body twist and closed-in rim, fired to dark brown sheen 3¾" × 4", $2,500

Bulbous bisque vase of white clay w/dimpled shoulder and folded rim; four small chips inside rim, 5" × 5½", $3,500

Squat bisque vase of red clay w/folded sides and closed-in rim, 3¾" × 5", $2,500

Bisque vessel w/deep in-body twist, 3" × 3¾" $3,000

Bulbous cabinet vase w/folded rim, covered in fine sparkling gunmetal glaze; minor nick to rim, 3" × 3", $2,150

Panther inkwell in cobalt blue glaze; firing line to base, 3½" × 3" × 4½", $1,750

Small ovoid pitcher in gunmetal glaze, 4" × 3¾", $1,550

Log cabin inkwell of white and red clay, cabin glued to base, 3" × 4¼" × 3½", $750

Puzzle mug w/snake handle in mottled brown and gunmetal glaze, 3½" × 5½", $625

Joe Jefferson mug, 1896, dedicated to H. R. Durant, Atlanta, GA, in sheer olive glaze, 3¼" × 4¼", $1,400

Pinched and folded pitcher in rare amber and green-speckled purple leathery matte glaze; minor nicks and two small chips (restored) on rim, 4½" × 5½", $10,500

Two-tiered flaring vessel w/cupped, folded rim, the base covered in gunmetal and green-speckled amber glaze, and the top brown; restoration to rim chips, 4¼" × 4½", $8,000

Tapering vase w/in-body twist, in mottled lavender, green, and blue vellum glaze, 6" × 3¾", $17,000

Bulbous vessel w/deep in-body twist around flat crimped rim, in green, brown, and gunmetal mottled glaze; stilt-pull chips to rim, 3¼" × 6¼", $12,000

Bulbous pitcher in sponged cobalt, raspberry, green and amber glaze; restoration to small chip at rim and to handle, $5\frac{3}{4}$" × 5", $6,250

Tapering vase w/crimped rim, dimpled body, and ribbed base, in speckled brown glossy glaze, 4" × 3", $2,000

Cabinet vase w/collapsed rim, in mottled green, amber, and gunmetal glaze, $2\frac{1}{4}$" × 3", $1,500

Two-handled vessel w/scalloped rim, the exterior covered in raspberry and pink glossy glaze, the interior in amber and green; couple of minor flecks under rim, $3\frac{1}{4}$" × $5\frac{3}{4}$", $6,500

Small tapering vase w/deep in-body twist, in superior and vibrant bright green mottled glaze over gunmetal brown w/sponged-on gunmetal crystalline around top, 3" × $3\frac{1}{2}$", $6,250

Vessel w/spiraling ribbon handles, deep in-body twist, cupped rim, in brown-speckled lustered umber glaze, 5" × $4\frac{1}{4}$", $17,500

Cup w/folded and dimpled body in rare mottled matte green glaze, $4\frac{3}{4}$" × $4\frac{1}{2}$", $9,500

Pitcher w/ribbon handle and cupped top, in leathery gunmetal glaze, $4\frac{3}{4}$" × 3", $3,000

Pinched and folded pitcher of red bisque clay; rim has short tight line from firing and very small chip, $3\frac{3}{4}$" × $5\frac{1}{4}$", $3,000

Bulbous vase w/crimped rim and deep in-body twist, covered in gunmetal-speckled green and amber mottled glaze; restoration to small kiln kiss and to firing line under bottom, $6\frac{1}{4}$" × $5\frac{1}{4}$", $16,500

Tapered vase w/deep in-body twist at rim and serrated edge, in speckled dark green glaze; repair to small kiln kiss, $5\frac{3}{4}$" × 3", $3,500

Bulbous vase w/ruffled rim and in-body twist to base, covered in vibrant gunmetal glaze dripping over glossy speckled brown base, $4\frac{1}{4}$" × 3", $3,250

Large corseted three-handled vessel of buff bisque clay, $8\frac{1}{2}$" × 9", $2,500

Bulbous vase w/crimped rim of buff bisque clay; small nicks to rim and restoration to two chips at base, $5\frac{1}{2}$" × $5\frac{3}{4}$", $3,500

Three-handled vessel covered in rich mottled pink and green matte glaze, $4\frac{3}{4}$" × $5\frac{1}{2}$", $12,000

Bulbous vase w/collared rim and dimpled body, covered in speckled brown glossy glaze; restoration to hairline from rim, $4\frac{3}{4}$" × $5\frac{1}{4}$", $3,500

Tapered bud vase w/cupped rim, in brown gunmetal glaze; repair to rim and touch-ups to base, $8\frac{1}{2}$" × $3\frac{1}{2}$", $1,750

Bulbous vase w/sponged-on lustered green and gunmetal brown glaze, $6\frac{1}{4}$" × $5\frac{1}{2}$", $1,250

Vase of totemic shape, one half covered in gunmetal speckled brown glaze, the other in green on amber, $7\frac{1}{2}$" × $3\frac{1}{2}$", $3,500

Plaque w/applied fiddler crab covered in dark green glossy glaze; restoration to claws and tips of shell, $1\frac{1}{2}$" × 8" × $8\frac{1}{4}$", $3,000

Small cup pitcher w/pinched rim, in rare amber volcanic glaze; restored chip to rim and minor nick, $2\frac{1}{2}$" × $4\frac{3}{4}$", $1,500

Squat vessel covered in speckled brown and green glaze; repair to rim chip, $3\frac{1}{2}$" × $5\frac{1}{2}$", $800

Gourd-shaped vase w/closed-in rim, in gunmetal glaze; small bruise to base, $3\frac{1}{4}$" × $3\frac{3}{4}$", $825

Squat vessel in gunmetal brown glaze; repair to rim chip and a few small nicks to shoulder, $2\frac{3}{4}$" × $4\frac{1}{4}$", $625

Bulbous cabinet vase w/ripped scalloped rim, in black gunmetal glaze w/green and yellow interior; nicks to points, $2\frac{1}{2}$" × $2\frac{3}{4}$", $750

Bulbous vase w/folded rim, top covered in speckled mahogany glaze, the base in sponged green and amber; small restorations to rim nicks, touchup to kiln kiss on shoulder, 8" × 3", $8,000

Tyge w/three ribbon handles and cup rim under green lustered and gunmetal glaze; restoration to one handle, $4\frac{1}{2}$" × 5", $1,500

Bulbous cabinet vase w/folded rim, covered in fine sparkling gunmetal glaze; minor nick to rim, 3" × 3", $2,250

Fine George Ohr bulbous cabinet vase with folded rim, covered in fine sparkling gunmetal glaze. Minor nick to rim. G.E. OHR/Biloxi,Miss., 3" × 3", $2530

Tapered vase w/asymmetrically folded rim, exterior covered in gunmetal and yellow glaze, interior in bright orange; minute flecks to rim, 5¼" × 2¾", $2,500

Squat vessel w/collared rim, covered in speckled ochre and green glossy glaze; a few minor touch-ups to rim, 2¾" × 3¼", $1,250

Pitcher w/angular cut-out handle, the exterior covered in extremely rare violet dead matte glaze w/dark green veining, interior speckled green, 3¼" × 5", $2,500

Pitcher of beige bisque clay asymmetrically pinched and folded w/oxidized flashes; firing cracks, 5" × 7½", $2,500

Pitcher w/dimpled rim and angular cut out handle, in mottled brown glossy glaze w/random gunmetal accents, 4¼" × 5¼", $2,500

Pitcher w/angular cutout handle in mottled green and gunmetal lustered glaze; restoration to handle and rim chip, 4¼" × 4¾", $1,500,

## Overbeck Pottery

SHOPMARKS: (Pre-1937) Impressed joined letters *O B K,* occasionally over the letter *E* (design by Elizabeth), *H* (decoration by Hannah), and/or *F* (decoration by Mary F.).
(Post–1937) Impressed joined letters *O B K,* on occasion over the initials MF (Mary F. Overbeck).
Dating key: *H,* pre–1931; *E,* 1911–35; *F* or *MF* , 1922–55.
PRINCIPAL CONTRIBUTIONS: Decorated vases, bowls, candlesticks, and figurines.
FOUNDERS: Margaret Overbeck, born: 1863, died: 1911. Hannah Overbeck, born: 1870, died: 1931. Elizabeth Overbeck, born: 1875, died: 1936. Mary Overbeck, born: 1878, died: 1955, founded: 1911, closed: 1955.
STUDIOS AND SALESROOMS: Overbeck Pottery, Cambridge City, Indiana, 1911–55.

> "They lived unto themselves, with commitment only to themselves and their desire to create."
> —*Kathleen Postle*[1]

For the Overbeck sister, 1911 was a year of both triumph and tragedy. After two years' study under noted ceramics instructor Charles F. Binns, Elizabeth Overbeck had returned to the family home in Cambridge City, Indiana, to help her three sisters form the Overbeck Pottery. Their sprawling two-story house was transformed into an active pottery, with a basement workshop, a first-floor studio, and a kiln in a nearby building. Before the young pottery

could celebrate its first anniversary, however, Margaret Overbeck, the oldest of the sisters and characterized as the guiding spirit of the founding, died from injuries sustained in an automobile accident the year before.

The management of the firm fell upon the shoulders of Elizabeth and her two artistic sisters: Hannah, who had suffered all her life from a debilitating form of neuritis, and Mary Frances, who, like her sister Margaret, had studied under Arthur W. Dow at Columbia University before teaching art in the public school system. Hannah, an accomplished watercolorist, took charge of the Overbeck Pottery design and decoration, while Mary Frances assisted her and created many of the pottery's glazes. Elizabeth, in addition to developing glazes, oversaw the technical production, mixing clay shipped from Tennessee, Delaware, and Pennsylvania and working on the potter's wheel.

From the beginning, Overbeck pottery was distinctly unique. Although molds were made, they were not used until after 1936, when Mary Frances became the sole Overbeck potter. "The pottery was built upon a definite philosophy, with an aim to achieve not quantity, but quality from both technical

Rare Overbeck squat vessel carved with panels of stylized flowers under a matte green glaze. Stamped OBK/EH, 4" × 4", $3,450

and aesthetic standpoints."[2] Vases, candlesticks, bowls, tiles, and tea sets (with molded cups and saucers) constituted much of their early production; ceramic sculpture was undertaken later. Decorations consisted of carving or glaze inlay—matte during the Arts and Crafts period, evolving into brighter colors as public tastes changed.

Overbeck admirers generally prefer the early work executed during the Arts and Crafts period. Abstract examples with limited, subdued color but crisp design often seem austere to observers of other eras but are considered most desirable by advanced Overbeck collectors. Keen carving on simple forms, highlighted with a matte glaze, characterizes some of the most sought-after work. Undecorated forms, although attractive, are not as highly valued.

The well-known Overbeck figurines were initiated sometime before the death of Elizabeth in 1936 and continued for several years thereafter. Often molded and generally less than five inches high, "these figurines included ladies and gentlemen in old-fashioned costumes, grotesque and humorous figures of people, animals and birds."[3] Many were uniquely original and are highly valued today. Multifigured scenes were executed on rare occasion and rank among the most treasured by Overbeck collectors. After 1936, when responsibility for the operation fell to Mary Frances, production gradually slowed, and reliance on molded forms increased until, at her death in 1955, the family pottery was closed.

Overbeck's best work suffers little from minor damage. It is, after all, extremely rare and each example is one of a kind. A small chip to the rim will reduce value by about 20 percent. The figurines, modestly priced in any case, usually have minor chipping along the sharp, hand-tooled edges. These minor flaws reduce value by about 15 percent.

### SELECTED PRICES

Squat vessel carved w/panels of stylized Art Deco flowers under matte
    green glaze, 4" × 4", $3,000


# Pewabic Pottery

SHOPMARKS: Early: impressed PEWABIC below line of oak leaves. Later: circular die-stamped mark PEWABIC/DETROIT.

PRINCIPAL CONTRIBUTIONS: Art pottery vases and architectural tiles

FOUNDERS: Mary Chase Perry, born: 1867, died: 1961. Horace J. Caulkins, born: 1850, died: 1923, founded: 1903, closed: 1965

STUDIOS AND SALESROOMS: Pewabic Pottery, Detroit, 1903–65

"One of the chief prides of the Pewabic operation in addition to its work was that the methods of big business never overtook the intimacy of the pottery. The creative work was kept consistently in the hands of the artist, and the technical end of the operation was achieved with the simplest equipment needed for the job."
—*Paul Evans*[1]

Among the most important of the women who were active in Arts and Crafts ceramics was Mary Chase Perry,"an adventurous artist with a love of color and experiment."[2] Trained as an artist at the Cincinnati Art Academy from 1887 until 1889 (where she met Maria Longworth Nichols and Kataro Shirayamadani) and later with the renowned ceramic teacher Charles Binns, she returned to Detroit, where her mother lived, and, like many women artists of the period, engaged in china painting.

By 1900, however, she was experimenting with clay sculpture, having outgrown overglaze decorations and instead creating her own ceramics, using her neighbor Horace Caulkins's dental kiln to fire her first pieces. Working together, "they developed the Revelation kiln, a portable, kerosene-burning, muffle kiln that became standard for the china painting movement and was used by many of the leading art potteries."[3] As Anthea Callen observed in her work on women artists in the movement, "Her early work displayed the influences of William H. Grueby, who was responsible for introducing matte glazes into American art pottery, and of European Art Nouveau ceramics, often through the intermediary exponents of the style such as Louis Tiffany."[4]

In 1903 Perry and Caulkins formed a pottery company, taking the name Pewabic from a nearby river. Ironically, "it was only after many years that

Miss Perry learned Pewabic meant 'copper color in clay,' "[5] Miss Perry also developed a fascination with glazes. Joseph Herrick, a potter, was hired to throw the forms on the wheel, working from drawings Miss Perry provided, while she took charge of the decorating and the glazes. "Her [early] vases were decorated with conventionalized natural forms and matte glazes, but gradually her interests centered on the effects of glazes, and of necessity the forms of her pots became simpler in order to show off the rich colors and luster."[6] As a result of her personal preoccupation with glazes, "the forms lacked the evolution and continuity of Binns and Robineau. Nonetheless she produced a few masterpieces whose beauty derives largely from her range of extraordinary glazes, from elusive, iridescent glazes to cloudy, rich inglaze lusters."[7]

Clay was shipped to their basement studio from four states, plus England, to form a durable, near-white body after it had been fired at high temperatures in their kiln. Miss Perry soon developed a formula for an iridescent glaze that became a staple of Pewabic production. "She evolved deep blues and burning gold, among many others, and her late work is characterized by subtle overlays of dripping color and sparkling iridescence that made her glazes quite original for the period, and ensured her importance in the development of American ceramics."[8]

Perry and Caulkins enlarged their operation in 1907. Even while their works were being turned out in the basement of Horace Caulkins's house, they were receiving national recognition. In addition to their famous glazed vases, the pair began producing architectural tiles. Her friend and patron, Charles L. Freer, was responsible for introducing Miss Perry and Pewabic art

Fine Pewabic bulbous ribbed vase covered in a lustered lavender and green over gold base. A few small nicks to base. Circular stamp mark, 8" × 6", $2,530

tiles to leading architects in Detroit. Their first major commission, for St. Paul's Cathedral, was completed in 1908 and led to both critical and popular acclaim, plus additional commissions from architects Cass Gilbert, Greene and Greene, and others.[9]

In 1918, at the age of 51, Miss Perry married William B. Stratton. Her associate, Horace Caulkins, died in 1923, but she continued to run Pewabic Pottery alone, even though the Depression had closed the doors on so many other firms. Two major tile commissions, the National Shrine of the Immaculate Conception in Washington D.C. (1923–31), and the Detroit Institute of Arts (1927) helped ensure her continued success through tough times. In 1938 her husband was killed in a tragic streetcar accident, but Mary Perry remained undaunted. With the assistance of Ira and Ella Peters, she continued to run the Pewabic Pottery until her death in 1961 at the age of 94. Pewabic Pottery remained in operation until 1965, at which time it was deeded to Michigan State University.

From 1966 until 1981, Pewabic Pottery served as an educational facility for Michigan State University students, during which time it did not produce pottery or tiles on a commercial basis. After the formation of the Pewabic Society, a nonprofit organization, in 1981, the pottery expanded its role to include the production of both reproduction tiles and original work by a staff of potters. Today the pottery consists of an archives, gallery, and active pottery engaged in custom tile commissions using many of the same techniques, glazes, and molds popular during the Arts and Crafts era.

There are two primary collecting areas of Pewabic pottery, often attracting wholly different buyers. The early work, typified by matte glazes (usually green, but occasionally brown or blue-gray) is best if carved with organic designs. These are often carved with stylized, geometric decoration. The former are far more valuable, and quite rare. Minor damage has little impact on value.

There is a great deal of Pweabic's later, iridescent work, most of which is in tones of blue and green. Look for more vibrantly colored examples with gold luster or reddish hues. On all but the best of pieces, minor damage will reduce value by about 40—50 percent.

## SELECTED PRICES

Bulbous ribbed vase in lustered lavender and green over gold base; a few small nicks to base, 8" × 6", $1,750

Bulbous vase in lustered cobalt and green glaze, 5¾" × 6¼", $1,000

Bottle-shaped vase in lustered bronze, green, and blue glaze, 9½" × 5", $1,250

Bulbous vase in indigo, turquoise and green lustered glaze; a few shallow scratches, 13¼" × 6¾", $1,650

Four tiles: one molded w/king under oxblood glaze; one molded w/scarab in mustard; and two small cuenca tiles, one w/turtle and one w/scarab, $2\frac{3}{4}$ to $3\frac{3}{4}$" sq., $875

Squat bulbous vessel in fine copper and purple iridescent glaze; some scratches around rim, $3\frac{1}{2}$" × 4", $550

Two cabinet vases in amber lustered glazes, 3" and $3\frac{1}{4}$" dia., $625

Dinner plate decorated in squeezebag w/band of rabbits and trees in black and green on crackled ivory ground; a few minor glaze flakes, $10\frac{1}{2}$" dia., $1,000

Bulbous vase in thick Persian blue glaze dripping over gunmetal base, $5\frac{3}{4}$" × 3", $1,050

Dinner plate in squeezebag w/band of rabbits and trees in black and green on crackled ivory ground; a few minor glaze nicks, $9\frac{1}{4}$" dia., $1,000

Tall candlestick in lustered blue and black glaze with volcanic base; one hairline to base, 12" × $6\frac{1}{2}$", $1,250

Bulbous vase in unusual mustard and lavender iridized glaze; small chip to base, $6\frac{1}{4}$" × $5\frac{1}{2}$", $750

Classically-shaped vase, circa 1950, in fine lustered, dripping blue, green and gold mottled glaze, $8\frac{3}{4}$" × $4\frac{3}{4}$", $1,000

Bulbous vase w/flaring rim in blue, green and purple lustered glaze; small glaze chip to base, 8" × 8", $1,250

Classically-shaped vase in mauve iridescent glaze, 9" × 5", $1,050

Cabinet vase in fine turquoise glaze over a green and gold iridescent body, $3\frac{1}{2}$" × $3\frac{1}{4}$", $700

Coupe-shaped vase covered in dripping turquoise, mauve, and purple lustered glaze; two flat chips to base, 8" × $5\frac{1}{2}$", $1,000

Set of plates by Arthur Wesley Dow for dining room of Household Arts Department of Columbia University, New York, 1904, 2 dining plates, 6 salad plates, 6 bread plates, 8 saucers, single vegetable dish have green borderline meant to represent Palisades in New Jersey, and wavy brown line for the Hudson River; several nicks, chips and a few hairlines, $1,050

Vase w/squat base and cylindrical neck, in matte flambé glaze in greens and caramels dripping around base; bottom drilled for lamp base, $10\frac{1}{4}$" × 8", $1,750

Elongated vase in sand and lustered purple crystalline glaze; overfired around rim, 8" × $2\frac{1}{2}$", $1,050

Spherical vessel in lustered mauve and dripping copper and turquoise glaze, $3\frac{1}{2}$" × $4\frac{1}{2}$", $875

Exceptional and early Pewabic large vase embossed with nubs around the shoulder and covered in a rare dripping matte mustard glaze on a caramel ground. (Featured in the "From our Native Clay Exhibit," New York, 1985.) Stamped Pewabic with leaves, 11" × 8½", $11,250

Two bowls, one covered in speckled orange matte glaze, the other in lustered ochre, lavender and celadon, w/blue-green hare's fur interior; firing line, 4¾" dia., $500

Ribbed bulbous vessel in glossy teal glaze, 5½" × 5¼", $400

Miniature vase in crackled turquoise glaze w/blue plumes, 2", $250

Cylindrical vase w/squat base, 1942, in mottled and lustered purple and turquoise glaze; small glaze scale to rim, 3¾" × 3", $550

Shouldered vase in unusual gunmetal brown, celadon and dripping turquoise mottled glaze, 8¼" × 6", $1,750

Classically shaped vase w/lustered copper and gold glaze, 7½" × 4", $1,550

Bulbous vessel in unusual semimatte glaze w/lustered umber rim, 3½" × 3¾", $750

Bottle-shaped vase in good opaque and sheer crackled dripping turquoise glaze, 7" × 4", $875

Small flaring bowl in Persian Green and lustered red dripping glaze, 2" × 5½", $350

## Paul Revere Pottery and Saturday Evening Girls

SHOPMARKS: (P-1915) Paper label or painted, BOWL SHOPT/S.E.G./18 HULL ST./BOSTON, MASS.

Impressed or painted mark of Paul Revere on horseback over words *THE PAUL REVERE POTTERY/BOSTON.*

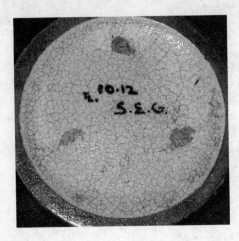

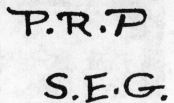

Letters *S.E.G.* or *P.R.P.,* often with year.

PRINCIPAL CONTRIBUTION: Art pottery, children's dishes, and tiles.

FOUNDERS: Edith Brown and Mrs. James Storrow. Founded: 1906, closed: 1942.

STUDIOS AND SALESROOMS: Paul Revere Pottery, Boston, 1906-15, Brighton, Massachusetts, 1915–42

> "To Miss Edith Brown is due a large part of the credit for the quality of the work produced. A distinctive character has been maintained both in design and technique, and too high praise can scarcely be awarded to the wares."
>
> —*C.F. Binns, 1916*[1]

The Paul Revere potters grew out of the concerns of two women—Edith Brown and Mrs. James J. Storrow, for the growing number of young immigrant women living in turn-of-the-century Boston. Miss Brown and Edith Guerrier, a Boston librarian, conceived the idea of having a group of young girls who met each week at the Saturday Evening Girls Club to decorate pottery that would then be sold to help support their settlement house activities. The girls set about learning the basis of ceramics, and in December 1906 Mrs. Storrow purchased a small kiln and hired an experienced potter to teach the young women how to glaze and fire their wares.

The Saturday Evening Girls Club had started their pottery experiment in 1906 in what little spare space their settlement house offered, and it soon became evident that the pottery was going to have to move to larger quarters if it ever hoped to sustain itself. Mrs. Storrow stepped forward once again, as she was to do for several years hence, and in 1908 provided a four-story brick structure for the girls and the pottery's director, Edith Brown. The building stood not far from the Old North Church; thus, the growing pottery took on a new name in honor of the Revolutionary War hero who had taken the cue for his famous ride not far from their site.

The Saturday Evening Girls Club continued to provide the decorators for the pottery, and it is estimated that "over two hundred girls worked on the pottery, although only about ten were active at anytime."[2] Most worked five days a week, plus half of Saturday in what has been described as ideal working conditions for sculpting and painting pottery. "The decorators at Paul Revere were girls just out of school, who after a year's training were able to undertake the more skilled aspects of the work such as the incising of designs on the ware in the biscuit stage or the application of colors."[3] The natural turnover in the staff required a great deal of training time, which served one purpose of the pottery—to train young women—but also helped to defeat another, that being to become and remain profitable. "The pottery in the next few years developed rapidly and grew steadily, but instead of making money it required thousands of dollars to subsidize it."[4]

In 1915 another major expansion was required. A new building was designed by Edith Brown and modeled after the Rookwood factory in Cincinnati. Once again, Mrs. Storrow came forward with the funds to finance the new structure and equipment in Brighton. The new pottery building allowed an increase in the number of employees to nearly 20 and in the number of kilns to four. As the size of the staff and facility increased, so did their line of pottery. Vases, lamps, bookends, paperweights, and candlesticks were complemented with dinnerware sets and tiles, including a popular series illustrating the ride of Paul Revere. "Most popular of all, however, were the children's breakfast sets, which consisted of a pitcher, bowl, and plate, all decorated with popular juvenile motifs of chicks, rabbits, ducks, and the like.

Paul Revere tile decorated in cuerda seca with the pottery's Hull Street house, mounted in a black enameled frame. Minor fleck to edge. Ink stamp, 3¾" sq, $1,380

Upon special order, monograms or initials could be incorporated in the design of these sets."[5]

Under the firm hand of Edith Brown and the benevolence of Mrs. Storrow, the pottery continued to produce high-quality wares, but the expenses involved in the hand-decorating process prevented it from ever surviving on its own. Edith Brown died in 1932, but a change in leadership could not prevent the economic depression that paralyzed the country from closing the Paul Revere Pottery. The kilns remained in reduced operation until finally, in 1942, two year before the death of its patron, Mrs. Storrow, the pottery closed.

Some of the art pottery produced at the Paul Revere Pottery features incised lines and painted decorations similar to that of Newcomb Pottery. "The design was outlined in black and filled in with flat tones in the manner of the period's illustrational style. Soft in color and texture, pieces most often were glazed in the popular Art Nouveau matte shades of yellow, blue, green, gray, white, and brown. A number of pieces were also decorated with a high-gloss glaze, in colors ranging from jade to metallic black."[6]

The earliest work, from the "bowl shop" period, is most desired by collectors. The glazes from this period are a distinctive dead, porous matte, and the designs gently incised into the surface are finely drawn. It is possible to date a piece of SEG from within a few years simply by noting the glazing and the crispness of the decoration. These early pieces are the most valuable.

Because of their utilitarian nature, most of these pieces were actually used, and damage is not uncommon. Nevertheless, even minor damage will reduce value by about 50 percent on even the best pieces.

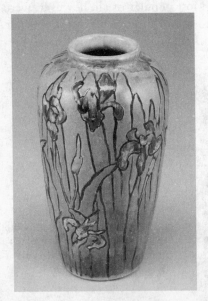

Exceptional Paul Revere ovoid vase, its entire surface decorated in cuerda seca with glossy purple and yellow irises with matte green leaves against a semi matte blue sky. In black glaze, June 24, 1938/AA, 8¾" × 4¾", $6,325

## SELECTED PRICES

Tile incised w/goat amidst grapevines in greens outlined in black, tight in-body line, glaze bubbles, 5¼" sq., $2,500

Tile decorated in cuerda seca w/pottery's Hull Street house; minor fleck to edge, 3¾" sq., $1,000

Bowl in mustard yellow glaze with a duck and landscape, w/"Elaine, Her Bowl," 1924, 2¼" × 5½" $350

Plate, 1917, decorated in cuerda seca w/geese and waterlilies in white and blue on a green matte ground, 8" dia., $1,000

Bowl, 1911, decorated in cuerda seca w/white rabbits on yellow ground; repair to rim chip, 2¼" × 5½", $500

Plate, 1914, w/cuerda seca decoration of green and brown trees on dark blue ground; tight hairline and minor touch-up to rim, 7½" dia, $450

Cereal bowl, 1909, decorated in cuerda seca w/hens and chicks in yellow and white; two very short tight lines, probably in firing, and slight wear to surface, 1¾" × 6", $850

Three-piece breakfast set, 1918, decorated in cuerda seca w/running rabbits in white on blue ground; hairline and chip repair to bowl, chip repair to plate, Plate 7"dia., $1,400

Tea caddy decorated in cuerda seca w/indigo irises on brown and green ground; small chips to lid, short tight line on jar, 4" × 3½", $1,500

Plate, 1910, in cuerda seca w/trotting pigs in ivory on yellow, ochre and ivory ground, 8½" dia., $2,550

Paul Revere tankard and six mugs, all in blue-green matte glaze; hairline to one mug, bruise to another, 7½" × 9½", $750

Paul Revere large swirling vase, 1920, in Robin's Egg blue semi-matte glaze, 8¾" × 7¼", $550

Paul Revere ovoid vase, 1924, painted w/band of puffy oak trees against blue sky, on blue-green semi-matte ground; restored chip to rim, 4¼" × 4", $875

Paul Revere tall vase w/closed-in rim, in green glaze over cobalt ground; restored hole at base, 10" × 5½", $875

Pair of very rare PRP bookends, 1926, each painted w/different snowy landscape of trees and clouds in dead matte glaze, on slate-gray ground; a few minor shallow flakes to edges, 4" × 5¼" × 2½", $625

Cereal bowl, 1909, w/band of green and gray on ivory ground, 6" dia., $350

Flaring bowl in lavender semi matte glaze, 1922, 8" dia., $150

Ovoid vase, 1917, decorated in cuerda seca w/band of oak leaves and acorns in green, brown, and turquoise on a blue-green ground, 6¼" × 3¾", $3,250

Flaring bowl in cuerda seca w/band of white trefoils on buff and blue
ground, 3¼" × 7¼", $1,250

Bowl in cuerda seca w/Greek key in light green, on blue-gray ground, 4½"
× 10½", $1,500

Pair of bookends, in cuerda seca w/two landscapes w/stylized trees, in dead
matte grays, ochre and black; several small and shallow glaze flakes, 4"
× 5" × 2½", $1,000

Three breakfast pieces w/black outlined decoration: small plate w/band of
ducks, egg cup w/band of rabbits, and milk pitcher w/band of geese on
blue-gray ground 6¼" dia., 1½" h, and 2¾" h, $875

Dinner plate w/ inscription "Eate thy Breade in Joye & Thankfulnesse," in
black on yellow matte, 9¾" dia., $550

Luncheon set, 1926, semimatte cobalt glaze w/sponged-on yellow, consisting of a coffee pot, teapot, and sugar pot (missing lid), six 10" luncheon
plates (hairline to one), five saucers (hairlines to two), five teacups (hairline to one and chip to another), 7" × 7" teapot, $750

Four items: a saucer, 1919, in cuerda seca w/band of trees in brown and
green on blue ground, a bowl in gray-green matte, a vase in gray matte,
and a creamer, 1922, in blue matte glaze vase, 8", $500

Three pieces: a teal bowl and matching pitcher, and a blue bowl w/pale
dripping glaze over rim, 4" tallest, $200

Set of five plates, each in yellow glaze w/white band around rim; line to rim
of one, bruise to another, 7½" dia., $300

Two child's pieces: a pitcher and plate, both decorated w/band of rabbits in
ivory against blue and green; glaze bubbles around plate, hairlines to
pitcher, 3¼" and 7½" dia., $300

Three bowls, all in blue glazes; hairline and small chip to largest, 7½" and
8½" dia., $300

## Rhead Pottery

SHOPMARKS: Impressed design or paper label, potter sitting at his wheel,
with words *RHEAD POTTERY/SANTA BARBARA.*

PRINCIPAL CONTRIBUTION: Decorated household vases, large garden ornaments.

FOUNDER: Frederick H. Rhead. Born: 1880, died: 1942, founded: 1913,
closed: 1917.

STUDIOS AND SALESROOMS: Rhead Pottery, Inc., Santa Barbara, California,
1913-1917.

Frederick H. Rhead came to America in 1902 after training with his father in England to become a potter. Over the course of the next 10 years he served as an artist and art director for the Avon Faience Company, Weller Pottery, Roseville Pottery, the Jervis Pottery, University City, and the Arequipa Pottery, designing important lines for each. In addition, he wrote and taught extensively.

Rhead and his wife, Lois, left the Arequipa Pottery in 1913 after a disagreement with the sanitarium directors. They moved to Santa Barbara, where Rhead established his own pottery firm. Two potters turned out large garden wares and small vases and bowls designed by Rhead that reveal a strong Oriental influence; the clay was native to California. Much of Rhead's fame came from his development of fine glazes, in particular a number of "black glazes of Chinese inspiration which resulted from fifteen years of personal research."[1] Like the pottery forms, decorations were designed by Rhead but often applied by assistants.

Unfortunately, Rhead's business ability did not equal his artistic powers. The small concern closed in 1917, but Rhead remained active in research, education, and the encouragement of new potters.

Rare Rhead (Santa Barbara) low bowl with closed-in rim decorated with light pink, red, and blue flowers with green foliage on a mauve ground, blue interior. Small chip and short line to rim, burst glaze bubbles on decoration, 2" × 8½", $900–$1,400

Ironically, his fabled "Black Chinese" glaze holds little sway with contemporary collectors. More important are his decorated pieces, showing the subtle, slip-trail lines of squeezebag decoration. This work is extremely rare, and minor damage does not significantly reduce value.

### SELECTED PRICES

Rhead/Santa Barbara vase depicting Mission Canyon, w/cluster of trees in squeezebag against carved mountaintop outline on shaded gray and brown matte ground, 9" × 4½", $13,000

Large vertical plaque in illustrative style w/pair of ducks in white, grays and blues against weeds and a blue sky, 9" × 12¼", $1,475

Large vertical plaque in illustrative style w/rooster in browns and blue-black, against a fence, mountains and blue sky, 9" × 12¼", $1,600

## Adelaide Alsop Robineau

SHOPMARK:  Incised initials *R P* (Robineau Pottery) within a circle.
(Early) Incised initials *A-R*. After 1908 the year generally is also found.
PRINCIPAL CONTRIBUTION: Small number of decorated porcelain wares exhibiting quality matte and crystalline glazes.
FOUNDER: Frederick Adelaide Alsop Robineau. Born: 1865, died: 1929, founded: ca. 1904, closed: ca. 1916.
STUDIOS AND SALESROOMS: Robineau Pottery, Syracuse, New York, ca. 1904–ca. 1916.

> "I have seen the Scarab Vase in all its stages of construction, and I know the labor and patience involved. Many times during the carving, Mrs. Robineau would work all day, and on an otherwise clean floor

there would be about enough dry porcelain dust to cover a dollar piece, and half an inch more carving on the vase."

—F. H. Rhead, 1917[1]

The significance of the contributions of Adelaide Alsop Robineau to the development of the art of porcelain design and glazes cannot be overstated or adequately summarized. Her life, her work, and her techniques are as complex as the design on the famous Scarab Vase. All contributed, as one study has been subtitled, to her "Glory in Porcelain."[2] Unfortunately, her output was extremely small; a true studio potter, she never entered into pottery production, preferring instead to invest innumerable hours in each work bringing it as close to perfection as humanly possible before selling it directly to a major museum. It has been estimated that Robineau completed fewer than 600 pieces of pottery during her career.

The initial outlet for young Adelaide Alsop's artistic abilities was china painting, deemed an acceptable profession for young women of her day. Her marriage to Samuel Robineau in 1899 spurred the realization of her dream of establishing a magazine dedicated to the artistic and technical aspects of china decorating. The first issue of *Keramic Studio* appeared in May of that same year and proved an immediate success; over the course of her career it provided artists and designers with articles from noted potters such as Charles Volkmar, F. H. Rhead, Charles Binns, and Mary Chase Perry, new of exhibitions, technical information, and color illustrations of important works. For Adelaide Robineau, it eventually provided her with the inspiration and financial freedom to establish her own small pottery.

Her early experiments let to a display of seven vases at Gustav Stickley's March 1903 Arts and Crafts Exhibition in his Syracuse showroom (the

Fine and rare Adelaide Robineau porcelain spherical lidded jar, 1920, the base covered in a mossy green flambé, the lid completely excised with a geometric floral design under a bronze glaze. Several short underglaze lines around rim from firing, and grinding bruise to edge of base, also in manufacture. Carved AR/44/1920, 4½" × 4½", $14,625

Robineau home included furniture from the Stickley workshops). With her husband's assistance, Adelaide continued to experiment, "eventually developing the unusual range of glazes, both fixed and flowing, crystalline and matte, for which she is known."[3] Her tenacity and skill led to numerous awards for her porcelains and recognition as a leading authority. She experimented successfully in a number of styles: Arts and Crafts, Art Nouveau, Oriental, and Art Deco. Though her limited production and enormous personal investment dictated that her rewards would arrive in forms other than monetary, she continued to experiment, teach, edit, write, and raise three children—even addressing the problem of women artists in 1913 by declaring: "It is because of the children and the home that we cannot and will not give up, that the women can never hope to become as great in any line as man. Art is a jealous mistress and allows no consideration whatever to interfere with her supremacy."[4]

Adelaide Robineau continued to work on her pottery until her death in 1929. As Martin Eidelberg observed, "For Robineau, the perfection of all-over excising became a foremost goal. In the compulsive realm of her thinking, time was her commodity to squander."[5] The famous Scarab Vase that she labored over at University City pottery in 1910 consumed over a thousand hours of her time. While critics may enjoy debating which among her many accomplishments was the most significant, all agree on one point: because of the extraordinary degree of skill it exhibits, every surviving example of her work is highly valued today.

Your chances of finding even a modest Robineau vase are slim. Decorated pieces, those with gently carved, excised designs, are rarer still. Because of the scarcity and quality of her work, minor damage does not significantly reduce value.

## SELECTED PRICES

Spherical vase in a bright cobalt crystalline glaze, $3\frac{3}{4}$" × 4", $7,500

Squat vessel in spectacular celadon and amber crystalline glaze, 4" × 6", $6,250

For Threshold Pottery, breakfast set: milk pitcher and cereal bowl, 1924, w/polychrome-enameled rooster motif on white crackled ground, 4"h, and 6" dia., $5,000

Spherical porcelain vase, 1921, in frothy blue-green and white glaze dripping over crackled olive green glaze; very short hairline to side, $5\frac{1}{2}$" × $5\frac{1}{2}$", $8,500

Porcelain closed-in vessel, 1906, carved w/geometric frieze above titanium matte body; hairline, 4' × 8", $32,500

Porcelain spherical vase, 1921, in frothy turquoise, white, green and red Flambé glaze; firing lines under base, 5" × 5", $17,000

Porcelain cabinet vase, 1904, in butterscotch Flambé glaze; minor bruise to rim, 2½" × 2", $1,150

Porcelain cabinet vase, 1904, in green and blue matte crystalline glaze, 2¼" × 2", $1,150

Spherical vessel covered in cobalt blue crystalline glaze, 3¾" × 4¼", $6,500

## Roblin Art Pottery Company

SHOPMARK: Impressed figure of a bear and/or *ROB-LIN*; occasionally with the initials *A. W. R.* and date. Occasionally with Linna Irelan's name or initials and her personal mark: a spider and its web.

PRINCIPAL CONTRIBUTIONS: Art pottery vases, mostly miniatures. Occasionally, decorated plates and small pitchers.

FOUNDERS: Alexander W. Robertson, born: 1840, died: 1925. Linna Irelan, born: unknown, died: unknown, founded: 1898, closed: 1906.

STUDIOS AND SALESROOMS: Roblin Art Pottery Company, San Francisco, 1898-1906

> "California is the only state in the Union that has all the clays necessary for the production of the finest grades of pottery."
> —*Alexander Robertson, 1905*[1]

The Roblin Art Pottery traces its beginnings back to Chelsea, Massachusetts, where James Robertson and his three sons, George, Alexander, and Hugh, were all active in the pottery business. In 1865 Alexander started his own pottery in Chelsea, producing a plain brown-glazed earthenware; brother Hugh joined him a few years later, forming the A. W. & H. C. Robertson Pottery Company in 1868. While the brothers may have experimented with early art pottery, the firm survived by manufacturing both simple and fancy flowerpots. In 1872 their father and their younger brother George, joined them, and under the inspiration and guidance of James Robertson, the new firm, Chelsea Keramic Art Works, soon began producing important art pottery and accompanying glazes.

The Robertsons continued to manufacture a commercial line of pottery, even selling undecorated, yet occasionally marked pottery blanks to other artists and experimenting with decorated tiles. George Robertson left the firm in 1878 to work with John G. Low at his fledgling tile works, and in 1880 James Robertson passed away. Alexander and Hugh continued to work together for the next four years, but in 1884 Alexander decided to move to California.

While it seems that Alexander Robertson went to California intent on opening a new pottery, it was not until he met Linna Irelan in 1891 that first serious steps were taken toward that end. The pair shared an unbridled enthusiasm for California clays and twice made unsuccessful attempts to establish a pottery that would rely on, and promote, native California minerals and materials. Finally, in 1898 the Roblin Art Pottery Company—the name representing the first three letters of Robertson's and Linna Irelan's names—was established in a small house in San Francisco.

The firm's output revealed the impact the Robertson family's Chelsea pottery had on Alexander, "Red, buff and white clays were used for the body, and all pieces were thrown by Robertson in shapes reminiscent of those he had produced at Chelsea. Often the vases were left in bisque or with only the interior glazed. Others were glazed, again using only native California materials."[2] Unafraid to experiment, the pair produced forms involving a wide variety of decorative techniques. Linna Irelan was primarily responsible for the decorating, including incising and carving the clay—"sometimes to an extreme . . . Robertson's own tastes were far more severe and classical, and frequently the only embellishment he would employ was finely executed handles, beading or application of a high-gloss glaze of a quality equal to the finest produced anywhere."[3] While plans to dramatically expand the small, quality operation seemed continually in the works, none had materialized by the time the San Francisco earthquake leveled much of the city. The Roblin Art Pottery was not spared, and at age sixty-six Alexander Robertson chose not to rebuild. He moved to Los Angeles with his son, Fred H. Robertson (1880–1952), who had joined the firm a few years earlier. He continued to research and experiment with California clays and glazes until retiring in 1915.[4]

Most of the Roblin ware that survived the earthquake is not impressive at first, and often second, glance. They are nearly all under 5" tall, and more than half of them are unglazed. Ornamentation, as described above, is usually minimal, with gentle tooling or fine beading around the top and bottom rims. Nevertheless, the consistency and quality of the ware rivals the best potteries in America.

The finest examples are decorated with slip relief work, usually by Ms. Irelan, typically depicting flowers and occasionally insects and scenes. At least one set of plates were made, decorated in slip relief with vignettes including an Arabian desert scene and, in sgraffito, frogs in a pond.

For some reason, most of the surviving Roblin pieces have not been damaged. An educated guess would suggest that most of what remains was in the estate of Dora Robertson and was packed away from danger for many decades before being purchased by a California collector/dealer, Robin Crawford, in about 1980.

**SELECTED PRICES**

Bulbous cabinet vase in crackled blue, gray and green glaze; opposing hairlines to rim, 4½" × 3", $300

# Rookwood Pottery

SHOPMARKS:  (Ca. 1880) Painted *ROOKWOOD* and initials *M.L.N.*

(1881–82) Variety of forms incorporating words *ROOKWOOD POTTERY,* often with year 1881 or initials *M.L.N.*

(1882–85) Word *ROOKWOOD* and the year.

(1886) Monogram *RP.*

(1887–1900) Monogram *RP* with one flame added each year.

(1901–67) Monogram *RP* with 14 flames over Roman numeral for the year.

PRINCIPAL CONTRIBUTIONS: Underglaze-decorated vases, bowls, lamps, and tiles in high-gloss and matte glazes.

FOUNDERS: Maria Longworth Nichols (Storer). Born: 1849, died: 1932, founded: 1880, closed: 1967.

STUDIOS AND SALESROOMS:  Rookwood Pottery, Cincinnati, Ohio, 1880–1967.

> "A vase made at Rookwood under the conditions existing there is as much an object of art as a painted canvas or sculpture in marble or bronze. And the artist's signature upon the vase is as genuine a guarantee of originality."
>
> —*Rookwood catalog, 1904*[1]

Just as the Grueby Pottery was not the first to develop the matte glaze but had often been credited with its invention, the Rookwood Pottery was not the first

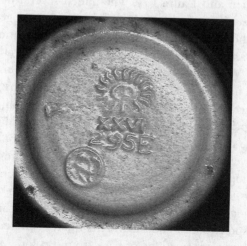

Fine and large Rookwood scenic Vellum plaque by Kate Van Horn, 1915, depicting a verdant river landscape. (Rich and unusual color combination for a Rookwood scenic plaque.) In original Arts and Crafts frame. Flame mark/XV/K.V.H. Plaque: 8¾" × 11", $6,325

to develop underglaze slip decorations; yet no other pottery in the Art Nouveau or Arts and Crafts era was able to develop it as artistically and promote it as successfully as this Cincinnati company. While most art potteries of this era were founded with more artistic ability than firm financial footing, the Rookwood Pottery was built on money. At the time she was born, Maria Longworth's grandfather owned much of downtown Cincinnati; her father extended the family's real estate holdings into the spreading suburbs. Described as "vivacious, attractive, ambitious for personal success, and . . . a careless money manager,"[2] by 1875 the 26-year-old Maria Longworth Nichols had discovered china painting and was preparing to begin experimenting with her own pottery. Five years later her father gave her both a building and the capital to buy equipment and hire a staff. Even the Rookwood name came from her father, as it was also the name of his country estate.

As the number of vases, pitchers, bowls, and household wares increased after 1880, so did the staff and the building. Among the first decorators were Albert R. Valentien and Laura Fry, who added several new shapes to the growing line. Were it not for the continued patience and generosity of Mrs. Nichols's father, however, the pottery could not have continued beyond the first or second years, let alone expanded. In 1883, perhaps at her father's suggestion, William W. Taylor was hired as business manager. Although (perhaps because) he had no pottery experience, he quickly instituted a number of cost-cutting measures, including discontinuing slow-selling shapes and revoking the kiln privileges of Louise McLaughlin and the Pottery Club; and by the end of the next year the improvement was evident. That same year Laura Fry discovered a new use for the mouth-blown atomizer that led in 1885 to the development of the first airbrush technique for applying underglaze decorations. As Martin Eidelberg aptly illustrated in *From Our Native Clay*, "The earlier vases show a heavily charged brush and rich impasto, while the later Rookwood Standard ware is finely rendered in thinned slips with subtle airbrushed transitions of background color. Although Japanese motifs and styles continued to play a part in Rookwood's output . . . , we can note how sophisticated it became and, by contrast, how charmingly naive it was at first."[3] By 1888 the pottery was showing a substantial profit, but Mrs. Nichols had remarried soon after the death of her first husband in 1885 and ever since had begun to lose interest in the venture. In 1890 her financial interest in the Rookwood Pottery was transferred to William Taylor.

Under Taylor's leadership a new pottery was built in 1891 atop Mt. Adams overlooking downtown Cincinnati. Senior decorators, such as Artus Van Briggle, Matt Daly, Kataro Shiraymadani, Albert and Anna Valentien, and William McDonald, were give private studios. Visitors were encouraged but controlled, affording the pottery valuable exposure and free publicity without disrupting the artists' work. "Most visitors were impressed," Herbert Peck related, "when it was explained that a single piece of Rookwood might pass through the hands of as many as 21 people before it reached perfection as a finished piece."[4] Floral decorations in rich, dark colors dominated as the most popular and the most prevalent motif in Rookwood Standard ware, which was awarded several medals at national and international expositions in 1892 and 1893.

While Taylor brought efficiency to Rookwood, he also encouraged experimentation. In 1892 the Gorham Manufacturing Company began applying silver overlay to selected Rookwood wares. By 1948 three additional high-glaze styles to complement Rookwood Standard had been introduced: Iris, Sea Green, and Aerial Blue. Two years later the first experiments with a matte glaze were being carried out by decorator Artus Van Briggle, whom Rookwood had sent to Paris to study for more than two years. Production for

Exceptional Rookwood iris glaze bulbous vase painted by O. G. Reed, 1900, with fleshy mauve poppies with yellow centers on a shaded mauve-to-amber ground. (Pan American Exposition paper label.) Flame mark/900B/O.G.R./W., 9½" × 6", $9,775

most of Taylor's tenure grew to an average of 10,000 to 15,000 pieces of art pottery per year in over 2,000 different shapes.[5] The vast majority were hand-decorated by artists who were described as a "close, happy, spirited group who thoroughly enjoyed their work and their play."[6]

In 1904 the Rookwood Pottery published a detailed catalog in an unsuccessful attempt to motivate mail-order sales. In it eight different styles were described and illustrated, including the following:

*Standard*—"noted for its low tones, usually yellow, red, and brown in color, with flower decoration, characterized by a luxuriant painting in warm colors under a brilliant glaze."

*Sea Green*—"characterized by a limpid, opalescent sea green effect. A favorite decoration is a fish moving under water."

*Iris*—"a light type with deliciously tender and suggestive color effects under a brilliant white glaze."

*Vellum*—"devoid of luster, without dryness, it partakes both to the touch and to the eye of the qualities of old parchment."[7]

William Taylor also introduced Rookwood tiles in 1901 in anticipation of an eventual decline in art pottery sales and a growing need for architectural faience. The tile department developed slowly and proved to be a drain on Rookwood resources for several years, despite important commissions from major hotels and the New York City subway expansion program. The pottery was shaken when Taylor died unexpectedly in 1913, but due to his foresight and the program he had established, it continued to prosper. By 1920 the pottery boasted 15 kilns and more than 200 employees; while the demand for expensive hand-decorated art pottery dwindled, its line of molded art wares proved popular.

The Depression, however, brought an end to prosperity at Rookwood. In 1932, staggered by an adverse Internal Revenue Service judgment, extensive boiler repairs, and plummeting sales, the directors laid off nearly all of the decorators. Despite additional drastic measures, in 1941 the Rookwood Pottery Company declared bankruptcy and was sold several times over the course of the next 30 years before production was finally halted.

## SELECTED PRICES

Painted matte ovoid vase by A. R. Valentien, 1901, decorated w/red poppies on green stems on dark blue ground, 12¾" × 6", $13,000

Art Nouveau silver-overlay ovoid vase by Ed Diers, 1904, w/wild roses in pink, yellow, and green covered in Iris glaze w/Gorham sterling silver mount, uncrazed, 9¼" × 3½", $25,000

Rookwood jewel porcelain bulbous vase by Jens Jensen, 1934, decorated with birds-of-paradise on a pink ground. Flame mark/artist's cipher, 4¾" × 4½", $1,840

Architectural faience two-tile frieze decorated in cuenca w/a ship on the ocean in front of large white clouds in a blue sky; chips to two corners on smallest, some efflorescence on the largest, 11¾" × 8¾"; 11¾" × 11½", $5,500

Architectural faience three-tile frieze depicting landscape w/mountains, lakes, and trees in polychrome cuenca; two small chips to corners (one restored), 12" × 37", $11,000

Architectural faience tile depicting a landscape w/mountains, lake, and trees in polychrome cuenca; ½" chip to one corner, 12" sq., $4,250

Colorful Iris bulbous vase by Carl Schmidt, 1908, painted w/blue and amber crocuses, 9" × 5", $3,500

Scenic Vellum bulbous vase by Charles McLaughlin, 1915, decorated w/winter landscape by a lake; 1" line to rim, 8¾" × 3¾", $1,150

Limoges-style humidor w/double lid by Maria Longworth Nichols, 1882, painted w/spiders and bats on mottled ground; glaze bubble to outer lid, 6" × 6", $2,250

Iris glaze bulbous vase painted by O. G. Reed, 1900, w/fleshy mauve poppies w/yellow centers on shaded mauve-to-amber ground, 9½" × 6", $7,500

Sea Green two-handled vase painted by Sallie Toohey, 1902, w/brown flowers on brown-to-green ground, 6¾" × 5", $3,500

Carved matte vase by Rose Fechheimer, 1905, deeply modeled w/oak branches in green, brown and burgundy on brown butterfat ground, 10½" × 4¼" $1,750

Incised matte ovoid vase by Elizabeth Lincoln, 1918, decorated w/bright red fruit and green and purple leaves on purple and umber butterfat ground, 10½" 5½", $1,500

Scenic Vellum vase by Cora Crofton, 1917, decorated w/silhouetted trees against orange sky; seconded mark for glaze inconsistency at base, restoration to opposing hairlines at rim, 9" × 3¼", $1,750

Scenic green Vellum vase by Sara Sax, 1911, decorated w/birds-eye view of an arid landscape w/cobalt river, 7" × 3", $6,250

Banded scenic Vellum cylindrical vase by Kataro Shirayamadani, 1911, elegantly painted w/flying Canada geese and bamboo on shaded blue, pink and green ground, 7½" × 3½", $9,500

Jewel Porcelain vase by Sara Sax, 1923, w/flaring rim decorated w/honeysuckle blossoms and leaves on yellow ground, 10" × 3¼", $3,000

Scenic Vellum ovoid vase by Elizabeth McDermott, 1916, w/one large tree by a pond in greens and peach; very light crazing, 8½" × 3¾", $2,500

Incised matte factory lamp base by Kataro Shirayamadani, 1903, decorated w/hydrangea on shaded yellow and green ground, complete w/original bronzed brass fittings, 13¼" × 5¼", $5,500

Banded scenic Vellum bulbous vase by Fred Rothenbusch, 1917, decorated w/snowy winter landscape on brown ground; seconded mark for tiny burst glaze bubbles, 18" × 10", $5,750

Scenic Iris tapering vase by Ed Diers, 1911, w/a hilly landscape of trees in brown, green and pale yellow on brown ground, 6" × 5", $3,250

Jewel Porcelain bulbous vase by Jens Jensen, 1934, decorated w/birds of paradise on pink ground, 4¾" × 4½", $1,750

Vellum bulbous vase by Ed Diers, 1930, painted w/blue crocuses on shaded blue ground, 6½" × 3½", $1,500

Sea Green bulbous vase by Matthew Daly, 1894, painted w/clusters of blue grapes on green ground; seconded mark for drips to background color, some abrasion to overglaze, 9" × 5", $2,500

Scenic Vellum tall vase by Kataro Shirayamadani, 1910, depicting a tropical scene w/palm trees and flying birds; overall crazing, 10½" × 4", $2,500

Modeled matte classically shaped vase by Elizabeth Lincoln, 1922, decorated w/poppies on red and green butterfat ground, 11" × 5¼", $1,500

Vellum ovoid vase by Lenore Asbury, 1923, decorated w/red sumac berries on blue ground, 8½" × 5", $1,500

Vellum corseted vase by Fred Rothenbusch, 1908, painted w/white wild roses on shaded blue and green ground; overall crazing, 8½" × 4½", $1,700

Jewel Porcelain footed vase by Elizabeth Barrett, 1944, w/pink hibiscus and green leaves on mauve ground, 12" × 7", $1,000

Standard glaze mug by Matthew Daly, 1891, decorated w/monkey hanging from a tree branch; restoration to hairline, 4½" × 4½", $500

Incised matte vase by Charles Todd, 1917, decorated w/bell-shaped flowers under red, green, and lavender frothy matte glaze, $7\frac{1}{4}$" × $8\frac{1}{2}$", $1,500

Incised matte vase by Charles Todd, 1915, decorated w/bell-shaped flowers under lavender and dripping green glaze, 9" × $6\frac{1}{4}$", $1,250

Incised matte vase by William Hentschel, 1915, decorated w/stylized pattern around shoulder in red and turquoise over a purple butterfat ground, $11\frac{3}{4}$" × 5", $1,500

Carved matte bulbous vase by C. S. Todd, 1917, w/wreath of bell-shaped flowers in blue and red on mustard ground, $8\frac{3}{4}$" × $4\frac{1}{2}$", $875

Squeezebag vase by Wilhelmine Rehm, 1934, w/rose matte antelope in relief on mottled blue matte ground, 6" × $3\frac{1}{2}$", $875

Painted matte bulbous cabinet vase by Harriet E, Wilcox, 1902, decorated w/yellow daffodils on green butterfat ground; restoration to spider lines on body and to chip at base, $4\frac{3}{4}$" × $3\frac{1}{4}$", $625

Wax matte ovoid vase by Elizabeth Lincoln, 1926, painted w/red flowers and green leaves on a shaded red and green butterfat ground, $7\frac{3}{4}$" × $3\frac{1}{2}$", $1,150

Wax matte tapering vase by Margaret McDonald, 1925, decorated w/wreath of blue dogwood against purple and blue butterfat ground, $7\frac{1}{2}$" × 4", $1,250

Wax matte by Wilhelmine Rehm, 1927, decorated w/purple magnolia, $6\frac{1}{2}$" × $3\frac{1}{2}$", $750

Iris glaze ovoid vase by Irene Bishop, 1903, w/amber maple leaves on shaded slate grey ground; overall crazing, $6\frac{1}{2}$" × $3\frac{3}{4}$", $900

Jewel Porcelain faceted vase by William Hentschel, 1923, painted w/branches of pink magnolia on ivory ground, 11" × $7\frac{1}{2}$", $3,500

Jewel Porcelain ovoid vase by Margaret McDonald, 1940, decorated w/branches and pods in polychrome on peach ground; restoration to drilled hole on bottom, $11\frac{3}{4}$" × 5", $900

Incised matte bulbous two-handled vase by Sallie Coyne, 1905, decorated w/red morning glories and green leaves on green butterfat ground, 7" × $4\frac{3}{4}$", $1,000

Jewel Porcelain baluster vase by Kataro Shirayamadani, 1945, decorated w/trumpet vines on an ivory ground, $8\frac{3}{4}$" × 4", $1,250

Faience architectural tile decorated in cuenca w/landscape of trees in blue, green and tan matte glazes, $17\frac{1}{2}$"sq., $2,000

Marine scenic Vellum vase by Carl Schmidt, 1922, on shaded pink to blue ground; light overall crazing, $7\frac{1}{2}$" × 3", $3,000

Vellum tapering vase by Carl Schmidt, 1905, w/white and lavender lady slipper orchids w/green leaves on shaded pink to green ground; fine crazing, $8\frac{1}{2}$" × $3\frac{1}{2}$", $3,250

Scenic Vellum vase by Sallie Coyne, 1915, w/misty landscape of tall trees in pastel colors; small bruise to base, 10" × $4\frac{1}{4}$", $1,250

Tapering Standard glaze pitcher by Kataro Shirayamadani, 1900, depicting floating draped skeleton bearing a lamp, w/silver-washed copper-overlaid rim and handle embossed w/half moon, wind-swept clouds and incense from the skeleton's burner; tight line to base, 9" × $4\frac{3}{4}$", $3,000

Silver-overlaid Standard glaze ewer by Josephine E, Zettel, 1891, decorated w/orchids on a shaded ground, w/Gorham silver floral overlay; some scratches to surface, $5\frac{1}{2}$" × 4", $2,100

Jewel Porcelain bulbous vase by Jens Jensen, 1926, decorated w/nudes and flowers in cobalt and black on a shaded taupe ground, X'ed for no apparent reason, $7\frac{1}{2}$" × 7", $2,000

Faience urn, 1905, embossed w/acanthus leaves in high relief and covered w/matte green glaze, clay body showing through; grinding chip to base, 27" × $13\frac{1}{2}$", $2,500

Standard glaze squat vessel by E. T. Hurley, 1899, w/yellow and orange pansies, $4\frac{3}{4}$", $350

Standard glaze light bottle-shaped vase, 1889, by A. M. Bookprinter w/yellow roses, $9\frac{1}{2}$", $750

Jug and stopper, 1906 w/geometric pattern in charcoaled matte green glaze; a few glaze nicks to rim of stopper, $7\frac{1}{2}$" × $4\frac{1}{2}$", $550

Standard glaze light urn ca, 1889, painted by Albert Valentien w/orange clover blossoms and green leaves on shaded ground; minimally crazed, 7" × $5\frac{3}{4}$", $500

Standard glaze small ewer, 1899, by Caroline w/maple leaves, 7", $450

Standard glaze light ovoid vase by Caroline Bonsall, 1901, decorated w/blue-green irises on shaded brown and green ground; minute burst to base, fine overall crazing, $7\frac{1}{2}$" × $3\frac{1}{2}$", $550

Standard glaze ewer by William P, McDonald, 1891, w/orange clover blossoms; restoration to handle, 10" × $6\frac{1}{2}$", $350

Standard glaze commemorative mug by Mary Nourse, 1895, "Commercial Club of Cincinnati, 1894," and painted w/orange carnations; silver band around handle is missing, 5" × $5\frac{1}{4}$", $350

Standard glaze ovoid vase by Lenore Asbury, 1894, painted w/narcissus; a few scratches, 7", $500

Iris glaze vase by Lenore Asbury, 1904, w/white waterlilies and green leaves on shaded pink and green ground; glaze miss and flaw in manufacture, fine overall crazing, 11½" × 4¾", $1,000

Tiger eye ewer by Albert Valentien, 1887, w/white orchids on shaded brown ground; a few shallow scratches, 12" × 5½", $1,150

Scenic Vellum plaque by Sara Sax, "Lake Louise," 1914, w/trees framing blue-green lake; fine overall crazing, in original frame, 9" × 12" (plaque), $6,250

Scenic Vellum plaque by Lenore Asbury, "The Pine Tree," depicting a river landscape in pastel tones in original frame, 11½" × 6¾" (plaque), $5,000

Sea Green vase, 1898, modeled w/aquatic plants in brown and blue on green ground; drilled hole on bottom, seconded mark for no apparent reason, 16" × 8¼", $4,000

Sea Green spherical vessel by Albert Valentien, 1895, painted w/seagulls flying over waves; four short hairlines from rim, firing lines around base, 6½" × 7", $750,

Iris glaze ovoid vase by O. G. Reed, 1903, w/golden blossoms on shaded lavender ground; seconded mark possibly for crazing, minor touch-up to rim, 11¾" × 4¾", $1,050

Iris glaze vase by Frederick Rothenbusch, 1904, decorated w/blue crocus on shaded celadon ground; hairline to rim, small bruises to base, overall crazing, 9½" × 4", $1,650

Iris glaze ovoid vase by Lorinda Epply, 1911, slip-painted w/cherry blossom branches on taupe ground; seconded mark for minor glaze inconsistency, 8½" × 3¾", $1,100

Standard glaze ovoid vase, 1900, by Carl Schmidt w/mushrooms, 7" × 3½", $1,250

Standard glaze baluster vase, 1899, painted by Sallie Toohey w/orange day lilies; 1" scratch near base, seconded for minor underglaze smudge, 15" × 6½", $750

Standard glaze puzzle mug, 1899, by Sturgis Lawrence Grutzner, portrait of a monk; a few scratches, 4¾" × 5", $625

Standard glaze bulbous vase w/flaring rim by Constance Baker, 1895, painted w/orange and yellow carnations, 11½" × 6¼", $850

Standard glaze bulbous vase w/flaring rim by Constance Baker, 1897, painted w/orange poppies, 10½" × 5½", $850,

Jewel Porcelain vase by Lorinda Epply, 1929, decorated in Chinese style w/four panels of birds and hollyhocks in blues and greens on ivory butterfat ground, 12" × 5", $3,500

Classically-shaped floor vase decorated in Limoges style w/a dragon, whale and carp sculpted in relief, in green, blue, cinnabar and shades of brown on a pearlized ground w/swirls of white and gold; restoration to several large body cracks, 32" × 20", $6,250

Silver-overlay Standard glaze double gourd-shaped bottle, ca. 1890, decorated w/an ear of corn and overlay of grapevines, monogrammed GWC; minor glaze flake and scratch to body, a couple of breaks to silver but no loss, 8½" × 4¾", $2,500

Black opal vase by Sarah Sax, 1927, w/floral boughs in muted yellow and purple on shaded cobalt ground, 9" × 6", $2,500

Standard glaze mug by Edith Felten titled "Conquering Deer," w/Indian chief (Sioux), 1901, 5" × 5", $1,650

Iris glaze vase by Ed Diers, 1911, painted w/Arts and Crafts landscape of ice-blue mountains and light green tall pines at dusk; light overall crazing, 14¾" × 7½", $20,000

Sea Green ovoid vase by Matt Daly, 1901, w/painted fish against green ground, 9½" × 5", $5,000

Iris glaze ovoid vase, 1901, painted by Carl Schmidt w/nest of swallows in gray, brown and white on shaded beige ground, 1½" crack from rim, overall crazing, 8½" × 3¼", $2,500

Sea Green ovoid vase by Sallie Coyne, 1902, w/brown and ochre dishes on shaded teal ground, 6" × 2½", $3,000

## Teco Pottery (The Gates Potteries)

SHOPMARK: Impressed TECO, with the letters arranged vertically. Many pieces are marked more than once. Occasionally, shape numbers are incised into the bottom of the pot.

PRINCIPAL CONTRIBUTION: Art pottery with strong architectural or organic qualities in solid-color glazes.

FOUNDER: William D. Gates. Born: 1852, died: 1935, founded: ca. 1886, closed: 1930.

STUDIOS AND SALESROOMS: American Terra Cotta and Ceramic Company, Terra Cotta, Illinois, 1886–1930.

"It is my earnest desire to put in each and every home a vase of my own make to become part of the home, and that I can so feel that I have in this way done something lasting, and have contributed to the homes and happiness of my generation."

—William D. Gates[1]

While many of the important figures in the art pottery movement descended from pottery families, William Day Gates was originally a practicing attorney in Chicago. And while many artistic potters of this era failed to manifest the business sense necessary to develop and maintain a profitable enterprise, Gates brought to his pottery the rare combination of necessary artistic and practical temperaments required to build a successful pottery business.

Gates opened the American Terra Cotta and Ceramic Company in 1886 in Terra Cotta, Illinois, 45 miles northwest of Chicago, with initial production focused on manufacturing decorative bricks, drainpipes, and architectural terra cotta. The plant was organized in an old grist mill built on the banks of a picturesque lake in hopes that the serene environment would serve as an inspiration to his potters. Gates's contribution to the art pottery market evolved slowly. As his experiments intensified, he built additional kilns and hired more chemists and designers, including two of his sons, but not, however, at the sacrifice of his profitable architectural terra cotta work. Although the name of his new art pottery line had been registered and experimental pieces made as early as 1895, it was not until 1901—20 years after he arrived in Terra Cotta—that Gates introduced his first line of art pottery to the public. He called it Teco Pottery, taking its name from the initials of the community in which it was produced.

From the beginning the majority of Teco pottery was made from molds, which Gates recognized as critical to the commercial production and profitability of the line. Not only did Gates refuse to apologize for producing molded forms, he advocated the technique, in a manner similar to that in which Frank Lloyd Wright and Gustav Stickley embraced the role of the machine in furniture production—as a means of providing the public with artistic wares at affordable prices. Gates designed some of the most elaborate

Fine and unusual Teco double gourd-shaped vase with four buttresed handles, covered in a smooth matte green glaze with charcoaling. Two small glaze flakes. Stamped Teco/237, 6¾" × 5½", $4,600

of the early vases himself; to set this pottery apart from the others, he also commissioned designs from several prominent artists and architects, including Hugh Garden, Fritz Albert, W. K. Fellows, and Max Dunning, many of whom may have been at Gates's pottery arranging for terracotta ornaments for their building projects. As Robert Ellison has noted, "Gates and some of his architect friends contributed designs with geometric, three-dimensional architectural elements, while the European-trained sculptors Fernand Moriau and Fritz Albert executed designs that were voluptuously organic or dynamically swirling.[2]

Some of the earliest Teco forms featured subtle red, tan, and yellow glazes, but when Grueby Pottery and its famous matte green glaze began to attract widespread attention around 1904, Gates introduced a similar green glaze that would dominate Teco production until 1912. (Ironically, the chemists at Gates's pottery were the first in America to develop a crystalline glaze,[3] but Gates apparently chose not to pursue it after the Louisiana Purchase Exhibition in St. Louis in 1904.) Sensing that the public would not distinguish (or could not afford to distinguish) between the expensive, hand-thrown Grueby and the inexpensive, molded Teco—both artistically pleasing and in similar green matte glazes—Gates gambled with his "Teco Green" and won. In 1911, the year in which the financially troubled Grueby Pottery ceased production of its acclaimed art pottery, the Gates operation was at the zenith of its production, advertising more than 500 variations of Teco.

Like William Grueby, however, William Gates generally refrained from utilizing underglaze decorations on his pottery. He preferred to let the form provide the decoration and the glaze determine the color. As the demand for both "Grueby Green" and "Teco Green" declined around 1910, Gates introduced additional glaze colors: rose, yellow, blue, purple, and several shades of brown. Grueby and Teco were both familiar subjects to readers of Gustav Stickley's magazine, the *Craftsman*. In observing the ads that Gates began placing in the magazine in 1904, Paul Evans remarks that "it is interesting to study the objects illustrated and see what started out with creative artistry steadily decline, like so many of its rivals, into mass-produced containers of uninspired design."[4]

Interest in even the later, less-interesting forms kept the Teco line in production until 1922. From then until 1930, when William Gates sold the Gates Potteries, production dwindled as the demand for art pottery, architectural terra cotta, and garden ornaments declined. The new owner changed the name of the pottery but may have continued to use the Teco trademark for some years thereafter.[5]

Most of today's Teco collectors prefer the early, strong, architectural pieces with rectilinear and geometric forms to the later, plainer, and smaller examples adapted for ease in production. Vases with handled buttresses, reticulated leaves, and pierced openings are highly sought-after, as are early forms that took their inspiration from natural plant forms. As one Teco catalog states, "Most happiness comes from the perception of the beautiful . . . and arises from either form or color. Both are exemplified in the highest degree in Teco pottery."[6]

In 1989, the Erie Art Museum in Erie, Pennsylvania, organized the first modern major exhibition of Teco pottery. Emerging from this exhibition was the definitive text, *Teco: Art Pottery of the Prairie School* (Erie Art Museum,

Fine and tall Teco tear-shaped vase embossed with linear band and four ribs and covered in a smooth green matte glaze with charcoaling. Stamped Teco, 11½" × 6¼", $6,500–$8,500

Erie, PA). Author Sharon Darling's compilation of full-page color photographs, historical ads, black and white photographs and detailed information on Gates and his noted designers makes this one of the single most important books to be written on American art pottery.

## SELECTED PRICES

Massive footed tapering vase embossed w/broad leaves and square buttressed handles under smooth matte green glaze w/charcoaling; restoration to three small nicks on edges and handles, 16" × 9¾", $15,500

Gourd-shaped vase in curdled matte green glaze w/charcoaling, 15½" × 7½", $1,750

Two-handled vase in smooth matte green glaze w/charcoaling, 5½" × 8", $1,250

Bulbous vase w/collar rim in smooth matte green glaze, 7" × 7", $1,250

Beaker shaped vase in smooth matte green glaze, 7" × 5½", $1,250

Bulbous vase in smooth matte green glaze w/charcoaling; restoration to chip at rim, 6" × 5½", $800

Tall corseted vase w/four whiplash handles in smooth matte green glaze w/charcoaling; hairlines to three handles, small bruise under the rim, 12" × 5", $1,000

Ovoid vase embossed w/tall leaves and daffodils under matte green glaze w/charcoaling, 9" × 4½", $1,050

Vase w/four buttressed handles and covered in smooth matte green glaze; minor bruise to edge, 7¼" × 4¼", $3,000

Ovoid vase w/two full-height buttressed handles, under matte green and charcoal glaze, 5½" × 3", $875

Cylindrical vase w/four full-height buttresses in matte green microcrystalline glaze; small fleck to base, touchup to one corner, 5½" × 3", $850

Large squat vessel w/four organic buttresses in matte green glaze; two grinding chips to foot ring, 5¾" × 9½", $1,900

Bulbous vessel w/horizontal ribs and two buttressed handles in matte green and charcoal glaze, 3½" × 3¾", $800

Ovoid vase embossed w/flowers and covered in matte green glaze, 9" × 4", $1,400

Ovoid vase w/four buttresses in matte green glaze w/ great charcoaling; minute fleck to tip of one buttress and minor bruise to base of two others, 5¾" × 2¾", $1,250

Four-sided vase w/closed-in, buttressed rim, in charcoaled matte green glaze, 9¼" × 4¼" sq, $3,000

Corseted vase w/four buttressed handles in medium green matte glaze; short abrasion and small glaze flake to rim, $7\frac{1}{4}$" × $4\frac{1}{4}$", $2,500

Vase w/four whiplash handles, matte green glaze w/some charcoaling, 12" × $4\frac{3}{4}$", $2,500

Bulbous vase w/two full-height buttressed handles in mottled green and charcoal matte glaze, 7" × $4\frac{1}{4}$", $2,500

Corseted vase w/four buttressed handles covered in smooth matte brown glaze, $7\frac{1}{2}$" × $4\frac{1}{4}$", $2,500

Pear-shaped vase w/two full height buttressed handles, in charcoaled green matte glaze; minor bruise to corner of one buttress, $5\frac{1}{2}$" × 3", $1,150

Bulbous vase w/two buttressed handles, in bright yellow leathery matte glaze, $5\frac{1}{2}$" × $4\frac{1}{2}$", $1,750

Vase w/flaring rim, decorated w/12 applied leaves forming a shoulder, in charcoaled matte green glaze; restoration to several small chips to rim tips, $11\frac{3}{4}$" × $4\frac{1}{2}$", $8,750

Corseted vessel w/four handles in matte green glaze w/charcoaled highlights; restoration to small chips and hairlines, $14\frac{1}{2}$" × 10", $5,500

Organic lobed bud vase in blue over green matte glaze, $\frac{1}{2}$" scratch to one lobe, 9" × 3", $2,625

Double gourd-shaped vessel w/four buttressed handles in matte green glaze; shallow, tight line to one handle, $6\frac{3}{4}$" × $5\frac{1}{2}$", $2,500

Tall lobed vase in leathery ivory matte glaze, 13" × 6", $2,500

Double gourd-shaped vase w/four buttressed handles in green glaze w/charcoaling, $6\frac{3}{4}$" × 6", $3,000

Tulip vase by F. Moreau w/four buttresses, in charcoaled matte green glaze; restoration to small chips at rim and base, $11\frac{3}{4}$" × $4\frac{3}{4}$", $1,500

Vase w/four buttresses joining a bulbous base to flaring rim in matte green glaze w/light charcoaling, $6\frac{3}{4}$" × $3\frac{1}{4}$", $1,250

Bulbous vase in rare green and brown matte speckled glaze, $5\frac{1}{2}$" × $5\frac{1}{4}$", $875

Experiemental bulbous vase w/two angular buttressed handles, in frothy green and brown matte glaze, 4" × 4", $625

Table lamp w/Teco spherical base w/four buttressed feet, in matte green glaze, w/its original green dome-shaped leaded glass shade w/copper rim, w/original copper fixture; drill hole to bottom in manufacture, $12\frac{1}{4}$" × $10\frac{1}{2}$", $12,500

Wall pocket embossed w/narrow leaves under charcoaled smooth matte green glaze; small glaze chip to top corner, 14" × $6\frac{3}{4}$", $1,500

## Tiffany Pottery

SHOPMARKS: Incised Letters *L.C.T.* Etched in glaze, L.C. TIFFANY or FAVRILE POTTERY or BRONZE POTTERY.

PRINCIPAL CONTRIBUTION: Decorative vases with floral themes.

FOUNDER: Louis Comfort Tiffany. Born: 1848, died: 1933, founded: 1898–1905, closed: 1919.

STUDIOS AND SALESROOMS: Tiffany Pottery, Corona, New York, ca. 1898–1919, Tiffany & Company (showrooms), New York, New York, 1905–current.

> "Mr. Louis Tiffany is busy experimenting in pottery, which no doubt means that he will finally produce something as artistic as his Favrile glass. In an interview with the manager, our representative was told that as of yet, Mr. Tiffany is in the experimental stage, but that he has been so charmed with the work of artist potters at the Paris exposition, that he came home with the determination to try it, and that he would probably produce something in the luster bodies."
> —*Kerimac Studio* magazine, December 1900[1]

Success breeds success, and in the case of Louis Comfort Tiffany, his success in the fields of metalware, lighting, jewelry, and glassware paved the way for his entry into the art pottery field. For many years some collectors have presumed that Tiffany's secret pottery experiments at his plant in Corona, New York, were intended to supplant his purchase of lamp bases from the Grueby Pottery Company, but research has indicated that Tiffany's interest lay not simply in duplicating Grueby's line (as many potteries did attempt) but in creating his own retail line of art pottery.[2]

Development of Tiffany's art pottery proceeded at a moderate pace between its initial conception around 1898 and its first public showing at the Louisiana Purchase Exposition in St. Louis in 1904. Even then there were only three examples in the pottery exhibit, each "ivory-glazed white semi-porcelain [made from] clay from Ohio and Massachusetts."[3] It was not until late the following year, however, that examples of Tiffany's *Favrile* pottery were offered for sale in his newly opened Fifth Avenue salesroom. The delay has been credited not to any lack of interest on the part of Louis Tiffany, but is reflective of the financial cushion other branches of his business provided his pottery experiments.

While Tiffany often referred to his pottery as *Favrile* ware, meaning "handmade," it appears that a large portion of the wares were cast in molds rather than thrown on a potter's wheel. Tiffany himself played an influential role in the designs of the vases and bowls, reflecting his personal interest in Oriental ceramics, his contact with European Art Nouveau designers of the era, and his decided preference for forms incorporating floral motifs. In some instances Tiffany designers would spray an actual plant or flower with shellac or a similar hardening finish, then coat it with plaster-of-Paris to form a naturalistic mold. On other examples details such as insects, birds, serpents, or flowers would be cast onto the base and then accented with additional handwork before firing. Among the most favored of the Tiffany ware today are those that were "treated sculpturally so that the decoration creates the form of the vase."[4]

Just as there was a wide range of shapes and floral decorations coming from the Tiffany pottery kilns, so were there a number of glazes. "Originally the color of *Favrile* pottery was almost exclusively a light yellow-green shading into darker tones and hence resembling 'old ivory,' the name sometimes applied to it," Paul Evans has noted.[5] After the early light yellow glaze came a mottled green by 1906, along with crystalline, textured, and matte surfaces in a number of colors. In a few instances bronze plating was applied over the form, not unlike that being popularized by Charles Clewell.

The line of Tiffany pottery, however, did not prove to be as successful as its founder had hoped. As a late entry into the art pottery field, Tiffany's tenure in the marketplace was shortened not by the quality of the work but by the changing climate of the Arts and Crafts movement, the dwindling art pottery market, and the intense competition among the various mass producers of art wares. Fine examples are today considered a rarity, due in part perhaps to the possibility that the company may have employed a stockroom practice similar to that applied to their glassware: "if it was not sold after being displayed at three retail showrooms, it was either offered to employees at a discount, given as a gift, or destroyed."[6]

Much of the existing Tiffany ware is bisque-glazed white on its exterior, and high-glazed green on its interior. It is possible that Louis Tiffany intentionally left his pottery unglazed until it was about to be sold and then glazed to the specification of the purchasers. Further, it is thought that, when he disbanded his pottery operation, the remaining pots were sold or otherwise released without the benefit of exterior glazing.

The best Tiffany ceramics are organic in form, with embossed vegetal decoration, covered with an old ivory or flowing green finish. Rarer still are bronze clad pieces with inset glass scarabs. One such example is in the collection of the Cooper-Hewitt Museum in New York City.

Minor damage has only minor impact on the pricing of the best pieces. Lesser examples, however, lose over 50 percent of their value from a single chip or short hairline.

It is also important to note that, because his incised LCT cipher is so easy to imitate, there are a number of fakes on the market. Some of these are new pots with an underglaze incised mark. Most, however, are older pots of dubious lineage with a wheel-cut cipher imparted through an existing overglaze.

## SELECTED PRICES

Vessel embossed w/lobed panels and covered in a gray, umber and indigo matte glaze, 6" × 5¾", $3,500

Porcelain bulbous vase covered in caramel and beige crystalline flambé glaze; short hairline and bruise to rim, 6" × 4", $625

Artichoke-shaped bisque vessel w/speckled green interior; missing tip to one leaf and several hairlines to rim, 6" × 5¼", $1,750

Tall bisque pitcher embossed w/leaves and cattails w/speckled glossy green interior; some short tight firing lines to rim, 12¼" × 5", $2,500

Squat bisque vessel embossed w/seaweed and fish w/smooth green glaze interior; several short tight lines to rim, 4" × 7", $2,500

*Favrille* coupe covered in dripping volcanic white matte over mahogany and bronze lustered glazes, 3¾" × 3", $1,650

Wisteria pod vase in mottled green microcrystalline glaze; restoration and loss to rim, 8" × 3¼", $3,500

White bisque squat vase w/molded leaves against chiseled ground; restoration to small shallow nick on rim, 3¼" × 4", $1,750

Ovoid bisque vase w/teal highlights, embossed w/three branches of berries; three hairlines to rim and restoration to two small chips at rim, 8¼" × 5¼", $800

Vase w/flat shoulder and textured surface in indigo, beige, ochre, and green matte glaze; drilled hole to bottom, abrasion to rim, 16¾" × 8", $1,500

Earthenware lamp base w/flat shoulder and textured surface, in indigo, beige, ochre and green matte glaze w/ bronze fittings; drilled hole to bottom, abrasion to rim, 16¾" × 8", $1,500

Squat vessel w/ribbed shoulder in thick mottled cobalt and green matte glaze; two chips to rim, several burst bubbles, 6¼" × 10¾", $1,250

Vessel w/closed-in rim and flat shoulder, incised w/medallion over wavy lines and in gunmetal crystalline glaze, the white clay showing through; shallow horizontal line at rim, 6¾" × 8½", $1,750

Squat vessel w/ribbed body in mottled amber semi matte glaze; hairline to shoulder and rim, 6" × 8¼", $1,250

# Van Briggle Pottery

SHOPMARKS: Incised conjoined double-A, with one or more of the following:

1901-20: Year and often form number (1-904).[1]

1901-05: Roman numeral denoting type of clay used.[2]

1904-20: Occasionally name or initials of potter.

1906-12: Date and occasionally
   COLORADO SPRINGS or abbreviation.

1922-26: Addition of VAN BRIGGLE/USA.

Post–1920: Addition of VAN BRIGGLE/COLO.SPRGS. and occasionally
   ORIGINAL (hand-thrown piece), HAND-CARVED (incised decoration), HAND DECORATED (slip decoration).[3]

1955–68: High-gloss glaze with ANNA [sic] VAN BRIGGLE.

PRINCIPAL CONTRIBUTION: Hand-thrown and molded vases and bowls in
   matte glazes.

FOUNDER: Artus Van Briggle. Born: 1869, died: 1904, founded: 1901, closed:
   current.

STUDIOS AND SALESROOMS: Van Briggle Pottery Company, Colorado
   Springs, Colorado, 1901-current.

"The history of the founding of the Van Briggle Pottery against the
odds of poor health, insufficient money, and untrained helpers is well-

known, but only a few intimate friends know how almost overwhelming the struggle. The Van Briggles were working day and often half the night and the kilns were turning out beautiful pottery. To make it in quantity to pay expenses, that was the problem."
—*Alice Shinn, describing the pottery of 1902[4]*

"He does not work for the sake of working, but rather with the purpose of producing a beautiful and perfect ware; of understanding every detail of vase building, so that he may create and teach; in a work, that he may be the competent head and master of his enterprise."
—*the* Craftsman, *1903[5]*

Artus Van Briggle died in 1904 at the age of 35. A gifted painter, an eloquent designer, and a determined creator of lost glazes, his potential for greatness could have been destroyed only by the disease that haunted him the final five years of his life. Stricken by tuberculosis while living in Ohio, Van Briggle left his friends and the studios where he had trained at Rookwood Pottery for over 12 years and in 1899 moved to Colorado Springs, where he hoped to continue his pottery experiments in the dry mountain air.

Van Briggle's last three years in Ohio had been divided among his painting, his decorating work at Rookwood, and his attempts to discover the lost secret of the famed Chinese,"dead glaze." By 1898 his attempts were successful, and his first Lorelie vase traveled with him the following year to Colorado. His first year was discouraging, but in 1900 his fiancée, Anne Gregory, arrived, and his arduous glaze experiments in a borrowed kiln began to show promising results. With the financial help of friend and patron Maria Nichols Storer (the founder and former owner of Rookwood), the young couple built

Exceptional and rare Artis Van Briggle for Rookwood proto-Lorelei, 1898, a shorter, broader, and more exquisite piece than the later piece, it is covered in a very light green satin glaze, the interior and accents in chartreuse green. (The earliest example of this form, Rodin's influence, under whom Van Briggle studied in Paris, is more apparent here than on the later versions made at his own factory. There are two others known, one of which is on display in the American Wing of the Metropolitan Museum of Art.) Painted in Van Briggle's hand, underneath brown glaze, A. VAN BRIGGLE 1898, 7¼" × 4½", $39,600

a small pottery in the yard behind Van Briggle's house. By the end of 1901 the pottery had produced nearly 300 new pieces, all of which sold immediately; thus encouraged, the Van Briggle Pottery Company was formally organized in 1902, and the resulting infusion of capital from the sale of stock enabled Van Briggle both to improve his facilities and to enlarge his staff.

Anne left her teaching job, and the two were married in June 1902, but despite continued artistic recognition the expenses and energies demanded by the hand-thrown pottery and delicate matte glazes took their toll on Van Briggle. The winters of 1902 and 1903 were spent convalescing in Arizona while the staff, under the direction of 19-year-old Frank Riddle and experienced potter Ambrose Schlegel, continued to turn out vases and bowls based on Van Briggle's sketches. Although Van Briggle was resigned to the use of molds, required for the firm to achieve financial success, it was not his intent "that molds were to be used for mass manufacture, which they were in the late period—to the extent that aging of the molds resulted in considerable loss of detail."[6] In early 1904 the pair returned to the pottery in Colorado Springs, but Van Briggle's health had deteriorated to the point that he was confined to bed. Anne Van Briggle assumed her husband's role as manager while he continued to sketch new designs until his death on July 4.

Anne Louise Gregory (1868–1929), an artist in her own right, proved a capable manager. Numerous awards and a new building with two enormous kilns soon followed. By 1908 production had increased in variety as well as in number (peaking at 6,000 items per year from 1909 to 1911),[7] as vases and bowls were complemented by lamps, tiles, candlesticks, bookends, flower frogs, and novelty items. Anne remarried that same year. By 1910, however, the pottery was struggling to remain solvent. With her new husband's encouragement, Anne left the pottery in 1912 to resume painting, at which time the pottery was leased, and in 1913 sold. Anne Gregory Ritter died of cancer in 1929.

The pottery struggled from 1912 until 1920 but survived two changes in ownership and a serious fire in 1919. The new owners in 1920, I. F. and J. H. Lewis, maintained control of the firm until 1969, during which time the pottery continued to expand with an extensive line of commercial art wares and novelty items that were distributed across the country and abroad. The vast majority of post–1920 production was both molded and mass-produced. At times the forms that Artus Van Briggle had designed were reissued. According to Paul Evans, "since 1920 there has been a steady deterioration in the quality of the design, execution, and glazes, the only reminder of the art pottery output being the addition of Art Pottery to the firm's name as the production of art pottery ended."[8] The few pieces hand-thrown after 1920 are generally incised with the word *Original*. A flood in 1935 destroyed much of the pottery and nearly all of its inventory of molds. The pottery was again sold in 1969 and has remained in operation ever since.

By far the most desirable of the hundreds of thousands of examples of vases and bowls bearing the Van Briggle trademark are those designed and executed while Artus Van Briggle was still alive. His early work often incorporated sculpted human or plant forms as low relief that "emphasizes the lines and contours of the vase which it beautifies."[9] A number of different colors were employed, often two or three incorporated into one piece; they were most often fired with Van Briggle's special "dead matte glaze" or a semi matte glaze. After his death the staff continued to produce limited numbers of his designs using molds; those dated prior to the sale of the pottery in 1913 are also among the most highly respected of the body of Van Briggle pottery work, as many of the early glaze formulas were perfected under Anne's leadership. As new designers were brought in, additional forms were produced, along with new glazes. Those dated between 1913 and 1920, when the pottery went through not less than three changes in ownership–are understandably more erratic and must be carefully evaluated on the basis of form, glaze, and quality workmanship.

Along with the misconception regarding the use of Roman numerals and early Van Briggle pottery (see Note 2), confusion has emerged surrounding the discovery of several pieces marked "Anna Van Briggle." Despite what many collectors and dealers would like to believe, these were not the work of either Artus or Anne Van Briggle (note the variance in the spelling). Instead, these were produced in mass quantity between 1955 and 1968 as a commercially motivated commemorative that is regarded today as not more than a novelty. Of slightly more interest are the pieces made in 1956 marked with the letter *G* enclosed in a circle. For approximately three months, these pieces were coated with a special high-gloss glaze containing specks of gold powder.

Van Briggle pottery is durable ware, and pieces seem to be either devoid of damage or shattered from a fall. The most common color found on early Van Briggle pieces are variations of green; the least valuable from any period are those in shades of blue. Look for examples using two or more glazes, with the secondary finishes highlighting embossed decoration. Because these matte glazes run in the heat of the kiln, make sure the additional colors adhere crisply to the embossed designs. Sloppy firings, no matter how rare, seldom achieve princely sums.

## SELECTED PRICES

Bottle-shaped vase, 1904, embossed w/spade-shaped leaves under leathery dark teal and red matte glaze, the white clay showing through, 8½" × 5½", $3,000

Tall two-handled ovoid vase, 1904, embossed w/trillium and covered in Persian rose matte glaze, 12" × 5¼", $3,500

Van Briggle tapering bud vase, 1906, embossed with abstract swirls under a sheer and frothy turquoise glaze, the brown clay showing through. AA/VAN BRIGGLE/COLO.SPRINGS/1906, 5½" × 3½", $2,070

Vase w/corseted shoulder, 1906, covered in fine, thick leathery red to teal matte glaze, 11¼" × 5", $2,500

Vase w/tapered shoulder, 1905, embossed w/poppy pods and leaves under sheer matte turquoise glaze, the brown clay showing through, 10" × 7¼", $3,000

Flaring vase w/sloping shoulder, 1905, in blue-green leathery matte glaze, 9¾" × 4¼", $1,150

Plate, 1903, embossed w/a swirling poppy blossom and leaves under bright green matte glaze, 8½" dia., $1,500

Elongated ovoid vase embossed w/stylized daisies, 1908-11, in matte turquoise glaze, the clay showing through, 10" × 3½", $1,750

Squat vessel, 1906, embossed w/stylized crocuses in red on a matte green ground, brown clay showing through, 3¼" × 4½", $1,100

Bottle-shaped bud vase, ca, 1904, embossed w/spade-shaped leaves under a leathery matte green glaze, 4½" × 3½", $1,500

Ovoid bud vase, 1903, embossed w/spade-shaped leaves under unusual fine matte brown glaze, 4¾" × 3¼", $1,750

Massive bulbous vase w/collared rim, 1919, embossed w/arrowroot leaves and covered in a purple and rose matte glaze, 17" × 12", $3,250

Vase, 1906, embossed w/stylized flowers under fine and unusual brown and celadon curdled matte glaze, buff clay showing through, 6½" × 3¾", $1,750

Bottle-shaped vase, 1907-11, embossed w/swirling leaves in sheer turquoise iridescent glaze against a crystalline indigo ground, buff clay showing through, 5" × 4", $1,750

Squat vessel, 1903, embossed w/stylized flowers under sheer light blue glaze, buff clay showing through; shallow spider lines to bottom, 4" × 4½", $1,750

Classically shaped vase, 1906, in leathery matte blue-green crystalline glaze, 8" × 5", $1,000

Bottle-shaped vase, 1906, embossed w/trillium under matte teal glaze, 5" × 3¾", $1,000

Two-handled urn, 1916, embossed w/narrow leaves and berries under matte green glaze, beige clay showing through; 1" bruise to rim and small grinding chip, 13" × 6½", $1,550

Squat vessel, 1916, embossed w/oak branches w/acorns under a green and burgundy matte glaze, 3¾" × 5½", $550

Clamshell form mermaid bowl, 1920s, w/a nautilus shell flower frog, both covered in blue and turquoise matte glaze; several dark crazing lines to both pieces, 8½" × 15½" × 12¾", $1,250

Tall vase, 1908-11, embossed w/iris and broad leaves under turquoise, green, and blue matte glaze, w/buff clay body showing through, 16½" × 8½", $8,000

Vase, "Climbing for Honey," 1920s, w/two bears hugging its rim, in blue and turquoise matte glaze, 16" × 5½", $2,000

Two-handled tapering vase, 1920s, embossed w/daisies and broad leaves under a Persian blue matte glaze, 9¼" × 7½", $500

Two-handled vessel, 1903, embossed w/arrowroot leaves under mottled chartreuse and brown matte glaze; old hairline to one handle, tight line to rim, 7" × 7", $2,000

Very rare two-color vase w/sloping shoulder, decorated w/stylized iris blossoms and leaves in an unusual iridescent copper and eggplant glaze; small chip to rim and base from manufacture, 10" × 4½", $12,500

Vase, 1903, embossed w/poppy pods and leaves, in sheer, frothy lime green matte glaze; clay showing through, 10¼" × 4½", $5,500

Dos Cabezas vase, 1908-11, embossed w/two Art Nouveau maidens, under mustard matte glaze; ¼" flat chip to fold, 7½" × 4¾", $7,500

Bulbous vase, 1903, embossed w/poppies under mottled red and sheer chartreuse glaze, buff clay showing through, 9¾" × 8", $8,750

Bulbous vase, 1903, embossed w/poppy pods under dark blue-green leathery matte glaze 9" × 6" $8,250

Bud vase, 1917, in mottled brown glaze, $7\frac{1}{2}$" × $2\frac{1}{2}$", $150

Faceted bottle, 1916, in blue and turquoise matte glaze, $\frac{1}{4}$" bruise to rim and some pitting, 7", $250

Two vases: one bulbous embossed w/leaves under green and brown glaze, the other a cabinet w/crocuses under turquoise and blue glaze, $5\frac{1}{2}$" and $2\frac{1}{2}$", $450

Two pieces in turquoise and blue glaze: one w/stylized daisies, the other squat w/dragonflies, 1920s, $7\frac{1}{2}$" and $2\frac{3}{4}$", $450

Cylindrical vase, 1916, in Persian rose glaze, 10" × $3\frac{1}{2}$", $350

Lorelei vase in turquoise matte glaze, 11" × $4\frac{1}{4}$", $250

Bulbous cabinet vase, embossed w/butterflies under turquoise and cobalt matte glaze, $2\frac{3}{4}$" × $2\frac{1}{2}$", $150

Flaring vase w/squat base, embossed w/crocus and covered in matte turquoise glaze, $5\frac{1}{2}$" × $4\frac{1}{2}$", $75

Figural center bowl and flower frog, the bowl w/ a half-naked maiden peering in, and frog w/a turtle, both covered in shaded turquoise glaze, 10" × 15", $500

Ovoid vase, 1903, w/two short handles at rim, in blackish-green leathery matte glaze, 8" × $3\frac{1}{2}$", $1,400

Bulbous vase, 1903, embossed w/crocuses under matte mustard glaze, 6" × $3\frac{1}{2}$", $2,500

Bulbous vase, 1906, embossed w/Jugendstil irises under fine and rare dark blue-green leathery matte glaze, 5" × $4\frac{1}{4}$", $1,750

Vase, 1903, crisply molded w/irises under periwinkle blue leathery matte glaze, buff clay showing through, $13\frac{1}{2}$" × 5", $7,500

Double gourd-shaped vase, 1904, embossed w/red dandelions on chartreuse matte ground, $8\frac{1}{2}$" × $7\frac{1}{2}$", $8,000

Three-color vase, 1906, embossed w/iris in lavender and green, buff clay showing through; couple of minor burst bubbles, $13\frac{1}{2}$" × $5\frac{1}{2}$", $5,000

Bulbous vase, 1908-11, embossed w/stylized flowers under matte mustard glaze, $5\frac{1}{4}$" × $5\frac{3}{4}$", $1,000

Elongated vase, 1903, embossed w/tobacco leaves under frothy sky blue glaze w/green stems; restoration to opposing hairlines from rim, 10" × 4", $1,750

Bulbous vase, 1907, embossed w/cornflowers and covered in fine, thick curdled brown matte glaze, $7\frac{1}{2}$" × $6\frac{1}{4}$", $1,250

Bulbous vase, 1908-11, embossed w/leaves under sheer green glaze, $3\frac{1}{2}$" tight hairline from rim, $4\frac{1}{2}$" × $3\frac{1}{4}$", $500

Spherical vase, 1903, covered in green and raspberry matte glaze, 3¾" × 4", $750

Ovoid vase, 1908-11, embossed w/spade-shaped leaves and panels under thick, leathery yellow and green matte glaze, 5" × 3¼", $1,250

Vase, 1915, embossed w/flowers and leaves under Persian rose glaze, 8¾" × 3", $1,500

Cylindrical vase, 1908-11, embossed w/daisies under dark teal blue glaze; short and shallow bruise inside rim, 7¼" × 3½", $875

Ovoid vase, 1914, embossed w/spade-shaped leaves under fine green and brown frothy glaze, 4¾" × 4", $500

Vase, 1915, embossed w/tulips under sheer turquoise glaze; shallow bruises to rim, 5¾" × 3", $625

Bulbous vase, 1905, covered in frothy matte green glaze, 15" × 10", $2,500

Bulbous vase, 1908-11, embossed w/heart shaped leaves under leathery green and cobalt matte glaze, 4" × 4½", $1,550

Copper-clad two-handled bud vase, 1908-11, embossed w/stylized flowers and leaves, 6½" × 3¼", $2,150

Cabinet vase, 1902, embossed w/poppy pods under rare cobalt and yellow striated matte glaze, 4¼" × 3", $2,000

Bulbous vase, 1902, embossed w/poppy pods under fine shaded matte green glaze, 4" × 4", $2,150

Squat vessel, 1903, embossed w/spade-shaped leaves under fine dark green matte glaze, buff clay showing through, 2" × 4½", $1,650

Bulbous vase, 1908-11, embossed w/leaves under matte green glaze w/red blush, 4½" × 5¼", $1,250

Advertising plaque, a, 1930, embossed w/"Van Briggle Pottery/Colorado Clay," in green and blue matte glaze; small chip to one corner and a few smaller chips along edges, 5¾" × 11½", $1,150

Bulbous vase, 1903, w/cupped rim and two loop handles, embossed w/leaves around base and covered in rare purple and green matte glaze, 9½" × 6", $2,500

Low bowl, 1908-11, embossed w/band of leaves under mottled green, purple, and blue matte glaze, 2" × 5½", $500

## Volkmar Pottery

SHOPMARKS: (Pre-1888) Letters *C* and *V* overlaid.
(1885–96) Impressed VOLKMAR & CORY.
(1896–1903) Impressed CHAS. VOLKMAR or CROWN.
    POINT WARE or stylized letter *V* (but without a year).

(After 1903) Stamped VOLKMAR KILNS/METUCHEN, N.J.

PRINCIPAL CONTRIBUTIONS: Art pottery and tiles with underglaze decorations.

FOUNDER: Charles Volkmar. Born: 1841, died: 1914, founded: 1882, closed: ca. 1911.

STUDIOS AND SALESROOMS: Charles Volkmar Pottery, Tremont (Bronx), New York, 1882–88. Menlo Park Ceramic Company, Menlo Park New Jersey, 1888–93. Volkmar & Cory, Corona (Queens), New York, 1895–1896. Crown Point, Corona (Queens), New York, 1897–1902. Volkmar Kilns or Charles Volkmar and Son, Metuchen, New Jersey, 1903–ca. 1911.

> "Volkmar's importance in the New York area is due to the fact that, besides exhibiting widely, he also taught classes at his pottery, first in Corona, Long Island, and, from 1903, in Metuchen, New Jersey."
> —*Robert Judson Clark*[1]

Charles Volkmar was born into an artistic family, his grandfather having been an engraver and his father a painter; thus, it was not surprising when Charles chose to follow in their footsteps. At age 18 he was an accomplished etcher and at 22 was studying in Europe, where he was to spend nearly 16 of his next 17 years working in the studios of numerous important potters, including the Havilland family's porcelain factory in Limoges, France.

Volkmar moved back to the United States in 1879, began teaching, and built a kiln in Greenpoint, New York, where he experimented with making Limoges-style tiles. One of his earliest commissions was a fireplace for the Salmagundi Club in New York City, for which he worked as both a potter and a pottery tutor for several years thereafter. The small Greenpoint (Long Island) kiln led to the establishment of his first complete pottery operation at his home in the Bronx around 1882. Volkmar concentrated his efforts primarily on decorative tiles, along with plaques and vases (molded and hand-thrown), in both the applied technique and underglaze. According to Paul Evans, "the decorative motif apparently most preferred by the artist was a landscape with water and some living creatures, often a duck, goose, or cow. In all, about twelve colors were used: yellow, orange, light and dark blue, red, pink, light and dark brown, a 'cold' and a 'warm' green and black."[2]

The popularity of Volkmar's decorated tiles led to his decision to expand in that direction by forming a partnership with J. T. Smith in Menlo Park, New Jersey, where they organized the Menlo Park Ceramic Company in 1888. The tiles of the firm were widely acclaimed, leading to commissions in

Volkmar gourd-shaped vessel covered in a mottled olive glaze. Chips to two feet and line to rim. Impressed mark, 5", $230

the Boston Public Library, the Rockefeller home in Tarrytown, New York, and the Fulton National Bank in Manhattan. The partners were unable to work together, however, perhaps due in part to Volkmar's independent spirit, and the firm was dissolved by 1893. Whatever the reason, Volkmar returned to New York and by the winter of 1895 had taken on another partner, Miss Kate Cory, an artist; together they designed and decorated award-winning art tiles, mugs, and plaques, often selecting popular historical subjects as their motifs.

Once again, however, success could not sustain the partnership. Volkmar may have insisted on major changes in their production, for after Miss Cory left in 1896, he phased out the traditional historical scenes and set out to achieve "rich but delicate color qualities, subdued in tone . . . as are only possible to secure in the underglaze treatment of pottery."[3] An exhibition in New York City elicited praise from a number of publications for his "simple shapes and single colour glazes [done] with admirable restraint. His greens, blues, and yellows are pure, colorful, and even to a high degree."[4]

As Martin Eidelberg noted in the Princeton Exhibition catalog in 1972, "by the turn of the century Volkmar was following the general tendency towards mat or dull glazes although he seems, curiously, not to have been entirely happy with this development."[5] Eidelberg also observed that prior to 1900, "Volkmar was making landscape tiles . . . thus paralleling, if not preceding Rookwood, whose work in this genre is better known. The soft, mat glazes well suited to the poetic mood of the scene; reveal his development away from his earlier, underglaze work."[6]

Volkmar's work is as rare as it is uneven. He clearly hit his stride as a ceramic artist once he began designing with matte glazes, however. His matte decorated tiles, usually depicting somber night landscapes, are his best work. Most of his matte glazed vases are simple forms with fine, spinach green finishes. These are of interest to collectors more because of their love of his work than for their artistic merit.

Most of the remaining Volkmar decorated tiles have either firing flaws, such as uneven glazing or under glaze lines from clay separations. His painted tile work is sufficiently rare to encourage buying in all but the worst of condition.

**SELECTED PRICES**

Centerpiece bowl, 1928, in thick, crackled Persian glazes, turquoise interior and blue exterior, $6\frac{1}{2}$" × $13\frac{1}{2}$", $1,000

Bulbous pitcher w/collared neck, in cucumber green matte glaze, $4\frac{1}{2}$" × 4", $250

Spherical vase covered in frothy sky blue glaze, $5\frac{1}{2}$" × $5\frac{1}{4}$", $350

## Walley Pottery

$W \mathcal{J} W$

SHOPMARK: Impressed letters $W J W$

PRINCIPAL CONTRIBUTIONS: Hand-thrown vases, bowls, and mugs in a variety of quality glazes.

FOUNDER: William J. Walley. Born: 1852, died: 1919, founded: 1898, closed: 1919.

STUDIOS AND SALESROOMS: Walley Pottery, West Sterling, Massachusetts, 1898–1919.

"To me there is more true art in a brick made and burnt by one man than there is in the best piece of molded pottery ever made."
—*William J. Walley, 1906*[1]

After a series of discouraging setbacks, art potter William J. Walley purchased a deserted pottery in West Sterling, Massachusetts, in 1898 and founded a one-

Fine and rare W. J. Walley bulbous vase with tooled and applied leaves under a turquoise feathered semi matte glaze, the red clay showing through. Restoration to inch-long bruise to rim, and grinding chips. Stamped WJW, $5\frac{3}{4}$" × 6", $1,380

man operation demonstrating his concern for quality art pottery over quantity. Utilizing clay dug near his pottery, Walley turned, decorated, glazed, and fired his work by himself, declaring "I am just a potter trying to make art pottery as it should be made."[2] He experimented with both matte and glossy glazes, most often in green, red, and brown, producing a small number of vases, bowls, and mugs that are highly sought-after today for both their rarity and their quality glazes.[3] The pottery closed at his death in 1919.

While even Walley's most mundane work shows the hand of an accomplished potter, ordinary pieces far outnumber great ones. The majority of his work, though hand-thrown and unique, is adorned only with glaze. His best pieces are decorated with applied and tooled leaves, reminiscent of the nearby Grueby Pottery. The majority of Walley's work is under 8" tall, and advanced collectors look for larger pieces with matte glazes over tooled, organic decoration. Such pieces are eagerly sought in all but shattered condition.

### SELECTED PRICES

Ovoid bottle in fine mottled apple green glossy glaze; minor fleck to rim, 7¼" × 5½", $1,500

Two-handled vessel w/tooled and applied leaves and thumbrests to handles, under a fine mottled matte green glaze; restoration to two hairlines to rim, one to handle, 6¾" × 7", $1,500

Squat bowl covered in fine matte brown glaze w/green pooled around the rim, 4½" × 6½", $1,250

Tyge in brown and green semi-matte glaze w/speckled blue interior, 5¾" × 6", $625

W. J. Walley bottle-shaped vase covered in a sheer light green and gunmetal glaze. Impressed WJW, 6½", $546

Squat flower frog vase in brown and green matte glaze; a couple of very minor nicks, 5" dia., $625

Squat vessel w/flat shoulder covered in rich brown and green matte glaze, 2½" × 5", $625

Squat vessel covered in green Flambé glaze over red clay, 3" × 6", $500

Bulbous vase w/tooled and applied full-height leaves in mottled turquoise glaze, brown edges of leaves showing through, 5½" × 5½", $1,500

Vase w/flat shoulder and tooled stylized leaves in green and mahogany mottled glaze; touch-up to minor kiln kiss on side, small nick below, 5½" × 3½", $1,050

Spherical vessel w/collar rim in mahogany and yellow mottled glaze; two chips to bottom ring, 7" × 6¾", $1,550

## Walrath Pottery

SHOPMARK: Incised WALRATH POTTERY around letters *MI* (Mechanics Institute).

PRINCIPAL CONTRIBUTION: Limited line of matte-glazed art pottery featuring conventionalized decoration.

FOUNDER: Frederick E. Walrath. Born: 1871, died: 1920, founded: ca. 1903, closed: ca. 1918.

STUDIOS AND SALESROOMS: Walrath Pottery, Rochester, New York, ca. 1903ca. 1918.

"Frederick Walrath . . . has successfully solved the difficult problem of incorporating flowers and leafage into the decoration of pottery with-

Fine and rare Walrath cylindrical vase decorated around the rim with a landscape of stylized trees with clouds and moon, in dark green, oatmeal, orange, and blue. Incised Walrath Pottery, 7" × 4¼", $14,625

out any suggestion of realism, without detracting in any way from the artistic ensemble."
—*International Studio, 1911*[1]

While Frederick Walrath is considered by scholars to be a studio potter rather than the owner of an art pottery, that distinction has certainly had no effect on the demand for his rare and characteristic Arts and Crafts-style pottery. Although he worked in 1907 and 1908 for the Grueby Pottery and had a brief stint at Newcomb College, most of Walrath's career thereafter was dedicated to teaching young potters at the Mechanics Institute in Rochester, New York (1908–18). There he was able to produce his noted "two-color wares . . . [in which] decorative motifs were generally conventionalized versions of plants, trees and flowers."[2]

Walrath's flowing matte glazes were recognized in 1912 in the *Craftsman* magazine and, like the pottery produced at Marblehead, have been prized by Arts and Crafts collectors ever since. "The similarity between the works of Arthur Baggs [at Marblehead Pottery] and Frederick Walrath can be traced to the fact that both had been students of Charles F. Binns at Alfred University. The simple, well-proportioned shapes of the vessels and the multi-toned, sober mat glazes give them a strength that accords well with the spirit of the Arts and Crafts movement after 1900. The conventionalization of natural motifs and the arrangement of horizontal bands and vertical accents contribute to the architectural sensibility of these works."[3]

Walrath concluded his career, which ended prematurely at the age of 49, as chief ceramist at Newcomb College Pottery from 1918–20.

Unusual Walrath pitcher, matte painted with stylized yellow lemons and light green leaves on a dark green matte ground. (From the Estate of Dr. Marion Nelson.) Incised Walrath Pottery, 4¾" × 7", $2,990

Walrath's decorated work is extremely rare, owing to the nature of the small studio in which he worked. He seemed in control of the delicate matte painting that was his trademark, and the vast majority of pieces appear crisply fired. This resulted in a soft and lovely ware, for which there would be many more contemporary collectors were more of it to be had.

In spite of this quality and scarcity, relatively minor damage has measurable impact on pricing. It is for this reason that better examples with minor damage seem underpriced as of this writing.

Walrath also produced sculptural work, mostly of scantily clad women. While these are interesting and consistent in quality with his decorated vases, they are relatively inexpensive.

### SELECTED PRICES

Bowl in mottled blue matte glaze, 3" × 9", $250

Corseted vase, matte painted w/stylized trees in brown and green on matte green ground; two short tight hairlines from rim, small stilt-pull chip, 7" × 4½", $5,500

Cider pitcher matte painted w/yellow fruit and green leaves on brown ground, 5" × 7", $1,250

Small bulbous vase in layered glaze of frothy ivory vellum dripping over celadon, blue and red; two small chips to rim, 3¾" × 3¼", $625

## Wheatley Pottery Company

SHOPMARKS: Incised *T.J.W. & CO.* or signature *T.J. WHEATLEY,* often with the year.

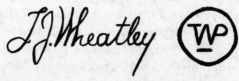

Fine and unusual Wheatley
bulbous vase decorated with three
climbing lizards and covered in a
feathery medium matte green
glaze. Restoration to drill hole on
side. Remnant of paper label,
12¼" × 6¾", $1,380

(1903–27) Paper label with letters *WP* enclosed in a circle beside the words
*WHEATLEY/CINCINNATI, O.*

PRINCIPAL CONTRIBUTION: Early high-relief and underglaze art pottery

FOUNDER: Thomas J. Wheatley. Born: 1853, died: 1917, founded: 1903,
closed: 1927

STUDIOS AND SALESROOMS: T. J. Wheatley & Company, Cincinnati, Ohio,
1880–82. Wheatley Pottery Company, Cincinnati, Ohio, 1903–27

Thomas J. Wheatley will be remembered more as an early pioneer in underglaze decoration than as a manufacturer of art pottery. In 1880, the year in
which he started his first individual pottery, Wheatley was granted a controversial patent for a method of applying underglaze colors and slips to a damp
from; regardless of the actual source for this technique, the patent proved inef-
fective in restricting the use of the technique. In 1882 Wheatley ended his association with the Cincinnati Art Pottery, which he had helped form in 1880. His
two-year-old firm failed that same year, as the Cincinnati market was unable
to absorb the growing number of underglaze wares being produced.[1]

Wheatley formally reentered the Cincinnati pottery scene in 1903 with
the formation of the Wheatley Pottery Company. Although the firm remained in business under that name until 1927, the production of art pottery
was practically eliminated by 1910, when a fire destroyed much of the plant.
Loss of the fragile Wheatley paper label has complicated the process of identifying the art pottery of the firm, which was "characterized by a colored matt
glaze over relief work, chiefly in dark shades of green, yellow and blue."[2]

Most of Wheatley's pottery was probably marked with the trademark, die-stamped "WP" cipher, but the rich matte glazes that covered his pieces usually coated the bottoms as well. Nevertheless, his finishes were unique enough to serve as a mark for all but beginning collectors. His pieces were molded and so the same form can be found repeatedly. This usually results in substantial loss of value for only minor damage.

As of this writing, the Wheatley market is depressed because of two major collections having been sold at the same time. While this does little to encourage collectors with large Wheatley holdings, it does represent an excellent buying opportunity for those looking to add such pieces to their collections.

## SELECTED PRICES

Chamberstick w/embossed leaves and scroll handle under thick leathery matte green glaze; chip and flake to bobèche, 4" × 6", $500

Vase w/four flaring buttresses, in curdled matte green glaze; minor glaze nick to one foot, 8¼" × 9", $1,500,

Tile impressed w/stylized flower and petal medallion in rose, yellow, and blue glazes, 6" sq, $350

Lamp base w/four cube handles embossed w/Native American symbols above full-height leaves and covered in matte green glaze, w/font cap; restoration to rim, blocks, and base, 17" × 11", $1,400

Vase w/closed-in buttressed rim, w/stylized flowers and broad leaves in charcoaled green matte glaze; several short, tight lines and small restored chip to rim, stilt-pull chip, 11½" × 7¼" $1,500

Wheatley architectural vase with four buttressed feet under embossed leaves and buds, under a matte ochre glaze. Chip to one foot. WP mark, 10½" × 8½", $1,900–$2,400

Sand jar w/grape leaves and vines sculpted in high relief from rim and covered in feathered medium green matte glaze; restoration to several glaze nicks, 24" × 15", $2,500

Lamp base embossed w/poppy pods and covered in frothy matte green glaze w/new hammered copper fittings and Japanese split bamboo shade lined w/new coral silk, 23" × 14", $1,400

Architectural vase w/four buttressed feet and embossed leaves and buds under matte ochre glaze; chip to one foot, 10½" × 8½", $1,000

Large vessel w/squat base, decorated w/stylized flowers and tooled leaves, in partially-feathered light green matte glaze; restored base, 10¼" × 9¼", $625

Large vase decorated w/tooled leaves to body and rim in pulled medium green matte glaze; two chips at rim, burst bubble at neck, short bruise to high point near base, 12½" × 8¾", $3,000

Shouldered vase w/four buttressed handles in feathered light and dark matte green glaze; restoration to edge of one handle, 12¼" × 8½", $1,650

Vessel w/tooled leaf and poppy pods, three buttressed poppy pod feet, in feathery dark green matte glaze; nick to shoulder, touch-up to bruise near base, 11½" × 8¾", $1,250

Floor vase w/two buttressed wing handles, w/crisply molded leaves and buds in thick brown oatmealy glaze; restoration to grinding chips, 20½" × 10½", $3,500

PART 2

# ARTS AND CRAFTS FURNITURE

# EVALUATING ARTS AND CRAFTS FURNITURE

*by Bruce Johnson*

Every collector in every field faces the challenge of distinguishing a carefully designed, well-crafted, quality piece from one that at first glance may share several characteristics, but which falls short in the final analysis. Collectors of early American furniture, while they don't have the opportunity to see as much furniture as Arts and Crafts collectors do, at least know that the majority of their poorly constructed pieces have already failed and been discarded. We, on the other hand, have to realize that since the majority of Arts and Crafts furniture is less than 100 years old and was made of tough, durable white oak, most of the bad has survived alongside the good. Our objective, then, is to know how to distinguish well-designed, well-proportioned, and well-constructed Arts and Crafts furniture from that which was formerly known as "Mission oak."

The term "Mission oak" originated in California, where, near the turn of the century, parishioners often made simple, almost crude chairs and tables for their missions. At a time when furniture stores, mail-order catalogs and manufacturers were touting late Victorian "fancy furniture"–mass-produced chairs, rockers, sideboards, and dressers with elaborate, tacked-on carvings, thin veneers disguising inferior woods, and weak joinery with little chance of surviving even moderate use–the romantic notion of heavy, handmade, honest furniture designed to last decades rather than months found a growing and appreciative audience. An enterprising chair manufacturer called the new style "Mission" and it stuck.

Over the course of the first three decades of the 20th century, this new style of furniture evolved from three sources: (1) crafts firms and manufacturers, such as Gustav Stickley and Charles Limbert, who were dedicated to the principles of the Arts and Crafts movement and who, as a result of their beliefs, paid careful attention to design, craftsmanship, and materials; (2) furniture manufacturers, both existing and new, who attempted to cash in on the new style of furnishings by mass-producing a line of furniture that at first glance appeared to be Arts and Crafts, but that did not adhere as closely to the principles that guided Stickley and others like him; and, (3) the home craftsman who, following plans published in books such as *How to Make Mission Oak Furniture* or in magazines such as Gustav Stickley's the *Craftsman*, made his own Arts and Crafts furniture.

As you can imagine, then, the range in quality of design, craftsmanship, and materials is tremendous—and not always predictable. Even Gustav Stickley had an occasional bad day at the drafting table. It didn't happen often, but there are pieces bearing his shopmark that most collectors would immediately recognize as being awkward in scale or proportion. Over in Grand Rapids, Michigan, his younger brother Albert, who brought with him from New York the rights to the name Stickley Brothers, proved that he was one of the most prolific furniture manufacturers of the Arts and Crafts era, but not always the most fastidious. Albert and his designers were constantly pouring out a stream of new designs, some of which, 80 years later, are recognized as being among the best of their type. Others, however, especially those that attempt to combine elements of two different styles in one form, such as his Tudor Mission line, continue to gather dust in antiques shops.

And on rare occasion a spectacular piece will surface from a home without any clue as to its designer or craftsman. Pleasing to admire, with perfectly fitted joints and carefully selected boards, it serves as a reminder that one of the basic tenets of the Arts and Crafts philosophy was the involvement of

Gustav Stickley single-door china cabinet, the overhanging top with backsplash over a 12-pane glass door, with 4-pane glass side panels and hammered copper V-pull. Good original finish and condition. Paper label and branded mark on back, 63" × 36" × 14", $6,900

homeowners not only in the selection of their furnishings, but, when possible, in their creation as well.

My first exposure to Arts and Crafts furniture came many years ago in the basement of a home in Iowa City, where I came face to face with 12 stern-looking Roycroft chairs lined up against a wall like twelve Puritan deacons. I was hooked. I immediately began disposing of my budding collection of Victorian Golden Oak and buying everything and anything that was brown and plain. In the process I quickly amassed a collection of "Mission oak" aberrations, including an early sofa bed with a folding spring adapted from a bear trap. As my collection grew and my bank account dwindled, I began to read whatever I could find on the American Arts and Crafts movement and gradually recognized that I had fallen prey to the temptation to buy first and research later.

The first lesson I learned was the difference between "Mission oak" and "Arts and Crafts" furniture. Mission oak originally included the entire range of plain, brown oak furniture. Later, the style developed and, in the hands of designers such as Gustav Stickley, LaMont Warner, and Frank Lloyd Wright, evolved into a more sophisticated, more comfortable, and more pleasing line of well-constructed furniture. The term "Arts and Crafts" was adopted to distinguish this better line of furniture from the more common, inexpensive, poorly constructed "Mission oak." Today, while a few general antiques dealers still refer to all Arts and Crafts furniture as "Mission oak," collectors recognize that the best of this era deserves the title of "Arts and Crafts."

How, then, do we distinguish between Mission oak and Arts and Crafts furniture, and, just as important, how do we recognize the best examples of Arts and Crafts furniture?

## 1. "IS IT SIGNED?"

This seems to be the question most often asked by every Arts and Crafts collector. One of the distinctive characteristics of Arts and Crafts furniture makers was their preference to "sign" their work. The signature (also referred to as their shopmark) generally took the form of a printed paper label, decal ,or metal plate, although in some instances, most notably the Roycrofters and Charles Rohlfs, the mark was carved deeply into the wood. Other firms, including the Charles Limbert Company and, late in his career, Gustav Stickley, branded their work, perhaps to ensure that it could not be easily erased or altered.

It is critical to realize that while a signature will tell us who made a particular piece of furniture, it will not tell us how well it was made. In some instances, in fact, firms appeared to have put more time into the design of their shopmark than they did into the design of their furniture.

Counterfeit shopmarks have surfaced on rare occasion, but they have not become a serious concern. As will be discussed more completely later in this text, the most respected and sought-after firms also signed their work through their construction techniques: the size, number, shape, and location of elements such as pegs, keyed tenons, internal braces, hardware, joints, tacks, arches, corbels, seat cushions, and slats. Placing a counterfeit Gustav Stickley paper label or decal on an ordinary Mission oak rocking chair is not going to fool even the novice collector, especially one armed with one of the readily available reprint catalogs of his work or reference books such as this one.

The shopmark, as more than one collector has remarked, should confirm what is first concluded by studying the construction and design elements in the piece. If the two don't match, then it's time to inspect the shopmark more closely.

At the other end of the spectrum, the lack of a shopmark does not mean that we can never know who made it. Shopmarks were important to Arts and Crafts furniture makers, but they were not essential. Furniture stores of this era, like today, were apt to carry the works of more than one furniture manufacturer. By signing their work, each manufacturer took a step toward making it easier for the customer to recognize and remember who made a particular bookcase, desk, or Morris chair.

Missing shopmarks can generally be attributed to one of three sets of circumstances. The first and most serious is that the piece may have been stripped and refinished. Decals and paper labels are fragile and were often destroyed when the piece was chemically stripped or mechanically sanded in the refinishing process. If the piece under consideration does not have a shopmark, inspect it carefully for evidence that it might have been refinished (stripper scars on the backs and undersides of rungs and arms, runs and drips in the finish, sanding scratches around joints, etc.), for the lack of an original finish will affect its value more than the lack of a shopmark.

In addition, we must keep in mind that the task of attaching a decal, metal tag, or paper label to a completed piece of furniture did not fall to the most skilled cabinetmaker in the shop. In all likelihood, it could have been the job of the foreman's 12-year-old son to attach the shopmarks to each piece before it was loaded onto a railway car parked on the track next to the factory. Chances are more than one piece of furniture made its way past him unmarked in the mad rush to fill the car at the end of the day before the doors were closed.

And collectors who lose sleep trying to figure out how a form that did not appear in a Stickley catalog until 1909 could surface with a shopmark believed to have been used just in 1903 need only envision the conversation that might have taken place between the 12-year-old in charge of sticking on decals and his foreman when the boy discovered he had run out of the new 1909 shopmarks. "Just slap on one of the old ones," must have been the growled reply, "they all say 'Stickley.'"

Finally, the third category is one that can cause the most controversy, for oftentimes a custom-made piece designed and crafted either for one special customer or as an experiment may not have been signed, for it would not have been destined for a furniture store showroom. Identifying these unsigned pieces is further complicated by the fact that since they were a special order, they may not have ever been photographed or included in a catalog. Here, again, the true signatures are the recognizable construction and design details unique to one particular furniture manufacturer.

Shopmarks can help confirm who made a particular piece of Arts and Crafts furniture, but the discovery of one should not blind you from seeing more important aspects of the piece. Years ago I drove several hours to a dealer's shop to buy a Gustav Stickley spindle rocking chair. The dealer had repeatedly told me over the phone that the chair was signed three times: two decals on the wood and one paper label under the cushion. In his excitement, however, he forgot to mention that the chair was missing two spindles.

## 2. WHAT IS THE CONDITION OF THE FINISH?

Arts and Crafts furniture has had the misfortune to endure both the Great Depression and the Second World War, as well as a period of time after that when the American public was enamored with lighter woods and new forms, including the introduction of the infamous coffee table.

Considered too strong to wear out and too heavy to throw out, thousands of pieces of Arts and Crafts furniture were either stripped and encased in a glossy polyurethane varnish or painted white. Some of the less fortunate examples, such as library tables and sideboards, were also cut down for coffee tables and stereo cabinets. Leather cushions were replaced with floral upholstery fabrics and tall headboards chopped off to make beds seem more contemporary.

As a result, the true rarity in Arts and Crafts furniture today is a well-designed, well-constructed form that retains its original finish and that has not been structurally altered or repaired.

Assessing the condition of an Arts and Crafts finish can be quite chal-
lenging. The most popular finish of this era was shellac, which, while it dries
quickly and has a warm, reddish-orange patina, is susceptible to alcohol, extended periods of direct sunlight, and water. For that reason, during the Arts
and Crafts era and since then it was often strengthened with a coat of paste
wax after the final coat had dried.

Since it is nearly impossible and very impractical to determine the age of
a coat of paste wax, this benign and reversible finish is accepted by museum
curators and collectors as an acceptable means of protecting an original shellac finish. Unlike other finishes, including linseed oil, lacquer, tung oil, and
varnish, paste wax can be removed using mineral spirits without damaging
the shellac beneath it

Recognizing a paste wax finish can be difficult, for when properly applied it hardens to form a thin barrier atop the shellac. It can be buffed to a
satin, semi-gloss or high-gloss sheen. With experience, a paste wax finish can
be recognized by its feel and its faint odor.

When an original finish has been protected with a coat of lacquer, oil,
new shellac, or varnish, it is said to have been "topcoated." Like wax, with experience each of these can be identified by their feel, their odor and their appearance. Varnish, for instance, has more body and more gloss than a tung oil
or linseed oil finish, each of which has a distinct odor and very little body or
sheen. Both shellac and lacquer, which is generally applied today with spray
equipment, have a distinctive texture reflective of the spraying process. Regardless of the type of finish, an original finish that has been topcoated will
be penalized by collectors.

Chances are, then, that the next piece of Arts and Crafts furniture that
you acquire will have a finish that will fall under one of these three categories:

*Original Finish:* No evidence, such as runs or drips, of anyone having
tampered with the finish; some loss of color or finish in expected areas,
ie., the tops of posts, the ends of arms, edges and corners, around drawer
and door pulls, the tops of front rungs, etc.; the finish will often appear
dry and lifeless; minor chips on corners and feet will reveal raw, un-
stained wood.

*Recommended Approach:* If the piece is extremely dirty, wipe it down
carefully with a soft cloth dipped in nothing stronger than mineral
spirits. Test an inconspicuous spot first, checking to make sure that
your cloth is picking up nothing more than dirt and grime. The
finish should appear cleaner, but not lighter in color. After the solvent has evaporated, apply a thin coat of a quality furniture paste
wax according to the manufacturer's directions. Do not use any wax

advertised to "clean and wax." These contain solvents capable of dissolving an original shellac finish. Also, do not use steel wool or a synthetic scrubbing pad, for either can leave scratches in the original finish.

*Daily Care:* Do not display in direct sunlight, for the ultraviolet rays of the sun can fade the original color. Dust as necessary using a soft cloth moistened lightly with a nonhardening oil, such as lemon oil (scented mineral oil). Never spray an aerosol polish, dusting agent, or furniture cleaner directly onto the finish, for the chemicals contained in it can soften and pit an original finish.

*Restored Finish:* The wood shows no evidence of having been chemically stripped or sanded, but the original finish has been topcoated with a permanent new finish, such as lacquer, linseed oil, tung oil, shellac, or varnish. Evidence would include runs and drips, especially on the underside of tops, rungs, and arms; the lack of expected wear in a piece nearly 100 years old; and an unnatural gloss or sheen.

*Recommended Approach:* The reason why collectors and curators disapprove of a permanent finish (as opposed to paste wax, which is reversible) over an original finish is because the new finish bonds with the original shellac, making it impossible to remove the new finish without damaging or removing the original finish. Since the day may come when we have the technology to do just that, it is recommended that you do not strip, dissolve, or sand off the new topcoat. Instead, dull any unnatural high-gloss sheen with a coat of paste wax applied carefully with a pad of #0000 steel wool. After the wax has hardened, buff it only to a satin sheen.

*Daily Care:* Same as above.

*Replaced Finish:* A new finish is relatively simple to identify, for refinishers rarely bother to strip, sand, stain, or finish the undersides of rungs, seats, drawers, and backs. Ample evidence should remain, including runs, drips, sanding scratches, and patches of a darker original finish around joints, and hardware and in corners. In addition, a decal shopmark will either have been completely removed or badly damaged in the process. In some instances the refinisher may have protected the shopmark, leaving a telltale dark box of original finish over and around it.

*Recommended Approach:* Once a piece has been refinished, you have the option of refinishing it a second time without automatically decreasing its value. If the piece was poorly stripped, stained, or finished—and if you or someone you know has the skills and knowledge to do a better job–then a proper refinishing will increase its value over what it had been, but never to what it would have been had it never been refinished. Instructions for duplicating an Arts and Crafts finish are beyond the scope of this book, but are readily available in Arts and Crafts woodworking and woodfinishing books and articles.

## 3. WHAT IS THE CONDITION OF THE WOOD?

In addition to the finish, an Arts and Crafts collector needs to be able to assess the condition of the wood. When it fell out of favor after World War II, much of our Arts and Crafts furniture was relegated to basements, porches, garages, and barns, where it often stood for years on damp floors. Unsealed wood, such as the bottom of legs and rockers, acts as a sponge, absorbing moisture from even a concrete or brick floor. Left untreated, damp wood eventually rots. The quick solution for many people who pull pieces from barns and basements is to saw off the damaged area, but removing as little as an inch of original wood from a chair or table cuts its value in half.

For that reason, be sure to inspect the feet of any piece you are considering. Saw marks, fresh wood, and sharp edges are obvious signs of foul play, but so is the absence of some normal wear, perhaps even a small amount of softening or a chip or two caused by being dragged across a floor.

Tables and sideboards that were cut down in a misguided attempt to modernize them may have since been restored, which is great–as long as the repairs and new parts are clearly identified and the piece is priced accordingly. But as a piece of furniture changes hands, information is often lost, so it is important that you be able to identify new wood and repairs.

In nearly every instance the restorer will work diligently to duplicate the color, the finish, and the original wear on the visible portions of a new leg, arm or rocker, but if you inspect the piece from the underside or the inside, you are apt to spot a small section of new wood, a fresh glue line, or shiny screw heads,—anything that would give you reason to ask more direct questions, including if the seller is willing to guarantee in writing that the piece is 100 percent original. If not, pass on the piece. Over-restored antiques reach a certain level of value beyond which they never seem to pass.

One of the major differences between an original piece and one that has been restored is that original pieces continue to increase in value year after year, while restored pieces hit a glass ceiling at which point the collectors would prefer to spend a little more money to get an original. Unfortunately, there is no standard formula by which you can gauge what percentage of the price you would pay for an original, unrestored piece would be acceptable for one that has been repaired. The price you are willing to pay is going to be affected by the rarity of the piece, the extent of the damage and the quality of the craftsmanship.

Fine and early Gustav Stickley flat-arm Morris chair (#332), with slats to the floor and original brown woven fabric tufted cushions. Excellent original finish and condition. Full box decal, 40" × 31½" × 36¼", $14,000–$18,000

One question worth asking yourself is this: If I found the same piece tomorrow in near-perfect condition, would I be able to easily sell this one for what I am about to pay for it?

### 4. IS IT RARE?

Historians and collectors have been studying Arts and Crafts furniture long enough to know that certain forms were produced in a greater quantity than others. Dining room chairs, rocking chairs, and library tables, for instance, appear more frequently than china cabinets, dressers, and large dining room tables.

Within the inventory of a particular craftsman or manufacturer we also find forms ranging from the extremely rare to the commonplace. Collectors who limit themselves to Gustav Stickley furniture made between 1901 and 1903 know, for instance, that these early pieces are extremely rare; these collectors have to wrestle with questions regarding condition and restoration more than the collector who elects to pursue Gustav Stickley furniture from his later (1904–15) years, when his workers churned out hundreds of examples rather than just a few.

Rarity alone, however, does not guarantee increased value. It has to be coupled with demand. Gustav Stickley experimented with a line of maple Arts and Crafts furniture, manufacturing many of the identical forms he was offering in oak in a wood that was every bit as durable, expensive, and respected, but which lacked the dramatic flake and grain of quartersawn oak. Sales figures for the maple furniture must have been disappointing to Stickley, for his maple furniture appears infrequently. Technically, it would be considered far more rare than the same forms in oak, but the maple leaves most Arts and Crafts collectors cold, so few collect it. Without the demand, a rarity becomes simply a curiosity—a footnote rather than a chapter in history.

You cannot learn about rarity and demand by studying a particular form, for you would have no idea whether you are looking at one of a kind or one of a thousand. Only by reading books, articles, and auction catalogs on the furniture, the designer, or the manufacturer you collect can you distinguish which forms are considered rare and desirable, which are considered common and desirable, and which are neither.

## 5. WAS IT WELL-CONSTRUCTED?

Manufacturers of mass-produced, late-Victorian furniture fell prey to the temptation to disguise poor workmanship with applied carvings, gaudy hardware, and highly figured veneers. In contrast, most Arts and Crafts furniture was made from solid oak rather than veneer, relied on the natural grain of the wood rather than applied carvings for its decoration, was strengthened with wooden pins (called "pegs") in key joints, featured durable leather cushions and heavy-guage, hand-hammered hardware, and utilized design components, such as arches, brass tacks, corbels, and leather tops, as primary visual elements.

Unfortunately, not all manufacturers of Arts and Crafts furniture adhered to the high standards of such firms as Charles Limbert, the Roycrofters and the Stickleys. Many firms that had previously manufactured poor-quality Victorian furniture also manufactured poor-quality Arts and Crafts furniture. When evaluating any example of Arts and Crafts furniture, then, watch for the following:

*High-quality lumber:* Although the vast majority of Arts and Crafts furniture was made from oak, examples can also be found in hard maple, ash, chestnut and mahogany. Regardless of the wood, the best examples will be made from boards that are free of knots and blemishes and that provide more than adequate support.

Oak boards could be cut in one of two ways. The least expensive method, called plain sawing, produced wide boards with a traditional wavy grain. When first quartered and then cut at an angle, the same log could produce boards with a more dramatic grain pattern highlighted with "flakes," which prompted people to also call it tiger oak. Because of the extra handling required, quartersawn oak was more expensive to cut and produced only narrow boards. However, quartersawn oak is less apt to split, warp, or twist than the wider, plain-sawn boards, and is considered a sign of quality when found in Arts and Crafts furniture.

*Pegged joints:* A typical joint in nearly every style of furniture consists of a tenon cut into the end of one board which slips into a matched mortise (a square or rectangular opening) cut, drilled, or chiseled into an adjacent board. During the Arts and Crafts era, many craftsmen and firms revived the ancient practice of also pinning the two boards together with a wooden peg through the mortise-and-tenon joint. The peg served two purposes: if the glue released its bond between the tenon and the mortise, the peg held the two together, and the top of the peg, which was generally sanded flush with the wood, provided some decoration on what would otherwise be a length of plain wood. Like quartersawn oak, then, pegged joints are considered a sign of quality craftsmanship.

*Exposed tenons:* If a tenon extends completely through the mortise and appears on the opposite side of the board, it is called an exposed tenon. While an exposed tenon is slightly stronger than a standard tenon, its primary purpose is to provide visual relief on what might otherwise be an uninteresting board. In rare instances a tenon will extend two to three inches beyond the board, enabling the Craftsman to secure it with a wooden wedge, making this a "keyed" tenon.

Collectors need to know, however, that some firms nailed or glued on small blocks of wood in an attempt to imitate a true exposed tenon. Upon close inspection, a false tenon can be identified either by the difference in grain pattern between it and the board it appears to have belonged to or by the presence of nail heads in the exposed tenon or a glue line around it.

*Corbels:* Originally considered an architectural element attached to the tops of porch columns, the corbel was often incorporated into Arts and Crafts chairs as a curved bracket that helps support the wide arm. Like exposed tenons, corbels actually served as much as a decorative element as they did a structural necessity.

*Hardware:* While even the mass-manufacturers of Arts and Crafts furniture switched from the thin, stamped hardware of the late-Victorian era to a heavier gauge of copper, brass or iron for their Arts and Crafts lines, the better quality pieces produced by firms such as Gustav Stickley and the Roycrofters featured hand-hammered hardware. One notable exception was the Charles Limbert Company, which purchased a lighter gauge of hardware from the Grand Rapids Brass Company.

*Splined tops:* As any woodworker can attest, the weakest joint is a simple butt joint that is totally dependent on the glue for its strength. A stronger joint for boards forming a tabletop is called a tongue-and-groove, wherein a tongue formed from the length of one board fits snugly into a matching groove cut the length of the adjacent board. The tongue-and-groove joint is commonly found in examples from the better Arts and Crafts furniture manufacturers, but a few, including the L. & J. G. Stickley Company and the Charles Limbert Company, went one step further. The craftsmen in these workshops often cut a narrow slot the length of each board, then, before gluing the two boards together, inserted a thin strip of wood called a spline into the two channels. The spline provided a physical bond between the two boards and additional gluing surface, making it the strongest joint possible between two boards on a tabletop.

## 6. IS IT WELL-DESIGNED?

Judging the design of any piece of furniture is far more subjective than any of the criteria yet discussed, for a form that may seem pleasing and proportional to one eye may jar another's nerves.

While architects and designers have often attempted to reduce good design to a formula, the ultimate test of the success of a particular form is whether or not it is pleasing to admire. The difference between a chair that springs from a good design and one that appears awkward may be as little as an inch in any direction. All of the elements of a piece of furniture–ranging from the number of inches of overhang on the top to the spacing of the slats, the height of the back in proportion to the width of the front, the location of the rungs, the curvature of the arch–must work together in total harmony in order for the piece to be considered a pleasing design.

Even if all of the other elements are present, including quality materials, handcraftsmanship, an original finish, even rarity, if the proportions of the piece leave it looking awkward or out of balance, the piece suffers. As a case

Fine and rare L. and J. G. Stickley crib settle (#222), with vertical slats to back and sides, tapering posts, and beveled rail with (new) dark brown leather drop-in seat and three loose cushions. Original finish with light overcoat to some areas, excellent condition. "The Work of..." label, 76" × 36" × 31", $12,650

Rare Gustav Stickley postcard desk with overhanging rectangular top, full gallery with two small cabinet doors and open slots, over two drawers. Refinished, replaced hardware. Red decal, 40½" × 43" × 25½", $4,600

in point, the craftsmen in the small Roycroft Furniture Shop produced heavy, durable furniture made from the finest lumber and exhibiting pegged joints and keyed tenons, but they lacked the leadership of an experienced designer. For that reason, Roycroft furniture is more often respected for its craftsmanship and rarity than its pleasing proportions.

So, when it comes to design, pull the piece away from any distractions, walk around it, study it from every direction, and listen to what your eyes and your mind tell you.

# THE ARTS AND CRAFTS FURNITURE MANUFACTURERS

## Byrdcliffe Arts and Crafts Colony

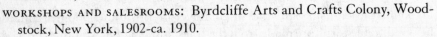

SHOPMARK: Branded mark with the word BYRD-CLIFFE and the year 1904 around a lily and enclosed in an octagon.

PRINCIPAL CONTRIBUTIONS: Furniture, pottery, textiles, and metalware.

FOUNDER: Ralph Radcliffe-Whitehead. Born: 1854, died: 1929, founded: 1902, closed: ca. 1910.

WORKSHOPS AND SALESROOMS: Byrdcliffe Arts and Crafts Colony, Woodstock, New York, 1902-ca. 1910.

> "Now I think not of such large beginnings, but of quietly finding out something which I shall be capable of doing as an individual, trusting that when I am master of that, I shall not fail to gather one or two around me."
> —*Ralph Radcliffe-Whitehead, ca. 1892*[1]

While Arts and Crafts entrepreneurs such as Gustav Stickley, Charles Limbert, and Elbert Hubbard elected to work within the factory system in their attempts to elevate the status of the *Craftsman* through an improved working environment, a few inspired and independently wealthy individuals established small utopian craft communities during the Arts and Crafts era. In light of the almost insurmountable difficulties they faced, all seemed doomed to failure from the start, but Byrdcliffe Colony, founded by Ralph Radcliffe-Whitehead, had a particularly bright flowering before it, too, withered and died.

Ralph Radcliffe-Whitehead inherited his family's English textile manufacturing fortune at the age of 32 and, freed of the responsibility of providing a living for himself, spent several years traveling. Inspired by an encounter with John Ruskin, the Oxford scholar, Arts and Crafts philosopher, and author, Whitehead made plans to establish an artisan colony "on a Ruskinian mountainside with a stream, some pine trees, and a view of the ocean in the distance."[2]

His first step toward the fulfillment of his dream was the purchase of 1,300 acres of land outside Woodstock, New York, in 1902. He christened it Byrdcliffe, combining portions of his name with that of his second wife, Jane Byrd Whitehead.

"Byrdcliffe was to be a place," author Coy Ludwig observed, "where the fusion of ideas and the teaching and production of crafts could take place among compatible, intelligent friends in an inspiring rural setting."[3] With his family fortune at his disposal, Whitehead poured thousands of dollars into Byrdcliffe, building more than 30 structures, including houses, a dining hall, artist studios, a dormitory for students, and a furniture workshop equipped with the most modern machinery. He and his associates, Hervey White and Bolton Coit Brown, planned to ship their furniture by rail to retail outlets in New York City, but their output, while unique and well-built, was extremely small. It is quite possible that fewer than 50 pieces were ever completed.[4]

It appears that what little furniture was made at Byrdcliffe was constructed between 1903 and 1905, although the branded shopmarks on the furniture always bear the date 1904. The only style of shopmark discovered consists of an octagon surrounding a stylized lily, the word *Byrdcliffe*, and the date 1904. The principal furniture designers were Zulma Steele and Edna Walker, both Pratt graduates, who favored hand-carved floral themes, often highlighted with naturalistic colors, including greens and reds. The pores of the oak and poplar furniture were generally left unfilled and the wood unfinished so as not to detract from the beauty of the natural pattern of the grain.

Fine and rare Byrdcliffe magazine stand, 1904, with rectangular top, two lower shelves, and side panels carved with hollyhocks. Original finish, excellent condition. Branded mark, 35¾" × 14" × 11", $14,950

As Byrdcliffe scholar Robert Edwards has noted, "Even though White-head had intended to make the colony pay for itself, he gave little thought to the portability of the furniture produced. Many of the cabinets were over six feet tall, and the oak used in their construction ensured a weight so great as to prevent easy transportation to the nearby Kingston freight depot. As a re-sult, more than half of the pieces known were relegated to shadowy corners of the corridors at 'White Pines,' where they remained for eighty years."[5] By 1905 Whitehead had become disenchanted with his dreams of Arts and Crafts furniture production at Byrdcliffe and closed the woodshops, turning his attention, instead, to pottery and weaving.

The few pieces of Byrdcliffe furniture that did leave the mountainside colony around 1904 encountered many of the same marketing problems as did the products of Morris and Company in the 1880s. The handcraftsman-ship involved in carving the panels and staining the wood inflated the price beyond that of its competition—and the budgets of all but a few potential buy-ers. "Though some Byrdcliff furniture lacks refinement in proportion, and all is simple," interprets Robert Edwards, "it remains an instructive manifes-tation of the Arts and Crafts idea that beauty found by the craftsmen in their daily lives was more important than the finished product."[6]

While the colony never achieved self-sustainment, Whitehead's fortune kept it open for several years after the close of the cabinet shops. The artists, designers, teachers, and students eventually departed, leaving Whitehead with the skeletal remains of a glorified country estate. He died in 1929, one year after his oldest son was lost at sea. His wife, Jane, continued to live at Byrdcliffe, selling off portions of the estate as needed to support herself and their other son, who lived there in quiet seclusion from the time his mother died in 1952 until he, too, passed away at Byrdcliffe in 1976.

Although Whitehead's experiment failed to meet his expectations, "the Byrdcliffe experiment attracted many talented people to the area, beginning a tradition that to this day makes Woodstock an important center for artists."[7]

## SELECTED PRICES

The rarity of Byrdcliffe furniture, plus the individual nature of each piece, makes establishing a price guide both impractical and quite possibly mis-leading, for the value of any example will be influenced by factors beyond the scope of this study.

Any examples of Byrdcliffe furniture that surface will need to be care-fully researched and analyzed in order to determine their fair market value.

Bench, double-back: oak, with four carved back panels above twin uphol-stered slip seats, 60" wide, $2,500–$3,500,

Blanket chest: poplar, stained dark green, each post with carved lilies, stained naturalistic colors, wrought-iron hardware, 29" × 50" × 22", $20,000–$30,000

Desk: mahogany, with one drawer on one side, three drawers on the other, carved mottos in Latin, Greek, and Italian, 28" × 37" × 24", $6,500–$9,500

Dining suite: oak, rectangular table with four carved legs joined by H-stretcher, 29" × 66" × 35"; four dining chairs with carved back panels and upholstered slip seat, $5,000–$7,500

Hanging cabinet: poplar, stained light green, small door on left with carved red iris, one shelf, closed back, branded inside door, 18" × 39" × 8", $15,000–$20,000

Magazine stand: rectangular top with two lower shelves, side panels carved with hollyhocks, 35" × 14" × 11", $5,500–$7,500

Magazine stand: cherry, two shelves beneath overhanging top, flared sides, painted lilies as decoration, 30" × 13" × 11", $12,000–$16,000

## Harvey Ellis

SHOPMARK: Illustrations only: initials "H. E." over the last two digits of the year, all enclosed in a furniture circle see Gustav Stickley.

PRINCIPAL CONTRIBUTIONS: Inlay furniture designs, architectural drawings.

FOUNDER: Harvey Ellis. Born: 1852, died: January 2, 1904.

STUDIOS AND WORKSHOPS: Harvey and Charles S. Ellis, Rochester, New York, 1879–85, 1895–1903.

*Various Firms:* LeRoy Buffington, St. Paul, Minnesota; J. Walter Stevens, St. Paul, Minnesota; George R. Mann, St. Louis, 1885–95; Gustav Stickley's Craftsman Shops, Syracuse, New York, 1903–04.

> "Care has also been taken properly to adjust the movable furnishings to the size of the room: as apparent space may be rapidly diminished by the introduction of pieces too large and too massive."
> —*Harvey Ellis, the Craftsman, October 1903*[1]

They worked together fewer than nine months, but the collaboration between the frail, itinerant architect Harvey Ellis and the robust, headstrong Gustav Stickley left an indelible impression on the Arts and Crafts movement that is still felt today. When they met at an Arts and Crafts exhibition in March of 1903, Ellis was but a few months from his death, a victim of

Fine and rare Gustav Stickley sideboard designed by Harvey Ellis with backsplash and plate rest over six drawers with hammered copper pulls, an arched apron, and lower shelf. Original finish, replaced back paneling, minor nicks to legs. Red decal, 42" × 54" × 21", $11,500

chronic alcoholism. Stickley's empire was just beginning to take shape: both his new furniture designs and the *Craftsman* magazine were steadily gaining popularity, and once again he was ready to expand, this time into the field of residential architecture.

Stickley, however, who never had the opportunity to finish high school, had no formal training or practical experience as an architect. His attempts at designing bungalows that he felt were appropriate for his massive Arts and Crafts furniture inevitably reflected his own personal bias toward interior design rather than critical aspects of the exterior structure. Finding an available architect who shared his enthusiasm for the Arts and Crafts ideals and who could provide plans and articles for the *Craftsman* could well have been difficult in 1903; Stickley undoubtedly felt fortunate that Ellis, even with his nomadic reputation, would leave his brothers' established practice to join him in Syracuse. As the Rochester *Times* reported at the end of May 1903, "Mr. Harvey Ellis, one of the most successful architects and one of the best-known and most talented of Rochester's artists has accepted a position with Mr. Gustav Stickley of Syracuse, who will hereafter control Mr. Ellis' designs and work."[2]

What the newspaper did not report, however, was that the talents and career of Harvey Ellis had been victimized by his bouts with alcohol addiction. An appointment to West Point at the age of 18 lasted only six months before he was dismissed. After a trip to Europe he served a brief apprenticeship in

Albany before opening an architectural office with his brothers, Charles and Frank, in Rochester in 1879. He was still in his twenties when it became apparent that his genius for design and his talent as an artist were to be diluted by his lifelong addiction to alcohol. After a disagreement with Charles in 1885, Harvey left the firm and chose to become a journeyman architect, traveling around the country, occasionally working for architectural firms in need of an experienced draftsman, apparently unconcerned about whose name and whose reputation were built on his work. It was left to later scholars to determine from visual analysis which buildings Harvey Ellis had designed while serving under various New York and Midwestern architects. LeRoy Buffington in St. Paul, Minnesota, for whom Ellis did extensive work, recalled that he "gave Harvey, at the end of every day, amounts varying from a quarter to several dollars; and whatever the sum, in the morning it was gone."[3] Ellis, though intensely private, could joke at his own expense. "You must remember," he replied to a friend who once complimented him on how well he looked, "that I've been preserved in alcohol for twenty years."[4]

In 1895 Ellis returned to Rochester once again to work with his brothers. This time he was sober and apparently stayed away from alcohol until "a few months before his melancholy death, weakened by disease, he sought its aid to give him strength for his daily task."[5] His interest and energies were soon drawn away from their architectural practice and into the emerging Arts and Crafts movement; in 1897 he played a crucial role in the founding of the Rochester Arts and Crafts Society, the first of its kind in New York. His efforts were rewarded by its members, who elected him their first president. As a friend reminisced a few years after his death, Ellis loved "to talk about anything under the sun except himself to anyone who would listen. . . he was easily and without effort the center of a charmed attention."[6] The Society's first show reflected Ellis's infatuation with Japanese art. "His love for things Japanese (at a time when most of us had never seen a Japanese print)," a friend later wrote, "influenced all of his later work, and particularly his color."[7]

When Gustav Stickley announced that he was sponsoring an Arts and Crafts exhibition in Syracuse in the spring of 1903, Harvey Ellis took personal responsibility for arranging for the exhibition to travel to Rochester for a subsequent showing in April. The two worked closely together on the exhibition and decided that Ellis, though it was reported that he was drinking heavily again at the time, should come to work for Stickley in Syracuse around the first of June. According to Stickley's daughter, "Gustav took care of Harvey, but he also recognized Ellis' design genius . . . [and] above anyone else at the United Crafts, Harvey understood Gustav's ideas about furniture."[8]

Given that Stickley had no formal training as an architect and that Ellis had never ventured into serious furniture design, it would appear that Ellis was hired to design Craftsman houses for Stickley's magazine. As he delved into his projects with renewed enthusiasm, the design of interiors, walls, and furniture seemed a natural extension of his work as an architect. The July issue featured an Ellis article, "A Craftsman House Design," with the trademark Ellis emphasis on color and his hope that "the owner is fortunate enough to possess, or can obtain two or three Japanese prints of a good period and by approved masters, such as Hokusai, Hiroshige, Toyokuni, or Utarmaro."[9] The furniture pictured is definitely of Gustav Stickley design, but the first glimpse of Harvey Ellis's own furniture designs appears later in the same issue in "A Child's Bedroom." Here can be found the arched toe boards inspired by Charles Rennie Mackintosh, the first sign of any inlay or bowed sides, the Voysey-like thin, overhanging tops, and a lighter, more sophisticated look than Stickley had been designing. As the year progressed, Ellis' architectural and furniture drawings continued to evolve issue by issue until, in the January 1904 publication, several pages of photographs of Harvey Ellis-designed furniture appeared. If Ellis had the opportunity to see this important issue, it was on his deathbed, for he had been hospitalized in December and died shortly afterward, on January 2. It fell to Gustav to write the article accompanying this new line of Craftsman furniture and to explain how the presence of inlay fit within his earlier declaration to "do away with needless ornamentation."

"It is used. . . to relieve and mark interesting what otherwise would have been a too large area of plain, flat surface," Stickley wrote, but as if not totally convinced, he continued, "It, in every case, emphasizes the structural lines; accenting in most instances the vertical elements, and so giving a certain slenderness of effect to a whole which were otherwise too solid and heavy."[10] While his reasoning may have been weak, Stickley was correct in his realization that the designs of Harvey Ellis brought a needed sense of lightness and reduced emphasis on the structural elements—exposed and keyed tenons, trumpet-flared stretchers, and massive legs—that had characterized Stickley's powerful pre–1903 designs.

The inlaid furniture that Harvey Ellis designed for Gustav Stickley bears no special signature different from that used by Stickley on all of his Arts and Crafts furniture produced in 1903 and 1904. Many of those pieces produced in 1903 bear the red decal featuring the name Stickley encompassed in a red box. Also in 1903 and on into 1904, a variation of the red decal was used in which the entire logo is contained within a box. While no special mark was used to indicate which pieces were designed by Ellis, the characteristics of his work, from the inlay to the bowed sides to the sweeping arches, are more identifiable than any decal could be. In those rare instances in which a watercolor or painting of Harvey Ellis's surfaces, his own mark—the initials H and E above the last two digits of the year, all encompassed in a circle—may be found. Some paintings and his architectural drawings, if

Harvey Ellis designed attenuated inlays of floral patterns with pewter, copper, nickel, and fruitwood.

signed, will bear his name clearly printed or written in longhand, often followed by the month and the year.

Through his research into Gustav Stickley's business records, author David Cathers was able to determine that drawings for the inlay designs would have first been executed in Stickley's drafting room in Syracuse, either by Ellis or LaMont Warner, another talented designer working for Stickley. The drawings would then have been sent to the marquetry firm of George H. Jones, where, using exotic woods, copper and pewter, skilled craftsmen created the inlaid patterns on backgrounds of solid or veneer oak, mahogany, or maple, then shipped them to Syracuse to be incorporated into the furniture which Ellis or, quite possibly, Warner had designed.[11]

Regardless of how Stickley felt about the philosophical justification for the presence of inlay in his Arts and Crafts furniture, economic considerations prevented the line from ever being put into production. Only a few exhibition and floor samples with inlays of pewter and exotic woods were produced in oak, and their rarity has made them the most valuable of all of the work produced by either Gustav Stickley or Harvey Ellis.

Students of Arts and Crafts design, however, recognize that the attention drawn to the inlaid furniture has overshadowed the more important contribution Ellis made both to Gustav Stickley's development and to the entire Arts and Crafts furniture movement. Ellis softened the impact made by the massive furniture of Stickley and his imitators by eliminating keyed tenons; replacing severe, straight aprons with sweeping curves, heavy chamfered backs with laminated panels, and straight sides with gentle bows; reducing both the number of pegged joints and the emphasis on heavy, hand-hammered hardware; and installing thin, overhanging tops and narrow chair stretchers. In short, Ellis brought style and sophistication to the basic Arts and Crafts furniture designs that Gustav Stickley had introduced and that his competitors continued to imitate. Although the inlay was discontinued shortly after his death, Harvey Ellis's more important contributions remained evident in Gustav Stickley's designs to the end of the Arts and Crafts movement. Stickley continued to produce examples of Ellis-designed furniture (minus the inlay) until the close of his factory in 1916; these pieces still command premiums from collectors. Around 1912 Stickley also released a few bedroom pieces made of curly maple and featuring Ellis-inspired inlay redrawn by LaMont Warner and produced in the shops of George H. Jones, but they have thus far failed to generate the interest demonstrated in the earlier inlaid oak furniture.

In the February 1904 issue of the *Craftsman* there appears a brief obituary, presumably written by Stickley. In it he declares that "Mr. Ellis was a man of unusual gifts; possessing an accurate and exquisite sense of color, a great facility in design and a sound judgment of effect. . . . Altogether, he is to be regretted as one who possessed the sacred fire of genius."[12]

## SELECTED PRICES

Although actual figures have never been discovered, it has been reported that the inlaid furniture designed by Harvey Ellis was never put into full production at the *Craftsman* Workshops. As might be expected, inlaid chairs appear most frequently, although still only rarely. In most other instances, the number of examples of each form ranges from two to fewer than a dozen. Unlike Stickley's spindle furniture, which has proved to be more available than once thought, the inlaid pieces will always remain the rarest of Stickley's furniture. Determining the difference, however, between a $3,000 Ellis chair and a $30,000 example is beyond the scope of this study. Before buying or selling any Harvey Ellis-designed furniture, consult with an unbiased expert who does not stand to benefit from the transaction.

Note: individuals who recognize the premium placed on Harvey Ellis furniture have demonstrated a tendency to attribute any piece of Gustav Stickley Arts and Crafts furniture with an arch or some inlay to his drafting table. Beware of paying extra for a piece that has been attributed to Ellis but that cannot be substantiated.

Armchair: inlaid central slat in back, flanked by pair of narrow slats, open arms, arched seat aprons, shoe feet, drop-in leather seat, red decal, 47" high, $35,000–$45,000

Armchair: three inlaid back slats beneath a double crest rail, open arms, drop-in seat with arched seat aprons, red decal, 43" high, $10,000–$15,000

Bookcase: #700, single door with three sections of leaded panes at the top over three vertical panes, overhanging top, arched toe board, exposed tenons, 58" × 36" × 14", $12,000–$16,000

China cabinet: #803, single door beneath overhanging top, bowed sides, chamfered board back, arched toe board, early red decal, 60" × 36" × 15", $10,000–$15,000

Desk, drop-front: rectangular fall front with three inlaid panels, flanked by two narrow doors above three drawers and open shelf, arched toe board, overhanging top, fitted interior, early red decal, 46" × 42" × 12", $50,000–$100,000

Desk, drop front: #706, rectangular fall front with three inlaid panels, open shelf below, overhanging top, arched toe board, fitted interior, red decal, 44" × 30" × 13", $20,000–$30,000

Music cabinet: larger square top section with two inlaid doors over a rectangular lower section with quartersawn-paneled cupboard door, bracket feet, red decal with "Stickley" outlined, 48" × 20" × 17", $25,000–$35,000

Music cabinet: pair of inlaid cupboard door panels below an overhanging top, four vertical compartments below, arched toe board, early red decal, 50" × 24" × 15", $25,000–$35,000

Piano: upright form with inlaid panels flanking central music rest, additional inlaid banding, 62" × 55" × 29", $50,000–$75,000

Rocking chair: curly maple, three inlaid vertical back slats, no arms, arched seat aprons, drop-in leather seat, red decal, ca. 1912, 34" × 17" × 26", $4,000–$6,000

Rocking chair: high back with three inlaid vertical slats, two horizontal top bars, open arms, arched aprons, early red decal under arm, 39" × 24" × 28", $8,000–$12,000

Screen: three panels, each with inlay in top section, cloth panels, arched crest, red decal, 67" × 20", $60,000–$80,000

Side chair: #338, three inlaid back slats, rush seat, arched aprons, 39" high, $7,000–$10,000

## George Grant Elmslie

SHOPMARK: Does not appear on furniture.

Principal Contributions: Architectural and furniture designs.

FOUNDER: George Grant Elmslie. Born: 1871, died: 1952.

STUDIOS AND WORKSHOPS: Louis Sullivan, Chicago, 1890–1909; Purcell, Feick and Elmslie, Minneapolis and Chicago, 1910–1913; Purcell and Elmslie, Minneapolis and Chicago, 1914–1922.

"After the motif is established the development of it is an orderly procession from start to finish, it is all intensely organic, proceeding from

main motif to minor motifs, interblending, interrelating and to the last
terminal, all of a piece."
—*Purcell and Elmslie, January 1913*[1]

The seeds of the Prairie school movement, an Arts and Crafts offshoot that
emphasized a relationship between the long, horizontal lines of the Midwest
prairie and the homes and furnishings that would be erected there, were
sown largely from the Chicago offices of the great architect Louis H. Sullivan. Of all the future Prairie school architects who trained under Sullivan's
watchful eye—including Frank Lloyd Wright, William Gray Purcell, Parker
Berry, and William Steele—none remained with him as long or was as greatly
influenced by his designs as—George Grant Elmslie.

At the age of 13, the Scottish-born Elmslie arrived in America and four
years later was sharing a drafting table with a 21-year-old architect named
Frank Lloyd Wright. The two aspiring architects worked in the offices of
Joseph Silsbee, as did another soon-to-be famous architect, George Washington Maher. By 1890, however, all three had left Silsbee: Maher departed in
1888 to establish his own practice, and two years later Elmslie and Wright
both left to take drafting positions with the firm of Adler and Sullivan. In
1893 the brash Wright left after Sullivan confronted him about the architectural commissions Wright had solicited independent of the firm. In contrast
to the fiery Wright, Elmslie remained with Sullivan for nearly 20 years, until
Sullivan's erratic, alcohol-induced behavior drove him away just as it had
Sullivan's partner, Dankmar Adler, in 1895.

In 1910 Elmslie joined a pair of younger architects, William Gray Purcell (1880–1965) and George Feick (1881–1945), whom he had known and
worked with on occasion during his last years with Sullivan. Purcell had
worked briefly for Sullivan in 1903, but left Chicago to travel and gain additional experience. He and George Feick had formed a partnership in Minneapolis in 1907, but six years later Feick chose to pursue other interests, at
which time the name of the firm changed to Purcell and Elmslie. The popularity of their partnership is evidenced by the fact that in 10 years, from 1910
through 1920, Purcell and Elmslie executed more than 70 commissions,
many of which included the interior furnishings of the buildings they had
designed.[2] Much of their work was residential and was built in the Minneapolis region; like most Prairie school architects, Purcell and Elmslie "involved themselves in the total design of their buildings from furniture to
landscape."[3]

Even though Purcell maintained the firm's office in Minneapolis while
Elmslie supervised a branch in Chicago, the two had strong ideological
bonds. That coupled with what has been described as Elmslie's "extraordi-

nary modesty" when it came to taking credit for his work, often has made it difficult for scholars to distinguish between the individual designs of the two architects. Researchers have determined that Elmslie, while still working for Sullivan, played an influential role in some of Purcell's pre–1910 designs. It was during that same time period, 1907–09, that three of Louis Sullivan's most important commissions were completed: the Babson House (Riverside, Illinois, 1907), the National Farmers' Bank (Owatonna, Minnesota, 1908), and the Bradley House (Madison, Wisconsin, 1909). By this time Elmslie had risen to become Sullivan's chief draftsman and designer and as such would have been "responsible for detailing and supervising the famous architect's last important commissions."[4]

Other scholars have been more outspoken regarding the extent to which these three commissions reflect Elmslie's creative involvement, claiming that Elmslie "should be credited with most of the design, ornamentation, and furniture"[5] for these important projects, most notably "the Bradley House furnishings including the ornamental glass windows, lamps, tables and chairs."[6] In a letter written to the owner of the Owatonna Bank shortly after he and Sullivan severed their working relationship, Elmslie declared that Sullivan "did none of the work you see on your building, none whatsoever."[7] As an interesting note, the furniture designed by Elmslie for both the Babson House and the Owatonna Bank was supplemented at the time with desks and chairs from the Craftsman Shops of Gustav Stickley.

Although Elmslie was a multifaceted interior designer, working in stained glass, draperies, linens, clocks, and metalware, it is his furniture for which he is best remembered today. For the Bradley House (1909) he designed a tall-back chair with a "central V-shaped splat pierced with an intricate motif of interlaced floral and geometric forms. He liked the effect so much that he created variations of these chairs for several of his clients as well as for his own house."[8] His continued insistence on decorative ornament in the backs of this series of dining chairs ran counter to what many other Prairie school and Arts and Crafts designers were doing, most notably Wright and Stickley, but it served to unify the overall plan for the residence, as the pattern in the chair was repeated in the leaded glass windows, the rugs, and even the linens used on the table.

Regardless of his negative feelings for Sullivan at this time, it also seems obvious that Elmslie's intricate floral and geometric designs are reflective of the lasting impression left by his former employer and teacher, who years earlier had begun combining "luxurious foliage with striking geometric patterns"[9] in his ornament. Elements of Wright's influence can be seen in the slight outward curve of the rear feet and the central back slat extending nearly to the floor, as well as elements of the general Arts and Crafts furniture movement: quartersawn oak, drop-in leather seats, rectilinear design, and wide stretchers.

As Marian Page has observed, "There is no doubt that Elmslie was a highly gifted ornamentalist, and the individuality and appeal of much of Purcell and Elmslie furniture is based on ornament. In fact, ornament is one of the essential elements contributing to the overall harmony of their interiors."[10]

## SELECTED PRICES

The rarity of Elmslie furniture, plus the individual nature of each piece, makes establishing a price guide both impractical and quite possibly misleading, for the value of any example will be influenced by factors beyond the scope of this study. Examples do surface will need to be carefully researched and analyzed in order to determine their current fair market value.

## Greene and Greene

SHOPMARK: Branded script SUMNER GREENE/ HIS TRUE MARK.
PRINCIPAL CONTRIBUTIONS: Architectural, furniture, and lighting designs.
FOUNDERS: Charles Sumner Greene, born: 1868, died: 1957. Henry Mather Greene, born: 1870, died: 1954.
STUDIOS AND WORKSHOPS: Greene and Greene, Architects, Pasadena, California, 1893–1922; Henry Greene, Pasadena, California, 1922–30; Charles Greene, Carmel, California, 1916–34.

> "Here things were really alive–and the Arts and Crafts that all the others were screaming and hustling about are here actually being produced by a young architect, this quiet, dreamy, nervous, tenacious little man, fighting single-handed until recently against tremendous odds."
>
> — *C. R. Ashbee, architect, 1909*[1]

> "The idea was to eliminate everything unnecessary, to make the whole as direct and simple as possible, but always with the beautiful in mind as the first goal."
>
> — *Henry Greene, 1912*[2]

Often classified along with Frank Lloyd Wright within a select group of architects who also designed furniture, Charles Greene and his brother Henry found in California the inspiration, the materials and the clients that enabled them to design and create some of the finest Arts and Crafts homes and furniture of the 20th century.

The two brothers grew up in St. Louis and for three years attended Washington University's Manual Training High School, where each student was required "to study woodworking and metalwork with emphasis on understanding the inherent nature of wood and metal as well as the use of tools and machinery, along with a regular liberal arts curricula."[3] Both went on to study architecture at M.I.T. and joined influential Boston firms, but in 1893 they traveled together to Pasadena, California, to visit their parents and stayed to open their own architectural office.

It was not until 1900, however, and the emergence of the Arts and Crafts movement in America, that Charles Greene began designing furniture. When the first issues of the *Craftsman* magazine appeared in October 1901, both brothers were so impressed with Gustav Stickley's new line of furniture that they ordered their next client's furniture directly from the magazine's first two issues. The bungalow concept championed by Stickley, with an emphasis on unity of architectural design and interior furnishings, appealed to the brothers. Charles's first commercial furniture designs in 1903 are reflective of those of Gustav Stickley both in design and in his selection of oak as his primary working material; but, as Randell Makinson has pointed out in his book on the brothers, "influenced as he was by Stickley's work, he added his own personal touch in the subtle variations."[4] Unlike many turn-of-the-century furniture manufacturers who were content to copy the designs of Stickley, Charles Greene used the Arts and Crafts concepts

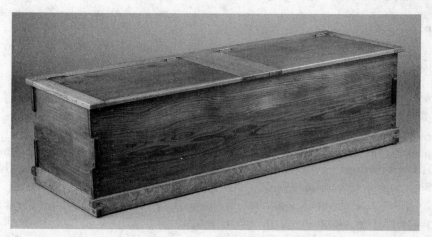

Fine and rare Greene & Greene oak and yellow pine double blanket chest from the Pratt Residence, Ojai, California, its unusually mortised corners fastened with square dowel pegs, topped by two lift-top doors. Good original finish and condition, 18½" × 65" × 23¾", $28,875

exemplified by Stickley in both his magazine and his furniture as a foundation for his more imaginative and creative work. As Makinson so aptly states:

"What wrenched Charles from his earlier precedents and established a recognizable Greene and Greene style was his effort to blend subtly curved forms into an otherwise linear composition and, by combining an honest use of joinery giving interest and variation, arriving at a less harsh overall effect. He accomplished this with such finesse that there was no need for applied decoration. . . . The departure from the total use of the straight line removed the harsh architectural character often associated with furniture designed by architects and, instead, created pieces with a scale and appearance more humanly pleasing."[5]

The execution of the imaginative plans flowing from the drafting table of Charles Greene (though subject to Henry's more disciplined and practical review, for Henry also served as their office manager) fell to two other highly skilled brothers. Peter and John Hall, who emigrated from Sweden as boys, were self-taught woodworkers and contractors who had settled in Pasadena and who, beginning in 1906, transformed Charles's and Henry's drawings into finished furniture and completed houses. It was also about this time that Greene and Greene began using mahogany rather than oak as the firm's principal wood; square ebony pegs began replacing oak dowels, and graceful Oriental designs began playing a major role in the brothers' renditions.

Demand for their services increased significantly the number of employees in both the Greene and Greene drafting rooms and the workshops of Peter and John Hall, as well as the delay in the completion of their projects. "Do you wish me to make a will telling who is to have the house if it is finished?" a client once inquired.[6]While Henry managed the office and supervised on-site construction, Charles would often be found in the Hall woodshop, working alongside the other craftsmen and devising new forms of joinery to give him additional freedom in design. His structural trademark—the raised, square ebony peg—actually disguised screws purposely placed in oversize holes to permit the boards to expand and contract without either splitting or warping. Additional decorative pegs were occasionally added to complete the design.

The full development and exercise of the creative talents Charles possessed—in designing furniture, lighting, stained glass, woodcarving, ironwork, even carpets, linens, and small accessories—was dependent on wealthy, imaginative, and patient clients. Between the years 1907 and 1909, five such clients in California commissioned Greene and Greene to design their homes and furnishings: the Robert Blacker house (1907), the David Gamble house

(1908), and the Freeman Ford house (1908) in Pasadena; the William Thorsen house (1909) in Berkeley; and the Charles Pratt house (1909) in Ojai.

The range of creativity and level of craftsmanship demonstrated in the furnishings of these homes is simply astonishing and certainly without equal. In the skillful hands of Peter and John Hall, the designs of Charles Greene passed beyond furniture forms into sculptured art. The finest Honduras mahogany, rosewood, walnut, and teak were often inlaid with subtle fruitwoods, contrasting ebony, fine silver, or semiprecious stones. Makinson's research into the Halls' finishing methods revealed that "soft stains were rubbed repeatedly with boiled linseed oil and Japan dryer until the friction produced the heat necessary for the final finish."[7]

Both the number and the size of the commissions declined after completion of the famous Greene and Greene "ultimate bungalows." Fewer clients seemed prepared to offer Charles Greene the unlimited budget he required, and the general sway away from natural woods in the Arts and Crafts style to period reproductions eliminated all but a few sizable commissions. Charles was drawn to the community of artists living around Carmel, California, and moved his family there in 1916, effectively ending the working partnership he and Henry had established in 1893 and which they officially dissolved in 1922. Both continued to work on smaller commissions the remainder of their productive years, retiring shortly after 1930.

Like the early furniture of Frank Lloyd Wright and George Grant Elmslie, Greene and Greene furniture was designed for specific clients and never intended to be marketed by retail merchants, thus the need to "sign" each piece was never a pressing concern. In 1912, however, Charles registered a branded trademark which, at that time, he stated had been in use since 1910 (it does appear on furniture from the 1909 Pratt House). After receiving trademark status, Charles went back to at least one of the other homes the firm had built prior to 1909 and branded numerous pieces of his furniture. In the sample he provided the patent office, the words "His True Mark" appear along with the signature "Sumner Greene" (Charles had apparently decided no longer to be called by his first name). Although it was used inconsistently and on furniture spanning only a few years, the brand is readily apparent, often appearing in two or three places on the underside of his furniture.

As with all Arts and Crafts furniture, however, a brand or decal can be reproduced and, for that reason, should not be used as the primary means of identifying any purported piece of Greene and Greene furniture. At least two pieces of furniture that, to the trained eye, were obviously not designed by Greene and Greene have surfaced bearing a counterfeit Sumner Greene brand.

Of the five "ultimate bungalows" designed between 1907 and 1909, in only one, the Gamble House, are the furnishings and fixtures still intact and the house open to public viewing. During the 1940s and 1950s the furniture in the Blacker, Ford, and Thorsen Houses was sold or dispersed and still surfaces occasionally. In the case of the Thorsen House, more than 40 pieces of Greene and Greene furniture went to one heir and have since been placed in a permanent, joint exhibition sponsored by the Gamble House (University of Southern California) and the Huntington Library and Art Galleries in San Marino, California. There they joined, among others, a display of Greene and Greene dining room furniture from the Robinson House. In 1985 trustees of the Pratt House suddenly consigned nearly a dozen pieces of Greene and Greene furniture to Christie's auction house in New York, where one inlaid fall-front desk immediately soared to a record-setting $242,000.

Greene and Greene furniture is considered to be among the most important and scarcest of the Arts and Crafts movement, and it certainly displays the most unique and complex construction techniques. While their shopmark may again be duplicated, thus far no counterfeiter has been willing to make the commitment necessary to duplicate accurately both the designs of Charles and Henry Greene and the workmanship of John and Peter Hall.

### SELECTED PRICES

The rarity of Greene and Greene furniture, plus the individual nature of each piece, makes establishing a price guide both impractical and quite possibly misleading, for the value of any example will be influenced by factors beyond the scope of this study. The number of examples of Greene and Greene furniture sold publicly declined substantially after 1989. Without comparable sales, it is dangerous to attempt to establish price ranges for collectors. Before completing any major transactions, collectors are advised to carefully research both the piece and the current market.

## Lifetime Furniture (Grand Rapids Bookcase & Chair Company)

SHOPMARK: Decal, paper label, or brand LIFETIME/ FURNITURE in rectangle, occasionally over GRAND RAPIDS BOOKCASE & CHAIR CO./HASTINGS, MICH.

PRINCIPAL CONTRIBUTIONS: General line of Mission oak furniture

FOUNDER: A. A. Barber. Founded: 1911, closed: undetermined

WORKSHOPS AND SALESROOMS: Grand Rapids Bookcase Company, Hastings, Michigan, 1896–1911. Barber Brothers Chair Company, Grand Rapids, Michigan, ca. 1900–11. Grand Rapids Bookcase & Chair Co., Hastings, Michigan, 1911-undetermined

Rare Lifetime three-door bookcase with gallery top, six panes to each door and hammered copper hardware. Good original finish and condition, minor staining to top. Stenciled #47/7604, 44¼" × 55" × 12" $5,175

> "During the Medieval period Master Craftsmen, when joining together parts that were subject to a severe strain, knew no other way than by the use of the mortise and tenon joint, locking it together with cross pins. The Manufacturers of Lifetime furniture know of no other way as good."
>
> —Lifetime Catalog, *ca. 1911*[1]

At the turn of the century, Grand Rapids, Michigan, was the home of scores of furniture companies, most of which had prospered making inexpensive reproductions of standard styles of furniture. When studying the history of these firms, two events seem to repeat themselves: fires and mergers. Uncontrolled dust and inadequate wiring often caused furniture factory fires, and the mergers of various firms was fueled by the financial necessity of offering precisely what a fickle public demanded.

In 1911 two neighboring Grand Rapids furniture companies, the Grand Rapids Bookcase Company and the Barber Brothers Chair Company, merged to form a new company—the Grand Rapids Bookcase and Chair Company. The firm was headed by A. A. Barber, an enterprising salesman who had previously worked as a sales representative for several Grand Rapids furniture manufacturing companies, including his own. The new company was located in Hastings, just outside Grand Rapids, in a modern factory boasting several innovative production features. Barber, however, continued to lease showroom space for his furniture in the Blodgett Building in Grand Rapids, which Charles Limbert had transformed into a central retail outlet for area manufacturers.

Both parent companies had been producing a line of Arts and Crafts furniture since 1903, and their Mission oak line under their new company name was called Lifetime Furniture. In Lifetime's first catalog, reprinted in 1981 by Turn of the Century Editions, the unidentified author of the introduction borrowed a well-known phrase from William Morris, the founder of the Arts and Crafts movement, when he declared that the Lifetime designers have "incorporated only that which is useful and beautiful."[2] Morris, who throughout his life had steadfastly protested the role of the machine in furniture production, may have rolled over in his grave, however, when the author continued: "A thorough and systematic organization has been perfected and division of labor has been carefully systematized. Every modem machine and appliance that can be utilized to increase production and efficiency has been installed."[3]

Barber, the firm's president, called the new Mission oak line "Cloister Furniture," in an apparent attempt to associate his furniture with the high level of handcraftsmanship associated with medieval England. He even went so far as to picture at the front of the catalog a thoughtful monk, diligently watering a lush bed of flowers, implying, perhaps, that their furniture was somehow inspired or even constructed by dedicated monks in a secluded abbey.

The Cloister line of Lifetime furniture included several designs originally popularized by Gustav or L. & J. G. Stickley, including, to mention a few of the more obvious, a trestle library table, a drawer-over-door cellarette, a drink stand, a magazine rack, and a bow-arm Morris chair. Many of their large case pieces, however, featured distinctive design elements, such as exposed tenons on the fronts rather than the sides of bookcases, rocking chairs, and china cabinets. They often incorporated a sweeping, arched toe board across the fronts of bookcases and other case pieces, giving them a look not unlike that associated with the Stickleys. However, whereas Gustav and L. & J. G. Stickley used small individual panes of glass in each door (as many as twelve per door), Lifetime bookcases and china cabinets are more apt to be found with one large pane of glass set behind a gridwork of mullions, giving the appearance of several individual panes with but a fraction of the effort or cost.

In the preface to its 1911 catalog the firm guarantees that "in Lifetime construction the front and back rails of all settees, chairs and rockers are tenoned on the ends, each tenon passing into a mortise in the post in its respective position. Holes are then bored through the post passing through the tenon. . . . Straight grained oak pins are then covered with glue and driven snugly into the holes. The posts are fastened into the arms in a like manner;

in fact every joint that receives the least strain is fitted with this mortise and tenon pinned construction."[4]

Generally speaking, the quality of construction of most Lifetime furniture is admirable. Grand Rapids authority Don Marek states that "at its best, their Arts and Crafts furniture rivaled the quality of the largest makers."[5] Unfortunately, the majority of their best designs, original or imitations, lack the grace and delicate balance of proportion required to make the leap from functional furniture to furniture that is also artistic and that, as Morris had recommended in 1880, "you know to be useful or believe to be beautiful."

One of the distinctive design elements often found on Lifetime furniture is an extremely wide and large corbel placed at the point where the arm of a chair or settle joins the rear post. The corbel serves no important structural purpose, but exists to soften visually the impact of the sharp 90-degree angle created by the two boards. The company produced a large number of settles and armchairs, the majority of which are characterized by sturdy, nearly massive posts and boards. In addition, a large number of Lifetime drop-front desks have also surfaced, many of which are uninspiring in design; a few, however—most notably those with rectangular sides, exposed tenons on the front posts, and arched aprons—command a great deal of respect.

A. A. Barber, though not a great designer, certainly was a smart businessman. Even when the Arts and Crafts movement was at the height of its popularity, the Grand Rapids Bookcase and Chair Company still issued "two catalogs yearly, one illustrating our line of Cloister Styles in Lifetime Furniture, and another that will illustrate our large and comprehensive line of Mahogany and Oak Dining Room Furniture in Period and Modern Styles."[6] Here was a captain who was determined not to go down with the Arts and Crafts ship.

The Lifetime shopmark, according to the catalog, "can always be found either in the form of a colored transfer or burned into the wood with an electric branding iron,"[7] although paper labels have also been discovered.[8] In any instance, the shopmarks are relatively easy to locate and identify, often appearing on the interior rather than the backs of bookcases and china cabinets. Earlier Barber Brothers Chair Company shopmarks appeared as paper labels, and the Grand Rapids Bookcase and Chair Company occasionally used a metal tag to identify its furniture.

Lifetime hardware is often hand-hammered copper, similar to that found on L. & J. G. Stickley bookcases and china cabinets, yet not as heavy or as impressive as that of Gustav Stickley. Other pieces bear hardware similar to that used by several Grand Rapids firms and that appear to have been purchased from the Grand Rapids Brass Company.[9]

While it is already evident that most Lifetime furniture will never attract the following or earn the respect accorded that of Gustav Stickley, L. & J. G. Stickley, the Roycrofters, Charles Limbert, or the best of the Stickley Brothers, it does stand at the top—in terms of both quantity and quality—of the other Mission oak manufacturers. For that reason, the sharp collector will continue to inspect each piece of Lifetime furniture carefully, for on occasion a piece will emerge combining the necessary elements of proportion, design, quality materials, and sound construction that make it a proud addition to any collection.

### SELECTED PRICES

Model numbers correspond with those in the *Lifetime Furniture Catalog* (New York: Turn of the Century Editions, 1981). Unless otherwise noted, all pieces are considered to have been constructed of oak and to have their original finish exhibiting normal wear. Prices reflect leather seats and cushions that are either original, but badly worn or have been replaced with appropriate materials.

Armchair: #624 ½, three vertical slats in the back above two horizontal
  slats, open arms, drop-in spring seat, 37" × 20", $200–$250

Armchair: #689 ½, two vertical slats in the back, three under each arm, exposed tenons on tops of arms, corbels, drop-in spring seat, 36" × 20",
  $250–$300

Bookcase: #7604, triple door with six panes each, gallery top, keyed tenons
  on sides, raised straight toe board, metal hardware, 44" × 55" × 12",
  $2,350–$3,000

Bookcase: #7625, double door with one large pane each, exposed tenons on
  front, eight adjustable shelves, 56" × 42" × 12", $1,000–$1,250

Chair, side: #113, three vertical slats in back, drop-in leather seat, 36" × 16"
  × 16", $85–$95, set of four, $425–$475

China cabinet: #6478, double door with one large pane each, overhanging
  top, three adjustable shelves, interior mirror above top shelf, 59" × 44" ×
  13", $1,200–$1,500

Desk: #8567, gallery top over drop front and long drawer, wide board sides,
  lower shelf, arched toe board and sides, 45" × 28" × 16", $450–$550

Desk: #8570, drop front, rectangular sides with exposed tenon stretchers top
  and bottom, two drawers beneath drop front, fitted interior, hammered
  hardware, paneled sides, decal, 43" × 42", $900–$1,100

Dresser: #4007, two half drawers above two long, splashboard on overhanging top, metal hardware, slight arch to sides, straight toe board, no mirror, 38" × 48" × 22", $800–$900

Footstool: #403, tray top with loose cushion, narrow stretchers, 15" × 16" × 15", $175–$200

Morris chair: #569, five slats under each flat arm, posts tenoned through arms front and back, seat apron tenoned through posts, adjustable wooden rod, four corbels under arms, 42" × 23", $1,750–$2,000

Morris chair: #584, open flat arms, exposed tenons in tops of arms, drop-in spring seat and loose back cushion, corbels, adjustable wooden rod, 41" × 21", $900–$1,000. Rocking chair: #623, three horizontal slats in back, open arms, no corbels or exposed tenons, drop-in spring seat, 39" × 20", $175–$225

Rocking chair: #689, two wide vertical slats in back, three under each arm, exposed tenon on top of each arm, corbels, drop-in spring seat, 36" × 20", $250–$325

Server: #5160, overhanging top with open plate rail, one long drawer with metal hardware, open lower shelf resting on side stretchers, 38" × 39" × 18", $750–$850

Settle: #614 ¾, even-arm, with 10 vertical slats in back, three under each arm, exposed tenons on front posts, drop-in spring cushion seat, 36" × 73" × 24", $2,600–$3,000.

Settle: #688 ¾, drop-arm with wide slats under arms and head rail, exposed tenons, spring cushion seat, 34" × 72" × 28", $2,600–$3,000

Sideboard: #5272, overhanging top supporting mirrored panel and shelf, three short drawers over one long drawer over two cabinet doors, hammered hardware, exposed tenons on front posts, 55" × 60" × 23", $1,200–$1,500

Table, dining: #1069, circular overhanging top with apron atop octagonal pedestal with four radiating feet, five leaves, 30" × 54", $1,250–$1,500

Table, lamp: #930, circular top over small circular shelf atop straight cross stretchers, exposed tenons, 30" × 24" diameter, $450–$550

Table, lamp: #917, circular overhanging top over apron, supported by four flared legs with arched cross-stretchers, exposed tenons, 27" × 18" × 18", $800–$900

Table, library: #8557, overhanging top above single drawer with hinged interior writing surface, metal pulls, open lower shelf, no exposed tenons, 30" × 36" × 24', $400–$500

Taboret: #257, square overhanging top with cut corners, lower shelf supported by arched stretchers, 18" × 16" × 16", $450–$475

# Charles Limbert

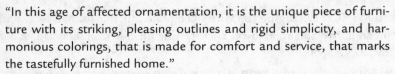

SHOPMARKS:  Paper label or brand of craftsman working at
a bench, with the words LIMBERTS ARTS CRAFTS
FURNITURE/MADE IN GRAND RAPIDS/MICHI-
GAN (After 1906) Addition of the words TRADE MARK
and replacement of MICHIGAN with AND HOLLAND

PRINCIPAL CONTRIBUTIONS: General line of Arts and
Crafts furniture.

FOUNDER: Charles P. Limbert. Born: 1854, died: 1923,
founded: 1894, closed: 1944.

WORKSHOPS AND SALESROOMS:  C. P. Limbert & Co., Grand Rapids, Michigan, 1894–1944. Holland, Michigan, 1906–44

> "In this age of affected ornamentation, it is the unique piece of furni-
> ture with its striking, pleasing outlines and rigid simplicity, and har-
> monious colorings, that is made for comfort and service, that marks
> the tastefully furnished home."
> —*Charles Limbert, 1905*[1]

The furniture bearing the shopmark of Charles Limbert often demands a
category of its own, for unlike so many of the manufacturers of Arts and
Crafts furniture, the source of its designs does not always lead directly back
to Gustav or L. & J. G. Stickley.

Charles Limbert, like many other prominent Arts and Crafts furniture
makers, began his career by designing, producing, and selling the period reproductions that were popular in the two decades immediately after the 1876
Centennial celebration. At the age of 35, however, he left a secure future with
the large Chicago furniture firm of John A. Colby and Company and moved
to Grand Rapids, Michigan, rapidly becoming known as the furniture capital of the world. There he and former co-worker Philip Klingman formed
the Limbert and Klingman Chair Company and in 1890 began manufacturing their own line of period reproduction chairs.

Just two years later the partners agreed to dissolve the firm, and Limbert
returned to a career in sales, representing a number of furniture manufacturers in his leased Grand Rapids showroom. Two years later, however, in
1894, Charles Limbert returned to furniture production with the announcement of the formation of C. P. Limbert and Company. The first few years
may have been rough ones for the 40-year-old entrepreneur, for from 1896
until at least 1905 he continued to serve as a major sales representative for the
Indiana-based Old Hickory Furniture Company.

Fine and rare Limbert single-door china cabinet with arched backsplash, three glass panes to door over one large, and open shelf on either side supported by long corbels, with three interior shelves. Good original finish. Faint stenciled number. On casters, 59" × 44½" × 16½", $6,325

When the popularity of Arts and Crafts furniture began to blossom in the early years of the new century, Limbert began producing his own line of "Dutch Arts and Crafts" furniture. Much of his early furniture was experimental in nature, at times incorporating elements of both the waning Art Nouveau style and the severe rectilinear form characterizing the emerging Arts and Crafts movement. His continued interest in outdoor furniture and the Old Hickory Company undoubtedly influenced his 1902 line of ash "summer furniture" with its trademark exposed carriage-bolt construction. Though not highly regarded by collectors today, Limbert's summer furniture, described as "well made, attractive, strong and comfortable [that looks]

Rare and oversized Limbert armchair with angled back, corbels under flat paddle arms, scooped apron, and brown leather-upholstered seat and back cushions. (Back cushion not pictured.) Original medium-brown finish, worn on arms. Branded mark, 32½" × 31½" × 34", $3,105

Limbert Ebon-Oak armchair from the Mission Inn, inlaid with mission bell motif to backslat and geometric forms with post with brown leather drop-in seat. (Purchased from the Mission Inn.) Original finish, good condition, 41" × 28" × 25½", $5,462

especially well in natural ash, light green and weathered finish,"[2] remained in production for more than a decade.

The years 1902 to 1910 saw major advancements in Limbert's line of interior oak furniture. His Arts and Crafts furniture of that period reveals a man unafraid of experimentation, as it often incorporates elements of Art Nouveau, English medieval, Japanese, Glasgow school, and Austrian secession styles. As Grand Rapids author Don Marek summarizes, Limbert's "early pieces are a little heavier and almost crude, with more elements from folk traditions and more experimentation (many of the more unusual pieces are from 1902–1904). The 1904–1910 period is characterized by increasing sophistication and the prominence of Glasgow School, Viennese and Prairie school influences."[3]

To illustrate, by 1905 Limbert had begun to phase out his use of Art Nouveau-influenced stained glass in the doors of his case pieces, had introduced a line of inlaid furniture, and had switched his emphasis to cutouts inspired by Charles Rennie Mackintosh of the Glasgow School and Josef Hoffmann in Vienna. The popular success of the Limbert production was reflected not only in his freedom to experiment with various forms, but in the physical expansion of his factory. Until 1906 Limbert furniture was both manufactured and displayed in Grand Rapids. That year, however, in an effort to locate "an environment more conducive to artistic effort and a higher quality of craftsmanship,"[4] Limbert established a new factory in the small rural town of Holland, Michigan. The plant continued to expand, prompting the local newspaper in 1912 to characterize "the Limbert company as one of the most progressive in the country. The business is on a sound financial footing and Holland foresees nothing but success for the enterprise."[5]

What Charles Limbert began to foresee, though, was a swing in public tastes away from Mission oak. Hordes of imitators had flooded the market with furniture that Limbert described as early as 1909 as being "poorly-constructed, ill-proportioned and uncraftsmanlike."[6] Unlike Gustav Stickley and many other Arts and Crafts manufacturers, Limbert was prepared for a change. His new line of oak Arts and Crafts furniture was lightened, both in color and in structure, and upholstered fabrics began to replace the dark leather. As if to assure his customers that this lighter look was not to be mistaken for a reduction in quality, in 1915 Limbert reintroduced a line of inlaid Arts and Crafts furniture. The "Ebon-Oak" furniture featured thin lines and small squares of ebony inlay, occasionally accented with copper. The following year Limbert introduced his first period reproductions in nearly two decades and by 1918 had phased out the 16-year-old line of Limbert's Arts and Crafts furniture.

Even though his health was beginning to fail, Limbert oversaw his factory's transition from Mission oak furniture to a variety of period reproductions. While on a winter trip to Hawaii in 1921 he became ill and never fully recovered. In late 1922 the lifelong bachelor reluctantly retired, and he died the following July at the age of 68. The company he founded in 1894, though, remained in business for 21 more years, until 1944, its 50th anniversary.

Limbert appears to have been among the first of the Arts and Crafts manufacturers to use a permanent branded shopmark in place of the traditional, but fragile, paper label or decal. His pre–1906 furniture bears a paper label, which can be identified by the location reference only to Grand Rapids. Sometime after 1906 and the opening of his Holland factory, the paper label was changed and a branded mark added, both of which include the words "Grand Rapids and Holland." In a few instances, small copper tags similar to those used by Stickley Brothers have been discovered on Limbert armchairs.

Unlike the Stickleys in New York, Limbert refrained from affixing his shopmark to the stretchers of chairs and tables. Armchairs and settles will invariably have a branded mark on the underside of the arm; tables will have either a brand or a paper label attached to the underside of the top. Case pieces with drawers will most often have a shopmark on the inside of a drawer; those without drawers, such as bookcases and china closets, will most often have either a brand or a paper label on the back. In nearly every case, the brand or paper label will be approximately two inches wide by three inches high and easily recognizable, for all feature a craftsman poised next to a workbench as he planes the edge of a board.

In those instances when either the paper label has been destroyed by a careless refinisher or a piece had left the factory without a brand, Limbert furniture can usually be distinguished from that of his competitors. With the exception of his summer furniture, Limbert Arts and Crafts furniture exhibits the quality of material and degree of craftsmanship associated with that of either Gustav or L. & J. G. Stickley. His hardware, unfortunately, appears to have been purchased from the Grand Rapids Brass Company and is neither as substantial nor as artistic as that of Gustav or L. & J. G. Stickley. Like the Stickleys, Limbert often used graceful, curved brackets beneath chair arms and overhanging tops and gently arched aprons and toe boards on tables and case pieces to lessen the severity of the rectilinear form. His tops are occasionally splined for greater stability between glue joints, and keyed tenons and pinned joints are often found; but the feature unique to some of the most highly desirable Limbert furniture is the cutout.

Will Bradley's series of household interiors drawn for *Ladies' Home Journal* from 1901–02 introduced the American public to a number of English and European Arts and Crafts elements that were to become characteristic of much of their forthcoming furniture: exposed tenons, strap hinges, pinned joints, and extensive use of cutouts. Limbert's adaptation of various square, rectangular, and spade-, arrow-, and heart-shaped cutouts can be traced back to the furniture of Mackintosh, Baillie Scott, and Voysey, plus Bradley's popular line of illustrated interiors. The combination of quality craftsmanship and materials, plus this unique design aspect, can enable a collector to identify many examples of Limbert furniture without a shopmark.

Limbert furniture appears in a variety of wood tones, from a dark ebony to a much lighter reddish-brown color. It appears that all of his oak Arts and Crafts furniture was fumed with ammonia, although as in most Arts and Crafts furniture factories, hand staining was also utilized to achieve an even color. The most popular finish, according to one catalog, was

> "autumn leaf brown. . . produced by placing White Oak, which contains tannic acid, in air tight boxes, and bringing it in contact with strong ammonia fumes for a number of days, until the fumes have thoroughly penetrated through the pores of the wood, and come in contact with the tannic acid, when a chemical change takes effect and discolors the wood through and through. After the furniture made of this wood is finished by our special process and waxed, a finish has been produced which is at once clear, translucent and smooth. This color never wears off or shows white on the edges or corners, as the wood is thoroughly impregnated with the ammonia fumes."[7]

His finishes have proved to be as durable as those of Gustav or L. & J. G. Stickley.

As Deborah Norberg observed early in the current Arts and Crafts revival, "Though by no means profoundly innovative, the Limbert production was nonetheless more original than the majority of straight line furniture and was designed and hand-crafted in an effort to provide quality goods to satisfy its middle-class patronage."[8] While collectors of early Limbert furniture might disagree with her assessment of Limbert's creativity in designs, it is true that he offered a line of less expensive Arts and Crafts-style furniture, including plank-seat chairs, open arm settles, and uninspiring tables. Until it became evident that the swing away from the Arts and Crafts style was inevitable, however, he continued to produce another line of high-quality, artistic furniture, including buffets and china cabinets with overhanging tops supported by long, graceful corbels, oval tables with cutout bases, and a number of pleasing taborets.

Thus, while Charles Limbert never attempted to match the rhetoric of either Gustav Stickley or Elbert Hubbard, nor did he stoop to the depths of their unscrupulous imitators. His furniture struck a middle chord by demonstrating that it could please both the Arts and Crafts enthusiast and the casual observer who admires the style without needing the Stickley shopmark.

Unless otherwise noted, all examples listed below are considered to be made of oak and retaining an original finish exhibiting normal wear. Prices reflect leather seats and cushions which are either original, but badly worn, or replaced with appropriate materials.

## SELECTED PRICES

Armchair: #933, three vertical slats in back, open arms, corbels, wide stretchers, drop-in spring seat, 43" × 27" × 28", $250–$335

Armchair: #1643, four vertical slats in back, three under each arm, arched front apron, exposed tenon on each arm, long corbels, drop-in spring seat, 38" × 30" × 26", $500–$750

Bookcase: #357, single door with two vertical panes, overhanging top supported by four long corbels, splashboard, flaring base with arched toe board, adjustable shelves, 57" × 30" × 14", $3,000–$4,000

Bookcase: #358, double doors, each with two vertical panes, overhanging tops supported by four long corbels, splashboard, flaring base with arched toe board, adjustable shelves, 57" × 48" × 14", $3,500–$4,500

Bookcase: #359, triple doors, each with two vertical panes, overhanging top supported by four long corbels, splashboard, flaring base with arched toe board, adjustable shelves, 57" × 66" × 14", $4,000–$5,000

Chair, side: #951, five vertical slats in back beneath curved crest rail, double side and front stretchers, scooped plank seat, 37" × 17" × 20", $125–$175; set of four, $500–$750

Chair, side: #851, same as #951, but with wraparound leather seat, 37" × 18" × 21" , $200–$300; set of four, $800–$1,000

Chest of drawers: #486 ¼, four half-drawers over four long drawers, all with metal hardware, through tenons at top and bottom of front and back posts, 60" × 40" × 22", $2,000–$3,000

China cabinet: #448, overhanging top with plate rack, double doors, each with three small panes over one large pane, adjustable shelves, arched toe board, 62" × 46" × 17", $2,750–$3,750

Desk: #1151, recessed flat top over two half-drawers, each over a smaller drawer flanking knee compartment, lower open shelf, exposed tenons, brass knobs, 30" × 42" × 28", $850–$1,250

Desk: #732, drop front over two short drawers over three long, each with brass knobs, arched toe board and sides, gallery top, 42" × 43" × 19", $1,250–$1,750

Dresser: #479 ½, three short drawers over two long drawers, all with metal hardware, arched apron, recessed top, attached mirror, exposed tenons, 80" × 49" × 23", $1,500–$2,000

Footstool: #201, "cricket" side panels with teardrops and heart cutout supporting leather-top surface, 12" × 20" × 12", $400–$600

Magazine stand: #300, four open shelves between canted sides, oval cutout on each lower side, buttons disguising screws, 37" × 20" × 14", $800–$1,200

Magazine stand: #301, gallery top over two shelves over arched toe board, single slat in each side, 29" × 16" × 11", $800–$1,200

Morris chair: #521, flat arms over single wide slat with three square cutouts, stretchers flush with floor, long corbels under arms, drop-in spring seat, loose back cushion, 43" × 34" × 43", $4,500–$6,500

Pedestal: #269, square top supported by square post and four full-length tapering corbels, 36" × 13" × 13", $1,750–$2,250

Rocking chair: #932, three vertical slats in back, open arms with long corbels, drop-in spring seat, 35" × 27" × 27", $400–$600

Rocking chair: #1656, five vertical slats in tall back, curved crest rail, three slats under each arm, exposed tenons on arms, drop-in spring seat, 43" × 28" × 29", $1,000–$1,500

Server: #456, overhanging top with closed plate rail, two short drawers over one long, each with brass knobs, open lower shelf, 41" × 42" × 18", $1,500–$2,000

Settle: drop-arm, ebony inlay on front posts, two caned back sections, front posts tenoned through arms, supported by corbels, eight slats in back, arched apron, drop-in spring seat, 38" × 47" × 25", $2,250–$2,750

Settle: #570, drop-arm with wide crest rail over nine wide slats, five slats under each arm, exposed tenons, drop-in spring seat, 29" × 76" × 32", $3,000–$4,000

Settle: #618, drop-arm with 11 slats in back, open arms supported by long corbels, stretchers near floor, drop-in spring seat,40" × 76" × 29", $2,500–$3,500

Sideboard: early design with four doors with Art Nouveau-inspired stained glass, three lower drawers, four keyed tenons per side, chamfered board back, 53" × 64" × 23", $5,000–$7,000

Sideboard: #1380, mirrored back panel with top shelf, two half-drawers over one long drawer over two cabinet doors, arched apron, 51" × 45" × 19", $2,000–$3,000

Table, dining: #1480, circular top supported by center pedestal and four pairs of slanted legs, each pair joined by arched stretchers, exposed tenons, four leaves, 30" × 54", $3,500–$4,500

Table, dining: #419, circular overhanging top supported by five legs, no stretchers, corbel on outside of each leg, four leaves, 30" × 54", $2,200–$2,700

Table, lamp: #110, circular top, cross-stretcher base on tapering legs, 29" × 24", $800–$1,200

Table, lamp: #214, square recessed top with arched aprons, two with small caned sections, single vertical slat beneath caned aprons, lower shelf, 30" × 11" × 11", $600–$800

Table, library: #1140, overhanging top, single drawer with square wooden pulls, corbels on each leg, lower shelf, exposed tenons, 29" × 42" × 30", $750–$1,000

Table, library: #146, oval overhanging top above four legs with cross-panel shelf and square cutouts, 30" × 45" × 30", $2,500–$3,500

Table, octagon: #120, overhanging top over four splayed legs, each with spade shaped cutout, flat cross-stretchers tenoned through each leg and secured with pair of wedges, paper label beneath top, 30" × 45" × 45", $4,000–$6,000

Taboret: #251, square overhanging top with cut corners, supported by four corbels, solid sides, each with a trapezoidal cutout, 24" × 17" × 17", $3,000–$4,000

# George Washington Maher

SHOPMARKS: None appearing on furniture
PRINCIPAL CONTRIBUTIONS: Architectural and furniture designs.

FOUNDER: George Washington Maher. Born: 1864, died: 1926.
WORKSHOPS AND STUDIOS  George W. Maher, Chicago, 1888–1926.

> "There must be evolved certain leading forms that will influence the
> detail of the design; these forms crystallize during the progress of the
> planning and become the motifs that bind the design together."
> —*George Washington Maher, 1907*[1]

While the Prairie school movement that coincided with and was inspired by
the Arts and Crafts philosophy is most often associated with the work of
Frank Lloyd Wright, other architects, including George Washington Maher,
carried the architect's role beyond simply planning the exterior structure to
include the design of the interior furnishings as well.

Led by the flamboyant Wright, the Prairie school architects found a willing clientele in the affluent Chicago suburbs between 1900 and 1915 and created one of the first truly American styles of architecture. Ironically, three of
the most important Prairie school designers—Frank Lloyd Wright, George
Grant Elmslie, and George Washington Maher–served simultaneous ap-
prenticeships under Chicago architect Joseph Silsbee. Maher left in 1888, at
the age of 23, to form his own practice; Wright and Elmslie went on to work
for Louis Sullivan before they, too, struck out on their own. While all of the
Prairie school architects stressed unity of site, materials, and design–internal
and external–Maher soon developed his unique "motif rhythm" theory.

In each commission he sought "to receive the dominant inspiration from
the patron, taking into strict account his needs, his temperament, and environment, influenced by local color and atmosphere in surrounding flora and
nature. With these vital impressions at hand, the design naturally crystallizes
and motifs appear which being consistently utilized will make each object,
whether it be of construction, furniture or decoration, related."[2]

Maher's motif generally consisted of a plant form in conjunction with a
repeating geometric shape. Among those with which he worked between
1901 and 1906 were a thistle and an octagon, a hollyhock and a simple band,
a poppy and a straight line, and a tulip and an arch. Both his early houses and
the furniture he designed for them were massive and solidly built; as one re-
porter noted, "everything seemed to have been designed to withstand an
earthquake."[3]

In 1904, Maher traveled to St. Louis for the Louisiana Purchase Exposition, where he had the opportunity to study closely the German and Austrian
furniture exhibits that proved popular with both the critics and the general
public.[4] What he saw there, combined with the emerging influence of Frank
Lloyd Wright over the entire Prairie school, was to affect all of his future

work. "Maher veered away from the overwhelming monumentality and elaborate carving of earlier work and began to design with a lighter hand, emphasizing architectural details and favoring geometric patterns rather than excessive floral decoration.[5] Maher's subsequent work also began to reflect the designs of Englishman C. F. A. Voysey, for as Edward S. Cooke, Jr., has observed, "many of Maher's residential structures for the period of 1905 to 1915 combine Voysey-influenced domestic forms with a midwestern horizontality."[6]

Like nearly all of the Prairie school architects, Maher's furniture is closely tied to each house he designed. His early work reflects a Victorian influence, with elaborate carvings and sinuous lines, while his later furniture designs reveal that the carving was dropped and severe geometric forms adopted. Voysey's influence and that of the Austrian secessionist style can be found in many of Maher's later Prairie designs, which combine a rectilinear framework with segmented arches and a wide base that seems rooted to the ground. Richard Guy Wilson, in an essay entitled "Arts and Crafts Architecture," describes Maher as one of the "Prairie school independents. . . whose interpretation of the midwest displays the same geometry and reliance on nature for detail [as Frank Lloyd Wright] but in a very personal way."[7]

Maher's motif-rhythm theory was more evident in the design of the furniture than in the structure of the home, as in the John Farson House (1897), wherein the chairs featured an elaborately carved lion's head under each arm as well as on the upper rear posts. After 1904 his furniture designs began to focus more on geometric patterns and less on ornate carvings and floral decorations, culminating, many believe, in his finest Prairie school design: Rockledge.

Rockledge was designed for a Minnesota businessman who wanted a summer home overlooking the Mississippi River. Maher drew on both the natural colors found at the site and the segmental arch as the key elements for his motif rhythm. The furniture he designed for Rockledge incorporated both: the wood was tinted a greenish-brown and featured segmented arches above the back splat and each of the wide side slats. The flaring legs, segmented arches, and overall design reveal more of an Austrian influence than the Oriental that is so often found in Wright's work. The 1987–88 "Art That is Life" exhibition gave thousands of people the opportunity to view examples of the wide range of talents of George Washington Maher, as an armchair, a tall-case clock, a table lamp, a pair of andirons, and a rug—all of which he designed for Rockledge—were included in the traveling display and discussed at length in the exhibition catalog, initiating what clearly was long-overdue recognition for his furniture designs.

## SELECTED PRICES

The rarity of the furniture designed by George Maher, plus the individual nature of each piece, makes establishing a price guide both impractical and quite possibly misleading, for the value of any example will be influenced by factors beyond the scope of this study. Without comparable sales, it is dangerous to attempt to establish price ranges for collectors. Before completing any major transactions, collectors are advised to carefully research both the piece and the current market.

# Joseph P. McHugh & Co.

SHOPMARK: Paper label, decal, or brass tag with JOSEPH P. MCHUGH/ MISSION FURNITURE; also impressed diamond outline around THE McHUGH (MISSION) FURNITURE, MADE IN NEW YORK.
PRINCIPAL CONTRIBUTION: Limited line of early Mission oak furniture
FOUNDER: Joseph P. McHugh. Born: 1854, Died: 1916.
WORKSHOPS AND SALESROOMS: The Popular Shop, New York, ca. 1884–1916.

> "In the early part of 1894, an interior decorator of San Francisco sent me a simple rush-seated chair similar to some used by a local architect to take the place of pews in a church of that city; certain details of the form and construction attracted me, and I set about making a variety of pieces which suggested the motive of the single model."
> —Joseph McHugh, 1900[1]

While neither the name nor the furniture of Joseph P. McHugh is widely known today, this New York City retailer has the dubious distinction of being the first person to coin the phrase "Mission furniture." In 1894 Joseph P. McHugh moved what was to be known as The Popular Shop to the corner of Fifth Avenue and West 42nd Street in Manhattan. He had grown up and been trained in his family's dry-goods store and learned early in his career the difference good publicity can make to a business. Through his efforts The Popular Shop proved as popular as its name, as McHugh made regular trips to England and Europe, bringing back upholstery fabrics, wallpapers, pottery, William Morris chintzes, and Liberty and Company metalware and furniture for his Fifth Avenue clientele.

Shortly before his introduction to the "simple rush-seated chair" that was to make him famous, albeit briefly, McHugh had experimented with manufacturing his own line of wicker furniture. But when his friend A. Page Brown, a San Francisco designer, shipped him one of the chairs for a church

McHugh game table with circular top, cross-banding to apron, keyed-through tenon ornamentation (two serving as drawer pulls and two decorative) with arched cross-stretchers mortised through the legs. Original finish, crack to applied tenons. Partial paper label, 30½" × 44½", $1,995

interior he and two other architects, A. C. Schweinfurth and Bernard May-beck, had designed,[2] Joseph McHugh saw the opportunity to create and market a totally new line of furniture. "The name McHugh mission furniture, which I used to distinguish the style, seemed appropriate, in view of the purpose for which the single chair had been used, and the part of the country from which it had been sent to me,"[3] McHugh explained a few years later. McHugh displayed the first samples of his "McHugh mission furniture" in his Manhattan showrooms, where it proved popular. The impending success of an extensive line of Mission furniture led McHugh to hire a major designer, Walter J. H. Dudley, in 1896. Dudley, a trained architect and an accomplished artist, was instructed "to develop a line of furniture based on the simple, structural chairs in the Swedenborgian Church in San Francisco."[4]

It was that same year, 1896, that Elbert Hubbard in East Aurora, New York, had local carpenters building plain, simple furniture for his expanding operation, but Hubbard wasn't as quick as McHugh to realize the potential popularity of the emerging style. By 1899, though, Hubbard had begun to advertise his line of Roycroft furniture "made after the William Morris fashion."[5] Gustav Stickley was developing his own line of furniture at that time, but much of it was still in a transitional stage between Art Nouveau and Arts and Crafts. By 1900, however, both Stickley and Hubbard were ready to compete with McHugh for the developing Mission oak market.

While Stickley and Hubbard both soon had their own publications in which they advertised and promoted their products, McHugh was adept at reminding the public that he had been the first to introduce Mission furniture. The May 1900 issue of *Ladies' Home Journal* featured the designs of McHugh and Dudley and helped make him one of the most successful and widely publicized furniture manufacturers of the times. McHugh and Company's early designs met with critical as well as popular approval. His furniture exhibit at the 1901 Pan-American Exposition in Buffalo was only a short distance away from the booth shared by Stickley's United Crafts and the Grueby Faience Company of Boston, affording visitors their first opportunity to view a large assemblage of Mission oak furniture. While it is widely known that the exposition gave Stickley vital public exposure, Joseph P. McHugh and Company walked away with that and more—a silver medal for his Mission furniture.

As has been pointed out, "McHugh's furniture was praised in 1901 as epitomizing an effort to capture the simplicity and harmony preached by William Morris and his followers."[6] But whereas the furniture designs of Gustav Stickley, the Roycrofters, and later those of Charles Limbert and L. & J. G. Stickley continued to improve, to evolve into more sophisticated forms, McHugh was unable to maintain both a consistency and the necessary high standards of workmanship to compete with the others, then or now. As David Cathers observed, "while being first may have been important to McHugh, the fact is that his mission designs were inept and their execution substandard."[7]

McHugh utilized a variety of types of shopmarks—a brand, an oval paper label, and a brass tag—but each bore basically the same words: "Joseph P. McHugh/Mission Furniture." The so-called McHugh chair, though not the only style made by the company, is indicative of its early designs. The massive legs and posts are unpegged, and the feet end in a mild variation of the Mackmurdo foot, also used both by Stickley Brothers and the Roycrofters. The seat of the McHugh chair may be either rush or leather. The Michigan Chair Company offered a similar chair in its 1898 catalog, but whereas the McHugh chair features a front stretcher slightly higher than the other three, the Michigan Chair Company version has all four stretchers at the same level.

McHugh lived long enough to see Gustav Stickley's empire crumble, to read of Elbert Hubbard's untimely death, and perhaps to sense that when the definitive history of the Arts and Crafts movement in America is finally written, Joseph P. McHugh will have become an important footnote.

## SELECTED PRICES

Other than the well-known and widely distributed McHugh chair, relatively few signed examples of McHugh furniture have surfaced. Those few have inspired only a lukewarm response, appealing for the most part to Arts and Crafts collectors interested more in the historical role than the intrinsic design. Until additional examples are identified and tested on the market, a comprehensive price guide will remain elusive.

Chair, side: the McHugh chair, two horizontal slats across the back between two massive posts, square legs ending in tapering, flared feet, rush seat, 36" × 17" × 18", $500–$750.

Table, card: flip top above a single drawer, supported by four square, tapering posts with straight cross-stretchers, 28" × 30" × 30", $425–$475

Table, card: 40" circular top with X-design in supporting sides, $800–$1,200

## George Mann Niedecken

SHOPMARK:  None appearing on his furniture

PRINCIPAL CONTRIBUTIONS:  Interior architectural and furniture designs.

FOUNDER  George Mann Niedecken. Born: 1878, died: 1945

STUDIOS AND WORKSHOPS:  Frank Lloyd Wright, Oak Park, Illinois, ca. 1904. Niedecken-Walbridge Co., Milwaukee, Wisconsin, 1907-ca. 1940

> "In keeping with the Prairie school philosophy of the natural use of materials, wood was seldom stained, painted, shellacked or varnished . . . only waxed to bring out its deeper beauty . . . to protect the wood and yet retain a very important quality of wood–its tactile beauty"
> — author Donald Kalec on Niedecken furniture[1]

He called himself an "interior architect." Craftsman, artist, interior decorator, and furniture designer, George M. Niedecken believed consummately in the total unification of design of a home's interior and exterior appearance. As author Virginia Jones Maher points out, "the ability to integrate the design of a building with its interior decoration and furnishings into a harmonious whole is the hallmark of George M. Niedecken's style."[2]

For many years it was incorrectly assumed that George Niedecken was simply the cabinetmaker who had built much of the furniture that Frank Lloyd Wright had designed between 1902 and 1911. To his credit, George Niedecken undoubtedly was familiar with the skills required of a cabinetmaker, for he oversaw the manufacture of much of the furniture he and other architects, including Wright, had designed; but his contributions to both the Arts and Crafts movement and the Prairie school of architecture go far beyond that of a contract woodworker.

After studying at the Wisconsin Art Institute and the Art Institute in Chicago, a young George Niedecken spent nearly three years (1899–1902) traveling in Europe and England, where he studied the work of important Arts and Crafts designers, including William Morris, as well as Art Nouveau artists in Paris and Arts and Crafts architects in Vienna, many of whom were to influence his later designs. He returned to Milwaukee in July 1902 and resumed painting, displaying his work in exhibitions he helped to organize. In addition, he was commissioned to paint murals and he began to specialize in custom-designed furnishings. Among the architects with wh,om he collaborated were Frank Lloyd Wright, George Elmslie, William Drummond, William Purcell, and Percy Bentley.

It was his relationship with Wright, however, that highlighted his career. Wright "cultivated a working relationship with Niedecken that spanned fifteen years and a dozen commissions."[3] In 1904 Niedecken was hired by Wright to design and paint the sumac dining room frieze in the Susan Dana House in Springfield, Illinois. The two developed a working friendship that almost led, according to John Walbridge, Niedecken's brother-in-law and eventual business partner, to a formal partnership.[4]

The work Niedecken did for Wright and other Chicago-area architects led to the establishment of a business partnership between Niedecken and John Walbridge, in 1907. Niedecken served as the firm's designer; Walbridge handled the business affairs. The partners offered a variety of services, from upholstery and refinishing of existing furniture to custom-designed furniture, fabrics, draperies, rugs, and lighting fixtures. They continued to collaborate with Wright on many of his interiors, at times transforming his rough sketches into finished drawings ready to be taken to a cabinetmaker. When needed, Niedecken designed pieces of furniture himself for Wright's clients.

In 1907, when both his reputation and his architectural business were blossoming, Wright hired the firm of Niedecken-Walbridge to assist with the furnishings of the Frederick C. Robie and the Avery W. Coonley houses in Chicago. At this point the partnership had not yet established its own woodworking shop, so the finished furniture plans were turned over to the F. H. Bresler firm for execution under George Niedecken's close supervision. By 1910, though, Niedecken and Walbridge were no longer subcontracting furniture construction to local cabinet shops, but had set up their own workshop and studio with as many as 25 artisans executing designs in furniture, lighting and stained glass. They completed the furniture for the Robie House and also began making furniture for William Purcell, George Elmslie, William Drummond, and other Midwestern architects. One of the most famous pieces that the Niedecken-Walbridge furniture shop built was the tall-case clock with mahogany and brass inlay designed by George Elmslie in 1912 for the Babson House in Riverside, Illinois. The hands and gold face for the clock were provided by none other than Roben R. Jarvie of Chicago. "Niedecken's custom-designed furniture during this period reflected the independent, modern style of Prairie school architects," author Maher has noted, "generally characterized by monumental simplified forms, solid construction, and thorough craftsmanship."[5]

Wright left Chicago in 1909, but he and Niedecken later worked together on the design of the furniture for the Allen House in Wichita, Kansas (1917–18) and the Bogk House in Milwaukee (1917–18), all of which was produced by the Niedecken-Walbridge furniture factory. The furniture reveals a Niedecken touch that was not typically Wright: decorative inlay.

"Whereas Wright chose to stress the plane geometry of his early furniture by adding linear wood strips, Niedecken's own contemporary style often relied on inlay to achieve the same effect. It is significant that Niedecken's own furniture shop, set up in 1910, was headed by Dutch immigrant Herman Tenbroeke, who specialized in veneered cabinetwork. . . . Niedecken apparently derived geometric inlay not from the oriental sources that inspired Wright but from the innovative architects associated with the Arts and Crafts movement in Vienna."[6]

As Edward S. Cooke, Jr., has noted, Niedecken, both through the work he did for Wright and other Prairie school architects and through the plans he designed for his own individual clients, "was one of the first to give definition to a new profession: that of the interior architect".[7] Niedecken's work reveals an ability to work in a variety of styles and woods, depending on the needs and desires of his client, but his personal Prairie school designs reveal the influence both Wright and the Austrian school of design exerted on him. Like Wright, Niedecken embraced the machine in the design and execution of his furniture plans, utilizing its ability to quickly cut precision dovetails, doweled joints, and splined miters, but as Chicago-based author Sharon Darling has pointed out, "At first view Prairie style furniture gave the illusion of simplicity; in fact it was quite complex. While its relatively straight lines allowed the use of modern woodworking machinery, a great deal of additional handwork was also required."[8]

The furniture produced by Niedecken-Walbridge was well constructed, utilizing both mortise-and-tenon and doweled joints, dovetailed drawers, mitered corners, tongue-and-groove joinery, and internal splines. Both the insides of drawers and the backs of case pieces were finished as if they were going to be on display. Unlike Wright, Niedecken was as concerned with the comfort of his furniture as he was with how it fit within the overall plan. Whereas Wright would later joke about his inability to design comfortable chairs, Niedecken's redesign of Wright's chairs for the Bogk House "involved shortening and contouring the backs to bring them more in line with human anatomy."[9]

Like most of the Prairie school architects and interior designers, Niedecken's work is identified not through shopmarks but by studying documents and photographs of the rooms in which it appeared. Unlike the furniture of any of the Stickleys or other furniture manufacturers, the clients' tastes generally took precedence over that of the architect's in the design of their furniture. While Wright proved to be the exception to this and many other rules, George Niedecken's work reflects the variety of styles inherent in the number of architects and private clients he served. One observer has surmised that, in part at least, "Niedecken's willingness to temper his creativity to conform with an architect's comprehensive plan stemmed from contact with Wright's dominant personality and exceptional conceptual powers."[10]

Niedecken proved that not only could he work in a wide range of styles, from Art Nouveau to Prairie to Georgian Revival, but that he could master them as well. "Whether called upon to decorate a colonial mansion or a historical Prairie residence, Niedecken faced the same challenge of interrelating facade, woodwork, fabrics, cabinetry and seating furniture."[11]

## SELECTED PRICES

The rarity of the furniture designed by George Niedecken, plus the individual nature of each piece, makes establishing a price guide both impractical and quite possibly misleading, for the value of any example will be influenced by factors beyond the scope of this study. Very little Niedecken furniture has surfaced since 1988, making it both difficult and dangerous to attempt to establish price ranges for his furniture. Examples will need to be carefully researched and analyzed in order to determine their fair market value.

## Charles Rohlfs

SHOPMARK: Incised or branded, the letter R within the outline of a saw, occasionally with the year underneath

PRINCIPAL CONTRIBUTIONS: Uniquely designed oak interior furnishings and accessories. Born: 1853, died: 1936, founded: ca. 1890, closed: ca. 1925

STUDIOS AND WORKSHOP: Charles Rohlfs Workshop, Buffalo, New York, ca. 1890-ca. 1925

> "In other words my feeling was to treat my wood well, caress it perhaps, and that desire led to the idea that I must embellish it to evidence my profound regard for a beautiful thing in nature. This embellishment consisted of line, proportion and carving."
> —*Charles Rohlfs, 1925*[1]

Fine and rare Charles Rohlfs double candleholder, 1903, with Gothic dark oak frame, cutout panels of stylized flames, and hand-wrought copper bobeches. Excellent original finish. Branded CR 1903, 18" × 21" × 4½", $3,737

A few miles away from the village of East Aurora, New York, where Elbert Hubbard and his colony of artisans were busily producing a line of severely plain and straight-lined Mission oak furniture, Charles Rohlfs and seven or eight German craftsmen were meticulously designing, carving, and producing a limited number of privately commissioned pieces. And while the Roycrofters and Charles Rohlfs worked in close proximity to one another, both utilizing quartersawn white oak and designing furniture with exposed structural details, in many cases the similarities end there.

Charles Rohlfs was born in New York City and as a youth learned the trades of both barrel maker and a cast-iron stove designer. While in his mid–20s he left the factory environment to take to the stage, where he quickly established a reputation as a fine Shakespearean actor. Soon thereafter he fell in love with Katherine Green, a popular writer of detective novels and daughter of a prominent socialite who refused to accept Rohlfs as a son-in-law as long as he remained an actor.[2]

Within a few years Rohlfs had decided to forgo a career in the theater, and in 1884 he married Katherine Green. As Rohlfs recalled years later, he and Katherine had hoped to furnish their home in Buffalo with antiques, but since they could not yet afford them, he drew on his basic woodworking skills and began designing and constructing furniture in a makeshift attic workshop. Even his earliest projects reveal that Charles Rohlfs had a rare talent for design that enabled him to successfully blend elements of the flowing

Art Nouveau style with the linear look and structural expressiveness characteristic of Arts and Crafts furniture. His love for his work, his admiration and devotion to both his subject and his material, and his dedication to his craft are revealed in one statement: "If I make a chair, I am a chair."[3]

Unhappy with his job in a Buffalo foundry, Rohlfs pursued his woodworking hobby, transforming it, as he turned 40, into a new career. By 1898 he had moved his shop out of the attic of his home and into a commercial building, but "instead of mass-producing a 'line' of furniture, Rohlfs believed in maintaining the high quality of art in his work by limiting production to pieces, suites, and ensembles that were unique."[4] Rohlfs and his furniture gained international acclaim at the 1901 Pan-American Exposition in Buffalo, where a new line of oak furniture by an Eastwood, New York, furniture maker by the name of Gustav Stickley was also being introduced. Subsequent expositions in St. Louis, Canada, and Europe brought honors and commissions from around the world, from Buckingham Palace to the home of Marshall Field, as well as inclusion in London's Royal Society of Arts. Nevertheless, Rohlfs steadfastly refused to enlarge his small staff of craftsmen and woodcarvers.

Like most Arts and Crafts designers, Rohlfs worked primarily in oak, often pegging joints and utilizing keyed tenons. Unlike any of the same major designers and manufacturers, however, Rohlfs's furniture is often decorated with elaborate carvings, motivated in traditional Art Nouveau style by natural plant forms. According to his son, Rohlfs was once inspired by the smoke curling up from the bowl of his pipe, and he preserved that image in the carvings on the side of a chest of drawers he designed for their home.[5]

Exceptional Charles Rohlfs tall-back hall chair, 1900, with carved and cutout details, faceted pegs and a semicircular seat. Old, very light overcoat and chip to finial. (Pictured in publication, 1900.) Branded CR/1900, 57" × 18" × 15", $31,625

Like Charles Greene on the West Coast, Rohlfs worked in the Arts and Crafts style, but his creative talents were never bound by convention. While most Arts and Crafts designers shunned the added decorative effect of carving, Rohlfs approached it as an art form, often letting the grain of the wood determine the direction his carving took. "If you have the feeling for this work," he later explained, "the carving will look after itself."[6]

Much of Rohlfs's early furniture was either darkly stained or fumed oak, as was the reigning fashion. Unlike the Roycrofters or any of the Stickleys, though, Rohlfs appeared to be constantly testing current fashion, incorporating curved cutouts and flowing lines into his designs at a time when rectilinear forms without elaborate ornamentation were prevalent within the movement. While most of the major Arts and Crafts furniture manufacturers used flush pegs to strengthen critical joints, Rohlfs drew attention to his pegs by letting them protrude above the wood. In addition, Rohlfs used raised pegs for their decorative effect, as he also did brass tacks and wood buttons. The buttons, however, often disguised screws used in place of dowels or tenons—a practice other important firms generally avoided and that has been attributed to Rohlfs's lack of extensive training in joinery.[7]

When Rohlfs's work, like that of all of the Arts and Crafts designers, fell out of style between the late 1920s and the early 1970s, it was scattered across the country as households to which it originally had been commissioned were disposed of and heirs sold off the contents. Robert Judson Clark and the organizers of the 1972 landmark exhibition "The Arts and Crafts movement in America: 1876–1916" were the first to call attention to Rohlfs's role as an important Arts and Crafts furniture designer;[8] respect and demand for his work has increased tremendously since then. As would be expected, important examples from Rohlfs's workshop surface only on rare occasions and are almost always recognized immediately because of their distinctive style. The combination of quality Art Nouveau carving and curved lines within an obviously well-constructed, often startling Arts and Crafts form is difficult for even an inexperienced collector to overlook.

While large case pieces, generally made on commission, are considered extremely rare, smaller forms intended to be sold to the public—from stamp boxes and candlesticks to chairs and rockers—continue to surface. Much of the Rohlfs furniture that was not intended for use in his own home was signed with a shopmark as unique as his furniture. The letter *R*, carved or burned into the wood, was encompassed by the rectangular outline of a wood saw. In many instances the year in which the piece was made will also be incised into the wood next to his shopmark, leading people unfamiliar with Rohlfs's work to refer occasionally to a piece as being "dated Roycroft furniture." Examples have been found in which the carved Rohlfs shopmark and date have been highlighted with either red or white paint, making them even easier to distinguish.

Although some people have difficulty understanding how the fanciful and often elaborate designs of Charles Rohlfs can be included with the severely plain and unadorned work of Arts and Crafts spokesmen such as Gustav Stickley, Elbert Hubbard, and Frank Lloyd Wright, his independent and creative spirit, his demand for quality craftsmanship, and his respect for the nature of his materials represent the very essence of the Arts and Crafts movement. As Coy Ludwig concluded, "Rohlfs furniture is the work of a self-assured individualist. His high ideals were nurtured by the courage of his conviction to pursue them, and his work genuinely deserves the name by which it is commonly called: art furniture."[9]

## SELECTED PRICES

Since Charles Rohlfs and his assistants worked primarily on private commissions, their furniture is considered both rare and extremely valuable. Rohlfs also designed smaller accessories for his assistants to complete, such as candlesticks and stamp boxes, which surface on a regular basis and for which price ranges are included. Very few important pieces of Rohlfs furniture have reached the public market in recent months, making it both difficult and dangerous to attempt to establish price ranges for his furniture. Examples will need to be carefully researched and analyzed in order to determine their fair market value.

Candleholder: mahogany, with a triangular column resting on a triangular base, a copper bobèche on the column, incised shopmark and 1902 painted red, 4 ½" × 11", $500–$750

Candleholder: oak, with a triangular column resting on a triangular base, a copper bobèche set on the column, incised shopmark and 1902 painted red, 4 ½" × 11", $1,000–$1,500

Candlestick: a triangular form with overhanging top drilled and fitted for candle, behind which is a triangular copper reflector, triangular shaft with cutouts on triangular base, incised shopmark and 1901, 25" high, $3,000–$4,000

Chafing set: an earthenware chafing dish sitting on a copper scrolled platform on a triangular oak base, incised shopmark, 20" high, $2,500–$3,500.

Chair, side: octagonal rear posts joined by four horizontal slats, seat apron arched with cutouts, raised pegs, loose cushion seat, incised shop mark and 1901 painted red on rear apron, 47" high, $20,000–$25,000.

Chair, side: single wide slat in back with pierced ovals and incised carving, seat apron cut out and carved, curved cross-stretcher base, incised shopmark, 38" × 18", $15,000–$20,000

Dirk Van Erp boudoir lamp with hammered copper "bean pot" base with single socket and conical four-paneled mica shade. Great patina, a few very small and shallow dents. D'Arcy Gaw mark with name removed, 11" x 10", $25,000

Fine and rare Roycroft bridal chest with broad wrought-iron hinges clasp and handles. Quartersawn oak grain-painted to resemble rosewood. Fine original finish, possibly original lock. Carved orb and cross mark, 19" x 46" x 21 1/2", $15,000

Fine and rare L. & J. G. Stickley two-door china cabinet with overhanging rectangular top, leaded glass panes over single pane to doors and sides, with three interior shelves. Good original finish. Handcraft decal, 66" x 44" x 16", $9,200

Exceptional George Ohr pinched and folded pitcher covered in a rare amber and green-speckled purple leathery matte glaze. A couple of minor nicks and two small chips (restored) on rim. Script signature, 4 1/2" x 5 1/2", $17,250

Exceptional George Ohr tapering vase with in-body twist, covered in a mottled lavender, green and blue vellum glaze. Script signature, 6" x 3 3/4", $25,875

Very rare and early Van Briggle two-color vase with sloping shoulder, decorated with stylized iris blossoms and leaves in an unusual iridescent copper and eggplant glaze. We have seen three other examples with this glazing, all dated 1904. Small chip to rim and base from manufacture. (Modeling of flowers is unusually sharp, showing hand-tooling after mold.) Incised AA, 10" x 4 1/2", $14,950

Rare and exceptional Grueby three-color squat vessel, 1914, decorated with tooled and applied waterlilies and lilypads in yellow and green against a leathery dark green ground. (Very crisp decoration with perfect glazing.) Very short tight bruise to rim. Circular pottery mark/ JE/1-14, 4 1/4" x 9 1/2", $54,625

Exceptional Marblehead cylindrical vase by Hannah Tutt, with stylized fruit trees in amber and brown on a matte gray ground. (Crisp decoration, unusual color. A great piece). Impressed ship mark, and HT, 4 1/4" x 3 3/4", $20,700

Exceptional Rookwood Iris glaze bulbous vase painted by O. G. Reed, 1900, with fleshy mauve poppies with yellow centers on a shaded mauve-to-amber ground. (Pan American Exposition paper label.) Flame mark/900B/O.G.R./W, 9 1/2" x 6", $9,775

Fine, rare and early Dirk Van Erp hammered copper bulbous pitcher with leaded interior, hinged lid, riveted loop finial and ear-shaped handle. Fine original reddish-brown patina, shallow dent to lid. Closed box mark, with remnant of D'Arcy Gaw, 11 3/4" x 9 1/2", $4,000

Fine Rookwood incised matte ovoid vase by Elizabeth Lincoln, 1918, beautifull decorated with bright red fruit and green and purple leaves on a purple and umber butterfat ground. Flame mark/XVIII/943C/LNL, 10 1/2" x 5 1/2", $3,450

Exceptional and rare Roycroft hammered copper box designed by Dard Hunter, with hinged lid and overlay of nickel silver squares. Restoration to hinge, new pin. Orb and cross mark, 1 3/4" x 6 3/4" x 3 1/2", $14,950

Heintz sterling-on-bronze desk lamp with helmet shade and overlay of berries and leaves. Shade has wear/cleaning to patina. Mark hidden by felt, 11" x 7 3/4", $747

Rare and early Tobey Furniture (Chicago) chaise lounge, ca. 1901, with square posts and hard leather sling seat. Excellent original finish and condition, with original hard leather sling seat, reinforced with new leather on the back. (Pictured in Chicago Furniture - Art, Craft and Industry 1833-1983 by Sharon Darling, from the 1901 catalog New Furniture in Weathered Oak. An example is in the Collection of the Chicago Historical Society.) Unmarked, 34" x 33" x 45 1/2", $2,000

Fine and rare Limbert cafe chair with spade-shaped cutout to plank back, two square cutouts to each side, sloped arms and new black leather upholstery to seat cushion. Minor touch-ups to good original finish. Branded mark, 34" x 26" x 21", $3,500-$4,500

Exceptional and rare Roycroft hammered copper fernery designed by Dard Hunter with a band of nickel silver pierced with small squares, with four riveted legs. Cleaned original finish. Orb and cross mark, and MW in shield, 3 3/4" x 7 1/4", $14,950

Fine and rare Shop of the Crafters clip-corner library table with cut-out plank legs inlaid with ebonized and exotic woods, and cross-stretchers. Excellent original condition, stenciled model number, 29" x 40" x 40 1/2", $6,900

Karl Kipp hammered copper plate
with stylized quatrefoil and rolled
borders to rim. Cleaned patina. Die-
stamped mark, 9 3/4" dia., $400

Fine and rare Fulper "Cattail" vase embossed
with intertwined cattails and covered in a
glossy blue-gray and Moss flambé glaze.
Rectangular ink mark, 13" x 4 3/4", $3750

Fine Grueby tile decorated in cuenca by
Marie Seaman with a pink tulip on a green
matte ground, mounted in a bronze Tiffany
trivet base. Light wear to surface, fine original patina to mount. Tile marked MS, mount
is unmarked. Tile: 6" sq., $5,000

Fine and rare Teco vase with flaring rim, decorated with twelve
applied leaves forming a shoulder,
and covered in a charcoaled matte
green glaze. (A great example in
excellent condition). Restoration
to several small chips to rim tips.
Stamped Teco, 11 3/4" x 4 1/2",
$10,350

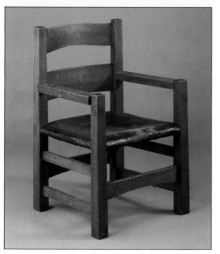

Extremely rare and early Gustav Stickley arm-chair with inverted-V crestrail, broad second slat, arched front and back stretchers, flaring legs and burgundy leather-upholstered seat. Original finish, some looseness. Unmarked, 37 1/2" x 23 1/4" x 21 1/2", $19,550

Adelaide Robineau spherical vase covered in a bright cobalt glaze with blooming crystals. Hairline to base. Incised AR, 3 3/4" x 4"  $6,000

Fine and rare Charles Rolhfs double pedestal desk, 1902, with four drawers to one side and bookshelf/cabinet to the other, with strap hinges, rough-sawn panels, and carved R medallion. Complete with tallback swiveling desk chair, carved with matching medallion and date, fleur-de-lis finial and tacked-on original red leather seat. Both pieces have an excellent original black finish with light overcoat and original green interior. Missing support for cabinet shelf and several rivet heads, some wear around feet of chair. Carved CR/1902. Desk (on casters): 32 3/4" x 60" x 32 3/4"; chair: 59" x 26" x 21", $28,750

Fine and rare Gustav Stickley hammered copper canister table lamp with two handles and electrified oil font, and original silk-lined wicker shade. Excellent original patina. Als Ik Kan stamp mark, 18 1/2" x 14", $5,000

Fine Wheatley vase with four flaring buttresses, covered in a rich, curdled matte green glaze. Minor glaze nick to one foot. Incised WP/640, 8 1/4" x 9", $1,840

Fine and rare Susan Frackelton gourd-shaped salt-glaze stoneware vase, ca. 1905, decorated with abutilon blossoms alternating with stylized leaves and vines, in indigo on an ivory ground. (An unusually beautiful example). Chip and nick to rim. Signed SF/IX/984, 6 3/4" x 3 3/4", $20,700

Fine, large and rare Fulper table lamp, with a two-socket baluster base and mushroom-cap shade inset with organically shaped blue, green, and red leaded-slag glass pieces, the entire piece covered in Chinese blue flambé glaze. Shade has a few very minor scratches and four short hairlines between leaded glass pieces, probably from firing, with original porcelain sockets. Rectangular ink mark. Base 18", shade 15", $12,500

Chair, swivel: wide back panel with pierced cutouts, carved rear posts and arm supports, incised shopmark and 1902, 46" high, $5,000–$6000

Chest: overhanging hinged top with carving, copper hardware, curved aprons, raised pegs, incised shop mark and 1906, 24" × 48" × 24", $30,000–$40,000

Frame, picture: rectangular form, incised shopmark on back, 16" × 26", $1,000–$1,500

Sewing cabinet: overhanging top over single paneled door with cutout apron, two keyed tenons on either side, fitted interior with sliding trays, incised shop mark and 1907 on door, 25" × 17" × 17", $7,500–$10,000

Stamp box: hinged top opening to reveal four square compartments, curved sides, incised shopmark and 1901 colored red, 2" × 6", $500–$750

Taboret: octagon overhanging top over an eight-sided base with hinged door to storage compartment, each side with cutouts and raised pegs, incised shopmark inside door, 29" × 32" × 32", $8,000–$10,000

## The Rose Valley Association

SHOPMARK: Branded mark, ROSE VALLEY SHOPS, and a rose and the letter V enclosed by a buckled belt.

PRINCIPAL CONTRIBUTIONS: Furniture, pottery, and the *Artsman* magazine.

FOUNDER: William L. Price. Born: 1861, died: 1916, founded: 1901, closed: ca. 1909.

FURNITURE WORKSHOPS: The Rose Valley Shops, Rose Valley, Pennsylvania, 1901–06.

"the art that is life. . . ."

—*William L. Price, 1903*[1]

Among the experimental utopian crafts communities that were inspired by John Ruskin and William Morris was the Rose Valley Association outside Philadelphia. Architect Will Price founded the colony in 1901 after having secured financial backing from prominent Philadelphia philanthropists, including the influential Edward Bok, founder of the *Ladies' Home Journal* and an early supporter of the Arts and Crafts movement. Price established the Rose Valley Shops amid the ruins of a bankrupt textile factory, a move that proved to be as prophetic as it was symbolic.

Though idealistic, Price was not devoid of practical considerations, "situating his experiment within commuting distance of Philadelphia, where he maintained his architectural practice and where most of the original Valley residents worked."[2] The corporation papers for the Rose Valley Shops indicated Price's intention to "manufacture structures, articles, materials and products involving artistic handcraft."[3] It was clear from the beginning that one of the principal endeavors at Rose Valley was going to be the production of handcrafted furniture. Price installed several workbenches and a minimum number of woodworking machines, for it appears that most of the relatively small number of examples that were produced at Rose Valley were made primarily by hand. Price employed an average of four to six craftsmen, generally European woodcarvers, who, in turn, attempted to train some of the residents, since Price believed that "Americans had already lost their craft skills to machinery."[4]

The furniture designs that Price provided for the Rose Valley woodworkers featured extensive hand-carving, often in a Gothic or Renaissance style. Keyed tenons were often incorporated, enabling many of the pieces to be disassembled for shipping. As Robert Edwards observed, "In some instances, three-dimensional figures formed the fully functional mortise pins of the tables and chairs that were the mainstay of Rose Valley production. Comparatively few case pieces were made and all of the known examples of the five hundred pieces estimated to have been made are of quartered oak finished with dark Cabot's stain."[5]

Problems soon surfaced at Rose Valley as Price, his associates, and his woodworkers "wrestled with the compromise reality forces upon the ideal. Woodworkers had no creative control over the products' designs nor were they accepted as peers by the residents of the community (where most workers did not reside)."[6] They were excluded from the other activities at Rose Valley, including the plays, publication of the *Artsman* (1903–07), and cultural events that highlighted life in the utopian community.

Price arranged for an exhibit of Rose Valley crafts and furniture at the prestigious 1904 Louisiana Purchase Exposition in St. Louis, which, along with ads and features in magazines such as Bok's *Ladies' Home Journal*, helped increase demand for the community's work, which was also sold through a retail outlet in Philadelphia. Nevertheless, as Edwards reveals, "workers were content neither with pity nor with the damp stone mill in which they worked. After five years, the woodworking shop closed amid complaints about poor working conditions."[7]

The few examples of Rose Valley furniture that surface can be recognized both by their high quality of workmanship and the Rose Valley shopmark: a branded rose and the letter *V* encompassed by a buckled belt and the inscription "Rose Valley Shops." Although its designs may not be considered strictly Arts and Crafts, the inspiration, motivation, and handcraftsmanship that were behind each example were clearly derivative of the principles of both John Ruskin and William Morris.

Rose Valley Association stained oak trestle table with reticulated sides, ca. 1910, 30" × 48" × 30", $15,000

## SELECTED PRICES

The rarity of the furniture designed and produced at Rose Valley, plus the individual nature of each piece, makes establishing a price guide both impractical and quite possibly misleading, for the value of any example will be influenced by factors beyond the scope of this study. Very little Rose Valley furniture has surfaced recently, making it both difficult and dangerous to attempt to establish price ranges for the furniture. Examples will need to be carefully researched and analyzed in order to determine their fair market value.

Chair, side: carved and pierced back panel with leather stretched between the two carved uprights, leather seat with brass tacks, 39" × 15" × 15", $2,000–$3,000

Table, library: rectangular top constructed of four boards joined with butterfly joints, sides with Gothic carving, through tenons and carved keys holding lower shelf, $15,000–$20,000

## The Roycroft Shops

SHOPMARK: Carved letter R within a circle topped by a cross; carved wood ROYCROFT in Gothic lettering

PRINCIPAL CONTRIBUTIONS: Oak furniture, metalware, and books

Fine Roycroft architectural bookcase from the Roycroft Inn in East Aurora, NY, with overhanging cornice top, glass-paned door and four adjustable shelves over a single drawer, with copper hardware. Excellent original finish, chip to back of top. Carved ROYCROFT and stamped with Inn registration number R084, 67" × 34" × 16", $19,550

FOUNDER: Elbert Hubbard. Born: 1856, died: 1915, founded: 1895, closed: 1938.

WORKSHOPS AND SALESROOMS: The Roycroft Shops, East Aurora, New York, 1895–1938.

> "We would ask you not to class our products as 'Mission,' or so called 'Mission Furniture.' Ours is purely Roycroft–made by us according to our own ideas. We have eliminated all unnecessary elaboration, but have kept in view the principles of artistic quality, sound mechanical construction and good workmanship."
> —*Elbert Hubbard, 1906*[1]

The story of Elbert Hubbard and the Roycrofters is one many people are familiar with, for more information has survived regarding his life and the evolution of the Roycroft community he founded than any other figure in the Arts and Crafts movement except Frank Lloyd Wright. Among his many talents, two served him best: a natural knack for promotion and a charisma that attracted talented individuals and artists to his fold. Hubbard's untimely death aboard the *Lusitania* in 1915 ended the stormy and controversial career of an enterprising soap salesman turned publisher, who, according to one of his respected peers "started more people to thinking in the last fifteen years than any man who has been talking or writing, or both, in this country."[2]

In 1892, in the midst of a successful career with the John Larkin soap company, Elbert Hubbard, married and fathered three boys, sold his stock in the firm for $75,000[3] and left to pursue other interests. During the next two years he enrolled briefly in Harvard, wrote an unsuccessful novel, and traveled extensively. In 1894 he hiked across England, where he claimed to have met William Morris, then returned home to devote his talents to the Arts and Crafts movement and a new career.

Elbert Hubbard embarked on a Morris-inspired publishing career that blossomed under his prolific pen and promotional campaigns. By 1895 he had established his press in East Aurora and named it after two 17th century brothers, Thomas and Samuel Roycroft, printers who had lived in London. His new shopmark, an orb-and-cross, had been used by a 14th-century monk, Cassiodorus. He and other monks had inscribed it at the end of each book they meticulously handcopied to signify that each work was "the best they knew how."[4] Hubbard combined the two—the letter R from the Roycroft brothers and the orb-and-cross from the monks—to create the Roycroft shop-mark that was to become a prominent element in all of their work.

As his regular publications, *Little Journeys* and the *Philistine*, grew in popularity, so did his need for additional staff and space. Local carpenters were hired in 1896 to construct and furnish a book bindery and soon there-after a leather shop, a larger print shop, and eventually the Roycroft Inn. The simple, straight-lined furniture the carpenters produced for the buildings quickly became popular with visitors to the Roycroft campus, and Hubbard, never one to let opportunity slip away, was offering it for sale by 1897.[5] An early advertisement stated that "no stock of furniture is carried—the pieces are made as ordered, and about two months will be required to fill your order. Every piece is signed by the man who made it."[6]

Hubbard's first love was always the printed word, and it does not appear that he played a major role in the design or production of Roycroft furniture. As with many of his projects, Hubbard attracted talented craftsmen to his East Aurora workshops, including Santiago Cadzow, Albert Danner, Victor Toothaker, and Herbert Buffum, all of whom contributed in various ways to Roycroft design and production. As David Cathers observed, Hubbard may have occasionally injected his opinions, but "the enormous variety in designs found in Roycroft furniture indicates that no one designer ever dominated its appearance."[7] That fact is unfortunate, for Roycroft designs often fail to equal the high quality of materials and level of workmanship evidenced in all of their work. Uncompromisingly severe, Roycroft furniture often lacks the warmth and almost personal nature other firms achieved through a careful use of tapering corbels, sweeping arches, and lighter finishes. Their massive-ness and sheer weight are enough to convince even those unfamiliar with cabinetry that these are quality pieces, but the bullish, masculine character of most Roycroft furniture, along with its relative rarity, has prevented it from becoming as widely collected as that of Gustav Stickley.

The Roycrofters encouraged visitors to the Inn and readers of their cata-logs to commission special orders. This is evident from the number of pieces of furniture that surface with a particular person's name carved into them,

Rare Roycroft vanity with pivoting bevel-edged mirror, single drawer with copper drop pulls, on tapering legs with Mackmurdo feet. Original finish, excellent condition. Carved orb and cross mark, 56" × 39" × 17½", $4,312

and in a line from their catalog: "We do not confine ourselves to the designs shown herein, but will if you wish, make special pieces to your order, embodying your own ideas."[8]

What Hubbard, no doubt, did have a hand in was the promotional descriptions of their furniture: "Roycroft furniture resembles that made by the old monks, in its simple beauty, its strength and its excellent workmanship. We use no nails—but are generous in the use of pegs, pins, mortises and tenons. Our furniture is made of the solid wood—no veneer. We use only the best grade of quarter-sawed oak and African or Santo Domingo mahogany. The oak is finished in our own weathered finish, a combination of stain, filler and wax polish, that produces a satisfying and permanent effect."[9] While Roycroft furniture is distinguished by its exceedingly high quality of materials and workmanship, their finishes have not proved to be as durable as those of Gustav Stickley or Charles Limbert. For that reason many pieces have been refinished, but collectors have demonstrated that they are willing to pay a premium for those pieces that have retained their original finish.

Roycroft furniture is by far some of the heaviest and the most massive produced in this era. Whereas even Gustav Stickley, late in his career, began to attempt to reduce both the weight and the cost of his furniture using veneers, plywood panels, thinner woods, and more advanced production techniques, the Roycrofters continued to use thicker woods, bulbous feet, keyed tenons, and coppered glass doors in a shop where it was claimed, though not substantiated, that "each piece was made by one man and each man could make any piece."[10] Hubbard's solution to the cost problem was simple: whereas a flat-arm Gustav Stickley Morris chair (No. 332) cost $33 in 1910, a similar Roycroft model (No. 045) was priced in 1912 at $55–a difference representing more than two weeks' pay for an average worker.

Since they never attempted to establish a furniture factory capable of producing hundreds of pieces a week, the Roycroft Furniture Shop's level of production lagged far behind that of other well-known manufacturers. As a result, large case pieces are considered extremely rare and, when in excellent, original condition, very valuable. Large bookcases, flat-topped desks, buffets, and china cabinets are among the hardest to find; dining chairs, library tables, and rocking chairs are among the most common. One form that appears quite often is a small bookstand, often referred to as a *Little Journeys* table. It was designed after 1915 to hold the fourteen-volume complete works of Elbert Hubbard's *Little Journeys* series. The table is distinguished by four keyed tenons on each side and is marked with a small metal tag bearing the orb-and-cross. Once considered unimportant by most Roycroft collectors, these small, convenient tables have since become more popular than the Elbert Hubbard books they were intended to promote.

Each piece of furniture that left the Roycroft Shops was a literal advertisement for Hubbard's enterprises. The Roycroft shopmark or, on special commissions, the entire word in Gothic script was boldly emblazoned across the front of each piece in letters large enough to be read from across the room, a barely silent reminder from Elbert Hubbard himself that this is not just a piece of furniture; this is ROYCROFT furniture.

Early Roycroft library table with overhanging top and lower shelf double-keyed through the legs. New finish, seam separation, minor cupping, small edge chips. Carved ROYCROFT on apron, 29½" × 50" × 33", $2,990

## SELECTED PRICES

Model numbers correspond with those in the catalog reprints *Roycroft Furniture* (New York: Turn of the Century Editions, 1981) and *Roycroft Handmade Furniture* (East Aurora, NY: House of Hubbard, 1973). Unless otherwise indicated, all examples are made from oak and retain their original finish exhibiting normal wear. Prices reflect leather seats and cushions which are either badly worn or have been replaced with appropriate materials. Pieces signed with the word ROYCROFT carved in the wood are considered more desirable by many Roycroft collectors and up to 15 percent more valuable.

Armchair: #106, five vertical slats across back, open arms, tacked leather seat, tapered feet, 40" × 22" × 20", $1,000–$1,500

Armchair: #28, two horizontal slats in back, open arms butting front posts, tacked leather seat, 38" × 25" × 22", $800–$1,200

Bench, "Ali Baba": #46, halved oak log, flat side finished, underside bark, with four splayed legs, cross-stretcher keyed through side stretchers, 20" × 42" × 11", $7,500–10,000

Bench, piano: rectangular overhanging top over beveled legs and lower shelf tenoned through side stretchers, 36" × 16", $6,000–$9,000

Bookcase: #84, single door over single drawer, copper hardware, straight toe board, arched sides, adjustable shelves, 67" × 32" × 14", $10,000–$15,000

Bookcase: #82, double doors, each with 12 panes of glass, two drawers, copper pulls, overhanging top with arched splashboard and letter rack, two keyed tenons at bottom of each side, 62" × 52" × 14", $15,000–$20,000

Bookrack: #0116, two fixed ends joined by flat board, orb incised in side, 6" × 15", $400–$600

Bookstand: *Little Journeys*, rectangular overhanging top, two open shelves with exposed keyed tenons and shoe foot base, 26" × 26" × 14", $400–$600

Box, "Goody": mahogany lidded box with iron hardware, 9" × 25" × 12", $500–$750

Cellaret: #1, overhanging top over two half-drawers over two doors with strap hinges, copper hardware, two keyed tenons on each flared side, 32" × 40" × 18", $12,500–$17,500

Chair, child's: #37, four vertical slats across back, tacked leather seat, Mackmurdo feet, 29" × 14" × 13", $1,000–$1,500

Chair, side: #27, two horizontal slats in back, drop-in leather seat, 37" × 17" × 18", $400–$600

Chair, side: #30, single wide vertical slat in back, tacked leather seat, bulbous feet, stacked stretchers, 44" × 17" × 17", $1,000–$1,500

Chair, side: incised "GPI" (Grove Park Inn) on crest rail, single vertical slat in back, tacked leather seat, open half-arms, stacked stretchers, 41" × 25" × 18", $2,000–$3,000

Chest of drawers: #113, two half-drawers over four long, splashboard, paneled sides, copper hardware, 60" × 42" × 24", $3,000–$3,500

China cabinet/server: #8, overhanging top with plate rail, one long drawer over two leaded glass doors, copper hardware, tapered feet, paneled sides, 45" × 42" × 20", $10,000–$15,000

Desk, drop-front: #91, strap hinges on the front, oval metal pulls on long drawer, tapering legs with bulbous feet, fitted interior, 46" × 36" × 18", $3,500–$4,500

Dresser: #108, two half-drawers over two long drawers, all with copper hardware, attached mirror, 34" × 43" × 25", $3,750–$4,750

Magazine pedestal: #80, square overhanging top over flared sides, each with four keyed tenons, five fixed shelves, arched sides, 63" × 18" × 18", $10,000–$15,000

Morris chair: #45, large paddle arms over four vertical slats, adjustable bar, drop-in cushion, Mackmurdo feet, 41" × 37" × 40", $6,500–$8,500

Rocking chair: #39A, five vertical slats across back, no arms, drop-in seat, 35" × 19" × 18", $500–$750

Rocking chair: #39, single curved slat in back, open arms, tacked leather seat, 38" × 21" × 19", $750–$1,000

Rocking chair: #51, four slats under each arm, loose cushion back and seat, 39" × 25" × 22", $2,000–$3,000

Server: #10, overhanging top with plate rail, long drawer with copper hardware, open shelf below, tapered feet, 36" × 44" × 22", $3,000–$4,000

Server: #11, half-round table, overhanging top supported by three legs, 36" × 48" × 24", $3,000–$4,000

Table, dining: #112, overhanging top over wide apron, supported by four square legs ending on × cross-stretchers, 30" × 54", $5,000–$7,500

Table, lamp: #102, circular top, no apron, supported by four tapering legs ending in bulbous feet, lower circular shelf rests atop straight cross-stretchers, 23" × 23", $1,500–$2,000

Table, lamp: #73 ½, circular top and apron supported by four curving legs, 30" × 30", $2,000–$3,000

Table, library: overhanging rectangular top supported by four legs joined by crossing stretcher arrangement, 30" × 42" × 30", $2,000–$3,000

Table, library: #18, overhanging rectangular top over one long drawer with copper hardware, five vertical slats on each side, lower shelf through-tenoned and keyed twice at each end, bulbous feet, 30" × 48" × 30", $2,500–$3,500

Table, library: #72, overhanging top, lower shelf with keyed tenons, 28" × 30" × 22", $2,500–$3,500

Table, library: #74, circular top with apron, four tapering legs with straight cross-stretchers, bulbous feet, incised orb in leg, 30" × 36", $2,500–$3,500

Taboret: #50, overhanging top over four flared sides, each with circular cutout extending to floor, narrow stretchers, 21" × 16" × 16", $3,500–$4,500

## The Shop of the Crafters

SHOPMARK: Paper label SHOP OF THE CRAFTERS/ AT CINCINNATI/OSCAR ONKEN CO. SOLE OWNERS around drawing of lantern.

PRINCIPAL CONTRIBUTIONS: Inlaid oak furniture.

FOUNDER: Oscar Onken. Born: 1858, died: 1948, founded: 1904, closed: 1920.

WORKSHOPS AND SALESROOMS: The Shop of the Crafters, Cincinnati, Ohio, 1904–20.

"The Crafter movement seeks to obliterate overdecoration, purposeless, meaningless designs and to install, instead, a purity of style, which will express at once, beauty, durability and usefulness. Working in harmony with this idea Professor Paul Horti has introduced a touch of inlay work of colored woods or metal, that enlivens the strong simple lines of Mission furniture."
—*Catalog introduction, ca. 1906*[1]

Although the Pan-American Exposition held in Buffalo, New York, in 1901 marked the first official introduction of American Arts and Crafts furniture through the exhibits of Gustav Stickley and Joseph McHugh, it was the 1904 Louisiana Purchase Exposition held in St. Louis that gave people from across the entire country the opportunity to inspect Arts and Crafts furniture, glassware, and metalware from firms and individuals such as Charles Rohlfs, Louis C. Tiffany, Arthur Stone, and the Rose Valley Shops, plus pottery designed by Artus Van Briggle, Grueby, Teco, Newcomb, and Rookwood. The St. Louis Exposition drew national attention, including coverage in a young periodical, the *Craftsman*. Among the thousands of viewers of the various displays,were two young architects, Frank Lloyd Wright and Charles Sumner

Fine and rare Shop of the Crafters massive sideboard
with arched mirror backsplash over four drawers
with hammered copper pulls, two cabinet doors
inlaid with stylized floral motif, and an open cabinet,
on casters. Good original finish, scratch to top.
Paper label, 58" × 54" × 25", $4,887

Greene, and a businessman from Cincinnati, Ohio, by the name of Oscar Onken.

In 1904 Oscar Onken was a successful retailer who had started a picture frame business more than 20 years earlier and expanded it into the manufacture of moldings and the sale of mirrors, etchings, and artwork. He had secured a prestigious downtown Cincinnati location to serve as his retail outlet, and a manufacturing plant he established on the outskirts supplied much of his merchandise. In 1903 he incorporated the Oscar Onken Company in preparation for a major expansion of his enterprise.

Onken's journey to the exposition in St. Louis was to have a dramatic impact on the next 15 years of his life. As scholar Kenneth Trapp has observed, Onken was enamored of the "contemporary designs of furniture and interiors from Germany and the Austro-Hungarian Empire that were first introduced to a large American audience at the Louisiana Purchase Exposition."[2] Unlike most casual visitors, however, Onken was not content simply to return to Cincinnati with illusive visions. Before leaving St. Louis he introduced himself to the acclaimed Budapest designer Paul Horti (1865–1907), who was an exhibitor at the exposition and who had already received numerous awards and recognition for his avant-garde furniture designs. The two quickly reached an agreement by which Horti, who had formerly worked for Charles Limbert in Grand Rapids, Michigan, was to begin designing furniture for the Oscar Onken Company.

By the fall of that same year ads were appearing in the *Saturday Evening Post* for Oscar Onken's new venture: The Shop of the Crafters, "Makers of Arts and Crafts Furniture, Hall Clocks, Shaving Stands, Cellarettes, Smokers' Cabinets and Mission Chairs."[3] Subsequently, ads also began appearing in other popular magazines, such as *Scribners, Harpers*, and *Literary Digest*. By 1906 Onken was prepared to issue his first catalog, featuring an extensive line of Arts and Crafts furniture for every room in the home.

The Shop of the Crafters at Cincinnati, as it was often referred to, featured "Furniture of Austrian Design" with a distinctive and unique flair. Horti often incorporated inlaid "marquetry panels of colored imported Austrian woods,"[4] which Onken described as being "out of the usual and not to be duplicated."[5] Unlike many of the firms that entered the Arts and Crafts market after it had been popularized by pioneers like Gustav Stickley and Elbert Hubbard, the Shop of the Crafters was not content to duplicate Craftsman furniture design. While their striking European flavor may have seemed a bit unorthodox for a severe American interpretation of the Arts and Crafts ideal, their designs were a refreshing change from the flood of Stickley imitators that were entering the market at the same time.

Onken brought to his new line of furniture two distinct skills. In addition to being an experienced businessman with sound promotional ideas, he also experimented with and developed a number of furniture finishes, including, as his catalog recommends, his "dull waxed finishes, such as Weathered, Fumed, Flemish, Austrian or Early English shades."[6] His advertisements and promotional material made reference to his work force, "comprised of a number of skilled Germans who represent the best handiwork of our day,"[7] reminiscent of Charles Limbert's proud references to his skilled staff of Dutch craftsmen and Albert Stickley's Russian coppersmiths.

In addition to stressing the quality handcraftsmanship of his German workers, Onken also appealed to the American desire to remain fashionable by European standards. As Trapp explains, Onken's advertisements implied that "by using Mission furniture purchased, of course, from the Shop of the Crafters, Americans could create rooms consonant with European high style to demonstrate that they were au courant in matters of international design."[8]

Trapp goes on: "The furniture that Onken manufactured, such as shaving stands, cellarettes, smokers' cabinets, and pieces for the library, traditionally the refuge of men, appealed directly to a male clientele. Moreover, the use of oak and leather and large metal fittings, the emphasis on muted earthen-colored stains and the massive forms of some of the furniture give it a distinct masculine character that accorded with the cultural norms of the turn of the century."[9]

The furniture produced by the Shop of the Crafters exhibits a variety of Arts and Crafts features. Most often it was produced in oak, although some mahogany, "dull or polished," was offered. In addition to Horti's unique inlay, pieces often displayed keyed tenons (though on occasion they were false tenons), Limbert-style cutouts, Art Nouveau-inspired stained and leaded glass, and variations of Mackmurdo-style feet not unlike those already in use by the Roycrofters and Stickley Brothers. Their advertisements described the hardware as being "old copper trimmings . . . old brass drawer pulls" and leather tops "heavily studded with old brass nails."[10] The Shop of the Crafters furniture also often featured strap hinges and beveled square brass knobs. Interestingly enough, elements of the Victorian era also appear occasionally, including claw feet, fancy drawer pulls, and applied trim.

The Shop of the Crafters shopmark apparently remained consistent throughout the 16 years the firm produced Arts and Crafts furniture. A gold paper label with black lettering reading "Shop of the Crafters" appears above a simple lantern, below which are found the words "at Cincinnati/Oscar Onken Co. Sole Owners."

Although its Arts and Crafts furniture production had ceased by 1920, the Oscar Onken Company remained in business until 1931. Onken passed away in 1948, at the age of 90, and was remembered in his obituaries not as the founder of the Shop of the Crafters but as "a prominent businessman and philanthropist, active in some of Cincinnati's most distinguished clubs and organizations."[11] The Shop of the Crafters furniture remained in the shadows for several decades, even after the recent revival of interest in the Arts and Crafts movement. Had it not been for the 1983 facsimile of its 1906 catalog and the research done by scholars such as Kenneth Trapp, the Shop of the Crafters might have been denied the recognition that it so well deserves. Fortunately, it received additional attention when an inlaid china cabinet, attributed to Paul Horti, was selected for "The Art That is Life" exhibition that premiered in Boston in 1987,[12] sustaining Oscar Onken's belief that "handmade things are slow in the making, and they are made by hand that style and distinction may be preserved, and that they may look as well fifty years hence as when first made."[13]

## SELECTED PRICES

A comprehensive price guide for the Shop of the Crafters furniture will be dependent on the identification of additional examples. While interest in the Shop of the Crafters furniture is growing, it remains to be seen how the market will respond to the additional pieces that are expected to surface as the furniture from this firm receives additional exposure. Until that time collectors are advised to consider carefully both the condition and the attractiveness of the design of any Shop of the Crafters furniture.

Armchair: #321, solid back with four vertical cutouts, inlaid panel in center, open arms, flared legs, attached leather seat, $500–$750

Bookcase: #360, single door with Art Nouveau-inspired leaded and stained glass, gallery top, copper hardware, molded base, 60" × 29" × 12", $1,500–$2,000

Cellarette: #264, overhanging top with copper tray, single solid door with strap hinges, solid sides with lower cutouts, shoe feet, interior with revolving bottle rack, paper label, 35" × 22" × 16", $800–$1,200

Chair, side: #320, solid back with four verticle cutouts, inlaid panel in center, flared legs, attached leather seat, 43" × 18", $250–$275; set of four, $1,200–$1,400

China cabinet: #326, single wide door flanked by four narrow doors, lower two with vertical inlaid panels, overhanging top, molded block base, 63" × 42" × 16", $1,750–$2,250

Clock: Van Dyke model with six leaded-glass panels, exposed tenon construction, brass numerals and bands, 74" × 20" × 13", $800–$1,200

Desk: #279, shaped crest over drop front and leaded-glass side doors, surface support over single drawer with dowel pulls, lower shelf, 46" × 42" × 18", $750–$1,000

Floor lamp: #153, Art Nouveau-inspired stained-glass shade with four panels, supported by four arms, flared base with three open shelves and oval cutouts, paper label, 72" × 24" × 24", $1,250–$1,750

Mirror, hall: #222 ½, center mirror flanked by inlaid peacock feathers, crest rail with small cutouts, five hat hooks, 26" × 40", $1,750–$2,250

Morris chair: #13, one wide slat under each arm, massive front legs, adjustable rod, two loose cushions, $1,500–$2,000

Morris chair: #333, flat arms supported by sides with multiple vertical cutouts, front legs inlaid, front apron arched, cushion seat and back, $3,500–$4,500

Rocking chair: #32, inlaid slat in back flanked by two plain slats, three slats under each arm, massive front posts tenoned through tops of arms, long corbels with false through tenons on each front post, loose cushion seat, $800–$1,200

Settee: #34, back divided into two matching sections, each with middle inlaid slat flanked by four plain slats, three slats under each arm, massive front posts tenoned through tops of arms, long corbels with false through tenons on each front post, two loose cushions, $1,000–$1,500

Sideboard, inlaid: #323, arched mirror and gallery surface, long drawer over two inlaid cabinet doors centering three half-drawers and open shelf, molded base, 58" × 54" × 25", $3,500–$4,500.

Table, library: #116, overhanging top supported by sides with large rectangular cutouts, lower shelf, 30" × 48" × 30", $800–$1,200

## Stickley Brothers, Inc.

SHOPMARKS: (Early) Oval paper label MADE BY
STICKLEY BROS. CO./GRAND RAPIDS, MICH.
(Later) Brass tag or decal QUAINT FURNITURE/
STICKLEY BROS. CO./GRAND RAPIDS, MICH.;
branded QUAINT with stylized letters S and B.

PRINCIPAL CONTRIBUTIONS: General line of Arts and Crafts furniture, plus
metalware and lighting.

FOUNDERS: Albert Stickley, born: 1862, died: 1928. John George Stickley,
born: 1871, died: 1921, founded: 1891, closed: ca. 1940.

WORKSHOPS AND SALESROOMS: *The Stickley Brothers Company, Binghamton,
New York, 1884–1890. Stickley Brothers, Inc., Grand Rapids, Michigan,
1891-ca. 1940.*

> "A chair ought to be well built and its structural qualities should be ex-
> emplified in two ways: first, the greatest possible amount of structural
> strength and dignity should be obtained with the smallest amount of
> wood; next, the wood must be handled expertly as wood, and not
> made to simulate properties of any other material."
> —Albert Stickley, 1909[1]

Unusual Stickley Brothers settle with four-sided posts topped with finials,
column-shaped slats to back and sides, the top rails cut out and carved in a
stylized floral motif, with new brown leather drop-in seat. Refinished, good
condition. Unmarked, 41" × 75" × 30", $6,900

Had the five Stickley brothers–Gustav, Albert, Charles, Leopold, and John–been able to control their strong, independent spirits and to combine their individual talents–Gustav's eye for design, Albert's marketing techniques, Charles's production talents, Leopold's management skills, and John's sales ability–they could well have built a furniture empire that would have survived long after Arts and Crafts furniture fell out of favor. Instead, they eventually formed their own competing furniture companies which flourished while the Arts and Crafts movement was in full bloom, but which eventually withered as furniture styles changed.[2]

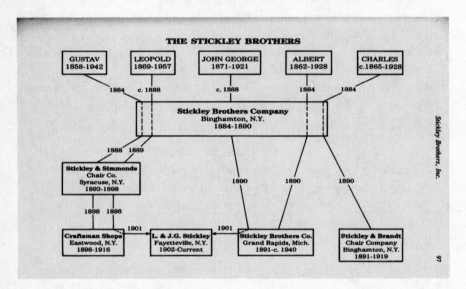

The Stickley children did not have an easy childhood. Their parents, Leopold and Barbara, had emigrated from Germany, married in America, and settled on a small farm in Wisconsin, where they struggled to support a growing family. Financial hardship took its toll on the marriage, and the couple separated in 1875, leaving Barbara to raise the six children who still remained at home.[3] She moved her family from their home in rural Wisconsin to Brandt, Pennsylvania, where Gustav, Albert, and Charles went to work in their uncle's small chair factory. By 1882 Gus had become foreman of the factory, which reportedly could manufacture thousands of chairs a year.[4] Albert, now 20, undoubtedly learned every aspect of the chair manufacturing business in the Brandt plant.

In 1883 the three older brothers formed what was to be known as the Stickley Brothers Company, which sold and later manufactured popular reproduction period chairs. Their business grew rapidly, and by early 1888 it appears that all five brothers were working together in the Stickley Brothers firm. That same year, however, Gustav left to pursue other projects, coaxing

Unusual Stickley Brothers drink stand with square inset top and three round-bottom slats to each side. Good original finish and condition. Paper label and stenciled number, 24¼" × 15" sq., $920

Leopold to join him the following year, Albert, Charles, and John kept the family business going in Binghamton, New York. In 1891 another division occurred. Charles and Schuyler Brandt, their uncle and financial backer, took over the operation in Binghamton, which was soon to be renamed the Stickley and Brandt Chair Company, while Albert and John moved to Grand Rapids, Michigan, taking with them the name Stickley Brothers Company. The two brothers worked together in Grand Rapids until 1900, when John moved back to New York to establish yet another Stickley furniture factory in partnership with brother Leopold. Leopold had previously been working as a foreman in Gustav's Eastwood, New York, factory, overseeing the production of a new line of Arts and Crafts furniture.

By 1901, then, the picture was nearly in focus: Gustav was designing and manufacturing Arts and Crafts furniture in his Eastwood shops; Charles was a partner and general manager of Stickley and Brandt in Binghamton; Leopold and John George were making plans to form the L. & J. G. Stickley Company in Fayetteville, New York; and Albert had maintained the name Stickley Brothers Company in Grand Rapids. Within five years, all four firms would be nationally recognized manufacturers of Arts and Crafts furniture—and rivals with one another in a highly competitive market.

While Gustav quickly became the most widely publicized of the five Stickley brothers, Albert worked very diligently in his older brother's long shadow. He was among the first American furniture manufacturers to reverse the centuries-old tradition of importing furniture from England. From 1897 until 1902 he shipped unfinished furniture from his Michigan base of operations to his London factory, where it was assembled and finished by 75 workers before being sold to the English public.

Marketing was not the only area in which Albert Stickley was unafraid to experiment. In the early years of the new century, before Harvey Ellis had an opportunity to introduce his inlaid designs to Gustav Stickley in 1903, Timothy A. Conti was executing exquisite inlay for Albert Stickley, often in forms directly influenced by both Japanese art and the innovative English and Scottish schools of design. As early as 1901 Albert was also producing high-quality furniture featuring circular, heart-shaped, and abstract cutouts, a clear reflection of his admiration for the work of the British designers C. R. Mackintosh and Charles Voysey.

Albert's adoption of the British term for the Arts and Crafts style of furniture – "Quaint" – as part of his trademark is another indication of the impact the British designers had on the Stickley Brothers firm. Just as Gustav believed the furniture of this period would someday be referred to as Craftsman furniture, D. Robertson Smith, a major designer for Albert Stickley, predicted in 1902 that "this new school of furniture and decoration. . . will most likely be called 'Quaint,' for that is what it has been called in the country to which we are indebted for it, namely, Scotland."[5]

It is apparent from the Stickley Brothers furniture that has surfaced in recent years that Albert was far more than just another furniture designer attempting to capitalize on the popularity of Mission oak. He hired and utilized some of the best furniture designers of the day, including Smith, who remained with the firm from 1902 until 1915, and Arthur Teal, who had studied in Scotland before joining Albert in 1904. At the same time that his designers were creating costly inlaid, carved, and cutout furniture, however, Albert Stickley's workers were also producing lines of less ornate, less expensive furniture, much of which was purchased for use in meeting halls, offices, and other businesses, "as well," according to his advertisements, "as for the club, the cafe [and] the hotel."[6]

In the introduction to his 1908 catalog, Albert Stickley declares that "Quaint Furniture in Arts and Crafts has made ideals possible which might otherwise have been impossible – has brought within the means of those with even the most modest of incomes the possibility of artistic homes."[7] Even so, at a time when a typical factory worker was being paid an average of $10 per week, a standard Stickley Brothers ladderback side chair was selling for $8, and a five-legged, round oak dining room table for $38. Gustav Stickley, in his 1910 catalog, advertised a similar chair for $6.50 and a table for $47. In contrast, Sears, Roebuck & Company was then selling pressed-back dining room chairs with leather seats for $3 and a five-legged dining room table for only $12.

Stickley Brothers furniture was produced primarily in oak, though a number of pieces were turned out in mahogany after 1907. "Quality is always sought," the 1908 catalog states, "even in the most trivial details. All drawer ends are solid black walnut. The joints are all the old fashioned tongue-and-groove kind."[8] Many pieces have a unique concave lower leg, apparently a modification of the Arthur Mackmurdo foot design, which the Roycrofters also often duplicated. Despite Albert's romantic description of his copper workers—whose "experience is augmented by the teachings of their fathers and their fathers' fathers, all copper workers for generations"[9] rarely will Stickley Brothers hardware equal the weight and quality of that found on Craftsman furniture. Comparisons with hardware advertised at the same time by the Grand Rapids Brass Company leads to the conclusion that, like several other Arts and Crafts firms, Stickley Brothers purchased hardware in large quantities from specialty metal shops.[10]

Like his brothers, Albert Stickley adopted the practice of affixing a shopmark to much of his furniture. Of the brand, paper label, gold decal, and metal tag shopmarks Stickley Brothers used, only the early oval paper label does not carry the trade name "Quaint." The decal, paper label, and metal tag make bold and clear reference to the factory location in Grand Rapids, proof that Albert Stickley did not intend customers to confuse his shopmark or his furniture with that of any of his brothers in New York.

What has happened on more than one occasion, however, is that a damaged Stickley Brothers paper label has mysteriously lost those portions containing the words "Brothers" and "Grand Rapids, Mich." The result can be a paper label simply reading "Stickley"—and a price tag that would be more appropriate on a piece of Gustav Stickley furniture. Fortunately, if a collector becomes familiar with the shopmarks of both Gustav and Albert Stickley, such incidents will not prove confusing. Many times the outline of the oval label or unique brass tag will still be evident in the wood even though the shopmark itself may be missing.

While Albert Stickley was a successful Mission oak manufacturer, the majority of the Stickley Brothers' most pleasing designs are those that appear to be copies or slight modifications of his older brother's Craftsman furniture. After 1904 Stickley Brothers furniture designs failed to progress with any consistency. And as the 1908 catalog demonstrates, when Albert's craftsmen ventured off into their own designs, such as their buffets and china cupboards, Quaint furniture often suffered from either a degree of misproportion, a disturbing lack of harmony, or mediocre workmanship.

The large volume of utilitarian furniture bearing the Stickley Brothers shopmark has adversely affected the firm's current reputation and status as designers and manufacturers of quality Arts and Crafts furniture. The fact that Albert was able to survive the swing away from Mission oak furniture after 1915 is a tribute to his business ability, but the ready availability of the transitional furniture (characterized by spiral-turned legs) his firm produced

Stickley Brothers two-drawer library table with overhanging rectangular top, copper drop pulls, slatted sides, double stretcher, on Mackmurdo-style feet. Original finish to base, refinished top. Unmarked, on casters (one broken), 29½" × 46" × 29¾", $1,380

between 1914 and his death in 1928 has tarnished his reputation as an Arts and Crafts manufacturer.

Astute collectors, however, have recognized that much of the early Stickley Brothers furniture is destined to increase in both demand and value. Early inlaid and cutout designs have already begun selling above their pre-sale estimates at major Arts and Crafts auctions. As additional research is conducted, such as that presented in 1987 by Don Marek in his book *Arts and Crafts Furniture Design: The Grand Rapids Contribution 1895–1915*, much of the early, high-quality furniture produced by Albert Stickley will undoubtedly step out of the shadow cast by his older brother.

## SELECTED PRICES

Model numbers, when applicable, correspond with those in the catalog reprint *Quaint Furniture* (New York: Turn of the Century Editions, 1981). Unless otherwise indicated, all examples are made from oak and retain their original finish exhibiting normal wear. Prices reflect leather seats and cushions that are either badly worn or have been replaced with appropriate materials.

Armchair: #873, three vertical slats in back, open arms, drop-in seat, 37" × 19" × 19", $175–$250

Armchair: #389 ½, three slats under each arm, loose cushion back and seat, arms notched around front posts, 38" × 19" × 21", $300–$350

Bookcase: double doors with one large pane each, overhanging top with flared supports, hammered copper pulls, canted feet, 58" × 42" × 12", $1,100–$1,500

Bookcase: #4690, double doors, each with two small panes above one large, recessed top, exposed tenons on front posts, straight toe board, metal pulls, 56" × 36" × 13", $1,100–$1,500

Bookcase, revolving: four corner posts extending through top, four-sided center section pivoting on cross-stretchers, 32" × 25" × 25", $800–$900

Chair, side: #412 ½, three vertical slats in back, wraparound leather seat, concave feet, 37" × 19" × 16", $90–$100; set of four, $400–$500

China cabinet: #8745, arched crest rail with plate rack, overhanging top, double doors with single large pane each, adjustable shelves, metal hardware, 61" × 32" × 14", $1,400–$1,800

Clock, tall: four corner posts joined by stretchers, sides and back consisting of thin slats, open face with brass numerals, brass pendulum and weights, 79" × 20" × 15", $500–$600

Costumer: double posts supported by four flared feet, copper hooks on posts and joining stretchers, 70" × 16" × 20", $550–$650

Desk: #6500, drop front with decorative strap hinges, gallery top, two short drawers over two long, lower open shelf flanked by two pairs of cutouts in sides, exposed tenons in sides, metal pulls, 48" × 36" × 14", $900–$1,000

Footstool: #674–5265, upholstered insert, narrow stretchers, rectangular framework, 12" × 18" × 12", $200–$250

Footstool: leather-covered, with seven spindles on each narrow end, 12' × 20' × 16", $1,100–$1,300

Magazine stand: three spindles on either side with four open shelves, each with backsplash, 39" × 26" × 13", $700–$800

Morris chair: #343, three vertical slats under each arm, supported by four corbels, front posts tenoned through tops of arms, two loose cushions, adjustable back, 38" × 21" × 22", $1,750–$2,000

Morris chair: #780 ½, open arms, front posts tenoned through tops of arms, no corbels, stretcher around seat, drop-in spring cushion seat, adjustable back, 36" × 21" × 20", $600–$750

Rocking chair: #790, three short vertical slats in back over lower back upholstered section, drop-in seat, open arms, front posts tenoned through tops of arms, 36" × 19" × 20", $250–$300

Rocking chair: #910, four short vertical slats in back over two horizontal slats, open arms, no corbels, drop-in spring seat, 35" × 20" × 20", $250–$300

Rocking chair: four vertical slats across back, three beneath each arm, front posts tenoned through arms, floor-length corbels, drop-in spring seat, 37" × 28" × 30", $350–$450

Settle: #905–3865, even-arm, with narrow vertical slats cut out with repeating arches, slightly canted sides, cushion seat on slats, 36" × 84" × 29", $2,500–$3,000

Sideboard: #8610, open plate rail with five short slats on overhanging top, two upper drawers over open shelf over two lower drawers, metal hardware, 46" × 54" × 21", $800–$1,100

Sideboard: overhanging top supporting paneled plate rail, two split drawers over two half-drawers centered by two cabinet doors, arched corbels on legs, 46" × 60" × 22", $950–$1,200

Stand, drink: #2615, circular overhanging copper top over four flared legs, arched aprons, 28" × 18", $900–$1,200

Table, dining: #2640, overhanging top supported by five square legs, wide apron, three leaves, 30" × 54", $1,100–$1,500

Table, lamp: #2504, circular overhanging top supported by four legs, lower square shelf resting on cross-stretchers, exposed tenons, 30" × 26" diameter, $450–$500

Table, lamp: circular top notched around four legs, lower square shelf, concave feet, 30" × 20" diameter, $350–$400

Table, library: #2606, overhanging top over single long drawer with metal hardware, two vertical slats at either end, lower shelf, 30" × 24" × 36", $850–$950

Taboret: #314 ½, circular overhanging top supported by three flared legs joined by triangular lower shelf, exposed tenons, 18" × 15" diameter, $350–$450

## Charles Stickley and Stickley and Brandt

SHOPMARKS: (Early) Rectangular decal with STICKLEY & BRANDT CHAIR COMPANY/signature, CHARLES STICKLEY/GENL. MGR.
(Later) Impressed signature CHARLES STICKLEY.

PRINCIPAL CONTRIBUTIONS: Chairs, rockers, and dining room furniture.

FOUNDERS: Charles Stickley, born: ca. 1865, died: ca. 1928. Schuyler C. Brandt, born: unknown, died: ca. 1913, founded: 1891, closed: 1919.

WORKSHOPS AND SALES ROOMS: The Stickley Brothers, Binghamton, New York, 1884–91. Stickley and Brandt Chair Company, Inc., Binghamton, New York, 1891–1919.

"You can visit the prominent Furniture stores in the large cities, and you will hear on every hand that "Stickley's Furniture" has a reputation for quality. Good furniture is a permanent investment and one of the requisites of comfortable living—not a luxury, but a necessity."
—*Stickley-Brandt Furniture Company catalog, 1908*[1]

The forgotten brother of the Stickley family, Charles, has remained something of a mystery for Arts and Crafts historians. His career has been pieced together primarily through fragmented references found among the records of his more publicized brothers, such as in a 1906 *Furniture Journal* magazine article, which reported that around 1874 "three of the boys were old enough to work and the chair factory [of their mother's relatives] needed hands. It was a far cry from Stillwater [Minnesota] to Binghamton, but the trip was made, and Gustav, Charles and Albert Stickley were put to work in the factory. . . . In the course of events Gustav became the general foreman of the factory; Charles became skilled in the weaving of rush fibre seats, then much used in chair making, while Albert showed skill in decorating old Boston rockers, which were among the products of the factory."[2] Charles, who would have

Charles Stickley trestle table with broad lower shelf keyed through double planks. Good original finish and condition with some staining to top. Unmarked, 28½" × 48" × 30", $920

been around 14 at the time, undoubtedly learned a great deal while working in the bustling chair factory over the course of the next 10 years.

By 1884 the three older Stickley brothers, perhaps with a loan from their mother's family, had established a new furniture business, selling a variety of styles of chairs to both the wholesale and the retail trade from a storefront in Binghamton, New York. Two years later, again, perhaps, with family assistance, the Stickley Brothers Company expanded, adding the machinery necessary to produce their own line of simple Colonial chairs. When Gustav left in 1888 to pursue other interests, Charles and Albert remained in Binghamton and continued to run the Stickley Brothers Company.

In 1890, when Albert and John George Stickley decided to move to Grand Rapids, Michigan, to establish a new Stickley Brothers Company, Charles chose to remain in Binghamton, where, in December of 1891, the Stickley and Brandt Chair Company was incorporated. Charles, 31, was named the new general manager. His uncle, Schuyler Brandt, was listed as president in the firm's incorporation papers, but given that business directories during the time the Stickley and Brandt Chair Company was in business cite Brandt's home address as Oak Park, Illinois, it would appear that Charles Stickley was solely responsible for the daily operation of the company.

Despite the defection and eventual competition of the other brothers, Stickley and Brandt continued to grow. In 1900, according to Binghamton public records, the company purchased a larger and better-equipped facility and soon had "one of the best factories in the city with a large force of men."[3] In 1905, Charles was listed as the factory superintendent and manager. It appears that at that time the Stickley and Brandt Chair Company was still selling period reproduction furniture, for the record goes on to state that they were "turning out an excellent line of chairs and fancy furniture which is sold in large quantities in all parts of the country."[4]

If they were not manufacturing Mission oak-style furniture in 1905, they were soon after. It is difficult to interpret what was meant by "large quantities" of furniture, but when the number of surviving examples of signed Stickley and Brandt furniture is compared with that of Gustav, L. & J. G., or Albert Stickley, it would appear that Stickley and Brandt produced a limited line of Mission oak furniture. As both the 1904 and 1908 catalogs reveal,[5] the Stickley and Brandt Chair Company was also a large mail-order distributor, with over 72 types of chairs (most manufactured by other firms) to choose from: fancy golden oak, Queen Anne, Art Nouveau, even wicker, but no Mission oak. In addition, Stickley and Brandt offered fancy parlor and bedroom suites and served as sales representatives for both Macy sectional bookcases and the Hoosier Kitchen Cabinet Company.

Like his brother, Charles Stickley instructed his workers to affix a shopmark to the Arts and Crafts furniture they produced. At least two forms have surfaced, the first of which is a yellow rectangular decal trimmed in red and bearing the words "Stickley & Brandt Chair Company" above the signature of Charles Stickley and his title "GENL.MGR." The Stickley and Brandt decals have been found on Mission oak arm chairs and rocking chairs with heavy structural features: wide slats, exposed wide tenons, double pegged joints, wide arms, and massive (2' × 4') front legs. The decal has most often been found on the rear seat apron of these particular chairs.

In what would appear by design to be later, lighter chairs, in which there were no pegs or exposed tenons and no unusually massive boards, the decal was replaced by an incised script signature of Charles Stickley. In nearly every instance the signature was stamped into the center of the rear apron of the chair. The exact date at which the Stickley and Brandt Chair Company decal was replaced by the Charles Stickley signature is unknown, but it may have been around 1913, shortly after Schuyler Brandt's death.

Although he obviously changed the shopmark at some time during the reign of Arts and Crafts furniture, Charles Stickley either could not or chose not to change the name of the original corporation, for Binghamton court records indicate that the firm of Stickley and Brandt Chair Company, Inc., declared bankruptcy in 1919—nearly four years after Gustav Stickley's Craftsman empire had crumbled.

It is interesting to speculate why, in 1918, when Leopold, John George, Albert, and a reluctant Gustav formed the Stickley Associated Cabinetmakers, Inc., Charles either declined their invitation or was not asked to join the new firm. In any event, by 1928 John George, Albert, and Charles had all passed away, Gustav was living with his daughter in quiet retirement, and only Leopold remained active in the furniture business, overseeing the production of Colonial reproductions until his death in 1957.

It cannot be denied that Charles Stickley, along with numerous other manufacturers, openly duplicated many popular Craftsman designs, but not all of the workmanship exhibited on his furniture deserves to be characterized as inferior. While verifiable examples of the work of Stickley and Brandt are relatively scarce compared with works by any of the other Stickleys, examples of the firm's early chairs, rockers, and settles reveal the use of quartersawn oak, pegged joints, massive front legs, leather upholstery, and exposed tenons. Although in these examples their designs may suffer in comparison with those of Gustav Stickley, no apology need be made for their workmanship.

In other examples, one particular china cupboard closely resembling Gustav Stickley's model No. 803 exhibits materials and workmanship equal to that displayed in the *Craftsman* Shops' original version. In another example, a set of four ladder-back side chairs stamped with Charles Stickley's signature and clearly modeled after a standard Craftsman design (No. 370) featured quartersawn oak, authentic leather upholstery, a durable original finish, and sturdy construction, even though none of the joints were pegged.

Although Charles Stickley occasionally produced quality Mission oak furniture, a large part of his work suffered from a lack of consistency. Too often, it seems, when the workmanship excelled, the design faltered; when the design excelled, the workmanship faltered. For that reason, each piece of Charles Stickley or Stickley and Brandt furniture must be closely examined and evaluated on the basis of the design, the materials, and the workmanship. When all three are in harmony, the result may well be a fine example of Arts and Crafts furniture.

## SELECTED PRICES

Although the Stickley and Brandt Chair Company remained in business longer than Gustav Stickley did, fewer examples of its Mission oak furniture have surfaced than of any of the other Stickley brothers. Arts and Crafts furniture production was not the firms primary concern but represented only a small portion of its large wholesale chair distribution. As was stated earlier, Stickley and Brandt and Charles Stickley Mission oak furniture varies considerably in the quality of materials, design, and workmanship; thus, the collector should use only the few representative prices included in this study as a basis from which to begin a careful appraisal. Unless otherwise indicated, all examples are made from oak and retain their original finish exhibiting normal wear. Prices reflect leather seats and cushions that are either badly worn or have been replaced with appropriate materials.

Armchair: three wide vertical slats across the back, open arms, massive front posts with exposed tenons from the seat apron, drop-in spring seat, 34' × 29' × 22", $800–$1,200

Armchair: four vertical slats in back, open arms, plank seat, impressed signature on rear seat apron, 36" × 26" × 21 ", $175–$250

Bookcase: double door, each with eight panes formed by gridwork of mullions over large sheets of glass, gallery top, straight toe board, 56" × 48" × 12", $2,000–$3,000

Chair, side: three horizontal slats across the back, wide stretchers, wraparound leather seat, 36" × 17" × 16", $85–$95; set of four, $400–$450

China cabinet: (similar to Craftsman #803) overhanging top, single door with large pane of glass, arched toe board, Gustav Stickley hardware, 60" × 36" × 15", $2,000–$2,500

Desk, drop-front: slant front opening to reveal fitted interior, narrow splashboard across top, two short drawers over one long, open base, 39" × 30" × 14", $500–$750

Rocking chair: three vertical slats across the back, open arms, massive front posts with exposed tenons from the seat apron, drop-in spring seat, 34" × 29" × 26", $400–$450

Sideboard: overhanging top supporting tall, paneled plate rail, three drawers centered by two cabinet doors over long drawer, Gustav Stickley hardware, 53" × 56" × 22", $2,000–$2,500

## Gustav Stickley and the *Craftsman* Workshops

SHOPMARKS: (1902–1903) Red decal: joiner's compass around words ALS IK KAN with STICKLEY in script enclosed in a rectangle below it (see Shopmark A)

(1903–1904) Red decal: same as before, but with entire decal also enclosed in a rectangle (see Shopmark B)

(1904–1912) Red decal or black ink: joiner's compass around words ALS IK KAN with GUSTAV STICKLEY in script below it, no rectangle (see Shopmark C)

(1912–1916) Black brand: joiner's compass around words ALS IK KAN with STICK-LEY in script below it, no rectangle (similar to Shopmark C, but without word GUSTAV)

*Paper Labels:* (1905–1907) Large paper label: joiner's compass and words CRAFTSMAN WORKSHOPS-GUSTAV STICKLEY in block letters, all in dark circle; GUSTAV STICKLEY in script over EASTWOOD, N.Y.

(1907–1912) Large paper label with "CRAFTS-MAN" across top; joiner's compass with

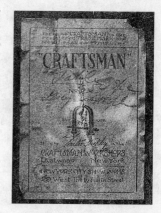

GUSTAV STICKLEY in script; Eastwood and N.Y. City addresses (see Shipmark D).

(1912–1916) Large paper label with CRAFTSMAN across top; joiner's compass with STICKLEY in script; only Eastwood, N.Y. location included.

PRINCIPAL CONTRIBUTIONS: Oak furniture, metalware, lighting fixtures.

FOUNDER: Gustav Stickley. Born: 1858, died: 1942, founded: 1898, closed: 1916.

WORKSHOPS AND SALESROOMS: The Stickley Brothers, Binghamton, New York, 1884–88. Stickley & Simmonds, Syracuse, New York, 1893–98. The United Crafts, Eastwood, New York, 1898–1904. Craftsman Workshops, Eastwood, New York, 1905–16.

> "In the beginning there was no thought of creating a new style, only a recognition of the fact that we should have in our homes something better suited to our needs and more expressive of our character as a people than imitations of the traditional styles, and a conviction that the best way to get something better was to go directly back to plain principles of construction and apply them to the making of simple, strong, comfortable furniture."
> —*Gustav Stickley, 1909*[1]

Gustav Stickley, unlike the vast majority of American furniture manufacturers who produced a line of Mission oak, not only believed in the principles of

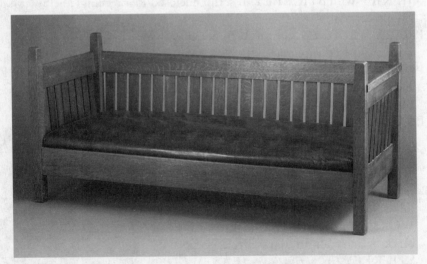

Fine Gustav Stickley settle #222 with tapering posts, tightly spaced canted slats to back and sides, and leather-upholstered drop-in seat. Fine original finish and condition, minor veneer chips and lifting on legs. Red decal, 36" × 80" × 32", $11,500

the movement founded by Ruskin and Morris, but also helped to spread the word of the reform movement throughout the country. Regardless of whether it began as a conscious decision, from 1900 until his bankruptcy in 1915, "he designed a new kind of American furniture, promulgated the Arts and Crafts philosophy to an educated and influential segment of the public and created a domestic architecture in which both his furniture and his philosophy were at home."[2]

Gustav Stickley was a stubborn and steadfast man with a creative and fiercely independent spirit. He demonstrated from the beginning of his career that he was unafraid to walk away from financial security in search of his beliefs and a form in which he could express them. Once discovered, he held to them doggedly, even in the face of financial ruin; yet he was also able to recognize that the early Arts and Crafts movement founders "have striven for a definite and intentional expression of art that was largely for art's sake and had little to do with satisfying the plain needs of the people. "[3]

Though initially trained by his father in Wisconsin to be a stonemason, Stickley began his career as a furniture maker at the age of 17 in his uncle's modest chair factory in Brandt, Pennsylvania. Lured by the prospect of self-employment, Gustav encouraged two of his brothers, Albert and Charles, to start with him in 1883 the Stickley Brothers Company in nearby Binghamton, New York. Four years later, about the time that their success as manufacturers and retailers of period reproduction furniture would have been assured, Gustav broke away to experiment with a variety of projects and careers, but returned to period furniture production in 1893 in yet another partnership.

Gustav Stickley tall spindle-back armchair with spindles to the floor and long corbels under the arms and tan leather loose cushion on sling seat. Excellent original finish, normal wear to front stretcher, one replaced spindle to back. Small red decal, 39½" × 27" × 22", $4,887

Five years later that partnership also dissolved, and after a year's sojourn in England and Europe, Gustav Stickley returned to establish what would eventually be known as the Craftsman Workshops in Eastwood, New York. His travels abroad had taken him into the homes and studios of many of the leading designers of the Arts and Crafts movement, and he returned to the United States determined to establish his personal interpretation of the medieval guild system. His idealized vision of United Crafts evolved into the Craftsman Workshops, a more conventional factory system, but Gustav nevertheless strove to design and produce "furniture which would be simple, durable, comfortable and fitted for the place it was to occupy and the work it had to do."[4]

Gustav Stickley's first public exhibition of his Arts and Crafts furniture took place in 1900 at the semiannual Grand Rapids furniture show and led to a brief arrangement in which he provided, without public recognition, furniture for the Tobey Furniture Company, a Chicago furniture manufacturer and retailer. Examples of this early Stickley furniture can be identified only by comparison with that pictured in the Tobey ads[5] or by a Tobey paper label, since Gustav had not yet begun affixing his own shopmark to his work. (See The Tobey Furniture Company.)

The line of furniture that he soon thereafter began selling under his own shopmark displayed heavy structural features, such as keyed tenons and chamfered boards, as well as pegged joints, forged or hammered hardware, wide chair stretchers, and flaked quartersawn oak. In 1903, however, Stickley hired the itinerant architect Harvey Ellis, whose subsequent furniture designs "brought a new sense of lightness and color to the Craftsman Workshops."[6] Although Ellis died tragically just nine months later, his influence

Gustav Stickley double-door bookcase with gallery top, eight glass panes to each door with hammered copper V-pulls, and three interior shelves, the top and bottom mortised through the sides. Refinished, small chip to apron. Red decal and Craftsman paper label, 56¼" × 42¾" × 13", $5,175

Gustav Stickley plant stand #660 with a square top over a broad apron and flaring legs. Refinished, reglued top, base somewhat loose. Remnant of paper label, 20" × 18" sq., $600–$900

can be traced through Stickley designs for the next 12 years. (See Harvey Ellis.)

As a result of his experience with Ellis, an ever-changing public taste, and his own design evolution, Stickley's later furniture had less emphasis on structural details. Exposed tenons diminished in size and number; keyed tenons were almost eliminated; legs and chair stretchers were reduced in size; and plywood panels replaced chamfered board backs. For a few years, beginning in 1905, spindles replaced slats in a number of chairs and settles, though hand-hammered hardware, pegged joints, leather upholstery, and quarter-sawn oak remained standard on nearly all Craftsman furniture. In the years just prior to his bankruptcy in 1915, many of Stickley's designs suffered from too much reduction in structural expression: curved aprons were replaced by stagnant straight boards, strap hinges were dropped altogether, chair stretchers shrank, and keyed and even exposed tenons became scarce. Although it has been argued that his furniture thus became pure in form, much of it pales in comparison with his earlier "simple, strong and comfortable furniture."[7]

Perhaps the most famous of all Arts and Crafts shopmarks, the Gustav Stickley joiner's compass appeared in one form or another on nearly all of his furniture produced between 1902 and 1916. Within each compass appear the Flemish words "Als ik kan," loosely translated, "As best I can." Prior to 1904, only his last name appeared on the red decal; but when his youngest brothers, Leopold and John George, continued to expand their Arts and Crafts line of furniture only a few miles away, Gustav added his first name to the Craftsman shopmark, where it remained until 1912, the same year L. & J. G. Stickley suddenly changed its red shopmark to one totally different from that of Gustav's (see L. & J. G. Stickley). Although Gustav must have felt that the

Gustav Stickley hardware.

new shopmark would erase any confusion on the part of the public, when he dropped his first name from his shopmark, he also switched from using decals to a permanent brand.

Stickley's shopmark appears repeatedly in certain locations on his furniture. Side chairs, footstools, and settles often reveal one on either the inside or

Early Gustav Stickley magazine stand with paneled sides and four shelves under an arched apron. Refinished, missing tacks. Unmarked, 35¼" × 15" × 14¼", $2,415

Fine and rare Gustav Stickley blanket chest with paneled top and sides joined by wrought-iron strap hardware. Excellent original finish. Red 1902-03 "in-box" decal, 18" × 34¾" × 19¾", $31,625

the outside of the rear stretcher. Rocking chairs, armchairs, and adjustable Morris chairs may have a decal underneath either arm or on a rear stretcher. Library tables and desks may have either a red decal inside the drawer or a brand on the outside of the drawer. Case pieces, such as bookcases and china cupboards, will often have a red decal centered near the top of the back and may be accompanied by a large rectangular paper label. Labels also appear on the bottoms of upholstered seats and tables after 1904, but many of them, like many of the red decals, were later destroyed by upholsterers and refinishers.

Undoubtedly, the most highly valued Gustav Stickley furniture is that from the experimental line of inlaid furniture designed by Harvey Ellis between June and December 1903. The inlay proved to be too expensive to put into production and may have come too close to compromising Gustav's desire "to do away with all needless ornamentation."[8] In 1905 the Craftsman Workshops began producing a line of patented spindle furniture. The new line included Morris chairs, footstools, a library table with spindles at either end, a settle, and several varieties of chairs, most of which were produced until 1909, but fine examples are considered relatively scarce.

Other highly desirable characteristics sought in Craftsman furniture include arched aprons, stretchers, and toe boards; wide, overhanging tops; strap hinges across buffet doors; settles and chairs with sides the same height as the back; bookcases and china cupboards with gently bowed sides; and desks and tables with original leather tops. Library tables, rocking chairs, and dining chairs are the most commonly found examples of Craftsman

Rare and early Gustav Stickley chest of drawers with V-shaped backsplash, two short drawers over four long ones with hammered copper pulls, chamfered sides. Mint original condition. Blackened paper label and red decal, 52½" × 52½" × 21¾", $36,800

furniture; bedroom furniture—especially tall chests of drawers and full-size beds—are among the most difficult to locate.

One of the lingering unanswered questions regarding Craftsman furniture involves plant production. Whereas Morris and Ruskin advocated handcraftsmanship, their American counterparts—most notably Gustav Stickley, Frank Lloyd Wright, and Elbert Hubbard—recognized that woodworking machines not only could eliminate much of the drudgery associated with cabinetmaking but could also reduce the time, materials, and cost involved in furniture production, thus making their furniture available to people of moderate incomes. Publicly, Stickley and Hubbard emphasized the

Fine and early Gustav Stickley for Tobey circular table, the top carved and incised with a celandine poppy motif, over cutout cross stretchers keyed through carved, floriform legs. (Very rare design marking the transition from the Art Nouveau to Arts & Crafts aesthetic.) Mint finish, good condition with reglued top. Partial paper label with catalog reference, 24" × 20", $11,500

handcraftsmanship that went into each piece of furniture they produced, preferring not to draw attention to the number of electric planers, tenoners, shapers, and mortisers in their factories.[9] In contrast, L. & J. G. Stickley claimed that its furniture was "built in a scientific manner, [and] does not attempt to follow the traditions of a bygone day."[10]

Regardless of the impression left by either his magazine articles or his catalog introductions, the fact remains that for the largest part of 16 years Gustav Stickley employed approximately 200 craftsmen working six days each week in a well-equipped furniture factory.[11] Calculating precisely how many Morris chairs, simple footstools, or double-door bookcases would have been made in that span requires additional information yet unavailable. When other factors are taken into consideration however, such as Stickley's continued factory expansion; the gradual elimination of time-consuming inlay, spindles, keyed tenons, chamfered backs, and arched toe-boards; the impressive number of major retail stores across the country that sold Crafts-man furniture; the number of designs offered each year in his catalogs; and the fact that at a time when the average factory worker made less than $500 per year, Gustav Stickley drew more than that amount each month[12]—it be-comes evident that the *Craftsman* Workshops were both efficient and prolific. With a few notable exceptions, today's perceived scarcity may be due to the fact that much of Stickley's furniture remains unrecognized, continuing to serve the practical roles for which it was intended in homes where parents or grandparents purchased it either new or used little more than 70 years ago. Too substantial to throw out, too well-made to wear out, it may have been relegated to the basement, back porch, or storage room and in some cases painted or refinished. But chances are the majority of what was originally

Rare and early Gustav Stickley window bench with rails mortised through the sides, keyed-through broad lower stretcher and tacked-on leather covered seat.
Unmarked, 26½" × 25" × 18½", $5,175

Set of ten Gustav Stickley "V-back" side chairs with vertical backslats and tacked-on new brown leather seats. Original finish with differing degrees of edge wear and tightness. Red box decal, 36" × 18¾" × 16¾", $17,500–$22,500

produced, whatever that number, is still in existence. And as Gustav Stickley predicted in 1910. "in fifty or a hundred years [it] will be worth many times its first cost, for the time is coming when good oak furniture will be as valuable on account of its permanent worth and also of its scarcity."[13]

## SELECTED PRICES

Model numbers correspond with those appearing in the *Stickley Furniture Catalogs* (New York: Dover Publications, 1979) and the *Collected Works of Gustav Stickley* (New York: Turn of the Century Editions, 1981). Unless otherwise indicated, all examples are made from oak and retain their original finish exhibiting normal wear. Prices reflect leather seats and cushions which are either badly worn or have been replaced with appropriate materials.

Armchair: #310 ½, three horizontal slats in back, wide front stretchers, wraparound leather seat, open arms, 36" × 20" × 19", $250–$350

Armchair: #354 ½, five wide vertical slats across back under V-back headrail, wraparound leather seat, open arms, front posts tenoned through tops of arms, 37" × 20" × 19", $650–$850

Armchair: #318, five wide vertical slats across back, open arms, front posts tenoned through tops of arms, drop-in spring seat, 38" × 21" × 19", $500–$750

Armchair: #324, five vertical slats under each arm, front posts tenoned through arms, fixed back with four horizontal slats and loose cushion, drop-in spring seat, 41" x22" × 25", $2,000–$3,000

Armchair, office: #361, swivel seat with wraparound leather, leather back, open arms, 35" × 22" × 19", $1,250–$1,750

Bookcase: #715, single door with 16 panes, gallery top, four exposed tenons per side, straight toe board, arched sides, 56" × 36" × 13", $4,000–$6,000

Bookcase: #716, double doors with eight panes each, gallery top, four exposed tenons per side, straight toe board, arched sides, 56" × 42" × 13", $5,000–$7,000

Bookcase: #717, double doors with 12 panes each, gallery top, four exposed tenons per side, straight toe board, arched sides, 56" × 48" × 13", $5,500–$7,500

Bookcase: #718, double doors with 12 panes each, gallery top, four exposed tenons per side, straight toe board, arched sides, 56" × 54" × 13", $5,500–$7,500

Bookcase: #719, double doors, with 12 panes each, gallery top, four exposed tenons per side, straight toe board, arched sides, 56" × 60" × 13", $6,000–$8,000

Chair, side: #306 ½, three horizontal slats across back, wide stretchers front and rear, wraparound leather seat, 36" × 16" × 16", $1250–$300; set of four, $1,500–$2,000

Chair, side: #308, wide H-shaped slat in back, drop-in seats, 39" × 17" × 15", $300–$350; set of four, $1,750–$2,250

Chair, side: #353, three vertical slats in back, wraparound leather seats, arched seat aprons, wide stretchers front and rear, 39" × 16" × 16", $400–$600; set of four, $2,500–$3,500

Chest of drawers: #909, two half-drawers over three long, with wooden knobs, overhanging top with splashboard, on legs, 42" × 36" × 20", $2,750–$3,550

Chest of drawers: #913, six half-drawers over three long, with wooden knobs, overhanging top with back splashboard, bowed sides, arched apron, Harvey Ellis design, 51" × 36" × 20", $8,000–$11,000

China cabinet: #820, single door with 12 panes, overhanging top with splash board, straight apron, 63" × 36" × 15", $6,000–$8,000

China cabinet: #815, double doors with eight panes each, gallery top, exposed tenons on sides, arched toe board and sides, 65" × 42" × 15", $10,000–$15,000

Costumer: #53, double posts on shoe feet, through tenons on both tapered posts, three hammered hooks on each side, 72" × 13" × 22", $2,250–$2,750

Desk, "Chalet": #505, drop front beneath gallery top, with closed lower shelf, shoe feet, keyed tenons on either side, 46" × 23" × 16", $1,200–$1,600

Desk: #720, overhanging top with upper section composed of slots and two small drawers, two regular drawers with metal hardware, 38" × 38" × 23", $1,500–$2,000

Desk: #732, veneered drop front, gallery top, two half-drawers over two long, arched sides, exposed tenons, 42" × 32" × 14", $2,000–$3,000

Dresser: #911, two half-drawers over two long, arched toe board, bowed sides, attached mirror, overhanging top, 67" × 48" × 22", $3,000–$4,000

Footstool: #300, wraparound leather seat, four stretchers, 15" × 20" × 16", $500–$750

Footstool: #302, wraparound leather seat on four short flared feet, 5" high, 12" × 12", $300–$350

Liquor cabinet: #86, lift top revealing copper-lined interior, single drawer over door opening to interior with rotating bottle rack, 42" × 24" × 17", $3,000–$4,000

Magazine stand: #72, overhanging top, three open shelves, arched sides, Harvey Ellis design, 42" × 21" × 13", $3,000–$4,000

Magazine stand: #500, overhanging top, relief carving of tree on either side, four open shelves with leather strips, unsigned, 43" × 12" × 12", $800–$1,200

Morris chair: #332, flat arms over five vertical slats, exposed tenons on each leg and arm, drop-in seat, loose cushion back, 40" × 23" × 27", $6,500–$9,500

Morris chair: #336, open bow arms supported by short corbels, arched seat aprons, three horizontal rails around seat cushion, drop-in spring seat, loose cushion back, 40" × 30" × 36", $10,000–$15,000

Morris chair: #346, open flat arms, legs tenoned through tops of arms, two corbels under each arm, drop-in spring seat, loose cushion back, 41" × 21" × 23", $2,000–$2,500

Morris chair: #369, slant arms with five slats under each, exposed tenons on each leg and arm, four long tapering corbels, drop-in spring seat, loose cushion back, 40" × 23" × 27", $9,000–$12,000

Rocking chair: #305 ½, three horizontal slats in back, no arms, wraparound leather seat, wide stretchers front and rear, 31" × 16" × 16", $250–$350

Rocking chair: #309 ½, three horizontal slats in back, open arms, wraparound leather seat, wide stretchers front and rear, 32" × 20" × 19", $500–$750

Rocking chair: #311 ½, five vertical slats under V-back headrail, wrap-around leather seat, exposed tenons on arms, 34" × 25" × 28", $750–$1,000

Rocking chair: #323, five vertical slats under each arm, drop-in spring seat, loose cushion back, exposed tenons on arms, 40" × 22" × 25", $2,000–$3,000

Rocking chair, child's: #345, three horizontal slats in back, open arms, original wrap around leather seat, 26" × 18" × 12", $750–$1,000

Server: #818, two or three drawers with metal pulls, overhanging top with splashboard, lower open shelf, 39" x48" × 20", $3,000–$4,000

Settle: #208, even-arm, eight slats across back, three under each arm, exposed tenons on each post, drop-in spring seat, 29" × 76" × 32", $7,000–$9,000

Settle, bench: #212, 12 slats across back, open arms, exposed tenons on tops of arms, wide front stretcher, wraparound leather seat, 36" × 48" × 21", replaced leather $1,250–$1,500; original leather $3,000–$4,000

Settle, hall: #205, even-arm, five slats across back, one wide slat under each arm, exposed tenons on each post, drop-in spring seat, 30" × 56" × 22", $3,500–$4,500

Sideboard: #814, overhanging top above three short drawers flanked by two doors with strap hinges, over long bottom drawer, open plate rail, metal hardware, straight toe board, 49" × 66" × 24", $4,500–$5,500

Sideboard: #816, overhanging top above long drawer above three short drawers flanked by two doors, open plate rail, straight toe board, 48" × 48" × 18", $2,750–$3,750

Sideboard: #819, overhanging top supporting attached mirror, with three short drawers over one long, 50" × 52" × 20", $3,500–$4,500

Table, dining: #632, circular top supported by five square legs without stretchers, apron, six leaves, 30" × 54", $3,000–$4,000

Table, dining: #634, circular top supported by five square legs joined with stretchers, exposed tenons on outside legs, apron, six leaves, 30" × 54", $12,000–$15,000

Table, dining: #638, drop-leaf style with cut corners on leaves, two swing-out legs, exposed tenons, 29" × 40" × 42" (open), $2,500–$3,500

Table, dining: #656, circular top supported by center pedestal, four flared feet, apron, six leaves, 30" × 54", $4,000–$5,000

Table, lamp: #604, circular top over four legs joined by two arched cross-stretchers, no apron, 26" × 20", $1,500–$2,000

Table, lamp: #607, circular top over four legs joined by arched cross-stretchers, lower circular shelf, apron, 29" × 24", $1,750–$2,250

Table, lamp: #611, square top with cut corners, four legs joined by cross-stretchers supporting lower square shelf, no apron, 29" × 24" × 24", $1,500–$2,000

Table, library: #615, rectangular overhanging top, two drawers with metal pulls, two corbels on each leg, exposed tenons on legs and side stretchers, open lower shelf, 30" × 48" × 30", $1,500–$2,250; with original leather top, $3,000–$4,000

Table, library: #653, overhanging top above single drawer with metal pull, open lower shelf, 29" × 48" × 30", $1,500–$2,000

Table, trestle: #637, rectangular overhanging top over double side legs, lower shelf, two exposed and keyed tenons on each side, 29" × 48" × 30", $1,500–$2,000; with original leather top, $3,000–$4,000

Taboret: #601, circular overhanging top supported by four legs joined by arched cross-stretchers, 16" × 14", $600–$800

Taboret: #602, same as #601, 18" × 16", $750–$1,000

Taboret: #603, same as #601, 20" × 18", $800–$1,200

Umbrella stand: #54, four tapering posts with stretchers top and bottom, copper drip pan, 29" × 12" × 12", $650–$950

## L. & J. G. Stickley Furniture Company

SHOPMARKS: (1902–06) Rectangular decal, THE ONONDAGA SHOPS / L.&J.G. STICKLEY / FAYETTEVILLE, N.Y.

(1902–06) Oval paper label with large S and THE ONONDAGA SHOPS

(1906–12) Red decal of handscrew with L.&J.G. STICKLEY on jaws

(1912–18) Red and yellow rectangular decal around THE WORK OF L.&J.G. STICKLEY

(1912–18) Branded mark, THE WORK OF L.&J.G. STICKLEY

(1918) Red and yellow circular decal with joiner's compass and handscrew encircled by STICKLEY HANDCRAFT CRAFTSMAN/ SYRACUSE & FAYETTEVILLE, N. Y.

PRINCIPAL CONTRIBUTION: Extensive line of Arts and Crafts furniture
FOUNDERS: Leopold Stickley, born: 1869, died: 1957. John George Stickley, born: 1871, died: 1921, founded: 1902, closed: current
WORKSHOPS AND SALESROOMS: The Onondaga Shops, Fayetteville, New York, 1902–04. L. & J. G. Stickley, Inc., Fayetteville, New York, 1904–current

"Fumed by ammonia in air-tight compartments and stained in tones that show beautiful undertints, the furniture is next given, through sanding and waxing, a smooth bloom-like texture, so that the arm or back of your chair is delightful to the touch. . . ."

"Where hinges and pulls are needed, as upon chests of drawers and bookcases, these metal fixtures are of copper handwrought in simple designs. The copper is hammered to obtain texture and is dulled and modulated in color by various processes until the soft tones of old metal are secured."
    —*Catalog introduction, 1912*[1]

Of the scores of furniture manufacturers who contributed to or capitalized on the popularity of the Arts and Crafts movement, there may well have been only one man who truly displayed the ability to recognize and to insist on the highest quality materials, craftsmanship, and professional design, yet who also brought to his enterprise an astute marketing plan, a keen focus and a shrewd sense of business: Leopold Stickley. The younger brother of Gustav,

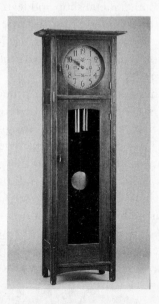

Fine and rare L. and J. G. Stickley tall case clock with beveled, overhanging top, large acid-etched copper face, glass-panel door with copper hardware, and brass works, weights and pendulum. Excellent original finish, color, condition, and wood choice, minor repair to front leg. Etched mark on face L. and J. G. Stickley/Fayetteville NY/Handcraft, 80½" × 21½" × 13", $50,000–$60,000

Leopold was one of the first to be involved with the introduction of Arts and Crafts furniture, which he produced for nearly three decades. He was able to survive the swing away from Arts and Crafts without compromising his high standards of production.

Unlike their older brother Gustav and their popular competitor Elbert Hubbard, Leopold and John George Stickley were solely occupied with the business of making furniture. They were neither Arts and Crafts philosophers, editors, nor writers. Leopold was a sharp businessman who managed the firm's factory in Fayetteville, New York, only a few miles away from Gustav Stickley's Eastwood plant where he had trained. John George Stickley was considered one of the best furniture salesmen of his day. In later years he oversaw the firm's main sales office in New York City until his early death at age 50 in 1921.

The two youngest Stickley brothers joined forces in 1902. Prior to that Leopold had worked from 1894–95 for Gustav at Stickley & Simonds and for brother Charles from 1898–99. He then went to work as plant supervisor in Gustav's new furniture factory, where he stayed for two years (1899–1901.) John George Stickley also trained with one of his older brothers, having spent nine years in partnership with brother Albert in the Stickley Brothers Company in Grand Rapids, Michigan, for which he continued to serve as New York City salesman until 1905. In 1902 Leopold and John began producing a line of Arts and Crafts furniture under the trademark of the Onondaga Shops, named after the New York county in which Fayetteville is located. Their immediate success is reflected in the rapid expansion of both their facility and their furniture line; in 1904 they incorporated and continued to enlarge their factory, constructing both a metal shop and leather shop soon thereafter. Early the following year they exhibited for the first time at the semiannual Grand Rapids trade show. Shortly afterwards it was reported in one of the important furniture trade journals that "the only trouble they are experiencing is an inability to fill orders."[2]

A few miles away Gustav Stickley must have been both proudly and painfully aware of his younger brothers' success, for in 1904 he redesigned the *Craftsman* shopmark, including his first name to help distinguish between the two companies. The confusion must have continued, however, fueled not only by the firms' close proximity to one another and their similar names but by the adoption, in 1906, by Leopold and John of a red shopmark similar to that of their brother. Gustav must have felt that the L. & J. G. Stickley "Handcraft" decal was an infringement on his red joiner's compass trademark and may have requested that they redesign it. In 1912, for whatever reason, L. & J. G. Stickley dropped the red Handcraft decal and replaced it with a yellow decal and a branded mark, both of which clearly read "THE WORK OF L.&J.G. STICKLEY."

L. and J. G. Stickley hat box dresser with backsplash, two-door cabinet over two small drawers and three full-width drawers, all with wooden pulls. Refinished, very good condition. "The Work of..." decal, 49¾" × 36" × 28",  $4,025

The L. & J. G. Stickley firm issued five catalogs between 1905 and 1922, the year it began to gradually phase out the Arts and Crafts line. All five catalogs reveal the debt the majority of their brothers' furniture designs owe to those of Gustav Stickley, especially early in their careers, which is not surprising in light of the fact that Leopold had trained under Gustav during the time that Gustav developed and introduced his first line of Arts and Crafts furniture. During those two years he would have assimilated the philosophy, the design, and the construction techniques that propelled Craftsman furniture to the top of the Arts and Crafts furniture world. Family members recalled that Leopold sketched some of the early Onondaga Shops designs himself, which were then transformed into working plans by the firm's experienced designers. Peter Hansen, one of its best-known designers in later years, had also once worked for Gustav.[3]

In some instances the L. & J. G. Stickley firm made only subtle changes (the length of the corbel, the sweep of an arch, the arrangement of drawers, etc.) in what had obviously originated as a Craftsman design. A comparison of the L. & J. G. Stickley server No. 741 with the slightly earlier Gustav Stickley No. 818, both of which are pictured and discussed in detail by David Cathers in *Furniture of the American Arts and Crafts movement*,[4] illustrates the extent to which Gustav Stickley often influenced the designs of L. & J. G. Stickley. The large number of L. & J. G. Stickley pieces bearing more than just a coincidental resemblance to those from the *Craftsman* shops have, unfortunately, overshadowed many of their own designs and improvements on those of Gustav's. (Note: For a complete examination of the design relationship between the two firms, see Donald Davidoff and Stephen Gray, *Innovation and Derivation: The Contribution of L. & J. G. Stickley to the Arts and Crafts movement* {Morris Plains, NJ: Craftsman Farms Foundation, 1995}.

L. and J. G. Stickley/Onondaga Shops Morris chair with vertical slats and side panels carved with tobacco leaf motif. Good original finish, replaced seat foundation and cushions. Unmarked, 40" × 29¾" × 34", $3,000–$4,500

Unlike most of Gustav Stickley's imitators, however, Leopold and John George did not resort to sloppy workmanship or inferior materials. The majority of their furniture was made from Kentucky quartersawn white oak and was pegged at crucial joints. In a few instances they experimented with false exposed tenons but appear to have concluded that it required nearly as much time to imitate an exposed tenon as it did to make one. Although their hardware may not have been as impressive as Gustav's, it certainly was better than that of every other major Arts and Crafts firm.

Leopold and John George Stickley were proud of their "scientific manner" of furniture construction, using "all the resources of moden invention."[5] In their 1910 catalog the brothers implied that they had been the first to adapt the spring seat from the fledgling automotive industry to Arts and Crafts chairs, rockers, and settles[6]—an innovation Gustav, in turn, incorporated into his large chairs around 1909. Whereas Gustav often veneered two sides of the legs of his Morris chairs and dining room tables, Leopold developed an interlocking design wherein "four pieces of solid oak, with a tiny core, [are] all so tightly welded together that no cracking is possible."[7] The firm also utilized thin splines in assembling the tops of tables, dressers, and buffets, stating in its catalog introduction that "no splitting is possible." Regardless of the validity of these claims, both the interlocking post system and the use of splines between boards may help distinguish between what might otherwise be two very similar designs from the shops of either Gustav or L. & J. G. Stickley.

The craftsmen in both shops, however, were permitted to make minor changes as deemed necessary, as is reflected in variations between the dimensions listed in the catalogs and those found on some of the pieces. In addition,

Fine L. and J. G. Stickley cellarette with arched backsplash, pull-out copper shelf and two-door cabinet with hammered copper strap hinges and ring pulls. Original finish to base, top refinished. "The Work of ..." decal, 35½" × 32" × 16", $13,800

a great deal more experimentation went on in these shops than in modern furniture factories. For instance, while the interlocking leg system is commonly associated with L. & J. G. Stickley, it has also been found on some signed Gustav Stickley library tables.

L. & J. G. Stickley furniture is generally well marked, but their early paper label and their later decals can both easily be destroyed by a careless refinishing. In these instances identification is dependent on comparisons of designs and dimensions illustrated in the original catalogs, many of which have been reproduced and widely distributed. Even without a catalog, an astute collector will recognize the unique L. & J. G. Stickley hand-hammered copper hardware found on many of the case pieces built after 1906. Another design characteristic that was often repeated was the long, tapering corbel,

L. J. & G. Stickley hardware.

Fine and rare L. and J.G. Stickley double-door china cabinet with 12 panes to each door over a two-door cabinet with hammered copper strap hinges and tab pulls. Original finish with overcoat, drill holes through back to accommodate interior lighting, veneer lifting, along with some chips and repairs. "Work of..." decal inside door, 70" × 47" × 16", $18,400

located under the arms of rocking chairs, settles, and armchairs, that ends with a unique flare.

Between 1916 and 1918, perhaps in an attempt to restore Gustav's tarnished image in the Arts and Crafts furniture industry, Leopold and John George bought controlling interest in Gustav's bankrupt factory and formed, along with Gustav and Albert (who remained in Grand Rapids), Stickley Associated Cabinetmakers. The reunion was short-lived; before the year had ended, so had the relationship. Gustav left to live with his daughter, and Leopold and John began the gradual transformation from the production of Arts and Crafts furniture to "Cherry Valley" Colonial reproductions. Their last Arts and Crafts furniture was produced around 1922; since then the factory has continued to manufacture quality reproductions of classic Early American designs bearing the Stickley name branded in the wood.

In 1989, the Stickley Company unveiled a line of Arts and Crafts furniture modeled after authentic examples of both Gustav and L. & J. G. Stickley furniture. In some instances the examples are replicas; in others, such as entertainment centers and coffee tables, the forms are new. While many people have expressed a concern over the possibility of a new example being sold to an unsuspecting collector who might think it was old, the Stickley Company signs each piece with a new shopmark deeply branded into the wood. In nearly every case, internal construction techniques differ from those employed from 1900 to 1923, making it nearly impossible for an educated collector to be fooled. And while many initially expressed concern over the potential impact the Stickley line of high-quality "new" Arts and Crafts furniture might have on the the antique market, it now seems apparent that the growing Arts and Crafts market has the capacity to support both.

## SELECTED PRICES

Model numbers correspond with those in the *Stickley Craftsman Catalogs* (New York; Dover Publications, 1979) and *The Mission Furniture of L. & J. G. Stickley* (New York: Turn of the Century Editions, 1983). Unless otherwise indicated, all examples are made from oak and retain their original finish with typical wear. Prices reflect leather seats and cushions that are either in badly worn condition or that have been replaced with appropriate materials.

Armchair: #818, four horizontal slats across the back, open arms, wide front stretcher, corbels, drop-in spring seat, 39" × 23", $500–$750

Armchair: #836, four vertical slats in tall back, open arms, drop-in spring cushion seat, flat arms with exposed leg tenons, 44" × 23", $500–$750

Armchair: #450, six vertical slats across the back, five under each arm, front posts tenoned through tops of arms, corbels, drop-in spring seat, 40" × 24", $1,750–$2,250.

Bookcase: #641, single door with 16 panes of glass, four keyed tenons on each side, gallery top, 55" × 30" × 12", $4,000–$6,000

Bookcase: #645, double doors, with 12 panes of glass each, four keyed tenons on each side, metal pulls, chamfered board back, 56" × 49" × 14", $5,000–$7,500

Chair, side: #350, three horizontal slats in back, wraparound leather seat, wide stretcher front and rear, 35" × 17", $200–$250; set of four, $800–$1,200

Chair, side: #820, four vertical slats across back beneath scooped crest rail, drop-in spring cushion seat, wide stretchers front and rear, 36" × 20", $350–$450; set of four, $1,400–$1,900

China cabinet: #761, overhanging top over single door with one large sheet of glass, arched sides and toe board, copper pull, 60" × 36" × 16", $4,000–$6,000

China cabinet: #746, double doors with 12 small leaded glass panels in the top of each, large single pane below, overhanging top, arched toe board, adjustable shelves, 58" × 44" × 16", $6,000–$9,000

Desk, drop-front: #613, overhanging top above slanted lid and single long drawer, fitted interior, lower shelf, arched sides, 40" × 32", $1,250–$1,750

Desk, flat-top: #502, overhanging top over single drawer and book shelf at either end, 30" × 48" × 28", $800–$1,200

Desk, flat-top: #610, overhanging top supporting compartment of slots across back, two short drawers over knee compartment, wooden knobs, 38" × 40" × 22", $1,000–$1,500

Dresser: #99, overhanging top with splashboard, two short drawers over three long, arched sides and toe board, wooden knobs, 38" × 40" × 22", $2,500–$3,500

Footstool: #391, leather-wrapped seat with two narrow stretchers at ends and one wide stretcher along each side, 18" × 19" × 16", $400–$600

Footstool: loose cushion set in rectangular frame with concave sides, stretcher base, 15" × 20" × 16", $300–$400

Magazine stand: #46, with four shelves, open back, three slats on either side beneath arched crest rail, arched toe boards, 42" × 19" × 12", $1,250–$1,750

Morris chair: #830, open flat-arm style, adjustable bar, front legs tenoned through arms, drop-in spring seat, loose cushion back, 41" × 25", $1,500–$2,000

Morris chair: #471, flat arms with six slats under each, front posts tenoned through tops of arms, four long corbels, adjustable bar, drop-in spring seat, cushion back, 41" × 26", $2,500–$3,500

Morris chair: #498, slant arms with five slats under each arm, exposed tenons on front legs and tops of arms, adjustable rod, drop-in spring cushion seat, loose cushion back, 41" × 28", $6,000–$8,000

Morris chair rocker: #831, open arms, front posts tenoned through tops of arms, long corbels on front posts, adjustable rod, 38 " × 25", $2,250–$2,750

Rocking chair: #823, four vertical slats across the back beneath scooped crest rail, open arms with exposed tenons on tops, wide front stretcher, drop-in spring seat, 36" × 23", $500–$750

Rocking chair: #837, tall-back version with four vertical slats, open arms with exposed tenons on tops, corbels, drop-in spring seat, 44" × 23", $750–$1,000

Server: #741, splashboard and overhanging top over three drawers and lower open shelf, copper hardware, 38" × 44" × 18", $2,500–$3,500

Settle, bench: #263, seven slats across the back beneath a scooped crest rail, arms slanted slightly over two vertical slats, corbels, drop-in spring seat, 37" × 72" × 25", $3,000–$4,000

Settle: #215, even arms with five vertical back slats, two under each arm, slightly curved apron, drop-in spring cushion seat, 36" × 54" × 24", $3,000–$4,000

Settle: #281, even arms with 16 back slats and five side slats, drop-in spring cushion seat, 34" × 76" × 31", $4,500–$6,500

Sideboard: #707, overhanging top supporting closed plate rail, two half-drawers over two doors, slightly arched apron, copper hardware, 44" × 48" × 20", $2,500–$3,500.

Sideboard: #731, overhanging top supporting paneled plate rail, four short drawers centered by two cabinet doors with strap hinges over long drawer, arched toe board, 49" × 72" × 25", $5,000–$7,500

Table, dining: #720, overhanging circular top supported by five tapering legs, three leaves, 30" × 48", $2,500–$3,500; 54", $3,000–$4,000; 60", $3,500–$4,500

Table, dining: #713, circular top supported by pedestal of four curved supports mounted on four wide feet, apron, 30" × 54", $3,500–$4,500

Table, lamp: #576, square top with cut corners, no apron, lower square shelf on arched cross-stretchers, 29" × 24" × 24", $1,200–$1,600

Table, lamp: #538, overhanging circular top with narrow skirt, straight cross stretchers, 29" × 30", $1,000–$1,500

Table, lamp: #577, circular top with lower circular shelf on cross-stretchers, 29" × 30", $1,200–$1,600

Table, library: #543, circular top with narrow skirt, circular lower shelf on cross-stretchers, 29" × 48", $1,250–$1,750

Table, library: #521, overhanging top over long single drawer with metal pulls, two long tapering corbels on each leg, lower shelf with through-tenons, 29" × 42" × 28", $1,250–$1,750; with leather top, $2,500–$3,500

Table, trestle: #593, overhanging top supported by dual column sides, lower shelf with big key tenons, shaped feet, 29" × 48" × 30", $1,250–$1,750

Taboret: #558, four legs protruding through octagonal overhanging top, arched cross-members, 17" × 15" × 15", $800–$1,200

## The Tobey Furniture Company

SHOPMARKS: (Pre–1900) Circular tag, TOBEY HAND-MADE FURNITURE / ESTABLISHED 1856/ CHICAGO
(1900-01: furniture designed by Gustav Stickley) Circular label, THE NEW FURNITURE/ THE TOBEY FURNITURE COMPANY/ CHICAGO
(After 1902) Metal tag, RUSSMORE/ THE TOBEY FURNITURE COMPANY/ TRADEMARK CHICAGO
PRINCIPAL CONTRIBUTION: Early distributor and producer of Arts and Crafts furniture
FOUNDERS: Charles Tobey, born: 1831, died: 1888. Frank Tobey, born: 1833, died: 1913, founded: 1856, closed: 1954

WORKSHOPS AND SALESROOMS: Charles Tobey, Chicago, 1856-1857. Charles Tobey & Brother, Chicago, 1858-1869. Thayer and Tobey Furniture Company, Chicago, 1870-74. The Tobey Furniture Company, Chicago, 1875–54.

> "It is but a beginning—the first slight harvest in this new field of furniture. Now that it has met with success, nothing will hinder its development. New pieces—pieces hitherto impossible to find—are being made, and it will be our constant endeavor to produce a variety of furniture that will be thoroughly practical, not too good for daily use, moderate in price, in demand by people of culture and taste, and that will help to make life better and truer by its perfect sincerity."
> —*Tobey advertisement, 1900*[1]

When Charles Tobey arrived in Chicago in 1855, he and his brother Frank, who arrived shortly thereafter, were on the brink of becoming an American success story in what was then the fastest growing city in America. They began with Charles's first furniture store, expanding it when Frank arrived from Massachusetts. The Panic of 1857 forced several Chicago companies into bankruptcy, but the two brothers weathered the economic storm, managing even to buy the inventories of several firms that went out of business— a move that proved profitable when Chicago's financial misfortunes were suddenly reversed by the Civil War. The firm soon expanded into furniture production, securing large contracts to fill Chicago's new hotels with hundreds of bedroom suites. Twelve years after they had arrived in Chicago, Charles and Frank Tobey owned a store on bustling State Street, where they

Gustav Stickley "Tree of Life" trapezoidal magazine stand with square top, slanted sides with carved tree motif, and four shelves. Refinished, filled tack holes on shelf edges. Unmarked, 43½" × 12½" sq., $1,150

continued to prosper, furnishing homes across the city with a variety of styles of furniture, draperies, and wallpapers.

The company continued to expand both its facilities and its furniture line. In the 1880s it was simultaneously selling high-quality Victorian bedroom suites in native black walnut and imported mahogany, a line of Colonial reproductions, oak Eastlake parlor sets, and the newest rage: horn furniture—perhaps utilizing the sprawling Chicago stockyards as a convenient source. Charles Tobey died in 1888, but his younger brother Frank proved to be a capable and innovative president. That same year he and a Norwegian woodworker, Wilhelm Christiansen, founded the Tobey & Christiansen Cabinet Company, a custom furniture factory that quickly developed a reputation as one of the finest in the country. Under Christiansen's capable leadership, the firm produced high-quality furniture in a variety of woods and styles that attracted wealthy clients and many of Chicago's growing number of important architects. "Furniture made in the cabinet shop, identified as Tobey Hand-Made Furniture by the use of metal tags after 1898, was distinguished by excellent craftsmanship and perfection of detail. Made from hardwoods like mahogany, maple, and oak, Tobey's pieces were finished on all sides, with as much attention lavished on the surfaces that stood against the wall as on the visible surface."[2]

It was at this same time that Frank Tobey also hired George F. Clingman, who first worked as a wholesale buyer and occasional designer but who eventually became the firm's manager. It was Clingman who later claimed to have sketched the first Mission-style furniture prior to 1900.[3] In July 1900, however, he traveled to Grand Rapids for the semiannual furniture trade show, where he saw Gustav Stickley's new line of furniture that incorporated elements of both the waning Art Nouveau and the emerging Arts and Crafts styles. Clingman immediately purchased Stickley's entire line and negotiated an exclusive arrangement wherein the Tobey Furniture Company would market Gustav Stickley's furniture. As Clingman recalled years later, "I took a piece of paper out of my pocket, or in fact several pieces, and told him that if he was going to make a success of the furniture that he was making it would be necessary for him to make some more important pieces than he was making at that time. On this paper I drew out several large sofas with square posts with flat arms with loose pillow seats and backs; some broad arm rockers and chairs, several styles of tables and one or two screens, and from these Gustave Stickley made what he now claims to be the originator of, that is his so-called arts and crafts furniture. . . [but] instead of Gustave Stickley being the originator of this kind of furniture I claim the honor of being the first to introduce to the public generally this plain, simple kind of furniture."[4]

The concern over who was the first to introduce the Arts and Crafts-style furniture did not become an issue until several years later, when its success was assured. In July 1900 Gustav Stickley was content to permit the Tobey Furniture Company to advertise and sell his line of furniture without any reference to him or his shops in Eastwood, New York; at that point economic survival took precedence over shopmarks. The ads that appeared that fall in *House Beautiful* magazine and the *Chicago Tribune* bore a new Tobey paper label: "The New Furniture" encompassed by four branches. The name of Gustav Stickley never appeared in any of the advertisements.

Identification of the Stickley-designed pieces in the Tobey ads that appeared that fall has been made possible through the publication of Gustav Stickley's first catalog, which was originally printed just before the Grand Rapids Exhibition in July 1900.[5] Clingman simply clipped Stickley's drawings out of his catalog, retained the same names and dimensions and added the prefix "3" to each model number. One of the most common of these early and now rare pieces is the Chalet magazine cabinet, which featured a carved plant form on either side, reflecting the comment in the Tobey ad stating that "such ornament as it bears is incut carving. . . something from nature, a flower or a leaf, as its motive, and all the carving is in bold line."[6] Although the ad also declared that "each piece of 'new furniture' bears our special trademark here shown,"[7] most of the pieces that came from Stickley's Eastwood shops either never received the paper labels or did not retain them over the course of the next century. Identification is most often made using the illustrations and dimensions listed in Stickley's catalog.

Stickley soon grew disillusioned with the terms he and Clingman had agreed to and by that same December was no longer shipping furniture to the Tobey salesrooms on State Street. The ads for Tobey's New Furniture continued through 1901, however, leading author Sharon Darling to first suggest that "it is possible that the original contract with the Tobey Company was fulfilled by Leopold Stickley,"[8] who, incidentally, had left Gustav's employment that same December to begin organizing his own furniture manufacturing company in nearby Fayetteville, New York, with his brother John George.

Back in Chicago, Clingman and Christiansen were busy initiating a new line of Mission oak furniture for the Tobey Furniture Company. Introduced in 1902, the Russmore line featured several new designs, along with some that were obviously inspired by Gustav Stickley. The major difference, though, was apparent to the trained observer: whereas Gustav Stickley preferred the more expensive and more durable quartersawn white oak, the Russmore line was constructed of plain-sawn oak "to meet the growing demand for a type of furniture of artistic simplicity in design, richness in finish, durability in construction, and of low price."[9] At first glance Russmore furniture can be confused with that of Gustav Stickley, especially if the brass plaque has been removed, but a closer examination will often reveal a lack of pegging of key joints, the use of thinner boards, less expensive construction techniques and, as mentioned, plain sawn oak lumber. While the Russmore line may have appealed to the growing numbers of young people who were clamoring for Mission oak furniture for its homes, Gustav Stickley was not left out of the Chicago scene. Not far from Tobey's State Street showrooms, Marshall Field and Company introduced their line of Mission oak-style furnishings in 1902—with an entire showroom of Gustav Stickley's Craftsman furniture.

While the Tobey Furniture Company had an auspicious beginning, introducing the early Arts and Crafts furniture of Gustav Stickley to a large audience, it, like several other Midwest furniture manufacturers and distributors—Sears, Roebuck & Company, the Hartman Furniture Company, S. Karpen & Brothers, and the Chicago Mission Furniture Company— was motivated not by the writings of William Morris or John Ruskin but by the potential for profit in a new fashion. More often than not, that motivation is reflected in the workmanship, design, and materials of the furniture the company produced, leaving the collector to determine the level of quality achieved by each piece encountered. In the case of the Tobey Furniture Company, it is the search for those rare early pieces designed and executed by Gustav Stickley, not the Russmore line of inexpensive Mission oak furniture, that will ensure continued, though limited, recognition.

## SELECTED PRICES

Unless otherwise indicated, all examples are made from oak and retain their original finish with typical wear. Prices reflect leather seats and cushions that are either in badly worn condition or that have been replaced with appropriate materials.

Armchair: slant arm rising sharply from front posts to rear, posts tenoned through tops of arms, leather swing seat from front seat apron to crest rail, unsigned, 46" × 26" × 30", $750–$1,000

China cabinet: double doors with eight false-mullion panes each, overhanging top, adjustable shelves, straight toe board, Russmore brass tag on back, 60" × 42" × 15", $800–$1,200

Magazine stand: designed and produced by Gustav Stickley, square overhanging top supported by six small corbels, splayed sides featuring incised plant form, arched at bottom, four fixed shelves, unsigned, 43" × 12" × 12", $900–$1,100

Magazine stand: similar to previous entry, but with inferior carving, plain sawn oak, and Russmore brass tag, 41" × 12" × 12", $250–$300

Plant stand: #3137 or #137, flush top with high-gloss green Grueby tile set in, top notched around four corner posts, lower square shelf, unmarked, 24" × 14" × 14", $15,000–$20,000

Trestle table: overhanging top supported by dual-column sides ending in shoe feet, lower shelf with two keyed tenons per side, unmarked, 29" × 48" × 35", $1,000–$1,500

## Frank Lloyd Wright

SHOPMARK: None appearing on Arts and Crafts or Prairie style furniture; red square on architectural drawings

PRINCIPAL CONTRIBUTIONS: Architectural and furniture designs.

FOUNDER: Frank Lloyd Wright. Born: 1867, died: 1959.

STUDIO AND WORKSHOPS Frank Lloyd Wright, Architect, Oak Park and Chicago, Illinois, 1887–1910. Spring Green, Wisconsin, 1911–59. Scottsdale, Arizona, 1933–59.

> "This is the modern opportunity—to make of a building, together with its equipment, appurtenances and environment, an entity which shall constitute a complete work of art, and a work of art more valuable to society as a whole than has ever before existed."
> —*Frank Lloyd Wright, 1908*[1]

> "I have done the best I could with this 'living room chair' but, of course, you have to call for somebody to help you move it. All my life my legs have been banged up somewhere by the chairs I have designed."
> —*Frank Lloyd Wright, 1954*[2]

Long before people had begun to recognize such names as Gustav Stickley, Elbert Hubbard or Dirk Van Erp, that of Frank Lloyd Wright was known to nearly everyone in America. His name was synonymous with the Prairie school of architecture, a movement within the Arts and Crafts movement that stressed the importance of unity of site and of structure. And for Frank Lloyd Wright, the structure did not stop at the front door. When permitted—and he was difficult to dissuade—Wright designed the lighting, the furniture and many of the accessories for each house for which he served as architect; he was even known to determine for his clients precisely how his furniture was to be arranged.

As one might expect from a career that spanned seven decades, the furniture, lighting fixtures, and stained-glass windows designed by Frank Lloyd Wright, like his buildings, fall into several different categories: Arts and Crafts, Prairie school, Art Deco, International, Usonian, and Modern. Unlike any of the other Arts and Crafts furniture designers, Wright not only survived the sudden swing in public tastes after World War I, he embraced it. The end of the Arts and Crafts and Prairie school movements coincided with the end of Wright's days of innocence and glory, but his endless stream of plans, projects, and visions for the future carried him from one style to another, through personal tragedy, public rejection, and, finally, nearing the end of his 72-year career, to recognition as America's greatest architect.

The stylistic development of the furniture of Frank Lloyd Wright parallels the buildings he designed, for Wright was the first Prairie school architect to insist that all of the furnishings of the home—woodwork, windows, lights, carpets, and furniture—are each a part of the more important whole and for that reason can only be designed by the architect. The Prairie school movement took root and flourished in turn-of-the-century Chicago, due in no small part to the influence of the young architect from Wisconsin. Wright's career had taken a major step forward when, in 1887, he was accepted into the prestigious architectural firm of Adler and Sullivan. Six years later, however, after a stormy argument with Louis Sullivan over Wright's moonlighting activities, Frank Lloyd Wright established his own firm in the Oak Park, Illinois, house and studio Sullivan had financed for him a few years earlier. From 1893 until 1915, when he moved to Tokyo to supervise the seven-year construction of the Imperial Hotel, Frank Lloyd Wright served as the spokesman and chief architect of the Prairie school movement.

"The decorative designs of the Prairie school architects were an outgrowth of the Arts and Crafts movement, ideologically and stylistically," observed David Hanks in a 1972 essay. "From the larger movement the Prairie architect derived an emphasis on unity of exterior and interior, the respect for natural materials, a desire for simplicity, the interest in Japanese art, and a geometric, rectilinear style."[3]

The furniture Wright designed for early Prairie school homes was, as one author has pointed out, "highly architectural and seemingly rooted to the floor as the houses are rooted to the earth."[4] Wright himself, years later, insisted that his furniture "should be seen as a minor part of the building itself even if detached or kept aside to be employed on occasion."[5] Perhaps the realization that Wright designed furniture for his homes and not for the general public will help explain why the volatile architect bristled at the suggestion that he was designing Mission oak furniture similar to that promoted by Gustav Stickley in the *Craftsman* magazine and by his friend Elbert Hubbard at the Roycroft Shops. Wright was well aware of the work of both Stickley and Hubbard, whom he visited on occasion, and in his typical outspoken manner pronounced it "plain as a barn door."[6]

To Wright's credit it should be pointed out that while Elbert Hubbard was yet a struggling writer and Gustav Stickley was still making reproduction Chippendale chairs on a farm in upstate New York, Frank Lloyd Wright, at the tender age of 26, had already designed the now famous set of

Arts and Crafts dining room furniture for his home in Oak Park (1893–95). By the time Gustav Stickley had placed his first spindle furniture designs into production in 1905, Frank Lloyd Wright had experimented with it 10 years earlier, had incorporated it into two major commissions—the Francis Little House (1902) and the George Barton House (1903)—and had moved on to conquer other challenges.

To Wright, oak seemed the natural choice for both the woodwork and the furniture of his Prairie school designs. While he may have disliked being associated with the more plebian Mission oak, Wright's furniture is clearly reflective of the Arts and Crafts movement, as evidenced by its simple, crisp, rectilinear design; his preference for natural or fumed oak under a varnish or wax finish; his choice of authentic leather upholstery; and his incorporation of narrow slats or square spindles. Where his custom-designed furniture differed from that associated with the major Arts and Crafts furniture manufacturers was in his calculated omission of pegged joints, hand-hammered hardware, and exposed tenons, a detail that on more than one occasion has confused collectors who have unexpectedly come upon a Frank Lloyd Wright-designed piece of furniture and have failed to recognize it.

Unlike Stickley, Limbert, or Hubbard, Wright was first and foremost an architect. Whereas the others employed cabinetmakers, Wright employed draftsmen. Rather than involve himself in furniture production, Wright sent his furniture plans to a number of custom furniture shops in the Chicago and Milwaukee areas, which explains the subtle differences in woodworking techniques and the omission of Wright's shopmark from his Arts and Crafts furniture.[7]

Identifying furniture designed by Frank Lloyd Wright requires an eye trained more for research than for recognizing the remnants of a hidden shopmark. Although his early furniture does not bear any shopmark, original drawings, blueprints, photographs, contracts, and letters have been used to identify his furniture. Although even a novice stumbling upon an early Wright high-back spindle chair would realize, simply by its sheer architectural impact, that it is a piece of major importance, identifying a copper urn, a small end table, a stained-glass window, a floor lamp, a modest side chair, or a library table as having originated from the drafting room of Frank Lloyd Wright requires an acquired familiarity with his career, his philosophy, and his designs.

Fortunately for the Arts and Crafts collector, Wright's prolific career has been well documented. No serious work on 20th-century architecture is complete without a major section on Wright and the Prairie school movement. Scores of newspaper and magazine articles trace both his stormy career and his sensational private life—a life that was marred by two exhausting divorces, bankruptcy, lawsuits, arrests, and the harrowing ax murders in 1914

FRANK LLOYD WRIGHT stained
oak chair from the Unity Temple,
42", $10,000

of his mistress and her two small children in his Spring Green, Wisconson, retreat. With the encouragement and assistance of his third wife, Wright undertook the writing of *An Autobiography*, first published in 1932 when Wright was in his 60s and when his most important contribution to modern architecture—the Guggenheim Museum in New York City—was still more than twenty-five years away.

Although the prices that fine examples of Frank Lloyd Wright Arts and Crafts furniture have brought in recent years are indicative of their relative rarity, the collector should not presume that he or she will never have the opportunity to inspect, let alone purchase, one of Wright's works. Between the years 1893 and 1909, when he left a lucrative practice and a growing family for a two-year sojourn in Europe with the wife of one of his clients, more than 100 of Wright's commissions were completed.[8] In nearly every instance, Wright designed the furnishings for each project, his wealthy clients concurring with his persuasive insistence that they replace their previous furniture with pieces Wright had designed exclusively for their home.

Dining room chairs and tables, desks, library tables, and armchairs are the most commonly discovered examples of early Wright furniture, because whenever possible, Wright incorporated built-in furniture—buffets, window seats, hall benches, and lamp tables—into his homes, both as an integral aspect of his philosophy of organic architecture and, indirectly or directly, as a way to prevent his present clients and future owners from replacing them with furniture from other designers. In at least one instance, however, one of Wright's clients was granted permission by the architect—grudgingly, it is reported—to furnish the secondary rooms with the less expensive Arts and

Crafts furniture of L. & J. G. Stickley. This instance led to the erroneous conclusion that the firm of L. & J. G. Stickley had been contracted by Wright in 1900 to execute his furniture designs for the Bradley House in Kankakee, Illinois.[9] Additional research has revealed, however, that Chicagoan John Ayers rather than the Stickleys deserves that credit.[10]

During the 1930s and 1940s, while Wright fought for national recognition and major commissions, both the Arts and Crafts and the Prairie school movements remained out of vogue. Many Wright houses, as they either passed to the next generation or were sold to new owners, were destroyed, remodeled, redecorated, or, as in the case of Wright's original Oak Park home and studio, transformed into multiple apartments. Now-priceless examples of Frank Lloyd Wright furniture were literally hauled out onto lawns to be sold, given away, or even thrown away. Today they occasionally surface as collections are dispersed, but it seems inevitable that within another decade all but a few lost examples will have found their way into permanent collections.

## SELECTED PRICES

The rarity of Prairie school and Arts and Crafts-style furniture designed by Frank Lloyd Wright, plus the individual nature of each piece, makes establishing a price guide both impractical and quite possibly misleading, for the value of any example will be influenced by factors beyond the scope of this study.

# J. M. Young Furniture Company[1]

SHOPMARKS: (1890–02) paper label "J.M. Young & Son, Camden N.Y."
(1902–16) white paper label (1" × 2") "J.M. Young & Sons, Camden, N.Y."
(1916–20) white paper label (2" × 3") "J.M. Young & Sons, Camden, N.Y."
(1920–26) oval black paper label (2" × 3") "J.M. Young & Sons, Chair Manufacturers, Camden, New York."
(1926–40s) oval black paper label (2" × 3") "J.M. Young's Sons, Chair Manufacturers, Camden, New York."
PRINCIPAL CONTRIBUTIONS: Extensive line of chairs, rockers, settles, footstools, Morris chairs, library tables, and small tables.
FOUNDERS: John McIntosh Young (1845–1926); George W. Young, born:1869, died:1951. Clarence E. Young: born 1880, died 1958.
WORKSHOPS AND SALESROOMS: Camden, New York, 1872—1979.

"It is a substantial, well constructed building better arranged for the comfort of the workmen especially in the matter of light and air space, than is common in factories where a great amount of machinery is required."

—*Camden* Advance-Journal, *1901*[2]

J. M. Young flat-arm Morris chair with four vertical slats to the floor and burgundy vinyl-upholstered seat and back cushions with white trim. Original finish, good condition. Paper label, 37½" × 30½" × 36½", $3,750–$4,750

For years it had been assumed that imitators of the furniture designs of Gustav Stickley and L. & J. G. Stickley would have been viewed with disdain by those whom they imitated, but the case of J. M. Young furniture appears to be to the contrary. Working without a trained furniture designer, the firm openly copied some of the finest examples of Stickley furniture, making minor adjustments and modifications, with, it would seem, the regular cooperation of those they sought to imitate.

James McIntosh Young arrived in the United States at the age of 20. He had already served an apprenticeship as a woodcarver in Scotland, so, upon his arrival in the burgeoning furniture town of Camden, New York, just north of Syracuse, he quickly found employment with the furniture company of F. H. Conant and Son. There he carved elaborate Victorian furniture and studied every facet of the furniture manufacturing business.

In 1872, at the age of 27, Young opened his own furniture business on the outskirts of Camden, but just six years later watched his workshop burn down in a disastrous fire. Undaunted, Young enlisted a business partner and soon reopened. In 1888, when his partner retired, the firm became known as the J. M. Young Furniture Company. The furniture James Young produced was similar to that which he had honed his trade on at F. H. Conant and Son's—heavily carved, fancy Victorian. Young's furniture proved to be both substantial and well-constructed and the company prospered. In 1899, John Young, like Gustav Stickley and Elbert Hubbard before him, made one of many trips back to the British Isles, where he may well have viewed furniture designed in the new Arts and Crafts style.

As they reached manhood, two of Young's sons joined him in the furniture business, reflected in the firm's new 1902 label, which read "J. M. Young

& Sons." Their furniture proved popular and the father and two sons gradually enlarged their factory. Even before launching their own line of Mission-
style furniture, they apparently subscribed to the American interpretation of
the Arts and Crafts philosophy, utilizing modern machinery while improving the working conditions for their craftsmen. As authors Michael Clark
and Jill Thomas-Clark have determined, "the company had its own drying
kilns, fuming chambers, steamers for bending wood and much of the equipment necessary to complete a product from start to finish."[3] James Young's
grandson, who worked in the factory, recalled that the firm's dozen or so
workers hand-fitted and hand-finished the furniture they produced. "One
must keep in mind," the Clarks observed, "that the Youngs, unlike the Stickleys, worked in the factory for all their professional lives; theirs was truly a
family-run, family-operated business."[4]

It appears that the firm followed Gustav Stickley's lead into the Arts and
Crafts style, for by 1904 the company had begun producing a line of Arts and
Crafts furniture, including a flat-arm Morris chair inspired by that intro-
duced in 1902 by Stickley. One difference that aids collectors today is the J. M.
Young substitution of a pair of metal hinges at the base of the adjustable back
rather than Stickley's swivel-peg design. To reduce manufacturing costs, the
Youngs also substituted false tenons on the front legs of their Morris chair in
place of actual through-tenons.

Young's earliest Arts and Crafts models, those manufactured prior to
1904, were clearly influenced by the furniture of Gustav Stickley, whose
workshops were only miles away. But as Gustav's younger brothers Leopold
and John George established a new business and began to develop their line
of Arts and Crafts furniture, the Youngs steadily began duplicating and
adapting more and more of their designs for chairs, rockers, and settles. It
even appears that the Young family and Leopold Stickley were visiting each
other's workshops and subsequently developed a close working relationship,
sharing construction techniques and finish formulas.[5]

The relationship between the two firms took an interesting turn when
Leopold discontinued making Arts and Crafts furniture in 1922 (his firm
continued to sell from its inventory for a few years after that date).[6] Surviving correspondence indicates that Leopold was searching for a firm to take
over the manufacture of the Arts and Crafts line. While it does not appear
that he and the Youngs ever signed a formal agreement, as Leopold Stickley
moved out of the Arts and Crafts arena, the Youngs expanded, utilizing,
without opposition, construction techniques, patterns, machinery, formulas,
and even salesmen formerly associated with L. & J. G. Stickley furniture.

J. M. Young's Sons (as it became known around 1926) continued to sell
Arts and Crafts furniture throughout the 1930s and 1940s, with much of its
furniture going to government agencies and corporations around the world.

The Arts and Crafts line was gradually phased out after World War II, but the firm remained in business until 1979.

The first label to appear on the firms line of Arts and Crafts furniture read "J.M. Young & Son, Camden, N.Y." and was used until 1902, when it was changed to "J.M. Young & Sons, Camden, N.Y." This white label was used until around 1916. A larger (2" × 3") label with the same wording appeared briefly from 1916 until 1920. That year a new black oval label in flowing script and bearing the words "J.M. Young & Sons, Chair Manufacturers, Camden, New York" was introduced. It was replaced in 1926 by a similar label noting a slight change in the company's name—"J.M. Young's Sons."

The vast majority of J. M. Young pieces are chairs, footstools, rockers, and settles. It does not appear that they were equipped to produce case pieces, such as bookcases, china cabinets and dressers, in large numbers. In many instances the furniture will appear at first glance to be that of either Gustav Stickley or, more often, that of L. & J. G. Stickley. Prior to the Clarks' research, it is believed that more than one piece of Young furniture was represented as being made by L. & J. G. Stickley. Upon close inspection, however, subtle differences will become apparent. Oftentimes the Young version will be slightly less robust, the hardware will be different, the exposed tenons will be routed into a post rather than passing completely through it, dovetails will be lacking in the drawers, and the arrangement of the stretchers (rungs) between chair legs will form a square rather than being offset.

While they did not offer a complete line of Arts and Crafts furniture, the J. M. Young family placed a special emphasis on quality of materials, high standards of craftsmanship, pleasing proportions, and traditional Arts and Crafts stains and finishes. A few of their forms are equal in every respect to those of Gustav Stickley and L. & J. G. Stickley—and those that don't quite match those standards often represent one of the best bargains in the Arts and Crafts market.

## SELECTED PRICES

Model numbers correspond with those appearing in the Dover publication *J. M. Young Arts and Crafts Furniture.* Unfortunately, the illustrations and photographs in this publication did not include dimensions, but an accurate comparison can be made by comparing details evident in the catalog (and explained in the text) with an actual piece of furniture. All examples listed below are assumed to be made of oak and in typical condition, exhibiting normal wear on both the wood and the finish.

Chair, arm: #152, five vertical slats, wide arms and corbels in style of Gustav
    Stickley, wraparound leather seat, $350–$400

Chair, side: #189, three horizontal slats, wraparound leather seat, no arms, wide front stretcher, $150–$200; set of four, $600–$800

Chair, side: #913, three vertical slats, drop-in padded seat, wide front stretcher, $150–$200, set of four, $600–$800

Footstool: #206, wraparound leather seat with arched aprons, four stretchers, $400–$450

Library table: #434, 48" top over single drawer with two pulls, four vertical slats under each end, lower shelf, $800–$950

Magazine stand: #240, four fixed shelves with arched aprons as base, three vertical slats on each end, open top, $900–$1,100

Morris chair: #186, flat-arm with four slats under each arm, four corbels, false tenons on legs, $1,750–$2,250

Rocker, arm: #264, horizontal back slats with loose back cushion and drop-in spring seat, four slats under each arm, $700–$800

Rocker, arm: #150, five vertical slats, wide arms and corbels in style of Gustav Stickley, wraparound leather seat, $400–$450

Rocker, arm: #154, five vertical slats in back, four under each arm, arched front apron, drop-in spring seat, $500–$600

Rocker, arm: #158 ½, five horizontal back slats, open arms and corbels in style of Gustav Stickley, drop-in loose cushion seat, $550–$650

Rocker, Arm: #288, three horizontal slats, scooped crestrail, open arms, drop-in spring seat, $450–$500

Rocker, arm: #364, five horizontal back slats, open arm, no corbels, drop-in spring seat, $300–$350

Rocker, arm: #424, five vertical slats, tall back, open arms with corbels, drop-in spring seat, $550–$600

Rocker, sewing: #188, three horizontal slats, wraparound leather seat, no arms, wide front stretcher, $150–$250

Settle: #230, eight wide slats across back, even-arm design, single wide slat under each arm, drop-in cushion, $2,500–$3,500

Settee (two-person): #416, wrap around leather covered back, drop-in spring cushion, open arms, $900–$1,200

Settee (two-person): #372, 11 vertical slats across back, open arms with corbels, drop-in spring cushion seat, $1,000–$1,200

Tabouret: #558, four legs mortised through 8-sided top, arched cross-stretchers, $500–$600

Table, Lamp: #180, circular top over recessed apron, smaller lower shelf on straight cross-stretchers, $450–$500

Table, Trestle: #182, 48" top over lower shelf with keyed through tenons, show feet design similar to L. & J.G. Stickley table, $800–$1,000.

## Other Mission Oak Furniture Manufacturers

"Do not confuse Limbert's Holland Dutch Arts and Crafts furniture with the many poorly constructed, ill-proportioned and uncraftsman-like specimens of straight line furniture with which the market is flooded at the present time, and called all manner of names, such as "Crafts Style," "Mission," etc., etc., simply because it is devoid of ornamentation. This is not Arts and Crafts furniture. Take the two words, "Arts" and "Crafts," and think of them separately and try to define each. You will see that the expression really means that which is beautiful, truly artistic, and expressive of the highest ideals and purest conceptions of a talented mind combined with the cleverness, ingenuity and mechanical ability of a well trained craftsman."

*—Charles Limbert*[1]

For years the American public simply classified all turn-of-the-century, straight-lined, brown furniture that had survived—primarily because it was too strong to wear out and too practical to throw out—as being "Mission oak." Furniture from once-respected designers such as Gustav Stickley, Frank Lloyd Wright and Harvey Ellis was lumped together with inferior, poorly constructed furniture intended to imitate rather than to emulate the best of the era. Once the Arts and Crafts style had carved out a foothold in the American public, manufacturers of a wide range of styles and quality of straight-lined, brown furniture had flooded the market with imitations, hoping to siphon off as much money as they possibly could before moving on to the next popular style—and much of it survived as well.

Some of these firms openly imitated the furniture designs of Gustav Stickley and L. & J. G. Stickley, right down to the precise dimensions of a Morris chair or magazine stand. Others made changes to the designs they copied, substituting plain-sawn for quartersawn oak, false tenons for exposed tenons, and veneer for solid lumber. Distinguishing a fine example of Arts and Crafts furniture from an inferior imitation is not a matter of memorizing a list of names and shopmarks, for many of these firms produced an erratic array of furniture, ranging from examples of pleasing proportions, quality materials, and excellent workmanship to those that are difficult to even look at, yet alone purchase and take home.

While some of these furniture firms were new, the majority had been producing period reproductions, fancy golden oak, or utility household furniture. For most, the switch to Mission oak was simple; few of these companies went to the lengths of the Stickleys, Charles Limbert, or the Roycrofters to manufacture consistently high-quality oak furniture.

Like the Stickleys, Limbert, and the Roycrofters, however, many of these companies adopted the practice of affixing a shopmark to their furniture. And they often changed their shopmarks for reasons we may never know. Unfortunately, since the quality varied tremendously even within the same firm, shopmarks do little but provide evidence as to which firm produced a particular piece. Determining the quality of that same piece remains a separate task. Signed and unsigned pieces have since been commonly called "generic Mission oak," a term that is not entirely accurate since most of this furniture was at some time signed or identifiable. An unsigned piece should no more be deemed poor quality than a signed piece should be considered worthy of a premium simply because a paper label managed to survive for 80 years. A label, decal, or brass tag can indicate only who made the piece, not how well it was made. In the final analysis, each piece must speak for itself.

Distinguishing between a well-constructed and a poorly constructed example of Mission oak furniture is relatively easy once the characteristics of low-quality Mission oak furniture are identified. In most cases, ample evidence will be found, including a number of the following:

- lack of pegged joints
- thin, lightweight hardware
- plain-sawn lumber
- ash or hickory rather than quartersawn oak
- square chair stretchers (rungs)
- flimsy drawer construction
- exposed screw heads or bolts
- no corbels under the arms
- false tenons
- awkward proportions
- imitation leather upholstery
- thin tops
- excessive use of veneers
- false mullions over a single sheet of glass
- gimmicks or novelties
- design characteristics from other furniture styles (Victorian paw feet, Queen Anne legs, barley-twist legs, scrollwork, etc.)

While even the most respected furniture manufacturers of the Arts and Crafts era may not have avoided each of these characteristics on every piece of furniture, the inexpensive imitations will inevitably exhibit several. Some of the most valuable examples of Gustav Stickley furniture were not pegged and his dining armchairs often did not have corbels under their arms, but when all of the factors are considered on each piece of furniture, it will become clear that the low-quality imitations suffer in comparison in not just one or two, but several respects.

The list of companies included in this category will probably never be complete, nor is any firm's inclusion indicative of the quality of its furniture. The works of several companies, such as Plail and Harden, are today sought by astute collectors aware that the high quality of their furniture has thus far been overlooked. As additional examples of such work surfaces—while furniture by the Stickleys, Limbert, and Roycroft grows more difficult to find—collectors will soon be turning to the less publicized manufacturers of quality Mission oak furniture.

A special note of gratitude must be awarded to a pair of diligent researchers and authors, Dr. Michael Clark and Jill Thomas-Clark. For more than 10 years they have undertaken the role of furniture sleuths, tracking down histories and shopmarks of scores of little-known Arts and Crafts furniture manufacturers. In addition, they have shared their research with fellow collectors through their books, their lectures, and their articles in *Style: 1900* and other publications. They willingly shared their information on obscure shopmarks for this edition and continue to research and document information that might have disappeared forever.

### AMERICAN CHAIR MANUFACTURING COMPANY
Brandt and Hallstead, Pennsylvania
ACTIVE: 1892—1930
Specialized in Arts and Crafts chairs and a matching armchair, rocker, and
    settle, noted for similarity to Harden suite
SHOPMARK: paper label "Made by the American Chair Mfg. Co. Hallstead, Pa.
NOTE: For more information, see Dr. Michael Clark and Ms. Jill Thomas-
    Clark "The Best of the Rest," *Style: 1900*, (Winter 1997).

### BARBER BROTHERS CHAIR COMPANY
Grand Rapids, Michigan
ACTIVE: early 20th century, became Lifetime ca. 1911
General line of Mission oak furniture
SHOPMARK: rectangular paper label

### BERKEY & GAY FURNITURE CO.
Grand Rapids, MI
ACTIVE: 1873-ca. 1930

Berkey & Gay lamp table with circular top incorporating seven butterfly keys, on faceted legs with cross-stretchers. Commissioned for Blythfield Country Club, Grand Rapids, Michigan, ca. 1910. Refinished, a little loose. Branded circular mark, 29¾" × 30" dia., $1,400–$1,900

General line of Mission oak furniture
SHOPMARK: BERKEY & GAY FURNITURE CO in circle

## BINGHAMTON CHAIR COMPANY
Binghamton, New York
ACTIVE: early 20th century
Mission oak chairs, Morris chairs, and rockers.
SHOPMARK: black circular paper label with yellow lettering, name of company plus "Morris Chairs, Rockers."

## BLACK RIVER BENDING COMPANY
Black River, New York
ACTIVE: founded 1860; reorganized 1895 with George Oakes as designer and general manager; ceased operations ca. 1916.
Chairs and tables in Mission oak style beginning in 1901; much imitates Gustav Stickley designs; wide range in quality of design and construction.
SHOPMARK: octagonal paper label, often with name "Kamargo Shops" included; also used rectangular paper label "Manufactured By Black River Bending Co., Black River, N.Y."
NOTE: For more information, see Dr. Michael Clark and Ms. Jill Thomas-Clark "The Best of the Rest," *Style: 1900* (fall 1991), pp. 19–22.

## BRIAR CLIFF
(see Craftsman's Shop of Ossining)

**BUFFALO CHAIR WORKS**
Buffalo, New York
ACTIVE: early 20th century
General line of Mission oak furniture
SHOPMARK: rectangular paper label with illustration of charging buffalo and "Best Made and Unrivaled in Finish"

**BUFFALO DESK AND TABLE COMPANY**
Buffalo, New York
ACTIVE: early 20th century
General line of Mission oak furniture
SHOPMARK: rectangular paper label with ornate outline

**CADILLAC CABINET CO.**
Detroit, Michigan
ACTIVE: early 20th century
General line of Mission oak furniture
SHOPMARK: paper label

**CATSKILL MISSION FURNITURE**
Woodstock, New York
ACTIVE: early 20th century
Small Mission oak furniture
SHOPMARK: CATSKILL MISSION FURNITURE/WOODSTOCK, N.Y.

**CHICAGO MISSION FURNITURE CO.**
Chicago, Illinois
ACTIVE: ca. 1904
Mission oak chairs and tables
SHOPMARK: paper label

**COLUMBIA PARLOR FRAME COMPANY**
Chicago, Illinois
ACTIVE: early 20th century
Line of Mission oak chairs, settles, and rockers
SHOPMARK: undetermined

**COME-PACKT FURNITURE COMPANY**
Toledo, Ohio
ACTIVE: early 20th century

Mail-order line of Mission oak furniture
SHOPMARK: decal, COME-PACKT in rectangle

## F. A. CONANT'S SONS
Camden, New York
ACTIVE: early 20th century
General line of Mission oak furniture
SHOPMARK: paper label

## CONREY & BIRELY TABLE CO.
Shelbyville, Indiana
ACTIVE: early 20th century
General line of Mission oak furniture
SHOPMARK: undetermined

## CORTLAND CABINET COMPANY
Cortland, New York
ACTIVE: early 20th century
Specialized in sideboards and china cabinets
SHOPMARK: circular black paper label with serrated edges "Manufacturers
    of Buffets and China Closets"; also rectangular paper label with model
    number

## CRAFTSMAN'S SHOP OF OSSINING
Ossining, New York
ACTIVE: early 20th century
General line of Mission oak furniture
SHOPMARK: BRIAR CLIFF

## CRON-KILLS COMPANY
Piqua, Ohio
SHOPMARK: oval red paper label with white lettering

## H. T. CUSHMAN MFG. CO.
North Bennington, Vermont
ACTIVE: early 20th century
General line of Mission oak furniture
SHOPMARK: undetermined

## DELAWARE CHAIR CO.
Delaware, Ohio

ACTIVE: early 20th century
Mission oak chairs
SHOPMARK: undetermined

## H. C. DEXTER CHAIR CO.
Black River, New York
FOUNDERS: David Dexter (1813–1880)
Henry Clay Dexter (1858–1946)
ACTIVE: 1838—ca. 1912
General line of Mission oak furniture derivative of the Stickleys (including some inlaid chairs), plus line of rustic birch-bark furniture; some furniture designed by Louis B. Ridenhour.
SHOPMARK: rectangular white paper label "H.C. Dexter Chair Co., Black River, N.Y."
NOTE: For more information, see Dr. Michael Clark and Ms. Jill-Thomas Clark, "The Best of the Rest," *Style: 1900* (vol. 12, no. 3, Summer 1999), pp. 19–22.

## C. F. DOLL FURNITURE COMPANY
Buffalo, New York
ACTIVE: early 20th century
General line of Mission oak furniture
SHOPMARK: rectangular blue paper label with clipped corners

## GEORGE C. FLINT COMPANY
New York, New York
SHOPMARK: rectangular paper label with name of company plus "FFF" (overlapping letters) and "Trade Mark"

## J. S. FORD, JOHNSON & CO.
Chicago, Illinois
ACTIVE: early 20th century
Line of Mission oak chairs and library tables
SHOPMARK: undetermined

## FRANCISCAN SHOPS
Apulia, New York
ACTIVE: early 20th century
General line of Mission oak furniture
SHOPMARK: paper label

**L. G. FULLAM & SONS**
Ludlow, Vermont
ACTIVE: early 20th century
General line of Mission oak furniture
SHOPMARK: undetermined

**GRAND LEDGE CHAIR COMPANY**
Grand Ledge, Michigan
ACTIVE: early 20th century
General line of well-constructed Mission oak furniture
SHOPMARK: Rectangular paper label with company name and city outlined
in black box

**GRAND RAPIDS BRASS & IRON BED CO.**
Grand Rapids, Michigan
ACTIVE: early 20th century
Mission-style brass and iron beds
SHOPMARK: undetermined

**GRAND RAPIDS CHAIR COMPANY**
Grand Rapids, Michigan
ACTIVE: 1872-undetermined
Extensive line of Mission oak furniture
SHOPMARK: brass tag

**GRAND RAPIDS DESK COMPANY**
Grand Rapids, Michigan
ACTIVE: 1893-undetermined
Limited line of Mission oak rolltop desks
SHOPMARK: embossed brass escutcheon

**GRAND RAPIDS FANCY FURNITURE CO.**
Grand Rapids, Michigan
ACTIVE: early 20th century
General line of Mission oak furniture
SHOPMARK: paper label

**GRAND RAPIDS FURNITURE MFG. CO.**
Grand Rapids, Michigan
ACTIVE: early 20th century

General line of Mission oak furniture, including unassembled mail order line.
SHOPMARK: undetermined

**GRAND RAPIDS TABLE COMPANY**
Grand Rapids, Michigan
ACTIVE: early 20th century
Mission oak tables
SHOPMARK: undetermined

**GRAY FURNITURE COMPANY**
Adrian, Michigan
ACTIVE: early 20th century
General line of Mission oak furniture
SHOPMARK: rectangular metal tag/decal with "Heirloom Line, Gray Furniture Co., Adrian, Mich. A.D. 1911"

**CHARLES A. GREENMAN CO.**
Grand Rapids, Michigan
ACTIVE: 1904-undetermined
General line of Mission oak furniture
SHOPMARK: undetermined

**W. H. GUNLOCKE CHAIR COMPANY**
Wayland, New York
ACTIVE: 1902—undetermined
FOUNDERS: W. H. Gunlocke, John Plail, Edwin Ecker, John Stahle, Charles Scales
Mission oak office chairs, clock cases, Morris chairs and steam-bent chairs, armchairs with caned backs.
SHOPMARK: rectangular paper label with clipped corners and red ink

**STANTON H. HACKETT**
Philadelphia, Pennsylvania
ACTIVE: early 20th century
General line of Mission oak furniture
SHOPMARK: undetermined

**HALE FURNITURE CO.**
Herkimer, New York
ACTIVE: early 20th century

General line of Mission oak furniture
SHOPMARK: rectangular black decal with gold lettering

## HARDEN FURNITURE COMPANY
Camden, New York
FOUNDER: Frank S. Harden
ACTIVE: early 20th century
General line of quality Mission oak furniture
SHOPMARK: red paper label "From The Harden Line, Factory No. 2,
    Camden, New York" (applied with tacks)

## HARDESTY MANUFACTURING COMPANY
Canal Dover, Ohio
ACTIVE: early 20th century
General line of Mission oak furniture
SHOPMARK: rectangular paper shipping label attached with tacks, name of
    company plus "Mission Furniture, Opera Chairs and Counter Stools"

## HARTMAN FURNITURE & CARPET CO.
Chicago, Illinois
ACTIVE: early 20th century

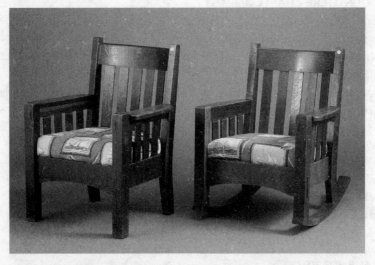

Harden armchair and rocker set with vertical slats to back and under
the arms, and fabric-covered drop-in seat cushions. Overcoated
original finish, good condition, 37½" × 29" × 23", $1,495

Mail-order line of Mission oak furniture
SHOPMARK: undetermined

## HONEOYE FALLS FURNITURE COMPANY
Honeoye Falls, New York
SHOPMARK: square paper label with blue text and box border

## HUBBARD & ELDRIDGE CO.
Rochester, New York
ACTIVE: early 20th century
Mission oak chairs, rockers, footstools
SHOPMARK: decal HUBBARD & ELDRIDGE CO/ROCHESTER NY
NOTE: No relationship to Elbert Hubbard of Roycrofter fame.

## IMPERIAL FURNITURE COMPANY
Grand Rapids, Michigan
ACTIVE: early 20th century
General line of Mission oak furniture
SHOPMARK: paper label or blue shield with "Imperial" in script below red
    crown

## JAMESTOWN LOUNGE COMPANY
Jamestown, New York
ACTIVE: early 20th century

Jamestown Furniture unusual tall-back hall chair in the style of Charles Rohlfs, with carved and cutout details, round rivets, and plank seat. Original finish to legs and back, seat is refinished. Unmarked, 56" × 16" × 13¾", $690

General line of Mission oak furniture
SHOPMARK: undetermined

**S. KARPEN & BROS.**
Chicago, Illinois
Founder: Solomon Karpen
ACTIVE: 1880–1952
Mission oak chairs, rockers, and parlor suites
Shopmark: metaltag,
    KARPEN/GUARANTEED/UPHOLSTERED/FURNITURE/CHI
    CAGO

**KENTON MANUFACTURING COMPANY**
Covington, Kentucky
Mission oak line designed by Louis B. Ridenhour
ACTIVE: ca. 1904 -
SHOPMARK: undetermined

**KIMBALL & CHAPPELL COMPANY**
Chicago, Illinois
ACTIVE: 1897 ca. 1920
Mission-style brass and iron beds
SHOPMARK: undetermined

**KNAUS MANUFACTURING COMPANY**
Constantia and Oneida, New York
ACTIVE: 1908—13 (Constantia); 1914–15 (Oneida)
FOUNDERS: William Knaus (plus two investors)
General line of Arts and Crafts furniture under line of "Craftmaster" pieces
    noted for similarity to those of the Stickleys.
SHOPMARK: (1908–13) rectangular metal tag "Knaus Mfg. Co. Manuf'ts of
    Craftsmasters Furniture, Constantia, N.Y."; (1914–15) circular metal
    tag "Knaus Meisterwerk Furniture."
NOTE: For more information, see Dr. Michael Clark and Ms. Jill-Thomas
    Clark, "The Best of the Rest" *Style: 1900,* Vol. 11, (Fall 1998), pp. 21–25

**LAKESIDE CRAFTS SHOP**
Sheboygan, Michigan
ACTIVE: early 20th century
General line of small Mission oak pieces
SHOPMARK: color circular paper label with man with wood plane

**LANGSLOW, FOWLER COMPANY**
Rochester, New York
ACTIVE: early 20th century
General line of Mission oak furniture
SHOPMARK: rectangular paper label with rounded corners

**LARKIN FURNITURE COMPANY**
Buffalo, New York
FOUNDER: John D. Larkin (1845–1926)
ACTIVE: 1901–1941
General line of household furniture
SHOPMARK: large paper label

**LESTERSHIRE FURNITURE COMPANY**
Lestershire, New York
ACTIVE: early 20th century
General line of Mission oak furniture
SHOPMARK: rectangular paper label with clipped corners, red ink

**LUCE FURNITURE CO.**
Grand Rapids, Michigan
ACTIVE: early 20th century
General line of Mission oak furniture
SHOPMARK: brass tag or rectagular shipping label with name of firm, plus
    word "LUCE" in red circle and "Manufacturers of Bedroom and Din-
    ing Room Furniture"

**MAJESTIC FURNITURE COMPANY**
Herkimer and Mexico, New York
ACTIVE: 1910–12
FOUNDERS: Group of local investors and Fred W. Flash, foreman and de-
    signer
A line of high quality Arts and Crafts furniture; especially noted for a series
    of tall back dining chairs that combined elements of both Frank Lloyd
    Wright and Gustav Stickley designs
SHOPMARK: rectangular paper label with rounded corners
NOTE: For more information, see, Dr. Michael Clark and Ms. Jill-Thomas
    Clark, "The best of the Rest," *Style: 1900* Vol. 12, (Summer 1999) pp.
    21–25.

**MCLEOD FURNITURE**
Grand Rapids, Michigan

ACTIVE: Early 20th century
Limited line of Mission oak furniture
SHOPMARK: decal with "McLeod" in script with office desk in background
over words "Grand Rapids"

## MICHIGAN CHAIR COMPANY
Grand Rapids, Michigan
ACTIVE: 1893-undetermined
Complete line of Mission oak furniture
SHOPMARK: circular paper label

## MICHIGAN DESK COMPANY
Grand Rapids, Michigan
ACTIVE: 1905-undetermined
General line of Mission oak furniture
SHOPMARK: undetermined

## MILLER CABINET COMPANY
Rochester, New York
ACTIVE: early 20th century
General line of Mission oak furniture
SHOPMARK: diamond-shaped label with blue lettering

## MUELLER & SLACK
Grand Rapids, Michigan
ACTIVE: early 20th century

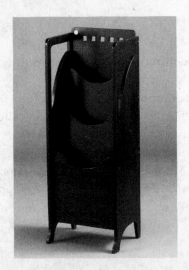

Michigan Chair Co. magazine
stand with cutout back and sides,
four compartments. Original dark
finish with overcoat, minor edge
roughness. Unmarked, 28" × 14" ×
9½", $1,092

Upholstered Mission oak furniture
SHOPMARK: undetermined

**MURPHY CHAIR COMPANY**
Detroit, Michigan
ACTIVE: early 20th century
General line of Mission oak furniture
SHOPMARK: rectangular decal with firm's name and model number

**MUSKEGON FURNITURE CO.**
Muskegon, Michigan
ACTIVE: early 20th century
General line of Mission oak furniture
SHOPMARK: undetermined

**NELSON-MATTER COMPANY**
Grand Rapids, Michigan
ACTIVE: 1885–1917
"Modern English" Mission oak bedroom suites
SHOPMARK: undetermined

**NORTHERN FURNITURE COMPANY**
Sheboygan, Wisconson
ACTIVE: early 20th century
General line of Mission oak furniture
SHOPMARK: rectangular shipping label tacked to back; also utilized a
   brand with the firm's name and location.

**OAK CRAFT SHOPS**
Portland, Michigan
ACTIVE: early 20th century
General line of Mission oak furniture
SHOPMARK: 1" × 2" paper label

**OAK-WORTH SHOPS**
Gouverneur, New York
ACTIVE: early 20th century
General line of Mission oak furniture
SHOPMARK: OAKWORTH label

**C. S. PAINE COMPANY**
Grand Rapids, Michigan

ACTIVE: 1900–undetermined
Upholstered Mission oak chairs and settles
SHOPMARK: undetermined

## PAINE FURNITURE COMPANY
Boston, Massachusetts
General line of Mission oak furniture
SHOPMARK: oval decal with company name, plus "Manufacturers and Importers of Fine Furniture"; also, circular paper label with company name plus "Makers of Fine Furniture"

## PHILADELPHIA FURNITURE COMPANY
Philadelphia, Pennsylvania
ACTIVE: early 20th century
General line of Mission oak furniture
SHOPMARK: oval stamp with black ink

## PLAIL BROTHERS CHAIR COMPANY
Wayland, New York
FOUNDERS: John Plail (1868–1938), co-founder and designer; Joseph Plail, co-founder and foreman
ACTIVE: 1906–33
Quality Mission oak chairs and settles, often in a multiple-slat barrel-back design; expanded to general line of quality Arts and Crafts furniture; John Plail was a noted wood carver and technician in steam bending wood
SHOPMARK: oval paper label, PLAIL BROS./WAYLAND, NY

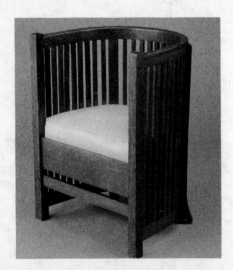

Fine and rare Plail Brothers barrel chair with spindles to the floor, and re-upholstered seat cushion in yellow vinyl. Original finish, break to back stretcher, chip to foot. Unmarked, 32½" × 24¼" × 20", $575

NOTE:  For more information, see *Style: 1900* (Vol. 9, No. 1, Spring 1996) "The Plail Brothers Chair Company," Dr. Michael Clark and Ms. Jill Thomas-Clark

## PORTLAND FURNITURE COMPANY
Portland, Michigan
ACTIVE:  early 20th century
Mission oak chairs
SHOPMARK:  undetermined

## POUGHKEEPSIE CHAIR COMPANY
Poughkeepsie, New York
SHOPMARK:  circular white paper label outlined in red with red lettering

## PREMIER MANUFACTURING CO
(also known as KNAUS BROS. AND ARVINE COMPANY)
Fayetteville, New York
FOUNDERS:  Norman and William Knaus, Fred Arwine
NOTE:  many of the principals in this business had formerly worked for the Stickleys;
line of Arts and Crafts furniture called "Craftstyle," which relied heavily on Gustav Stickley designs
ACTIVE:  1905–11
SHOPMARK:  Craftstyle

## QUAINT ART FURNITURE COMPANY
Syracuse, New York
ACTIVE:  1909–16
FOUNDERS:  David Carrick, Charles Litchison, Jr., George Perin (designer)
General line of Mission oak chairs, rockers, tables, and settles; considered of higher quality than the majority of lesser-known furniture firms; utilized splined joints on table tops and settle posts
SHOPMARK:  oval paper label attached with single tack with oval black line around company name; also, rectangular paper label attached with two tacks with name of company and style number, finish, etc
NOTE:  For more information, see Dr. Michael Clark and Ms. Jill Thomas-Clark., "The Best of the Rest" *Style: 1990* Vol. 9, (Summer 1996).

## QUAKER MISSION CRAFT
unknown
SHOPMARK:  white decal with red lettering

## JOHN D. RAAB CHAIR COMPANY
Grand Rapids, Michigan
ACTIVE: early 20th century
Mission oak chairs
SHOPMARK: undetermined

## RAMSEY-ALTON COMPANY
Portland, Michigan
ACTIVE: early 20th century
General line of Mission oak furniture
SHOPMARK: "OAKCRAFT" brand

## J. K. RISHEL FURNITURE COMPANY
Hughesville and Williamsport, Pennsylvania
Founded: ca. 1867 by James Laird; purchased 1878 by Dr. J. K. Rishel
Noted for matching bedroom suites and dining room suites in "Mission,
    Modern Mission and Swiss Austrian."
SHOPMARK: rectangular label/plate "Made By J.K. Rishel Co.,
    Williamsport, PA"
NOTE: for more information, see Dr. Michael Clark and Ms. Jill Thomas-
    Clark, "The J. R. Rishel Furniture Company," *Style: 1900* Vol. 2 (Fall
    1998); pp. 18–20.

## H. P. ROBERTSON COMPANY
Jamestown, New York
ACTIVE: early 20th century
General line of Mission oak furniture
SHOPMARK: rectangular paper label

## ROSS CHAIR MANUFACTURING COMPANY
Louisville, Kentucky
ACTIVE: early 20th century
General line of low-quality Mission oak furniture
SHOPMARK: rectangular paper label

## SHEBOYGAN FURNITURE COMPANY
Sheboygan, Wisconsin
ACTIVE: ca. 1910
Line of small Mission oak furniture: plant stands, wastebaskets, smoking
    stands, bookracks, etc
SHOPMARK: paper label

## SHEBOYGAN CHAIR COMPANY
Sheboygan, Wisconsin
ACTIVE: early 20th century
Mission oak chairs
SHOPMARK: square decal containing name and location, plus intertwined
S/C/C in a red square

## SIKES CHAIR COMPANY
Buffalo, New York
SHOPMARK: rectangular paper label with light lettering on black or blue
background

## SLIGH FURNITURE COMPANY
Grand Rapids, Michigan
ACTIVE: 1880–undetermined
Limited line of Mission oak furniture
SHOPMARK: brass tag; also paper label with name in triangle with red,
white and blue ink; also paper shipping label tacked onto piece

## SKANDA FURNITURE CO
Rockford, Illinois
ACTIVE: early 20th century
General line of Mission oak furniture
SHOPMARK: undetermined

## SKINNER AND STEENMAN
Grand Rapids, Michigan
ACTIVE: early 20th century
Line of Mission oak dining room suites
SHOPMARK: undetermined

## SWAN FURNITURE
Wadhams Mills, New York
ACTIVE: early 20th century
General line of Mission oak furniture
SHOPMARK: MAYFLOWER label

## SWEET AND BIGGS
Grand Rapids, Michigan
ACTIVE: early 20th century
Line of Mission oak chairs
SHOPMARK: undetermined

## THOMPSON MANUFACTURING CO
Holland and Grand Rapids, Michigan
ACTIVE: early 20th century
General line of smaller Mission oak furniture
SHOPMARK: paper label with red ink "Crafstyle (sic) Furniture"

## TRAVERSE CITY CHAIR COMPANY
Traverse City, Michigan
ACTIVE: early 20th century
Line of Mission oak chairs
SHOPMARK: undetermined

## MARTIN TROMP
Holland, Michigan
ACTIVE: early 20th century
Line of smaller Mission oak furniture
SHOPMARK: undetermined

## UDELL WORKS
Indianapolis, Indiana
ACTIVE: early 20th century
General line of Mission oak furniture
SHOPMARK: red rectangular decal

## C. A. WARNER & CO
New York, New York
ACTIVE: early 20th century
Mission oak tall clocks
SHOPMARK: undetermined

## WILKINSON & EASTWOOD
Binghamton, New York
ACTIVE: early 20th century
General line of Mission oak furniture
SHOPMARK: undetermined

## WISCONSIN MANUFACTURING CO
Jefferson, Wisconsin
ACTIVE: early 20th century
General line of Mission oak furniture
SHOPMARK: undetermined

## WOLVERINE MANUFACTURING CO
Detroit, Michigan
ACTIVE: early 20th century
General line of Mission oak furniture
SHOPMARK: large circular decal

## WOODCRAFT GUILD
Location unknown, possibly Sheboygan, Wisconsin
ACTIVE: early 20th century
Line of small Mission oak furniture
SHOPMARK: medallion-shaped decal with firm's name over color illustration of woodworker sawing a board with an old handsaw

# PART 3

# METALWARE AND ACCESSORIES

# EVALUATING ARTS AND CRAFTS METALWARE

*by Bruce Johnson*

The quiet revolution, as some might call the Arts and Crafts movement, was not limited to architecture, art pottery, and furniture. The goal of social reformers on both sides of the Atlantic was to create homes filled with beautiful but practical objects handcrafted by men and women working in pleasant surroundings and earning an amount equal to their skill and ability. Metalsmiths of this era, men and women such as Clara Barck Welles, Karl Kipp, Victor Toothaker, and Dirk Van Erp, rose to the challenge and created hand-hammered objects in copper, brass, and silver that would complement the handcrafted oak furniture of the era.

Copper was the metal of choice of most Arts and Crafts metalsmiths, for, like oak, it remained affordable for the middle class. In addition, copper could be worked easier than either brass, bronze or iron, making it possible for a shop like the Roycrofters in East Aurora, NY to turn out thousands of bowls, vases, bookends, desk sets, and lighting fixtures. Some shops, most notably Kalo outside Chicago and Arthur Stone in Boston, continued the Victorian tradition of working in sterling silver but adopted the principles of the Arts and Crafts movement in its execution, eliminating unnecessary ornamentation and producing forms that were at once beautiful, artistic, handcrafted, and simple.

Just as the oak boards that went into each piece of Arts and Crafts furniture were fumed with ammonia to give them the appearance of being much older than they actually were, the copperware of the Arts and Crafts movement was also chemically treated to transform it from a bright piece of shiny copper in to one with a warm, rich patina like that found on a piece made hundreds of years earlier. And like the furniture manufacturers of this era, individual metalsmiths and metal shops most often stamped their identifying mark on the bottom of each piece they produced.

Distinguishing a well-made example of Arts and Crafts metal from a

Fine and rare Roycroft hammered copper bud vase designed by Dard Hunter with four flaring buttresses and four nickel silver squares on woodgrain texturing. Excellent original dark patina, small dent to rim. Early orb and cross mark, 8" × 4½", $5,500-7,500

mediocre one, however, requires more than a familiarity with the most common marks. Within any shop the quality of work could vary depending on whether it was designed and produced by one of the more experienced metalsmiths or by one of the apprentices. When evaluating any piece of Arts and Crafts metalware, then, consider the following:

## 1. IS IT SIGNED?

Finding a shopmark on a piece of Arts and Crafts metalware is easier than finding one on a piece of Arts and Crafts furniture, and, since the marks were generally stamped into the metal, they are less apt to have been removed or damaged. The mark will indicate from which shop the piece came and, on occasion, when it was made, but not always who made it. The Roycrofters, for instance, used different shopmarks over the course of three decades, but none would indicate which pieces were made by which craftsman. Certain collectors will seek items from one particular shop and if that shop, like the Roycrofters or the Van Erp Studio, has a reputation for having designed and produced quality items, then the shopmark will affect the value of the piece. Provided, that is, it meets the other criteria.

Unfortunately, unsigned metalware will have a problem generating much interest unless it can be proved by comparison to signed or cataloged examples to have come from a particular shop. Most Arts and Crafts metalsmith shops were diligent about signing their work, so when an unsigned piece of unusual quality shows up it is generally accompanied by the question: Why wasn't it signed? In some cases the piece may not have been intended to be sold. If it were to be used in the firm's office or the owner's home, a shopmark might have seemed unnecessary to the craftsman completing it. Some shops also permitted craftsmen to make objects for their own homes on their own time; these were often identical to signed items made a few hours earlier but were intentionally left unsigned. Years later, many of these unsigned pieces surfaced through estate sales and since circulated as attributions.

Amateur metalsmiths generally did not have a shopmark, so most of their home work was left unsigned. In most instances the quality of craftsmanship and the design will clearly indicate that it was amateur work, but there will always be the possibility that an amateur metalsmith turned out an impressive, but unsigned, Arts and Crafts piece. Ironically, these pieces are actually more in tune with the original Arts and Crafts philosophy than many factory-produced pieces that command higher prices.

## 2. HOW HEAVY IS IT?

While silver collectors traditionally consider weight when evaluating a piece, collectors of Arts and Crafts copper do not need to invest in a scale. Arts and Crafts collectors have discovered, however, that some firms used a very thin gauge of copper while others opted to use a heavier gauge. All other criteria being equal (which usually they weren't as firms that used lightweight materials usually cut corners on design and craftsmanship, too), a heavy piece will bring more than a lighter piece.

## 3. HOW PLEASING IS THE DESIGN?

Major Arts and Crafts firms often employed a number of designers, some of whom were better than others at creating a design that could be coaxed willingly out of a flat sheet of metal. Good design is difficult to define, but easy to spot. The curve of a lamp base, the height of a candlestick, the flair on the

Pair of Roycroft hammered copper bookends with riveted, repoussé poppies. Original medium patina. Orb-and-cross mark, 5½" × 5", $747

neck of a bowl or any element on a piece can be soothing, natural, and inspi-rational—or they can be awkward, jarring, and as discordant as the wrong pitch. There is no formula to learn. Collectors can only study hundreds of ex-amples in books, in catalogs, and in person at museums and auctions. Note which ones command the most respect and study their forms to determine what secret the designer knew that set his or her work apart from others. Once you see it, you will never forget it. The greatest challenge to a new col-lector is being able to pass on a piece that is relatively inexpensive precisely because it is of poor design.

## 4. HOW WELL WAS IT CRAFTED?

During the Arts and Crafts era metalsmiths utilized at least three means of forming a piece. Starting with a piece of flat, unblemished, shiny copper, the craftsman would hammer it into shape using a variety of hammers and "stakes" mounted on his anvil or workbench. The hammering marks would purposely be left in the surface of the metal as proof that the piece had, in-deed, been "hand-hammered." It has been reported that metalsmiths could identify who in their shop had made a particular piece by the characteristics of the hammer marks, but, unfortunately, that information was rarely, if ever, recorded. Arts and Crafts collectors prize highly those pieces that show evidence of having been hand-hammered by a skilled craftsman.

Cost-conscious companies soon developed a means of achieving the hammered effect without additional hand labor; machines were invented that would produce a uniform hand-hammered effect on a sheet of copper or brass before it was ever turned over to the craftsman. Collectors can deter-

Heintz sterling-on-bronze tall vase with overlay of a rose on a verdigris ground. A few very small dents to base. Stamped HAMS/Patent 1912/Ovington Fifth Ave., 12¼" × 5", $805

mine whether a piece was hand-hammered or machine-hammered by inspecting the planishing marks closely. The machine-hammered marks will be nearly identical in pattern, depth, and dimensions; in contrast, marks left by a craftsman and his hammer will vary slightly from those around them. To a serious collector the difference is crucial.

The third method, referred to as "spun" copper, appeared as interest in the Arts and Crafts movement began to lose momentum in the late 1910s and early 1920s. Just as quickly as pegged joints became associated with outdated furniture, hand-hammered marks were deemed old-fashioned. In an effort to remain current, many shops began offering copper wares in a smooth, unhammered style. Spun-copper pieces were produced by pressing a flat piece of copper against a rapidly turning wooden form mounted on a lathe. Unfortunately, by this time the weight of the copper had also been reduced, and the net result was that these pieces rarely equaled the quality of workmanship, design, or materials of the earlier examples.

## 5. HOW WAS IT FINISHED?

Another consideration in evaluating Arts and Crafts metalware is the finish. Often referred to as the "patina" of the piece, the finish can have a dramatic effect on the value of any piece of metalware.

In some instances the piece may have been permitted to age naturally without benefit of a chemical process. From the workshop's standpoint, this was not always the most desirable, for copper ages slowly and unevenly. More often, the pieces were sent from the workshop to the adjacent finishing room, where they would be carefully polished to remove fingerprints and surface contaminants, then submerged in vats of chemicals which, depending on the ingredients, would alter the color of the metal. The major workshops offered a variety of finishes in an attempt to satisfy, within a certain framework, the tastes and styles of the day. The most popular of the Roycroft patinas was aurora brown, described as a "golden red brown finish." The Roycroft finishing rooms also developed several other finishes, including a rarely found blue-bronze patina, a limited line of Italian polychrome pieces featuring a greenish patina in the hammered areas, the more common Sheffield silver-plated wares, and the popular brass-plated copper items. At one time collectors were known to purposely remove the original patina and replace it with one considered more desirable, but today each type of finish has attracted its own group of collectors who value the merits of that particular type of finish.

As interest in Arts and Crafts metalware has grown, it has spurred an interest in duplicating the original patina that has often been destroyed by an enthusiastic yet uninformed owner who made the mistake of polishing the piece. In a few instances the repatination technique has been developed by craftsmen-chemists to such a fine art that even the most experienced collector cannot distinguish between it and an original. In all too many cases the repatination attempt leaves the piece with a mottled, unnatural-appearing patina rather than a uniform one. Distinguishing between the two is important, for even a fine example of repatination work will not make a piece as valuable as an original, untouched example. To illustrate, a vase valued at $300 in its original patina would be worth no more than $225 if it has been repatinated. Nevertheless, had that same piece been polished to a blinding brightness, it might be worth only $75 on the basis of its design alone. For that reason, repatination, like refinishing, can serve a useful purpose, so long as a repatinated piece is both identified as such and priced accordingly.

Many repatinated pieces can be identified on close examination. Experienced collectors have learned to look on the bottoms of pieces they suspect may have been repatinated, for if the bottom has a perfect, unscarred appearance, the piece was either never used or recently treated to a chemical bath. In a similar manner, high spots on the outside of the piece should show some evidence of wear. If the piece has a perfect patina, beware; even a seldom-used piece of metalware should show some evidence of having survived for as close to 100 years.

## 6. IS IT DAMAGED OR HAS IT BEEN REPAIRED?

Like furniture from this era, the condition of the metalware is also an important consideration when determining the value of a piece. Normal wear is both expected and appreciated as a sign that a piece has proved beneficial in many people's lives. It is not an indication that a piece should be repatinated, for that process should be reserved only for those pieces that have been polished. Minor dents, like normal wear, will not detract from the value of a piece as long as they do not detract from the beauty as well. Rare and important pieces can actually be seriously damaged in the attempt to remove a minor dent, for the stress applied to the metal can adversely affect the finish, especially if it is an early form of lacquer applied to the patina to retard additional darkening.

## 7. IS IT A RARE, DESIRABLE FORM?

Rarity and demand always play a role in the determination of the value of any antique. Roycroft letter openers were mass produced, even if by hand, and remain one of the least expensive of all of their wares. The same inexpensive letter opener with a cutout design in the handle or applied squares of German silver suddenly stands out from the rest and commands a price many times that of an ordinary and common letter opener. Roycroft designers and craftsmen Dard Hunter and Karl Kipp collaborated on a few lamps

Fine Kalo Shops hammered sterling silver ovoid pitcher. (Pictured in Sharon Darling, "Chicago Metal Work.") Stamped Kalo Sterling/Chicago/New York, 9" × 6½", $2,415

in 1909 and 1910, and the combination of the quality of craftsman and design, plus the reputation of the two designers, makes them both rare and desirable.

Determining which pieces from any shop are rare, however, is difficult, for production figures have never been discovered that would indicate exactly how many examples of each particular design were produced. Instead, to judge the relative rarity of a piece, collectors have to rely on the number of times that particular form becomes available. When an item appears for the first time at a major auction, it is bound to stir excitement in a crowd of bidders; but if the resulting publicity draws out a dozen more examples the following year, then the first price may never be equaled, let alone surpassed.

Collecting metalware of the Arts and Crafts era may perhaps be the most enjoyable of all the areas discussed in this study, for it has been widely distributed, both in its day and ours; much of it remains both inexpensive and practical; and it complements the other areas. Even if your interest is only in books from this period, hand-hammered bookends display them as they were meant to be seen. The metalware blends well with the art pottery of this era, especially that from shops that adopted Arts and Crafts designs, such as Marblehead, Walrath, Grueby, and Hampshire. And the heavy, often dark furniture of Roycroft, Stickley, and Limbert appreciates the glow of copper, brass, or silver to enliven its otherwise staid appearance. The complete Arts and Crafts collector is the well-balanced collector: philosophy, furniture, pottery, metalware—and information.

# METALWARE MANUFACTURERS

## Gorham Manufacturing Company

SHOPMARK: Outline of a lion, an anchor, and the letter G, all beneath outstretched eagle and word MARTELÉ.

PRINCIPAL CONTRIBUTION: Hand-hammered silver line with Art Nouveau embellishments.

FOUNDERS: Jabez Gorham, born: 1792, died: 1869. John Gorham, born: 1820, died: 1898, founded: 1831, closed: current.

STUDIOS AND SALESROOMS: Gorham Manufacturing Company, Providence, Rhode Island, 1831–current.

"A very fine ground effect is produced by finishing the article first, then peaning it in regular courses and then chasing devices in the rough surface, smoothing the chased parts. The effect has a remarkably fine appearance."

—*Diary of a Silversmith, 1876*[1]

When 21-year-old John Gorham joined his father, Jabez Gorham, in 1841 in what was then to be known for a brief period of time as Gorham & Son, he brought a desire for innovative expansion to the stable, conservative business foundation that his father had established. Against the advice of his father, who retired in 1847 rather than risk his savings in the firm's expansion, John Gorham borrowed the money to build a new factory, increased both his work and sales force, and expanded the company's line from silver spoons to hollowware, such as tea sets, bowls, and presentation pieces. Over the course of the next five decades Gorham was to encounter numerous setbacks, but each proved to be but a temporary hindrance to his goal—to make Gorham silver the most respected in the country.

One of his first important designers was George Wilkinson (1819–94), who created some of Gorham's most impressive high Victorian styles before his death. His place was then taken by William C. Codman (1839–1921), who was responsible for Gorham's entry into the Art Nouveau and Arts and Crafts styles of silver production. George Wilkinson had helped raise Gorham to where its chief competitor was Tiffany and Company, but it was Tiffany that captured world attention in 1876 with the introduction of hand-hammered silver. As author Charles H. Carpenter, Jr., observed, "The idea of leaving a hammered surface on a piece of silverware is a complete reversal of the traditional idea of smoothing out hammer marks in a finished object. Hammer marks of various kinds have been left on silverware since the beginnings of the craft, but it was usually thought that such marks were an indication that the piece had not been quite finished."[2] Although Tiffany acknowledged his indebtedness to the Japanese for the idea of hand-hammering, the fame was still Tiffany's. Gorham quickly introduced its own style of hammering, which differed from that of Tiffany; whereas Tiffany hammering appears uniform and controlled, Gorham silver reveals the freedom given each silversmith to select the size and pattern of hammering deemed appropriate to his particular piece.

By 1877, when the Arts and Crafts movement was still more than 20 years away, a growing number of silversmiths across the country had adopted the hammering technique introduced by Tiffany. The emergence of the Arts and Crafts movement found an audience philosophically receptive to hand-hammered metalware, and as Carpenter points out, "the hammered surfaces were not only beautiful in the way they broke up light into glittering reflections, they were also practical. Hammered silver didn't show finger marks as easily as plain, highly polished silver."[3]

Although the hand-hammered effect is most often associated with the Arts and Crafts movement, Gorham's first ventures into this technique were inspired by the Art Nouveau style. In 1890 the new Gorham Manufacturing plant was opened, and the company entered into a period of continued artistic and financial achievement. Although not considered at the time as important as its other projects, in 1893 Gorham experimented with applying silver overlay on Rookwood vases and ewers. The silver was not signed and the project was soon discontinued, making those surviving examples extremely valuable today.

In 1896 William Codman introduced what was to later be named Martelé (French for "hand-hammered") silver. The line was put into full production by 1900, reflecting Gorham's decision to "take a direction toward expensive, prestigious, handmade silverwares . . . a direct outgrowth of the English Arts and Crafts movement."[4] But while most other silversmithing firms were executing Colonial Revival forms in the hand-hammered Arts and Crafts technique, William Codman's craftsmen at Gorham applied the same technique to the Art Nouveau style. Although the Gorham factory was the most advanced of its kind, the Martelé line was made entirely by hand. Hammering was subtle, and a mild oxidation chemical was applied to highlight the carvings.

The Gorham Martelé line garnered numerous awards at the 1904 St. Louis Exposition, but as the Arts and Crafts movement progressed, desire for their "floral and naturalistic imagery. . . in the French Art Nouveau design"[5]—even in a hand-hammered technique—began to falter. By 1912 the line had been discontinued except for a few special commissions. William Codman, who personally designed the vast majority of the Martelé pieces, retired in 1914 at the age of 75. The Gorham company responded with a number of new designs, including an Art Deco line, and has enjoyed continued success.

### SELECTED PRICES

Centerpiece: Martelé sterling silver, oval form with raised, shaped edge with chased anemones and bud border with swag stems on scrolled raised foot, monogrammed interior, 4" × 13" × 11", $2,500–$3,500

Cigarette holders: beaded rim over band of chased hands holding cigars in repeating design, angled bowl on pedestal fitting into scored marble base, silver hallmarked, 4", $700–$900

Inkwell: #2342 Martelé sterling silver, square lid with leaves and poppies on oval form, with pen tray with vines on raised S-curve feet, 6" × 11", $2,500–$3,500

Pot: #9988 Martelé sterling silver, bud finial on fluted hinged lid, elongated lobed neck, spout and curved handle on sectioned melon-shape base, chased with violets and buds, raised scroll foot, 11", $2,250–$3,250

## Heintz Art Metal Shop

SHOPMARK: (1903–06) THE ART CRAFTS SHOP, BUFFALO, NY, PAT. JUL 21–03 impressed in metal (1906–12) PAT. APD. FOR (Note: this is considered a transitional mark utilized while the firm was obtaining patents for its overlay process.)

(1912–1930) initials H.A.M.S. in diamond over STERLING ON BRONZE and patent date (Note: This mark is generally impressed in the metal, but may be found as a paper label.)

PRINCIPAL CONTRIBUTIONS: Copper and bronze desk sets, bowls, and accessories with sterling silver overlay.
FOUNDER  Otto L. Heintz.
ACTIVE:  ca. 1903–30.
Art Crafts Shop: 1903–06.
Heintz Art Metal Shop: 1906–30.
STUDIOS AND SALESROOMS:  Buffalo, New York.

> "Beautiful colored effects have been produced after much thought and experiment and our efforts are now devoted almost entirely to three finishes."
>
> —*Otto Heintz, undated brochure*[1]

Long before the Arts and Crafts movement had taken root in America, two brothers, Charles and Louis Heintz, had started manufacturing Victorian jewelry in the mid–1870s under the name of Heintz Brothers in Buffalo, New York. By the turn of the century, the family business was being run by Edwin and Otto Heintz, who in all likelihood were the sons of Louis. While little is known about the family dynamics, by 1903 Otto Heintz had purchased another Buffalo business—the Arts and Crafts Company—and, over the course of the next three years changed the name first to the Art Crafts Shop and, finally, in 1906 to the Heintz Art Metal Shop.

When he purchased it, the Arts and Crafts Company was already producing a line of simple copper and bronze vases, bowls, and small items of

Tall Heintz sterling-on-bronze ovoid vase with goldenrod overlay on an excellent bronze patina. Stamped mark, 12½" × 5½", $805

Large and rare Heintz Sterling-on-Bronze mushroom-shaped table lamp with three sockets and overlay of berries and leaves. Wear to patina on top of shade. Stamped HAMS, with patent, 17" × 15", $10,925

undistinguished design and devoid of any silver overlay. Under Otto Heintz's direction, the craftsmen at the Heintz Art Metal Shop produced an array of bronze vases, desk sets, small boxes, and candlesticks, plus a few monumental table lamps. Unlike the Roycrofters or the Dirk Van Erp Studio, however, the craftsmen at the Heintz Art Metal Shop did not employ traditional Arts and Crafts hand-hammering techniques; instead, they "spun" the pieces by pressing flat sheets of bronze against a spinning form mounted on a lathe or cut them out using sheers and shaped them with a minimum amount of hand-hammering. As noted authority David Surgan points out, "Heintz Art Metal Shop items distinguish themselves from most Arts and Crafts period metalware in obvious ways: Heintz ware is made of bronze and not copper and it is decidedly not hammered; decoration and 'texture' are provided by the application of sterling silver overlays without the use of solder; and finally the patinas are both unique and noteworthy."[2]

What distinguished Heintz Art Metal from spun metal pieces made by other firms, the majority of which have garnered little attention from Arts and Crafts collectors, is the silver overlay, that the craftsmen carefully attached to the bronze using a unique heating process that Otto Heintz had patented by 1912. The pattern of the overlay was modeled to compliment the design of the piece, whether it be a slender bud vase, a bookmark, or a table lamp. The silver overlay took many forms, including geometric forms, Art Nouveau designs, birds, leaves, branches, plants, and flowers. In addition, the craftsmen at Heintz Art Metal developed a number of patinas, including Verde, a dark green favored by many Arts and Crafts collectors; Royal, an iridescent red; Bronze, a light brown color; and French gray, which had the same effect as silver plating. The firm also experimented with other patinas over the years.

Otto Heintz died unexpectedly in 1918 and the following year several of the key Heintz Art Metal employees, led by salesman Fred Smith, formed a new company, the Smith Metal Arts Company, not far away. Not surprisingly, their forms and silver overlay decorations closely resembled those of Heintz Art Metal, although the new company adapted its own "Silver Crest" mark. The Heintz Art Metal Shop remained in business for 10 more years, but eventually closed in 1930. The Smith Metal Arts Company, under Fred Smith's leadership, gradually began introducing new forms with unique patinas. "As the 1920s progressed," Kevin McConnell notes, "the Smith Metal Arts Company relied less and less upon imitation, eventually diversifying its line of bronze wares with a plethora of highly original designs and finishes."[3] Indicative of the firm's ability to adjust to changing tastes, it is still in business today, manufacturing high-quality desk sets.

While Arts and Crafts collectors initially shied away from Heintz Art Metal pieces, they have grown in popularity as prices for hand-hammered wares by the Roycrofters, Dirk Van Erp and other firms have escalated. Collectors have also come to appreciate the workmanship required by the silver overlay process and the quality patinas developed at the shop. As would be expected, collectors of Heintz Art Metal are willing to pay a premium for the green patinas which display well with the green art pottery of the period. When the combination of the Verde patina, a desirable form, and a strong presence of silver overlay comes onto the market in the form of a Heintz Art Metal vase or lamp, collectors are no longer shy about going after it.

Heintz sterling-on-bronze table lamp with squat base and silver floral bouquet overlay, the shade with cutout panels of the same motif over (new) mica, original verdigris patina. Stamp mark, 15½" × 11", $2,875

## SELECTED PRICES

Bookends: #7090D with variegated green patina and silver overlay of cattails, 5¾", $275–$375

Bowl: #3589 with brown patina and silver overlay of plant form, 2" × 8", $300–$400

Bowl: #3706 with green patina and silver pine tree overlay, 2" × 9", $375–$475

Calendar and Letter Rack: #1177 with silver overlay on front, brown patina, 3" × 5", $75–$150

Candlestick: Tiffany–style with brown patina, tulip–shaped socket, circular base with geometric overlay in silver, 14", $600–$700

Inkwell: #1177 with pen rest and silver overlay on inkwell lid, brown patina, 2½", $125–$200

Jardiniere: #3574A: bronze with brown patina and extensive silver overlay in vine and leaf pattern, 6", $1,350–$1,500

Lamp, desk: adjustable helmet shade with brown patina and overlay of goldenrod on shade and circular base, 10", $1,300–$1,500

Lamp, table: adjustable helmet shade with green patina and silver overlay on circular base and rim of shade, 13", $2,000–$2,500

Lamp, table: large mushroom form in dark brown patina with silver overlay of vine and leaf design on base and shade, 17" × 14", $12,000–$14,000

Picture frame: bronze with silver overlay of stems, leaves and flower petals around border, brown patina, 7", $600–$700

Vase, stick: tall cylindrical form with circular base, silver overlay of stems and leaves, brown patina, 12", $250–$350

Vase: bulbous form with silver overlay of leaves, dark brown patina, 3½", $225–$325

Vase: #3840 with green patina and silver overlay, 8", $650–$750

Vase: #3816 with dark brown patina, flared rim and sloping shoulders; silver overlay in floral design, 4½", $275–$375

Vase: #3668B, cylinder form with green patina and silver overlay of hollyhock stem, 6", $400–$500

Vase: tapering cylindrical form with flared base and rim, dark brown patina, silver overlay of wild rose, 12", $700–$800

Vase: #3543B with tapering form and silver overlay of single rose, green patina, 5", $325–$425

# The Jarvie Shop

SHOPMARK: Script signature JARVIE or MADE BY THE JARVIE SHOP.

PRINCIPAL CONTRIBUTIONS: Candlesticks and lanterns, hand-hammered bowls, trays, desk sets, and accessories.

FOUNDER: Robert R. Jarvie. Born: 1865, died: 1941, founded: 1904, closed: 1917.

STUDIOS AND SALESROOMS: The Jarvie Shop, Chicago, 1904–ca. 1920.

> "Determined to succeed—being a Scotchman—Mr. Jarvie purchased sheet iron and rivets, and at a temporary work bench set up in one corner of the dining-room of his apartment, began his serious work as a craftsman. Only the angels who hover above the earnest arts and crafts workers can tell why he was not driven forth from that building by the irate tenants below, when nightly the sound of his hammer was persistently heard."
> —*the Craftsman, 1903*[1]

Like Gustav Stickley the following year, when Robert Jarvie passed away in 1941 at the Scottish Old People's Home outside Chicago, he may well have considered his venture into the Arts and Crafts movement a failure. Like so

Rare and exceptional Jarvie four-piece hand-hammered polished brass coffee set, with riveted spouts and boar's tusks handles, monogrammed LPH. Marked Jarvie, 9" × 7", $23,000

many of the craftsmen whose shops—furniture, pottery, and metalware—flourished during the reign of the Arts and Crafts movement, he was unable to survive the change in public tastes that began around 1920 and continued to erode interest in handcrafted wares.

Jarvie was a 35-year-old Department of Transportation official for the city of Chicago when he entered two simple iron lanterns in a 1900 Arts and Crafts Society exhibition. They and several subsequent candlesticks displayed at the Art Institute Show in 1903 attracted the attention of both the press and the public, prompting the *Craftsman* to comment that "one has but to visit the department and the so-called art stores crowded with impossible creations of metal, gauze, silk, beads and paper, in order to appreciate the quiet but satisfying beauty of Mr. Jarvie's lampshades. The motive in all Mr. Jarvie's work is utility and simple beauty rather than a striving for striking effects."[2] After the close of the show Jarvie and his wife, Lillian Gray Jarvie, opened their first shop in their home and in 1902 issued their first catalog, containing lanterns, lamps, shades and candlesticks. Prior to 1902 Jarvie did not make it a point to sign his work; increased competition after that date may have been what prompted him to begin signing his work with his name in script.

By 1904 Jarvie had received enough encouragement and commissions to leave a secure future with the city and open the Jarvie Shop in the Fine Arts Building in downtown Chicago. Much of his early work consisted of iron lanterns with horn shades (procured from the nearby stockyards) and candlesticks ranging in style from Colonial to Art Nouveau cast from brass or copper and "brush polished, a process which leaves the metal with a dull glow."[3] As the observer from the *Craftsman* went on to describe, "Some pieces are cast in bronze and their unpolished surfaces are treated with acids which produce an exquisite antique green finish."[4] By 1906 his work was offered for sale in nearly 20 retail outlets nationwide.

The "Candlestick Maker," as he was soon called, designed a number of "slender candlesticks which so fluidly glided between a finely proportioned base and socket,"[5] and proved so popular that he was unable to meet the growing demand for his work. In addition to his famous brass and bronze candlesticks, he and a pair of young apprentices were kept busy producing a number of related copper and brass accessories, including inkwells, bowls, smoking sets, trays, bookends, and wall sconces. By 1910 Jarvie had widened his scope to include silver and gold, which led to a number of commissions for hand-hammered silver trophies, engraved silver pitchers and punch bowls, and a line of silver tea sets in the Colonial style of Paul Revere. His most important work of this era was a 1910 sterling silver presentation bowl commissioned by the Chicago Cliff-Dwellers Club.

In 1912 he moved his studio to a building near the Union Stockyards in Chicago and began to concentrate on his silver presentation work rather than

Fine and rare Jarvie brass omicron three-branch candelabra with curled riveted brackets inset with torch-shaped inserts. (Discovered in a basement in Orange County, California). Original untouched naturally ocurring patina, a few scratches. Incised Jarvie, 10½" × 7", $24,150

his Arts and Crafts candlesticks. Two talented immigrant silversmiths, Knut Gustafson and John Petterson, went to work for Jarvie around this time. It was at this time Jarvie also collaborated with Prairie school architect George Grant Elmslie on a number of trophies.[6]

Despite glowing reviews, such as one in the *Craftsman* declaring that "the graceful outlines and soft luster of the unembellished metal combine to produce dignity as well as beauty,"[7] by 1917 Jarvie was forced to close his shop and take a job as a salesman for one of Chicago's popular silver firms. Now, all of the work of Robert Jarvie is actively sought by Arts and Crafts collectors. Especially prized are matched pairs of copper, brass, or silver-plated candlesticks, although even individual candlesticks attract a great deal of attention from Arts and Crafts collectors, for, as one reviewer noted in 1903, "the possessor of one of the Jarvie candlesticks must feel that nothing tawdry or frivolous can be placed by its side."[8]

Jarvie bronze presentation box designed by Robert Jarvie and George Elmslie for the A.M.P.A. (American Meat Packing Association) convention of 1912, its lid and base decorated in a signature Elmslie motif. Original patina. Die-stamped "Made by Robert Jarvie/Union Stockyards/Chicago," 1¾" × 4¼" × 2", $1,250–$1,750

**SELECTED PRICES**

Production at Jarvie's shop remained limited; thus, examples of his work are considered both rare and, in many cases, extremely valuable. While candlesticks are the most often discovered examples of his work, the difference between a $300 pair of brass candlesticks and a $3,000 pair of similar-appearing candlesticks is too subtle to be described in this study. As in all metalwork, style, patina, and rarity are the determining factors in evaluating Jarvie's work. Advanced collectors should be consulted before buying or selling important Jarvie pieces.

## The Kalo Shop

SHOPMARKS: (Early) Word KALO.
(Later) Words HAND BEATEN or HAND WROUGHT AT THE KALO SHOP(S)/STERLING/CHICAGO and/or NEW YORK and/or PARK RIDGE[1].
DATING KEY: PARK RIDGE (1905–14), NEW YORK (1914–18), HAND BEATEN (1905–1914), HAND WROUGHT (after 1914)[2].
PRINCIPAL CONTRIBUTIONS: Copper and silver bowls, trays, desk sets, jewelry, and silver dining ware.
FOUNDER Clara P. Barck. Born: 1868, died: 1965 (retired 1940), founded: 1900, closed: 1970.
STUDIOS AND SALESROOMS: Kalo Shop, Chicago, 1900–70
New York (salesrooms only), 1914–18.

> "Beautiful, Useful, and Enduring"
> —The Kalo Shop motto

One woman–Clara Barck Welles–while not a household name even in Arts and Crafts circles, may well have ultimately been responsible for the training of more Arts and Crafts silversmiths than anyone else associated with the movement. What eventually grew to become Chicago's most prolific source of handmade silver tableware began in 1900 as 32-year-old Clara Barck's small leather shop on Dearborn Street. From the beginning it was her intention to establish a business that would both teach and train young women who had an interest in arts and crafts. When, in 1905, she married metalsmith George S. Welles, the "Kalo girls"—and young men—soon had the opportunity to add metalwork and jewelry design to their repertoire.

While their early metalwork concentrated on copper bowls, trays, desk sets, and jewelry, Clara Welles soon expanded their small but growing operation into handmade silverwork. Simple sterling silver bowls, candlesticks, tea and sugar sets, pitchers, and flatware in the current Arts and Crafts style

Fine Kalo Shops hand wrought
sterling silver octagonal pitcher
with angular handle and applied
initial "L", the bottom engraved
"January 10, 1914." Small dent to
one panel. Die-stamped mark, and
numbered, 9½" × 8", $4,312

featuring a hammered surface found a number of ready buyers, even long
after the initial fervor had cooled. As Sharon Darling observed in her detailed study, "A few pieces of Kalo hollowware made before 1914 displayed
flaring side handles and were set with stones in the manner favored by
Charles R. Ashbee and other silversmiths of the British Arts and Crafts
movement. Such designs were soon abandoned, however, in favor of soft
curves which gave objects a gently rounded look."[3]

As the firm's reputation for quality grew, the staff was besieged with ap-
plications from aspiring silversmiths, both male and female. At any given
time workers in the shop would consist of students, apprentices, and trained
employees, many of whom later established their own silver shops in
Chicago. Awards and recognition soon followed, and the shop's fame, both
artistic and popular, spread across the country. While many of its popular

Fine Kalo Shops handwrought
sterling silver syrup dispenser and
underplate, both with applied
initial "L." A couple of small dents
to dispenser. Die-stamped mark,
and numbered, 4½" × 6", $2,645

styles were continued for several years, the "substantial handwrought hammer-textured silverware designed by Mrs. Welles in plain, paneled, and fluted shapes, infrequently ornamented with chasing, was consistently expressive of the metal and revealed subtle shifts in styles and tastes."[4]

Clara Barck Welles retired in 1940 and in 1959 gave the Kalo Shops to four of her loyal employees.

## SELECTED PRICES

Bowl: wide hammered–copper form with curled edge, silvered interior, 3" × 9", $450–$600

Bowl: copper form with silver wash, 2" × 5", $300–$350

Bowl: #20H, sterling silver, three indentations around top, 3" × 4", $350–$450

Bowl: #P12M, hand–hammered silver, linear design around top, 2" × 6", $450–$550

Bowl: sterling silver, showing a conventionalized repoussé design repeated five times, 3" × 4", $600–$700

Box, stamp: sterling silver, ebonized fruitwood finial with beaded base on squat cylindrical form, with applied initials, 2" × 2", $300–$350

Cup, child's: silver with two embossed ducks on one side, applied curved handle, 3" × 4", $275–$325

Ice bucket: with liner, octagonal form tapering to footed base, corresponding liner with tab handles and pierced bowl, 5", $900–$1,100

Ice tongs: sterling silver, simple handle with cut–corner detail and a chased rib border, shaped pierced bowls, 8", $200–$300

Pitcher: sterling silver, paneled octagonal cylindrical form slightly indenting to a molded base, raised flat spout, rolled rim, square hollow handle, 9", $1,200–$1,300

Spoon, serving: sterling silver, painted bowl with long, flaring handle, embossed Y at the handle end, 14" × 1", $200–$225

Spoon and bowl: sterling silver, #7, 10" long, $400–$500

Tea set: tall teapot with ribbed body, ribbed creamer and sugar bowl, platform bases, large oval scalloped tray, ivory handle and finial, 19" × 12", $3,000–$4,000

Tray, serving: silver, circular, with attached center ring, 11", $500–$700

Tray: #3, sterling silver, hand–hammered, three indentations around top in clover leaf shape, 6", $400–$600

Tray: serving, sterling silver, with three lobes on each end, 5" × 14", $500–$700

# Karl Kipp (The Tookay Shop)

SHOPMARK: The initials KK (first one reversed) enclosed in a circle.

PRINCIPAL CONTRIBUTIONS: Hand-hammered copper bowls, vases, and accessories.

FOUNDER: Karl Kipp. Born: ca. 1881, died: undetermined, founded: 1911, closed: 1915.

STUDIOS AND SALESROOMS: Roycroft Copper Shop, East Aurora, New York, 1908–11, 1915–31. Tookay Shop, East Aurora, New York, 1911–15.

"The rare coloring of these pieces adds to their individuality and charm."
—Tookay advertisement, the Craftsman, 1912[1]

The secret to the success of the Roycroft enterprise lay not in Elbert Hubbard's skills in the field of either design or business management, but in his charisma and his ability to attract talented artisans, designers, and artists to East Aurora. Nowhere is this more evident than in the case of Karl Kipp and the ultimate success of the Roycroft Copper Shop. In 1908 the 27-year-old Karl Kipp walked away from a career in banking and moved his family to East Aurora, New York, where he asked to work in one of the craft shops in Elbert Hubbard's Roycroft colony of artisans.[2] Hubbard first assigned Kipp to the bookbindery, which had been in operation since before the turn of the century, as Hubbard's primary interest always had been and continued to be

Pair of Kark Kipp hammered copper Princess candlesticks with riveted double-stem shaft on faceted base. Good original patina. Stamped KK, 8", $1,092

publishing. While Hubbard's own skills lay in his flowery style of persuasive writing and speaking, he was quick to recognize and promote talented individuals. By 1908 many metalshops—from Gustav Stickley's Craftsman Shops outside nearby Syracuse to Arthur J. Stone's silversmiths in Gardner, Massachusetts—were producing hand-hammered silver, copper, and brass wares, but Hubbard's small blacksmith shop had grown only to where it was producing copper pulls for the limited line of furniture and trim for the doors and interiors. Recognizing Kipp's natural sense for design, metal-work, and management, Hubbard soon appointed him head of the new Roycroft Copper Shop. From the bookbindery next door Kipp brought with him Walter Jennings, and the two men set about expanding the blacksmith shop at Roycroft into a copper shop of national importance.

With no prior experience and no one in East Aurora to train him, Kipp demonstrated a remarkable natural talent for design. From the very beginning his work revealed a familiarity with the designs of the Vienna seces-sionists, led by Josef Hoffmann, whose work was illustrated in current magazines and art books that Elbert Hubbard provided and encouraged his craftsmen to read. Within one year the Roycroft Copper Shop was able to re-lease a catalog of the wares Kipp and Jennings had designed and their grow-ing staff had produced. What is striking about some of these early designs is their advanced degree of sophistication: Kipp had incorporated cutout squares into geometric motifs reflective of Josef Hoffmann's designs as flu-ently as a craftsman who had worked with metalwares for several years rather than for only a matter of months.

In 1909 Dard Hunter, another Roycroft convert, returned from a sabbat-ical in Vienna and met Kipp for the first time. Hunter had become a Roy-crofter in 1903 but was away from his duties in the book-design and stained-glass departments studying in Europe when Kipp arrived in East Aurora. The two became good friends and together designed and created a number of unique lamps and lighting fixtures. Their collaboration in the Roycroft Shops was brief, however, for Hunter left in early 1910, but not be-fore he had added to Kipp's education in modern design. Subsequent issues of the *Fra* magazine introduced metalwares with square silver overlay and candlesticks on chamfered squares or rectangular bases that became standard in Roycroft production for several years.

The Roycroft Copper Shop grew rapidly under Kipp's leadership, but in 1911 he and Walter Jennings left the Roycroft campus to form the Tookay Shop a short distance away. The reasons for their sudden departure have never been made clear; the two men may have differed with Elbert Hubbard over the Copper Shop operation or may simply have been convinced that they could duplicate the success of the Roycroft Copper Shop on their own without watching the majority of the profits go to Hubbard.

Whatever the reason, the Tookay Shop was in operation by 1912, when the first advertisements began appearing in the *Craftsman* magazine—a double annoyance, no doubt, to Elbert Hubbard. Kipp's new shopmark, two *K*'s back-to-back, began appearing on his designs, many of which were executed in pewter and silver, perhaps in an attempt to distinguish his new work from that being manufactured in the Roycroft Copper Shop. There the workers he had trained continued to produce copper wares based on his previous designs and stamped with the familiar orb-and-cross. Kipp and Jennings were on their way to establishing a successful business with a sales outlet in New York City when World War I erupted. On May 7, 1915, a German submarine torpedoed the *Lusitania*, sending Elbert and Alice Hubbard, along with more than a thousand others, to a watery grave. The shock swept through the country and the Roycroft campus. Thirty-two-year-old "Bert" Hubbard assumed control of his father's operation and almost immediately went to Kipp and Jennings to ask that they return to the Roycroft Copper Shop. It is uncertain whether Kipp and Jennings had grown somewhat disillusioned with self-employment or were beginning to feel the effect of the shortage of copper and brass caused by the war effort, but the pair returned that same year.

While Bert Hubbard never pretended to be the charismatic leader his father was, his business sense was just as keen. With Kipp and Jennings back in the Copper Shop, he instituted a national sales campaign for Roycroft metalwares. Rather than limiting sales to visitors to the campus and readers of their publications, Hubbard offered established retail stores across the country the opportunity to sell a wide range of Roycroft products in their showrooms, including books, leather items, and metalwares.[3] As a result, production in the Copper Shop increased dramatically. Kipp continued to create designs for the staff of nearly 35 apprentices and experienced metalsmiths, who churned out thousands of bookends, desk sets, bowls, vases, candlesticks, and ash trays. Although designers such as Dirk Van Erp criticized the restraint placed on the artistic freedom of the Roycroft metalsmiths, the emphasis remained on the production of uniform, quality metalwares rather than time-consuming experimental designs.

When the Arts and Crafts movement began to give way to new styles in the early 1920s, Kipp responded with a number of new designs. Unfortunately, a reduction in the thickness of the copper sheets ordered detracted from some of his designs, yet they still reveal a man in tune with the times. Some of Kipp's Art Deco bookends, for instance, preceded those of several of the best-known metalware designers of that era. Once the Depression set in, however, it became evident that bankruptcy was inevitable. Sales declined, and gradually most of the Copper Shop employees were released. Karl Kipp retired from the Roycroft Copper Shop in the early 1930s and chose not to reopen the Tookay Shop.

## SELECTED PRICES

While Roycroft collectors have long known of Karl Kipp, the general public, including a large number of Arts and Crafts collectors, has not. As yet, no one has come forth with any biographical information or critical analysis regarding Kipp that would further document his role in Arts and Crafts metalwork design. Although Tookay Shop collectors have their own personal price guides for determining how much they will pay for a particular design, the information and examples necessary to establish a reliable price guide have not yet reached the marketplace. Until they do, collectors will need to evaluate carefully each piece they encounter. At present those pieces with the double-K mark tend to run parallel in price to the identical Kipp designs bearing the Roycroft orb-and-cross, but because the Tookay Shop output remained small, spanning only four years, those designs with the double-K mark are likely to soon begin to increase in value at a faster rate.

## The Roycrofters

SHOPMARKS: The letter R within a circle topped by a cross[1].

(post-ca. 1915) Addition of the word ROY-CROFT.

PRINCIPAL CONTRIBUTIONS: Copper vases. bowls, bookends, desk sets, candlesticks, and lamps.

FOUNDER: Elbert Hubbard. Born: 1856, died: 1915, founded: 1895, closed: 1938.

STUDIOS AND SALESROOMS: The Roycroft Shops, East Aurora, New York, 1895–1938.

> "Beautiful objects should be owned by the people. They should be available as home embellishments and placed within the reach of all. The Roycroft artists in metal believed this so they designed and created hand-hammered copper vases, trays, bowls, candlesticks, lighting fixtures and a hundred and one other objets d'art —individual pieces of craftsmanship that were lasting, beautiful and worthwhile."
> —*Roycroft catalog, 1919*[2]

If there was one Arts and Crafts firm that, by the sheer number of quality items its craftsmen and craftswomen produced, came to symbolize for the vast majority of collectors and general antiques dealers what the Arts and Crafts movement was all about, it was the Roycroft Copper Shop. Here was a firm that from 1910 until 1938 produced thousands of hand-hammered,

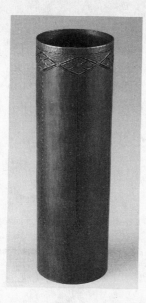

Fine Roycroft hammered copper cylindrical vase, with tooled quatrefoils on tall stems. Excellent original dark patina. Orb-and-cross mark, 10" × 3¼", $2,185

hand-patinated, useful and beautiful, as William Morris dictated, desk sets, bowls, vases, candlesticks, and lamps, the majority of which were of pleasing design and constructed by hand from quality materials in a pleasant workshop setting. And, as a result, for many of us, a piece of Roycroft copper represents the first item we discovered in our quest to build an Arts and Crafts collection.

By 1910 the Arts and Crafts movement in America and its principal players were well established in their respective studios and workshops. Names such as Grueby, Stickley, Teco, Rookwood, Limbert, and Roycroft had grown familiar to the thousands of readers of magazines such as *House Beautiful, Ladies' Home Journal, Studio, Beautiful Homes*, and the *Craftsman*. Many were continuing to expand their popular lines, and in East Aurora, Elbert Hubbard was preparing to add yet another dimension to the growing Roycroft production.

For nearly 10 years his artisans had produced books, leather crafts, and oak furniture, much of it embellished with hammered copper pulls and strap hinges created in the small metal shop near the Roycroft Inn, but metalware production had been hampered by a lack of internal leadership and direction in design. As described in the landmark 1972 exhibition headed by Robert Judson Clark,

"Local residents were employed [in the Roycroft Shops], but significantly large numbers of people came to East Aurora from across the country to find work. An apprentice system was set up, and workers learned various crafts, migrating from shop to shop. The cultural

Roycroft large acid-etched silver vase with squat base and tall flaring neck. Orb-and-cross mark, 16" × 9", $1,092

life included lectures, frequently by Hubbard, concerts and organized sports. While Hubbard wrote, edited his magazines, and made lecture tours, his admirable wife Alice kept the books and supervised the business."[3]

Hubbard, although a man of many ideas, was neither trained nor self-taught in the design aspect of either furniture or metalware. Aware, no doubt, of the Craftsman Shops' line of hammered bowls, trays, and lighting fixtures illustrated in Gustav Stickley's catalogs and monthly magazine, Hubbard could not begin large-scale production until he found the man who could provide the designs and organization necessary to compete with Stickley and the growing number of metalsmiths working in the popular Arts and Crafts style.

For Hubbard and the Roycroft Shops that man was Karl Kipp, a young banker who, like many Roycroft converts, had journeyed to East Aurora willing to work in whatever capacity his skills could best be utilized. Kipp arrived in September 1908 and was assigned to the bookbindery, but was soon singled out by Hubbard to organize and direct the Roycroft Copper Shop. From the bookbindery Kipp selected Walter U. Jennings to assist him, and by the time the 1910 catalog went to press, the Copper Shop had begun production of a number of hammered copper desk sets, a smoker's set, a nut bowl set, candlesticks, and vases. According to Mary Laura Gibbs, "Kipp conceived each design and then turned the prototype over to an assistant, who made the special tools to execute the details more rapidly."[4] Characteristic of these early Kipp designs were small square cutouts, appearing in the

Exceptional and rare Roycroft
hammered copper oversized desk
blotter with two riveted corners,
and two pen trays flanking an
inkwell. (The first one we've seen.)
Fine original patina, missing
inkwell liner, excellent new green
leather blotter. Orb-and-cross
mark, 18½" × 28", $2,760

handle of the nut spoon, in the letter opener, and in the sides of the smoking set's tray, or a silver square applied to the copper forms.[5]

The year 1909 also marked the return of Dard Hunter (1883–1966) to the Roycroft campus. Hunter, who later emerged as a world authority on paper-making, had been introduced to the book designs of William Morris, not by Elbert Hubbard but by Hunter's father, a small-town Ohio newspaper publisher. Like Kipp, Hunter journeyed to East Aurora to meet and work with Elbert Hubbard but at an earlier age. When the twenty-year-old Hunter arrived in East Aurora in 1903, book design and production at Roycroft was well organized but lacked sophistication. Hubbard's extensive library included a number of current German publications, which influenced Hunter's subsequent Roycroft designs and his decision to journey to Vienna in 1908.

During his early years at Roycroft, Hunter was also involved with stained-glass design, and "by 1906 he was making windows, lampshades and lighting fixtures of leaded glass for the Roycroft Inn and Shops."[6] Hubbard appointed Hunter head of the stained-glass department at Roycroft and in 1908 encouraged and possibly financed Hunter's sabbatical in Europe. The designer returned in 1909 and immediately set about incorporating much of what he had seen of the work of the Vienna Secessionists into his stained-glass designs. By that time the Roycroft Copper Shop had been organized by Karl Kipp, undoubtedly much to Hunter's delight, and the pair quickly collaborated on several lighting fixtures—Hunter designing the stained-glass shades, Kipp taking charge of the bases—which appeared in the 1910 catalog. These rare ceiling and wall fixtures with Kipp's silver squares or cutouts and Hunter's simple geometric glass patterns are among the most valued of all Roycroft production.

Dard Hunter returned to Vienna in 1910 and never worked for Elbert Hubbard again. Karl Kipp continued to manage the Copper Shop for an additional year, leaving in 1911 and taking his top assistant, Walter Jennings, with him across the small town of East Aurora to establish, in direct competition with Elbert Hubbard, the Tookay Shop. Kipp's and Jennings's reasons for leaving were not made public, but since Hubbard was never known for

Large Roycroft hammered copper vase with flaring, rolled rim and riveted strap to bulbous base. Original patina on neck, new patina under riveted brace. Early orb-and-cross mark, 15" × 6¾", $3,220

being generous with his payroll, financial and family responsibilities and the lure of self-employment may well have been critical factors in their decisions.

As evidence of his organizational abilities, the Roycroft Copper Shop survived the departure of Karl Kipp and continued to expand production. In 1912 and 1913 the shop, under the supervision of Victor Toothaker, renowned illustrator and designer, executed several hundred ceiling fixtures, table lamps, dresser and desk pulls, and related accessories for the renowned Grove Park Inn outside Asheville, North Carolina. In 1915, however, the world and the Roycroft family of artisans were stricken with the news of the sinking of the *Lusitania*. Elbert and Alice Hubbard were among the more than 1,000 travelers who drowned in the North Sea after the precipitous German submarine attack. Their son, Elbert Hubbard II (1883–1970), affectionately called Bert, took over the Roycroft operation at age 32 and immediately persuaded Karl Kipp and Walter Jennings to return to the Roycroft Copper Shop.

Kipp remained at the Roycroft Copper Shop until the Depression brought with it bankruptcy proceedings. Walter Jennings, who had resigned a secure management position with a knitting mill in 1908 to move his wife and three small children to East Aurora and become a Roycrofter, stayed with Bert and the Roycroft Copper Shop until 1933. He then worked for approximately seven years with another former Roycroft coppersmith, Arthur Cole, who had left several years earlier to establish his own shop, the Avon Coppersmith, in Avon, New York. In the early 1940s, however, Jennings returned to East Aurora finally to establish his own copper shop.

The Roycroft Shops ultimately fell victim to the Great Depression, though formal bankruptcy did not take place until 1938. Over the course of the next 40 years a number of unsuccessful owners were able to preserve the key structures on the campus but not without the loss of many of the original Roycroft furnishings. Today the Roycroft Inn and the other buildings of the East Aurora campus have been preserved, and restored and are continuing the Arts and Crafts tradition. Efforts were furthered by the organization of a group of artisans and Roycroft collectors, historians, and preservationists in 1976 under the name "Roycroft Renaissance." Their Roycroft reproductions and other items designed and produced in the Roycroft spirit are marked with an orb-and-cross similar to the original mark but encompassing a pair of *R*'s to distinguish it clearly from the early mark.

National distribution of Roycroft metalwares was assured in 1915 when Elbert Hubbard II decided to supplement the gift shop and mail-order sales with Roycroft displays in established retail stores across the country. The opportunity was immediately grasped by a number of prestigious stores, including Marshall Field in Chicago, Lord & Taylor in New York, and Stix, Baer & Fuller in St. Louis. By 1924 the list of retail outlets had grown to more than 320, with distribution spread to every state in the country.[7] In a move that his father would have appreciated, Elbert Hubbard II did not offer to place the items, which included Roycroft books, leather crafts, and copper wares, on consignment but instead sold them to the participating store at a 33 percent discount. Any items that failed to sell in the store were eventually reduced in price or given to local employees rather than being returned to East Aurora, thus enabling collectors 50 years later to find examples from the Roycroft Shops in every part of the country.

As Charles Hamilton summarized in his book *Roycroft Collectibles*, "It

Roycroft hammered copper small American Beauty vase. Fine original dark patina. Orb-and-cross mark, 7" × 3¼", $1,700

wasn't until about 1909 that a truly well organized and talented Copper Shop group began turning out the fine specimens of the craft. But from then on, until Roycroft folded in 1938, their output was amazingly large for a hand-crafted line. The variety of products grew and grew and the quality was superb. They worked in copper, brass, silver, silver plate, and etched silver and brass."[8] Among the more commonly found Roycroft items are the standard hammered copper ashtrays and smoking sets (even though Elbert Hubbard campaigned on the Chautauqua circuit against smoking), vases, bowls, and desk accessories. What has failed to ignite much interest among Arts and Crafts collectors are the smooth copper pieces produced after 1920; the silver-plated pieces, some of which are marked "Silverplate" and/or "Sheffield," also have only a small following unless the design of the piece is particularly exciting and unique. Many of the standard copper items were brass-plated, and as a result years of hard use may have worn the plating off the high spots, exposing the bright copper beneath it and reducing its value in the eyes of many collectors.

Among the more desirable of the Roycroft metalwares are bud vases with Steuben glass inserts from the Corning Glass Company, as well as Roycroft lamps with Corning's Steuben lampshades, stained glass, or mica. As more and more collectors have attempted to assemble Arts and Crafts room settings, the value of nearly all Roycroft lamps has increased, the only exception, as with all examples, being those pieces that have been polished. Like Stickley's Craftsman Shops, the Roycrofters treated their metalwares chemically to produce a patina resembling that found on pieces that have been exposed to the air for several decades. Polishing removes not only the original patina but also the additional patina the piece has acquired since it was first sold. As

Fine Roycroft heavy gauge hammered copper tapering vase, with cutout silver band overlay to rim and base. Original patina. Orb-and-cross mark. Minor dimple to base, 7" × 3½", $1,610

every experienced Roycroft collector will attest, restoring both patinas—and the value of the piece—is virtually impossible.

Roycroft metalwares remain the most popular of all of the Arts and Crafts shops, for they are attractive, useful, available, and, for the most part, reasonably priced.

## SELECTED PRICES

Ashtray: hammered copper, stacking set of three with stylized flower form, 4", $300–$350

Ashtray: hammered copper with cigarette rest, 1" × 4", $100–$125

Ashtray: hammered copper on oak pedestal, copper strap handle on match-box holder over shallow round bowl. round oak base, 29", $500–$600

Bookends: hammered copper, tall rectangular form with stylized repoussé flower and tooled border, one open frame, one with full panel, 8" × 6", $200–$300. Bookends: hammered copper, semicircular arch on rect-angular plate, 3" × 6", $125–$175

Bookends: overlapping graduated triangles in copper on brass ground, Art Deco style, 5" × 4" × 3", $200–$300

Bookends: hammered copper with large, heavily embossed poppy on each, 6" × 5", $500–$750

Bookends: hammered copper with heavily embossed poppies, brass wash, 5" × 5", $400–$600

Bookends: hammered copper with dark patina, floral decoration, 3" × 3", $125–$150.

Bowl: hammered copper, wide, deep form in dark brown patina, 5" × 10", $150–$200

Bowl: hammered copper with brass outer wash, 1" × 7", $125–$150

Bowl: hand–hammered copper with brass highlights, 3" × 6", $150–$225

Bowl: hammered copper with crimped design top, 3" × 4", $125–$175

Bowl: hammered copper, 1" × 5", $100–$125

Bowl with ladle: hammered copper, three–footed form with broad planishing marks, bowl 3" × 7", $350–$400

Box, cigar: hammered copper, applied medallion with initials on rectangular hinged lid with tooled border, cedar–lined, 2" × 9" × 6", $500–$750

Candlesticks: hammered copper, flattened rim and socket on cylindrical stems and wide floriform bases, pair, 8", $300–$350

Candlesticks: hammered copper, angled flattened rim and deep socket on cylindrical standard and flattened disk base, pair, 10", $200–$300

Candlesticks: hammered–copper design with two square rods riveted to a square base, pair, 7", $500–$750

Candlesticks: hammered copper, each with four feet that continue into long strips to form the body, riveted at top and bottom with circular bobèche, 12" × 4", $700–$800.

Candlesticks: silver on copper, with bobèches resting on two squared shafts supported by a pyramidal, four–sided base, pair, 8" × 3", $300–$350

Crumber: hammered copper with silver wash, two–piece set with stylized decoration, $50–$75

Desk set: five pieces of hammered copper with radially hammered pattern, consisting of a letter holder, calendar holder, letter opener, inkwell, and blotter, 3" × 5" × 1", $400–$600

Desk set: four pieces, hammered bronze and copper with textured honey-comb finish, consisting of inkwell with hinged lid, calendar stand, tray, letter opener, $400–$600

Lamp, desk: #903, hammered copper, round dome with mica panels on square standard and base, 14", $2,000–$3,000

Lamp, desk: hammered copper, wide, domed shade with four straps and hand of mica, resting on a flaring cylindrical shaft and broad, circular base, fully riveted, 15" × 10", $2,500–$3,500

Lamp, desk: hammered–copper helmet shade supported by cylindrical copper shaft, ending in flared circular base, 16" × 7", $1,200–$1,700

Lamp, table: hammered copper and leaded glass, conical shade of long, thin triangular channels of green–yellow glass ending in small rectangles of pink and green, broad, circular foot, 20" × 16", $15,000–$20,000

Lamp, table: four–piece hammered–copper base, center shaft, and three legs ending in Greek key feet on triangular platform, three–socket ball con-nector, with tapering, six–sided mica shade, 17" × 10", $7,500–$10,000

Lamp, table: hammered brass and copper, cylindrical shaft and tapering, domed shade in brass and copper, 16" × 7", $3,000–$4,000

Letter opener: hammered copper with curled handle, 7", $100–$150

Sconces, wall: hammered copper, arrowhead backs, incorporating candle sockets, pair, 8", $300–$450

Smoking set: hammered–copper oval tray, attached match holder, three loose canisters with riveted sides, 14" × 6", $400–$600

Tray: hammered copper, 8" diameter, $125–$175

Tray, serving: hammered copper with double handles, 11" diameter, $300–$350

Vase: hammered copper with brass wash, heavy–gauge cylindrical, tooled stylized flowers and green stems, 10" × 3", $500–$750

Vase: American Beauty #211, hammered copper, cylindrical neck extending from bulbous base and ending in flared rim, covered with brass–wash patina, 7", $1,000–$1,500

Vase: American Beauty #210, same as above, 12", $1,500–$2,000

Vase: American Beauty #201, same as above, 19", $3,000–$3,500

Vase: American Beauty #201, same as above, but with Grove Park Inn inscription, 22", $3,500–$4,500

Vase: hammered copper, cylinder, with four angled, tooled buttresses riveted to the body, nickel–silver square alternating between the top of each buttress, 8" × 4", $4,500–$6,500

Vase: hammered copper, with gently closing top, decorated with pierced and applied nickel–silver banded design, 6" × 3", $1,200–$1,700

## Shreve & Company

SHOPMARKS: (1883–1909) Bee within a shield (1909–1922) Bell within a box, SHREVE & CO.

PRINCIPAL CONTRIBUTION: Quality hand-hammered silver with applied strapwork.

FOUNDER: George C. Shreve. Born: ca. 1825, died: 1893, founded: 1852, closed: current.

STUDIOS AND SALESROOMS: Shreve & Company, San Francisco, California, 1852–current.

> "When President Theodore Roosevelt visited San Francisco, the citizens presented him with a 10-inch high golden bear, cast from solid gold from Shreve's."
>
> —*Shreve employee*[1]

The California Gold Rush of 1848 and statehood two years later attracted thousands of fortune-seekers from across the United States. While most never found the mother lode, they remained to open new businesses, such as the Shreve jewelry store founded in 1852 by George C. Shreve and his half-brother Samuel in San Francisco. Beginning as a jewelry store rather than a manufacturing operation, Shreve & Company grew to become one of the most successful silversmith operations in the state after 1883. Its output was both substantial and varied, ranging from custom made flatware, souvenir spoons, and hollowware to platters and tea sets.

When the earthquake of 1906 destroyed most of its plant, it forced

Shreve & Company to retool and enabled it to introduce new lines in the popular Arts and Crafts style. The company's first catalog after the earthquake revealed a wide variety of silver wares, including a number of flatware patterns. While not generally known for their innovative designs, the Shreve & Company Arts and Crafts silver retained the high standards of quality for which the firm had been known for several decades. Many of the new designs were actually standard silver forms adapted to the Arts and Crafts style by adding strapwork and rivets to the exterior. As one observer noted, "the decorative rivets have their counterpart, occasionally seen on Mission-style furniture, in pegs that serve no structural purpose."[2] The strapwork evokes medieval images that were also mirrored in the strap hinges that Gustav Stickley designed at the Craftsman Shop and that the Roycrofters utilized in East Aurora. Although Shreve & Company's attempt to fulfill the demand for Arts and Crafts–style silver on the West Coast was not always an artistic success, its high standards of craftsmanship and materials never suffered. By 1968 the firm eventually returned to what it had been over a hundred years earlier—a very successful retail jewelry business.

## SELECTED PRICES

Basket: sterling silver, with decorative scalloped handle, and with two engraved and reticulated coats of arms on either side of its undulating rim, stemming from an oval base, 8" × 14" × 10", $1,250–$1,750

Bowl: sterling silver, wide mouth with beaded rim on round form with applied silver balls, footed base, 5" × 9", $1,500–$2,000

Breakfast set: sterling silver, one–pint coffee, creamer, open sugar, and shaped edge oval tray, cylindrical form flaring at base, straight spout, strapwork borders, $3,000–$4,000

Creamer and sugar: strap detail around rim, double C–scroll handle on squat bulbous form, 2" × 4", $700–$800

Pitcher: sterling silver, with stylized leaf and rivet design, 11" × 9", $1,000–$1,200

Plate, cake: sterling silver, shaped shallow plate with strapwork edge on cylindrical stem flaring toward domed base, 5" × 10", $500–$600

Tray, bread: sterling silver, oval with shaped edge and flat strap border, hammered texture, 14", $800–$950

## Stickley Brothers

SHOPMARK:  Model number impressed in metal, generally with STICKLEY BROTHERS paper label.

PRINCIPAL CONTRIBUTIONS: Line of hand-hammered copper metalware, including candlesticks, jardinieres, bowls, umbrella stands, ash trays, and urns

FOUNDERS: Albert Stickley, born: 1862, died: 1928. John George Stickley, born: 1871, died: 1921, founded: 1891, closed: ca. 1940

STUDIOS AND SALESROOMS: Stickley Brothers, Inc., Grand Rapids, Michigan, 1891-ca. 1940

While most Arts and Crafts collectors are well aware of the Stickley Brothers' contribution to Arts and Crafts furniture, many do not know that they may have handled an unsigned example of Stickley Brothers metalware. According to its 1908 catalog, the Stickley Brothers Company, under the leadership of Albert Stickley,[1] offered their customers a line of "Russian hand-beaten copper."[2] Grand Rapids author Don Marek estimates that the company's metal work was introduced in 1904, citing a tray, "probably inspired by English work, as was Gustav Stickley's similar design,"[3] as an example of the commendable work of the firm's metalsmiths. While examples of every item illustrated have not yet surfaced, the catalog depicts a variety of lighting devices, including chandeliers (referred to as "electroliers"), table lamps, candlesticks, and electric sconces. In addition, a number of umbrella stands, jardinieres, plaques, boxes, pitchers, and desk accessories in copper or brass were offered.

Like Stickley Brothers furniture, surviving examples reveal a variety of designs, reflecting influences of both the European Art Nouveau and the English Arts and Crafts, as well as Old World and Colonial styles, plus differences in quality of material and workmanship. As collector and author Terry Seger writes, "at its best, it was as good as any of the era. Their tall candlesticks (#146) are of the finest design and quality. The candlesticks (#177) are reminiscent of the Roycrofters' very best work."[4]

Influenced, perhaps, by brother Gustav's success, Albert Stickley apparently had established a copper shop along the Grand River outside Grand Rapids by 1904. There he employed a large force of immigrant coppersmiths,

Rare and massive Stickley Brothers hammered copper two-handled jardiniere with rolled rim and stylized fruit and plant decoration in repoussé. New patina. Stamped 400, 12½" × 18½", $6,325

Pair of fine and tall Stickley Brothers hammered copper candlesticks, each with two buttressed, riveted handles joining the socket to a delicate baluster-shaped shaft. Small drill hole to one base, original medium patina (one lighter). One stamped 14, 18" × 5¾", $4,025

many of whom had recently arrived in the United States from Russia. It appears that he continued to buy the hardware for his furniture from commercial sources and instructed his metalworkers to produce lamps, vases, ewers, trays, and similar decorative objects. Seger has observed that "they produced a large variety of copper and slag-glass table lamps. Many of these lamps have appeared on the market and their variety in design seems endless."[5] While Stickley Brothers' copper is not as heavy as that of either Dirk Van Erp or Gustav Stickley, it is similar to the gauge of copper utilized by the Roycrofters. Unfortunately, the quality, except on rare occasions, is not as good as the Roycrofters.

Stickley Brothers' copper was often left unmarked or was marked with a paper label, which soon peeled off. That which can be authenticated is identified by either comparison to objects illustrated in the catalog or recognition of the single-, double-, or triple-digit number die-stamped in the exact center of the bottom of the piece. Signed examples are not as common as those from the Roycroft and the Craftsman shops; thus, determining a value is totally dependent on the design, condition, and quality of each individual piece.

## SELECTED PRICES

While metalwork bearing the Stickley Brothers paper label is relatively scarce, it is just beginning to stir interest on the part of collectors. The earlier copper wares are considered more valuable than their later, domestic wares, but neither has garnered as much attention as any of the other shops dis-

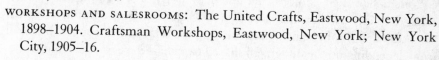

cussed in this section. Leaving room for an exceptional rare piece, the larger examples remain in the $1,000–$1,500 range, with most of the smaller items falling in the $300–$500 category.

## Gustav Stickley and the Craftsman Workshops

SHOPMARK: Impressed joiner's compass around motto, ALS IK KAN.

PRINCIPAL CONTRIBUTIONS: Copper trays, bowls, desk sets, and lamps.

FOUNDER: Gustav Stickley. Born: 1858, died: 1942, founded: 1898, closed: 1916.

WORKSHOPS AND SALESROOMS: The United Crafts, Eastwood, New York, 1898–1904. Craftsman Workshops, Eastwood, New York; New York City, 1905–16.

> "Having begun with the necessary drawer and door pulls, hinges and escutcheons, done from simple designs which were in harmony with the furniture, it was natural that we should go on with the making of other things along the same lines, as in the Craftsman scheme of interior decoration and furnishing there is a well-defined place for the right kind of metal work."
>
> —*Gustav Stickley, 1910*[1]

Gustav Stickley's desire to go into "the right kind of metalwork" never resulted in the level of production achieved at the Roycroft Copper Shop, but while the output of copper trays, bowls, vases and lamps at Craftsman Workshops was small, the quality was never compromised. Given the amount of furniture that was being produced at Craftsman Workshops, it would also appear that the metalworkers had all they could handle in making the necessary drawer and door pulls and strap hinges. Though having professed at one point to personally preferring wood knobs over hand-hammered hardware, Gustav Stickley did not sacrifice any cost when it came to either the hardware on his Craftsman furniture or the copper, brass, and iron accessories his metalsmiths also produced. Without exception, the hardware accompanying Stickley's Arts and Crafts furniture is the best of its genre; of all of the other furniture manufacturers, only the Roycrofters approached the quality of the Craftsman hardware. While L. & J. G. Stickley were content with smaller copper pulls, Charles Limbert and Albert Stickley more often than not purchased mass-produced hardware from the Grand Rapids Brass Company.[2] Although production figures have never come to light, it would appear that the Craftsman Workshops' metalworkers were not as prolific as the Roycrofters, who garnered a steady income from the sale of their metalwork to visitors on the Roycroft campus and in outlets around the country. The Craftsman Workshops trays, bowls, lamps, and sconces that have survived, however, reflect the high degree of both materials and craftsmanship invested in each piece.

The Craftsman catalogs of both 1904 and 1910 illustrate the emphasis Stickley placed on lighting fixtures.[3] As America was blowing out candles and flipping on light switches in the first decade of the new century, furniture, metalware, and even pottery companies were scrambling to fill the need for electric lamps and ceiling fixtures. While Stickley's 1904 catalog offered four styles of copper serving trays, two copper wall plaque designs, and no vases, customers had their choice of no less than 33 types of lighting fixtures: six using candles, nine dependent on oil, and 18 electric. (See Lighting chapter.)

Although Craftsman metalwork might utilize either copper, brass, or iron, depending on the design, all shared two characteristics that continue to cause confusion years later. First, the planishing marks made by the metalsmith's hammer were purposely left in the surface. Collectors accustomed to smooth silver and polished brass may have assumed such marks were evidence of crude, untrained work, but those familiar with the Arts and Crafts era's attempt to recapture the spirit of medieval craftsmanship realize that the marks were no reflection on the skill of the coppersmith. Second, metalwork of the period was treated in the shop to give it a dark patina that normally would require years of exposure to the air. As Stickley described in the *Craftsman* magazine, "If a very dark finish is desired, the copper may be

Fine and rare Gustav Stickley hammered copper coal scuttle with riveted arrow motif iron handles. Excellent original patina. Impressed circular stamp "Gustav Stickley, The Craftsman Workshops," 24" × 15", $10,925

heated long enough to turn it black and then rubbed with the powdered pumice stone, which will brighten the raised places on the metal, leaving the sunken places dark. The tray should not be lacquered as age gives the best possible finish, and this is prevented by lacquering."[4] Owners who have discovered metalwork made during the Arts and Crafts era and who have also incorrectly assumed that the tarnishing was unintentional have caused permanent damage by polishing it. Only a few craftsmen have been able to duplicate an Arts and Crafts patina consistently.

The Craftsman Shops nine-piece copper desk sets that were being offered by 1910 have provided current Arts and Crafts collectors with additional opportunities to purchase a hand-hammered example impressed with the famous joiner's compass mark. While most Craftsman trays, plaques, and rare lighting fixtures are highly coveted collector's items, individual pieces from the desk sets—inkwells, letter openers, letter holders, calendars and pen trays—continue to surface at auctions, flea markets, and antiques shops, where they generally sell for reasonable prices.

Just as he provided furniture plans for the home craftsman, Stickley published numerous articles in the *Craftsman* magazine illustrating for his readers the basics of metalsmithing. In addition, he offered to provide sheets of copper or brass, mica for lampshades, and for those who were also building their own Mission oak furniture "the same metal trim which we use ourselves, so that when they make Craftsman furniture in their own workshops from designs which we furnish them, they need not be at a loss for the right metal trim."[5]

Gustav Stickley hammered copper and iron table lamp with cylindrical oil font base, rolled, riveted legs, glass chimney and original split bamboo shade lined in new silk, 26" × 16", $8,625

Rare and important Gustav Stickley cast-iron hanging fixture designed by Harvey Ellis with original cylindrical opalescent glass shade, curled feet, and overhanging top with stylized pod finial. New patina. Unmarked. Fixture only: 14½" × 10", $25,875

## SELECTED PRICES

Ashtray: #271, hammered copper form with four repoussè balls, 7", $250–$300.

Candlestick: hammered copper cylinder set in bowl base, finger–grip on cylinder, removable bobèche, 9", $800–$900

Lamp, floor: hammered copper harp atop oak pedestal with four flared supports at bottom, 57", $3,000–$4,000

Lamp, table: hammered copper base with deep hammering, wicker shade, 25", $3,000–$4,000

Lamp, table: #504, oak and copper base with cloth–lined wicker shade, pyramid base, 23", $3,000–$4,000

Letter opener: hammered copper, scooped top for hand, 11", $300–$400

Plaque, wall: hammered copper with four repoussé spade motifs along border, recessed center, 15" diameter, $2,500–$3,500

Sconce, wall: #400, hammered–copper bracket with three–link chain, suspended Steuben glass shade, 10", $1,500–$2,000

Tray: circular, hammered copper, no handles, 9", $500–$750

Tray: circular, hammered copper, no handles, 13", $750–$1,000

Tray, serving: circular, hammered copper, with repoussé flower motifs and four pierced handles, 20", $1,500–$2,000

Umbrella stand: #383, hammered copper cylindrical form with flared rim, double handles, repoussé spade motif, 25", $2,000–$3,000

Vase: #26, flared form top and bottom, 11", $1,500–$2,000

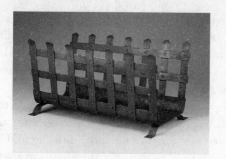

Exceptional and rare Gustav Stickley log holder of riveted wrought-iron straps covered in a fine iron patina. Als Ik Kan stamp, 15½" × 29" × 17", $10,925

## Arthur J. Stone

SHOPMARKS:  (Pre–1906) Metalsmith's hammer conjoined with the letter S.

(1906–37) Metalsmith's hammer conjoined with the word STONE.

(After 1937) Addition of the letter H within a shield.

PRINCIPAL CONTRIBUTION: Wide range of domestic silver items in the Arts and Crafts style.

FOUNDER: Arthur J. Stone. Born: 1847, died: 1938, founded: 1901, sold: 1937.

STUDIOS AND SALESROOMS: Arthur J. Stone, Silversmith, Gardner, Massachusetts, 1901–37.

> "Pieces. . . are all raised from the flat by hammering except when the parts are too small to make this process practical. The work is designed, directed, and ornamented by Mr. Stone. It is stamped with his mark and also the initial of the hammerer."
> —Advertising leaflet, 1914[1]

Trained in England as a silversmith and influenced by the writings of John Ruskin and William Morris, 37 year-old Arthur J. Stone came to America in 1884 and went to work for a number of silver manufacturing firms. In 1901, at the age of 54, Stone's lifelong dream was realized when he opened his own silversmith shop in Gardner, Massachusetts. His work immediately attracted the attention of members of the Boston Arts and Crafts Society, who bestowed numerous awards on Stone, leading to a silver award at the Louisiana Purchase Exposition in St. Louis in 1904. One of his entries, a copper and silver jardiniere, characterized his emerging style with its "curving outline, the faint hammer marks on the surface, and the encircling repoussè wreath of oak leaves and inlaid silver acorns."[2]

While much of his earliest work was in the form of presentation and ecclesiastical silver, as word of his skill spread, Stone had to hire apprentice and journeymen silversmiths to assist him in producing a wide range of domestic silver wares: tea sets, bowls, boxes, trays, and vases. Stone was respected as much as a teacher of young silversmiths as a designer and craftsman; he instituted a profit-sharing plan with his employees and permitted key assistants to add their initials below that of the firm's shopmark on their work.

Stone preferred working with his own designs, opting to incorporate the best elements of earlier styles and techniques into a unique rendition that captured both his philosophy and the spirit of the Arts and Crafts movement. His decoration remained subtle; he preferred not to detract from the form itself. Some of his most coveted work features gold inlay. Stone's interest in botany is legendary, as he was known to traverse nearby fields and streams in search of new forms with which to embellish his work. His personal involvement with both his clients and their commissions brought them back time and time again.

Arthur Stone suffered a stroke in 1926 but remained active as the firm's chief designer. As a credit to his talent, "the spare, ascetic quality of Stone silver insured his shop's success when Arts and Crafts metalwork styles and textures became unfashionable."[3] The reputation established by Arthur Stone enabled the firm to continue past his death in 1938.

## SELECTED PRICES

Bowl: sterling silver, wide-mouthed form with chased band incorporating triangle and scroll medallion on flared foot, 5" × 8", $1,500–$1,750

Bowl: sterling silver, fine–lobed round form with triple rib border, 1" × 8", $800–$900.

Bowl: copper, wide mouth on squat bulbous form, designed with tooled scroll feather and loop design, 3" × 5", $600–$800

Box, pill: sterling silver, straight–sided oval form, 1" × 2", $225–$250

Dish: ivory finial on rounded square cover fitting into corresponding lower half, 4" × 7", $700–$800

Napkin ring: sterling silver, chased and openwork decoration with berries and leaves, 2", $150–$175

Pepper shaker: baluster form with urn finial on diamond–patterned cover, rib detail at shoulder, 4", $225–4,250

Pitcher: sterling silver, flat molded rim with curved lip on wide mouth, scroll handle, squat body swelling toward bulbous base, ring foot, 7", $1,000–$1,500

Pitcher: sterling silver, molded curved rim in ribbed pear–shaped body and flared molded base, hollow curved handle, 10", $1,500–$2,000

Platter: sterling silver, molded rim, oval form with shaped, ribbed inner edge, 18", $1,000–$1,500

Platter: sterling silver, molded rim, oval form with shaped, ribbed inner edge, 16", $1,000–$1,250

Spoon: serving, antique pattern, 9", $200–$225

Spoon: martini, antique pattern, 12", $125–$150

Tray: sterling silver, molded wavy edge on oval form with stylized pad feet, 5", $450–$500

## Tiffany Studios

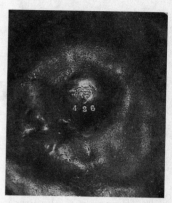

SHOPMARK: Impressed TIFFANY STUDIOS / NEW YORK.

PRINCIPAL CONTRIBUTIONS: Stained-glass windows, glassware, lamps, and metal accessories.

FOUNDER: Louis Comfort Tiffany. Born: 1848, died: 1943, founded: 1902, closed: 1938.

STUDIOS AND SALESROOMS: Louis C. Tiffany & the Associated Artists, New York, 1879–1885. Tiffany Glass Company, New York, 1886–02. Tiffany Studios, New York, 1902–38.

"Louis Comfort [Tiffany's] relative avoidance of silver as an art material may have had a psychological implication—perhaps one that is almost too obvious. His father and his father's firm were world famous for their silverware, and it would have only been natural for him to want to make it on his own as an artist—in another field."
—*Charles H. Carpenter, Jr.*[1]

Louis C. Tiffany was raised in a world of riches—most notably of silver. His father, Charles Lewis Tiffany (1812–1902), was well on his way to having created an empire made of silver and jewels when Louis was born. As a young man he traveled extensively and studied art in Europe, returning in 1879 to establish a popular interior decorating firm that was hired in 1883 to furnish a portion of the White House for President Chester A. Arthur. Tiffany continued to travel and to explore new avenues of artistic expression. In Paris he was enthralled by the work of Emile Galle and became close friends with Samuel Bing; on his return to New York he redirected his focus and by 1896 had introduced both his famous stained-glass lamps and his line of *favrile* (handmade) glass. (See Lighting chapter.)

Many of the bases for his decorative stained-glass shades were purchased from art pottery firms, most notably Grueby but also Wheatley and Hampshire. The majority, however, were of bronze, cast in an Art Nouveau

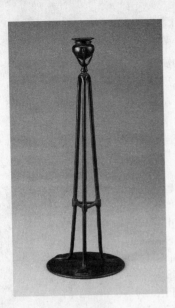

Fine Tiffany Studios tall bronze candlestick with tripod shaft on a circular base and prong-set bobèche with flaring rim, original dark verdigris patina. Stamped TIFFANY STUDIOS/NEW YORK/1211, 24" × 8" dia., $4,312

style. In 1902, on the death of his father, Louis C. Tiffany was named vice-president and artistic director of Tiffany & Company, which had continued to excel in Victorian silver. That same year the name of the Tiffany Glass Company was changed to Tiffany Studios to reflect its wide range of production. The Tiffany fortune had been built on the carriage trade, but the intent of Tiffany Studios was the "mass production of beautiful household objects that brought affordable art into the middle class house."[2]

While Tiffany experimented with art pottery[3] and continued to produce stained-glass lamps, his line of *favrile* glass overshadowed all phases of his expanding operation during the first decade of the 20th century. Tiffany's interest in metalware was a complete contrast—in both style and materials—to that of Tiffany & Company. Silver production at Tiffany Studios was restricted to special commissions, and even then the intent of the decoration and subtle hammering was to reduce the traditional mirrorlike surface of the silver. Met-

Fine Tiffany Furnaces bronze hinged box with Dore finish, its lid decorated with a border of enameled blue-violet flowers and green leaves. Repair to both hinges. Stamped LOUIS C. TIFFANY FURNACES, INC./FAVRILE/139, with Tiffany Studios monogram, 2" × 6¼" × 4", $1,725

Unusual Tiffany Studios bronze and green slag glass desk tray overlaid with grape vine pattern, with attached penholder, covered inkwell, and matchholder. Old cleaning to patina. Stamped TIFFANY STUDIOS NEW YORK, 2¾" × 9¼" × 5½", $2,875

alware production at Tiffany Studios centered on bronze, often in combination with glass. Small desk lamps, desk accessories, boxes, and bowls in a wide range of reasonably priced styles constituted the majority of the metalware production. Motifs ranged from abstract Art Nouveau to Egyptian and American Indian designs to natural forms, including dragonflies, flowers, and plants

Tiffany & Company did introduce a line of quality sterling silver intended to compete with both Kalo and Lebolt, two chicago-based firms that opened salesrooms in New York City. The pieces in this line featured light hammering marks and a noticeable lack of decoration in hopes of appealing to the Arts and Crafts market. They are considered rare and quite valuable and are usually marked "Special Hand Work."

Louis C. Tiffany's involvement in Tiffany Studios declined after 1919, but he continued to experiment with his favorite medium, stained glass, until the studios closed in 1938.

### SELECTED PRICES

Bowl: bronze, shallow form with band of repeating pierced flowers, 9", $350–$450

Candlestick: #11489, bronze, removable bobèche, lobed socket with green glass on slender stem and disk foot, 17", $1,000–$1,500

Candlesticks: bronze, removable bobèche on bulbous socket resting on three fingers, tall slender stem on disk base, pair, 19", $2,000–$3,000

Humidor: etched metal over glass panel, 6" × 4", $500–$700

Inkwell: nautical design with dolphin corners, clamshell lid, $450–$550

Inkwell: zodiac pattern in dark bronze patina, $250–$300

Inkwell: etched metal in pine needle design over green slag glass, $350–$450

Lamp: #319, three–light, three lily shades supported by three arms extending upward from a circular base, base has original green/brown patina, 13", $10,000–$20,000

Lamp: leaded glass, shade consists of multiple shades of green and white, glass with swirling leaf design in yellow, 23" × 18", $15,000–$20,000

Lamp: #269, green–blue favrile glass molded as a scarab on two branches and domed ribbed base, 8" × 6", $4,000–$5,000

Pitcher, water: 10–sided cylindrical body mounted on flared foot, lightly hammered, marked "Special Hand Work," 9"h., $4,000–$5,000

## Dirk Van Erp

SHOPMARKS: (1908–09) Raised arm holding a hammer over the words THE COPPER SHOP.

(1910–77) Hammered outline of windmill over the words Dirk Van Erp in box beneath it, with one of the following variations:

(1910–11) Addition of name D' Arcy Gaw in the box, above that of Dirk Van Erp

(1911–12) Empty space above name of Dirk Van Erp; box intact.

(1913–14) Empty space above that of Dirk Van Erp; right side of box missing (this mark may have been used on occasion as late as 1977).

(1915–77) Addition of words SAN FRANCISCO either inside or beneath box with missing right side; occasionally with the addition of the words HAND WROUGHT.

PRINCIPAL CONTRIBUTIONS: Mica-shade copper lamps, bowls, vases, and accessories.

FOUNDER: Dirk Van Erp. Born: 1860, retired: 1929, died: 1933, founded: 1908, closed: 1977.

STUDIOS AND SALESROOMS: Dirk Van Erp Studio or The Copper Shop, Oakland, California, 1908–10. San Francisco, California, 1910–77.

> "He had it in his head and his hands. There was no lost motion whatsoever when he started to make a piece. [Either] it came out a very nice piece [or] it never got finished."
> —William Van Erp (1900–77), speaking of his father[1]

Designers of Arts and Crafts lighting faced a challenge that seldom affected their contemporaries in the field of furniture and art pottery: adapting to the change from oil-burning lamps to electric lighting. And for many years during the Arts and Crafts era, designers and metalsmiths had to be able to produce both styles of lamps. One in particular who was both a designer and a craftsman—Dirk Van Erp—demonstrated clearly that not only could he produce both oil-burning and electric lighting, but that his

Pair of Dirk Van Erp bookends with repoussé stylized floral design. Old cleaning to original patina. D'Arcy Gaw box mark, 5½" × 6", $2,300

designs, materials, and craftsmanship labeled him as the finest of the Arts and Crafts era.

Born in the Netherlands in 1860, Dirk Van Erp received his first training in metalsmithing in the family business, where he helped produce kitchen utensils and milk containers. The lure of unbridled opportunities in America attracted the young Van Erp, the eldest of seven children, and he traveled to California in 1886, where at the age of 26 he found employment in the San Francisco shipyards. While his experience as a metalworker provided him with a steady income in the shipyards, Van Erp eventually began producing metalwares in his home, utilizing brass shell casings, and by 1906 was consigning the finished products to area art dealers. Encouraged by the response, Van Erp opened a studio in Oakland in 1908 and soon hired Harry Dixon as his first employee. By 1910 he had moved his shop to San Francisco and taken on a partner, D'Arcy Gaw, a young interior designer from Canada who had been experimenting with electric lamps since 1902.[2] Although the partnership lasted only one year before Miss Gaw returned to Chicago to resume a career in interior design work, the collaboration proved to be instrumental in Van Erp's development. Miss Gaw's lamp designs provided Van Erp with the ideal format to display his skills as a coppersmith. "Substantial and functional, [the] lamp exemplifies inspired coppersmithing skills, particularly in the use of copper for both the base and the shade to create a unified composition."[3] While historians are unsure whether or not Van Erp was making lamps prior to Darcy Gaw's arrival, her presence and sense of design certainly "initiated the period of great lamp design at the studio."[4] Using mica panels in the shade, Van Erp created lamps that "give warm tones harmonizing with the softly reflective patinated copper base."[5] After Miss Gaw left San Francisco in 1911 to establish a design studio in Chicago, Van Erp continued to produce electric lamps for the next 20 years, occasionally using designs commissioned from other artists.

Dirk Van Erp was also assisted in his San Francisco studio by his daughter Agatha Van Erp, Harry Dixon (who went on to open his own shop in 1921), and later his son William. D'Arcy Gaw's departure in 1911 coincided with the arrival from Holland of Dirk Van Erp's nephew 21-year-old August Tiesselinck (see Other Metalware Shops and Studios). The young man im-

Fine and rare Dirk Van Erp "curtained" copper bulbous vase with dimpled and folded sides covered in a rare original red finish. (The only example of this hammering technique seen for sale, and one of only four known, perfectly executed and in pristine, original condition.) Windmill/San Francisco mark with partial D'Arcy Gaw visible, 5" × 6", $34,500

mediately went to work in Van Erp's workshop, learning the craft, designing new items, and teaching classes in metalsmithing.

In addition to the now-famous lamps, the studio produced a number of smaller copper accessories, including bowls, vases, and desk sets. In speaking of the brass shell casings that Van Erp occasionally transformed into vases and lamp bases, his son William remarked, " . . . my father loved the toughest jobs. He was the only one who worked the shells. He liked the tough jobs and he saved them for himself. He hammered from the hip, so to speak, without ever looking at a drawing, while everyone else used drawings or models. Each piece was a spontaneous event. For every vase that he completed, there were three or four that went into scrap drums."[6]

Although he still came to work each day, Dirk Van Erp officially retired in 1929, turning the daily operation of the studio over to his daughter, Agatha, who had revealed advanced skills as a lamp designer, metalsmith, and maker of shades, and his son, William. In 1933 Dirk Van Erp and his

Dirk Van Erp hammered copper squat vessel with rolled rim. Excellent original patina, one verdigris drip. Stamped open box mark/San Francisco/Dirk Van Erp, 5" × 6", $1,500

wife died on the same day and, a few months later, Agatha decided to move, leaving William with a tremendous burden. He was assisted in the studio, which retained its original name, by Charles Anderson, who had also been trained by Dirk Van Erp. As tastes changed, so did the designs at the Dirk Van Erp studio, but over the course of the next 40 years, while the styles and materials often varied, the insistence on handcraftsmanship never wavered. In 1977 William Van Erp died and the shop closed soon thereafter.

While nearly all of the work of Dirk Van Erp is sought by Arts and Crafts collectors today, his lamps rank the highest. By 1915, when output at the shop reached its peak, Van Erp had hired enough assistants so that lamp production was divided, with the apprentices assembling shades while the more experienced craftsmen hammered out the bases. As Bonnie Mattison has pointed out, "Patterns were used for both the bases and the shades. Even so, subtle variations of proportion and planishing distinguish each example of a given design."[7] Distinguishing between a multi thousand-dollar lamp and one of the more common $3,000 to $4,000 lamps requires careful attention to design, condition, technical details, and degree of rarity. Serious Van Erp collectors show a decided preference for his earlier work, which is identified through the shopmark box and the style of the lip of the shade. In Van Erp's pre–1911 lamps, the lip of the shade formed a very small, tight rim. After 1915 a definite horizontal band evolves, often as wide as one inch. The earlier lampshades also feature struts riveted to the outside of the cap at the top, whereas later the struts ended under the cap. Among the rarest of all of his lamps are his floor models and a unique hanging desk lamp.

In a similar vein, the large bowls and vases with a "warty" texture and "usually accompanied by 'fire-color, a brilliant red achieved by heating the

Exceptional and early Dirk Van Erp table lamp, designed by d'Arcy Gaw, of hammered copper with mica panels, 18", $75,000

Rare and massive Dirk Van Erp hammered copper jardiniere with an exceptional mottled red patina. Given to an employee by Alma Spreckles, a friend and patron of the Van Erps, then purchased from her estate in Windsor, California. (A rare example of Van Erp's best patina.) Windmill stamp/Dirk Van Erp/open box, 11½" × 16", $37,375

copper during the annealing process,"[8] also are considered rare and thus more valuable than the standard hand-hammered wares. These examples were not smoothed with the small planishing marks of the finish hammer but instead reveal the rough texture created by the ball-peen hammer used to form the shape. For those collectors desiring an example of Van Erp's work, smaller items, such as vases, trays, or letter openers, can still be purchased for reasonable amounts, especially if they are beginning to show wear or slight damage.

Speaking of the lamps in particular, scholar Robert Judson Clark touched on one important reason why the work of Dirk Van Erp was successful both during his lifetime and after: "Its shape and color, as well as the glow from the mica shade, were perfect complements for the oak furniture and paneled interiors of the American bungalow during the mature phase of the Arts and Crafts movement in this country."[9] Modern collectors have shown that they too recognize what a Dirk Van Erp lamp can mean to an Arts and Crafts interior.

## SELECTED PRICES

Since the distinctions between a $5,000 and a $60,000 Dirk Van Erp lamp may not be evident in a price guide description, his mica-shade lamps have purposely been omitted from this listing. Providing the mica is intact and the base unpolished, any Dirk Van Erp lamp has the potential of being worth a minimum of $5,000. The best advice for any collector preparing either to buy or to sell a Dirk Van Erp lamp is to have it first inspected and appraised by a qualified expert familiar with the implications of a rolled rim, riveted strut, and unbroken shopmark.

Basket: pierced, banded handle riveted to a boat-shaped base, 10" × 8", $1,500–$2000.

Bookends: hammered copper, with ribbon border, 3" × 4", $750–$1,000

Bowl: hammered copper, seven-sided, 2" × 10", $800–$1,200

Bowl: hammered copper with detailed round copper base, 3" × 6", $700–$1,000

Bowl: hammered copper with deep patination, ruffled edge, 2" × 5", $500–$750

Candlestick: four–sided form riveted to hexagonal base, ending with hexagonal bobèche and riveted candle cup, 9" × 5", $1,000–$1,500

Desk set: copper pen tray, inkwell, and stamp holder, $1,500–$2,000

Inkwell: hammered copper with mid-dark patina, geometric design on the four corners of the lid, 3" × 3", $500–$750

Jardiniere: hammered copper, large and bulbous form with rolled rim and tapered base, 10" × 12", $3,000–$4,000

Letter opener: hammered copper, with cutout design on handle, 8", $450–$650. Matchbox holder: hammered copper, 3" × 3", $300–$450

Tray: hammered copper, round form with tooled inner circle and loop handles, 12", $1,000–$1,500

Tray, serving: hammered copper with handles, stylized rounded corners, 22" × 12", $1,000–$1,500

Tray, serving: hammered copper, riveted handles on rectangular form, 10" × 24", $1,000–$1,500

Tray, smoking: hammered copper with cigarette rest and matchbox holder, 3" × 7", $500–$750

Vase: hammered copper in early style, 8" × 7", $2,000–$3,000

Vase: hammered copper with light brown patina, 10" × 11", $2,500–$3,500

Vase: hammered copper with red "warty" texture, flared base, bulbous top, rolled rim, covered with red–brown finish, 7" × 6", $5,000–$7,000

Vase: hammered copper with red "warty" texture, bulbous, squat form with rolled rim, 4" × 6", $3,500–$4,500

Vase: hammered copper in flaring cylindrical form, with stepped-in, rolled rim, 8", $2,000–$3,000

## Other Metalware Shops and Studios

"The word 'hand-wrought' means much or little of itself. It may stand only for sturdy usefulness, or for exquisite perfection of symmetry and design. It may accompany ignorant, careless workmanship or the skilled intelligence of long experience."
—Arthur J. Stone, 1934[1]

The proponents of the Arts and Crafts movement, from William Morris and John Ruskin in England to Gustav Stickley and Jane Addams in America, attempted to improve the life of the common worker through renewed recognition of the value of handcraftsmanship. From a purely business standpoint, Stickley's offer to provide plans and hardware for furniture, copper and mica for lamps, and encouragement for anyone interested in constructing his or her own Arts and Crafts furnishings may have seemed self-defeating, but his attitude was typical of the truly zealous reformers. As a result, inspired craftsmen and craftswomen all across the country began experimenting with the design and fabrication of their own furniture, pottery, and metalware. While most never rose to nor maintained the level of the well-known firms, examples of their work continue to surface. Many were attracted to metalware for obvious reasons. Unlike furniture it did not require a large workshop; unlike pottery it did not require a kiln. Tools, for the most part, were simple, often improvised. Those craftsmen who found the work rewarding and, in at least some part, financially promising opened their own studios or joined existing firms as apprentices or journeyman metalsmiths.

The sheer number of craftsmen and craftswomen whose work and whose lives were never well documented has dictated that a complete listing—let alone a detailed analysis—of their names, their locations, their shopmarks, and their work can never be amassed. As was emphasized in the introduction of this section, the evaluation of Arts and Crafts metalware is more dependent on the individual piece than on the name of the craftsman who produced it. Nevertheless, the compilation of information on the craftsmen of this era must continue.

One of the finest studies was conducted by Sharon Darling, entitled *Chicago Metalsmiths* (Chicago: Chicago Historical Society, 1977). The large number of Chicago craftsmen included below is indicative as much of Miss Darling's research as it is of Chicago's support of the Arts and Crafts movement at the turn of the century. In addition, a series of catalogs issued by ARK Antiques (Box 3133, New Haven, CT 06515) in recent years also contains photographs and information on scores of little-known Arts and Crafts metalsmiths. It can only be hoped that writers and researchers in every major city will undertake similar studies in order that they might share what information is available on Arts and Crafts craftsmen with today's growing number of collectors.

**APOLLO STUDIOS**
New York, New York
ACTIVE: ca. 1909–22
Brass and copper kits for amateur metalworkers, jewelry.
SHOPMARK: APOLLO STUDIOS/NEW YORK.

## ARTS CRAFTS SHOP

(also BUFFALO ARTS CRAFTS SHOP)

Buffalo, New York.

ACTIVE:  ca. 1902–06 (became Heintz Art Metal Shop).

FOUNDER:  Otto L. Heintz (dates unknown).

PRINCIPAL CONTRIBUTIONS:  Copper bowls, candlesticks, and accessories
with enamel decoration.

SHOPMARK:  ARTS CRAFTS SHOP/BUFFALO.

## AVON COPPERSMITH

Avon, New York

FOUNDER:  Arthur Cole (1898–ca.1970).

ACTIVE:  1930–70: Former Roycrofter who worked in hand–hammered
copper bowls, vases, bookends, etc.

SHOPMARK:  "The Avon Coppersmith" in circular border

As a teenager growing up in East Aurora, New York, Arthur Cole had the
opportunity to meet and talk with several of the Roycroft metalsmiths, including Karl Kipp, for whom he worked while going to high school. He is
pictured in photographs taken in the Roycroft Copper Shop. After serving
in the military, Cole attended Pratt Institute in New York before returning
to the Roycroft Copper Shop to work under Kipp. In 1929 Kipp and Cole
both resigned in protest against layoffs in the Copper Shop. In 1930 Cole
opened his own shop in Avon, New York, calling it the Avon Coppersmith
and worked until his health failed in 1970. Note: For more information see
or Michael Clark and Ms. Jill Thomas–Clark, "The Best of the Rest," *Style:
1900,* Vol. 2, (spring 1998), pp. 22–24.

## BELLIS, JOHN O

San Francisco, California.

Died: 1943

SHOPMARK:  JOHN O. BELLIS/STERLING

John Bellis trained as a jeweler around the turn of the century in San Francisco, then worked at Shreve & Co. as a silversmith before establishing his
own shop shortly after the historic earthquake of 1906. Much of his work
consists of spun silver pieces embellished with hammered strapwork and
rivets, a technique he undoubtedly learned at Shreve & Co. His hollowware
is considered both rare and desirable.

## BENEDICT ART STUDIO

East Syracuse, New York (purchased Onondaga Metal Shop in 1907 and renamed).

Eight-piece Benedict hammered copper nut set with large bowl, six serving bowls, and serving spoon. Some wear to patina. Unmarked. Largest: 3" × 8½", $287

FOUNDER: Harry L. Benedict (assumed ownership in 1906).

ACTIVE: Benedict Manufacturing Company, 1894–undetermined.

Benedict Art Studio, 1907 (formerly known as the Onondaga Metal Shop).

Hand–hammered trays, lamps, desk sets, bowls, and accessories in copper, iron, and brass.

SHOPMARK: letters BB and bee enclosed by diamond.

NOTE: The Benedict Art Studio did not appear to be manufacturing a line of Arts and Crafts items until after its owner purchased the Onondaga Metal Shop. For more information, see David Rudd, "Wrought In Syracuse: Onondaga Metal Shops and Benedict Art Studios," *Style: 1900,* Vol. 2, (spring 1998), pp. 58–61.


**BENNETT, BESSIE**

Chicago, Illinois

Dates unknown

ACTIVE: 1902–21 Arts and Crafts–style copper wares.

SHOPMARK: undetermined


**BERRY, ALBERT**

ARTS AND CRAFTS SHOP

Seattle, Washington

ACTIVE: 1913–ca. 1960s.

Quality hand–hammered copper wares, desk sets, often incorporating fossilized walrus tusk and, on rare occasion, gold.

SHOPMARKS: ALBERT BERRY in script under initials A.A. flanking a metalsmithing hammer; BERRY'S CRAFT SHOP/SEATTLE encircling large initial B.

Born in England in 1878, Albert Berry arrived in the United States when he was 10. He studied at the Rhode Island School of Design before landing a

Fine and rare Albert Berry four-piece carving set with elk horn handles, including two knives, carving fork, and sharpener, in hide-lined gift box "Gifts of Character/Berry's Arts & Crafts Shop/Seattle." Excellent original condition, normal wear to utensils. Stamped mark, $1,350–$1,750

position as a designer for Gorham and, later, Tiffany. By 1905 he had moved across the country to Alaska, where he and his wife studied the art of the Pacific Northwest Indians. Inspired by their work, he began incorporating ancient ivory into his copperwork. In 1913 they opened the Arts and Crafts Shop in Juneau, before moving to Seattle in 1918, where he continued to produce unique copper desk items, bowls, vases, lamps, and accessories accented with mica, shell, and fossilized walrus tusks.

NOTE:  For more information, see Joe Farmarco, "Berry Picking: A Personal Pursuit of the Crafts of Albert and Erwina Berry," *Style: 1900*, Vol. 2, (Spring 1998): pp. 64–70.

### BLANCHARD, PORTER
Boston, Massachusetts; Los Angeles, California
1886–1973
ACTIVE:  1909–73
SHOPMARK:  PORTER BLANCHARD or his initials, P. B.; outline of man hammering within a rectangle.
Born to a family of silversmiths, Porter George Blanchard was trained by his father in the Stone–style of smithing. By 1917, Porter was being described as both a silversmith and a designer of flatware and hollowware. He moved from Boston to California in 1923, where he helped found the Arts and Crafts Society of Southern California the following year. His business grew steadily, as he and a number of assistants produced high–quality flatware and hollowware in the Arts and Crafts style. Blanchard was recog-

nized during his lifetime with numerous awards and honors. He died in 1973, but his firm remained in existence until 1994.

## BOWLES, JANET PAYNE
New York, New York; Indianapolis, Indiana
1872/3–1948
ACTIVE: 1907–ca. 1939
SHOPMARK: stamped JANET PAYNE BOWLES
Born in Indianapolis, Indiana, Janet Payne married Joseph Bowles, an active proponent of the Arts and Crafts movement, in 1895 and soon thereafter learned the skill of metalsmithing from a Russian metalsmith. In 1907 the couple moved to New York City, where she opened a shop selling her handwrought jewelry. She returned to Indianapolis without him in 1912 and taught metalsmithing for the next thirty years, during which time she continued to make jewelry and sterling silver items of her own design. Many of these are now in the Indianapolis Museum of Art.

## BOYDEN COMPANY, FRANK S.
Chicago, Illinois
Founders: Frank S. Boyden (1861–1943), Fred C. Minuth (1884–1966)
ACTIVE: 1903–currently Boyden–Minuth Company
Jewelry, trophies, and ecclesiastical wares.
SHOPMARKS F.S. BOYDEN/CHICAGO; letter F within a large letter B.

## BRADLEY & HUBBARD
Boston, Massachusetts
ACTIVE: early 20th century
Bronze and slag glass lamps, desk sets, and accessories
SHOPMARK: BRADLEY & HUBBARD MFG. CO. around triangle enclosing outline of lamp.

## BRANDT METAL CRAFTERS
Chicago, Illinois
ACTIVE: ca. 1914–ca. 1923
Jewelry and housewares
SHOPMARK: BRANDT METAL CRAFTERS

## BREESE, EDWARD H
Chicago, Illinois
Dates unknown

ACTIVE: ca. 1921–1940
Jewelry and silverware in the Kalo Shop style
SHOPMARK: STERLING/HANDWROUGHT/E.H.B

**BROSI, FRED**
San Francisco, California
ACTIVE: early 20th century
High quality hammered copper wares in style of Van Erp
SHOPMARK: YE OLDE COPPER SHOPPE

**BURTON, ELIZABETH EATON**
Santa Barbara, California
Dates unknown
ACTIVE: ca. 1910
Bronze, brass, and copper table lamps
SHOPMARK: undetermined
NOTE: See article written by Gustav Stickley on Elizabeth Burton entitled
    "Nature and Art" in the *Craftsman*, July 1904, pp. 385, 387.

**CARENCE CRAFTERS**
Chicago, Illinois
Dates unknown
Silver, copper, and brass desk accessories; occasionally decorated with
    nickel; sterling silver jewelry.
SHOPMARK: CARENCE CRAFTERS/CHICAGO or C and C in a square

**CAUMAN, REBECCA**
Boston
ACTIVE: ca.1900–ca.1940
Boston metalsmith (b.1872) who trained at Massachusetts College of Art
and rose to the status of Master Craftsman in 1924 in the Boston Society of
Arts and Crafts; her specialties were copper, silver and pewter boxes and
covered bowls with lids decorated with a decorative finial.

**CELLINI CRAFT SHOP**
Evanston, Illinois
FOUNDER: Ernest Gerlach (1890–date unknown)
ACTIVE: 1914–current (retail store)
(Early) Copper bowls and silver dinnerware in Kalo Shop style.
SHOPMARK: (early) CELLINI SHOP/EVANSTON/HANDWROUGHT

## CHICAGO ART SILVER SHOP
Chicago, Illinois
Edmund Boker (1886–date unknown), Ernest Gould (1884–1954)
ACTIVE: 1912–currently Art Metal Studios
Art Nouveau copper, bronze, and silver housewares
SHOPMARK: STERLING/HAND–MADE/CHICAGO/ ART SILVER
 SHOP; initials S.A.S

## CHICAGO SILVER COMPANY
Chicago, Illinois
Knut L. Gustafson (1885–1976)
ACTIVE: 1923–45
(Early) Hand–hammered flatware and dinnerware
SHOPMARKS large letter C; initials S. C. CO encompassed by circle

## COPELAND, ELIZABETH
Boston, Massachusetts
1867–1957
ACTIVE: 1902–37
Jeweler and silversmith, occasionally incorporating semiprecious stones into
 her silverwork
SHOPMARK: initials E. C.

## COULTAS, WILHELMINA
Chicago, Illinois
Dates unknown
ACTIVE: 1910–23
Jewelry designer
SHOPMARK: undetermined

## CRAFTSMAN STUDIOS
Laguna Beach, California
ACTIVE: dates unknown
Machine-hammered, lightweight copper bowls and accessories.
SHOPMARK: anvil and hammer/HANDMADE/CRAFTSMAN/
 CRAFTSMEN INC, often with form number
A machine shop with no designers and from which no one of significance
emerged to go elsewhere.

## DEMATTEO, WILLIAM
Silversmith

## DIDRICH, C. H.

Chicago silversmith believed to have trained at Kalo before opening his own shop. His designs, plus the quality of his craftsmanship and the heavy gauge of silver that he used are all indicative of the training he would have received at Kalo.

## DIMES, RICHARD

Boston—area silversmith

## DIXON, HARRY

San Francisco, California

1890–1967

ACTIVE: 1908–1967

Hand—hammered copper items, including vases, trays, and candlesticks.

SHOPMARK: (1918–22) his name, the date, and the words SAN FRAN-
CISCO scratched in the bottom.

(1922–1932) HARRY DIXON over infused metalsmith with hammer over SAN FRANCISCO; other works signed with shopmark of studio where he was employed.

Harry Dixon served an apprenticeship under Dirk Van Erp, where he worked with August Tiesselinck. The two young coppersmiths also worked for Lillian Palmer, where they designed lighting in the Van Erp style for her. He was a student at the California College of Arts and Crafts in Berkeley from 1909 to 1914, where he also taught basic metalsmithing. After working for Lillian Palmer until 1922, he opened his own shop where he produced a line of high—quality items.

## DODGE, WILLIAM WALDO

Asheville, North Carolina

1895–1971

ACTIVE: 1924–1942

Sterling silver hollowware, flatware, trophies, and presentation pieces.

SHOPMARK: (earliest) ASHEVILLE SILVERCRAFT/HAND
WROUGHT/STERLING; (later) DODGE/BY HAND/
STERLING

Caught in a cloud of poison gas during World War I, William Dodge was sent to Asheville, NC, in the heart of the Blue Ridge Mountains, to recuper-ate. Though trained as an architect, Dodge learned the craft of silver-smithing and opened a shop in Asheville in 1924. For the next twenty years he divided his time among his many pursuits, including architecture, sculp-ture, wood carving, painting, and silver smithing. His hollowware and presentation pieces exhibit the characteristics of the Arts and Crafts movement, including a hand–hammered texture and a simple, elegant style.

### EK, SETH
Silversmith at Handicraft Shop in Boston, ca. 1905

### ENOS COMPANY
New York, New York
ACTIVE: ca. 1913
Copper and brass lighting fixtures (advertised in the *Craftsman*)
SHOPMARK: undetermined

### FOGLIATA, A.
Chicago, Illinois
Dates unknown
ACTIVE: ca. 1903–07
Jeweler and silversmith
SHOPMARK: undetermined

### FRIEDELL, CLEMENS
Pasadena and Los Angeles, California
1872–1963
ACTIVE: 1892–1953
SHOPMARK: CLEMENS FRIEDELL/PASADENA/HAND
WROUGHT
Clemens Friedell trained in Vienna as a silversmith, then worked for Gorham from 1901 until 1908 on the Martelé line, (see Gorham). In 1910 he established his workshop in Pasadena, where he and one or two assistants produced custom–made silver hollowware, plaques, and presentation pieces for a wealthy clientele. His work reflects both the Art Nouveau style practiced at Gorham and the more restrained Arts and Crafts philosophy, including hand-hammering and the incorporation of native plants into his designs. He is considered one of the finest silversmiths of the era

### FROST ARTS AND CRAFTS WORKSHOP
Dayton, Ohio
George W. Frost (dates unknown)
ACTIVE: early 20th century
Hand–hammered copper accessories (advertised in the *Craftsman* in 1908)
SHOPMARK: triangle encompassing company's initials.

## GEBELEIN, GEORGE CHRISTIAN
Boston
ACTIVE: 1903–09 Handicraft Shop; 1909–ca. 1940 Gebelein Silversmiths
Line of sterling silver inspired by Paul Revere.

## GERMER, GEORGE E.
Boston, Massachusetts
1868–1936
ACTIVE: ca. 1893–ca. 1920
Ecclesiastical silverwork
SHOPMARK: inscribed GEORGE E. GERMER/BOSTON, MASS./ date

## GLESSNER, FRANCES MACBETH
Chicago, Illinois 1848–1922
ACTIVE: 1904–1915
Hand–hammered silver items
SHOPMARK: the letter G encompassing a bee

## GYLLENBERG, FRANS J. R.
Boston, Massachusetts
1883–unknown
ACTIVE: ca. 1905–ca. 1929
Hand–hammered copper wares and sterling silver; worked at Handicraft
    Shop.
SHOPMARK: F.J.R.G.
Born in Sweden, where he may have served an apprenticeship, Gyllenberg
collaborated with Mary Katherine Knight at the Handicraft Shop in 1905;
he was accepted into the Boston Arts and Crafts Society in 1906 and was
given its highest honor, Medalist, in 1929. He formed a partnership with
Alfred Swanson and the two remained in business until ca. 1950.

## HALLMARK SILVERSMITHS, INC
Sterling silver hollowware

## HANDICRAFT GUILD
Minneapolis, Minnesota
FOUNDER: Ernest A. Batchelder (1875–1957)
Founded: 1902
Metalwork and jewelry by independent craftsmen, teachers, and students.
SHOPMARK: Handicraft Guild/MINNEAPOLIS

## HANDICRAFT SHOP
Boston and Wellesley Hills, Massachusetts
ACTIVE: 1901–ca. 1940
Jewelry, metalwork, and silversmithing by independent craftsmen and
craftswomen SHOPMARK: anvil and letters H and S, often with mark
of craftsman.
Founded in 1901 by Arthur Astor Carey and directed by Mary Ware Dennett, the Handicraft Shop was intended to provide workshop space for
craftspersons and designers in Boston. The first supervisor of the workshop
was Mary C. Knight (see entry), a former student of Dennett.

## HANCK, MATTHIAS WM.
Park Ridge, Illinois
1883–1955
ACTIVE: 1911–55
Jewelry and silver dinnerware
SHOPMARK: HANDMADE BY M.W.
HANCK/PARKRIDGE,ILL/STERLING

## HANDEL COMPANY
Meriden, Connecticut
ACTIVE: early 20th century
Bronze lamps
SHOPMARK: HANDEL and model number

## HEINRICHS, JOSEPH
New York, New York
ACTIVE: ca. 1910
Quality hand–hammered copper bowls and accessories
SHOPMARK: JOS.HEINRICHS/PARIS & NEW YORK/PURE
COPPER

## HULL HOUSE SHOPS
Chicago, Illinois
FOUNDER: Jane Addams (1860–1935),
ACTIVE: ca. 1898–ca. 1940
Copper, brass, and silver bowls, candlesticks, trays, and accessories
SHOPMARK: none

## JULMAT, THE
Park Ridge, Illinois

FOUNDERS: Julius O. Randahl (1880–1972), Matthias Wm. Hanck (1883–1955)
ACTIVE: ca. 1910
Hand–hammered housewares
SHOPMARK: THE JULMAT/HAND WROUGHT/PARK RIDGE, ILL/STERLING

### KNIGHT, MARY CATHERINE
Boston, Massachusetts
1876–unknown
ACTIVE: beginning ca. 1901
Silversmith (also worked as supervisor at Handicraft Shop); had worked as a designer at Gorham.
SHOPMARK: shield enclosing letter K and knight on horseback/ STERLING

### KOEHLER, FLORENCE
Chicago, Illinois
1861–1944
ACTIVE: ca. 1900
Metalsmith, jewelry designer, often working in Art Nouveau designs.
SHOPMARK: undetermined

### LAWRENCE, F. WALTER
New York silversmith

### LEBOLT & COMPANY
Chicago, Illinois
FOUNDER: J. Myer H. Lebolt (1868–1944)
ACTIVE: 1899–current
Jewelry and silver dinnerware; began producing handwrought silver in 1912, phased out during the 1940s.
SHOPMARK: letter L in diamond over LEBOLT/HANDBEATEN

### LEINONEN, KARL F
Boston, Massachusetts
1866–1957
ACTIVE: ca. 1903–ca. 1950
Silversmith and supervisor at the Handicrafts Shop.
SHOPMARK: Handicraft Shop mark and letter L
Karl Leinonen arrived in the United States in 1893, after having trained as a

silversmith in Finland. By 1901 he was supervising the metalsmiths at the Handicraft Shop in Boston, where he also took time to complete his own work. His silver was exhibited widely and is held in high esteem today.

### MAGNUSSEN, ERIK
Silversmith and designer, known to have worked at Gorham from 1925 to 1929.

### MARCUS & CO
Beginning as Starr & Marcus in 1864, this New York jewelry firm eventually had retail outlets in Paris, London and Palm Beach. Although best known for its jewelry, Marcus & Co. also produced a line of high-quality Arts and Crafts hollowware.

### MARSHALL FIELD CRAFT SHOP
Chicago, Illinois
Craft Shop
ACTIVE: ca. 1904–ca. 1950
Silver jewelry, dinnerware, trays, tea sets, bowls, etc
SHOPMARKS: MADE BY MARSHALL FIELD & CO.; MADE IN OUR CRAFT SHOP/MARSHALL FIELD & CO.; MF & CO/ ART-METAL CRAFT

### MARSHALL, FRANK J
Boston, Massachusetts
(1884–unknown)
SHOPMARK: none known
This noted Boston silversmith and enameler earned the distinction of being a Master Craftsman member of the Society of Arts and Crafts. Although he was recognized for his skills during his active years in numerous publications, including the *Craftsman*, Marshall apparently did not subscribe to the Arts and Crafts practice of signing his work. Historians and collectors have had to draw upon photographs of his work and family pieces in order to identify and recognize his design and technical characteristics.

### MERRILL SHOPS
Sterling silver

### MULHOLLAND BROTHERS
Park Ridge and Evanston, Illinois

FOUNDERS: Walter Mulholland (dates unknown) David E. Mulholland
  (dates unknown)
ACTIVE: 1912–1934
Silver dinnerware in Kalo Shop style; may have trained at Kalo; worked in
  sterling silver until 1919, at which time they switched to silver plate;
  produced work sold in Cellini Shop from 1916 to 1919.
SHOPMARK: letter M within outline of an anvil; MULHOLLAND, also
  CELLINI SHOP (retail outlet), and EVANSTON (1916–1919)

**MUNSON, JULIA**
New York, New York
Dates unknown
ACTIVE: ca. 1900
Metalsmith with Tiffany Studios
SHOPMARK: unknown

**NOVICK, FALICK**
Chicago, Illinois
1878–1957
ACTIVE: 1909–57
Hammered copper bowls, plus sterling silver trays in Kalo Shop style
SHOPMARK: STERLING/HANDWROUGHT/BY F. NOVICK/
  CHICAGO
Trained in Russia before arriving in Chicago in 1907, Novick worked in
both copper and sterling silver, opening his own shop in 1909. His designs
are occasionally reflective of his early training in Russia, but they also indicate he may have worked at or for the Kalo Shop at some point after arriving in Chicago. His expertise lay in the formation of trays, considered one of
the greatest challenges for any metalsmith. It is believed that he produced
copper bowls and trays in his shop for Kalo.

**OAKES, EDWARD E**
Boston, Massachusetts
1891–1960
Known primarily for his fine Arts and Crafts jewelry; designated Medalist
in the Boston Arts and Crafts Society in 1923.

**OLD MISSION KOPPER KRAFT**
San Jose and San Francisco, California
FOUNDERS: Fred T. Brosi (Italy, unknown–1935) Hans W. Jauchen (Ger-
  many, unknown–1970)

Fine Old Mission Kopper Kraft hammered copper table lamp with riveted bulbous base and flaring copper and mica four-panel shade. Original patina, base lightly cleaned. Stamped mark, 17" × 18" dia., $6,325

ACTIVE: ca. 1922–25 Copper lamps and accessories

SHOPMARK: OLD MISSION KOPPERKRAFT with outline of mission

Hans Jauchen and Fred Brosi were active in a number of metalsmith ventures before and after the brief tenure of Old Mission Kopper Kraft (possibly accounting for the large number of similar, unsigned examples). Their workshop was located in San Jose, but goods were retailed in San Francisco. Many of their designs capitalized on the popularity of San Francisco's most famous coppersmith, Dirk Van Erp. Old Mission Kopper Kraft manufactured, using molds, die–presses, and machines, mica shade lamps which appeared to have been handcrafted. In truth, they were only hand-assembled. As the value of Dirk Van Erp lamps have escalated, Old Mission Kopper Kraft lamps have once again benefited, often bringing prices higher than the quality of their design and workmanship.

### OLD NEWBURY CRAFTERS
Silversmiths

### ONONDAGA METAL SHOPS
East Syracuse, New York (later Benedict Art Studio)

ACTIVE: ca. 1901–06

Quality hand–hammered copper wares (possibly for Gustav Stickley and L. & J. G. Stickley), including candlesticks, wall plaques, and chafing dish stands

SHOPMARK: conjoined initials O M S

NOTE: For more information, see David Rudd, "Wrought in Syracuse: Onondaga Metal Shops and Benedict Art Studios," *Style: 1900,*. Vol. 2, (Spring 1998), pp. 58–61

### PALMER COPPER SHOP
San Francisco, California

Onondaga Metal Shops hammered copper chamberstick with cup-shaped bobèche, riveted angular handle, and flaring base. Old cleaning and verdigris to patina. Stamped OMS, 6¼", $172

FOUNDER: Lillian MacNeill Palmer (1871–1961)

ACTIVE: 1910–ca. 1928

Lamps

Lillian Palmer established the Palmer Copper Shop in San Francisco in 1910. She was joined by young August Tiesselinck (1890–1972) and Harry Dixon (1890–1967) by 1914, shortly after each left the employment of Dirk Van Erp. Tiesselinck and Dixon may well have been responsible for the line of lamps produced by the Palmer Copper Shop that bear a striking resemblance in form and quality to those of Van Erp. Palmer Copper Shop lamps are often characterized by their smooth–textured copperwork on the mica shades, which were often mounted on Japanese bronze vases and sold through retail merchants. Lillian Palmer is noted for her experimentation with lampshade designs and materials, including an extremely fine wire mesh, which, in the Arts and Crafts style, she hand–painted.

**PAYNE, ARTHUR F.**

(1876–1939)

Author of *Art Metalwork with Inexpensive Equipment for the Public School and the Craftsman* (1914).

Influential writer and teacher; worked in copper.

**PETTERSON STUDIO**

Chicago, Illinois

John Pontus Petterson (1884–1949)

ACTIVE: 1912–49

(Early) Silver dinnerware influenced by Jarvie.

SHOPMARK: THE PETTERSON STUDIO/CHICAGO; initials TPS enclosed in circle/HANDMADE

Born and trained in Norway, silversmith John Pontus Petterson immigrated to the United States in 1905. He worked under both Robert Jarvie and Tiffany & Co. before establishing his own shop. His work, which included flatware and hollowware, reflects the quality and design of the finest of the American Arts and Crafts movement.

## POND APPLIED ART STUDIOS
Baltimore, Maryland
Theodore H. Pond (1872–1933)
ACTIVE STUDIO: 1911–1914
Silversmith
SHOPMARK: dragonfly enclosed by KWO–NE–SHE and
    HAND/WROUGHT/ STERLING/POND

## PORTER, FRANKLIN
Silversmith
ca. 1930s

## POTTER, HORACE E
Cleveland metalsmith who studied first at the Cleveland School of Art in the late 1890s, then in Boston and at C. R. Ashbee's Guild of Handicraft. He appears to have returned to Cleveland full-time around 1905 to establish his own metalsmithing business, working primarily in sterling silver but also demonstrating a unique ability to work in other metals as well as ivory.

## PRATT, KATHERINE
Boston silversmith

## PRESTON, JESSIE M
Chicago, Illinois
Dates unknown
ACTIVE: 1900–18
Jewelry designer; high–quality candlesticks in style of Robert Jarvie
SHOPMARK: PRESTON/CHICAGO

## RANDAHL SHOP, THE
Park Ridge, Illinois
FOUNDER: Julius O. Randahl (1880–1972)
ACTIVE: 1907–10 (Kalo); 1911–50 The Randahl Shop

(Early) Hand–hammered bowls, tea sets, candleholders
SHOPMARKS  RANDAHL/HAND WROUGHT/STERLING; initials
    JOR with silversmith's hammer
This Swedish silversmith worked at the Kalo Shop prior to the establishment of the Randahl Shop. For many years his work was retailed through Marshall Field and Company. In addition, he executed numerous special commissions reflecting the Arts and Crafts tradition.

### ROGERS, MARGARET
Boston
Painter, craftsperson, jeweler, designer; achieved Craftsman level in Society of Arts and Crafts of Boston in 1905, Master Craftsman in 1910, and Medalist in 1915 (highest level).

### ROKESLEY SHOP
Cleveland, Ohio
FOUNDERS:  Carolyn Hadlow, Ruth Smedley, Mary Blakeslee
ACTIVE:  ca. 1907–ca. 1916
Jewelry, smaller metal items, silversmithing
SHOPMARK:  rectangle around ROKESLEY/STERLING

### SCIARROTTA, ALFREDO
Newport, Rhode Island
Silversmith

### SHAW, JOSEPHINE HARTWELL
Boston and Duxbury, Massachusetts
Dates unknown
ACTIVE:  ca. 1900–35
Acclaimed jewelry designer
SHOPMARK:  J.H. SHAW

### SMITH METAL ARTS (SEE ALSO HEINTZ ART METAL SHOP)
Buffalo, New York
FOUNDER:  Fred Smith
ACTIVE:  1919–present
Spun bronze items with silver overlay imitative of Heintz Art Metal, plus unique patinas.
SHOPMARKS  (1919–30) SILVER CREST (in script lettering) over SMACO; (after 1930) SMACO in triangle

## SORENSON, CARL

Philadelphia, Pennsylvania
Dates unknown
ACTIVE: ca. 1914
Hand–hammered copper desk accessories
SHOPMARK: large letter C encompassing smaller letter S

## STICKLEY, L. & J. G.

Fayetteville, New York
Leopold Stickley (1869–1957) John George Stickley (1871–1921)
ACTIVE: ca. 1902–present
Trays
SHOPMARK: triangle around LJGS
Scholars are not yet in agreement as to the degree to which Leopold and
John George Stickley delved into metalwork. They may have formed their
own metalshop for a brief period of time and/or they may have had a con-
nection with the Onondaga Metal Shops or, after 1904, the Benedict Studios
in nearby Syracuse. Since metalware does not appear in their catalogs, they
may have dropped the idea early in their careers.

## SWASTICA SHOP

Chicago, Illinois
ACTIVE: 1902–date unknown

Fine and rare Onondaga Metal
Shops hammered copper and
wrought-iron chandelier with
stylized cutouts to frame, and five
lantern fixtures with original yellow
glass cylindrical shades, complete
with hanging chain and ceiling cap.
Excellent original patina, a few
scratches to tops of lanterns, needs
wiring. Unmarked. Ring: 16" dia.,
$11,500

Jewelry, hand–hammered metalware, leathers, and crafts
SHOPMARK: undetermined

## SWEESTER COMPANY
New York, New York
ACTIVE: ca. 1900–15
Silver and gold jewelry
SHOPMARK: S & E inside rectangle

## T. C. SHOP
Chicago, Illinois
FOUNDERS: Emery W. Todd (dates unknown) Clemencua C. Cosio (dates unknown)
ACTIVE: 1910–23
Silver dinnerware, jewelry
SHOPMARK: THE TC SHOP/CHICAGO/HAND WROUGHT/STERLING or letters T C conjoined

## THATCHER SCHOOL OF METAL WORK
Woodstock, New York
ACTIVE: ca. 1911
Basic metalwork forms by students
SHOPMARK: undetermined

## TIESSELINCK, AUGUST
San Francisco, California
1890–1972
ACTIVE: 1911–72
Lighting, vases, decorative objects
SHOPMARK: (after 1920) Dutch wooden shoe above his conjoined initials AT, or his name and the year; (his pre–1920 work bears the shopmarks of Dirk Van Erp, Lillian Palmer, or none at all)

Like his famous uncle, Dirk Van Erp, August Tiesselinck was born in Holland, trained as a metalsmith, and emigrated to the West Coast. He arrived in 1911 and immediately went to work in Van Erp's San Francisco shop. The young, enthusiastic Tiesselinck helped improve the design of Van Erp's emerging line of copper and mica lamps, and helped teach Van Erp's two children, Agatha and William, the craft and art of metalsmithing. He left Van Erp's studio in 1914 to work as foreman at the Lillian Palmer Shop for two years, where he designed a line of copper and mica shade lamps. From

1920 to 1922 he operated his own shop, but returned to the Van Erp studio in 1922, where he served as foreman over Van Erp's fifteen employees. In 1926 he left again to embark on a 30–year teaching career. He continued to work as a metalsmith until his death in 1972.[2] Note: For more information see Isak Lindenauer, *August Tiesselinck: A Lifetime in Metal* (San Francisco: Isak Lindenauer, 1989).

### TIFFANY & CO.
New York
SHOPMARK: SPECIAL HAND WORK, plus standard Tiffany marks
By 1914 the growing popularity of the Arts and Crafts style motivated Tiffany & Co. to introduce a line of handwrought sterling silver bowls, pitchers, vases, and trays. Their entry into the field around 1914 may have been due to the opening of a Kalo retail store in New York City.

### TRAUTMANN, GEORGE H.
Chicago, Illinois
Dates unknown
ACTIVE: 1910–17
Lamps, sconces, chandeliers, lighting fixtures
SHOPMARK: G.H. TRAUTMANN/RAVENSWOOO, CHICAGO

### TRIO SHOP
Evanston, Illinois
ACTIVE: 1908–15

George H. Trautmann in collaboration with Christia Reade. Copper, micro screen, and mica lamp, 1914-17. Handwrought, 24" tall × 20" dia., $42,000

Hand–hammered metalware by independent craftsmen.
SHOPMARK: individual

### TROY SCHOOL OF ARTS AND CRAFTS
Troy, New York
ACTIVE: ca. 1907
Basic metalware forms, including desk accessories, by students.
SHOPMARK: individual

### TWITCHELL, GERTRUDE
Boston
ca. 1889–undetermined
ACTIVE: 1916–30s (Master craftsman of the Boston Arts and Crafts Society in 1927)
Enameled copper boxes, jewelry, sterling silver boxes, bookends.

### VAN ERP, WILLIAM AND AGATHA
San Francisco, California
ACTIVE: 1910–77
Lamps, vases, silver flatware, and decorative objects.
SHOPMARK: Dirk Van Erp windmill mark, generally with the addition of the words SAN FRANCISCO and HANDWROUGHT
Agatha (b.1895) and William Van Erp (1901–1977) grew up in their famous father's copper shop, where they trained under their father and their cousin August Tiesselinck. When Dirk Van Erp retired in 1929, William took over and ran the business until 1977. During this span of 48 years, his work reflects prevailing styles, executed in copper, bronze, silverplate, and sterling silver. Agatha Van Erp worked for her father, and taught metalsmithing, but never offered pieces for sale under her own shopmark. She retired shortly after her father's death in 1933.

### VANDENHOFF, GEORGE A.
New York, New York
Dates unknown
ACTIVE: ca. 1913
Artistic brass and copper novelties (advertised in the *Craftsman*)
SHOPMARK: undetermined

### VERMON COPPER COMPANY
(Location undetermined)
Dates unknown

Inexpensive copper accessories

SHOPMARK: conjoined letters V.C.C./ VERMON/HAND HAMMERED
COPPER and form number

### WATKINS, MILDRED G.
Cleveland, Ohio

1883–1968

ACTIVE: ca. 1903–ca. 1960

Jeweler and noted silversmith

SHOPMARK: sailboat and MILDRED WATKINS/STERLING

Watkins is considered to be one of the finest enamelers of the Arts and Crafts era. She graduated from the Cleveland School of Art where, after a brief time in Boston, she also taught. Working well into the 1950s, she revealed an exceptional ability to adapt her style to compliment that of the era, including Art Nouveau, Art Deco, and Modern.

### WEHDE, ALBERT
Chicago

ACTIVE: ca. 1910–ca. 1915

Jewelry in silver and gold

### WINN, JAMES H.
Chicago, Illinois

1866–ca. 1940

ACTIVE: 1895–1927 Jewelry in both Arts and Crafts and Art Nouveau
styles

SHOPMARK: WINN

### WOOLEY, JAMES T.
Boston, Massachusetts

Accomplished silversmith awarded the highest level (Medalist) in the Boston Society of Arts and Crafts in 1916; established his own shop in 1908 after having worked for Goodnow & Jenks from 1890 to 1906; created hollowware, including tea services, often in the Colonial Revival style.

### YNNE, MADELINE YALE
Chicago, Illinois

1847–1918

ACTIVE: 1893–1909

Hand–hammered gold, silver, and copper bowls and jewelry

SHOPMARK: unknown

## YELLIN, SAMUEL

Philadelphia, Pennsylvania

1885–1940

ACTIVE: 1906–40

Ornamental architectural detailing, grilles, gates, fire screens, lighting, and
railings.

SHOPMARK: SAMUEL YELLIN

This Polish–born blacksmith elevated the role of the blacksmith from utilitarian worker to craftsman. He came to America in 1906 and three years
later, at the age of 24, opened his own shop in Philadelphia. Many of his earliest commissions came from the drafting tables of the architectural firm of
McKim, Mead, and White, but by 1915, when he opened his new shop, the
Arch Street Metalworker's Studio, he was involved in the design, supervision, and production of numerous wrought–iron ornaments and decorative
accessories. He hand–picked his craftsmen, teaching them the techniques he
had learned in Europe. In the true Arts and Crafts style, he rejected cast
iron and, instead, advocated the hammer and the anvil as essential to proper
iron work. His work attracted the attention of Gustav Stickley, who featured him in a 1912 issue of the *Craftsman* magazine.

NOTE:  For more information, see Anna Fariello, "Samuel Yellin and the
Expression of Ruskin's Gothic," *Style:1900* 13, (February 2000).

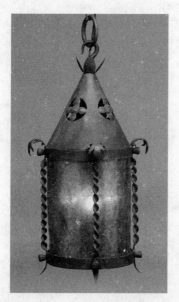

Large and rare Samuel Yellin
wrought-iron and mica lantern
with cutout floral motif and
twisted stems. Some surface rust,
original mica, dent to one panel.
Stamped SAMUEL YELLIN, 29" ×
16" dia., $4,600

**ZIMMERMANN, MARIE**
New York, New York
1878–1972
ACTIVE: 1903–ca. 1930s
Hammered metal bowls in copper, silver, bronze, gold, with various chemical patinas; jewelry, accessories; noted for her fine patinas and imaginative designs.
SHOPMARK: MARIE ZIMMERMANN/MAKER/around M Z cipher

PART 4

# LIGHTING, TEXTILES, AND COLOR WOODBLOCKS

# LIGHTING

*by David Rago*

Comprehending the many types of lighting fixtures manufactured during the Arts and Crafts era is difficult, for the Arts and Crafts movement coincided with a time of many important innovations in the lighting industry. In the late 1880s, most homes and businesses in America were illuminated by fluid lamps, fueled by a variety of liquids, including whale oil, turpentine (also called camphene), alcohol, naphtha, benzene, and kerosene. By the close of the Arts and Crafts movement, however, electricity had radically altered the design and production of lighting fixtures. As a result, Arts and Crafts manufacturers and craftsmen produced a wide variety of lighting fixtures—from candlesticks and kerosene table lamps to gas wall sconces and electric chandeliers.

The discovery of kerosene in 1859 provided Americans with an abundant, inexpensive fuel. From 1859 until 1879 more than 1,600 patents were granted for kerosene lamps alone.[1] The greatest obstacle for kerosene lighting manufacturers and consumers was the maintenance required by the smoke-producing fuel. Cleaning of the glass chimneys, trimming of the wicks, and changing of the oil was recommended daily for optimal performance. Among the list of early manufacturers of oil lamp burners and bases was Bradley and Hubbard, which had opened in 1854 in Meridan, Connecticut, a major metal manufacturing center. Their familiar "B & H" can be found on a variety of Victorian chandeliers, wall sconces, and floor and table lamps.

The development of early forms of propane gas as a fuel for interior lighting was actually taking place at the same time as kerosene lamps were being improved. As early as 1835, in fact, Philadelphia had installed one of the first gas-producing plants capable of providing its residents with gas distilled from heated coal. Problems remained, however, for this fledgling fuel. The greatest obstacle was the cost of the underground pipeline required to transport the gas from the plant to the homes. Safety was yet another concern, for a faulty valve, careless owner, or naive child could fill a house with

Exceptional Grueby Kendrick lamp base with a Tiffany Turtleback leaded-glass shade, the base with seven handles and tooled leaves covered in a superior matte green glaze, the shade with original verdigris patina and a halo of lustered Turtleback tiles on green slag glass. Originally an oil lamp, this was retrofitted at the Grueby factory to accommodate electric wiring. Two paper labels on base provide instructions: "Change to electric, three lights, chain sockets/bronze band at foot of base/cord to come there," and "Do not make a shade. Sold with turtleback sh. (sic)" Tiffany bronze beading at base complete but loose.
This was purchased by the consignor at Macklowe Galleries in New York City in 1972 for $2,500, an extraordinary sum at the time. It remains the best such example ever to come to market. Grueby price tag "$125," Grueby label and Grueby stamp. Shade and font stamped Tiffany Studios/New York. Vase: 12½" × 10"; Shade: 7" × 18" dia., $286,000

the highly explosive gas in a matter of minutes. Providing customers with a reliable and consistent flow of gas also proved to be a problem for gas companies. In the face of these problems with gas, most homeowners continued to buy kerosene lamps and ceiling fixtures for several years, despite their inconvenience.

By the turn of the century, as gas production and gas mantles were improved, gas lighting fixtures provided strong competition for both kerosene lighting and the recently invented electric bulb. "It was not until approximately 1913 that the new advantages of having one's home powered by electricity could justify the expenses involved in making that conversion. Until about 1920, gas gave electricity a fierce run for its money, but gradually found itself losing ground. Conversion to electricity did not just mean better lighting, it meant a whole new way of life."[2] The introduction of electricity and the limited application of petroleum gas as a fuel for lighting fixtures combined to limit the number of gas lighting fixtures designed after 1900. Since the gas had to be piped directly to the lighting fixture, gas table and floor lamps appear infrequently. Wall sconces and chandeliers constitute the majority of gas lighting fixtures produced. Manufacturers were more apt to design gas fixtures in a style more closely aligned to the more elaborate Victorian movement than to the less ornate Arts and Crafts. One of the exceptions was Bradley and Hubbard, who also marketed a line of simple, inexpensive gas lighting fixtures. Never known as an active proponent of the

Fine, early and rare Dirk Van Erp hammered copper desk lamp with candlestick base, four riveted armatures and four-paneled mica shade with vented cap, single socket. Fine original patina and mica. Closed box mark with D'Arcy Gaw/Dirk Van Erp, 15" × 12", $109,250

arts and Crafts movement, the firm's gas lighting fixtures were inspired by economic, and philosophic, simplicity.

Once the idea occurred to combine gas and electrical components in a single lighting fixture, the number and variety of fixtures increased dramatically. By 1900, combination lighting fixtures could be found in Victorian, Art Nouveau, and Arts and Crafts styles, as well as in a number of transitional designs and bizarre marriages. One of the first recognitions by lighting manufacturers of the Arts and Crafts movement was the incorporation of square brass tubing and square shades into ceiling and wall fixture designs. Hand-painted shades with Arts and Crafts motifs, as well as acid-etched shades with a Greek key design, also appeared on electric, gas, and combination fixtures. The vast majority of manufacturers, though, were responding to the demand for simple, less-expensive lighting fixtures deemed appropriate for middle-class owners of bungalows, shingle, and other moderately priced styles of homes. Few manufacturers paid more than token recognition to William Morris's and Gustav Stickley's calls for hands-craftsmanship, integrity of materials, and the elevation of the status of the craftsman.

Although scientists had experimented with crude forms of electricity since the early 1600s, it was Thomas Edison who, by 1879, first developed not only a durable, efficient electric bulb, but also a means of generating, storing, and transmitting electricity from its source to the home. Ironically, it remained for another inventor, Harvey Hubbell, to devise a means by which homeowners could turn their electric light fixtures on and off. "The first electric fixtures were left on continuously," one author reports. "There were no separated circuits and switches for individual fixtures. Electric companies advertised that they would come and change your light bulbs for you when they burned out. In 1891, Hubbell submitted an electric switch design for patent, and in 1896 his new pull socket was patented. It is still in use today."[3]

Thus, when the Arts and Crafts movement burst upon the scene in America around the turn of the century, homes were illuminated by a variety of fixtures: kerosene and candles (by far the least expensive and often the only alternative for rural areas), gas, electric, and combination gas and electric fixtures. For the next 20 years, all four of these styles of lighting fixtures would be in demand, but only one, the electric bulb, was destined to dominate. Thomas Edison secured the future of the electric bulb by inventing a number of household appliances that would also require electricity to operate, such as the coffee pot, heating pad, curling iron, clothes iron, and the electric motor. Since wall outlets had not yet been invented, early electric appliances had to be plugged into a special light bulb socket with a plug designed into it.

The first electric sconces and chandeliers were either adapted from existing gas fixtures or were designed in a similar, ornate style. Victorian ceiling fixtures—often called electroliers—featured from one to five lengths of metal chain attached to brass shade holders. In some instances the bulbs were left exposed, but in most cases the bulbs were partially covered by glass shades designed in a typically ornate Victorian style.

One of the first shade manufacturers to offer an alternative to the ornate, ruffled-edge Victorian shade was the Holophane Lighting Corporation. Intended for chandeliers, ceiling plates, and wall sconces, Holophane shades were designed to increase the intensity of the early, nine-watt bulbs through a series of decorative ribs. Introduced in America in 1898, Holophane shades were actually manufactured by the Heisey Company in Newark, Ohio, using

Fine, large and early Dirk Van Erp hammered copper table lamp with tapering base, four riveted arms, four-paneled shade and broad vented cap, double socket. Original patina and mica, replacement to base, scratch to cap. Unmarked, 18½" × 16" dia., $13,800

Roycroft hammered copper table lamp with four-sided base and flaring gold and purple iridescent faceted glass shade. New patina to base. Base marked with orb-and-cross, shade unmarked, 17¼" × 10½", $3,450

molds designed by Holophane employees. Most Holophane shades are signed with molded letters around the upper rim. "According to industrial accounts, the largest markets for the shades existed in Texas, Illinois, Michigan, and New York and the biggest buyer was General Electric."[4]

The prismatic crystal shades of the Holophane Lighting Corporation dominated the industry during the entire Arts and Crafts movement. Other companies attempted to imitate the ribbed crystal shades, including Phoenix, Wellington and Gill and Co., but the carefully guarded patents of the Holophane designs prevented them from becoming a serious threat. Even today Taiwan-produced shades bearing the Holophane name are being distributed, but their clarity is vastly inferior to the Heisey-made originals.

The Phoenix Glass Company in Monaca, Pennsylvania, was a major producer of electric light bulbs, and, in 1886, began marketing etched, frosted, white opalescent, and painted shades as well.[5] Hand-painted shades with Victorian, Art Nouveau, or Arts and Crafts motifs became popular during the early years of the 20th century, prompting several companies to begin hiring artists to hand-paint designs on glass shades. In addition, "hand-painted Czechoslovakian shades were imported into the U.S. prior to World War I and feature landscape scenes with cottages and mountains."[6] In keeping with the Arts and Crafts philosophy, customers also had the opportunity to purchase undecorated shades, which they could literally paint themselves. By 1910, Americans had literally hundreds of wood and brass electric lighting fixtures to choose from and several thousand varieties of styles of shades.

Handel table lamp with floriform bronze base topped by two sockets, and painted glass shade with landscape of trees. Excellent original condition. Base stamped HANDEL, fabric HANDEL on felt, shade with painted Handel 0489. Base: 20"; shade: 8" × 14" dia., $2,760

## Arts and Crafts Lighting Studios and Workshops

What this wide variety of lighting fixtures and shades lacked, however, was a high level of handcraftsmanship and artistic design. While Arts and Crafts lighting designers, such as Louis Comfort Tiffany, Gustav Stickley, Robert Jarvie, and Dirk Van Erp, could not hope to compete with these large, well-established companies in the field of inexpensive, mass-produced lamps and shades, they could offer high-quality, handmade lighting fixtures for the discriminating homeowner.

Louis Comfort Tiffany (1849–1933), son of Charles Lewis Tiffany, the wealthy New York silversmith and jeweler, was among the earliest American designers who strove to make beautiful objects affordable for the middle-

Bronze desk lamp with floriform finial on pivoting shaft, and flaring leaded glass shade. Original dark patina, several short cracks to glass, small dent to base, replaced socket. Unmarked, 12" × 14", $431

Tiffany table lamp with columnar bronze base, three sockets, and green opalescent leaded-glass shade. Mint original patina and all original parts. Base marked TIFFANY STUDIOS NEW YORK, 526; shade stamped TIFFANY STUDIOS NEW YORK, 1901. Base: 21½" × 8¾"; Shade: 7" × 16½", $14,375

class through carefully controlled mass production. After studying art in Paris as a young man, Tiffany focused his artistic and technical skills on the production of colored glass. After a brief yet successful partnership with textile designer Candace Wheeler, Lockwood DeForest, and Samuel Coleman from 1879 until 1883, Tiffany reorganized his business as the Tiffany Glass Studio.

Tiffany combined techniques he had developed with ancient methods of producing, coloring, and molding glass to create many unique effects. Not unlike the potter, Tiffany discovered that by coating the glass with a glaze-like material, then exposing it to certain gases, he could produce an iridescent glass characterized by a metallic sheen. By developing a stronger glass than had previously existed, Tiffany and his designers escaped many of the restrictions placed on their designs by the heavy, cumbersome lead caning. Special effects within the glass itself enabled them to create in their windows and lamps perspectives of depth and shadow previously found only on the artist's canvas.

During the 1890s, production of stained-glass windows, lamps, and other decorative arts increased dramatically at Tiffany's studio. Artists and technicians worked side-by-side at the glasshouse and studio, utilizing both machines and handcraftsmanship to create artistic, yet affordable table and floor lamps for the American people. First inspired by Art Nouveau designers such as Galle, Daum, and Lalique, Tiffany's *favrile* ("hand-made") shades were often designed for specific bases that his firm also produced, and could seldom be matched with a base made by another company. As Arts and Crafts motifs grew increasingly popular, Tiffany introduced additional styles of shades, including simple geometric patterns, vines, leaves, daffodils. Dragonflies and other organic designs in more subdued, earth-tone colors than were found in the firm's Victorian and Art Nouveau lamps.

In 1902, Tiffany reorganized his expanding businesses under the name of Tiffany Studios. It was also around this time that Tiffany began experimenting with art pottery bases for his lamps, quite possibly as a means of disguising the kerosene fuel canister. While some of the pottery bases have remained unidentified, a number of signed Tiffany lampshades and fittings have been found on Grueby vases. This rare combination has created one of the most sought-after examples of lighting for Arts and Crafts collectors today. A finely crafted Grueby vase designed by an artist of the caliber of George Kendrick or Ruth Erikson topped by a Tiffany Studios shade with an Arts and Crafts motif can climb into the $30,000 to $40,000 range even during a recession. The same shade and fittings on a non-Grueby vase may be worth only one-half to two-thirds as much.

As author Beth Cathers has noted, "Grueby's subtle monochromatic glazes were found to be an admirable complement to the muted palette of the leaded glass shades, especially those with geometric patterns, of that period. It was anticipated in 1906 that Tiffany Studios would phase out its use of Grueby bases and replace them with its own newly introduced range of ceramic wares; but this did not occur, as the firm was at the time in the process of converting its combustion light fixtures to electricity. This eliminated the need for bases to house fuel canisters. The result was a sharp decrease in the use of Grueby wares by lamp manufacturers."[7]

Other lamp companies copied Tiffany's idea, adapting vases from a number of art potteries to serve as bases, both for kerosene-burning and electric lamps. Duffner & Kimberly, Bigelow, Kennard & Co., and others utilized vases by Grueby, Hampshire, Teco, and other art pottery firms to enhance their lampshades. Unfortunately, once the shade and fittings have been removed, the vase, if it had been drilled to accommodate a lamp cord, is worth less than it would have been had it not been altered.

Though far more expensive than its competitors, Tiffany's art glass shades were an immediate success. By 1901, in fact, the Fostoria Glass Specialty Company in Fostoria, Ohio, was also producing "luster and decorated shades which are generally heavier than those of other companies. Early shades were marked with a paper label, until after 1912 when they began using the IRIS trademark."[8] The firm closed in 1917.

A former Tiffany employee, Martin Bach, founded in 1901 the Quezel Art Glass and Decorating Company in New York City. Active until 1924, Quezel shades appeared in an array of iridescent colors, as well as with floral motifs and colorful feathers (the quezel is a beautiful Central American bird). Most of its shades were signed with the name of the firm either etched or engraved into the rim.

Bach's son-in-law, Conrad Vahlsing, founded the short-lived Lustre Art Glass Company in 1920, which also produced art glass shades. Yet another art glass company that produced Arts and Crafts shades was Vineland Flint Glass company (1924–1931), founded by Victor Durand. Their crackle glass shades were most often marked with the letter "V" and the name DURAND.

Although, in 1903, a latecomer to the art glass field, the Steuben Glass Company quickly established a reputation as one of the finest producers of art glass shades. Its iridescent shades of blue, amber, green, and brown were popular with Arts and Crafts enthusiasts, including Elbert Hubbard and the Roycroft metalsmiths. By the middle of the Arts and Crafts movement, the Roycroft catalog included table lamps with either Steuben shades or Steuben glass bases. Examples of either are considered extremely rare today.

With the exception of Tiffany Studios, most art glass firms produced shades that could be matched with a wide variety of mass-produced lighting fixtures equipped with the standard 2¼" shade holders. Among the companies that produced bronze bases similar to (but far less expensive than) those made popular by Tiffany Studios was Edward Miller and Co., as well as the prolific and highly successful Bradley and Hubbard. Both firms originated in Meriden, Connecticut. As a result, shades from one particular company can be found on bases from a number of firms.

Duffner and Kimberly of New York City produced leaded glass shades for only five years, beginning in 1906, but they quickly achieved fame as a rival to Tiffany Studios. The similarities in design and workmanship to the lampshades of Tiffany Studios has been attributed to the possibility that one of the two founders may have worked for L. C. Tiffany prior to starting a new firm. Since their lampshades were not always signed, identifying Duffner and Kimberly shades can be difficult, but as one author has observed, "Some Duffner and Kimberly table lamps are characterized by a special circular locking mechanism which secured the shade to the top of the base."[9] After 1911, the firm was known only as the Kimberly Company.

As a more affordable alternative to handcrafted shades, companies began offering lamps incorporating large panels of slag glass, curved or flat, occasionally mounted behind metal silhouettes. In some instances, sheets of glass were mounted in oak frames atop Mission oak bases, while other companies imitated the bronze look of higher-quality lamp designers with less expensive metal frames and bases. Since few of these firms made it a practice to sign their work, most have to be identified through period advertisements. Among the more popular firms producing slag glass lighting fixtures were Bradley and Hubbard, the Carl V. Helmschmied Manufacturing Company, Edward Miller & Company, the U.S. Art Bent Glass Company, Williamson and Company, Moskan and Hastings, Crest and Company (Chicago), H. P. Peter (Chicago), Albert Sechrist Manufacturing Company (Denver), Alladdin (Chicago), and Bigelow and Kennard.[10] As would be expected, the quality of workmanship evident in each firm ranges widely, as they attempted to compete with one another at nearly every market level.

In the preface to his 1910 catalog, Gustav Stickley wrote, "Rooms finished with beams and wainscot in the Craftsman style needed the mellow glint of copper and brass here and there in lighting fixtures, lamps, and the like. As the glittering lacquered surfaces and more or less the fantastic designs of the machine-made fixtures were entirely out of harmony, we began to make lanterns of copper and brass after simple structural designs; electric and oil lamps of the same general character . . . letting their decorative value grow out of their fitness for that use and the quality of the design and workmanship."[11]

While we await a definitive study on Craftsman lighting fixtures, the catalogs and magazines which Stickley issued between 1901 and 1916 reveal a great deal about the lighting fixtures that his metalshop produced (see Gustav Stickley entries in *Furniture and Metalware* sections). In one of his earliest publications, the 1901 *Chips from the Workshops of the United Crafts,* we find illustrations of a few oil-burning table lamps. At least two appear to be Grueby pottery bases with conventional fittings and shades unlike those produced a few years later by the Craftsman Workshops. The oil lamps, and occasionally candlesticks, books, vases, and blotters, appear to be included in the illustrations simply as accessories rather than items that were for sale. The same appears to be true for a series of photographs taken of Craftsman furniture in 1902, wherein we find what appears to be another Grueby vase filled with conventional shade for an oil-burning lamp. Another picture

Fine, rare, and large Gustav Stickley forged iron table lamp #755, with four-sided base and shaft, and hammered copper and amber hammered glass shade with pendant amber glass squares, complete with hammered copper cap and six fixtures. Original patina, some squares re-foiled, one with replaced glass. Unmarked, 35½" × 27" dia., $80,500

taken that same year shows a distinctively colonial candlestick atop a Craftsman somno. In what may be the first example of Craftsman Workshop lighting, dressing table #632 was designed with an attached mirror flanked by two candlesticks of wrought iron or copper. A separate mirror, model #633, also came with two attached candlesticks in 1902, fashioned in the same handcrafted style of the hardware.[12]

By 1903, Craftsman lighting fixtures began replacing period oil lamps and candlesticks in the *Craftsman* magazine illustrations. The 1904 catalog exhibits photographs of a number of different oil-burning lamps, some of which appeared in Stickley's own catalog in 1905. Others apparently were being used only as props in 1904. In his first metalware catalog (1905), Stickley reflects the current popularity of art glass shades, for he offers more than 10 options incorporating yellow, green, and ruby glass panels "designed with a view of a perfect and harmonious effect in their use with our special hammered copper oil lamps."[13] His 1905 catalog reveals that nearly all of his table lamps were oil burning, while the wall sconces and ceiling fixtures (electroliers) were nearly all electric. Examples of early Craftsman oil-burning table lamps with art glass shades are extremely rare. Either they were produced in only small quantity or there was little demand for this soon-to-be obsolete form.

By 1905, Gustav Stickley was offering electric fixtures, but all but two were either wall sconces or ceiling fixtures. He did offer one "portable electric lamp"[14] with either a ruby or yellow opalescent glass shade, and an electric candlestick with a silk shade. His electroliers, available with three, four, five, or nine lights, are perhaps the best the Arts and Crafts movement produced. Constructed of a heavy gauge of iron, copper, or brass, Craftsman

Fine and rare Gustav Stickley hammered copper chandelier with cross-form riveted bracket, four pendant lanterns with clear "hammered" yellow glass panels, complete with original 8' 8" hanging chain and ceiling plate. Original patina and glass. Als Ik Kan stamped mark to ceiling plate. Fixture: 21" × 21½" dia., $19,550

Gustav Stickley harp desk lamp with riveted hammered copper strapwork to top, and lower keyed-through stretcher. Fine original finish, missing shade. Unmarked, 16¼" × 9½" × 7¼", $2,990

electroliers reflect the high-quality design, materials, and workmanship evident in Gustav Stickley's shops. The chains were always wrought iron, not oak, and the glass shades could be crystal, amber, or opalescent glass.

As Gustav Stickley continued to enlarge his selection of electric table lamps, gradually phasing out all but a few oil-burning lamps, an interesting development occurred. He gradually began producing lamps with wicker shades, often incorporating liners of "a heavy grade of Habutai silk in soft shades of green, red, dull yellow and orange."[15] While he kept a few opalescent glass shades in his inventory, the majority of his lamps were offered with wicker shades over a variety of bases of oak, clay, hammered copper, or iron. At the peak of his career in 1912, the Craftsman Workshops were offering the public an amazing number of styles of handcrafted lighting fixtures, including candlesticks, newel post lamps, more than a dozen styles of sconces and one-light lanterns, more than a dozen major electroliers, floor lamps, a few oil-burning table lamps, and nearly 30 different electric table lamps available with several choices of shades.

Regardless of the range of his lighting fixture designs, Stickley's prices often prevented middle-class homeowners from purchasing them. For example, model #50, a 21" table lamp with a hammered copper base and wicker shades, cost $18.50 in 1912. In the same catalog, a number of chairs, rockers, magazine stands, and small tables cost considerably less. Craftsman lighting fixtures surface only rarely today, especially in their original form. The majority of examples that do reach the market invariably exhibit the almost inevitable signs of age: copper bases have been over-polished, original wicker and glass shades have been discarded, or the wood has been refinished. Collectors will pay a premium, generally in the $4,000–$6,000 range, for com-

Rare Gustav Stickley hammered copper hanging exterior lantern with faceted overhanging top, trellis grid over hammered yellow glass, complete with original iron chain and faceted ceiling plate. Corrosion to lantern, ceiling plate in excellent condition, one replaced glass pane. Unmarked. Lantern: 13½" × 7" sq., $4,000–$6,000

plete examples of Craftsman Workshops table lamps without any alterations or unusual wear. Wall sconces, depending on the style, are generally valued in the $1,200–$2,800 range, and four-lantern electroliers in original condition can range from $10,000–$15,000.

In East Aurora, New York, the Roycrofters produced a number of lamps under the direction of Elbert Hubbard (see Roycrofters entries in Furniture and Metalware sections). Their earliest and most valuable lamps were de-

Fine and rare Gustav Stickley floor lamp with hammered copper harp and Quezel bell-shaped shade, on a footed base. Original finish and patina. Stamped mark, 57" × 12", $4,312

signed around 1905 by Dard Hunter, who had been sent by Hubbard to the New York firm of J. & R. Lamb to learn the technique of stained-glass work. Hunter remained with the Roycrofters only until 1910, during which time he created a small number of table lamps, wall sconces, and chandeliers for the Roycroft Inn and a few special commissions. Like the other Roycroft workshops prior to 1910, stained-glass production was limited to special orders. As the catalog stated "we shall be glad to submit special designs for lighting fixtures, adapted for electricity, gas or oil, and will give prompt attention to the designing of a particular article to be made especially for a place that needs it."[16] As a result, Dard Hunter lamps are considered quite rare and extremely valuable.

Around the time that Dard Hunter was preparing to leave East Aurora, another Roycroft convert, Karl Kipp, arrived and soon was made foreman of the copper shop (see Karl Kipp in Metalware section). Kipp, like Hunter, had a natural talent for design and within a few years had organized the Roycroft Copper Shop so effectively that its products were being shipped across the country. Among the scores of Karl Kipp-designed items were a number of lighting fixtures, including electroliers, wall sconces, electric lanterns, and table lamps. Nearly all of the Roycroft lighting designed after Kipp's arrival was composed primarily of metal, as opposed to the oak and stained-glass lamps that Hunter had executed.

While Kipp was undoubtedly the most talented designer working in the Roycroft Copper Shop, he was not the only one, for Victor Toothaker designed the Roycroft lighting for the Grove Park Inn outside Asheville, North

Exceptional, large and rare ROYCROFT brass-washed hammered copper table lamp with riveted baluster base and two ring handles, topped by a six-panel dome shade with acanthus leaf straps and mica rim. Early brass wash has been gently worn away from normal wear at stem of base to reveal copper highlights. (Riveted elements and acanthus leaf straps are indicative of the work of Victor Toothaker, who worked for both Gustav Stickley and Roycroft. This rare form is the only one we've ever seen). Orb-and-cross mark, 22¼" × 17½" dia., $20,700

Carolina, in 1912 and 1913. Kipp, in fact, left the Roycrofters in 1911 and did not return until after Hubbard's death in 1915. Those items that can be identified as having been designed by Karl Kipp (though actually produced by any of a number of Roycroft metalsmiths), such as the Princess candlesticks or examples decorated with small square cutouts or applied squares of German silver, are valued more highly by many collectors.

All but a few examples of Roycroft lighting are considered to be rare. Those that were placed into production and sold through mail-order catalogs and gift shops around the country, such as the small table lamps with hammered copper shades (models #C–901, C–902, and C–903), often surface after having been overpolished or after their original shades have been damaged or discarded. Roycroft table lamps in their original, intact condition and showing only normal signs of wear will generally start around $1,000 and will quickly escalate, depending on the rarity of the form. The addition of mica incorporated into the shade design increases the value of a lamp with a hammered copper shade. Small table lamps with Steuben glass shades are rarer than the same forms with hammered copper shades and generally sell for approximately 100 percent more. Large table lamps with mica or stained-glass shades, such as models #904 and #905, are among the rarest of Roycroft production lighting. These lamps will often sell in the $10,000–$15,000 range. As a general rule, collectors are advised to consider all intact Roycroft lighting as rare and should research each piece and the current market thoroughly before making any serious decisions.

A number of other firms active during the Arts and Crafts market did venture into the lighting arena on a small scale. As a result, several of these experiments and limited productions are considered quite scarce and quite

Exceptional and rare Roycroft hammered copper table lamp with three sockets, riveted baluster base with two angular drop handles, and conical shade designed by Dard Hunter of lavender and green leaded glass. Mint condition, excellent repatination to cap. Unmarked, 22½" × 18½", $20,000–$30,000

valuable. The Fulper Pottery, for instance, created a limited number of lamps with a pottery base and shade. To make them even more unusual, pieces of stained glass were inset into the clay shade. These lamps ranged in size from approximately 12" to nearly 24" in height. Their value is determined by a complex set of equations, including the size of the lamp, the color and type of glaze, the arrangement of the stained glass, and the proportions of the shade and base. These were prone to damage, due to a combination of fired clay and top heavy forms. Perfect examples are quite rare and always expensive. The Rookwood Pottery, among others, also produced a limited number of lamps, using their base and a glass shade. In each instance, the value of these lamps will be determined by the quality of the workmanship, the glaze, and the relationship between the shade and the base. In those lamps where the base and shade work naturally together, especially in terms of color, dimension, motif, and decoration, the value can reach record heights.

The number of arts and Crafts firms that either experimented with electric lighting fixtures, such as Charles Limbert, or that delved completely into the manufacturing of them, such as Old Mission Kopper Kraft and Heintz Art Metal, may never be completely known. The work of these latter two firms had been overlooked for years, even after the revival of interest in the Arts and Crafts movement. Both firms produced table lamps of copper and mica, and thus could not avoid comparison with those of Dirk Van Erp (see entry in Metalware). Van Erp carried the art of creating beautiful, yet functional lighting completely by hand to a level unrivaled in his day and after. Both the Old Mission Kopper Kraft in San Francisco and the Heintz Art Metal firm in Buffalo attempted to produce quality lamps using the same materials as Van Erp, but manufactured at a lower price. Ninety years later, as prices for Dirk Van Erp lamps soared to as much as $100,000 (and beyond), collectors began to take a closer look at the lamps produced by these two

Limbert faceted copper table lamp with bulbous base with two sockets and floral cutout shade inset with red slag glass. Fine original patina to base, normal cleaning to original patina on shade, 1" dent to base. Unmarked, 22½" × 23", $4,312

Fine and rare Limbert Windmill copper and brass table lamp, the octagonal base in the shape of a lighthouse with reticulated window panels lined with green slag glass, topped by an octagonal shade of caramel and green opalescent glass behind a repeating die-cut scene of windmills and children. Base fitted with four sockets (also one in base). Original patina. Unmarked, 25" × 27" dia., $8,625

firms. In the past few years, quality lamps form these two firms, and others have climbed into the $2,000–$4,000 range as collectors have scrambled to find examples while the prices remain within their reach.

## Mission Oak Lighting Fixtures

One of the most popular and least expensive styles of lighting fixtures manufactured during the Arts and Crafts era was the oak and slag glass fixture. Ceiling fixtures, wall sconces, and table lamps were mass produced in a number of variations on a common theme: an oak fixture encompassing inexpensive, colored glass. Ceiling plates, wall plates, and lamp bases were most often square with protruding square arms or posts. Ceiling lights often incorporated oak chains into their design in place of an oak center post. While some shades were made of metal, the majority were also oak, with elaborate, interlocking joints cut by machine. By far the most popular color of slag glass was

Exceptional, rare and large D'Arcy Gaw for Dirk Van Erp hammered copper table lamp with four sockets, extremely unusual four-panel flaring mica shade with bulbous cap and cupped rim, supported by four armatures riveted to a tacked-on shoulder, with bullet-shaped base. Excellent original patina, minor dent removed, repair to two panels (with minor light bulb marks), re-wired, missing one interior shade clip, missing interior cap. Closed box mark with D'Arcy Gaw/Dirk Van Erp, 22" × 22", $180,000

Arts and Crafts oak table lamp
with pyramidal shade inset with
yellow-green slag glass panes.
Good original condition.
Unmarked, 23¾" × 13½" sq.,
$575

amber, although many lamps were marketed in green, ruby, and other colors as well.

Very few of these lighting fixtures were signed with the name of their manufacturer. Most were mass-produced by firms that sold them either to retail stores or through mail-order catalogs. Although from a historical standpoint, it would be valuable to know which firms produced these lighting fixtures, experience has proved that it is the quality of the workmanship, design, and materials—not the name of the manufacturer—that determines the monetary value of each fixture. As a typical example, in its 1912–1913 catalogs, the Come-Packt Furniture Company offered, in addition to Arts and Crafts furniture, pianos, curtains, pillows, and sewing machines, 27 styles of "Bungalow and Mission Lighting Fixtures."[17] While some of their furniture was marked with the Come-Packt label, the majority of the lighting fixtures were not. Judging by the variety of styles of furniture and lighting fixtures displayed in its catalog, it may well be that the Come-Packt Company purchased a portion of its inventory from other firms. It is interesting to note that many of their light fixtures were offered with an optional beaded fringe. While few of these fragile fringes have survived, many lighting fixtures bear evidence of them. In many cases, they help explain what now appears to be an awkward shade design. Many shades without their original three- or four-inch beaded fringe appear to sit too high on the post or seem too small for their base. Once a beaded fringe is replaced, however, the proportions generally fall into place.

The appearance of many Mission oak lighting fixtures of questionable origin and workmanship may be explained in part by the reprint of the 1911 book *Lamps and Shades in Metal and Art Glass: Eighteen Complete Designs and Shades in Drawings and Full Directions for Their Making.*[18] Published by the Popular Mechanics Company, this small book gave thousands of hobbyists the encouragement and the information required to produce their own Mission oak lighting fixtures. Included were instructions for cutting, bending, soldering, and patinating metal shades, assembling electrical components, and working with art glass. Judging from the popularity of the book and its clear, simple instructions for chandeliers as well as table lamps, Arts and Crafts collectors can expect to discover scores of examples of home crafted lighting fixtures in their travels today.

## Painted Glass Shades

When Philip Handel and Adolph Eydam, two young, but experienced glass workers in Meridan, Connecticut, began advertising themselves as "decorators of opal glassware: lamp shades, vases, jardinières, plaques, salts, etc."[19] in 1886, electric lighting was still in its infancy. Four years later, however, the Eydam & Handel Company had opened a showroom in New York City, where demand for their hand-painted shades for electric lamps was growing rapidly. Adolph Eydam left the firm in 1892, at which time Philip Handel assumed total control. In 1903, with an infusion of capital from two new associates, the Handel Company Incorporated was formed, embarking on more than three decades of quality lamp production.

By the turn of the century, the firm had established a fine reputation for hand-decorated shades. With artists procured from other companies and blank shades purchased from Roederfer Brothers Bellaire, Ohio, Philip Handel had built one of the most important shade-decorating firms in America. Handel shades generally fall into one of two categories: "opal, or translucent glass examples of milky color, painted on the exterior only and chiefly used on

Fulper mushroom-shaped lamp covered in an exceptional cucumber green crystalline and gunmetal glaze, the shade inset with leaded blue-green slag glass. Restoration around rim of shade. Rectangular ink mark, 18½" × 15" dia., $9,775

Fine Handel desk lamp, the hexagonal shade with pine tree metal overlay inset with polychrome slag glass, on curved shaft with paneled bronzed base. Crack to one glass panel. Shade stamped HANDEL, fabric label to base, 17¼" × 14", $1,750–$2,250

library lamps or less expensive fixtures, and the interior, or reverse-painted 'Teroma' shades, which were created from clear blown glass blanks, and are regarded by today's collectors as the most desirable product of the Handel Company."[20]

According to authors De Falco, Hibel, and Hibel:

"the transformation of a blank into a decorative shade normally took one to two weeks and required the attention of up to a dozen individual craftsmen. The first stage for Teroma lamp shades was the creation of the patented "chipped ice" effect, achieved by sandblasting and then coating the shade with fish glue and placing it in a kiln fired at 800 degrees F. The contraction of the glue during the cooling stage tore away fragments of the glass surface, leaving a frosted, lightly textured effect when cleaned."[21]

At this stage the shade was ready to be transferred to the decorating department.

The design department at Handel was responsible for developing watercolor drawings, including the specifications for size, color, firings, and finish, for the decorators. While in later years they also produced stencils for use on simple, repeating patterns, the finest lamps from the Arts and Crafts era were painted freehand using a completed shade as a model. Once one of the experienced artists had painted and fired the model shade according to the specifications provided along with the watercolor by the design department, it was used as a guide by the artists in the decorating department. Individual flourishes and interpretations by the gifted decorators at Handel, whose list included Albert Parlow, Henry Bedigie, William Runge, and more than 40 other recognized artists, ensured that no two reverse-painted shades would be identical. "A complex shade could take several days to pass through the decorating stage, sometimes requiring the attention of more than one artist, as well as several firings at various stages of production."[22] One technique that produced spectacular three-dimensional results was the combination of both exterior and reverse painting on a single shade, which provided a depth unattainable with reverse or exterior painting alone.

The infusion of new capital in 1903 enabled the Handel Company to increase the number of shapes of shades that the firm decorated. While they stopped short of producing their own shades, Philip Handel and George Lockrow, the first two designers at Handel, provided the Roederfer Brothers glassworks with plaster models of the shapes that they desired. At the same time, the company also developed a casting shop, wherein they could design and produce their own lamp bases and metal components. The earliest bases used with Handel shades were supplied by the Miller Company of Meridan, Connecticut, but by 1903 their own foundry was producing a wide variety of styles of bases. The majority were produced using a molten metal with a high lead content (called "white metal"),[23] which was poured into metal molds. The Handel Company was justifiably proud of the many patinas which they could produce on their lamp bases. "All of Handel's metalwork was first given a plating of copper in order to prevent a reaction between the base metal and the surface material or atmosphere. This copper finish was sometimes left in a polished state, but normally the metal was patinated in a variety of bronze tones."[24] The only exceptions occurred during World War I, when a copper shortage forced the firm to switch to brass and silver for its plating.

Designs for Handel shades and bases were often inspired by nature, such as their woodland scenes and tree trunk bases, but the individual artist's interpretation and expression included traditional Victorian florals, fluid Art Nouveau elements, and classic Arts and Crafts motifs. Their famous scenic landscapes appeal to a wide variety of collectors of all three movements, making them the most popular—and often the most valuable—of all Handle lamps. Other shade designs include those inspired by the French Impressionists, Egyptian landscapes, Greek ruins, seascapes and sailing ships, flowers and vines, and colorful, exotic birds. Molded lamp base designs, which were carefully selected to match the motif of the shade, include classical urns, Chinese vases, tree trunks, overlapping petals, and simulated strap work and rivets, nearly all of which appeal to Arts and Crafts collectors today.

Handel shades are generally marked with the name of the firm as well as a style number and often with an artist's last name as well. Bases were also signed, either with a cloth label or stamped with the word HANDEL.

The Pairpoint Corporation (New Bedford, Massachusetts) was formed in 1894 by the merger of the Mount Washington Glass Company and the Pairpoint Manufacturing Company, which produced metalware items, including candlesticks and lamp bases. Much of the technology behind painted glass shades had originated in the Mount Washington Glass Company studios, where Harry and Alfred Smith had been producing crystal, art glass, and decorated glass shades for fancy kerosene lamps since 1871. As larger shades became fashionable in the 1880s, the firm began producing reverse-painted shades, originally designed to protect the painted decoration from wear. "A ten-inch diameter reverse-painted shade required a painting thirty inches in length equal in quality to an oil painting. In fact, many of the Pairpoint decorators were artists who produced works on canvas as well. One of these was Adolph Frederick who signed his Pairpoint lamps 'C. Durand.'"[25]

The merger of the two firms in 1894 led to a new line of electric table lamps with Pairpoint bases and reverse-painted shades. Unlike pottery decorators, the artists painting these special shades had to work in reverse. One problem they shared with their counterparts in the art pottery studios was that of not knowing exactly how their colors were going to react when fired in the kiln. Like those at Handel, some of the more complex Pairpoint scenes required additional firings as colors were added. The firing was necessary to ensure that the colors were baked onto the glass. Pairpoint shades were almost always signed by the artist and with the company's name as well. "Unsigned" Pairpoint shades often turn out to have been produced by a period competitor, such as the Consolidated Glass Company in Coraopolis, Pennsylvania. Pairpoint bases, which were produced in bronze, brass, and silver plate, were also well marked with the company's name.

In addition to scenic motifs, Pairpoint lampshades were produced in frosted ribbed designs and in what are called "blown-outs" or "puffies." These shades, as their names imply, feature unusual shapes, generally hand-decorated with floral motifs. One of their most popular models was a small boudoir lamp with a floral, puffy shade. As was often the case with Pairpoint lamps, the motifs were frequently more in keeping with the Victorian style than with the Arts and Crafts movement.

Other companies that produced hand-painted shades included the Pittsburgh Lamp, Glass, and Brass Company, whose shades were often marked "P. L. B. & G." The Pittsburgh Lamp, Glass, and Brass Company also manufactured shades decorated with high-quality transfers. Intended to imitate the look of a hand-painted shade for far less money, these transfers are often difficult to detect, especially by collectors unaware that not all shades of this style were hand-painted. The Pittsburgh Lamp, Glass, and Brass Company produced a great number of lamps, including sconces, hanging fixtures, and desk lamps, as well as the familiar table lamp. One of its most popular designs often distinguishes its shades from those of Handel or Pairpoint, depicting winter landscapes.

Other companies active in the field include the Jefferson Company Limited (Toronto, Ontario, Canada) and the Jefferson Lamp Company (Follansbee, West Virginia). Both of these unrelated firms offered quality reverse-painted lamps, signed and numbered on the interior shade rim. In the Midwest, the Moe Bridges Company (Milwaukee, Wisconsin) and Classique (Milwaukee, Wisconsin) attracted a large following. They, too, signed their lamps either with their name on the rim or with a label on the underside of the base. In Pennsylvania, the Phoenix Glass Company of Monaca, Pennsylvania also produced a line of reverse-painted lampshades.

By 1920, there were a number of companies offering painted, reverse-painted, and transfer lampshades, some in combination with one another. The transfer shades, while effective in creating the general effect of a hand-painted shade, suffer in direct comparison. Collectors must be aware that what may, at first glance, appear to be a hand-painted shade may actually be an applied transfer worth far less than the authentic artist-painted shade.

## Other Lighting Developments

As the illuminating powers of the light bulb were improved, manufacturers turned their emphasis away from magnifying the amount of light produced by a single bulb to ways to decrease the glare of the glass bulb. In 1916, near the close of the Arts and Crafts movement, the H. G. McFaddin Company patented a green cased shade under the brand name of Emeralite. Its slogan was "Be kind to your eyes."

Cased glass was produced by "blowing one layer of glass over another while the shade was still at a small size and then expanding the two layers together."[26] While cased glass had been invented years earlier, it was popularized by the Emeralite advertising campaign. In a matter of just a few years, Emeralite green cased-glass shades were a mainstay in businesses, offices, and libraries. Many cased-glass shades produced under the brand name of Emeralite and many of its competitors, such as Verdalite, Greenalite, and Ambrolite, were imported from Europe. Philosophically, they had little in common with the Arts and Crafts movement, but their abundance during the time period, plus their forest green shades, simple design, and low cost, accounted for their presence on hundreds of Mission oak desks and tables. Reproduction shades are bountiful today, but "a thin finished edge signifies the shade is old, as opposed to a broad rough edge found in the shades being blown in Italy and Taiwan."[27]

Toward the mid–1920s, one development in particular inadvertently symbolized the end of the Arts and Crafts movement. In addition to new shades in pastel colors, such as mauve pink and pale green, homeowners could also select pleated or taut parchment shades intended to be "placed on old brass and white metal lamp bases to give them a 'modern' look."[28] In Asheville, North Carolina, where, in 1913, the famous Grove Park Inn had been designed, built, and furnished in the Arts and Crafts style, the management ordered more than 600 parchment shades to replace more than 600 hand-hammered copper shades on all of its Roycroft table lamps.

While Arts and Crafts lighting has always been in demand, the intensity has increased in the past few years. As more and more collectors enlarge their collections, buying not just a piece or two of furniture and art pottery, but striving to create a total Arts and Crafts home environment, they find themselves in need of not another bookcase or sideboard, but of table lamps, ceiling fixtures, and wall sconces. As a result, this increased demand has led to an increase in value of nearly all Arts and Crafts lighting. Ordinary, unsigned slag-glass table lamps that sold for $75 in 1987 now command $500–$750. Roycroft helmet lamps which for year sold for $500, have now jumped to the $1,500–$2,500 category. And as many styles of Dirk Van Erp lamps have climbed into the $30,000–$50,000 range, collectors have begun to pay closer attention to the mica and copper lamps of the Lillian Palmer Copper Shop, Old Mission Kopper Kraft, Elizabeth Burton, and others. It may be several years before prices for Arts and Crafts lighting stabilize, thus the collector is urged to evaluate each example carefully, but to be prepared to move quickly when a bargain presents itself.

Additional information on Arts and Crafts lighting is contained in the *Metalware* section.

Exceptional and rare hammered copper table lamp, with shade by Elizabeth Burton incorporating five inset abalone shells surrounded by spade-shaped appliques, and riveted four-strap base by Christopher Tornoe. (Purchased directly from the Christopher Tornoe estate in Santa Barbara in the late 1980s.) Fine original red patina. Unmarked, 22" × 16½", $24,150

# ARTS AND CRAFTS TEXTILES

*by Bruce Johnson*

As the Industrial Revolution rumbled across England during the middle of the 19th century, it left in its wake hundreds of unemployed men and women who had formerly woven by hand rugs, draperies, tapestries, tablecloths, runners, napkins, and portieres. As the technology improved, manufacturers on both sides of the Atlantic quickly began to incorporate newly-designed machines into textile production, where engraved cylinders soon began rolling out yard after yard of less-expensive, printed fabric.

William Morris (1834–96) took it upon himself to revive the practice of hand-crafted textile production, "not only to recreate the beauty of medieval examples, but to recreate them under working conditions that would gratify their makers."[1] Inspired by anonymous medieval weavers of Persia, Italy, and India, the English philosopher and entrepreneur began designing a line of Arts and Crafts textiles in 1865. His daughter, May Morris, soon joined him, as did Edward Burne-Jones and John Henry Dearle, all of whom worked for the firm of Morris, Marshall, Faulkner & Co., renamed Morris & Company in 1875. May Morris, her sister, and her mother specialized in hand-printing high-quality fabrics using heavy cumbersome blocks, each with a designed carved into its surface. Many of the designs that were hand-printed onto the textiles, primarily tapestries, coverlets, and rugs, were derived from the wallpapers for which the firm had already become famous.

Along with the new array of machinery, manufacturers had also switched from vegetable dyes to less-expensive, more predictable synthetic dyes, which Morris found equally as disturbing. Instead, he resurrected 16th- and 17th-century formulas for vegetable dyes, which he felt were more natural and more pleasing than their synthetic counterparts. Among the older techniques he also reintroduced was discharge printing, wherein the cloth was first dyed, then the design was created by using bleach to erase portions of the background color. After it dried, second and third colors could be added by overprinting the fabric.

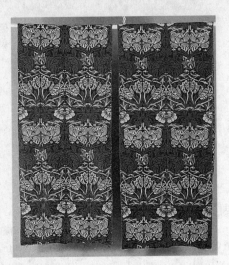

Pair of 19th-century William Morris-designed woven wool panels in the Tulip and Rose design, with stylized floriform motif in gold and black on a two-toned moss green ground. Some discoloration. Approx. dimensions for each panel, 130" × 32½", $2,300

Although the return to natural dyes and hand printing achieved William Morris's goal of involving each of his employees in the entire process, from design through production, the process proved slow and the product expensive. Even though only a select few could afford its fabrics, Morris & Company inspired other textile designers and manufacturers to adopt principles and practices in line with the Arts and Crafts philosophy. In addition, Morris was the first manufacturer to publicize the names of his designers, paving the way for international recognition for men such as C. F. A. Voysey, Walter Crane, and Lewis Day.

In keeping with the Arts and Crafts philosophy they espoused, Morris and his staff offered their customers the opportunity to complete needlework designs themselves with materials supplied by the firm. Interest in art needlework quickly spread across England, finding a ready audience in the women who had already learned needlework skills. Needlework societies and schools sprang up, providing women with the necessary training to earn a living through their needlework or simply to improve the aesthetic value of their homes with art they had created. Many companies offered individuals without the desire, the skills, or the time to embroider their own needlework the opportunity to purchase inexpensive fabrics machine-printed with Arts and Crafts motifs. Economic necessity did force Morris & Co. to utilize machines in the production of rugs, carpets, and some fabrics, but their tapestries, a personal favorite of William Morris, remained handwoven. By 1879 Morris had taught himself how to weave on a handloom, after which he began teaching the technique to his staff. Morris & Co. soon had three handlooms in operation, each capable of producing enormous, wall-sized tapestries. While output was limited, the Morris & Co. designs and the quality of the work revived tapestry production throughout Great Britain.

In nearby Scotland, the work of Morris & Co. exerted a great deal of influence on Jessie Newberry, who from 1894 until 1908 was a needlepoint artist and teacher at the Glasgow School of Art. From her work and that of other needlepoint designers evolved the "Glasgow style," characterized by the appearance of appliqué on homespun fabrics, such as linen, burlap, and muslin. The bold, simple designs, such as the familiar "Glasgow Rose," attributed to Jessie Newberry and later adapted by Charles Rennie Mackintosh and Dard Hunter, appealed to multitudes of people on both sides of the Atlantic Ocean. Their international exposure—and that of other designers in Scotland and England—must be credited to retail merchants and shops, such as Liberty & Company of London, who eagerly sought to fill the growing demand by their clientele for handcrafted textiles.

## Arts and Crafts Textiles in America

America was first officially introduced to English Arts and Crafts textiles at the 1876 Philadelphia Centennial Exhibition, where London's Royal School of Art Needlepoint displayed some of its finest examples. Among those who studied the exhibit was Candace Wheeler, an influential and wealthy woman with an interest in the arts, who the following year formed the Society of Decorative Art in New York "with the objective of providing women with the opportunity to produce high quality work that not only would be valued by society, but would also be both recreational and profit making."[2]

During the last quarter of the 19th century, Candace Wheeler proved to be "the most influential person in the production of American Arts and Crafts textiles."[3] She began by arranging for Englishwomen to travel to the

Arts and Crafts table runner embroidered with geometric flowers in red, blue, yellow and green on buff linen with crocheted ends, 53" × 19½", $115

United States to teach classes in art needlepoint, lace, and tapestries. Later, she also organized additional classes in woodcarving and painting. Many of these instructors brought with them copies of influential magazines, such as the *Studio*, which inspired American designers, both professional and amateur. Soon, a number of exhibitions of the work of these women artists were being held amid popular acclaim. Reflective of her close ties with Morris, Wheeler eventually left the group she had founded to help form the Women's Exchange, which she hoped would train more women to be able to earn a living through their needlepoint.

In 1879, Candace Wheeler, Lockwood DeForest, Samuel Coleman, and Louis Comfort Tiffany formed Associated Artists, soon to become the leading interior design studio in New York. Among their most prestigious clients was President Chester Arthur, who commissioned them to redecorate the White House. Wheeler's responsibilities in the firm included the design of tapestries and other woven textiles, where she and her staff excelled in producing enormous, naturalistic wall hangings. The firm disbanded in 1883, but Wheeler quickly organized a new studio, calling her all-woman firm the Second Associated Artists. Cheney Brothers, a silk mill in Connecticut, produced many of the woven silk textiles the Manhattan-based firm designed. The Second Associated Artists (which eventually was also called the Associated Artists) designed and produced a limited number of printed cotton textiles, as well as fabrics decorated through the discharge printing process revived by Morris. Its designs were often inspired by nature and they marked their work also marked with the letters "AA." The success of Candace Wheeler and Associated Artists signaled the beginning of the end of the British dominance in this field.

As the century drew to a close, additional schools, clubs, and societies were formed in cities across the country. While some needlework societies continued to draw their inspiration from British models, others, such as the Blue and White Society of Deerfield, Massachusetts, revived American Colonial designs. Founded in 1896 by Margaret Whiting and Ellen Miller, two artists who had been inspired by Colonial embroidery, its members utilized natural dyes on either linen or cotton fabric to create table runners, wall panels, curtains, tablecloths, and cushions. Miss Miller, a former teacher, and Miss Whiting, an artist, designed the patterns that were used to train small groups of women to become highly skilled embroiderers. While their work was exhibited and sold at numerous shows, the primary focus of the founders was the instruction of their students, who often completed the designs in their homes. Although their earliest work was confined to blue and white colors, they later included other colors and techniques, including appliqué, in their repertoire. If a work was deemed acceptable to Miss Whiting and Miss Miller, it was marked with the Society's shopmark: the letter "D" encompassed by a

Arts and Crafts runner embroidered with amber cornflowers on an oatmeal ground. Excellent original condition, a few minor stains, small pull to edge, 19½" × 53", $862

spinning wheel. The income from each sale was divided among the embroiderer, the designer, and the Society. In 1926, the Society closed when Miss Miller and Miss Whiting grew too frail to continue their instruction.

In New Orleans in 1902, Newcomb College offered classes in needlework under the guidance of Gertrude Roberts Smith (1869–1962). Like their successful art pottery, many of the designs in art needlework produced by the women at Newcomb College were inspired by southern flowers, plants, and trees. Exposure in national magazines, such as Gustav Stickley's the *Craftsman*, brought recognition and fame to the Newcomb College program. Although needlework production never equaled the volume of the school's art pottery, no less skill or talent was applied to the design and execution of Newcomb College textiles. Table runners, wall hangings, and book covers were exhibited alongside art pottery at major exhibitions that garnered numerous medals and awards for their Arts and Crafts programs. As author Dr. Jessie Poesch noted, "Flat patterns, clearly defined forms, and conventionalized motifs advocated by the arts and crafts aesthetic of the time are seen in this work. Linens and some native cottons were used as the base, and much of the thread was Persian silk, carefully selected and colored with Oriental dyes that would not easily fade."[4]

Art instructor William Woodward, recognizing the same difficulties William Morris had wrestled with in England several decades earlier, observed, "Abandoning the popular idea that the chief attraction in work lies in the hope in earnings, yet holding that art ideas cannot be truly separated from absolute utility, we must always recognize the dignity of the worker who feels a pride in making beautiful every work in his hands."[5] Surviving examples of needlework produced at Newcomb College are rare, and while several were marked with the initials of the college and/or the embroiderer, others have been identified through their design and motif.

Pair of Arts and Crafts woven cotton curtains with stylized irises in greens, yellow and white. Good condition, 74" × 46", $1,035

In the July 1903 issue of the *Craftsman*, Gustav Stickley introduced Craftsman fabrics and needlework to his readers. That same year he wrote an article about the Deerfield Society of Blue and White Needlework. As he later enlarged upon in his catalog *Craftsman Fabrics and Needlework*, one of the goals of his philosophical stance was the creation "of an atmosphere of restfulness, friendliness and home comfort."[6] Only in a unified interior in which the appropriate elements of color, texture, space, furnishings, and accessories have been carefully arranged could an ideal environment be achieved. Essential to each room was the unique combination of color, texture, and design offered only by textiles—table runners, pillows, portieres, and curtains. As an illustration, he points out that "the dull glow of a copper fireplace hood will be given a new and greater value by repeating it in a brilliant scarf or pillow of copper hued silk or velvet that gleams like a jewel against dull-toned leather."[7]

Like William Morris, his philosophic mentor, Gustav Stickley encouraged his readers to produce their own needlework if they could not afford

Rare and fine Gustav Stickley "China Tree" table runner with silk embroidered trees in shades of green on ecru linen. Small foxing stains, overall. (Excellent condition.) Unmarked, 87" × 14", $3,105

Craftsman fabrics or if they simply were attracted by the intrinsic rewards of taking part in the creative process. While he offered to supply fabrics, materials, and designs, just as often he was apt to encourage his readers to take his suggestions and designs at no cost from the *Craftsman* magazine and to obtain their materials from local sources.

Today, authentic Craftsman textiles are among the rarest and most valuable of all Arts and Crafts textiles to survive. Unlike his furniture and metalware, Stickley apparently did not insist that his shopmark, the joiner's compass, be embroidered on all Craftsman textiles. Realizing, perhaps, that its inclusion might distract from the design, it rarely appears, opening the door for many collectors to attribute lesser-quality textiles to the Craftsman Workshops. At the same time, this fact also enables astute collectors who have studied Stickley's catalogs to identify authentic, unsigned examples that others have overlooked. To confuse the issue even further, without a shopmark it is difficult to distinguish high-quality kit-work ordered from Craftsman Workshops from that executed under the supervision of Gustav Stickley.

By far the most reliable way to identify Craftsman fabrics is through comparison with both his verbal descriptions and illustrations in his magazine and catalogs. In *Craftsman Fabrics and Needlework*, he states that "the Craftsman method of decorating textiles is exceedingly simple, the object being to obtain good lines and broad effects in color and mass, without too much detail. Therefore, many of our designs are carried out by means of the appliqué of one fabric upon another, needlework being used only for outlines and for additional touches of decoration."[8] The fabric upon which much Craftsman needlework was often done was called Craftsman canvas, made from flax and jute. The two combined to give the fabric a rough texture, not unlike that of burlap, but the presence of jute, which deteriorates quickly even under ideal circumstances, explains why so little of their firm's work on this type of fabric has survived.

Like many later manufacturers, Stickley also utilized linen as a background fabric. According to his catalog, his craftspeople worked on a homespun linen in "a warm brownish gray... firmly and closely woven from a soft, loosely twisted thread,"[9] a handwoven linen, a Flemish linen, and colored linens, all of which were more durable than the Craftsman canvas containing jute. This same catalog indicates that block-printed linens were available for window curtains, as well as for cushions on wicker furniture. Block-printed or stenciled fabrics were considerably less expensive than those that had been hand-embroidered, a factor homeowners had to take into consideration when decorating several windows, doorways, or cushions. Craftsman fabrics displayed a number of what are now considered classic Arts and Crafts designs: the ginkgo leaf, the lotus, the poppy, the checkerberry, the pine cone, the rose, the dragonfly, the China tree, and others. The most common forms included table scarves, portieres, pillows, table covers, curtains, and square and circular centerpieces for tables.

By far the most commonly found examples of Arts and Crafts textiles are those that were produced at home from kits supplied by manufacturers. Many of these firms hired women designers who had been introduced to art needlework through Arts and Crafts schools and societies, such as the California School of Arts and Crafts. Established in 1907 by Frederick Meyer, this school produced a number of noted designers, artists, and illustrators, including Mary McCurdy, Edith Anderson, and Alma Vass. These three women are known to have worked for the Pacific Embroidery Company, which marketed textile kits for homeowners from 1909 to 1929.[10]

Through the efforts of diligent researchers, a number of companies that produced kits for homeowners have been uncovered. Among them are the Carlson Currier Company, the Richardson Silk Company, the H. E. Verran Company, Brainard & Armstrong, and the M. Heminway & Sons Silk Company.[11] As author Dianne Ayers has observed, many of these firms already had distribution systems established when the demand for Arts and Crafts needlework kits and materials increased. Once new designs were created and kits assembled, they were sold across the country through retail outlets, as well as through mail-order catalogs and advertisements in popular magazines.[12] Ironically, many of these firms have been identified through kits that were never completed. It was often the practice to stamp the company's name, the kit number, the thread color, and other information along one edge of the fab-

Arts and Crafts pillow with overall leaf design in red, brown and green on a beige ground, cotton ruffle. 21" × 19"  $115

ric. Upon completion of the needlework, the owner would then cut off this information and discard it. Only on unfinished material would this information survive for researchers. On rare occasion a catalog from one of these firms will also surface. As Ms. Ayers has observed from her study, "Arts and Crafts designs do not begin to appear in number until about 1905 and then most are simply labeled 'conventional' (no attempt being made to identify the floral or other inspiration for the design)."[13]

Author and textile collector Chris Walther observed that "the textile firms that may have had the greatest impact on the popularity of the early 20th century design reform were manufacturers of patterns and kits to be completed by home needleworkers."[14] His in-depth study of one such firm, The Belding Brothers & Company, reveals that the firm was founded in 1863 and grew rapidly, employing as many as 4,000 workers producing an array of textile products, including silk thread, fabrics, and yarn, but its first needlework patterns and kits in a distinctive Arts and Crafts style were not introduced until 1905.[15] "Between 1911 and 1914, Belding Brothers illustrated over forty different designs in the popular press, along with a number of patterns in other styles. The firm also published hundreds of other Arts and Crafts designs in its catalogs during these years."[16] By 1915, however, the number of Arts and Crafts motifs being offered had dwindled significantly. Even though firms like Belding Brothers were not Morris-inspired guilds, but rather manufacturers, "by allowing the home needleworker to finish her own work, Belding Brothers and other kit manufacturers contributed to a more democratic distribution of the Arts and Crafts aesthetic."[17]

Kits offered homeowners the opportunity to start at any of a number of skill levels. In most instances, the fabric arrived with the outline of the design lightly stenciled on one side. Included with the kit would be the embroidery thread and, if appropriate, the appliqué. Kits and instructions were also available for homeowners who wanted to experiment with making their own stenciled designs or blockprinting, though the process was slightly more complicated and certainly more messy. Since the majority of Arts and Crafts textiles that are discovered today were produced by homeowners with a wide range of skills, it is imperative that each be closely inspected. Among the details to be evaluated are: form, fabric, color, design, and workmanship. (Additional information included at end of this section.) The collector must remember that not all art needlework of this time period can be classified as Arts and Crafts. In fact, Victorian, Art Nouveau, Colonial, and transitional designs far outnumbered the Arts and Crafts kits that were offered in catalogs of the period. Classic Arts and Crafts motifs, such as the Glasgow rose, geometric patterns, stylized flowers and leaves, pine cones, and other designs found in the art pottery, metalware, and inlaid furniture of the Arts and Crafts movement, are highly prized by collectors attempting to create a unified interior.

One other form of Arts and Crafts textiles that does appear on occasion is the stenciled curtain. Less expensive than handstitching, stenciling enabled manufacturers and homeowners to cover large sections of fabric quickly. In some instances, stenciling was highlighted with some degree of needlework. Unfortunately, the combination of sun and rain destroyed many Arts and Crafts curtains and left others too frail to be used today. Even when found in good condition, owners should not subject Arts and Crafts fabrics to any direct sunlight, nor should they have them laundered or dry cleaned, for any of these acts would shorten the life expectancy of the fabric and its design.

Interest in Arts and Crafts textiles also revived interest in two much older forms: rag rug-making and American Indian rugs. For decades before the advent of the Arts and Crafts movement, colonial women had recycled worn-out fabrics into rag rugs using hand looms. When interest in hand-weaving was rekindled at the turn of the century, artisans took to the looms and rag rug-making was in vogue again. Ironically, the new generation of rag rug makers often forgot the historical precedence that inspired the first rag rugs and, rather than using worn-out fabrics, used new cotton cloth which gave them greater control over the color and pattern of their work. Noting this, scholar Gilliam Moss observes that "the rag rug became typical of the Arts and Crafts romanticizing of the past."[18]

Gustav Stickley and other proponents of the Arts and Crafts movement recognized the Native American Indian as symbolic of the true original craftsman. Stickley promoted Indian artifacts, including textiles, in the *Craftsman* magazine. Navajo rugs and blankets, woven on hand-looms, were sought by Arts and Crafts enthusiasts, who often used them as decorative wall hangings. As further evidence of their influence, Native American designs appeared on Arts and Crafts rugs, textiles, and art pottery produced during this era.

The appeal of Arts and Crafts textiles today remains much the as it was 90 years ago. Handwoven textiles symbolize the essence of the Arts and Crafts philosophy. On another level, they help to soften the severity of much of the furniture of this era, as well as to add color to rooms often dominated by browns and yellows. As furniture catalogs and interior illustrations reveal, tables were considered incomplete without a table runner. Regardless of the reason, Arts and Crafts textiles have emerged as one of the most popular accessories today.

## Evaluating Arts and Crafts Textiles

Due to the ease with which both amateur and professional artists could learn many of the techniques associated with Arts and Crafts textiles, nearly every Arts and Crafts school, club, society, and guild became involved at some level

Pair of fine Arts and Crafts linen curtain panels with crewel embroidery in shades of blue, gold and green depicting stylized papyrus motif on a natural linen ground. Each panel is 8' × 30". Excellent condition, $1,610

with textile design and production. In addition, thousands of homeowners created their own textiles using kits that were assembled and shipped to all parts of the country. As a result, only a very small fraction of the textiles that surface today can ever be attributed to a specific firm or designer. Provided other criteria are met, those that can be verified are destined to become quite valuable and should be handled with extreme care. In such cases a qualified textile conservator should be consulted in order to determine how the textile should be preserved, stored, and displayed. There are at least six criteria by which Arts and Crafts textiles can be evaluated. They are (in no specific order):

1. Form
2. Materials
3. Color
4. Design
5. Workmanship
6. Condition

## FORM

Arts and Crafts textiles take many forms, some of which were produced in large quantities, such as table runners, others of which were produced less often, such as book covers. Rarity alone, however, does not equate with value. Without demand for a specific form, regardless of how rare it may be, its value may never equal that of more common forms for which there is a greater demand.

Of the various forms, rectangular table runners, also called dresser scarves, are among the most common. Since they can be used in a number of rooms and on a number of pieces, require no extra effort for installation, and are easy to store, table runners are quite popular today. And since they were widely produced and have survived in large number, the other criteria will have more effect on their value than their form. Square and circular table covers appear only slightly less often. As would be expected, the larger examples (those more than 36" square or in diameter) are more difficult to find. One form that does appear only on rare instances are complete luncheon sets (4–6 placemats for plates, plus a centerpiece).

In a similar manner, large pillows (more than 18" square) are also difficult to locate, but smaller pillows appear quite frequently. Kits for small pillows were among the most popular with amateur needleworkers, while textile-producing firms, such as the Craftsman Workshops, were more apt to offer the larger, more detailed pillows. A single Craftsman Workshop appliqué pillow measuring 25" square generally cost $5 in 1908. In comparison, a Craftsman spindle side chair in the same catalog was priced at $7. Needless to say, price alone may have dictated that large Craftsman pillows may have been produced in a smaller quantity than even some of their rarer forms of furniture. Worth noting is an observation by Gillian Moss that large pillows with rounded corners are more apt to be American in origin, while pointed corners are more characteristic of the British."[19]

During the height of the bungalow craze, curtains and portieres may have been produced in large numbers, both by homeowners using kits and by firms such as Craftsman Workshops, but, 90 years later, their survival rate is extremely low. The majority that were installed eventually deteriorated from exposure to sunlight, moisture, and dirt before being discarded. Even those that were stored for several decades most often emerge too frail to be placed into service today. As a result, Arts and Crafts curtains are considered scarce, especially in good condition, but the restrictions on their current adaptability have discouraged many collectors from actively seeking them beyond bargain prices. Arts and Crafts furniture collectors have long known that bedroom furniture is among the most difficult to find. In a similar manner, Arts and Crafts coverlets and bedspreads are also considered rarities.

## MATERIALS

While Arts and Crafts textiles were produced using a wide range of fabrics—cotton, silk, canvas, linen, burlap, casement fabric, velour, etc.—collectors are more apt to evaluate textiles on the condition rather than the type of fabric found in the piece. Stains, tears, and repairs are more apt to decrease the value of a textile than whether it is linen, cotton, or silk. As a general rule, however, homespun linens and other fine woven fabrics in natural cream and tan colors are more desirable than rough burlaps.

## COLOR

Arts and Crafts collectors are apt to judge the color in a textile on three criteria: the amount of color, the appropriateness of the colors to an Arts and Crafts interior, and the clarity of the colors. As would be expected, textiles with three or four different colors would have been more difficult to produce, thus they do not appear as often. When they do, providing the piece has no problems, collectors will pay a premium for them. Simultaneously, the colors most often associated with the Arts and Crafts movement—Grueby green, Stickley's famous nut brown, amber, a muted orange, etc.—are those that collectors like to find on their textiles. Garish, unnatural colors do occur, especially on kits completed long after the ideals of the movement had faded away, and are considered less desirable.

Sunlight has always been one of the greatest enemies of Arts and Crafts textiles. Many of the experimental vegetable and synthetic dyes have a tendency to fade over the years, but if exposed for long periods of time to direct sunlight, they can nearly disappear. Oftentimes a table runner will emerge with bright, vibrant colors at one end and dull, lifeless colors at the other. An acceptable scenario is simple to construct: one end remained protected from the sun, while the other suffered through two or three hours of ultraviolet rays each day. The ideal textiles to discover are those that spent their entire lives in a cedar chest.

## DESIGN

Beneath the Arts and Crafts umbrella can be found a wide range of designs, ranging from transitional Victorian landscapes and sinuous Art Nouveau forms to colonial revival and American Indian themes. Also included are British, William Morris, and Viennese secessionist designs, as well as classic American motifs. More often than not the choice of which has the greatest appeal is highly subjective, for the personality of the collector and his or her plans for the interior design of a particular room will play major roles in determining which designs are more appealing than others. Those viewed as "classic" American Arts and Crafts designs—such as the Glasgow rose, Stickley's use of the ginkgo leaf or the china tree, Newcomb College's moss-draped tree, stylized dragonflies found in Tiffany lamps and Marblehead pottery— have the greatest appeal to the growing number of collectors in search of Arts and Crafts accessories.

## WORKMANSHIP

While it is not necessary to be able to identify by name the various stitches employed by both amateur and professional needleworkers, collectors need to be able to distinguish between the proper and improper execution of any particular stitch. Only by inspecting and comparing as many examples as possible in private collections, galleries, museums, and antiques shows can a collector learn to differentiate between a well-executed work and a poorly executed one. Ironically, the better the workmanship, the less obvious the needlework will be. Loose, awkward stitches are more apt to draw attention to themselves than are tight, neatly aligned stitches. Consistency in thread, spacing, and knots will distinguish an amateurish effort from that of a skilled needleworker.

Arts and Crafts collectors have demonstrated a preference for hand-stitched fabrics, but, in the future, stenciled curtains, portieres, and runners should also garner additional respect, provided they meet the other four criteria. Well-executed stenciled and block-printed pieces, especially curtains and portieres, deserve recognition. While they did not require as much labor as needlework pieces, they fulfilled an important function, especially on large sections of fabric, that needlework seldom, if ever, could.

## CONDITION

Like all antiques, the value of any textile is directly affected by its condition. Ink stains, tears, alterations, fading, unraveled stitches, brown spots, and other signs of age and use will quickly reduce the value of even a once-fine example. The more common forms, such as table runners, will generate little interest if they are in poor condition. Their value can be reduced as much as 75 percent if they surface with ample signs of age, for collectors have learned that more, not fewer, examples are apt to be found now that general antiques dealers have begun looking for them.

# Reproductions

The demand for textiles executed in classic American Arts and Crafts motifs has revived a former cottage industry—art needlework. In some instances, the individual employs the identical skills and techniques used a hundred years ago to create historically accurate curtains, luncheon sets, portieres, and table runners. Others may utilize sewing machines for some of the more monotonous work, while a few individuals have been exploring the possibility of producing less-expensive printed or even silkscreened designs on fabric.

In most instances, collectors turn to new textiles not to save money, but to be able to dictate the design and dimensions required by their windows and doors. It also gives them the opportunity to select a motif for a room and to have that motif repeated in whatever number of curtains, table runners, or luncheon sets they desire. While some purists oppose all reproductions, most will admit that without modern needlework artists, it would be virtually impossible to complete an Arts and Crafts interior using one specific motif. If a designer, architect, or homeowner wanted to carry a ginkgo leaf theme throughout a home in 1910, it was simply a matter of placing an order for either kits or completed fabrics with a textile firm—something most modern-day collectors enjoy being able to do as well.

At the present time, custom-designed and handwoven textiles are generally more expensive than those found in antiques shops, which should prevent unscrupulous individuals from attempting to sell new textiles as being old. The exception, of course, comes under the category of signed textiles, for collectors are prepared to pay a premium for authentic Craftsman, Newcomb College, and Associated Artists textiles. The best defense for a collector is to insist on having any questionable textile inspected by an experienced textile curator, who can determine the age of the textile by the threads in the needlework and the fabric itself. Another problem that has surfaced is that of unfinished kits being completed before they are sold as antiques. Since most unsigned textiles made from kits do not command extremely high prices, more often than not it is more profitable for a dealer to sell an unfinished kit as he or she found it. Again, however, if a highly desirable textile with an unusually high price is offered, it is best to insist that it be inspected if there is any question as to the age of any of the needlework.

## Values

With the exception of rugs, a category that demands its own treatment, Arts and Crafts textiles tend to fall into two price categories: inexpensive and very expensive. At the upper end of the scale are signed and authenticated examples of Craftsman, Newcomb College, and similar Arts and Crafts firms or schools. Table runners from these firms have sold for as much as $1,500–$2,500. Rare, classic designs in excellent condition from important Arts and Crafts firms are destined to continue to climb into this price range (and possibly beyond) regardless of what is happening to the rest of the market.

The remainder of Arts and Crafts textiles—those made from kits or by unknown firms and guilds—will have to be evaluated on the basis of the six criteria discussed earlier. Once the finer examples of pillows and table runners have made their way into an Arts and Crafts gallery, they can command prices in the $200–$400 range. Examples with minor problems, including an abundant supply, often sell in the $75–$200 range. Those with only a hint of an Arts and Crafts motif or in poor condition, as well as those finer examples

Pair of linen Arts and Crafts stenciled curtains with stylized poppies in brown and beige with green leaves on a red ground, together with a single matching panel. Good condition, 104" × 44½", $230

that are languishing in an antiques shop whose owners (or whose clients) have little interest in the Arts and Crafts movement, will often be marked at $25–$50 simply on the basis of their workmanship and condition.

The bargains in Arts and Crafts textiles remain in the general antiques shops and malls, where they will be hidden amongst 40 or 50 examples of lace doilies. While other dealers, pickers, and Arts and Crafts collectors will quickly scan a shop for a piece of Stickley furniture or Van Briggle pottery, few take the time required to patiently work their way through a dresser drawer of Victorian needlework in hopes of finding one lone example of an Arts and Crafts motif. This is where the $25 bargains are to be found, for chances are the dealer paid little more than that for an entire stack of needlepoint at a local estate auction or yard sale.

# COLOR WOODBLOCK PRINTS: THE ART OF THE ARTS AND CRAFTS MOVEMENT

*by Bruce Johnson*

One of the most often asked questions by new collectors is: What is the art of the Arts and Crafts movement?

Since the selection of art is and always has been of a very personal nature, people have been less apt to follow the recommendations of architects, interior designers, and authors in this area than they have been in others. As a result, no particular style of art dominated the Arts and Crafts movement. Frank Lloyd Wright collected Japanese prints and urged his clients to do the same. Harvey Ellis recognized black-and-white art photography as an appropriate element in Arts and Crafts interiors. For years, Gustav Stickley displayed in his home in Syracuse a landscape oil painting by Charles P. Appel, ca. 1905. American and European impressionists, as well as California and European plain air painters, also attracted a large following during the Arts and Crafts movement. While each of these art forms contains elements that appeal to Arts and Crafts collectors, past and present, none wholeheartedly embraced the tenets of the philosophical foundation of the movement as did color woodblock prints.

As their name implies, color woodblock prints are created using a series of handcarved wood blocks. The artist would begin by drawing a design on the face of a block of wood or, in some cases, a piece of linoleum. The wood around the design would then be carved away, leaving the design in what is called "relief" or raised. The artist would then apply either oil-based or water-based pigments to the raised portions before pressing a sheet of paper onto the block and rolling it firmly to transfer the color from the block to the paper. In most instances, the artist would carve a separate block for each color in the print.

In writing about Arthur Wesley Dow (1857–1922), America's most important woodblock print artist, author Nancy E. Green observed, "Although

Fine Edna Boies Hopkins color woodblock print on paper, depicting hollyhocks in pink, white, and green on a black ground, matted and framed under glass. (Hopkins was a friend of the French Impressionist Claude Monet, and his gardens at Giverny were the inspiration for many of her floral prints.) Pencil signed and numbered 31. Image: 10¾" × 7", $3,737

no specific fine art developed during the last decades of the nineteenth century to correspond to the beautifully crafted furniture, tapestries, floor coverings, and pottery that evolved during the Arts and Crafts period, Dow's color woodcuts. . . best capture the spirit of the finely crafted and the beautifully rendered."[1]

Woodblock printing can be traced back to Japan in the 8th century, where the technique of producing prints on paper using carved wooden planks developed over the course of the next 1,200 years. For several centuries, the woodblock printing technique, as practiced in Japan and Europe, produced black ink outlines intended to be handcolored. Woodblock prints appeared in Europe during the 15th century, where fabrics, religious tracts, and playing cards were produced using techniques first developed by the Japanese.

The process of woodblock printing in Japan involved a number of individuals, beginning with the artist who created the design. His artwork was handed to an engraver, whose task it was to transfer the design to a plank and then to remove, using simple carving tools, the excess wood. Most engravers preferred to work with even, tight-grained woods, such as cherry, pear, willow, or boxwood. Hardwoods, such as oak, walnut, and mahogany, proved difficult to carve and prone to chipping. Softwoods, such as pine and fir, were apt to split, though some artists incorporated the effect rendered on the paper by the long, wavy grain of pine boards into their designs.

Once the engraver had completed his work, the printer took over. The choice of paper he selected had a direct impact on the final work, for its color, flexibility, thickness, texture, and rate of absorbency had to be taken into consideration. After the 17th century, the printer also had a choice of colors to be applied to the raised portions of the wood. He could also affect the final print by the amount of pressure he applied to the back of each sheet of paper. In Japan, these three individuals—the artist, the engraver, and the printer— were also influenced by the publisher who sold the prints. With the large number of individuals involved in the creation of each print, technical errors and inhibited creativity were not uncommon.

The 17th century saw the rise of the plebeian class in Japan and the increased popularity of woodblock prints. "These prints were meant to be democratic substitutes," a Japanese historian observed, "for the hand-painted pictures treasured in aristocratic circles."[2] That same century, Suzuki-Harunoby, the father of the Japanese color print, introduced a second and third block of wood to the printing process, each of which transferred a different color to the paper. With the technical freedom to incorporate various combinations of color into each print, the golden age of Japanese color woodblock prints developed between 1765 and 1850. Landscape prints by artists such as Hokusai, Kuniyosi, and Hiroshige found admirers in Europe and America, as well as across the countrysides of Japan. Their goal was "not the mere photographic reproduction of Nature, but the adding of something artistic to her image."[3]

Following in the footsteps of Harunoby, Japanese woodblock artists Katusika-Hokusai (1760–1849) and Utagawa-Hirosige (1798–1858) achieved worldwide recognition both during their lifetimes and after. Thousands of their prints were distributed across Japan and Europe, although the Europeans and a small band of Americans held these two Japanese artists in higher respect than did most Japanese people. By the end of the 19th century, the color woodblock print had lost its luster in Japan. As one art historian observed, the woodblock print "had achieved the highest possible peak of development without having its artistic value recognized in Japan, then had come to an end and degenerated into a mere handicraft for faithfully reproducing original drawings, older prints, and paintings."[4]

In America, a small group of artists and collectors had discovered Japanese color woodblock prints during the latter half of the 19th century, but it remained for one artist, Arthur Wesley Dow (1857–1922) to revolutionize the ancient technique. "Before Dow," scholar Nancy Green points out, "japonisme had been filtered to America through the work of Whistler and the impressionists. Dow, however, took the Oriental aesthetic one step further, by adopting the Oriental medium of block printing as his own."[5] Born in Ipswich, Massachusetts, Dow received formal training as an oil painter, primarily of landscapes, at the Academie Julian and the Ecole Nationale des Arts Decoratifs in France. Upon his return to the United States in 1887, Dow grew disillusioned with the expectations and demands of Boston art critics. Anxious to find a new avenue for creative expression, Dow discovered the

Elizabeth Norton color woodblock print on rice paper, 1922, depicting a California mission with landscape in blue, green and yellow. Matted and framed. Pencil signed, dated, designed, and printed by the artist, with artist's chop mark. Image: 5½" × 4½", $575

color woodblock prints of Hokusai in a work on Oriental art in 1891. "One evening with Hokusai," he wrote, "gave me more light on composition and decorative effect than years of study of pictures."[6] As Nancy Green observed, "Over the next 30 years Dow propounded an art style based on formal Japanese elements. Through his writings, work, and teaching, he would change the way in which an entire generation of American art students would express itself."[7] Author Steven Thomas adds, "Four years of study and synthesis changed Dow and the face of American art forever. By 1895 he had developed an entirely new theory of art based on the integration of eastern and western artistic principles, which culminated in a show of his new Japanese-inspired color prints."[8]

One of the most revolutionary changes which Arthur Wesley Dow instituted in the 20th-century woodblock print was the elimination of a separate artist, engraver, and printer. Dow insisted not only on drawing the initial design, but in transferring it to the wood, carving the individual blocks, applying the color to each block, and producing the finished print. With complete control over the entire process, the artist could vary each print by adjusting the color, the type of paper, and the pressure exerted on each block and the paper atop it. "Dow did not feel that these prints were "reproductions," Thomas writes, "rather each print that was pulled from the block was a unique piece of art from its conception to its completion."[9]

Dow singled out three specific elements critical to the success of Japanese color woodblock prints: line, light, and harmony. "Though he copied the Japanese masters—Hokusai, Hiroshige, Hokkei—his own works were not slavish imitations; they elegantly incorporated the principles of line, *notan* [harmony], and color while maintaining an honest directness and restrained ornamentation, close tenets of the Arts and Crafts movement."[10] Dow combined elements of the Orient and of the West, creating landscapes steeped in the Oriental tradition of composition and an impressionist's approach to lighting.

Dow broke from the Japanese tradition of using tight-grained hardwoods. In their place he substituted pine, which he selected for the soft tones created by the texture of the wavy grain. Upon the completion of the original work of art, one block of wood was carved for each color to be printed. Dow's work was characterized by the thick, porous paper he preferred, as well as by the thin coat of watercolor he applied to each block. In general, his works were small and focus primarily on scenes found along Boston's North Shore. Printings were also small in number. Dow was more apt to experiment with various color possibilities utilizing the same series of blocks than he was to create large editions of one particular color combination. One of his most famous examples, *The Yellow House* (1910, 4.5" × 6.5") was entitled *The Clam House* (1910, 4.5" × 6.5") when the same blocks were printed in completely different colors.

Dow was not only an artist, but also wrote, taught, and lectured widely. In addition to running his own summer art school in Ipswich, he taught at the Pratt Institute, the Art Student's League, and Columbia University. The principles that he taught were assimilated into mediums other than color woodblock prints. Many Arts and Crafts potters, photographers, and weavers credit Dow with their approach to composition, color, and design. But it was in the world of printmaking that Dow influenced the greatest number of artists. Eliza Draper Gardiner, M. Louise Stowell, Georgia O'Keeffe, Max Weber, James and Edna Hopkins, Margaret Jordan Patterson, and scores of other well-known artists studied under the famous printmaker and teacher. As one of his students, Max Weber, wrote, "Mr. Dow was one of the greatest art educators this country was blessed with. His message was prophetic and innovative. He awakened interest in the eternal art of the Far East."[11]

Fine and rare Zulma Steele (1881-1979, Byrdcliffe colony artist, Woodstock, New York) color woodblock print depicting mountains and palm trees in greens and red. Light foxing. New mat and frame. Pencil-signed. Image: 5¼" × 7", $1,200-$1,600

As the following brief biographies of some of the more notable color woodcut artists will reveal, there was an affinity among this group of pioneer artists. Many followed Dow, attending either his private art school or enrolling at Pratt Institute in Brooklyn and the Teachers' College at Columbia University in New York when he taught there. Many artists also traveled together to Europe, and also were drawn to artist colonies on either coast, the most famous of which was at Provincetown, Massachusetts. The Provincetown Artists, as they came to be known, achieved worldwide recognition for the wide range of works of art that they created.

## Other Notable Color Woodcut Artists

### W. CORWIN CHASE AND WALDO CHASE
Inspired by English print artist Frank Morley Fletcher, these brothers created color woodblock prints in the Pacific Northwest.

### ELIZA DRAPER GARDINER (1871–1955)
After years of formal training as an artist, Gardiner attended Arthur Wesley Dow's first exhibition of color woodblock prints in 1895. Like Dow, she also taught, while continuing to develop her own style of color woodblock prints. Today she is recognized as one of the most important woodblock artists of the 20th century.

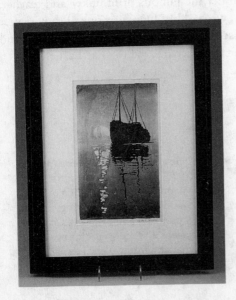

Waldo S. Chase color woodblock print, "Nomad," 1932, depicting a large boat with setting sun reflecting on water, in yellow, orange, and shades of blue. Mounted and framed, under glass. Pencil-signed, titled, and dated. Image: 12" × 7¼"  $1,265

Edna Boies Hopkins woodblock print on rice paper, ca. 1920, titled "Orange Arrangement," depicting a still life with lilies. (Hopkins, who studied in Japan, was an early member of the Provincetown Printers.) Matted. Pencil signed. Image: 16¼" × 14¼", $900–$1,200

### EDNA BEL (BOIES) HOPKINS (1872–1937)

The 27-year-old Edna Hopkins studied under Arthur Wesley Dow from 1899–1900. Her husband, James R. Hopkins, was also a woodblock artist and teacher. They traveled extensively in Japan and Europe before settling in the United States in 1914. She worked in Ohio, where her husband taught; she also worked with Margaret Patterson and Ethel Mars in New York and Provincetown. Her work was awarded a silver medal in 1915 at the Panama Pacific International Exposition.

### JAMES HOPKINS (1877–1969)

After traveling around the world in 1904 with his wife, Edna Bel Hopkins, then living in Paris until 1914, James Hopkins taught at Ohio State University for several years, where he rose to become head of the art department. Like his wife, he, too, embraced the color woodcut and Dow's principles of composition.

Helen Hyde polychrome woodcut of Japanese women, c. 1910. Image: 6" × 9", $500

### HELEN HYDE (1868–1919)

Helen Hyde was introduced to the color woodcut in 1896 at an Arthur Wesley Dow exhibition in San Francisco, where she had studied under Emil Carlsen before traveling to New York, Paris, and Berlin to continue her training. Her enthusiasm with color woodblock printing led her to Japan, where she moved in 1903.

### PEDRO DE LEMOS (1882–1954)

Born in Nevada, de Lemos studied at the Mark Hopkins Institute (San Francisco) with Arthur Mathews in 1900. He met Arthur Wesley Dow shortly thereafter and studied under him at Columbia University. In addition to making his color woodcuts, de Lemos taught at the San Francisco Institute of Arts, was director of the Museum of Fine Arts at Stanford University, and wrote extensively.

### ETHEL MARS (1876–CA. 1956)

Ethel Mars both studied and taught the art of color woodcuts among a number of influential artists, including Edna Bel Boies Hopkins, Maud Squire, James Hopkins, and Margaret Jordan Patterson. Although she was born in Illinois and worked until 1906 in Cincinnati, she lived most of her life in Europe. Margaret Patterson credited Ethel Mars with having taught her the technique of the color woodblock print.

### GEORGIA O'KEEFFE (1887–1986)

While not as well known for her color woodblock prints as for her other work, Georgia O'Keeffe attended Teachers' College at Columbia University under Arthur Wesley Dow from 1914 to 1916. There she both learned and practiced the art of color woodblock prints. Undoubtedly Arthur Wesley Dow's most famous student, O'Keeffe's early woodblock prints provide

Margaret Patterson watercolor, "Italian Riviera," in gilded wood frame. Two labels verso, one from the Boston Society of Watercolorists; pencil-signed Margaret Patterson and M. J. Patterson at bottom center. Sight: 14¾" × 17½", $1,500–$2,000

a glimpse into the philosophy and style that later emerged in her trademark flower motifs.

### MARGARET JORDAN PATTERSON (1867–1950)
Already known as one of the finest woodblock artists in America, Margaret Jordan Patterson studied under Dow prior to learning the technique of color woodcuts from fellow artist Ethel Mars. Like many artists of this era, she taught in the Northeast, traveled extensively in Europe, and was featured in major exhibitions.

### WILLIAM S. RICE (1873–1963)
William Rice was introduced to Japanese color woodcuts at the Panama Pacific Exposition of 1915, held in San Francisco. During the ensuing years he produced a number of his own color woodblock prints, taught printmaking at the University of California at Berkeley, and wrote the well-known text *Block Prints—How to Make Them* (1941).

### MAUD HUNT SQUIRE (1873–1955)
Maud Squire studied at the famous Art Academy in Cincinnati, where she met James Hopkins, Ethel Mars, and Edna Bel Boies. She learned the technique of color woodblock prints from Ethel Mars around 1906 and shortly afterwards moved to Provincetown, Massachusetts, a thriving colony of artists and writers. She and Mars moved to Europe in 1921, where she lived until her death.

Rare and early William S. Rice color woodblock print, "The Old Oaken Bucket—Valley Forge PA," ca. 1915, depicting an old farmhouse with well and bucket. (Rice, a Philadelphia native, moved to Stockton, California in 1901. Pennsylvania scenes, which are rare, were executed after his relocation.) Matted and framed, under glass, pencil-signed and titled. Image: 11½" × 9", $1,955

## M. LOUISE STOWELL (1861–1930)

M. Louise Stowell was a prominent founder and member of the Rochester Arts and Crafts Society, where, in 1897, she shared a studio with Harvey Ellis. She had met and been influenced by Dow in the early 1890s. She lived nearly her entire life in the Rochester area, dividing her time between her art and her teaching

## SELECTED PRICES

The criteria involved in determining the value of a work of art—especially works of an artist who has not appeared on the market on a regular basis over an extended period of time—are highly complex and seemingly subjective. While auction prices can be helpful, they often reflect the whims and emotions of a particular collector who has little regard for the market value of a work he or she covets. Color woodblock prints are now recognized by a significant number of collectors as appropriate accessories in an Arts and Crafts interior, but market values for many artists and their work will not be established with any sort of predictability for several more years. Until that time, collectors will have to study the market closely, including auction house results, gallery prices, and price guides, and then then have to establish personal price ranges for themselves and the works they wish to add to their collection

The prices quoted below reflect samplings of both recent pre-sale estimates at major Arts and Crafts auction galleries and the final bids. As always, they are intended to represent approximate ranges. The collector must keep in mind, however, that in a new area, such as color woodblock prints, even liberal ranges can quickly become outdated. Additional information on the artist, the work in question, and the general market should be compiled before making any major decisions. Finally, restrict your major transactions to reputable collectors, dealers, galleries, and auction houses that stand behind their claims

Gustave Baumann (1881–1971):
"Procession" ($13\frac{3}{4}$" × $12\frac{3}{4}$"), $2,500–$2,750
"Mountain Pool" ($13\frac{1}{2}$" × 17"), $1,200–$1,600
"Winter Corral" ($12\frac{3}{4}$" × $12\frac{3}{4}$"), $2,000–$2,250
"Provincetown" ($9\frac{1}{4}$" × 11"), $1,800–$2,000
"San Geronimo" ($7\frac{1}{4}$" × 6"), $2,000–$2,300

W. Corwin Chase:
"Moraine Park" ($6\frac{1}{2}$" × 5"), $500–$750

Untitled Pacific Northwest scene (6" × 8"), $500–$750
"Seattle Park" (13¼" × 7½"), $800–$950

Waldo Chase:
"Nomad" (12" × 7"), $750–$1,000

Leo F. Dorn (b. 1879):
"Cabin in Winter" (4" × 3"), $350–$450
"Clipper Ship at Sunset" (5" × 4"), $400–$500
"River in Winter" (2½" × 3½"), $300–$400

Arthur Wesley Dow (1857–1922):
(Check with reliable source for current value of any of Dow's work, all of which is highly sought after.)

Eliza Draper Gardiner (1871–1955):
"Lady Among the Poppies" (10½" × 10"), $1,500–$2,000
Untitled New Hampshire mountain landscape (10" × 7¾"), $800–$900
"Boy and Cat" (10" × 7½"), $800–$1,200

Frances Gearhart (1864–1958):
"Rain Tomorrow" (10" × 11"), $900–$1,100
"Above the Sea" (9¼" × 8½"), $800–$900
"Minarets" (9" × 6¼"), $750–$850
"Autumn Brocade" (12" × 9¼"), $1,000–$1,250
"Geraniums" (8" × 4¼"), $600–$800

Carl Heinrich:
"Dogwood Blossoms" (11½" × 11½"), $500–$600

Edna Boies Hopkins (1872–1937):
"Mountain Women" (10" × 9") $3,500–$4,000
"Apple Blossoms" (10½" × 7½"), $2,000–$2,500
"Dandelions" (10¾" × 7"), $2,000–$2,500

Helen Hyde (1868–1919):
"A Day in June" (14½" × 6½"), $875–$1,000

"The Family Umbrella" (7" × 6"), $750–$900
"The Puppy-Cat and the Baby" (4¼" × 7"), $600–$750

Jane Berry Judson (1868–1935):
"Twilight-Sheepscot River, Maine" (8¼" × 6¼"), $650–$750
"Blossom Time" (6" × 8"), $1,000–$1,200
"Our Village Street" (6" × 8"), $800–$900

Pedro J. de Lemos (1882–1954):
"Driftwood-Oakland Shipyard" (7½" × 8"), $900–$1,100
"Waiting for the Breeze" (8½" × 7¾"), $850–$1,050

Bertha Boynton Lum (1869–1954):
"Fox Women" (16" × 10") $1,250–$1,600
"Lanterns" (9½" × 5") $1,000–$1,250
"Rickshaw Riding" (3" × 9") $600–$750
"The Christmas Fairy" (8¾" × 1¾"), $800–$1,000
"Lung Fu Sou" (8¾" × 10"), $900–$1,100
"The Spirit of the Sea" (16¾" × 11"), $1,000–$1,200
"Mother of the Night" (15¼" × 10½"), $1,300–$1,500
"Japanese Children and Kites" (7½" × 13¾"), $600–$900

Lilian Miller (1895–1945):
"Cathedral Cliffs" (14¼" × 9½"), $650–$850

Elizabeth Norton (1887–1985):
California mission scene (5½" × 4½") $1,500–$2,000

Margaret Jordan Patterson (1867–1950):
"The Winding Road" (7½" × 10¼"), $1.500–$2,000
"Windblown Trees" (7" × 10¼"), $2,000–$2,500
"On the Canal" (8" × 6"), $2,000–$2,500
"Bleeding Heart" (7" × 10"), $2,500–$3,000
"Poppies and Convolvous" (7" × 10"), $2.500–$3000

William S. Rice (1873–1963):
"Millsmont Twilight" (6½" × 5½"), $850–$950

"Venetian Sail" (12" × 9"), $800–$1,000
"The Buoy" (5¾" × 4½"), $800–$1,200

Charles H. Richert (b. 1880):
"Manset Fish Wharf" (5" × 7"), $450–$550

Mary Burr Russell (1898–1977):
"Backstairs" (14½" × 13½"), $1,200–$1,500
"Castle on Hill" (11¼" × 7¾"), $1,000–$1,250
"European Town" (15" × 10¼"), $1,250–$1,500
"Judgement" (10" × 13¼"), $1,800–$2,000
Rudolph Ruzicka:
"Dock Slip" (7" × 9½"), $350–$475

Birger Sandzen (1871–1954):
"Aspen Grove at Sunset" (8" × 6"), $425–$550
"Evening Glow" (5" × 7"), $450–$550
"Poplars" (6" × 9"), $500–$650

Charles W. Smith (b. 1893):
"Junks" (16" × 11¾"), $750–$900

Zulma Steele (1881–1979):
Mountain scene (5" × 7"), $1,000–$1,350

Charles Turzak (1899–1985):
"Michigan Avenue Bridge" (12¼" × 8½"), $900–$1,100
"Randolph Street" (12¼" × 9"), $1,000–$1,500

Ernest W. Watson (1884–1969):
"Woodbine" (6¾" × 9¼"), $450–$550

# ENDNOTES

### An Introduction to the Arts and Crafts Movement in America

1. Beverly Brandt, *The Encyclopedia of Arts and Crafts* ( New York: E.P. Dutton, 1989), p. 8.

2. Design Council, *William Morris and Kelmscott* (London: The Design Council, 1981), p. 85.

3. Gustav Stickley, *Stickley Craftsman Furniture* Catalogs (New York, Dover Publications, 1979), p. 3.

4. Ibid..

5. Thomas M. Voss. *The Bargain Hunter's Guide to Used Furniture* (New York: Delta, 1980), p. 82.

## PART 1    ART POTTERY

### The Potteries

**Arequipa pottery**

1. Eloise Roorbach

**Cl Clewell Pottery**

1. Ralph and Terry Kovel, *The Kovels' Collector's Guide to American Art Pottery* (New York: Crown Publishers, 1974), p. 15.

2. Paul Evans, *Art Pottery of the United States* (New York: Charles Scribner's Sons, 1974), p. 57.

3. Ralph and Terry Kovel, *The Kovels' Collector's Guide to American Art Pottery (New York: Crown* Publishers, 1974), p. 15.

**Clifton Pottery**

1. See Lonhuda Pottery.

2. See Denver China and Pottery Company.

3. Paul Evans, *Art Pottery of the United States* (New York: Charles Scribner's Sons, 1974), p. 59.

4. Elisabeth Cameron, *Encyclopedia of Pottery and Porcelain: 1800–1960* (New York: Facts on File Publications, 1986), p. 82.

## Dedham Pottery and Chelsea Keramic Art Works

1. J. Milton Robertson, *Dedham Pottery Catalog* (1938), (Halifax, VA: Dedham Folio, 1987), reprint.

2. Paul Evans, *Art Pottery of the United States* (New York: Charles Scribner's Sons, 1974). p. 47.

3. J. Milton Robertson, *Dedham Pottery Catalog* (1938), (Halifax, VA: Dedham Folio, 1987), reprint.

4. Paul Evans, *Art Pottery of the United States* (New York: Charles Scribner's Sons, 1974). p. 49.

5. Ralph and Terry Kovel, *The Kovels' Collector's Guide to American Art Pottery* (New York: Crown Publishers, 1974), p. 31.

6. Martin Eidelberg, ed., *From Our Native Clay* (New York: Turn of the Century Editions, 1987), p. 96.

7. Ibid.

8. Lloyd Hawes, *The Dedham Pottery* (Dedham, MA: Dedham Historical Society, 1968), p. 38.

9. J. Milton Robertson, *Dedham Pottery Catalog* (1938), (Halifax, VA: Dedham Folio, 1987), reprint.

10. Ibid., p. ii.

## Denver China and Pottery Company

1. See Lonhuda Pottery, Weller Pottery, and J. B. Owens Pottery for additional information.

2. Paul Evans, *Art Pottery of the United States* (New York: Charles Scribner's Sons, 1974), p. 88.

## Frackelton Pottery

1. "The Frackelton 'Blue and Gray,'" the *Craftsman* (January 1903), p. 255.

2. Martin Eidelberg, ed., *From Our Native Clay* (New York: Turn of the Century Editions, 1987), p. 48.

## Fulper Pottery

1. Robert W. Blasberg, *Fulper Art Pottery: An Aesthetic Appreciation 1909–1929* (New York: The Jordan-Volpe Gallery, 1979), p. 72–73.

2. Evelyn Marie Stuart, "Vasekraft—and American Art Pottery," *Fine Arts Journal* (October 1913), p. 608; also quoted in Robert W. Blasberg's *Fulper Art Pottery*.

3. Wendy Kaplan, ed., *The Art That Is Life: The Arts and Crafts Movement in America, 1875–1920* (Boston: Museum of Fine Arts, 1987), p. 262; and Paul Evans, *Art Pottery of the United States* (New York: Charles Scribner's Sons, 1974), p. 113.

4. Wendy Kaplan, ed., *The Art That Is Life: The Arts and Crafts Movement in America, 1875–1920* (Boston: Museum of Fine Arts, 1987), p. 262.

5. Martin Eidelberg, ed., *From Our Native Clay* (New York: Turn of the Century Editions, 1987), p. 99.

6. Ibid.

7. Paul Evans, *Art Pottery of the United States* (New York: Charles Scribner's Sons, 1974), p. 110.

8. Wendy Kaplan, ed., *The Art That Is Life: The Arts and Crafts Movement in America, 1875–1920* (Boston: Museum of Fine Arts, 1987), p. 262–263.

9. Paul Evans, *Art Pottery of the United States* (New York: Charles Scribner's Sons, 1974), p. 11.

## Grueby Pottery

1. Mary White, quoted in "The Potters of America," the *Craftsman* (December 1914), p. 302. Although scholars have since proved that the Grueby Pottery was not the first to develop a matte glaze, Miss White's statement remains as evidence of the respect accorded the Grueby pottery and their matte glazes. Recent research has led many historians to conclude that the Hampshire Pottery deserves recognition as being the first to develop a matte glaze, but it was the combination of the Grueby matte glaze and their hand-modeled forms that led to the widespread popularity of both their pottery and the matte glaze.

2. "Faience" refers to any glazed earthenware or pottery, especially that of a fine quality with highly colored designs.

3. See *Keramic Studio* (February 1905), p. 216–217.

4. The Grueby Faience Company shared a booth with Gustav Stickley at the Pan-American Exposition in Buffalo, New York, in 1901. That year and the next Stickley advertised small tables featuring "the now-famous Grueby tiles" set in each top. Surviving examples are considered both rare and extremely valuable.

5. Robert W. Blasberg, *Grueby* (Syracuse, NY: Everson Museum of Art. 1981), p. 17.

6. Paul Evans, *Art Pottery of the United States* (New York: Charles Scribner's sons, 1974), p. 119.

7. Martin Eidelberg, ed., *From Our Native Clay* (New York: Turn of the Century Editions, 1987), p. 66.

8. Ibid, p 50.

## Hampshire Pottery

1. Albert Christian Revi, ed., *The Spinning Wheel Complete Book of Antiques* (New York: Grosset & Dunlap, 1972), p. 112.

2. Paul Evans, *Art Pottery of the United States* (New York: Charles Scribner's Sons, 1974), p. 129.

3. Elisabeth Cameron, *Encyclopedia of Pottery and Porcelain: 1800–1960* (New York: Facts on File Publications, 1986), p. 322.

4. Ralph and Terry Kovel, *The Kovels' Collector's Guide to American Art Pottery* (New York: Crown Publishers, 1974), p. 57.

5. Ibid.

6. Paul Evans, *Art Pottery of the United States* (New York: Charles Scribner's Sons, 1974), p. 130.

7. Albert Christian Revi, ed., *The Spinning Wheel Complete Book of Antiques* (New York: Grosset & Dunlap, 1972), p. 110.

8. Paul Evans, *Art Pottery of the United States* (New York: Charles Scribner's Sons, 1974), p. 130.

## Losanti Pottery

1. Hebert Peck, *The Book of Rookwood Pottery* (New York: Crown Publishers, 1968), p. 47.

2. Wendy Kaplan, ed., *The Art That Is Life: The Arts and Crafts Movement in America, 1875–1920* (Boston: Museum of Fine Arts, 1887), p. 250.

3. Paul Evans, *Art Pottery of the United States* (New York: Fiengold & Lewis, 1987), p. 148.

4. Martin Eidelberg, ed., *From Our Native Clay* (New York: Turn of the Century Editions, 1987), p. 50.

## Low Art Tile Works

1. Ralph and Terry Kovel, *The Kovels' Collector's Guide to American Art Pottery* (New York: Crown Publishers, 1974), p. 83–84.

2. Ibid., p. 28.

3. Elisabeth Cameron, *Encyclopedia of Pottery and Porcelain: 1800–1960* (New York: Facts on File Publications, 1986), p. 205.

4. Paul Evans, *Art Pottery of the United States* (New York: Fiengold & Lewis, 1987), p. 152.

5. Ibid.

## Marblehead Pottery

1. Jonathan A. Rawson, Jr., "Recent American Pottery," *House Beautiful* (April 1912), p. 149; also quoted in Wendy Kaplan, ed., *The Art That Is Life: The Arts and Crafts Movement in America, 1875–1920* (Boston: Museum of Fine Arts, 1987), p. 257.

2. Albert Christian Revi, *The Spinning Wheel Complete Book of Antiques* (New York: Grosset & Dunlap, 1972), p. 104.

3. Wendy Kaplan, ed., *The Art That Is Life: The Arts and Crafts Movement in America, 1875–1920* (Boston: Museum of Fine Arts, 1987), p. 256.

4. Paul Evans, *Art Pottery of the United States* (New York: Charles Scribner's Sons, 1974), p. 157.

5. Elisabeth Cameron, *Encyclopedia of Pottery and Porcelain: 1800–1960)* (New York: Facts on File Publications, 1986), p. 212.

6. Robert Judson Clark, ed., *The Arts and Crafts Movement in America: 1876–1916* (Princeton, NJ: Princeton University, 1972). p. 180.

7. Martin Eidelberg, ed., *From Our Native Clay* (New York: Turn of the Century Editions, 1987), p. 15.

8. Ibid.

## Merrimac Pottery

1. Irene Sargent, "Some Potters and Their Products," the *Craftsman* (July 1903), p. 249.

2. Ibid.

3. Martin Eidelberg, ed., *From Our Native Clay* (New York: Turn of the Century Editions, 1987), p. 68.

4. Paul Evans, *Art Pottery of the United States* (New York: Charles Scribner's Sons, 1974), p. 169.

## Newcomb Pottery.

1. In 1940 the Newcomb Guild was established and continued to use the Newcomb Pottery shop mark until 1948.

2. Paul Evans, *Art Pottery of the United States* (New York: Charles Scribner's Sons, 1974), p. 187.

3. Jessie Poesch, *Newcomb College: An Enterprise for Southern Women, 1895–1940* (Exton, PA: Schiffer Publishing, 1984), p. 18.

4. Ibid., p. 20.

5. Ibid., p. 53.

## Niloak Pottery

1. Albert Christian Revi, ed., *The Spinning Wheel Complete Book of Antiques* (New York: Grosset & Dunlap, 1972), p. 108.

2. Wendy Kaplan, ed., *The Art That Is Life: The Arts and Crafts Movement in America, 1875–1920* (Boston: Museum of Fine Arts, 1987), p. 387.

3. Ibid. p. 386.

4. Paul Evans, *Art Pottery of the United States* (New York: Charles Scribner's Sons, 1974), p. 191.

## Norse Pottery

1. Paul Evans, *Art Pottery of the United States* (New York: Charles Scribner's Sons, 1974), p. 194.

## George Ohr Pottery

1. Paul Evans, *Art Pottery of the United States* (New York: Feingold & Lewis, 1987), p. 29.

2. Ibid., p. 28.

3. Robert Judson Clark, ed., *The Arts and Crafts Movement in America: 1876–1916* (Princeton, NJ: Princeton University, 1972), p. 135.

4. Martin Eidelberg, ed., *From Our Native Clay* (New York: Turn of the Century Editions, 1987), p. 44.

5. See Wendy Kaplan, ed., *The Art That Is Life: The Arts and Crafts Movement in America, 1875–1920* (Boston: Museum of Fine Arts, 1987), p. 252; also Kirsten Hoving Keen, *American Art Pottery, 1875–1930* (Wilmington, DE: Delaware Art Museum, 1978), p. 44.

6. Kirsten Hoving Keen, *American Art Pottery, 1875–1930* (Wilmington, DE: Delaware Art Museum, 1978), p. 44.

7. *Crockery and Glass Journal* (December 30, 1909), p. 50; also quoted in Wendy Kaplan, ed., *The Art That Is Life: The Arts and Crafts Movement in America, 1875–1920* (Boston: Museum of Fine Arts, 1987), p. 252.

8. Kirsten Hoving Keen, *American Art Pottery, 1875–1930* (Wilmington, DE: Delaware Art Museum, 1978), p. 46.

## Overbeck Pottery

1. Kathleen Postle, *The Chronicle of the Overbeck Pottery* (Indianapolis, IN: Indiana Historical Society, 1978), p. 27.

2. Ibid., p. 51.

3. Paul Evans, *Art Pottery of the United States* (New York: Charles Scribner's Sons, 1974), p. 204.

## Pewabic Pottery

1. Paul Evans, *Art Pottery of the United States* (New York: Charles Scribner's Sons, 1974), p. 227.

2. Garth Clark and Margie Hughto, *A Century of Ceramics in the United States: 1878–1978* (New York: E. P. Dutton, 1979), p. 46.

3. Ibid.

4. Anthea Callen, *Women Artists of the Arts and Crafts Movement: 1870–1914* (New York: Pantheon Books, 1979), p. 86.

5. Ralph and Terry Kovel, *The Kovels' Collector's Guide to American Art Pottery* (New York: Crown Publishers, 1974), p. 170.

6. Anthea Callen, *Women Artists of the Arts and Crafts Movement: 1870–1914* (New York: Pantheon Books, 1979), p. 86.

7. Garth Clark and Margie Hughto, *A Century of Ceramics in the United States: 1878–1978* (New York: E.P. Dutton, 1979), p. 47.

8. Anthea Callen, *Women Artists of the Arts and Crafts Movement: 1870–1914* (New York: Pantheon Books, 1979), pp. 86–87.

9. Garth Clark and Margie Hughto, *A Century of Ceramics in the United States: 1878–1978* (New York: E.P. Dutton, 1979), p. 47.

## Paul Revere Pottery and Saturday Evening Girls

1. Anthea Callen, *Women Artists of the Arts and Crafts Movement: 1870–1914* (New York: Pantheon Books, 1979), p. 91.

2. Ralph and Terry Kovel, *The Kovels' Collector's Guide to American Art Pottery* (New York: Crown Publishers, 1974), p. 189.

3. Paul Evans, *Art Pottery of the United States* (New York: Charles Scribner's Sons, 1974), pp. 213–214.

4. Ibid.

5. Ibid.

6. Ibid, p. 216.

## Rhead Pottery

1. Elisabeth Cameron, *Encyclopedia of Pottery and Porcelain: 1800–1960* (New York: Facts on File Publications, 1986), p. 276.

## Adelaide Alsop Robineau

1. Peg Weiss, ed., *Adelaide Alsop Robineau: Glory in Porcelain* (Syracuase, NY: Syracuse University Press, 1981), p. 215.

2. Ibid.

3. Ibid., p. 19.

4. Adelaide Alsop Robineau, *Kerimac Studio* (May 1913), p. 1; also quoted in Peg Weiss, ed., *Adelaide Alsop Robineau:. Glory in Porcelain* (Syracuse, NY: Syracuse University Press, 1981), p. 29.

5. Martin Eidelberg, ed., *From Our Native Clay* (New York: Turn of the Century Editions, 1987), p. 52.

## Roblin Art Pottery Company

1. Paul Evans, *Art Pottery of the United States* (New York: Charles Scribner's Sons, 1974), p. 250.

2. Ibid, pp. 250–251.

3. Ibid, p. 251.

4. Elisabeth Cameron, *Encyclopedia of Pottery and Porcelain: 1800—1960* (New York: Facts on File Publications, 1986), p. 280.

## Rookwood Pottery

1. *Rookwood 1904 Catalog.*

2. Herbert Peck, *The Book of Rookwood Pottery* (New York: Crown Publishers, 1968), p. 2.

3. Martin Eidelberg, ed., *From Our Native Clay* (New York: Turn of the Century Editions, 1987), p. 23.

4. Herbert Peck, *The Book of Rookwood Pottery* (New York: Crown Publishers, 1968), p. 45.

5. Ibid., pp. 70–97.

6. Ibid., p. 65.

7. *Rookwood 1904 Catalog;* also Herbert Peck, *The Book of Rookwood Pottery* (New York: Crown Publishers, 1968), pp. 74–91.

## Teco Pottery

1. *Gates Pottery Catalog* (n.d., n.p.).

2. Martin Eidelberg, ed., *From Our Native Clay* (New York: Turn of the Century Editions, 1987), p. 54.

3. Ibid., p. 98.

4. Paul Evans, *Art Pottery of the United States* (New York: Charles Scribner's Sons, 1974), p. 280.

5. Ralph and Terry Kovel, *The Kovel's Collectors Guide to American Art Pottery* (New York: Crown Publishers, 1974), p. 262.

6. *Gates Pottery Catalog* (n.d., n.p.).

## Tiffany Pottery

1. *Keramic Studio,* II (December 1900).

2. Martin Eidelberg, ed., *From Our Native Clay* (New York: Turn of the Century Editions, 1987), pp. 57–61.

3. Ralph and Terry Kovel, *The Kovels' Collector's Guide to American Art Pottery* (New York: Crown Publishers, 1974), p. 268.

4. Martin Eidelberg, ed., *From Our Native Clay* (New York: Turn of the Century Editions, 1987), p. 59.

5. Paul Evans, *Art Pottery of the United States* (New York: Charles Scribner's Sons, 1974), p. 263.

6. Ibid.

## Van Briggle Pottery

1. Paul Evans, *Art Pottery of the United States* (New York: Charles Scribner's Sons, 1974), p. 283.

2. A previous and widely held theory attributed each of the Roman numerals to Artus Van Briggle, Anne Gregory (Van Briggle), and Harry Bangs. Painstaking research by authors Robert W. Newton, Lois K. Crouch, Euphemia B. Demmin, and Scott Nelson (*A Collector's Guide to Van Briggle Pottery,* published in 1986) shed addi-

tional light on the markings, revealing a document written by Artus Van Briggle in 1902 explaining that the Roman numerals referred to the type of clay used in the ware. Their evidence and conclusions have been accepted and promoted by respected scholar Paul Evans in the 1987 edition of his book *Art Pottery of the United States* (see Note 6).

3. Elizabeth Cameron, *Encyclopedia of Pottery and Porcelain : 1800–1960* (New York: Facts on File Publications, 1986), p. 337.

4. Scott H. Nelson et al., *A Collector's Guide to Van Briggle Pottery* (Indiana, PA: Halldin Publishing, 1986), p. 17.

5. Irene Sargent, "Chinese Pots and Modern Faience," the *Craftsman* (September 1903), p. 423.

6. Paul Evans, *Art Pottery of the United States* (New York: Charles Scribner's Sons, 1974), p. 300.

7. Scott H. Nelson et al., *A Collector's Guide to Van Briggle Pottery* (Indiana, PA: Halldin Publishing, 1986), p. 131.

8. Paul Evans, *Art Pottery of the United States* (New York: Charles Scribner's Sons, 1974), p. 300.

9. Irene Sargent, "Chinese Pots and Modern Faience," *the Craftsman* (September 1903), p. 424.

### Volkmar Pottery

1. Robert Judson Clark, ed., *The Arts and Crafts Movement in America: 1876–1916* (Princeton, NJ: Princeton University, 1972), p. 180.

2. Paul Evans, *Art Pottery of the United States* (New York: Charles Scribner's Sons, 1974), p. 310.

3. Margaret Whiting, *House Beautiful* (October 1900).

4. *International Studio* (November 1900).

5. Robert Judson Clark, ed., *The Arts and Crafts Movement in America: 1876–1916* (Princeton, NJ: Princeton University, 1972), p. 180.

6. Ibid., p. 181.

### Walley Pottery

1. Paul Evans, *Art Pottery of the United States* (New York: Charles Scribner's Sons, 1974), p. 316.

2. Ibid.

3. See Martin Eidelberg, ed., *From Our Native Clay* (New York: Turn of the Century Editions, 1987), p. 103.

### Walrath Pottery

1. Paul Evans, *Art Pottery of the United States* (New York: Charles Scribner's Sons, 1974), p. 400.

2. Ibid.

3. Martin Eidelberg, ed., *From Our Native Clay* (New York, Turn of the Century Editions, 1987), p. 38.

### Wheatley Pottery Company

1. Martin Eidelberg, ed., *From Our Native Clay* (New York: Turn of the Century Editions, 1987), pp. 10–11.

2. Paul Evans, *Art Pottery of the United States* (New York: Charles Scribner's Sons, 1974), p. 335.

## PART 2   ARTS AND CRAFTS FURNITURE
### The Arts and Crafts Furniture Manufacturers

#### Byrdcliffe Arts and Crafts Colony

1. Ralph Radcliffe-Whitehead, *Grass of the Desert* (London: Chiswick Press, 1892), p. 61.

2. Robert Edwards, *The Byrdcliffe Arts and Crafts Colony* (Wilmington, DE: Delaware Art Museum, 1984), p. 6.

3. Coy L. Ludwig, *The Arts and Crafts Movement in New York State:* 1890s–1920s (Hamilton, NY: Gallery Association of NY State, Inc., 1983), p. 45.

4. Wendy Kaplan, ed., *The Art That Is Life: The Arts and Crafts Movement in America,* 1875–1920 (Boston: Museum of Fine Arts, 1987), p. 229.

5. Robert Edwards, *The Byrdcliffe Arts and Crafts Colony* (Wilmington, DE: Delaware Art Museum, 1984), p. 10.

6. Ibid., p. 11.

7. Coy L. Ludwig, *The Arts and Crafts Movement in New York State:* 1890s–1920s (Hamilton, NY: Gallery Association of NY State, Inc., 1983), p. 45.

#### Harvey Ellis

1. Harvey Ellis, "A Simple Dining Room," the *Craftsman* (October 1903), p. 92.

2. *Times* (Rochester, NY, May 29, 1903).

3. Claude Bragdon, "Harvey Ellis: A Portrait Sketch," *Architectural Review* (December 1908), p. 20.

4. Ibid., p. 21.

5. Ibid., p. 19.

6. Ibid., p. 20.

7. Hugh Garden, "Harvey Ellis, Designer and Draughtsman," *Architectural Review* (December 1908), p. 38.

8. Barry Sanders, "Harvey Ellis: Architect, Painter, Furniture Designer," *Art and Antiques* (January-February 1981), p. 64.

9. Harvey Ellis, "A Craftsman House Design," the *Craftsman* (July 1903), p. 275.

10. Gustav Stickley, "Structure and Ornament," the *Craftsman* (January 1904), p 395–396.

11. David Cathers, "Gustav Stickley, George H. Jones & The Making of Inlaid Craftsman Furniture," *Style 1900* (February 2000), pp. 54–60.

12. Gustav Stickley (untitled), the *Craftsman* (February 1904), p. 520.

#### George Grant Elmslie

1. Marian Page, *Furniture Designed by Architects* (New York: Whitney Library of Design, 1980), p. 115.

2. Wendy Kaplan, ed., *The Art That Is Life: The Arts and Crafts Movement in America,* 1875–1920 (Boston: Museum of Fine Arts, 1987), p. 204.

3. Marian Page, *Furniture Designed by Architects* (New York: Whitney Library of Design, 1980), p. 114.

4. Sharon Darling, *Chicago Furniture: 1833–1983* (Chicago: Chicago Historical Society, 1984), p. 253.

5. Marian Page, *Furniture Designed by Architects* (New York: Whitney Library of Design, 1980), p. 112.

6. Ibid., p. 112–114.

7. Wendy Kaplan, ed., *The Art That Is Life: The Arts and Crafts Movement in America,*. 1875–1920 (Boston: Museum of Fine Arts, 1987), p. 208.

8. Sharon Darling, *Chicago Furniture: 1833–1983* (Chicago: Chicago Historical Society, 1984), p. 254.

9. Wendy Kaplan, ed., *The Art That Is Life: The Arts and Crafts Movement in America, 1875–1920* (Boston: Museum of Fine Arts, 1987), p. 194.

10. Marian Page, *Furniture Designed by Architects* (New York: Whitney Library of Design, 1980), p. 115.

## Greene and Greene

1. Marian Page, *Furniture Designed by Architects* (New York: Whitney Library of Design, 1980), p. 121.

2. Bruce Smith, *Greene & Greene Masterworks* (San Francisco: Chronicle Books, 1998), p. 27.

3. Marian Page, *Furniture Designed by Architects* (New York: Whitney Library of Design, 1980), p. 121.

4. Randell L. Makinson, *Greene and Greene: Furniture and Related Designs* (Salt Lake City, UT: Peregrine Smith Books, 1979), p. 20.

5. Ibid., p. 27.

6. Ibid.

7. Ibid., p.113–114.

## Lifetime Furniture

1. *Lifetime Furniture Catalog* (New York: Turn of the Century Editions, 1981). p. ii.

2. Ibid.

3. Ibid.

4. Ibid.

5. Don Marek, *Arts and Crafts Furniture Design: The Grand Rapids Contribution 1895–1915* (Grand Rapids, MI: Grand Rapids Art Museum, 1987), p. 56.

6. *Lifetime Furniture Catalog* (New York: Turn of the Century Editions, 1981), p. 109.

7. *Lifetime Furniture Catalog* (New York: Turn of the Century Editions, 1981), p. 109.

8. Don Marek, *Arts and Crafts Furniture Design: The Grand Rapids Contribution 1895–1915* (Grand Rapids, Ml: Grand Rapids Art Museum, 1987), p. 66.

9. Ibid., p. 63.

## Charles Limbert

1. Charles Limbert, *Limbert's Arts and Crafts Furniture Catalog,* ca. 1905, introduction.

2. *The Arts and Crafts Furniture of Charles P. Limbert*, introduction by Robert Edwards (Watkins Glen, NY: The American Life Foundation, 1982), p. 21.

3. Don Marek, *Arts and Crafts Furniture Design: The Grand Rapids Contribution, 1895–1915* (Grand Rapids, MI: Grand Rapids Art Museum, 1987), p. 49.

4. Deborah DeVall Dorsey Norberg, "Charles P. Limbert: Maker of Michigan Arts and Crafts Furniture," *The Herald* (Henry Ford Museum, Dearborn, MI, 5: October 1976), p. 28.

5. Ibid., p. 30.

6. Charles Limbert, "The Arts and Crafts Furniture," Furniture (October 1909), p. 31.

7. *Limbert's Holland Dutch Arts and Crafts Furniture* (New York: Turn of the Century Editions, 1981), pp. 15–16.

8. Deborah DeVall Dorsey Norberg, "Charles P. Limbert: Maker of Michigan Arts and Crafts Furniture," *The Herald* (Henry Ford Museum, Dearborn, MI, 5: October 1976), p. 33.

## George Washington Maher

1. Wendy Kaplan, ed., *The Art That Is Life: The Arts and Crafts Movement in America*, 1875–1920 (Boston: Museum of Fine Arts, 1987), p. 396.

2. Marian Page, *Furniture Designed by Architects* (New York: Whitney Library of Design, 1980), pp. 109–110.

3. Sharon Darling, *Chicago Furniture: 1833–1983* (Chicago: Chicago Historical Society, 1984), p. 252.

4. Gustav Stickley, "The German Exhibit at the Louisiana Purchase Exposition," the *Craftsman* (June 1904), p. 488–506.

5. Wendy Kaplan, ed., *The Art That Is Life: The Arts and Crafts Movement in America,* 1875–1920 (Boston: Museum of Fine Arts, 1987), p. 396.

6. Ibid.

7. Ibid., p.123.

## Joseph P. McHugh & Co

1. David Cathers, *Furniture of the American Arts and Crafts Movement* (New York: New American Library, 1981), p. 15.

2. Wendy Kaplan, ed., *The Art That Is Life: The Arts and Crafts Movement in America. 1875–1920* (Boston: Museum of Fine Arts, 1987), p. 124.

3. *American Cabinetmaker and Upholsterer* (July 14, 1900).

4. Coy L. Ludwig, *The Arts and Crafts Movement in New York State: 1890s–1920s* (Hamilton, NY: Gallery Association of NY State, Inc., 1983), p. 61.

5. David Cathers, *Furniture of the American Arts and Crafts Movement* (New York: New American Library, 1981), p. 88.

6. Wendy Kaplan, ed., *The Art That is life: The Arts and Crafts Movement in America*, 1875–1920 (Boston: Museum of Fine Arts, 1987), p. 185.

7. David Cathers, *Furniture of the American Arts and Crafts Movement* (New York: New American Library, 1981), p. 15.

## George Mann Niedecken

1. Virginia Jones Maher, "The Harmony of Total Design" (*Style: 1900,* 8, (summer 1995), p. 49.

2. Ibid., p. 44.

3. Rosalie Goldstein, ed., *The Domestic Scene* (1897–1927): George M. Niedecken, Interior Architect (Milwaukee, WI: Milwaukee Art Museum, 1981), p.11.

4. Ibid.

5. Virginia Jones Maher, "The Harmony of Total Design" (*Style: 1900,* vol. 8, no. 2, summer 1995), p. 49.

6. Rosalie Goldstein, ed., *The Domestic Scene* (1897–1927): George M. Nie decken, Interior Architect (Milwaukee, WI: Milwaukee Art Museum, 1981), p.47.

7. Wendy Kaplan, ed, *The Art That Is Life: The Arts and Crafts Movement in America,* 1875–1920 (Boston: Museum of Fine Arts, 1987), p. 237 .

8. Sharon Darling, Chicago Furniture: Art, Craft & Industry 1833–1983 (Chicago: Chicago Historical Society, 1984), p. 265.

9. Rosalie Goldstein, ed., *The Domestic Scene* (1897–1927): George M. Niedecken, Interior Architect (Milwaukee. WI: Milwaukee Art Museum. 1981). p.65.

10. Ibid. p.69.

11. Ibid., p. 70.

## Charles Rohlfs

1. Charles Rohlfs, "My Adventure in Woodcarving," *Arts Journal* (September 1925).

2. Coy L. Ludwig, *The Arts and Crafts Movement in New York State: 1890s–1920s* (Hamilton, NY: Gallery Association of New York State, 1983), p. 87.

3. Michael James, "The Philosophy of Charles Rohlfs: An Introduction," Arts and Crafts Quarterly (April 1987), p. 15.

4. Coy L. Ludwig, *The Arts and Crafts Movement in New York State: 1890s–1920s* (Hamilton, NY: Gallery Association of New York State, 1983), p. 87.

5. Judson Clark, *The Arts and Crafts Movement in America*, 1876–1916 (Princeton, NJ: Princeton University Press, 1972), p. 28–29.

6. Eve Warner, "Charles Rohlfs: In Step with a Different Drummer," *The New York-Pennsylvania Collector* (November 1986), p. 6.

7. Wendy Kaplan, ed., *The Art That Is Life: The Arts and Crafts Movement in America, 1875–1920* (Boston: Museum of Fine Arts, 1987), p. 98–99.

8. Judson Clark, *The Arts and Crafts Movement in America, 1876–1916* (Princeton, NJ: Princeton University Press, 1972), p. 28–81.

9. Coy L. Ludwig, *The Arts and Crafts Movement in New York State: 1890s–1920s* (Hamilton, NY: Gallery Association of New York State, 1983), p. 88.

## The Rose Valley Association

1. This phrase was adopted by William L. Price for the subtitle of his periodical the *Artsman*, which was published from 1903 to 1907.

2. Wendy Kaplan, ed., *The Art That Is Life: The Arts and Crafts Movement in America, 1875–1920* (Boston: Museum of Fine Arts, 1987), p. 223.

3. Ibid., p. 314.

4. Ibid., p. 225.

5. Ibid., p. 229.

6. Ibid., p. 229.

7. Ibid.

## The Roycroft Shops

1. *Roycroft Furniture Catalog* (New York: Turn of the Century Editions, 1981), p. 3.

2. Freeman Champney, *Art and Glory: The Story of Elbert Hubbard* (Kent, OH: Kent State University Press, 1983), p. 199.

3. Mary Roelofs Stott, *Rebel with Reverence: Elbert Hubbard* (Watkins Glen, NY: American Life Foundation, 1984), p. 20.

4. Nancy Hubbard Brady, ed., *The Book of the Roycrofters* (East Aurora, NY: House of Hubbard, 1977), p. 4.

5. David Cathers, *Furniture of the American Arts and Crafts Movement* (New York: New American Library, 1981), p. 87.

6. Nancy Hubbard Brady, *Roycroft Handmade Furniture* (East Aurora, NY: House of Hubbard, 1973), p. 57.

7. David Cathers, *Furniture of the American Arts and Crafts Movement* (New York: New American Library. 1981), p. 91 .

8. Nancy Hubbard Brady, *Roycroft Handmade Furniture* (East Aurora, NY: House of Hubbard, 1973), p. 1.

9. Ibid.

10. Ibid.

## The Shop of the Crafters

1. Stephen Gray, ed., *Shop of the Crafters Catalog* (ca. 1906). Introduction by Kenneth Trapp (New York: Turn of the Century Editions, 1983), p. 4.

2. Ibid., p. 69.

3. Ibid., p. 3.

4. Ibid., p. 6.

5. Ibid., p. 68.

6. Ibid., p. 4.

7. Ibid., p. 68.

8. Ibid., p .69.

9. Ibid.

10. Ibid., pp. 8, 16.

11. Ibid., p. 3.

12. Wendy Kaplan, ed., *The Art That Is Life: The Arts and Crafts Movement in America*. 1875–1920 (Boston: Museum of Fine Arts, 1987), pp. 21, 248.

13. Stephen Gray, ed., *Shop of the Crafters Catalog* (ca. 1906). Introduction by Kenneth Trapp (New York: Turn of the Century Editions, 1983), p. 68.

## Stickley Brothers, Inc

1. Albert Stickley, "The Merits of Arts and Crafts Furniture," *A Magazine of Education for the Home* (April 1909), p. 30.

2. The technical exception was Leopold Stickley, but his later line of Colonial reproductions marketed under the Cherry Valley trademark did not surpass the recognition or production of his earlier Arts and Crafts designs.

3. For an in-depth study of the early years of the Stickley family, see Marilyn Fish, *Gustav Stickley: Heritage & Early Years* ( North Caldwell, NJ: Little Pond Press, 1997).

4. Ibid., p. 27.

5. Don Marek, *Arts and Crafts Furniture Design: The Grand Rapids Contribution 1895–1915* (Grand Rapids, MI: Grand Rapids Art Museum, 1987), p. 52.

6. *Quaint Furniture Catalog* (New Yolk: Turn of the Century Editions, 1981), p. 5.

7. Ibid., p.4.

8. Ibid., p.5.

9. *Quaint Furniture Catalog* (New York: Turn of the Century Editions, 1981), p. 5.

10. Don Marek, *Arts and Crafts Furniture Design: The Grand Rapids Contribution 1895–1915* (Grand Rapids, MI: Grand Rapids Art Museum, 1987), p. 63.

## Charles Stickley and Stickley and Brandt

1. *Stickley-Brandt Furniture Company catalog* #A-II (dated 1908).

2. David Cathers, *Furniture of the American Arts and Crafts Movement* (New York: New American Library, 1981), p. 258–260.

3. Broome County Public Library (Binghamton, NY).

4. Ibid.

5. Henry Francis Du Pont Winterthur Museum (Wilmington, DE).

## Gustav Stickley and the Craftsman Workshops

1. Gustav Stickley, *Craftsman Homes* (New York Dover Publications, 1979), p. 158.

2. Mary Ann Smith, Gustav Stickley: the *Craftsman* (Syracuse, NY: Syracuse University Press, 1983), p. xvi.

3. Gustav Stickley, *Craftsman Homes* (New York: Dover Publications, 1979), p. 154.

4. *Stickley Craftsman Furniture Catalogs* (New York: Dover Publications. 1979), p. 3.

5. David Cathers, *Furniture of the American Arts and Crafts Movement* (New York: New American Library, 1981), p. 37.

6. Ibid., p.47.

7. Stickley *Craftsman Furniture Catalogs* (New York: Dover Publications, 1979), p. 3.

8. Gustav Stickley, *Craftsman Homes* (New York: Dover Publications, 1979), p. 158 .

9. Wendy Kaplan, ed., *The Art That Is Life: The Arts and Crafts Movement in America, 1875–1920 (*Boston: Museum of Fine Arts, 1987), p 230.

10. Stickley *Craftsman Furniture Catalogs* (New York: Dover Publications, 1979), p. 131.

11. Wendy Kaplan, ed., *The Art That Is Life: The Arts and Crafts Movement in America, 1875–1920* (Boston: Museum of Fine Arts, 1987), p. 235.

12. Ibid., p. 236.

13. Stickley *Craftsman Furniture Catalogs* (New York: Dover Publications, 1979), p. 9.

## L. & J. G. Stickley Furniture Company

1. *Stickley Craftsman Furniture Catalogs*, introduction by David Cathers (New York: Dover Publications. 1979), p. 130.

2. David Cathers, *Furniture of the American Arts and Crafts Movement* (New York: New American Library, 1981), p. 72.

3. Wendy Kaplan, *The Art That Is Life: The Arts and Crafts Movement in America, 1875–1920* (Boston: Museum of Fine Arts, 1987), p. 168.

4. David Cathers, *Furniture of the American Arts and Crafts Movement* (New York: New American Library, 1981), pp. 196–197.

5 *Stickley Craftsman Furniture Catalogs* (New York: Dover Publications, 1979), p. 131.

6. Ibid.

7. Ibid.

## The Tobey Furniture Company

1. *Chicago Tribune* (October 7, 1900).

2 Sharon Darling, *Chicago Furniture: Art, Craft and Industry 1833–1983* (Chicago: Chicago Historical Society, 1984), pp. 235–236.

3. Don Marek, *Arts and Crafts Furniture Design: The Grand Rapids Contribution 1895–1915* (Grand Rapids, MI: Grand Rapids Art Museum, 1987), p. 35 .

4. Ibid.

5. See Stephen Gray, *The Early Work of Gustav Stickley* (New York: Turn of the Century Editions, 1987).

6. *Chicago Tribune* (October 7, 1900).

7. Ibid.

8. Sharon Darling, *Chicago Furniture: Art, Craft and Industry 1833–1983* (Chicago: Chicago Historical Society, 1984), p. 235.

9. Ibid., p. 240.

## Frank Lloyd Wright

1. Frank Lloyd Wright, *In the Cause of Architecture* (1908).

2. Frank Lloyd Wright, *The Natural House* (1957), as quoted in Marian Page, *Furniture Designed by Architects* (New York: Whitney Library of Design, 1980), p. 106.

3. Robert Judson Clark, *The Arts and Crafts Movement in America 1876–1916* (Princeton, NJ: Princeton University Press, 1972), p. 59.

4. Marian Page, *Furniture Designed by Architects* (New York: Whitney Library of Design, 1980), p. 101.

5. Ibid., p. 94.

6. Frank Lloyd Wright, *An Autobiography* (New York: Longmans Green, 1932), p. 138.

7. David Hanks, *The Decorative Designs of Frank Lloyd Wright* (New York: E. P. Dutton, 1979), p. 41–42.

8. Robert C. Twombly, *Frank Lloyd Wright in Spring Green* (Madison, WI: State Historical Society of Wisconsin, 1980), p. 2.

9. Robert Judson Clark, *The Arts and Crafts Movement in America 1875–1916* (Princeton, NJ: Princeton University Press, 1972), p. 44.

10. David Hanks, *The Decorative Designs of Frank Lloyd Wright* (New York: E. P. Dutton. 1979), pp. 41–42.

## J. M. Young Furniture Company

1. The only in-depth research that has been done on the furniture of J. M. Young is that of authors Michael Clark and Jill Thomas-Clark. Their book, *J. M. Young Arts and Crafts Furniture* (New York: Dover Publications, 1994) includes historical and biographical information, details on construction techniques and finishes, and a compilation of illustrations of the firms most common forms.

2. Ibid., p. xii-xiv.

3. Ibid., p. xiv.
4. Ibid., p.xiv.
5. Ibid., p.xviii.
6. Ibid., p.xix.

## Other Mission Oak Furniture Manufacturers

1. Charles Limbert, *Limbert's Holland Dutch Arts and Crafts Furniture Catalog #112.*

## PART 3   METALWARE AND ACCESSORIES

### Gorham Manufacturing Company

1. Charles H. Carpenter, Jr., *Gorham Silver: 1831–1981* (New York: Dodd, Mead & Co., 1982), p. 108.
2. Ibid..
3. Ibid.
4. Ibid., p. 223.
5. Wendy Kaplan, ed., *The Art That Is Life: The Arts and Crafts Movement in America, 1875–1920* (Boston: Museum of Fine Arts, 1987), p. 156 .

### Heintz Art Metal Shop

1. David H. Surgan, "The Heintz Finishing Touch," *Style: 1900,* II (Spring, 1998), p. 32.
2. Ibid., p. 30.
3. Kevin McConnell, Heintz Art Metal (West Chester, PA: Schiffer Publishing, 1990), p. 20.

### The Jarvie Shop

1. "An Appreciation of the Work of Robert Jarvie," the *Craftsman* (December 1903), p. 272.
2. Ibid., pp. 274–275.
3. Ibid., p. 273.
4. Ibid., p. 273.
5. Sharon Darling, *Chicago Metalsmiths* (Chicago: Chicago Historical Society, 1977), p. 55.
6. Thomas K. Maher, *The Jarvie Shop* (Philmont, NY: Turn of the Century Editions, 1997), pp.22–23.
7. "An Appreciation of the Work of Robert Jarvie," the *Craftsman* (December 1903), p. 273.
8. "An Appreciation of the Work of Robert Jarvie," the *Craftsman* (December 1903), pp. 273–274.

### The Kalo Shop

1. For more information on dating Kalo works, see Sharon Darling, *Chicago Metalsmiths* (Chicago: Chicago Historical Society, 1977), p. 48.
2. Wendy Kaplan, ed., *The Art That Is Life: The Arts and Crafts Movement in America, 1875–1920* (Boston: Museum of Fine Arts, 1987), p. 279.

3. Sharon Darling, *Chicago Metalsmiths* (Chicago: Chicago Historical Society, 1977), p. 45.

4. Wendy Kaplan, ed., *The Art That Is Life: The Arts and Crafts Movement in America, 1875–1920* (Boston: Museum of Fine Arts, 1987), p. 279.

## Karl Kipp

1. "Craftsman Advertising Department", the *Craftsman* (September 1912).

2. For more information see Roycroft entries under Furniture, p. 229, and Metalware, p. 336, respectively.

3. For a list of the outlets see Charles F. Hamilton, *Roycroft Collectibles* (New York: A. S. Barnes & Co., 1980), pp. 63–67.

## The Roycrofters

1. Unsigned pieces, which can be positively identified by using a Roycroft catalog, are the result of a Roycroft tradition in which the staff members were permitted to work on pieces during their free time, as long as those pieces were for use in their own homes. Such pieces, along with apprentice work failing to meet Roycroft standards, would normally not be stamped.

2. Nancy Hubbard Brady, ed., *The Book of the Roycrofters* (East Aurora, NY: House of Hubbard, 1977), p. 10.

3. Robert Judson Clark, ed., *The Arts and Crafts Movement in America: 1876–1916* (Princeton, NJ: Princeton University, 1972), p. 45.

4. Ibid., p. 47.

5. Mary Roelofs Scott, *Rebel with Reverence* (Watkins Glen, NY: American Life Foundations, 1984), p. 66–69.

6. Wendy Kaplan, ed., *The Art That Is Life: The Arts and Crafts Movement in America, 1875–1920* (Boston: Museum of Fine Arts, 1987), p. 168.

7. Charles Hamilton, *Roycroft Collectibles* (New York: A. S. Barnes & Co., 1980), pp. 63–67.

8. Ibid., p. 58.

## Shreve & Company

1. Edgar W. Morse, *Silver in the Golden State* (Oakland, CA: Oakland Museum, 1986), p. 17.

2. Wendy Kaplan, ed., *The Art That Is Life: The Arts and Crafts Movement in America, 1875–1920* (Boston: Museum of Fine Arts, 1987), p. 283.

## Stickley Brothers, Inc

1. For more information on Albert Stickley and the formation of the company, see the Stickley Brothers entry in the Furniture section.

2. *Quaint Furniture: Arts and Crafts* (1908: reprint, New York: Turn of the Century Editions, 1981), p 5.

3. Don Marek, Arts *and Crafts Furniture Design: The Grand Rapids Contribution. 1895–1915* (Grand Rapids, MI: Grand Rapids Art Museum, 1987), p. 52. .

4. Terry Seger, "Stickley Brothers Metalwork: A Touch of Russia," (*Style: 1900* 2 (Spring 1998), p. 76.

5. Ibid., p. 78.

## Gustav Stickley and the Craftsman Workshops

1. *Stickley Craftsman Furniture Catalogs* (New York: Dover Publications, 1979), p. 82.

2. Don Marek, *Arts and Crafts Furniture Design: The Grand Rapids Contribution 1895–1915* (Grand Rapids, MI: Grand Rapids Art Museum, 1987), p. 63.

3. Stephen Gray, ed., *Collected Works of Gustav Stickley* (New York: Turn of the Century Editions, 1981); also *Stickley Furniture Catalogs* (New York: Dover Publications, 1979).

4. "Lessons in Metalwork," the *Craftsman* (October 1907), pp. 101–102.

5. *Stickley Craftsman Furniture Catalogs* (New York: Dover Publications, 1979), p. 82.

## Arthur J. Stone

1. Elenita C. Chickering, "Arthur J. Stone, Silversmith," *Antiques* (January 1986), p. 279.

2. Ibid., p. 278.

3. Wendy Kaplan, ed., Th*e Art That Is Life: The Arts and Crafts Movement in America, 1875–1920* (Boston: Museum of Fine Arts, 1987), pp. 282–283.

## Tiffany Studios

1. Charles H. Carpenter, Jr., *Tiffany Silver* (New York: Dodd, Mead & Co., 1978), p. 50.

2. Wendy Kaplan, ed., *The Art That Is Life: The Arts and Crafts Movement in America. 1875–1920* (Boston: Museum of Fine Arts. 1987), p. 152.

3. For more information see Tiffany Pottery.

## Dirk Van Erp

1. Bonnie Mattison, *California Design 1910* (Pasadena, CA: California Design Publications, 1974), p. 78.

2. Wendy Kaplan, ed., *The Art That Is Life: The Arts and Crafts Movement in America. 1875–1920* (Boston: Museum of Fine Arts, 1987), p. 275.

3. Ibid.

4. Scott Goldstein, "Inside the Dirk Van Erp Studio," *Style: 1900,* Vol. 12, (Fall 1999): p. 31.

5. Wendy Kaplan, ed., *The Art That Is Life: The Arts and Crafts Movement in America. 1875–1920* (Boston: Museum of Fine Arts, 1987), p. 276.

6. Scott Goldstein, "Inside the Dirk Van Erp Studio," *Style: 1900,* Vol. 12 (Fall 1999): p. 31.

7. Bonnie Mattison, California Design 1910 (Pasadena, CA: California Design Publications, 1974), p. 78.

8. Ibid., p. 79.

9. Robert Judson Clark, ed., Th*e Arts and Crafts Movement in America*. 1876–1916 (Princeton, NJ: Princeton University, 1972), p. 90.

## Other Metalware Shops and Studios

1. Wendy Kaplan, ed., *The Art That Is Life: The Arts and Crafts Movement in America, 1875–1920* (Boston: Museum of Fine Arts. 1987), p. 283.

## PART 4   LIGHTING, TEXTILES, AND COLOR WOODBLOCKS

### Lighting

1. Nadja Maril, *American Lighting: 1840–1940* (West Chester, PA: Schiffer Publishing, 1989), p. 23.

2. Ibid., p. 47.

3. Ibid., pp. 74–75.

4. Ibid., p. 86.

5. Ibid., p. 87.

6. Ibid., p. 91.

7. Beth Cathers and Tod Volpe, *Treasures of the American Arts and Crafts Movement: 1890–1920* (New York: Harry N. Abrams, Inc., 1988), p. 157.

8. Ibid., p. 99.

9. Ibid., 106.

10. Ibid., 107.

11. *Stickley Crafts Furniture Catalogs,* David Cathers, intro. (New York: Dover, 1979), p. 82.

12. Stephen Gray, ed., *The Early Work of Gustav Stickley* (New York: Turn of the Century Editions, 1987), p. 106–107.

13. Stephen Gray, ed., *The Early Work of Gustav Stickley* (New York: Turn of the Century Editions, 1981), p. 145.

14. Ibid., p. 154.

15. Stephen Gray, ed., *The Early Work of Gustav Stickley* (New York: Turn of the Century Editions, 1987), p. 150.

16. Stephen Gray, ed., *The Early Work of Gustav Stickley* (New York: Turn of the Century Editions, 1989), p. 10.

17. Victor M. Linoff, ed., *Illustrated Mission Furniture Catalog, 1912–1913. Come-Packt Furniture Company* (New York: reprint, Dover, 1991), pp. 59–62.

18. *How to Make Mission Style Lamps and Shades* (New York: Dover, 1982).

19. Robert De Falco, Carole Goldman Hibel, and John Hibel, *Handel Lamps* (Staten Island: H & D Press, 1986), p. 8.

20. Ibid., p.16.

21. Ibid., p.17.

22. Ibid., p.17.

23. Ibid., p.38.

24. Ibid., p. 41.

25. Nadja Maril, *American Lighting: 1840–1940* (West Chester, PA: Schiffer Publishing, 1989), p. 114.

26. Ibid., p. 127.

27. Ibid., p. 134.

28. Ibid., p. 139.

### Arts and Crafts Textiles

1. Hazel Clark, *The Encyclopedia of Arts and Crafts* (New York: E. P. Dutton, 1989), p. 71.

2. Ibid., p. 83.

3. Gillian Moss, oral presentation at Grove Park Inn Arts and Crafts Conference, Asheville, NC, February 24, 1991.

4. Jessie Poesch, *Newcomb Pottery* (Exton, PA: Schiffer Publishing, 1984), p.40.

5. Ibid.

6. Gustav Stickley, *Craftsman Fabrics and Needlework* (Madison, WI: Razmataz Press, 1989 reprint), p. 1.

7. Ibid., p. 8.

8. Ibid., pp. 10–11.

9. Ibid., p. 17.

10. Dianne Ayers. "A Primer on Arts and Crafts Textiles," *Arts and Crafts Quarterly* IV, 1. (1991): p. 6.

11. Ibid.

12. Ibid., p. 7.

13. Ibid., p. 6.

14. Chris Walther, "Arts and Crafts Needlework," *Style: 1900,* 14, (Winter 2001): p. 23. See also his article "Sources and identification of American Arts and Crafts Needlework Kits," *Style: 1900,* 12, (Summer 1999).

15. Ibid.

16. Ibid., p. 26.

17. Ibid., p. 27.

18. Wendy Kaplan, ed., *The Art That Is Life: The Arts and Crafts Movement in America, 1875–1920* (Boston: Museum of Fine Arts, 1987), p. 176.

19. Gillian Moss, oral presentation at Grove Park Inn Arts and Crafts Conference, Asheville, NC, February 24, 1991.

## Color Woodblock Prints

1. Nancy E. Green, *Arthur Wesley Dow and His Influence* (Ithaca, NY: Herbert F. Johnson Museum of Art, Cornell University, 1990), p. 5.

2. S. Huzikake, *Japanese Wood-Block Prints* (Japan: Board of Tourist Industry, 1938), p. 25.

3. Ibid., p. 60.

4. Ronald Robertson, *Contemporary Printmaking in Japan* (NY: Crown Publishers, 1965), p. 8.

5. Nancy E. Green, *Arthur Wesley Dow and His Influence* (Ithaca, NY: Herbert F. Johnson Museum of Art, Cornell University, 1990), p. 9.

6. Ibid., p. 8.

7. Ibid., p. 5.

8. Steven Thomas, "Glowing Spots of Color: The Growth of the Arts and Crafts Woodblock Print in America," *Style: 1900,* 2 (Summer 1999): p. 28.

9. Ibid.

10. Nancy E. Green, *Arthur Wesley Dow and His Influence* (Ithaca, NY: Herbert F. Johnson Museum of Art, Cornell University, 1990), p. 10.

11. Ibid., p. 17.

# SELECTED BIBLIOGRAPHY

Anderson, Timothy, Eudorah Moore, and Robert Winter. *California Design 1910*. Pasadena, CA: California Design Publications, 1974; Santa Barbara, CA; Peregrine Smith, 1980.

Anscombe, Isabelle, and Charlotte Gerre. *Arts and Crafts in Britain and America*. New York: Rizzoli International Publications, 1978.

*Arts and Crafts Quarterly* (periodical). Philadelphia: Rose Valley Press, 1903–1907.

*Artsman* (periodical), Philadelphia: Rose Valley Press, 1903–1907.

Bartinique, A. Patricia. *Gustav Stickley: His Craft*. Morris Plains, NJ: the Craftsman Farms Foundation, 1992.

Bavaro, Joseph, and Thomas Mosmann. *The Furniture of Gustav Stickley: History, Techniques, Projects*. New York: Van Nostrand Reinhold, 1982.

*The Book of the Roycrofters*. Roycroft Shop catalog: 1919 and 1926 (catalog reprint). East Aurora, NY: House of Hubbard, 1977.

Bowman, Leslie. *American Arts and Crafts: Virtue in Design*. Los Angeles: Los Angeles County Museum of Art, 1990.

Bragg, Jean Moore. *The Newcomb Style*. Lousianna, 2002.

Brandt, Frederick. *Late Nineteenth and Early Twentieth Century Decorative Arts*. Richmond: Virginia Museum of Fine Arts, 1985.

Brooks, H. Allen. *Frank Lloyd Wright and the Prairie School*. New York: George Braziller, 1984.

Callen, Anthes. *Women Artists of the Arts and Crafts Movement 1870–1914*. New York: Pantheon Books, 1979.

Cathers, David. *Furniture of the American Arts and Crafts Movement*. New York: New American Library, 1981.

Cathers, David, and Alexander Vertikoff. *Stickley Style: Arts and Crafts Homes in the Craftsman Tradition*. New York: Simon & Schuster, 1999.

———. *Genius in the Shadows: The Furniture Designs of Harvey Ellis*. New York: Jordan-Volpe Gallery, 1981.

Champney, Freeman. *Art and Glory: The Story of Elbert Hubbard*. Kent, OH: Kent State University Press, 1983.

Chickering, Elenita C., and Sarah Morgan Ross. *Arthur J. Stone 1847–1938 Designer and Silversmith* Boston, MA: The Boston Athenaeum, 1994.

Clark, Barth, Ellison, Robert, and Eugene Hecht. *The Mad Potter of Biloxi: The Art and Life of George Ohr*. New York: Abbeville Press, 1989.

Clark, Garth, and Hughto, Margie. *A Century of Ceramics in the United States 1878–1978*. New York: E.P. Dutton, 1979.

Clark, Michael E., and Jill Thomas-Clark, *J.M. Young Arts and Crafts Furniture*. New York: Dover Publications, Inc., 1994.

Clark, Robert Judson, ed. *The Arts and Crafts Movement in America 1876–1916*. Princeton, NJ: Princeton University Press, 1972.

Cole, G. D. H., ed. *William Morris: Selected Writings*. Centenary edition. London: Nonesuch Press, 1948.

Copeland, Peter A., Janet H. Copeland, eds. *The 1912 Quaint Furniture Catalog: Stickley Brothers Company, Grand Rapids, Michigan*. Parchment, MI: The Parchment Press, 1993.

*the Craftsman* (periodicals). Gustav Stickley, ed. Eastwood and New York: Craftsman Publishing, 1901–16.

Cummins, Virginia. *Rookwood Pottery Potpourri*. Silver Spring, MD: Leonard and Coleman, 1980.

Danforth Museum of Art. *On the Threshold of Modern Design: The Arts and Crafts Movement in America*. Framingham, MA: Danforth Museum of Art, 1984.

Darling, Sharon. *Chicago Furniture: Art, Crafts, and Industry, 1833–1933*. Chicago: Chicago Historical Society, 1984.

———. *Chicago Metalsmiths*. Chicago Historical Society, 1977.

———. *Teco: Art Pottery of the Prairie School*. Erie, PA: Erie Art Museum, 1989.

Davey, Peter. *Architecture of the Arts and Crafts Movement*. New York: Rizzoli International Publications, 1980.

Davidoff, Donald A., and Stephen Gray. *Innovation and Derivation, The Contribution of L. & J.G. Stickley to the Arts and Crafts Movement*. Morris Plains, NJ: Craftsman Farms Foundation, Inc., 1995.

Rago, David. *The Fulper Book*. New Jersey. Arts and Crafts Quarterly Press, 1993.

Doros, Paul. *The Tiffany Collection of the Chrysler Museum at Norfolk*. Norfolk, VA: The Chrysler Museum, 1978.

Edwards, Robert, ed. *The Arts and Crafts Furniture of Charles Limbert* (catalog reprint). Watkins Glen, NY: American Life Foundation, 1982.

———. *The Byrdcliffe Arts and Crafts Colony*. Wilmington, DE: Delaware Art Museum, 1985.

Eidelberg, Martin, ed. *From Our Native Clay*. New York: American Ceramic Arts Society and Turn of the Century Editions, 1987.

Evans, Paul. *Art Pottery of the United States, 2d ed*. New York: Feingold & Lewis Publishing, 1987.

Fish, Marilyn. *Gustav Stickley, Heritage and Early Years*. North Caldwell, NJ: Little Pond Press, 1997.

Freeman, John Crosby, *The Forgotten Rebel, Gustav Stickley and His Craftsman Mission Furniture*. Watkins Glen, NY: Century House, 1965.

Garner, Philippe. *Twentieth-Century Furniture*. New York: Van Nostrand Reinhold, 1980.

Gray, Stephen, ed. *The Mission Furniture of L. and J. G. Stickley* (catalog reprint). New York: Turn of the Century Editions, 1983.

———. *The Early Work of Gustav Stickley* (catalog reprint). New York: Turn of the Century Editions, 1987.

———. *Lifetime Furniture* (catalog reprint). New York: Turn of the Century Editions, 1981.

———. *Limbert's Holland Dutch Arts and Crafts Furniture* (catalog reprint). New York: Turn of the Century Editions, 1981.

———. *Roycroft Furniture* (catalog reprint). New York: Turn of the Century Editions, 1981.

———. *Quaint Furniture: Arts and Crafts* (reprint of Stickley Brothers catalog). New York: Turn of the Century Editions, 1981.

———. *Arts and Crafts Furniture: Shop of the Crafters at Cincinnati* (catalog reprint). New York: Turn of the Century Editions, 1983.

Gray, Stephen, and Robert Edwards, eds. *The Collected Works of Gustav Stickley* (catalog reprint). New York: Turn of the Century Editions, 1981.

Hamilton, Charles, *Roycroft Collectibles*. New York: A. S. Barnes and Co., 1980.

Hamilton, Charles, Kitty Turgeon, and Robert Rust. *History and Renaissance of the Roycroft Movement*. Buffalo, NY: Buffalo & Erie County Historical Society, 1984.

Hanks, David. *The Decorative Designs of Frank Lloyd Wright*. New York: E. P. Dutton, 1979.

———. *Frank Lloyd Wright: Preserving and Architectural Heritage—Decorative Designs from The Domino's Pizza Collection*. New York: E. P. Dutton, 1988.

Henderson, Philip. *William Morris: His Life, Works, and Friends*. New York: McGraw-Hill, 1967.

Hecht, Dr. Eugene. *George Ohr, After the Fire: An American Genius*. Lambertville, New Jersey: Arts and Crafts Quarterly Press, 1994.

Hunter, Dard. *My Life with Paper*. New York: Alfred Knopf, 1958.

Huxford, Sharon, and Bob Huxford. *The Collector's Encyclopedia of Weller Pottery*. Padcah, KY: Collector Books, 1979.

Kaplan, Wendy, ed. *The Art That Is Life: The Arts and Crafts Movement in America, 1875–1920*. Boston: Museum of Fine Arts, 1987.

Keen, Kirsten Hoving. *American Art Pottery 1875–1930*. Philadelphia: Falcon Press, 1978.

*Keramic Studio, a Monthly Magazine for the China Painter and Potter* (periodical). Syracuse, NY: Keramic Studio Publishing, 1899–1930.

Koch, Robert. *Louis C. Tiffany's Glass, Bronzes, Lamps*. New York: Crown Publishers, 1971.

Kornwolf, James M. H. *Baillie Scott and the Arts and Crafts Movement*. Baltimore: John Hopkins Press, 1972.

Kovel, Ralph and Terry Kovel. *The Kovels' Collector's Guide to American Art Pottery*. New York: Crown Publishers, 1974.

Kurland, Catherine, and Lori Zabar. *Reflections: Arts and Crafts Metalwork in England and the United States*. New York: Kurland-Zabar, 1990.

Lambourne, Lionel. *Utopian Craftsmen: The Arts and Crafts Movement from the Cotswolds to Chicago*. Salt Lake City, UT: Peregrine Smith, 1980.

Lamoureux, Dorothy. *The Arts and Crafts Studio of Dirk Van Erp*. San Francisco: San Francisco Crafts and Folk Art Museum, 1989.

Lindenauer, Isak. *August Tiesselinck: A Lifetime in Metal (1890–1972)*, San Francisco, Isak Lindenauer Antiques, 1989.

Ludwig, Coy. *The Arts and Crafts Movement in New York State: 1890s–1920s*. Layton, UT: Peregrine Smith, 1983.

Maher, Thomas K. *The Jarvie Shop: The Candlesticks and Metalwork of Robert R. Jarvie*. Philmont, NY: Turn of the Century Editions, 1997.

Makinson, Randell. *Greene and Greene: Architecture as a Fine Art*. Salt Lake City, UT: Peregrine Smith, 1977.

———. *Greene and Greene: Furniture and Related Designs*. Salt Lake City, UT: Peregrine Smith, 1979.

Manson, Grant Carpenter. *Frank Lloyd Wright to 1910: The First Golden Age*. New York: Van Nostrand Reinhold, 1958.

Marek, Don. *Arts and Crafts Furniture Design: The Grand Rapids Contribution 1895–1915*. Grand Rapids, MI: Grand Rapids Art Museum, 1987.

McConnell, Kevin. *Roycroft Art Metal*. West Chester, PA: Schiffer Publishing, 1990.

Miller, Donald. *Samuel Yellin Metalworkers Three Generations*. Asheville, NC: Southern Highland Craft Guild, 1998.

Montgomery, Susan. *The Ceramics of William H. Grueby*. Lambertville, NJ. Arts and Crafts Quarterly Press, 1993.

Naylor, Bayer, et al. *The Encyclopedia of Arts and Crafts: The International Arts Movement, 1850–1920*. New York: E. P. Dutton, 1989.

Nelson, Scott, Lois Crouch, Euphemia Demmin, and Robert Newton. *A Collector's Guide to Van Briggle Pottery*. Indiana, PA: Halldin Publishing, 1986.

*The Newark Museum Collection of American Art Pottery*. Newark, NJ: Newark Museum, 1984.

Page, Marion. *Furniture Designed by Architects*. London: The Architectural Press, 1983.

Poesch, Jessie. *Newcomb Pottery*. Exton, PA: Schiffer Publishing, 1984.

Rago, David and Suzanne Perrault. *American Art Pottery*. New York. Knickerbocker Press, 1997.

Rago, David and Suzanne Perrault. *American Art Pottery: Treasure or Not*. Mitchell Beazley, 2002.

*Roycroft Handmade Furniture* (1912 catalog reprint) East Aurora, NY: House of Hubbard, 1973.

Rubin, Jerome and Cynthia Rubin. *Mission Furniture*. San Francisco: Chronicle Books, 1980.

Scott, Mary Roelofs. *Elbert Hubbard: Rebel with Reverence*. Watkins Glen, NY: American Life Foundation, 1984.

Shifman, Barry. *The Arts and Crafts Metalwork of Janet Payne Bowles*. Indianapolis, IN: Indianapolis Museum of Art, 1993.

Smith, Bruce, Alexander Vertikoff. *Greene and Greene Masterworks*. San Francisco: Chronicle Books, 1998.

Smith, Mary Ann. *Gustav Stickley: The Craftsman*. Syracuse, NY: Syracuse University Press, 1983.

*Stickley Craftsman Furniture Catalogs* (Gustav Stickley 1910 catalog and L. & J. G. Stickley 1912 catalog reprint). New York: Dover Publications, 1979.

Stickley, Gustav. *Craftsman Fabrics and Needlework* (catalog reprint). Madison, WI: Razmataz Press, 1989.

——. *Craftsman Furniture* (1912 catalog reprint). Asheville, NC: Bruce Johnson, Knock on Wood Publications, 1989.

Stickley, Gustav, ed., *Craftsman Homes*. New York: The Craftsman Publishing Co., 1909; Dover Publications, 1979.

——. *More Craftsman Homes,* New York: The Craftsman Publishing Co., 1912; Dover Publications, 1912.

*Style: 1900* (a periodical produced quarterly). Lambertville, N.J: Style:1900 Press, 1986 to present.

*Tiller, a Bimonthly Devoted to the Arts and Crafts Movement* (periodical). Bryn Mawr, PA: The Artsman, 1982–1983.

Twombly, Robert. *Louis Sullivan: His Life and Work*. Chicago: The University of Chicago Press, 1986.

Via, Marie, and Marjorie Searl, eds. *Head, Heart and Hand: Elbert Hubbard and the Roycrofters*. Rochester, NY: University of Rochester Press, 1994.

*William Morris and Kelmscott*. London: The Design Council, 1981.

Wright, Frank Lloyd. *An Autobiography*. New York: Duell, Sloan, and Pierce, 1943.

# INDEX

# ABOVT THE AVTHORS

David Rago began dealing in American art pottery and artifacts of the Arts and Crafts movement in 1972. In partnership with his wife, Suzanne Perrault, he is currently the owner of David Rago Auctions, of Lambertville, New Jersey, and co-owner of Rago Modern Auctions, Craftsman Auctions, and 333 estate auctions. These companies specialize in 20th century decorative art and furniture.

Rago has appeared as an appraiser on the PBS staple *Antiques Roadshow* since its first year. He is currently a member of the *Antiques Roadshow* Speaker's Bureau, and serves on the *Roadshow* Appraiser's Ethics Committee.

Rago has authored five books on 20th-century art, spanning from Mission to Modern decorative art and furniture. He also publishes two quarterly magazines servicing collectors and dealers of Period art. The first, *Style: 1900,* is in its 16th year of publication and has a readership of over 35,000. The second, *Modernism Magazine*, is in its fourth year of publication and has already attracted over 20,000 readers. Both are full color, graphically consistent periodicals and are available on newsstands and by subscription Style:1900.com and Modernismmagazine.com.

He also serves as an independent appraiser for 20th-century decorative art, providing both on-site and from-photo evaluations for a fee. He can be reached at info@ragoarts.com.

Bruce Johnson has been collecting Arts and Crafts furniture, pottery, and metalware since 1979. He and his two sons, Eric and Blake, live on a small horse farm outside Asheville, North Carolina, where he hosts the national Arts and Crafts Conference and Antiques Show at the historic Grove Park Inn each February. The author of more than eight books and hundreds of articles, Johnson also writes a regular Arts and Crafts column for *Style: 1900*.

Readers who have additional information on firms, shopmarks, or craftsmen and craftswomen of the movement are invited to write Bruce Johnson, 25 Upper Brush Creek Rd., Fletcher, NC 28732. Collectors who wish to receive information on the next annual Arts and Crafts Conference may request it by writing to Mr. Johnson at this same address.